THEORIES OF COUNSELING AND PSYCHOTHERAPY

theories of counseling and psychotherapy

C. H. PATTERSON
University of Illinois

HARPER & ROW
PUBLISHERS   New York   Evanston   San Francisco   London

TO *Frances*

Theories of Counseling and Psychotherapy, Second Edition

Standard Book Number: 06–045056–8
Library of Congress Catalog Card Number: 72–10051

CONTENTS

V

PREFACE

This revision of *Theories of Counseling and Psychotherapy* incorporates a number of changes.

First, several chapters have been omitted from this edition: Salter's "Conditioned Reflex Therapy," the reinforcement theory of the Pepinskys, and Phillips' interference theory approach.

All of these deletions are from the section on learning theory approaches to counseling. This is the area in which there has been the most activity in the past decade. Yet it was a difficult task to find current replacements for older approaches. In spite of the tremendous amount of writing and research in behavior therapy, no recent systematic and theoretical treatment was available. *Learning Foundations of Behavior Therapy* by Frederick Kanfer and Jeanne Phillips is a comprehensive survey of behavior therapy. Although not clinically oriented, and without case histories or interview protocols, this book was chosen for the summary of the most recent developments in behavior therapy.

In addition, a chapter on gestalt therapy, based upon the writings of Fritz Perls, has been added.

All the chapters that have been retained have been revised. The chapter on Thorne's eclectic system is almost entirely new, utilizing his writings since the publication of the first edition. Its placement has been changed from Part I to a new Part VI because of its comprehensive, eclectic nature.

The chapter on Wolpe has been revised to include his 1969 book, *The Practice of Behavior Therapy.* "Bordin's Psychological Counseling" is based upon his 1968 second edition. Revision of the other chapters consists mainly in editing changes.

In debating the form that the revision would take, the author

vii

considered abandoning the organization into parts along a rational-affective continuum and eliminating the brief chapters introducing each section. Discussion with student groups who had used the book, however, indicated that they unanimously felt that these introductions were helpful and should be retained. The final chapter presents a continuum of helping relationships with the cognitive-affective dimension as one of the underlying variables.

In addition to the reviewers listed in the Preface to the first edition, I am grateful to Dr. Frederick Kanfer for reading the chapter on learning foundations of behavior therapy and reviewing the Introduction to Part II. Dr. Erving Polster read the gestalt chapter and offered suggestions.

The student should perhaps be cautioned that the summary presentations in this book are not a substitute for reading the original sources and are not adequate as a basis for attempting to apply or practice any of the methods described.

Mrs. Anna Jane Bretzlaff again contributed with her typing, which was shared by Mrs. Pat Rowland.

C. H. PATTERSON

PREFACE
to first edition

Students in counseling or psychotherapy should be exposed early in their preparation to the major approaches or points of view. The purpose of the introductory or basic principles course is, in my opinion, to introduce the student to the various points of view in counseling or psychotherapy, to the "schools" or theories that are prevalent, rather than to limit him to a single point of view or to a text that presents no systematic point of view. In later courses it may be desirable or permissible to emphasize, or limit the course to, a particular approach. But somewhere the student must become familiar with the various approaches. It would therefore appear to be an appropriate function for the first or basic course to survey the major existing approaches to counseling or psychotherapy.

Accomplishing this presents a problem, however. In a single course, whether for an academic quarter or for a semester, it is manifestly impossible to require the student to read some twelve or fifteen different books, which would be required to introduce him to the major approaches to counseling or psychotherapy. In some instances there is no single book that adequately represents the point of view.

It is, of course, possible for the instructor to present the varying points of view in lectures. But it would appear to be desirable to have relatively brief introductions to various approaches available to the student. There is a place in the counseling field for a book that does what Hall and Lindzey do with *Theories of Personality* and what Hilgard does with *Theories of Learning* in the areas of personality and of learning. It is the purpose of this book to meet this need.

It will be apparent to many that some major points of view have been omitted. The most obvious gap is in the area of psychoanalysis. As indicated in the Introduction to Part III, the omission is deliberate. Students usually obtain some acquaintance with Freudian psychoanalysis and its variants (Adler and Jung) as well as the neoanalytic approaches (for example, Horney and Sullivan), in basic courses in psychology. In addition, abbreviated presentations of these approaches are available. If the instructor wishes students to review these approaches, he thus has several sources available in which he can assign reading. In some courses the instructor may desire the student to become familiar with a particular approach in more detail than is available in this book and may therefore assign the original source. In such a case, the chapter covering the particular approach may be omitted.

There are a number of ways in which a book such as this may be approached. It is difficult for a single person, with the biases that each of us has, to present various points of view. One way of minimizing bias is to have collaborators, each representing a different approach. The writing of such a book would be difficult, however, unless the collaborators were responsible for separate chapters. Another approach, one that would reduce if not eliminate bias, would be a book with a general editor in which different points of view were presented by acknowledged representatives. Such a book presents problems, however, particularly with regard to the consistency of the presentations. A third approach is one in which a single person writes the book and has it read by some colleagues or other experts in counseling or psychotherapy. The nature of the presentation could vary, however. In one, the theories might be summarized from the writer's point of view, that is, in an expository or even critical or evaluative manner. In a second kind of presentation, the author could attempt to give a nonevaluative summary of the theories as they are propounded by their originators or representatives.

It is the latter kind of presentation that has been attempted in this book. Each chapter is written not as the present author would describe a given approach, but as the point of view would be summarized by an adherent, insofar as this is possible. The author has attempted to be nonevaluative in the presentations. It is one of the advantages of such a method of presentation that it is possible to avoid, or to minimize, phrases such as "so and so claims" or "as so and so would say." This presentation does involve much condensing through paraphrasing, and frequent quotations are used to preserve accuracy as well as to express the flavor of the approach.

That the author has been at least fairly successful in avoiding biased presentations is evidenced by the fact that his summaries have been accepted by the authors or developers of each approach. Each summary was presented to the original author or the person identified most closely with the approach, who was asked to read it for accuracy and clarity of presentation, and to make suggestions for corrections and revisions. These suggestions were incorporated into the revision.

The major dissatisfactions expressed were related to the brevity of the summaries and to recent changes in the approach or the author's thinking. An attempt was made to incorporate these changes into the revision. The original authors were not given the final section of each chapter, the summary and evaluation, since the writer reserved the right to express his own reactions there.

I am indebted to the following writers for reading and commenting on the presentations, and in some cases for permission to reprint case summaries or typescripts: Edward S. Bordin, Albert Ellis, Viktor E. Frankl, Thomas M. French (for Alexander's psychoanalytic psychotherapy), Roy R. Grinker, Sr., George A. Kelly, Neal E. Miller, Harold B. Pepinsky, E. Lakin Phillips, Carl R. Rogers, Julian B. Rotter, Andrew Salter, Frederick C. Thorne, E. G. Williamson, and Joseph Wolpe.

I wish to acknowledge the courtesy of the following publishers in permitting the inclusion of excerpts from books published by them: Appleton-Century-Crofts, Basic Books, Capricorn Press, Houghton Mifflin Company, Journal of Clinical Psychology Press, The Macmillan Company, McGraw-Hill Book Company, Prentice-Hall, Ronald Press, the *American Journal of Psychotherapy,* and the *International Journal of Neuropsychiatry.*

I am indebted to George Middendorf of Harper & Row for the suggestion that I undertake this book. Discussions with a number of colleagues verified the impression that there was a place and a need for such a book.

As always, and as has been the case before, I also owe a great debt to my family for their tolerance of my absorption in the writing of this book. And of course no book could be written without the help of that indispensable person in the modern world of scholarship, as well as business, the typist. In the present instance Mrs. Anna Jane Bretzlaff carried the burden.

C. H. PATTERSON

INTRODUCTION

Counseling and psychotherapy are both used in the title of this book because it appears to be impossible to make any clear distinction between them. If experts in counseling and psychotherapy were asked to list the theories that should be considered under each heading, there would probably be great overlapping in the lists. The difficulty in determining which are theories of counseling and which are theories of psychotherapy is taken as one evidence of the lack of clear or significant differences between them. The position taken by the writer is that there are no essential differences between counseling and psychotherapy.[1] Students in courses in which either counseling or psychotherapy appears in the title would be expected to be familiar with most of the theories included in this volume.

The difficulty in, or impossibility of, separating counseling and psychotherapy is apparent when one considers the definitions of each offered by various authors. The definitions of counseling would in most cases be acceptable as definitions of psychotherapy, and vice versa. There seems to be agreement that both counseling and psychotherapy are processes involving a special kind of relationship between a person who asks for help with a psychological problem (the client or the patient) and a person who is trained to provide that help (the counselor or the therapist). The nature of the relationship is essentially the same, if not identical, in both counseling and psychotherapy. The process that occurs also does not seem to differ from one to the other. Nor do there seem to be any distinct techniques or group of techniques that separate counseling and psychotherapy.

When objectives are considered, however, there may appear to be some differences. The objectives of counseling have been identified by the Committee on Definition, Division of Counseling Psychology of the American Psychological Association, as "to help individuals toward overcoming obstacles to their personal growth, wherever these may be encountered, and toward achieving optimum development of their personal resources." [2] Most psychotherapists would accept these as goals of psychotherapy also. Tyler, attempting to distinguish counseling from psychotherapy, states that it is *not* the job of counselors "to remove physical or mental handicaps or to get rid of limitations." [3] This is presumably the job of the therapist. But this statement appears to disagree with that of the Committee cited above, and in the writer's opinion would not be acceptable to most counseling psychologists. Tyler goes on to note that the activity of the therapist "is aimed essentially at change in developmental structures rather than at fulfillment," while counseling does not attempt to "repair damage done to [the client] in the past, to stimulate inadequate [sic] development of some stunted aspect of his personality," but is the process of "helping a person attain a clear sense of personal identity," along with acceptance of limitations. Again, it would appear that many would reject these restrictions on counseling and would accept the goal of counseling as a goal of psychotherapy.

The distinction that it seems is being made by many, including Tyler as well as Vance and Volsky, is that counseling applies to work with so-called normal individuals, whose problems are related to the development of their potential, while psychotherapy refers to work with individuals who are deficient in some respect. [4] This leads to an artificial distinction in terms of severity of disturbance on a continuum of adjustment-maladjustment. When a client has a serious emotional disturbance, or is handicapped in functioning "normally" because of emotional disturbance, the process is called psychotherapy and is seen as a remedial process to bring the individual up to "normal." When the client is not seriously disturbed but rather has the problems of the so-called normal person, which interfere with the development of his potential, then the process is called counseling. It should be obvious, as Tyler recognizes, that no sharp line can be drawn between the two. So-called counselors practice psychotherapy, while psychotherapists practice counseling, for it is clear that a therapist cannot and does not make a determination that the client, after a period of psychotherapy, is now functioning at a minimal "normal" level and should therefore be transferred to a counselor for help beyond this point. In any case, the counselor or psychotherapist takes a client where he is and allows him to go as far as he can go or desires to go. The counselor is not limited to working with "normal" clients, nor does he limit his efforts with a client to what Tyler calls attempts to "bring about the best utilization of what the person already has," [5] with acceptance of his limitations, without concern about, or even with avoidance of, personality weaknesses and personality change. Thus, a distinction in terms of severity of disturbance or of the kinds of clients dealt with is an artificial one.

A second difference is also artificial or unessential. This is the distinction in terms of the setting in which services are provided. If the setting is a medical one, what is done is called psychotherapy, while if the setting is nonmedical, it is called counseling.

A further distinction is sometimes made in terms of the nature or content of the problem that the client brings to the counselor. So-called reality-oriented (or "conscious") problems, such as educational and vocational problems and choices, have been considered to be the province of counseling, while problems that are inherent in the personality of the individual ("unconscious" problems) are the province of psychotherapy. This line of thinking has lead to the suggestion that cognitive, rational approaches are appropriate for dealing with reality or conscious problems, while problems involving the unconscious require a different approach. Again, however, no clear line can be drawn, and if there is concern only with the rational solution of so-called reality (non-ego-involved) problems, then this is not counseling, but teaching. Nor is the providing of information, which may be a part of counseling, itself counseling. This attempted distinction has led to an unwarranted extension of the term "counseling" to include functions that actually involve individual instruction or information giving. Counseling, in the opinion of the writer and in agreement with most definitions that have been offered, deals with or includes the conative or affective realm—attitudes, feelings, and emotions, and not simply ideas. When there are no affective elements involved, then the process is not counseling, but is probably teaching, information giving, or an intellectual discussion.

It is concluded that there are no essential differences between counseling and psychotherapy in the nature of the relationship, in the process, in the methods or techniques, in goals or outcomes (broadly conceived), or even in the kinds of clients involved. For convenience, or for practical or political reasons, counseling often refers to work with less seriously disturbed clients or with clients who have rather specific problems with less accompanying general personality disturbance, usually in a nonmedical setting; while psychotherapy refers to work with more seriously disturbed clients, usually in a medical setting. This book, therefore, makes no distinction among theories on this basis and does not attempt to classify or dichotomize them into one category or the other.

THE NATURE OF THEORY

We have indicated that certain theories of counseling and psychotherapy will be presented. But what constitutes a theory of counseling or psychotherapy? How many theories are there?

A formal theory has certain characteristics. First, there is a set of stated postulates or assumptions. These assumptions state the premises of the field with which the theory is concerned. The assumptions must be related to each other and must be internally consistent, and the relationships must be specified. Second, there is a set of definitions of the terms or concepts in the theory. These definitions relate the concepts to observational data and thus make possible the study of the concepts in research or experimentation.

The statement of the assumptions and definitions makes possible the construction of hypotheses. Hypotheses are essentially predictions of what should be found if the theory has validity. That is, given certain assumptions and definitions, certain things should follow or be true. Hypotheses state, in a form that can be tested, what these things are.

Not only does a theory predict new facts or relations, it should also organize and integrate what is known in a meaningful framework. Whether this organization of existing knowledge comes with the formation of the theory or follows its formulation is not clear. Many writers appear to think of organization as a late development or result of the theory. However, the assumptions and postulates of a theory do not come out of the thin air; they are developed upon the basis of observation and experience. That is, the existing facts and knowledge are the bases for the assumptions and definitions of a theory. The process of theory construction, testing, modification or reconstruction, and further testing is thus a continuing process.

Several formal criteria of a good theory have been proposed: [6]

1 *Importance*   A theory should not be trivial, but should be significant. It should be applicable to more than a limited, restricted situation, such as the behavior of rats in a T maze or the learning of nonsense syllables. It should have some relevance to life or to real behavior. Importance is very difficult to evaluate, however, since the criteria are vague or subjective. Acceptance by competent professionals or recognition and persistence in the professional literature may be indicative of importance. Also, if a theory meets other formal criteria, it is probably important.

2 *Preciseness and clarity*   A theory should be understandable, internally consistent, free from ambiguities. Clarity may be tested by the ease of relating the theory to data or to practice, or the ease of making predictions from it and specifying methods of testing them.

3 *Parsimony or simplicity*   Parsimony has long been accepted as a characteristic of a good theory. This would involve a minimum of complexity, and few assumptions. Maddi questions this assumption, however, suggesting that one cannot determine which of two theories is most parsimonious until everything is known about the area to which the theory applies. He also questions its value on the grounds that the most parsimonious theory on the basis of current data might not be the best theory: "it is distinctly possible that a theory which looks parsimonious in explaining today's facts may be actually such an oversimplification in terms of explaining all human functioning as to be

wholly inadequate to cope with tomorrow's facts without major over-haul." [7] Nevertheless, it might be maintained that the phenomena of the world and of nature are relatively simple in terms of basic principles. Hall and Lindzey propose that parsimony is important only after the criteria of comprehensiveness and verifiability have been met. "This becomes an issue only under circumstances where two theories generate exactly the same consequences." [8]

4 *Comprehensiveness*   A theory should be complete, covering the area of interest and including all known data in the field.

5 *Operational*   A theory should be capable of being reduced to procedures for testing its propositions or predictions. Its concepts must be precise enough to be measurable. A strict operationism can be restrictive, however, as Maddi points out, when a concept is defined by a restricted or limited measurement operation.[9] The concept should first be defined and then a method of measurement chosen or developed. Not all the concepts of a theory need to be operational; concepts may be used to indicate relationships and organization among concepts.

6 *Empirical validity or verifiability*   The preceding criteria are rational in nature. Beyond meeting these criteria, a good theory must be supported by experience and experiments involving the testing of predictions. That is, in addition to its consistency with, or ability to account for, what is already known, it must generate predictions that are confirmed by new data.

7 *Stimulating*   The capacity of a theory to lead to predictions that can be tested, leading to the development of new knowledge, has often been referred to as its fruitfulness. A theory can be fruitful even if it is not capable of leading to specific predictions. It may provoke thinking and the development of new ideas or theories, sometimes because it leads to disbelief or resistance in others.

There is a final criterion of a good theory, which is seldom mentioned or recognized. That is that it should be useful to practitioners in organizing their thinking and practice, providing a conceptual framework for their practice. Practitioners too often think of theory as something that is irrelevant to what they do, unrelated to practice or to real life. Yet, as Kurt Lewin, the developer of topological psychology, is reputed to have said, "there is nothing as practical as a good theory." [10]

If we looked for a theory of counseling or psychotherapy that met all of these criteria, we probably would not find one. Nor would we find such a theory of personality or of learning. Existing theories are at a primitive stage, and the criteria constitute goals toward which theorists should strive. Most theories of counseling or psychotherapy are not cast in a formal form, though some are attempts at a formulation in terms of a set of related postulates or assumptions, with their corollaries. In many instances, theoretical concepts are implicit rather than explicit. Explicit statements of points of view in counseling vary from specific statements concerned with only one aspect or element of the counseling process or relationship to very general expositions. Frank writes that

> Some formulations [of psychotherapy] try to encompass all its aspects. Many of these have been immensely insightful and stimulating and have illuminated many fields of knowledge. To achieve all-inclusiveness, however, they have resorted to metaphor, have left major ambiguities unresolved, and have formulated their hypotheses in terms that cannot be subjected to experimental test.
>
> The opposite approach has been to try to conceptualize small segments of the field with sufficient precision to permit experimental tests of the hypotheses, but these formulations run the risk of achieving rigor at the expense of significance. The researcher is faced with the problem of delimiting an aspect of psychotherapy that is amenable to experimental study and at the same time includes the major determinants of the problem under consideration. He finds himself in the predicament of the Norse god Thor, who tried to drain a small goblet only to discover that it was connected with the sea. Under these circumstances there is an inevitable tendency to guide the choice of research problems more by the ease with which they can be investigated than by their importance. One is reminded of the familiar story of the drunkard who lost his keys in a dark alley but looked for them under the lamppost because the light was better there. This has led to a considerable amount of precise but trivial research.[11]

It appears that counselors and psychotherapists have been so engrossed in practice that little attention has been given to the development of formal theories. Nevertheless, although not formally stated, there are, in every practice or approach to counseling, implicit assumptions. They are often not clearly stated, or perhaps not stated at all. But they are there. Theoretical discussions of counseling or psychotherapy frequently allude to assumptions and hypotheses, sometimes confusing the two. Many of these theoretical discussions are in a sense after-the-fact explanations or rationalizations and have not been developed formally for research. They are thus usually not clearly or systematically stated. Nevertheless, they are embryo theories and should be capable of being explicitly formulated as formal theories.

It is not the purpose of this book to attempt to formulate such theories on the basis of the literature. Its purpose is rather to present existing theories in the forms in which they occur. Thus, the word "theory" is used rather loosely, as it must be if the book is to have any content at all. The phrase "point of view" is probably more appropriate.

THE POINTS OF VIEW AND THEIR ORGANIZATION

Once the concession is made to include points of view or approaches to counseling rather than formalized theories, the candidates for inclusion become numerous. We might attempt either to reduce all theories or approaches to a few central ones or to deal with only the major theories. The Pepinskys, in 1954, classified theories into five major categories: the trait-and-factor centered approach, the communications approach, self theory, the psychoanalytic approach, and the neobehavioral approach.[12] It is perhaps possible to subsume most of the major approaches under these rubrics. The various learning theory approaches of Dollard and Miller, Salter, Shoben, and Wolpe, for example, might be included under the neobehavioral category. And the various neoanalytic theories might all be included under the psychoanalytic approach.

To some extent this is the procedure adopted here; that is, the various approaches have been grouped into categories that have some similarity to those of the Pepinskys. But the organization of the approaches, or their ordering, presents a problem. Is it possible to impose any organization upon the various approaches, or are they too heterogeneous to order in any way? One possible manner of organization would be to arrange them on the commonly used continuum of directiveness, from highly directive to highly permissive approaches. There are other bases for organization. One such basis, probably not entirely independent of the directive-permissive continuum, is a continuum from highly rational to highly affective approaches, from theories that are highly cognitive to those that are highly conative in their emphases. Bordin suggested such a continuum, from an "emphasis on an intellectual process of reasoning out the problem" to "the emphasis upon stimulating the client to further and deeper expression of his attitudes through such methods as accepting and clarifying responses," as a dimension of the counseling process.[13] This continuum was accepted as a basis for organizing the various points of view.

At the cognitive end of such a continuum are those theories or approaches to counseling that are rational, logical, or intellectual in nature. Perhaps the most extreme example of this would be the rational psychotherapy of Albert Ellis. Further along the continuum would fall the more psychological approaches, the learning theory and conditioned response theories of John Dollard and Neal Miller, Andrew Salter, and Joseph Wolpe. Still further along would be the various analytic approaches. Toward the other extreme would be the self theories or phenomenological approaches, with existentialism perhaps at the most extreme end of the continuum.

For convenience, this continuum has been divided into five parts, which make up the five sections of the book. These are designated as (1) rational approaches to counseling, (2) learning theory approaches to counseling, (3) psychoanalytic approaches to counseling, (4) perceptual approaches to counseling, and (5) existential approaches. A sixth section has been included to accommodate the eclectic position of Frederick Thorne. Within the sections, however, no attempt has been made to order the theories or approaches in terms of the underlying continuum; indeed, it would probably not be possible to do so in most instances. In some cases the assignment of a theory to a particular section might be questioned. Some might place Dollard and Miller among the psychoanalytic approaches. Kelly's approach is in some respects quite cognitive or rational in its orientation. Any attempt to group or classify approaches to counseling or psychotherapy must result in arbitrary assignments in some cases. It might thus be questioned whether it is necessary or desirable to group the approaches at all. The present writer confesses to a need for some organization in their presentation, and feels that some organization is better than none and that some basis for grouping and ordering groups is better than no basis.

A question arises as to how many points of view, or variants of a point of view, should be included. There are, of course, necessary limitations of space. But the author has attempted to include, even though sometimes rather briefly, those positions that are dealt with in an extended manner (usually at book length) in the literature of the field. Thus, the student is introduced to most of the current writers in counseling or psychotherapy. Obviously, every book dealing with counseling or psychotherapy could not be represented here. The criterion for selection was whether the author presented either what might be considered a systematic point of view or a significant variant of a particular approach. Even so, it is obvious that I have neglected to include every possible point of view or variant, if for no other reason than that I am sure I have missed some through ignorance of their existence.

RELATION TO OTHER PSYCHOLOGICAL THEORIES

Theories of counseling cannot be clearly separated from theories of learning, theories of personality, or general theories of behavior. Counselors deal with behavior. The fact that they work with clients who exhibit behavior that is more or less disturbed, abnormal, or unsatisfactory in some respects, either to themselves or to society or to both, does not change the fact that it is behavior with which the counselor is concerned. Moreover, the aspect of behavior that is the primary focus of the counselor falls in the area of personality in its individual and social aspects. In addition, the goal of counseling is the changing of behavior or personality in some respect or to some extent. Different approaches to counseling vary in the specific nature and extent of behavior change toward which they are directed, but all accept behavior change of some kind, including changes in attitudes, feelings, perceptions, values, or goals, as the objective of counseling. Since learning may broadly be defined as change in behavior, then counseling is, of course, concerned with learning and thus with theories of learning.

In fact, it is difficult to distinguish between theories of learning, theories of personality, and theories of counseling. All are concerned with behavior and are thus theories of behavior. Hall and Lindzey differentiate between theories that deal with any behavioral event of significance to the human organism (general theories of behavior) and those that are limited to certain aspects of human behavior (single-domain theories).[14] It is difficult, however, to make the separation clearly. Hall and Lindzey state that personality theories are general theories of behavior, and they admit that theories of learning may also be considered theories of behavior. But so may theories of counseling. Even theories of perception may be theories of behavior, since perception is central to all behavior. Behavior, in short, is all of one piece, and any theory dealing with a major aspect of behavior is or must become a general behavior theory. Theories concerned with the various aspects must be consistent among themselves and together must constitute a general theory of behavior. Eventually, a theory of learning, a theory of personality, a theory of perception, and a theory of counseling or psychotherapy must all be parts of a general theory of behavior.

The discussion of theories of counseling, therefore, inevitably involves the areas of personality and learning. Every theory of counseling has, and must have, a theory of personality and of learning behind it. Usually, the related theories of personality and learning are implicit rather than explicit. When they are explicit, they usually have developed from the theory of counseling or psychotherapy, as in the case of client-centered counseling, although it may, of course, be the case that a theory of counseling is consistent with an independently developed theory of personality. At any rate, theories of personality and theories of counseling are interrelated, although there is not necessarily a theory of counseling for every theory of personality that has been identified or developed.

Thus, insofar as the authors of the various approaches presented deal with personality theory it will be included as a part of the summary of the approach. There will be no attempt, however, on the part of the writer to provide a personality theory to accompany an approach that is lacking in an explicit theory. It is not the purpose of this book to go beyond what has been developed by those concerned with the various approaches to counseling.

PHILOSOPHICAL IMPLICATIONS

Allport notes that "theories of learning (like much else in psychology) rest on the investigator's conception of the nature of man. In other words, every learning theorist is a philosopher, though he may not know it." [15] This applies perhaps even more forcefully to counseling theorists. It is, therefore, necessary to include in our discussions the philosophical bases that are implicit or explicit in the various counseling theories. Again, no elaborate philosophical formulation will be developed for each theory considered. But it does seem to be necessary to consider the assumptions regarding the nature of man underlying the various theories, as well as the goals or objectives of counseling that are accepted or advocated by them. In many cases, of course, very little formal consideration was given in the original presentation of the approach, and this will be reflected in the summaries in this book.

NATURE OF THE PRESENTATIONS

It seems desirable that in the discussion of the various theories some common method or outline should be followed. It is difficult, however, to develop a detailed outline that would be appropriate for all theories. The categories selected are, therefore, few, broad, and general.

The general procedure is to identify the theory in terms of its major proponents, giving some background or orientation to the approach. Then the major concepts, or the essential elements, of the approach are discussed. These would include the philosophical background or implications and the related theories of personality and learning or of behavior and its change. Next, the goals of counseling and the counseling process are considered, followed by consideration of the techniques, or the behavior, of the counselor, which implement the concepts in the process. Then, when possible, one or more illustrative examples of the approach are presented. Finally, a summary and general evaluation concludes the discussion.

The evaluation is not a full-scale critique of the theory, but rather a summary of the major contributions of each approach and a consideration of some of the major objections or criticisms that have been or might be raised against it.

The presentations are intended to be descriptive rather than polemic. The reader who is familiar with the author's point of view will perhaps be able to recognize areas where bias may be still present. I have, like Hilgard, "approached the task with the desire to be friendly to each of the positions represented, on the assumption that each of them has been proposed by an intelligent and sincere person or group of persons, and that there must be something which each of them can teach us." [16] The final chapter, of course, represents my own attempt at evaluating or drawing out differences and similarities among current approaches to counseling. The purpose of the book is not to present a critique or comparison of the various theories, or to attempt to develop a single theory by integrating aspects of various approaches. The purpose is to present in a relatively brief, objective form the various current points of view in counseling or psychotherapy. This is difficult to do without danger of misrepresentation because of brevity, misunderstanding, or biased perception. It is hoped that this danger has been minimized by having the presentations read by the representatives of the various approaches. The writer, however, accepts the responsibility for what appears in the following chapters.

Unlike the works of Hilgard and of Hall and Lindzey, this book does not attempt to review the research associated with the various theories presented. There are a number of reasons for this. First, to attempt to cover the research in counseling and psychotherapy would be prohibitive in terms of the space requirements. Second, although there has been considerable research in the field of counseling and psychotherapy, very little of it has been directly associated with a particular theory or point of view. There seems to have been, in general, a separation between theory and research, on the one hand, and practice and research, on the other, so that advocates or practitioners of a particular orientation, unlike those in the field of learning, have not engaged in research related to the theory espoused or practiced. The major exception is the research of Rogers and his associates on client-centered counseling. This may be related to the fact that, for the psychologist, there is not much one can do about a personality theory or a theory of learning except research; while counseling and psychotherapy are applied fields, and practitioners seem to have little time, or perhaps inclination, for research.

REFERENCES

[1] Patterson, C. H. *Counseling and psychotherapy: theory and practice.* New York: Harper & Row, 1959. Chap. I; Patterson, C. H. Counseling and/or psychotherapy. *Amer. Psychologist,* 1963, **18,** 667–669; Patterson, C. H. Distinctions and commonalities between counseling and psychotherapy. In G. F. Farwell, N. Gamsky, & Phillips M. Coughlan. Scranton, Pa.: International Textbook, in press.   [2] American Psychological Association, Division of Counseling Psychology, Committee on Definition. Counseling psychology as a specialty. *Amer. Psychologist,* 1956, **11,** 282–285.   [3] Tyler, Leona E. Theoretical principles underlying the counseling process. *J. counsel. Psychol.,* 1958, **5,** 3–10. [4] Vance, F. L., & Volsky, T. C. Counseling and psychotherapy: split personality or Siamese twins. *Amer. Psychologist,* 1962, **17,** 565–570.   [5] Tyler, Leona E. Minimum change therapy. *Personnel guid. J.,* 1960, **38,** 475–479. [6] Hall, C. S., & Lindzey, G. *Theories of personality.* (2nd ed.) New York: Wiley, 1970; Maddi, S. R. *Personality theories: a comparative analysis.* Homewood, Ill.: Dorsey, 1968; Stefflre, B., & Matheny, K. *The function of counseling theory.* Boston: Houghton Mifflin, 1968.   [7] Maddi, S. R., *ibid.,* p. 456.   [8] Hall, C. S., & Lindzey, G., *op. cit.,* p. 13.   [9] Maddi, S. R., *op. cit.,* p. 454.   [10] Lewin, K. Science, power and education. In G. W. Lewin (Ed.), *Studies in topological and vector psychology,* 1944.   [11] Frank, J. D. *Persuasion and healing.* Baltimore: Johns Hopkins, 1961. Pp. 227–228.   [12] Pepinsky, H. B., & Pepinsky, Pauline. *Counseling: theory and practice.* New York: Ronald, 1954.   [13] Bordin, E. S. Dimensions of the counseling process. *J. clin. Psychol.,* 1948, **4,** 240–244. [14] Hall, C. S., & Lindzey, G., *op. cit.,* p. 17.   [15] Allport, G. W. *Patterns of growth in personality.* New York: Holt, Rinehart and Winston, 1961, p. 84. [16] Hilgard, E. R. *Theories of learning.* (1st ed.) New York: Appleton-Century-Crofts, 1948. P. v.

PART ONE

Rational Approaches to Counseling

1

Introduction

Rational theories of counseling or psychotherapy are those that tend to take a logical, intellectual approach to the process and/or to the solution of the client's problems or difficulties.

These theories tend to be relatively simple in nature. They also tend to be eclectic; that is, a variety of techniques is likely to be accepted or adopted. Although this may be rationalized on the basis that different problems or different clients require different methods or techniques, the choice of techniques is usually made on the basis of common sense or empiricism. The empiricism does not rest on experiments as much as on experience.

Rational approaches to the counseling process are usually based on an analogy between medicine and counseling or psychotherapy. Thus, these approaches usually place great emphasis upon diagnosis. In fact, it is assumed that treatment cannot be attempted until some diagnosis is reached, since, logically, the diagnosis would be the basis for differential treatment.

Edmund G. Williamson adopts this medical model, although there is no detailed system of diagnostic categories in Williamson's approach. Diagnosis is rather a statement of the client's problem in its individual aspects. Nevertheless, the need for classification appears to be felt, and Williamson refers to the categories proposed by Bordin[1] and Pepinsky.[2] Although, as judged by their use by counselors, the value of these categories has never been substantiated, they persist,

3

and several recent attempts have been made to revise them.[3] This is an illustration of the appeal of the medical model. But there is as little agreement on diagnostic categories in the area of counseling problems as there is in the area of psychopathology. The medical model has increasingly been called into question.[4]

Albert Ellis, on the other hand, is not concerned with diagnosis. His approach is rational because it applies logic and rational argument to the solution of the client's problems. While there is no emphasis on the client's learning a problem-solving approach that he can apply to other problems, this would be one of the goals of such an approach. Weitz has also presented this view of counseling.[5]

The two approaches summarized in the following chapters—those of Williamson and of Ellis—present the counselor as essentially a teacher who applies a rational, problem-solving process in an individual teaching relationship. To be sure, neither limits counseling to intellectual problem solving. Both recognize the influence of conation upon the cognitive processes. But in both the emphasis is upon counseling or psychotherapy as a cognitive process.

The nature of American culture would appear to be conducive to a logical approach to counseling and psychotherapy because of the emphasis upon science. Frank points this out and in doing so also indicates the weakness of this approach in psychotherapy. The scientific ideal, he says, "values objectivity and intellectual comprehension, and these features may not be entirely advantageous for psychotherapy. They tend to result in an overevaluation of the cognitive aspects. From the patient's standpoint 'insight' in the sense of ability to verbalize self-understanding may be mistaken for genuine attitude change. From the therapist's standpoint, the scientific attitude may lead to undue stress on the niceties of interpretation and avoidance of frankly emotion-arousing techniques . . . even though there is universal agreement that in order to succeed, psychotherapy must involve the patient's emotions."[6]

REFERENCES

[1] Bordin, E. S. Diagnosis in counseling and psychotherapy. *Educ. psychol. Measmt.*, 1946, **6**, 171–172.   [2] Pepinsky, H. B. The selection and use of diagnostic categories. *Appl. Psychol. Monogr.*, 1948, No. 15.   [3] Byrne, R. H. Proposed revisions of the Bordin-Pepinsky diagnostic constructs. *J. counsel. Psychol.*, 1958, **5**, 184–188; Sloan, T. J., & Pierce-Jones, J. The Bordin-Pepinsky diagnostic categories: counselor agreement and MMPI comparisons. *J. counsel. Psychol.*, 1958, **5**, 189–193; Robinson, F. P. Modern approaches to counseling diagnosis. *J. counsel Psychol.*, 1963, **10**, 325–333.   [4] Patterson, C. H. Is psychotherapy dependent upon diagnosis? *Amer. Psychologist*, 1948, **3**, 155–159; Menninger, K., Ellenberger, H., Pruyser, P., & Mayman, M. The unitary concept of mental illness. *Bull. Menninger Clin.*, 1958, **22**, 4–12; Menninger, K., Mayman, M., & Pruyser, P. *The vital balance.* New York: Viking, 1963; Szasz,

T. S. *The myth of mental illness.* New York: Hoeber Medical Division, Harper & Row, 1961. See also Patterson, C. H. Counseling and diagnosis. *J. counsel. Psychol.,* 1964, **11,** 297–298.   [5] Weitz, H. *Behavior change through guidance.* New York: Wiley, 1964.   [6] Frank, J. D. *Persuasion and healing.* Baltimore: Johns Hopkins, 1961. Pp. 219–220.

2

Williamson and the Minnesota point of view

What has become known as the Minnesota point of view in counseling is chiefly associated with the name of Williamson, although others have, of course, contributed to its development.

Edmund Griffith Williamson (1900–   ) has been associated with the University of Minnesota for over forty years, having begun there as a graduate student under Donald G. Paterson in 1926, after receiving his B.A. at the University of Illinois in 1925. He received his Ph.D. in 1931 and in 1932 became the first Director of the University Testing Bureau. In 1939 he became Coordinator of Student Personnel Services and in 1941 was named Dean of Students. From Assistant Professor of Psychology in 1932 he moved to Associate Professor in 1938 and became Professor in 1941. In June, 1969, he retired. He is a Diplomate in Counseling Psychology of the American Board of Professional Psychology.

The first major expression of the Minnesota point of view was Williamson and Darley's *Student Personnel Work*.[1] A year later Paterson, Schneidler, and Williamson published *Student Guidance Techniques*,[2] which summarizes the point of view developed in the earlier volume, but is mainly a technical discussion of the testing instruments that form the basis for the counseling process. The next year Williamson elaborated the approach in *How to Counsel Students*.[3] In 1950 Part I of this book, "An Outline of Clinical Techniques," was revised as a separate

6

volume entitled *Counseling Adolescents.*[4] Since that time a long series of journal articles have dealt with aspects, elaborations, and developments of Williamson's approach.[5-20]

BACKGROUND AND DEVELOPMENT

The Minnesota approach to counseling is the only one that has developed from an essentially vocational counseling base, emphasizing problems of educational and vocational adjustment. While Williamson has been the principal spokesman for the Minnesota position, many others have contributed to it. The foundation was laid by D. G. Paterson in his studies of individual differences and test development during the 1920s.[21] This work continued during the 1930s in connection with the Minnesota Stabilization Research Institute, resulting in the publication of a series of bulletins, and was then summarized by Paterson and Darley.[22]

In the early years of the present century, Parsons described vocational guidance as providing youth with: "(1) a clear understanding of [himself, his] aptitudes, abilities, interests, ambitions, resources, limitations, and their causes; (2) a knowledge of the requirements and conditions of success, advantages, compensations, opportunities, and prospects in different lines of work; (3) true reasoning on the relations of these two groups of facts." [23] Paterson, in his introduction to Williamson and Darley's book, deplored the fact that vocational counselors had become preoccupied with the second aspect of Parsons' concept of vocational guidance, providing information about occupations to clients, and had neglected the first aspect. "Strangely enough," he notes, "the vocational guidance movement as it has developed historically has paid less and less attention to the problem of analyzing the individual and has paid more and more attention to the problem of accumulating and disseminating information about occupations." [24]

Paterson and his colleagues and students worked at providing an objective, scientific basis for Parsons' formulation. Psychologists and counselors owe much to them for the development of tests of aptitudes and abilities.[25] Nor was the second of Parsons' factors neglected. The description and definition of jobs was recognized as needing elaboration, with the result that the Minnesota Occupational Rating Scales,[26] first published in 1941, were developed. Paterson and his colleagues' goal was to develop an actuarial approach to counseling in which the empirical, statistical relationships of client characteristics and job (or college or course) requirements could be used in counseling in the form of probabilities. The terms "clinical diagnosis" and "clinical counseling" were used to designate the process of working within this framework. These terms apparently were selected to indicate that the counselor does more than administer tests: he deals with the total individual.

Clinical counseling and the clinical counselor must not be confused with clinical psychology or the clinical psychologist. Paterson was concerned with the practical problems of adjusting to work. His lifelong interest was vocational psychology, and he was critical of those clinical or counseling psychologists whose only concern was psychotherapy with personality problems and who disdained working with vocational problems or who felt competent to do vocational counseling on the basis of a knowledge of the Rorschach test and a course in occupational information.

Although closely related to research that was concerned with the assessment of occupational aptitudes and abilities and the requirements of jobs, including those at the semiskilled and unskilled levels, the Minnesota approach to counseling, as developed by Williamson, was formulated in a student personnel program in a large university. This setting, as well as the clientele, that is, students at the adolescent and late adolescent or early adult age levels, influenced the nature of the approach, as will become apparent in the later material. The combination of the vocational-occupational background and the educational setting distinguishes this approach from all the other points of view in counseling that we shall consider or, for that matter, that exist.

The Minnesota point of view has developed over the years, with increasing recognition of, and concern for, problems other than educational and vocational ones, under the influence of developments in psychotherapy. Psychotherapy is not considered to be the same as counseling, however; the former, as Williamson has stated, "in the past has centered attention almost exclusively and somewhat narrowly upon the pathology and medical treatment of emotional disruptions, traumas, and anxieties." [27]

The changing and developing nature of Williamson's approach to counseling makes it difficult to present in a systematic or unified way. Williamson has written prolifically on many aspects of counseling since the publication of his 1950 book. He has been sensitive to developments in the field of counseling and psychotherapy, and his point of view has expanded and developed under these influences. He emphasizes its developing nature rather than claiming to present a finished product.

This element of change and development makes it difficult to present Williamson's point of view. While the 1950 book was a somewhat systematic presentation of his position at that time, subsequent developments have not been brought together in any integrated presentation. The present chapter uses as a basis and framework the 1950 publication. The student should be familiar with this, if only for its historical significance. An attempt has been made to incorporate later developments into this framework. This may not result in an adequate picture of Williamson's present position, but one purpose of this chapter is to present to the student the 1950 position, which has not been superseded by an integrated statement of a current position that would warrant separate treatment.

PHILOSOPHY AND CONCEPTS

The Minnesota approach is related to the educational framework in which it has developed. Chapter I of *Counseling Adolescents* is titled "Counseling As Education." While the Minnesota point of view is essentially rational and logical in its approach to counseling, it is not associated with intellectualism or essentialism in education. It is identified with what Williamson calls personalism,[28] or with concern for the whole individual. While knowledge of the world is a major objective of education, knowledge useful to the student in achieving and maintaining personal adjustments is also included. According to Williamson, "the basic purpose of education is not only to train the intellect but also to assist students to achieve those levels of social, civic, and emotional maturity which are within the range of their potentialities.[29]

It is here that counseling joins with instruction in "a comprehensive program geared to the strategic objective of helping each individual to select and grow toward personal goals, of which one is the full development of each individual member of our democratic society." [30] The goals of education and of counseling are the same—"the optimum development of the individual as a whole person and not solely with respect to his intellectual training." [31] Thus, "counseling is as fundamental a technique of assisting the individual to achieve a style of living satisfying to him and congruent with his status as a citizen in a democracy as are the instructional techniques used by the teacher, in classroom and laboratory, to achieve stipulated academic or educational goals in the field of knowledge." [32]

The function of counseling is thus clearly more than "delivering the student to the classroom in the optimum condition for profiting from instruction." [33] Counseling is broader than psychotherapy, which is often restricted "to the emotion-feeling-evaluation aspects of personality development," [34] to self-conflicts often considered in isolation from the client's actual life, and is often limited to the client's evaluations of, and reactions to, his experiences rather than being concerned with actual behavior in social situations. Counseling, on the other hand, is concerned with the interaction of personality and the surrounding culture. However, "the *substantive* conditions faced by the adolescent in the adult world are only a part, and often a minor part, of his transitional adjustment." [35] While there is a factual content, these conditions also involve his emotional reactions and evaluations of himself. Thus, "counseling must deal both with the content of the adjustments and also with the individual's attitude toward and valuations of his adjustment." [36] Counseling is not psychotherapy but "a different concept, one that embraces and integrates vocational and educational guidance with personality dynamics and interpersonal relationships." [37]

In his most recent book, an interpretative history of vocational counseling, Williamson brings together his views on theory and philosophy in counseling.[38] While it is more in the nature of questioning current theories and assumptions than presenting a systematic approach, it is nonetheless his most systematic treatment of this area. He states that there are three major dimensions of a theory about the nature of counseling: (1) the basic purpose, or objective, of counseling relative to human development, (2) the principal means to this end goal, (3) the implicit and necessary assumptions concerning human nature and its development as influenced by the counseling process and techniques.

The Nature of Man

There are five basic questions that counselors must face. Answers are only provisional and must be continuously reexamined; "it is essential that counselors, as educational and societal philosophers, learn to live with question marks." [39]

1   What is the nature of human nature, the nature of man? Counselors must be optimistic in the belief that "through education, man can become himself, in a deep and elaborate manner that will bring satisfaction of accomplishment. Perhaps this is the true meaning of existence—that *man continues to strive to become himself*." Specifically, "counselors must believe that man is capable of learning to solve his problems, especially if he learns to utilize his abilities." [40] Man is a rational being who is able to think and use science in furthering his own development and human progress. "I wish to be counted among those who have very strong prejudices in favor of man's rational processes, in contrast with any intuitive capacity he may possess." [41]

But while the counselor is optimistic, he must recognize that "man is born with the potential for both good and evil and that the meaning of life is to seek good and reject—or at least control—evil. The degree to which one becomes a full human being is thus determined by the measure of enlightened self-control attained and deployed in the direction of 'full humanity.' " [42]

2   What is the nature of human development? Since man has the potentiality for evil, he is not capable, in the pattern established by Rousseau ("man is born good and society corrupts him"), and as assumed by the self-actualization movement, of developing autonomously. He needs other persons to achieve the full development of his potentiality. Self-actualization requires the assistance of other people. In fact, "one can argue that man would not be as good as he is; that is, he would not have self-actualized his potentiality, if it were not for society, and an interdependent society at that, with one individual helping others in the Dewey concept of doing some social good." [43] Williamson quotes Herberg's statement that "the human self emerges only in the community and has no real existence apart from it." [44]

3   What is the nature of the "good life" and "the good"? The nature of the good life has been a problem of all ages. It is a question that should not be answered with finality, but only provisionally. It cannot be accepted that "the nature or form of one's full potential and

self-actualization will thus be the 'best possible' or the 'good' form of human nature. Indeed man seems to be capable both of becoming his 'best' bestial and debasing self, as well as those forms of 'the best'that are of high excellence." [45] One dimension of "the good" is *arete*, the concept of excellence in all aspects of human development.

4   What is the nature of the determination of the "good life"? Who determines what is good? Again, there are various answers. Teachers and parents, in attempting to dictate the form of the good life, may block the student's search. It may be that the search itself will prove to be the good life.

5   What is the nature of the universe, and what is man's relationship to that universe? Here each of us, each counselor and counselee, must formulate his own conception or personal cosmology.

Assumptions Concerning Effective Counseling Relationships

1   The goal of counseling is often assumed to be to help the individual grow in the direction of optimum development in all aspects of his personality. This sometimes seems to imply that there are no external restraints. It may leave out of consideration the social aspects of development, placing emphasis upon the individual and his autonomy in opposition to outside pressures for conformity. Individual growth and self-actualization as the goal of counseling may be questioned, however. While "counseling may be thought of as a method of freeing individuals from their limitations and thus facilitating their development . . . such counseling is not an instrumentality for growth through demolishing all barriers restricting free development in any and all directions, irresponsibly and without regard for the development of others." [46] One may question the assumption that "any and all forms of growth contain within themselves their own, and sufficient, justification," and ask, "Do we believe that the fullest growth of one individual inevitably enhances the fullest growth of all other individuals?" [47] Thus, "absolutistic and autonomous self-direction," or autonomous individualism, cannot be accepted as the goal of counseling. The belief may be questioned that it is "basically evil, immoral, and undemocratic to interfere in any way with what many conceive to be the individual's basic freedom to become himself without proscriptions." [48] And the "implicit assumption that the 'best' potentiality will be actualized under optimum counseling relationships" [49] may be questioned.

The problem of the individual and society is thus raised. The goals of counseling cannot be limited to the individual or his self-actualization, since the result may be a self-centered person with little concern for others. The counselor must therefore be concerned with society in order to guard against the development of extreme or isolated individualism and antisocial individuality. While self-understanding and self-direction are desirable, it must be "socially enlightened self-understanding and self-direction." [50]

Since human nature is potentially both good and evil, "it is the purpose of education in Western society to actualize the good and to minimize the evil in man's potentiality. . . . I believe that an educator could readily support the hypothesis, if not the conclusion, that man is not capable of developing his full potentiality alone and without much assistance. Indeed, in all human societies, education is a necessary means to helping him actualize himself fully, as is counseling within education. That is, civilization and society are necessary to full self-actualization and counseling within education is one of many means to that end goal." [51] Since the individual does not possess "full and adequate resources within himself . . . he needs help from the outside, not only to release his own growth potential, but as much to add to the dimensions of that potential." [52] The counselor must therefore assume a responsibility to assist the client to develop his full or best potentiality: "the art of counseling, within Western education, is the forging of effective ways of helping students to become what they ought to want to become—their best possible selves—without violating their moral right of self-determination in choosing their own life goals." [53]

Counselors thus have a role in determining the good life for their counselees. "Surely one need not document the hypothesis that *some forms of becoming are more worthwhile than are others.*"[54] "The function of counseling is aiding students to desire to strive to achieve full human potentiality." [55] Since excellence is an attribute of the good life, "the purpose of counseling is held to be a means of facilitation of human development identified with the standard of excellence in all aspects of living." [56]

2   Counseling, like education, assumes the uniqueness of individuality. But this should not mean atomistic individuals. Individuals are interdependent; group membership is necessary for the development of uniqueness. "Individuality comes to fruition *only within the context of relationships with other individuals.*" [57]

3   Counseling, as generally defined, assumes "the desirability, if not the necessity, of the voluntary or self-chosen counseling relationship as opposed to 'required' counseling." [58] But this, like all generalizations, should be limited. The counselor has the responsibility to motivate those students whose need, and even desire, for counseling lead them to resist it. "My own counseling experience, especially with disciplinary cases, leads me to believe that much effective counseling can be achieved even with reluctant or nonvoluntary clients." [59]

4   A related assumption states that counseling is only necessary when the student faces a problem that he cannot resolve by himself. Counseling is thus remedial. But counseling should also include those who may not be progressing in their development.

5   Another assumption is that the counseling relationship is neutral as regards value orientation and commitment, and that the counselor is nonevaluative. But the counselor who is concerned with the goals of counseling indicated above cannot remain neutral or

abstain from making judgments, even if he should desire to do so. He is influenced by his own values and those of society, as well as by the client's values. He must be concerned with the values of the society in which he lives and the values of the institution in which he works. Moreover, he has a professional obligation to be concerned with the values represented in the goals of counseling. As education is involved with the development of, and commitment to, values in students, so should the counselor, as a member of an educational institution as well as of society, be involved with this in his clients.[60]

Life is a search for a hierarchy of value commitments. Counseling theory "should order, and also give hierarchy to, the various values involved in human existence; but the hierarchy should be 'loose' impositions upon each student of the varied and various styles of living held to be the societal hierarchy of values," [61] within which the individual's moral right to choose is not unduly or unreasonably restricted. These values include reason, honorable conduct, cooperation, courage, independence, charity, generosity, sensitivity, constructive and benevolent attitudes, and a high level of aspiration for self-perfection.[62] Others, perhaps more general, include concern for others, the pursuit of excellence in all things, the sovereignty of rationality, and the search for full humanity.[63]

To the extent that he is committed to values and goals *"as an educator*, the counselor does indeed *sit in judgment*, in an evaluative mood. The very fact that he is operating within an educational institution would in itself indicate to the student that the counselor is on the side of full utilization of abilities." [64]

6   The assumption that "unconditional acceptance" of the counselee will lead to his developing his full potential, becoming a "fully functioning person," has been transposed from psychotherapy to counseling. Reasons for questioning this assumption have already been mentioned.

7   It has been assumed that counseling is concerned with the totality of human development. However, examination of counseling as it is practiced indicates that it is centered upon "whatever the student himself perceives as his problem," [65] and with such specific things as the choice of an adult career. Dimensions of personality such as taste, standards, human behavior, and logical and inductive thinking have not been given attention in the literature.

8   Whereas we have up to now focused largely upon a vocational choice, today, under the influence of Super, Tyler, and Roe this concept of counseling has been broadened to include the concern for vocational development through a series of life stages.

9   In part as a reaction against the formalism of the rationalist movement in education, other aspects of "full humanity" have been included in counseling. However, "in some circles counseling is restricted to psychotherapy with regard to technique and self-perception." [66]

10   But the objective of counseling does not end with accept-

ance and understanding of the self, with concern with feelings and emotions. "Man is, we now believe, a feeling individual . . . and helping clients 'feel good' is a basic goal of counseling. But for me, a most essential and distinctive feature of counseling is its problem-solving dimension with respect to objective difficulties in the external world and also with regard to associated, subjective, affect disturbances. In our culture, man not only is trying to 'feel good' but he also seeks to become and to maintain himself as a rational, problem-solving being." [67] Counseling is thus a "thinking" relationship, applying human reason to the problems of human development, although the methods for implementing counseling as an intellectual process as well as an affective relationship remain to be explored.

Emotions may interfere with rationality and may have to be dealt with before clear thinking is possible. But we must not stop counseling at this point: "Counseling really begins at the feeling state in which the person is able to use his rational powers in an effort to understand himself. . . . Perhaps some counselors are saying that affect is the thing that is wrong, fix it and the client is thereafter able to take care of himself. However, I think that one can read the history of human development, individual or collective, and arrive at a different formulation: namely, that while affect can get out of order, yet man is essentially trying to become a rational, problem-solving organism." [68] One of the value commitments of counselors, and one which clients should achieve through the counseling relationship, is the "sovereignty of reason." "May it not be true that in our understandable and sympathetic concern for the affective development of students and their healthy participation in activities that we have underemphasized things intellectual? I, for one, have found in the literature of counseling very, very little reference to the sovereignty of reason." [69]

11   The concept of insight as important in human development has been borrowed from psychotherapy. This assumption requires reexamination. "Is insight rational self-enlightenment, or is it self-perception as cognition, or is it a feeling of enlightenment? Or what is it?" [70]

12   We have taken for granted the concept of individuality and opportunity for full development of each individual. We must recognize that this is not reserved to a cultural elite, but is becoming universal, so that counseling for self-development is available to everyone.

13   It is sometimes assumed that everyone has a motivation toward optimum well-roundedness. But there is also a conflicting urge toward restriction of development to that which is maximally pleasurable or to activities that one performs well or best. We may thus be in danger of abandoning the concept of breadth in Western education and of developing narrowness and specialization. Counseling must be reexamined in the light of this conflict.

14   The assumption that each individual has a moral obligation to develop fully his potentiality "raises questions about whether individuals have a right not to choose to actualize their best potential-

ity." [71] Dewey stated that "if democracy has a moral and ideal meaning, it is that a social return be demanded from all and that opportunity for development of distinctive capacities be afforded to all." This assumption may not be "built into the universe." Education has had a societal obligation. "We now need to examine the related assumption that counseling as a part of education must not, therefore, be grounded upon a contrary and contravening assumption of utilization of the counseling relationship only for self-development in the narrow sense of the concept." [72]

15   Counseling seems to be premised on the concept of stable life development as an inner-to-outer unfolding of potentialities. While there is some evidence of stability and continuity once maturity is reached, an alternative formulation needs to be considered—that is, that the unfolding may not be smooth, but uneven, with new directions emerging from unknown potentials.

16   Perhaps the most important of all assumptions of counseling is the concept of human development as a purposive striving for *arete*, which "involves the overriding backdrop of 'standards' of development which are judged and evaluated not only in terms of what the student defines as his desired standard of living but also in terms of 'higher' standards which are characteristic of humanity in its full potential." [73]

17   A final basic assumption, implicit in prior assumptions, is respect for the worth and dignity of the student being counseled, based upon knowledge of the unending struggle of man to realize his full humanity. "It may very well be that the counselor has a promising and unique opportunity within the warm, friendly intimacy of the counseling relationship to accept the individual for what he is *potentially* worth, rather than for *what he actually is*," and "also in the hopeful expectation" that his student clientele "will want to become all that they can become, the 'best' of their potentialities." [74]

The Nature of Counseling

Counseling is perhaps implicitly defined in the discussion above. Williamson, however, has given many definitions of counseling, some of which may make the concept more explicit. "Counseling is one of the personalized and individualized processes designed to aid the individual to learn school subject matter, citizenship traits, social and personal values and habits, and all the other habits, skills, attitudes, and beliefs which go to make up a normally adjusting being. Broadly speaking, it is the function of counseling to assist the adolescent in high school and college to learn effective ways of identifying and then achieving desired and desirable goals, often in spite of certain obstacles to learning." [75] Later definitions recognize the aspect of the development of self-understanding and autonomy: "Counseling is an individualized, personalized, and permissive assistance in developing skill in attaining and re-attaining socially enlightened self-understanding and self-direction." [76] A somewhat later definition is as follows: "Counseling is a peculiar type of relatively short-term human relationship between a 'mentor' with some considerable experience in problems of human development and in ways of facilitating that development, on the one hand, and a learner, on the other hand, who faces certain clearly or dimly perceived difficulties in his efforts to achieve self-controlled and self-manipulated forward-moving development." [77] And later, referring to Wheelis' book *The Quest for Identity*, he suggests that "counseling is a way of facilitating man's quest for identity, his striving for self-understanding and the expression of his aspirations," and notes that "the counseling interview, generally rather than only in psychotherapy, is now perceived as a type of human relationship (warm, friendly, empathic), through which a person learns to perceive himself as he actually is and to live with and accept himself with all his faults and shortcomings as well as his positive capabilities and potentialities." [78]

The concept of counseling has thus been broadened from concern with specific problems or classes of problems, such as educational and vocational difficulties, to a concern with the total individual as a person facing the problem of discovering his identity and realizing his greatest potential in all areas of his life. This concept brings the vocational guidance and therapy emphases together.

The Minnesota approach is thus concerned with the total development of the individual so that he may function at his optimum potential. Educational and vocational development and adjustment or success are only aspects, though important aspects, of the total individual. This point of view is based on a philosophy of education that emphasizes concern with the total individual and with the development of values as well as of the intellect.

THE COUNSELING PROCESS

The development of the Minnesota approach in an educational setting has had an influence on the conception of the nature of the counseling process. The counselor is essentially a teacher. The curriculum is the client and

> his own style of living, his mistakes and his "correct" responses in relationships with others. . . . The interactions of the counselor and the counselee are, therefore, those of teacher and learner, and it is a highly personalized teaching and learning process. . . . The role of the counselor is clear, then—to teach or help the individual learn to understand and accept himself in terms of capabilities, aptitudes, and interests; to identify his own motivations and techniques of living; to appraise them in terms of their implications or consequences; and, when appropriate, to substitute more adequate behavior to achieve desired life satisfactions that the individual has set as his personal goal.[79]

The client's role is to learn how to understand himself and to use his intelligence, or rationality, to change or correct his responses in order to achieve a rational, satisfying life.

In a later publication, the teaching nature of counseling is expressed as follows:

> I have long held the conviction that one of the major functions of counseling, especially the counseling interview, is that of helping students to modify their subjective and often error-ridden skills in self-appraisal of potentialities, aspirations, and self-concept with the aid of the "scientific method" of fact identification. In a real sense, I see a parallel between methods of self-appraisal and the use of the counseling interview as a means of teaching students—Dewey's major emphasis on teaching the scientific method (not facts of sciences) of separating fact from nonfact via the subject matter of classrooms. In both situations, interview and classroom, we help students to learn scientific methods of discovering understanding and knowledge. In the one case, the interview, discovery of knowledge about the self is the subject matter and, in the other, we utilize the raw data of scientific observations about "natural" phenomena of nature.[80]

In a 1961 discussion of the uses of the counseling interview, Williamson lists four important uses.[81] The first three—the collection of necessary information about counselees, the appraisal of potentiality, and the remediation of problems—appear in earlier writings. The fourth is that of helping the individual to achieve his full potentiality in all areas, not only the vocational. Used for this purpose, the counseling interview is seen as a particular kind of interpersonal, or human, relationship which is a benign, benevolent caring for the individual. It is this kind of relationship that seems to motivate the individual to become himself in his full potentiality. Eight facets of this relationship are pointed out: (1) The counseling interview is individualized. (2) The one-to-one relationship is highly personalized. (3) It is a helping relationship, with the counselor caring about the student. (4) The relationship is developmental, with a forward thrust: it looks to the future. (5) The counseling interview is life-centered; that is, it is concentrated upon the individual's development in terms of his self-concept, or self-percept. (6) The interview has an affect context, having emotional elements that are not to be eliminated, but are to be used as energizing or motivating forces. (7) The counseling relationship stresses the dignity and worth of the individual as a person in his own right. Such an attitude motivates the client to develop his full potentiality. (8) The interview centers attention and effort on man's capacity to think, to solve his problems by rational means. "I like to think of the personal interview in counseling as an intellectual exercise in thinking about self problem-solving in a very profound sense. It is a thinking exercise, not merely an effort to get rid of today's problems but rather a high adventure in applying reason to one's self. Left to their own efforts, some students seldom seem to learn to reason about themselves."[82]

The counseling relationship is a close, highly personal, one-to-one relationship. "The counselor really 'cares' for the counselee in a personal way—to be sure, not as intimately and deeply as a parent cares for the personal development of a child, but nevertheless far more personally than we usually experience in the casual or day-to-day relationships of life." [83]

Counselors are "not in the business of aiding students to develop just any and all kinds of individuality for which they have potential . . . but are in the business of influencing students to develop in one direction rather than another." [84] In the area of values, "there are legitmate, proper, and sound ways for counselors to 'influence,' *but not to determine*, the value commitments adopted by students . . ." [85] The counselor cannot avoid introducing his own values, for they influence his reactions to the client's statements. The standards and values of society and of its institutions, such as the school, also enter into the interview through the counselor or the client. The counselor must be aware of these orientations. But clients also "need to learn to identify and understand the implications of their moral and ethical codes and other value orientations in order to act responsibly." [86] Values should not be imposed on clients, however, and the counselor must avoid conflict with the home and the church in this area. "A counselor may, as a teacher sometimes does, illustrate the range of possible value choices by explaining as objectively as possible his own, or others', value approach to life's questions." But

> in counseling about values, as in the case of vocational and educational counseling, we limit ourselves to helping a student understand the options open to him, one with his capabilities and responsibilities, and their implications for him. At that point, within the framework of institutional and societal responsibilities and limitations, the student is free to make his own choice from these or other options. . . . I have long held that the exercising of such a right [of free choice] does not preclude "direct" assistance from counselors, or anyone else, prior to and after choices have been made. . . . I have suggested that we accept the "teaching" of values as a function of counselors, but that we remain aware of the risk of imposing a set of values upon the student and thus depriving him of his right to and responsibility for self-determination.[87]

This procedure with respect to values is similar, then, to the procedure used in other areas of counseling, such as educational and vocational choice.

The concept of counseling as the application of science or of objective facts or knowledge to the problems of the individual thus influences the nature of the counseling process or relationship. The democratic principle of freedom of choice is respected, but the counselor has an obligation to assist the student or client in making the best choices. For example, he supplies information that is lacking. If he accepts the value of objective tests, then he must utilize the results in counseling and see that the client has these data available to him. Paterson thus states that "the newer method of guidance is based upon the assumption that students are often unable to diagnose their own aptitudes and interests and that, therefore, they need the assistance of a trained diagnostician." [88] Williamson and Darley write that "the identification of the complex factors entering into students' choices and the judicious interpretation of their significance are a task in logic and psychology often involved and difficult even for a seasoned adult. . . . Self analysis, still widely used under one disguise or another, is not a dependable analytic tool in diagnosis, however useful it may be in treatment or counseling." [89] Williamson later states that "much advising is based upon the assumption that students are able to diagnose and understand their own needs and aptitudes. . . . If students were able to understand themselves, there would be little need for counselors except as dispensers of information and as sympathetic listeners." [90]

In discussing the uses of the interview, Williamson lists as one use the appraisal of potentiality. He says: "We help the individual appraise himself *in comparison with external requirements,* whether they be school, vocational, or societal. Thus we help him to 'measure' himself against the requirements of the external society." The counselor may add his own appraisal. "The appraisal of the individual student in terms of the information given or collected before and during the interview would seem to me to be a most significant contribution on the part of the counselor to the counselee's approximation to full understanding. For counselors, as external observers, to reflect what we think a student is, *phrased as a tentative hypothesis,* seems to me to be one of our major contributions in aiding the student." [91]

The counselor is thus engaged in an influencing process, but the process is one in which the counselor assists the client in making decisions, or choices, or developing a system of values, without pressure on the client or denial of his right to self-determination. If there are affective elements present, these are dealt with, but this is not the end of counseling. There is an extension of counseling with a rational problem-solving approach to the specific problems with which the client is faced.

With this general description of the counseling process as background, we now turn to a more detailed consideration of the phases, or steps, in the counseling process.

In 1937 Williamson and Darley listed six steps in the clinical counseling process.[92] They were repeated by Williamson in his 1939 book and again in the 1950 revision. These steps are (1) analysis, (2) synthesis, (3) diagnosis, (4) prognosis, (5) counseling (or treatment), and (6) follow-up. Although one of the steps is designated specifically as counseling, it appears that the others are all part of the counseling process as broadly conceived.

The logical nature of the progression of the steps is apparent. The analogy to the science and practice of medicine is also obvious.

Williamson and Darley's 1937 publication, however, contains a section discussing this analogy which does not appear in the later publications.[93]

Our discussion will follow the lines of the 1950 statement describing the six steps in the work of the clinical counselor. It is pointed out that in actual clinical practice, the counselor "uses a flexible procedure rather than adhering rigidly to a sequence of procedures." [94] The sequence may not follow the exact order listed; there may be overlaps and reversals. The counselor "may be counseling a student's emotional problems at the same time he is diagnosing a vocational problem." [95] Each step is incomplete by itself and depends upon others. Moreover, each step is a tentative formulation, "subject to the validity test of the individual's own experiences; i.e., ultimately the validity of all diagnosis is to be found in the individual's subsequent experiences." [96]

Williamson refers to the kind of counseling with which he is concerned, which includes the six steps listed above, as being "derived from a clinical methodology of a more *scientific* rather than a *curative* type of counseling. Essentially we are beginning to see that the two systems are designed to be appropriate and effective with different types of problems." [97] In curative, or therapeutic, counseling, where the goal is to lead the client to obtain insight into and understanding of himself, these six steps may not be necessary. The counselor or therapist may achieve his goal by being warm and accepting and by reflecting and clarifying the client's attitudes. He may not need to interpret, make suggestions, or reason with the client. The client may have the capacity to resolve his own problems under such conditions. The counselor's role is mainly one of permissiveness and passivity. It may not be necessary for the counselor to diagnose or understand the causes of the client's difficulty.[98]

The second, or scientific, approach "assigns to both counselor and counselee the role of a learner, a role of collecting, sifting, evaluating, and classifying relevant facts to arrive at a description (or an approximate description) which will provide *both* with 'insight' or perception of the nature and circumstances of the condition concerning which the client needs counseling." [99]

In this approach "the client takes full responsibility for participating in *learning about himself* with the counselor performing the secondary role of a 'teaching assistant' who aids in the learning process of the client-pupil. . . . In this second approach we find a congenial place for all those sciences and educational practices which give student and counselor more accurate and more precise self-understanding." [100]

The first four steps of the counseling process are intended essentially to prepare for the counseling interviews, or treatment, although the interview itself may be employed here too. Also, counseling may proceed in relation to some problems at the same time that analysis or diagnosis may be occurring in relation to other problems. "Much more time is required to prepare adequately for counseling than to discharge the counseling process itself." [101]

Analysis

The purpose of analysis is "to acquire an understanding of the student in relation to the known requirements of his present and future adjustments." [102] Analysis consists of the collection of information and data about the student or counselee. "Before a student can be effectively counseled, the student and counselor must collect *dependable*, i.e., reliable, valid, and relevant information, from which to diagnose aptitudes, interests, motives, physical health, emotional balance, and other characteristics which facilitate or inhibit satisfactory adjustment in school and at work." [103]

Six general analytical tools are (1) cumulative records, (2) the interview, (3) the time distribution form, (4) the autobiography, (5) the anecdotal record, and (6) psychological tests. The case study as an analytical tool is a method of integrating all the data and consists of a comprehensive record including family history, health history, educational history, vocational and work history, and social-recreational interests and habits.

As many data as possible are collected before the interview. "A trained counselor does not rely solely upon the impressions resulting from a short interview with a student." [104] Nor should the interview be

> misused to collect routine information which may make the student restless and reluctant to return for counseling. To avoid this danger, especially in the case of educational and vocational counseling, many counselors request that students fill out check lists and case history forms before appearing for an interview. These forms may provide the counselor with data regarding the student's background and also with an insight into his frame of mind and what he thinks are his problems and their causes. By inspecting such data before seeing the student, the counselor can gain better understanding of the student's psychology and, therefore, begin his interviewing at the point of the student's own thinking." [105]

Thus, while objective data about the student are gathered, the counselor is concerned with the student's ideas and attitudes. "The manner in which the student approaches his problems not only reveals his life style, but also determines his reactions to the analysis and diagnosis. These attitudes of the student toward his own problems and toward ways and means of achieving optimum adjustment constitute one of the most important of all analytical data." [106]

The importance of these data is their bearing on the cooperation of the student. "If the student possesses cooperative attitudes, then he may work with the counselor." [107] The student's attitudes also indicate to the counselor his beliefs and knowledge about counseling. "Then the counselor stimulates a discussion-exposition of the evidence for and against the student's beliefs and a comparison of the student's beliefs with the principles and procedures of clinical work. . . . One of the tasks of the personnel worker is to change the student's expectancy of magic into an appreciation of the complexity and clinical nature of counseling procedures." [108]

The purpose, therefore, of understanding the student's attitudes and beliefs is to enable the counselor to correct misconceptions by the way in which he structures the interview. But the counselor should do more than this. He should engage in an analysis with the student in which he attempts to correct the tendency of students and their parents to give

> equal weight to irrational attitudes and desires as compared with more dependable techniques of analysis. Many students believe that their "liking" for a vocation and their "conviction" of aptitude for that vocation are equal in weight to more objective evidence as indicators of the possession of aptitude. . . . His desires for success are thought to be evidence of aptitude equal in importance to, or more important than, an actual tryout or measurement of aptitude. Many students believe that they can go into a "Buddhistic huddle" with themselves and, by a process of psychological legerdemain and irrational thinking, wipe out lack of aptitude, thus becoming qualified for a desired goal. . . . Thus we see that the counselor needs to explain to the student the rules of evidence—that certain things are admissible as evidence of aptitudes, e.g., that desires for success alone are not evidence of aptitude. . . . He must first devote time to explaining . . . the logic of choosing a vocation. This logical process involves collecting, reviewing, evaluating, rejecting and accepting the evidence of experience, school grades, psychological tests, and other data.[109]

Williamson concludes that "these analytical procedures are indispensable if the counselor and the student are to arrive at a diagnosis of the student and if counseling is to result in appropriate and satisfying adjustment." [110]

Synthesis

While synthesis is retained in Williamson's 1939 and 1950 presentations as the second step in the process, it is not given any more attention than to be defined as "the summarizing and organizing of the data from the analysis in such a manner as to reveal the student's assets, liabilities, adjustments, and maladjustments." [111] Not much more space was given to this step by Williamson and Darley in 1937.[112]

Synthesis appears to be essentially the ordering and arranging of the data obtained in analysis to make them more useful for the next step, diagnosis.

Diagnosis

"Diagnosis is only one of several parts of guidance; but it is the necessary first step." [113] The collection and synthesis of data provide the material for diagnosis. Diagnosis is the finding of consistencies and patterns leading to "a terse summary of problems, their causes, and other significant and relevant characteristics of the student, together with the implications for potential adjustments and maladjustments." [114] Diagnosis consists of the interpretation of the data in terms of the problems indicated and of the assets and liabilities, the strengths and weaknesses of the student. It is arrived at by a process of logic involving inference, and is thus the opposite of analysis. But it is a clinical process, although results of personnel research and experiment are used. The application of results such as those of prediction studies to the individual student is a clinical process. The clinical method weighs, integrates, and synthesizes all the data into a judgment, or diagnosis, specific to the individual.

Diagnosing involves three major steps. The first is the identification of the problem. This is descriptive in nature and not just the application of a label. Nevertheless, diagnostic categories, such as those of Bordin or of Pepinsky, may be useful. Bordin's diagnostic categories are five in number: (1) dependence, (2) lack of information, (3) self-conflict, (4) choice anxiety, (5) no problems.[115] Pepinsky proposes the following five: (1) lack of assurance, (2) lack of information, (3) lack of skill, (4) dependence, (5) self-conflict.[116]

The second step is discovering the causes. This involves a search for relationships, past, present, and potential, that may lead to an understanding of the causes of the symptoms. When there is little or no scientific research or knowledge relating symptoms to causes, the counselor "falls back upon hunches and intuition, which is another way of saying that he makes the shrewdest guess possible as to the causes and then checks himself by logic, by the student's reactions, and by the tryout of a program of action based upon the assumed diagnosis." [117] Logic may also be used in arriving at causes, but care must be taken to distinguish between causality and simple association.

The third step is prognosis. While Williamson indicates that this is an element in all diagnoses, he also states that diagnosis and prognosis are separate steps in clinical work particularly where there is no prior research or experience to indicate the outcome of a problem or condition. When the outcome is known, the prognosis is incorporated into the diagnosis; for example, a diagnosis of "low intelligence" becomes "too low for difficult school work," or "almost certain failure will result if this student tries to become a doctor as he now desires to do." [118] The diagnosis and prognosis are both relevant to the goals that the student is attempting to achieve. The possibility and ease of change are taken into account in the prognosis. While diagnosis relates to the past and the present, prognosis is concerned with the future and is therefore a prediction.

Caution must be used in diagnosing, and the counselor should not jump to conclusions. Nevertheless, "no counselor should fail to make a diagnosis simply because of lack of certainty. All sciences and professions make progress only by trying out hypotheses, hunches, and predictions to see if they work and why they fail to be correct." [119] Diagnoses are always provisional and may be modified or rejected during counseling, with new ones being formulated and again tested in counseling.

Since human behavior is complex, a detailed diagnosis may not be possible, and basic causes of problems may not be apparent. "Therefore, the counselor should not be distressed, *provided the client really achieves satisfactory adjustment,* when he closes the case with less than complete diagnostic understanding. But for the sake of future studies of the effectiveness of therapy, he should formulate a diagnosis to the best of his ability with the facts made known to him by the client." [120]

The counselor should test the validity of his diagnoses, using the methods suggested above in the discussion of discovering causes. He may apply the criterion of consistency, or congruence to the case data. He may check with other counselors, individually or in staff clinics. The enthusiastic cooperation of the student in carrying out a program of action is perhaps the most effective check on the validity of the diagnosis. On the other hand, "the counselor should not expect students always or readily to agree with his diagnosis of their problems." [121] A final method of checking the diagnosis is to determine whether counseling is effective. But it must be recognized that in many cases the nature of the problem and other conditions make success in counseling impossible, although the diagnosis may be correct.

While diagnosis is primarily an activity of the counselor, he does not work alone. Diagnosing is *"a cooperative undertaking with the student taking major responsibility in the understanding of himself insofar as he is intellectually able and emotionally willing to do so."* [122] When the student is unable to do this, the counselor assumes the major responsibility while assisting the student to reach the stage of taking the responsibility himself.

Counseling

Counseling is that part of personnel work in which a counselor helps the client to marshal his own resources, the resources of an institution and of the community, to assist the client to achieve the optimum adjustment of which he is capable . . . the term covers first of all a relationship which might be referred to as guided learning toward self-understanding. . . . Second, counseling covers certain kinds of re-education or relearnings which the individual desires and needs as means to his life adjustments and personal obejctives. . . . Third, counseling may involve the counselor's personalized assistance to the counselee in understanding and becoming skilled in the application of the principles and techniques of general semantics to his daily living. In the fourth instance, the term is used to cover a repertoire of techniques and relationships which are therapeutic or curative in their effects. . . . In a fifth type of counseling, some form of re-education does follow therapeutically induced catharsis.[123]

Williamson was, in the early part of his career, concerned mainly with the first three types of counseling. According to this point of view, counseling, while it is the treatment aspect or phase of the total process, is not limited to, or the same as, psychotherapy. It is, as was pointed out earlier, a teaching-learning, or educational relationship. Counseling as "*a generalized method of learning to deal with all kinds of situations*" [124] attempts to apply the cause-and-effect method of analysis to all phases of life and behavior. The definitions of counseling quoted above are essentially consistent with the earlier 1950 definition. However, more attention is given in the later statement to the fourth type, therapeutic counseling, especially as a preliminary of the fifth type.

The purpose of counseling is "to aid the individual to formulate and answer the following questions about himself:

"How did I get this way—what factors caused this behavior?

"What will *probably* be the future developments if this present situation continues?

"What alternative actions or modifications could be produced and by what means?

"How can I effectively upset the above predictions? How can I produce desirable changes in my behavior?" [125]

Counseling is thus more than therapy—it is "a generalized method of life adjustments." [126] It is an attempt to assist students to "become prepared to solve their adjustment situations *before* they become so involved with self-conflicts and evaluations that deep and complicated therapy is needed." [127]

Follow-up

Follow-up "includes what the clinician does to assist the students with new problems, with recurrences of the original problems, and what is done to determine the effectiveness of counseling." [128] This step in the counseling process receives no extended treatment by Williamson.

IMPLEMENTATION AND TECHNIQUES

Five categories of counseling techniques are proposed in the 1950 book: (1) forcing conformity, (2) changing the environment, (3) selecting the appropriate environment, (4) learning needed skills, and (5) changing attitudes. After defining these five kinds of techniques, however, Williamson proceeds to a discussion of particular techniques without regard to their classification. The techniques considered are limited to those that are used in the counseling interview.

Since counseling is regarded as broader than psychotherapy (that is, it is not confined to evaluational and conflict types of adjustment), it includes a wider variety of techniques than does psychotherapy. It embraces "a wide variety of specific techniques, from which repertoire the effective counselor selects, *for his part in counseling,* those which are relevant and appropriate to the nature of the client's problem and to other features of the situation." [129]

The concern with individual differences manifests itself in the techniques of counseling. Williamson states that "there are no techniques appropriate to the counseling of all students," so that no text can give "full directions for counseling a particular case." [130] "*The counselor's techniques must be adapted to the individuality of the students.* There is no standard technique of advising appropriate to *all* students . . . . We cannot ignore the fact that each student's problems demand flexibility and variation in our attempts at counseling." [131]

Techniques are thus specific to individuals and problems. "Each technique is applicable only to particular problems and particular students. There are no general techniques, but rather particularized techniques to be used *only* if the student has a problem for which those procedures are appropriate. . . . Techniques are specific to different problems and to different students. The effective counselor avoids indiscriminate counseling. Rather, the counselor adapts his specific techniques to the individuality and problem pattern of the student, making the necessary modifications to produce the desired result for a particular student." [132]

Techniques of counseling are discussed under five headings:

1. *Establishing rapport*   Certain factors provide a foundation for rapport. These include the counselor's deserved reputation for competence, respect for individuality, and the keeping of confidences, and his treatment of the student prior to the counseling interview.

When the student enters the office, "the first thing to do is to put him at ease by greeting him cordially *by name,* shaking hands, and avoiding any semblance of impatience or ill humor." [133] Personal attention and understanding are important. With many students the interview should begin with casual conversation concerning the student's known interests and activities. With other students a more direct, open approach is effective. Flexibility of techniques is desirable. The student should be put at ease, and the counselor must be careful to keep him at ease. In a later publication Williamson indicates that the counselor should be kindly but not obsequious in his manner; he is friendly, warm, and treats the student as an equal.[134]

2. *Cultivating self-understanding*   The student must have an understanding of his assets and liabilities, and must be helped to want to utilize his assets and to overcome his liabilities. This requires that

the counselor interpret data such as test scores in a simple yet professional way. The use of technical terms such as "percentile rank" and the showing of test profiles to the student should be avoided. Low scores may be passed over.

In interpreting and translating the diagnosis and in explaining the evidence leading to the diagnosis, the counselor must make certain, as he proceeds, that the student is following him in the marshaling of the evidence leading to the diagnosis. The counselor proceeds no more rapidly in his explanation than the student can follow. The counselor does not enumerate in detail all the steps in his own diagnosing, nor does he touch upon all the evidence. He telescopes his thinking, presenting only that evidence that appears to be relevant to the diagnosis and to the desirable programs of action. This means that he mentions facts that point to, or from which he infers, his diagnosis and mentions, for purposes of persuasion, those liabilities that rule out certain lines of action.[135]

3 *Advising or planning a program of action* The counselor begins with the student's choice, goal, point of view, or attitude and then points out the favorable and unfavorable data from the diagnosis, marshaling the evidence both for and against it. He then weighs the evidence and explains why he advises the student as he does. The student should be ready to recognize and accept the advice because he has been prepared for it by the counselor's presentation of the data and the evidence.

This process may require more than one interview, particularly with those students who have emotional attitudes and reactions to their aptitudes. "Indeed, if a student with a problem of choosing an occupation still hesitates to make a choice after the counselor has interpreted the case data, then the counselor may suspect that emotional blockings are at the base of the vocational problem. These conflicts must then be cleared up before the student can be counseled effectively regarding his choice of an occupation." [136]

The counselor should "state his point of view with *definiteness,* attempting through *exposition* to enlighten the student." [137] If the student seems unwilling to go along, he may be told to think it over and return later. The counselor avoids being dogmatic, but he should not appear indecisive, since this may lead to the student's losing confidence in the validity of the information. He must maintain a balance between definiteness and open-mindedness.

The counselor works cooperatively with the student. While he accepts the suggestibility of the student as the basis for rapport, he does not misuse this suggestibility; he avoids allowing his prestige and the student's blind faith in tests to lead the student to accept his advice without critical review of the evidence. The counselor recognizes that advice is tentative, being based upon limited data, and encourages the student to try out his own ideas as well as those of the counselor, even though they may be inconsistent with the diagnosis.

The counselor is not afraid of direct advising, since he realizes that the student often is not able to recognize the implications of the data, or may be unwilling to recognize them. There are three methods that the counselor may use in advising a student after the presentation of the data.

In *direct advising* the counselor—openly and frankly—states his own opinion. This approach may be used with tough-minded students who ask for a frank opinion and with students who persist in an activity or choice that the counselor believes will lead to serious failure.

The *persuasive method* is useful when the data clearly indicate a definite choice. The counselor marshals the evidence reasonably and logically to lead the student to see the outcomes of alternative actions.

The *explanatory method* is the most desirable and satisfactory method of counseling. The counselor carefully and slowly explains the diagnostic data and points out possible situations that will utilize the student's potentialities. It is a careful and detailed reasoning of the implications of the data.

4 *Carrying out the plan*   Following the student's choice or decision, the counselor may provide direct assistance in its implementation. This may include either remedial work or planning a program of education or training.

5 *Referral to other personnel workers*   Since no counselor is qualified to work with a student in all areas, he must recognize his limitations, know the sources of specialized help, and make referrals to these sources.

Williamson's later writings appear to be essentially consistent with the 1950 formulation, though there seems to have been a change away from persuasion and logical reasoning toward less directive methods. There is still the distinction between the two kinds of counseling, the vocational and the psychotherapeutic.[138] Psychotherapeutic counseling, utilizing catharsis and insight, leads to ego integration, removal of repressed self-conflicts that prevent growth or lead to maladaptive growth, and self-understanding.[139] Such "relationship therapy" may be needed before the client can face his problems clearheadedly.[140]

But self-understanding is not enough. The counselor must go beyond this to assist the client in resolving the practical problems that face him. In this process the counselor is essentially a teacher; in using problem-solving methods in counseling, he is teaching the student the nature and use of this approach in relation to his problems. Sometimes this may be direct teaching, using explanations, suggestions of possible hypotheses, and assistance in searching for facts. At other times it may consist of listening. But there is no exhortation, propaganda, or persuasion.[141] Particularly in the area of values, while the counselor may be tempted to use logical argument,

> the most effective and acceptable counseling method aids students in applying to the problem of values those techniques,

analyses, clarification, and understanding which we hope they will habitually apply to the solution of other developmental problems. That is, the counselor helps the individual to use his intellect and his emotions to analyze his developmental situation and to identify the pivotal point of the issue—in this case, values as sources of behavior motivation and determination. Then the counselor, as teacher, helps the counselee to identify and to evaluate alternative value systems and to examine the consequences of alternative answers to moral and ethical questions. The counselor's role as teacher is thus emphasized, as is the student's role as one who explores issues, chooses, and acts upon values, and subsequently experiences the consequences of his choices.[142]

In an article entitled "The Counselor As Technique," Williamson suggests that the counselor is an available role model for youth to consider. As a possible model, the counselor should express his philosophy of human development—a hopeful, optimistic one—in his behavior. His behavior should exemplify reason and intellect—"those academic virtues that symbolize personal commitment to the high mission of educating youth"—and should indicate that he is carrying on his own independent intellectual life, that he is a "broadly informed and cultivated educator" as well as competent in his own field. In the counseling interview, too, he should exemplify "the relevancy of research design and rigorous thinking to the student's efforts at full self-understanding." [143]

The use of intellectual analysis and reason, however, is not on a formal, impersonal basis. As was indicated earlier, the counselor is warm, friendly, and genuinely interested in and caring for the client, and the relationship is a close, personal, human relationship. The Minnesota approach is thus not a one-sided approach, impersonal, coldly logical, in which the client's feelings and emotions are ignored. While it makes a distinction between psychotherapy and counseling, the latter is also an affective relationship; the importance of affective, or emotional, elements in the external problems facing the client are recognized.

EXAMPLES

The following are transcriptions of two interviews with a student referred to the University of Minnesota Counseling Bureau "apparently for thorough discussion of his problem." He was on academic probation. Both interviews were conducted prior to testing, and thus do not illustrate the discussion of test results and the conclusion of counseling. These are the only transcriptions of interviews included in Williamson's publications, however. The interviews were conducted by a staff member of the Counseling Bureau. Williamson points out that staff members are encouraged to develop their own styles and points of view, as well as techniques, and that the interviews were not selected to represent any particular point of view.[144] He continues: "Certainly there is no indication that they are representative of the so-called 'Minnesota point of view' and they are certainly not representative of my point of view." In a later statement, however, in response to a request for suggestions of other materials illustrating his point of view, Williamson writes, "I believe that essentially the published interviews in my book represent reasonably well my approach, as you refer to it, and certainly represent in general terms as much as any single case can the generalized approach of our contingent on the campus.[145]

Other published transcriptions of interviews representing a point of view similar to Williamson's will be found in *A Casebook of Counseling*.[146]

Initial Interview [147]

STUDENT   I talked with Dean Peterson, and he said I should come and talk to you . . . uh . . . I want to try and find out what I could do to increase my . . . I mean improve my record . . . and I'd like to have some advice. . .

COUNSELOR   You mean you're having trouble . . . with . . . studying?

ST   Yes . . . with my school exams . . .

CO   Uh-huh. What seems to be the trouble . . . can you . . .

ST   Well, uh . . .

CO   Tell me a little about it?

ST   I don't know . . . it seems . . . I . . . study . . . I mean . . . I . . . do enough studying . . . can't seem to uh . . . make the grades . . .

CO   Uh-huh.

ST   Well, I have one difficulty in spelling . . . I'm trying to overcome that . . . taking the spelling lab . . . this quarter . . .

CO   Uh-huh.

ST   And see if that will improve it . . . affect it any . . .

CO   You don't think it's the time then . . . you think you're studying enough . . .

ST   I think I'm studying enough, yes . . . uh-huh . . . (pause) But uh . . . I don't know if it's my study . . . the way I study . . . or what it is . . .

CO   Uh-huh. Do you think you do a pretty good job of studying when you are studying with time limits?

ST   Well, it seems to me . . . I don't know I . . . try to, but . . . just doesn't seem to uh . . . comprehend too much . . .

CO   Do you have some trouble understanding what you read?

ST   Yes, uh-huh, (long pause)

CO   How about your reading uh . . . from when you first learned how to read . . . and so on . . . have you uh . . .

ST   Well, uh . . .

CO   Been able to comprehend right along?

ST   Well, not too much . . . I took . . . reading lab last quarter, too . . . I'm . . . I'm . . . always a slow reader . . .

CO   You are very slow?

ST   Uh-huh. Then I took this reading lab fall and winter quarters. I think that . . . helped me a lot.

CO   You're talking about the reading lab over in the rhetoric uh . . .

ST   Yes.

CO   Courses on the Ag Campus?

ST   On the Ag Campus, yes.

CO   Do you think anything happened there much that . . . that has helped you?

ST   Well, I . . . I can read a little faster now . . . and I seem to comprehend . . .

CO   Uh-huh. You're not quite satisfied still . . . with the way you do.

ST   That's right.

CO   Uh-huh. Sometimes a problem like that is of long standing and you can't hope to build yourself up in a very short time . . . when it is something that has been building up all through your school years. (long pause) Sometimes it's related to other things also . . . I mean it might not be just reading difficulty . . . it might be a lack of interest in your subject . . .

ST   Well, that might be . . . because like . . . now chemistry is giving me a hard time. Then there is uh . . . well, I don't know . . . it shouldn't, like some subjects, like in animal subjects . . . animal husbandry . . . subjects and on the Main Campus I should be interested in those . . .

CO   You just find that they aren't as interesting as you . . .

ST   That's right . . .

CO   As you think they should be (long pause) Did uh . . . Mr. Peterson tell you anything about what we might do here? What we might talk about?

ST   No, he didn't. He said I should come over and talk to you . . .

CO   Uh-huh. There are several possibilities . . . what we might do . . . one might be to take some tests . . . uh . . . you've probably had quite a few reading tests . . . if you've been taking some of that work. It might be that other tests, not just reading tests, would give us a picture there. For example, an interest test. (pause) Have you ever had anything like that?

ST   Uh . . . these uh . . . aptitude tests uh . . . and . . . are those in the same order or . . .

CO   Uh, yes. Some of them would be what I'm talking about . . .

ST   I . . . took those in my senior year in high school.

CO   Did you?

ST   Uh-huh.

CO   Was that an interest test? (pause)

ST   I don't know. I can't recall what they . . . they called it . . . an interest test or what it was . . .

co   Uh-huh. (pause) We give many different kinds of tests . . . and they are sometimes lumped together and called aptitude tests . . .

st   Oh, I see.

co   But each one might really be telling you something different about yourself.

st   Uh-huh.

co   One might give you an idea of your general ability to handle college work, and another might give you an idea of your background in math and science . . . (pause) . . . and it would be then a combination . . . of all those that might be considered aptitude. Have you ever seen any test results for yourself?

st   I uh . . . not . . . I haven't seen the results . . . I think my IQ is . . . it's pretty low . . . let's see, I talked to my high school superintendent. I think he said it was 98 . . . I think it was.

co   When was that?

st   That was my senior . . . uh . . . senior or sophomore year I took this aptitude . . .

co   Uh-huh.

st   I mean, I've . . . that doesn't mean too much . . . does it?

co   You mean does that have any bearing on college?

st   Yes, and is it . . .

co   Well, we don't usually talk too much about IQ in terms of college work. We have some other tests that are designed to give you an idea of where you rank with college students . . . and they would perhaps be better. You've never seen how you came out on anything like that?

st   No, I haven't.

co   Would you like to look at your results? I think I have some here for you.

st   I . . . I would.

co   Do you remember taking that science test and the algebra test last September when you entered?

st   Uh-huh. Yes, I do . . .

co   Those results might be the kind of thing that we're talking about. (pause) Here they are on the sheet here . . .

st   Uh-huh.

co   In this column it indicates where you ranked . . . on a percentage basis . . . compared to entering agriculture freshmen. This number places you on a rank on a scale from 1 to 100.

st   Uh-huh.

co   If you were then at the 50 on that, that would mean that you were right at the average.

st   Uh-huh . . . (pause) So I'm below average . . .

co   The ranking there would be below average. (pause) Those tests, by the way, have been given to quite a few students over the years in that college and they have an idea of how you might be able to handle the work in that college from how you do on these tests.

st   Uh-huh.

CO   Scores . . uh . . . (pause) . . . like this would be the kind of scores . . . that persons make who have difficulty in making a satisfactory record . . . in that college. (long pause—client sighs toward the end of pause)

ST   The answer, I mean, I always did have a hard time and it was through my high school and . . .

CO   Uh-huh. Do you find that you have that same sort of trouble in your college chemistry?

ST   Yes, I think I do.

ST   Uh, huh. (long pause) Uh . . . do you think that's because of the background . . . that I didn't have too uh . . . good a background in those subjects?

CO   Well, yes. Either that or you didn't master it well . . .

ST   Uh huh.

CO   There are those two possibilities (pause). You know there are all kinds of abilities and academic ability is just one kind of ability. It might be that you don't stand too well in that kind of ability. It may be that there are others for you. What sort of things do you think that you can do well?

ST   You mean in subjects?

CO   Or anything.

ST   (Pause) Well, I don't know. (pause) I don't believe I understand what you mean.

CO   That's kind of a hard question to answer. (pause) What I mean is are there things that you like to do better than school work or that you feel that you do better than school work?

ST   Well, I mean there isn't much else . . . I mean, there's . . . I've lived on the farm all the time . . .

CO   Uh-huh. Do you like that kind of work?

ST   Oh, yes . . . (pause) that's about the only work I ever did . . . I mean, it's in fact, I know I like that . . .

CO   Uh-huh. What did you do?

ST   Oh . . . just general farm work uh . . . all around the farm.

CO   Like any of it better than any other part?

ST   Oh, the machinery part I like better . . . tractors . . .

CO   Did a lot of work on tractors?

ST   Oh, yes, I have . . . (long pause)

CO   That's an example of a kind of ability that's different from school work ability . . . mechanical skill . . .

ST   Uh-huh.

CO   Working with machines and understanding them . . . it seems to be a very different kind of ability from academic or scholastic or college ability, we might say. (pause) Have you ever considered going into some kind of work that involves that sort of skill?

ST   Well, like uh . . . certain mechanical work?

CO   Uh-huh.

ST   I was . . . I uh . . . I haven't thought much about that but . . .
like going to Dunwoody and taking up some mechanical courses . . .
a person could do that . . .

CO   You haven't considered it for yourself?

ST   No, I haven't like . . . I mean, I haven't written in there and asked
for their bulletin or anything . . .

CO   Uh-huh. We have some tests here for that purpose too, tests that
would give you a little better idea, maybe, of where you stand in that
kind of aptitude or skill. They would be different from this kind of test
that you've taken before. (pause) It might possibly be that you would
like to do something on that order just to see where you stand and
explore alternatives . . .

ST   Uh-huh.

CO   To the course that you're in now . . .(pause)

ST   I could do that . . . I might find this course I'm taking now . . .
it's too hard . . . (laughs)

CO   You're beginning to think that . . . that it may be too rough for
you . . .

ST   Yeah . . . I think so . . . (pause) I mean, I think I'll uh . . .
transfer to something else . . . after the spring quarter is over . . .

CO   What is your official status with the college now?

ST   You mean my . . . honor point ratio? That's a .56 and I haven't
raised it any . . .

CO   Does that mean that you're on probation?

ST   Yes, uh-huh. (long pause)

CO   Have you talked over any other possibilities with Mr. Peterson or
anybody?

ST   No, I haven't . . . no, I just saw him that one day and he said I
should have an appointment up here. (pause)

CO   Well, what we sometimes do is, as I said, start out with a kind of
test and then by talking with you about what alternatives look possible
to you, then sometimes we can reach an answer on the thing as to what
possibility would be best. (pause) You said that you had started thinking about transferring to something else . . . what things have you
considered?

ST   Well, uh . . . either . . . go to Dunwoody or else . . . uh . . . I've
talked to one of the students . . . his . . . his roommate . . . he took
up mortuary science and I . . . I just had those two things in mind . . .

CO   You haven't considered anything else or have you narrowed it
down to these two things?

ST   Well, uh . . . no, I just considered . . . I think those two . . .

CO   Those are the only ones you've been thinking about at all. Do you
have very much information about . . .

ST   No, I haven't . . .

CO   Those possibilities?

ST   Not at the present, no.

CO   Well, we have information about Dunwoody . . .

ST   Uh-huh.

CO   In our files. We can give you a little idea of the courses that are available there, and I think that we would suggest going and seeing the place and maybe talking . . .

ST   Yes . . .

CO   With them, in addition to looking over the bulletin. (pause)

ST   Now this . . . mortuary science uh . . . that's a . . . just two years, isn't it?

CO   It's a year in the General College . . .

ST   General College and a year up here . . .

CO   And then the mortuary science course in extension. Have you seen the bulletin on that?

ST   No, I haven't uh . . . do you have it?

CO   Yes. The General College bulletin gives the pre-mortuary science course.

ST   Uh-huh.

CO   And then the mortuary science is written up in the Extension bulletin . . . (pause) Maybe we can look at them next time . . . I . . . don't locate them right now . . .

ST   Yes . . . uh-huh.

CO   And if you would like, you could get them for yourself over at the Administration Building. Do you know where it is on this campus?

ST   Yes, it's over there by the . . .

CO   Ask at the information booth which is in the middle of the lobby.

ST   Uh-huh.

CO   And you can get the bulletins that you wish there. You'd want the one for the General College . . .

ST   Yes.

CO   And the one for Extension. You may ask for others, too, by the time we get through talking.

ST   Well, is that . . . that . . . mortuary science, is that . . . is it as difficult as . . . most of the other subjects?

CO   You mean as in any other courses?

ST   Yes.

CO   At the University?

ST   Uh-huh.

CO   Well, that's a problem that's kind of hard to say yes or no to, because it depends on you.

ST   Uh-huh.

CO   The general idea is that it is not as difficult because it is not as long . . .

ST   Uh-huh.

CO   A course. (pause) But it would depend on you as to whether it would be difficult for you or not.

ST   I mean . . . that General College . . . this one . . . uh . . . fellow . . . his roommate . . . he went to a teachers' college for a year and took up General College and then he transferred back up here. I guess he said he's finding it . . . it isn't difficult for him . . . yet, we're two different people again . . .

co   And different courses.

st   Uh-huh. (pause)

co   Well, what would you like to do? Would you be interested in seeing what material we have on Dunwoody?

st   Yes, I would.

co   And would you like to maybe take one or two tests, and come back and talk about them later?

st   I think that's fine . . . yes . . .

co   I'll show you the ones that I have in mind . . .

st   Uh-huh.

co   They might be things like dexterity tests giving you an idea of how able you are using your hands, and mechanical comprehension . . . that kind . . .

st   Uh-huh.

co   Of thing. Then perhaps an over-all interest test, and perhaps an over-all ability test. (long pause)

st   I think I'd like that choice . . .

co   You think you'd like to do that?

st   Uh-huh, I think so.

co   O.K. Then I'll check the card for those that we've been talking about.

st   Uh-huh.

co   I wonder, would you be interested in a reading test? And maybe a study habits inventory while we're . . .

st   Sure.

co   Doing it? I'm sure that this reading test is different from the one you take over there . . . (pause) Are you classed as a freshman still?

st   Yes, Uh-huh . . .

co   Then we'll put freshman on the card so you'll be compared to freshmen.

st   Uh-huh.

co   Some of these are long and others are short . . .

st   Uh-huh.

co   I can give you an idea of how long it will take you in all and then we can arrange when you might be able to come back.

st   Uh-huh.

co   It will probably be about uh . . . (pause) . . . 6 hours or so of testing in all and our testing room is open all the time between 8 and 12 and 1 and 5, Monday through Friday. One or two of them will require appointments but most of them won't require any appointment and this means you can come then just at your own convenience between those hours I mentioned.

st   Uh-huh.

CO   Do you think maybe that you'll have time to come over a couple of times within the next week or so?

ST   Oh, yes.

CO   Uh-huh.

ST   In the afternoons from one on . . .

CO   Uh-huh, then maybe we could see each other about . . . uh . . . this same time next week or a week from now.

ST   Uh-huh.

CO   Let's fill them out too then . . . (referring to card and asking spelling of name)

ST   That's right.

CO   Do you have a middle name?

ST   Arlington.

CO   And what is your home address?

ST   Miles City, Minnesota.

CO   How do you spell that?

ST   (Spells)

CO   You're not a veteran, are you?

ST   No, I'm not.

CO   And how old are you?

ST   Nineteen.

CO   And you graduated from high school . . .

ST   Yes.

CO   In?

ST   1947.

CO   Darby High School?

ST   Yes.

CO   Miles City, Minnesota?

ST   Uh-huh. (pause)

CO   O.K. This card is put at the entrance to the testing room and it authorizes you to take the tests. When you come in, you ask for your card at the entrance to the testing room. I'll show you where it is as we go out.

ST   Uh-huh.

CO   I wonder if you would like to look at the material that I mentioned on Dunwoody this afternoon . . . do you have time now?

ST   Oh, yes, I still have time.

CO   When do you have a class?

ST   I have a dental appointment at 4.

CO   At 4?

ST   Uh-huh.

CO   Well, we'll go out and arrange for the next appointment and then I'll show you where that information is.

ST   Uh-huh.

CO Do you think there's anything else that we should talk over right now or does that kind of cover it for the moment?

ST I think that covers most of it . . . I can't think of any more . . .

CO Uh-huh.

Second Interview

CO I think I'll shut this window, if it's all right with you. It's kind of chilly.

ST That's all right. (pause)

CO Well, do we have anything to talk about today?

ST Well, I don't know, I just . . . uh . . . you said something about those tests . . . I was supposed to take those tests.

CO Uh-huh. You didn't have a chance to do those . . .

ST No, I haven't had a chance to . . .

CO Uh-huh. Well, maybe, we made the appointment a little too preliminarily, did we?

ST Well, I think so.

CO You haven't had a chance to take any one of them yet?

ST No, I haven't.

CO Uh-huh. Do you have anything you'd like to talk about today? Have you gotten any ideas . . .

ST Well . . .

CO Since we talked the last time?

ST Uh . . . I looked over Dunwoody . . . and . . .

CO Uh-huh.

ST I don't know . . . that surveying may be all right. I may try to get into that.

CO Uh-huh. That looked kind of good to you?

ST Uh-huh. I think so.

CO Have you been down there or did you just look over . . .

ST No.

CO You're talking about the things . . .

ST I just looked through . . .

CO I was showing you . . .

ST Yes . . . uh-huh.

CO Uh-huh.

ST I'm planning to go down there as soon as possible . . .

CO Uh-huh.

ST And talk to them down there.

CO Do you know anybody to ask for down there?

ST No, I don't.

CO Well, there are several people that you might ask for if you want a name. Sometimes it makes it a little easier to . . .

ST Uh-huh.

co   Say, I want to talk to so and so. A Mr. Carlson is the one that most of us know the best.

st   Uh-huh.

co   He's been out here to tell us about Dunwoody and so on. He's one of the assistant directors.

st   I see.

co   Part of his job is to just see people who are interested in finding out what the school is about.

st   Uh-huh.

co   So you might ask for him, if you like, or there's a Mr. Michaels who also does the same thing.

st   Uh-huh.

co   You may ask for him. What you're going to do is to get more of an idea of what it is, isn't that right?

st   Yes, uh-huh. (pause) And . . . uh . . . these tests . . . do I come in any time?

co   Uh-huh. Any time between 8 and 12 and 1 and 5, Monday through Friday.

st   And what I'll do is just . . . walk in the testing room then . . .

co   Uh-huh, and this card is placed in the file there at the entrance to the testing room.

st   Uh-huh.

co   So that all you have to do is go ask for your card and they give you the tests we've checked.

st   Oh, I see.

co   When do you think you might be able to do that? Do you have any time in the near future?

st   I'd suppose I could do one today.

co   Uh-huh.

st   This afternoon.

co   Uh-huh. (pause) You've got quite a few . . . shall we hold off and make the appointment to look at the test results about two weeks from now? Do you think that'll give you enough time? Or we could make it later than that . . .

st   Oh, I think that'll be all right.

co   Two weeks from today, you think, maybe?

st   Uh-huh.

co   O.K. We might put it on the book that way because we get so jammed up . . .

st   Uh-huh.

co   That way you'll know that we have an appointment.

st   Uh-huh. (pause)

st   Then I just come in any time I . . . just to finish them all . . . before . . .

co   Uh-huh.

st   Two weeks from today.

co   Uh-huh. And if you can't finish all but one, that'll be O.K.

st   Oh, yes, uh-huh.

co   You can get a good bunch of them done by then, don't you think?

st   Oh, I think so.

co   Uh-huh. Would you like to start right now . . .

st   Yes, I could . . .

co   And let this be the end of our interview for today, or do you have something else you'd like to . . .

st   No, I haven't.

co   O.K. Maybe by the time you come in again you will have had a chance to talk to the people down at Dunwoody . . .

st   Uh-huh. I'll try . . . yes.

co   We can talk about that at the same time.

st   Uh-huh. Shall I just go in there and start the tests?

co   Yes, I'll go down there with you.

st   O.K.

Following the testing, the counselor summarized his interview as follows:

> In going over the tests, particularly as the result of the discussion of the Strong Vocational Interest Test and some of the material on the Individual Record Form, Carl stated that he has come to the conclusion that he will check into the training at Dunwoody in the next few weeks. He is still considering Industrial Education as one other alternative. He has some doubts on that still, however, and thinks he might best be suited for something like the air conditioning and refrigeration course at Dunwoody or perhaps the surveying course. He seemed to gain a good deal of reassurance from the way all the test results came out and stated that he felt he had learned a good deal which was helpful about himself through the testing and discussion here.
>
> Vocational indecision appears to be lessening through the client's understanding better his standing in the course he has attempted.
>
> Techniques used were mainly questioning, test interpretation, information giving, and reflection. Rapport seemed to be good and, as I stated earlier, the boy stated his satisfaction with the outcome of the counseling.[148]

SUMMARY AND EVALUATION

The Minnesota point of view attempts to apply a scientific approach to counseling by the use of measurement and prediction. The process consists of gathering objective data about the client, synthesizing the data into a diagnosis, predicting outcomes from the data (prognosis), and planning a program of action derived from the data. The counselor engages in a tutorial relationship with the client, assisting the client in obtaining data or providing him with necessary information, presenting and discussing alternatives, and attempting to aid the client to reach the best choice, decision, or solution. The choice or decision is the client's, and the counselor avoids undue influence upon the client.

While the emphasis is upon counseling as a rational, problem-solving process, the influence of emotions is not ignored. However, the concern with emotions alone, leading the client to the resolution of self-conflicts, to self-understanding, or to feeling better, is considered to be psychotherapy. The techniques used in this process are listening and catharsis, and the establishing of a relationship. Counseling, on the other hand, goes beyond self-understanding and attempts to help the client deal with external or situational problems, to make decisions regarding actions. It is here that the rational, problem-solving methods or techniques are emphasized, although the influence of affect, or emotions, is not ignored.

This distinction between psychotherapy and counseling is similar to that made by other writers.[149] It is difficult to maintain a distinction between psychotherapy and counseling on the basis of an emotional-rational dichotomy, however. Williamson actually recognizes the overlap, since his counseling is concerned with affective elements. The problem develops from the apparent difference in techniques. In psychotherapy the counselor may be passive, or less active, and not provide data or information or propose alternatives, as he does when dealing with educational-vocational problems. On the other hand, as Williamson recognizes, the counselor must be concerned with emotions in educational-vocational counseling. The present author has attempted to reconcile this apparent difference elsewhere.[150] The resulting approach to vocational-educational counseling appears to be similar to Williamson's approach as developed in his recent publications. When the client is lacking in information, or when he is ignorant of possible alternatives, these may be provided by the counselor.

Williamson's approach, however, is somewhat more directive and didactic. It would appear that Williamson has less confidence in the client's ability to engage in problem solving without direct guidance or teaching by the counselor. This may be related to his concern that the individual cannot be trusted in the process of self actualization because he may actualize a selfish, antisocial self rather than his best self. There is no question that man cannot develop as a person in isolation, that he requires others to actualize his potential. The issue seems to be whether man's best potential will develop under optimum counseling relationships (or other good human relationships), or whether it is necessary to guide and control development to prevent the expression of the best bestial and debasing self, or the evil Williamson believes is inherent in man. There seems to be a recurring vacillation or contradiction between the emphasis upon the individual and his freedom and potentiality for good, and the need for guidance and control that evidences an implicit distrust in the individual.

This concern with guidance and control has persisted throughout Williamson's publications since the 1950 book. Perhaps it is related to the educational setting in which the approach developed, where there are, of course, always examples of students' immaturity and difficulty in taking responsibility for themselves. We have perhaps created a dilemma for ourselves in that our educational system too often encourages or produces dependence, so that when a student comes for counseling he assumes a dependent position, to which many counselors feel they must respond by assuming responsibility and allowing the dependence to continue in the counseling relationship.

This lack of complete confidence in the positive growth forces in the client is the source of the techniques of guidance, direct teaching, encouragement, etc. The counselor must exercise his influence to assure that the client actualizes his *best* potentialities, or commits himself to the *right* values. He is thus in a dilemma, since he must do this without exerting undue pressure through persuasion, exhortation, propaganda, etc. The right of the client to make his own choices must be preserved. So the counselor, in addition to being warm, understanding, and friendly in his technique and style "should establish clearly his expertness" and "should also indicate that he has a penetrating understanding of humans, their capabilities and potentialities, motivations and aspirations." [151] The approach thus appears to be caught between Scylla and Charybdis.

The emphasis upon objective data and measurement is, of course, laudable. But there is a real question as to whether such data are dependable enough (in terms of reliability, validity, and completeness) to warrant their use in as positive a way in counseling as this approach advocates. There appears to be an overconfidence in the use of such data. Williamson does point out their fallibility and the errors of measurement involved, and cautions the counselor about this. Yet the discussion of the counseling process clearly shows the dependence of his approach upon such data and seems to place greater confidence in them than is perhaps justified.

The emphasis upon objective data and the rational approach to its use in counseling seems to underestimate the importance of the student's affective, or emotional, reactions. It is doubtful that any problem involving the individual himself, or in which he is ego-involved, can be approached in a purely rational manner; or that the affective aspects can be dealt with separately; or that one approach to counseling—the rational—can be used until emotional, or affective, elements interfere, at which time the client can be referred for psychotherapy to remove the emotional block. Problems of vocational choice are no exception. They are not free from ego involvement. There is, of course, a place in counseling, particularly in vocational counseling, for the presentation and discussion of facts and information. But the point is that these so-called objective facts are often not accepted objectively by the client, but instead elicit an emotional reaction. These reactions must be recognized and dealt with by the counselor. This requires a therapeutic approach rather than a rational approach, which is recognized as not being effective against emotional attitudes.

The affective, or emotional, aspects of counseling are given more recognition in Williamson's recent writing, but the essentially rational, problem-solving, teaching nature of counseling is still basic to his outlook. There still seems to be the separation of the rational and the emotional, with counseling dealing with the former and psychotherapy with the latter.

His point of view thus recognizes the importance of the affective aspects of behavior, but there seems to be inadequate consideration of this in the counseling process and a relegation of consideration of affective problems to psychotherapy. While recognizing that students do not think rationally, he insists upon rationalizing the counseling process, which may be viewed as a process of forcing the student to think rationally about his problems and his choice. Williamson writes that "to assume that every adolescent is capable of logical and psychological thinking, when both experience and experiment have shown clearly that even adults do not or cannot think clearly, is to ignore some well-established facts. . . . Yet we need not assume that the counselor's role is one of passively listening to illogical self-analysis, psychological blindness in abilities, and irrational attempts to cover up deficiencies by attempting the impossible." [152] Instead of dealing with the irrational thinking, he reasons and marshals the evidence against such thinking. But if there is anything we have learned in psychology, it is that such techniques are not effective against emotionalized attitudes and thinking.

The emphasis upon objective data is, therefore, too narrow an approach to counseling in two respects. First, it does not adequately consider and deal with the affective reactions of the client. And second, it leaves out of consideration a kind of data that is of crucial importance in any decisions or choices that the student makes. These are the student's own perceptions of himself and the world, of the so-called objective facts. It is eventually these *perceptions* that determine choices or decisions, rather than the objective fact themselves. Williamson is aware of the influence of the client's perceptions, including his self-perceptions. He recognizes that self-perceptions are important in understanding the client. But there seems to be inadequate emphasis in the counseling process upon such data as compared to the objective, external data. He writes that "the self-percept as applied in the counseling situation tends to center too much attention upon the individual student as an isolated autonomy." [153] He also states that the idea that the internal frame of reference is sufficient for counseling "ignores the fact that the individual's perception of self is often distorted or incomplete." [154] But Williamson offers no method of dealing with distorted perceptions other than to confront them with external appraisal data: "We need to keep in mind that the student is less than fully in possession of understanding about himself when he does not accurately perceive external appraisal of himself." [155] It is perhaps that Williamson leaves the dealing with distorted perceptions to psychotherapy.

A related problem is the emphasis upon diagnosis. Counseling cannot be effective, according to Williamson, if it is based upon an inaccurate diagnosis. Yet it is doubtful if anything approaching an adequate diagnosis can be made in the present state of our knowledge and with the instruments currently available. Incomplete, inadequate diagnoses are probably the rule rather than the exception.

A final characteristic of Williamson's point of view that requires comment is the lack of a systematic approach to counseling. There are no general principles to guide the counselor in the choice and use of techniques. Instead, everything depends upon the individual client. It is maintained that "there should be a relationship of appropriateness or relevance between the nature of the student's problem and the kind of counseling technique used in the counseling relationship." [156] Yet, with the exception of the differentiation of the techniques of counseling and psychotherapy, there is no consideration of indications or contraindications for the use of various techniques. No criteria are given for the use of specific techniques. Instead, the experience of the counselor is relied upon, even when it is recognized that such experience is far less valid than experiments. Thus, while the scientific value of data that enter into counseling is emphasized, the counseling process and techniques are not based upon any scientific or experimental evidence. "The counselor recognizes that dependable evidence is lacking which would establish a particular technique as a *certain* producer of a desirable adjustment. Rather, the counselor has knowledge of certain techniques which produced effective results in a similar case; therefore, he tries them out with appropriate modifications. If they prove ineffective, he tries something else and continues this trial and rejection until he finds something which clicks with the student. . . . Counseling is still in the trial-and-error stage of treatment . . ." [157]

Thus, we see that there is a peculiar inconsistency in the approach. On the one hand, there is the attempt to be objective and scientific, while on the other, there is the admission that counseling is in a trial-and-error stage. There is no attempt to relate the process and techniques of counseling to scientific knowledge about students or clients as individuals or as members of groups. Nor is there even any suggestion that research could raise counseling from the trial-and-error stage into an orderly, systematic process. These comments are not meant to say or imply that there is no place in counseling for objective data, or that in counseling some clients a rational, logical approach to problems is not possible or desirable. But they are meant to say that this approach is limited and insufficient. The counselor must be able to recognize and accept affective reactions and attitudes, and to deal with them with more than a rational, logical technique.

The summary of Williamson's approach to counseling has been perhaps the most difficult of any presented in this book. While this difficulty is no doubt related to the changing and developmental nature of his approach, there are other elements that also enter in. One of these relates to the ambiguity of much of the recent literature.

Numerous value-laden terms are used without adequate definition or differentiation. In some instances unjustified meanings are attributed to certain terms, such as self-centeredness as implicit in self-actualization. Straw men are thus set up to be demolished. The reviewer admits to being unable to pin down Williamson's position on many points. He seldom takes a clear position, or he appears to vary in his position in different publications, although this may perhaps only be a result of loose usage of terminology. A lack of systematic organization in presenting a point of view is apparent in his recent book and results in some repetitiousness. Thus, in order to avoid as much as possible any misrepresentation, direct quotations have been used more frequently in this summary than in most other chapters.

REFERENCES

[1] Williamson, E.G., & Darley, J. G. *Student personnel work: an outline of clinical procedures.* New York: McGraw-Hill, 1937.   [2] Paterson, D. G., Schneidler, Gwendolen G., & Williamson, E. G. *Student guidance techniques: handbook for counselors in high schools and colleges.* New York: McGraw-Hill, 1938.   [3] Williamson, E. G. *How to counsel students: a manual of techniques for clinical counselors.* New York: McGraw-Hill, 1939.   [4] Williamson, E. G. *Counseling adolescents.* New York: McGraw-Hill, 1950.   [5] Williamson, E. G. A concept of counseling. *Occupations,* 1950, **29**, 182–189.   [6] Williamson, E. G. Discipline and counseling. *Education,* 1954, **74**, 512–518.   [7] Williamson, E. G. The fusion of discipline and counseling in the educational process. *Personnel guid. J.,* 1955, **34**, 74–79. (Reprinted in G. F. Farwell & H. J. Peters (Eds.), *Guidance readings for counselors.* Chicago: Rand McNally, 1960, and in H. G. McDaniel and others (Eds.), *Readings in guidance.* New York: Holt, Rinehart and Winston, 1959.) [8] Williamson, E. G. Value orientation in counseling. *Personnel guid. J.,* 1958, **37**, 520-528.   [9] Williamson, E. G. Some issues underlying counseling theory and practice. In W. E. Dugan (Ed.), *Counseling points of view.* Minneapolis: University of Minnesota Press, 1959. Pp. 1–13.   [10] Williamson, E. G., Rogers, C. R., Warweg, Claire, Gum, M., & Dugan, W. E. Counseling theory and techniques: a panel discussion. In *Ibid.,* pp. 27-48.   [11] Williamson, E. G. Value commitments and counseling. *Teachers Coll. Rec.,* 1961, **62**, 602-608. [12] Williamson, E. G. A critical review of the high school guidance program today. In E. G. Kennedy (Ed.), *Current status and future trends in student personnel.* Pittsburg, Kansas: Kansas State College of Pittsburg, 1961. Pp. 6–20.   [13] Williamson, E. G. Uses of the counseling interview. In *Ibid.,* pp. 31–44. [14] Williamson, E. G. The counselor as technique. *Personnel guid. J.,* 1962, **41**, 108–111.   [15] Williamson, E. G. The societal responsibilities of counselors. *Illinois Guidance and Personnel Association Newsletter,* 1963, Winter, 5–13.   [16] Counseling as preparation for self-directed change. *Teachers Coll. Rec.,* 1964, **65**, 613–622   [17] Current views on counseling theory and techniques. In *Perspectives in Personnel: Proceedings of the Third Annual Student Personnel Conference.* Stillwater, Oklahoma: Oklahoma State University, 1964. Pp. 1–17.   [18] Williamson, E. G. Discipline—another dimension of counseling. In *Ibid.,* pp.

18–36.   [19] Williamson, E. G. Vocational counseling: trait-factor theory. In B. Stefflre (Ed.), *Theories of counseling.* New York: McGraw-Hill, 1965. Pp. 193–214.   [20] Williamson, E. G. Value options and the counseling relationship. *Personnel guid. J.,* 1966, **44,** 617–623.   [21] Paterson, D. G. *Physique and intellect.* New York: Appleton-Century-Crofts, 1930; Paterson, D. G., Elliott, R. M., Anderson, L. D., Toops, H. A., & Heidbreder, Edna. *Minnesota Mechanical Abilities Tests.* Minneapolis: University of Minnesota Press, 1930.   [22] Paterson, D. G., & Darley, J. G. *Men, women, and jobs.* Minneapolis: University of Minnesota Press, 1936.   [23] Parsons, F. *Choosing a vocation.* Boston: Houghton Mifflin, 1909. P.5.   [24] Williamson, E. G., & Darley, J. G. *op. cit.,* p. viii.   [25] See, for example, Paterson, D. G. Elliott, R. M., Anderson, L. D., Toops, H. A., & Heidbreder, Edna, *op. cit.*   [26] Paterson, D. G., Gerken, C. D'A., & Hahn, M.E. *Revised Minnesota Occupational Rating Scales.* Minnesota Studies in Student Personnel Work, No. 2. Minneapolis: University of Minnesota Press, 1953.   [27] Williamson, E. G. A concept of counseling, *op. cit.*   [28] Williamson, E. G. *Counseling adolescents.* New York: McGraw-Hill, 1950. Pp. 37–39.   [29] *Ibid.,*p. 38.   [30] *Ibid.,* p. 4.   [31] *Ibid.,* p. 25.   [32] *Ibid.,* p. 3.   [33] Bradshaw, F. F. The scope and aim of a personnel program. *Educ. Res.,* 1936, **17,**121. Quoted in Williamson, E. G. *Counseling adolescents.* New York: McGraw-Hill, 1950. P. 45.   [34] Williamson, E. G. *Counseling adolescents.* New York: McGraw-Hill, 1950. P. 9.   [35] *Ibid.,* p. 20.   [36] *Ibid.* [37] Williamson, E. G. Value orientation in counseling, *op. cit.*   [38] Williamson, E. G. *Vocational counseling.* New York: McGraw-Hill, 1965.   [39] *Ibid.,* p. 181.   [40] *Ibid.,* pp. 183, 182.   [41] *Ibid.,* p. 170.   [42] *Ibid.,* p. 183. [43] Williamson, E. G. The societal responsibilities of counselors, op. cit. [44] *Ibid.;* also, Williamson, E. G. *Vocational counseling.* New York: McGraw-Hill, 1965. Pp. 184–185.   [45] Williamson, E. G. *Vocational counseling.* New York; McGraw-Hill, 1965. P. 185.   [46] Williamson, E. G. A concept of counseling, *op. cit.*   [47] Williamson, E. G. Value orientation in counseling, *op. cit.* [48] Williamson, E. G. Some issues underlying counseling theory and practice *op. cit.,* pp. 2–3.   [49] Williamson, E. G. The societal responsibilities of counselors, *op. cit.*   [50] Williamson, E. G. A concept of counseling, *op. cit.* [51] Williamson, E. G. The societal responsibilities of counselors, *op. cit.* [52] Williamson, E. G. Some issues underlying counseling theory and practice, *op. cit.,* p. 3.   [53] Williamson, E. G. The societal responsibilities of counselors, *op. cit.* See also Williamson, E. G. *Vocational counseling.* New York: McGraw-Hill, 1965. P. 196.   [54] Williamson, E. G. *Vocational counseling.* New York: McGraw-Hill, 1965. P. 194.   [55] *Ibid.,* p. 168.   [56] *Ibid.,* p. 156. [57] *Ibid.,* p. 206.   [58] *Ibid.*   [59] Ibid., p. 207.   [60] Williamson, E. G. Value orientation in counseling, *op. cit.*   [61] Williamson, E. G. *Vocational counseling.* New York: McGraw-Hill, 1965. Pp. 157–158.   [62] Williamson, E. G. Value orientation in counseling, *op. cit.*   [63] Williamson, E. G. Value commitments and counseling, *op. cit.*   [64] Williamson, E. G. *Vocational counseling.* New York: McGraw-Hill, 1965. P. 194.   [65] *Ibid.,* p. 209.   [66] *Ibid.,* p. 210.   [67] Williamson, E. G. Value orientation in counseling, *op. cit.*   [68] Williamson, E. G. Some issues underlying counseling theory and practice, *op. cit.,* p. 12.   [69] Williamson, E. G. Value commitments in counseling, *op. cit.* [70] Williamson, E. G. *Vocational counseling.* New York: McGraw-Hill, 1965. P.

210.   **[71]** Williamson, E. G. The societal responsibilities of counselors, *op. cit.*   **[72]** Williamson, E. G. *Vocational counseling.* New York: McGraw-Hill, 1965. P. 212.   **[73]** *Ibid.,* p. 213.   **[74]** *Ibid.,* pp. 195, 214.   **[75]** Williamson, E. G. *Counseling adolescents.* New York: McGraw-Hill, 1950. Pp. 2–3. **[76]** Williamson, E. G. A concept of counseling, *op. cit.*   **[77]** Williamson, E. G. Value orientation in counseling, *op. cit.*   **[78]** Williamson, E. G. Value commitments and counseling, *op. cit.*   **[79]** Williamson, E. G. Value orientation in counseling, *op. cit.*   **[80]** Williamson, E. G. Uses of the counseling interviews, *op. cit.,* p. 33.   **[81]** *Ibid.,* pp. 32–42.   **[82]** *Ibid.,* pp. 41–42. **[83]** Williamson, E. G. Value orientation in counseling, *op. cit.*   **[84]** Williamson, E. G. Some issues underlying counseling theory and practice, *op. cit.* **[85]** Williamson, E. G. Value commitments and counseling, *op cit.*   **[86]** Williamson, E. G. Value orientation in counseling, *op. cit.*   **[87]** *Ibid.*   **[88]** Paterson, D. G., Schneidler, Gwendolen G., & Williamson, E. G., *op. cit.* **[89]** Williamson, E. G., & Darley, J. G., *op. cit.,* pp. xix–xx.   **[90]** Williamson, E. G. *Counseling adolescents.* New York: McGraw-Hill, 1950. P. 54.   **[91]** Williamson, E. G. Uses of the counseling interview, *op. cit.,* pp. 33-36.   **[92]** Williamson, E. G., & Darley, J. G., *op. cit.,* Chap. 6.   **[93]** *Ibid.,* pp. 180–183. **[94]** Williamson, E. G. *Counseling adolescents.* New York: McGraw-Hill, 1950. P. 102.   **[95]** *Ibid.*   **[96]** *Ibid.,* p. 104.   **[97]** *Ibid.,* p. 107.   **[98]** *Ibid.,* pp. 105–107.   **[99]** *Ibid.,* p. 109.   **[100]** *Ibid.*   **[101]** *Ibid.,* p. 127.   **[102]** *Ibid.,* p. 150.   **[103]** *Ibid.,* p. 127.   **[104]** *Ibid.*   **[105]** *Ibid.,* p. 139. **[106]** *Ibid.,* p. 146.   **[107]** *Ibid.,* pp. 146–147.   **[108]** *Ibid.,* pp. 147–148. **[109]** *Ibid.,* pp. 148–149.   **[110]** *Ibid.,* p. 150.   **[111]** *Ibid.,* p. 101.   **[112]** Williamson, E. G., & Darley, J. G., *op. cit.,* pp. 171–172.   **[113]** Williamson, E. G. *Counseling adolescents.* New York: McGraw-Hill, 1950. P. 54.   **[114]** *Ibid.,* p. 178.   **[115]** Bordin, E. S. Diagnois in counseling and psychotherapy. *Educ. psychol. Measmt.,* 1946, **6,** 171–172.   **[116]** Pepinsky, H. B. The selection and use of diagnostic categories. *Appl. Psychol. Monogr.,* 1948, No. 15.   **[117]** Williamson, E. G. *Counseling adolescents.* New York: McGraw-Hill, 1950. P. 187. **[118]** *Ibid.,* p. 189.   **[119]** *Ibid.,* p. 191.   **[120]** *Ibid.,* p. 203.   **[121]** *Ibid.,* p. 206.   **[122]** *Ibid.,* p. 180.   **[123]** *Ibid.,* pp. 209–210.   **[124]** *Ibid.,* p. 213.   **[125]** *Ibid.*   **[126]** *Ibid.*   **[127]** *Ibid.,* p. 215.   **[128]** *Ibid.,* p. 101. **[129]** *Ibid.,* pp. 219–220.   **[130]** Williamson, E. G. *How to counsel students.* New York: McGraw-Hill, 1939. P. viii.   **[131]** *Ibid.,* p. xvi.   **[132]** Williamson, E. G. *Counseling adolescents.* New York: McGraw-Hill, 1950. P. 220. **[133]** *Ibid.,* p. 225.   **[134]** Williamson, E. G. The counselor as technique, *op. cit.*   **[135]** Williamson, E. G. *Counseling adolescents.* New York: McGraw-Hill, 1950. P. 229.   **[136]** *Ibid.,* p. 230.   **[137]** *Ibid.*   **[138]** Williamson, E. G. Value orientation in counseling, *op. cit.;* Personal correspondence. December 27, 1962.   **[139]** Williamson, E. G. A concept of counseling, *op. cit.*   **[140]** Williamson, E. G. Value orientation in counseling, *op.cit.*   **[141]** *Ibid.* **[142]** *Ibid.*   **[143]** Williamson, E. G. The counselor as technique, *op. cit.* **[144]** Williamson, E. G. Personal correspondence. August 30, 1962.   **[145]** Williamson, E. G. Personal correspondence. October 9, 1962.   **[146]** Callis, R., Polmantier, P. C., & Roeber, E. C. A *casebook of counseling.* New York: Appleton-Century-Crofts, 1955.   **[147]** From *Counseling adolescents* by E. G. Williamson. Copyright 1950. McGraw-Hill Book Company. Used with permis-

sion of McGraw-Hill Book Company. Pp. 511–519, 533–535. **[148]** *Ibid.,* p. 536. **[149]** See Patterson, C. H. *Counseling and psychotherapy: theory and practice.* New York: Harper & Row,1959. **[150]** Patterson, C. H. *An introduction to counseling in the school.* Part III. New York: Harper & Row, 1971; Patterson, C. H. Counseling: self-clarification and the helping relationship. In H. Borow (Ed.), *Man in a world at work.* Boston: Houghton Mifflin, 1964. Pp. 434–459. Compare with Williamson, E. G. Vocational counseling: trait-factor theory. In B. Stefflre (Ed.), *Theories of counseling.* New York: McGraw-Hill, 1965. Pp. 193–214. **[151]** Williamson, E. G. The counselor as technique, *op. cit.* **[152]** *Ibid.,* pp. 257–258. **[153]** Williamson, E. G. Some issues underlying counseling theory and practice, *op. cit.,* p. 5. **[154]** *Ibid.* **[155]** *Ibid.* **[156]** Williamson, E. G. A concept of counseling, *op. cit.* **[157]** Williamson, E. G. *Counseling adolescents.* New York: McGraw-Hill, 1950. P. 221.

3
Rational-emotive psychotherapy: Ellis

Perhaps the most extreme of the attempts to introduce logic and reason into counseling or psychotherapy is the approach of Albert Ellis, which was first called rational psychotherapy and was later designated as rational-emotive psychotherapy.

Albert Ellis (1913–) received his bachelor's degree (B.B.A.) at the City College of New York in 1934. He obtained his M.A. in 1943 and his Ph.D. in 1947, both at Columbia University. He began private practice in the field of marriage, family, and sex counseling in 1943. Becoming interested in psychoanalysis, he obtained training in this field and underwent a three-year analysis. He has held positions briefly as clinical psychologist in a mental hygiene clinic attached to a state hospital and in a state diagnostic center, as Chief Psychologist of the New Jersey Department of Institutions and Agencies, and as Instructor at Rutgers University and New York University, but the main part of his professional life has been spent in private practice. For several years he has been Executive Director of the Institute for Rational Living, Inc. He is a Diplomate in Clinical Psychology of the American Board of Examiners in Clinical Psychology. Recently, he has been involved in carrying his approach into group therapy.

49

BACKGROUND AND DEVELOPMENT

In his early practice of marital counseling, Ellis was concerned essentially with giving authoritative information. However, he became aware that the problems brought to him involved more than the lack of valid information or knowledge; his clients also were psychologically or emotionally disturbed. He then turned to psychoanalysis for help, and after his training and personal analysis, began practicing orthodox psychoanalysis. Although he feels he was as successful as other analysts (he claims 50 percent of all his patients, and 70 percent of the neurotics, were significantly helped), he was dissatisfied with the results and, more important, was dissatisfied with the theory and techniques of psychoanalysis. Apparently, one element was the lack of correspondence between the passivity and inactivity of the orthodox analysis and Ellis' personality and temperament. "Why," he writes, "when I seemed to know perfectly well what was troubling a patient, did I have to wait passively, perhaps for a few weeks, perhaps for months, until he, by his own interpretive initiative, showed that he was fully 'ready' to accept my own insight? Why, when patients bitterly struggled to continue to associate freely, and ended up by saying only a few words in an entire session, was it improper for me to help them with several pointed questions or remarks?" [1]

As a result, Ellis changed to a neo-Freudian approach and then to psychoanalytically oriented psychotherapy, becoming more active and directive. Although he feels that his effectiveness increased (63 percent of all patients and 70 percent of neurotics showing significant improvement), and results were achieved in less time and with fewer interviews, he was still dissatisfied. Even though his patients achieved insight into their behavior and its origins, they did not necessarily change their behavior or improve.

Ellis then became interested in learning theory (that is, conditioning) and attempted to apply it in deconditioning his patients by directing them to engage in pertinent activities. Again, he felt that this activity-directive eclectic therapy was more effective, but he still was not satisfied.

His rational approach began to develop at this point (in 1954). He became convinced that irrational, neurotic early learnings persisted, rather than being extinguished as they should be if they were not reinforced, because individuals persisted in reinforcing them by reindoctrinating themselves and in resisting therapy and its insights. Ellis then turned to teaching his patients to change their thinking to agree with a rational approach to their problems. He feels that about 90 percent of those treated by this method for ten or more sessions show distinct or considerable improvement.

This approach was developed in a series of articles, beginning in 1955[2-8] and culminating in the book *Reason and Emotion in Psychotherapy*, which incorporates the earlier statements. Ellis also promised a "Casebook of Rational Emotive Psychotherapy" and several volumes supporting his approach with research and clinical evidence of its effectiveness. These have not as yet materialized.

PHILOSOPHY AND CONCEPTS

Ellis claims no originality for the concepts that make up his system. While he discovered many of them through his own experience, he recognizes that they had already been formulated by many ancient and modern philosophers, psychologists and psychotherapists, and social thinkers.

Rational-emotive therapy makes certain assumptions about the nature of man and about the nature and genesis of his unhappiness or emotional disturbances, among which are the following:

1   Man is uniquely rational, as well as irrational. When he is thinking and behaving rationally, he is effective, happy, and competent.

2   Emotional or psychological disturbance—neurotic behavior —is a result of irrational and illogical thinking. Thought and emotion are not separate or different functions. Emotion accompanies thinking and is, in effect, biased, prejudiced, highly personalized, irrational thinking.

3   Irrational thinking originates in the early illogical learning that the individual is biologically disposed toward and that he acquires more specifically from his parents and his culture.

4   Human beings are verbal animals, and thinking usually occurs through the use of symbols or language. Since thinking accompanies emotion and emotional disturbances, irrational thinking necessarily persists if the emotional disturbance persists. This is just what characterizes the disturbed individual. He perpetuates his disturbance, he maintains his illogical behavior by internal verbalization of his irrational ideas and thoughts. "For all practical purposes the phrases and sentences that we keep telling ourselves frequently *are* or *become* our thoughts and emotions." [9] This continuing self-stimulation is the reason that the disordered behavior and emotions are not extinguished. It is also the reason that simple understanding of the origins of the disturbance, obtained through psychoanalysis, is not sufficient to eliminate the disturbance.

5   Continuing states of emotional disturbance, being a result of self-verbalizations, are thus determined, not by external circumstances or events, but by the perceptions and attitudes toward these events that are incorporated in the internalized sentences about them. Ellis finds the origin of this concept in Epictetus, who wrote: "Men are disturbed not by things, but by the views which they take of them." He also quotes a similar idea from Hamlet: "There's nothing either good or bad but thinking makes it so." [10]

6   Negative and self-defeating thoughts and emotions must thus be attacked by reorganizing perceptions and thinking so that thinking becomes logical and rational rather than illogical and irrational. The

goals of counseling or psychotherapy are to demonstrate to the client that his self-verbalizations have been the source of his emotional disturbance, to show that these self-verbalizations are illogical and irrational, and to straighten out his thinking so that his self-verbalizations become more logical and efficient, and so are not associated with negative emotions and self-defeating behavior.

Ellis identifies eleven ideas or values that are irrational, superstitious, or "senseless," and that are universally inculcated in Western society and "would seem inevitably to lead to widespread neurosis." [11]

1 *It is essential that one be loved or approved by virtually everyone in his community* This is irrational because it is an unattainable goal, and if one strives for it, one becomes less self-directing and more insecure and self-defeating. It is desirable that one be loved; however, the rational person does not sacrifice his own interests and desires to this goal, but expresses them, including the striving to be a loving, creative, productive individual.

2 *One must be perfectly competent, adequate, and achieving to consider oneself worthwhile* This again is an impossibility, and to strive compulsively for it results in psychosomatic illness, a sense of inferiority, an inability to live one's own life, and a constant sense of fear of failure. The rational individual strives to do well for his own sake rather than to best others, to enjoy the activity rather than to engage in it solely for the results, and to learn rather than to be perfect.

3 *Some people are bad, wicked, or villainous and therefore should be blamed and punished* This idea is irrational because there is no absolute standard of right or wrong and very little free will. "Wrong" or "immoral" acts are the results of stupidity, ignorance, or emotional disturbance. All men are fallible and make mistakes. Blame and punishment do not usually lead to improved behavior, since they do not result in less stupidity, more intelligence, or a better emotional state. In fact, they often lead to worse behavior and greater emotional disturbance. The rational individual does not blame others or himself. If others blame him, he tries to improve or correct his behavior if he has been wrong, and if he hasn't, he realizes that blaming in others is an indication of disturbance in them. If others make mistakes, he tries to understand them and, if possible, to stop them from continuing their misdeeds; but if that is not possible, he tries not to let their behavior seriously upset him. When he makes mistakes, he admits and accepts this but does not let it become a catastrophe or lead him to feel worthless.

4 *It is a terrible catastrophe when things are not as one wants them to be* This is irrational thinking because to be frustrated is normal, but to be severely and prolongedly upset is illogical, since (a) there is no reason why things should be different from what they are in reality, (b) getting upset not only rarely changes the situation, it usually makes it worse, (c) if it is impossible to do anything about the situation, the only rational thing to do is to accept it, and (d) frustration need not result in emotional disturbance if one does not define the situation in

such a way as to make obtaining one's desires a necessity for satisfaction or happiness. The rational person avoids exaggerating unpleasant situations and works at improving them if he can or accepts them if he can't. Unpleasant situations may be disturbing, but they are not terrible or catastrophic unless we define them as such.

5 *Unhappiness is caused by outside circumstances, and the individual has no control over it*   Actually, outside forces and events, while they can be physically assaulting, usually are psychological in nature and cannot be harmful unless one allows oneself to be affected by one's attitudes and reactions. One disturbs oneself by telling oneself how horrible it is when someone is unkind, rejecting, annoying, etc. If one realized that disturbances or emotions consist of one's own perceptions, evaluations, and internalized verbalizations, they could be controlled or changed. The intelligent person will realize that unhappiness comes largely from within, and while he may be irritated or annoyed by external events, he will recognize that he can change his reactions by his definitions and verbalizations of these events.

6 *Dangerous or fearsome things are causes for great concern, and their possibility must be continually dwelt upon*   This is irrational because worry or anxiety (a) prevents an objective evaluation of the possibility of a dangerous event, (b) will often interfere with dealing with it effectively if it should occur, (c) may contribute to bringing it about, (d) leads to exaggerating the possibilities of its occurrence, (e) cannot possibly prevent inevitable events, and (f) makes many dreaded events appear worse than they are. The rational person recognizes that potential dangers are not as catastrophic as he fears, and that anxiety does not prevent them, but may increase them and may be more harmful itself than the feared events. He also realizes that he should do those things that he fears to do in order to prove that they are not actually frightful.

7 *It is easier to avoid certain difficulties and self-responsibilities than to face them*   This is irrational because avoiding a task is often harder and more painful than performing it, and leads to later problems and dissatisfactions, including loss of self-confidence. Also, an easy life is not necessarily a happy one. The rational individual does without complaint what he has to do, although he intelligently avoids unnecessary painful tasks. When he finds himself avoiding necessary responsibilities, he analyzes the reasons and engages in self-discipline. He realizes that the challenging, responsible, problem-solving life is the enjoyable life.

8 *One should be dependent on others and must have someone stronger on whom to rely*   While we all are dependent upon others to some extent, there is no reason to maximize dependency, for it leads to loss of independence, individualism, and self-expression. Dependency causes greater dependency, failure to learn, and insecurity, since one is at the mercy of those on whom one depends. The rational individual strives for independence and responsibility for himself, but he does not refuse to seek or accept help when he needs it. He recognizes that risks, while

possibly resulting in failures, are worth taking, and that failing is not a catastrophe.

9 *Past experiences and events are the determiners of present behavior; the influence of the past cannot be eradicated* On the contrary, what was once necessary behavior in certain circumstances may not be necessary at present. Past solutions to problems may not be relevant in the present. The presumed influence of the past may be used as an excuse for avoiding changing one's behavior. While it may be difficult to overcome past learnings, it is not impossible. The rational individual, while recognizing that the past is important, also realizes that he can change the present by analyzing past influences, questioning those acquired beliefs that are harmful, and forcing himself to act differently in the present.

10 *One should be quite upset over other people's problems and disturbances* This is erroneous because other people's problems often have nothing to do with us and therefore should not seriously concern us. Even when others' behavior does affect us, it is our definition of its implication that upsets us. Becoming distraught over the behavior of others, while implying that we have power to control them, actually lessens our ability to change them. In any event, we suffer in the process and neglect our own problems. The rational person determines whether the behavior of others warrants becoming disturbed about, and if so, then attempts to do something that will help the other person to change. If nothing can be done, he accepts it and makes the best of it.

11 *There is always a right or perfect solution to every problem, and it must be found or the results will be catastrophic* This is irrational because (a) there is no such perfect solution, (b) the imagined results of failure to find such a solution are unreal, but the insistence on finding one leads to anxiety or panic, (c) such perfectionism results in poorer solutions than are actually possible. The rational person attempts to find various possible solutions to a problem and accepts the best or most feasible, recognizing that there is no perfect answer.

These fallacious ideas are almost universal in our society, and when they are accepted and reinforced by continuous self-indoctrination, they lead to emotional disturbances or neurosis, since they cannot be lived up to. The disturbed individual is unhappy because he is unable to achieve his unreasonable shoulds, oughts, and musts. "For once a human being believes the kind of nonsense included in these notions, he will inevitably tend to become inhibited, hostile, defensive, guilty, ineffective, inert, uncontrolled, unhappy. If, on the other hand, he could become thoroughly released from all these fundamental kinds of illogical thinking, it would be exceptionally difficult for him to become intensely emotionally upset, or at least to sustain his disturbance for any extended period." [12]

While the Freudians are right in pointing out the influences of early childhood on emotional disturbances, these are only secondary causes and could not continue to be influential if the individual did not acquire any of the basic illogical ideas listed above. It is not his early experiences alone that cause the disturbance, but his attitudes and thoughts about them, which are engendered by the illogical ideas.

Ellis discusses the relationship of his position to certain philosophies and philosophical issues. His early designation of his approach as rational therapy was abandoned because it led to confusion with other "rational" therapies and with the classical rationalist philosophy, which he does not accept. He is, however, sympathetic to modern or neorationalism, which applies reason and logic to science and to the search for truth, and which is opposed to supernaturalism, mysticism, dogmatism, etc. He is also in sympathy with most of the goals for living of the modern existentialists and accepts the following themes from Braaten: "(1) Man, you are free, define yourself; (2) Cultivate your own individuality; (3) Live in dialogue with your fellow man; (4) Your own experiencing is the highest authority; (5) Be fully present in the immediacy of the moment; (6) There is no truth except in action; (7) You can transcend yourself in spurts; (8) Live your potentialities creatively; (9) In choosing yourself, you choose man; and (10) You must learn to accept certain limits in life." [13]

Rational-emotive therapy accepts the fact that human events are largely controlled by causal factors beyond the individual's will, but believes that the human being has the possibility, difficult though it may be, of taking action now that will change and control his future. This recognition of the individual's ability to determine, in good part, his own behavior and emotional experience is expressed in the A-B-C theory of personality incorporated in rational-emotive therapy: A is the existence of a fact, an event, or the behavior or attitude of another person; C is the reaction of the individual—emotional disturbance or unhappiness—that is presumed to follow directly from A. However, it is not A that is the cause of C, but B, which is the self-verbalization of the individual about A, his definition or interpretation of A as awful, terrible, horrible, etc. The recognition of this relationship leads to the possibility of changing and controlling one's attitudes and behavior in reaction to circumstances.

THE THERAPY PROCESS

In view of the above philosophy and concepts regarding the nature of emotional disturbance, it follows that the process of counseling, according to Ellis, is the curing of unreason by reason. While there are other ways of controlling emotions—by electrical or chemical means, by sensorimotor techniques, or by doing something out of love or respect for someone else—counseling or psychotherapy does so by using the cerebral processes. Man, as a rational being, is able to avoid or eliminate most emotional disturbance or unhappiness by learning to think rationally. This is what occurs during the therapy process.

The task of the therapist is to help the client get rid of illogical, irrational ideas and attitudes and to substitute logical, rational ideas and attitudes for them. The first step in the process is to show the client that he is illogical, to help him understand how and why he became so, and to demonstrate the relationship of his irrational ideas to his unhappiness and emotional disturbance. Ellis recognizes that most therapeutic approaches do this, but they (1) do it passively and indirectly and (2) stop there.

In the second step rational-emotive therapy goes beyond this step by showing the client that he is maintaining his disturbance by continuing to think illogically, that is, that it is his present irrational thinking that is responsible for his condition, and not the continuing influence of early events.

The third step is to get the client to change his thinking, to abandon his irrational ideas. While some approaches depend upon the client to do this himself, rational-emotive therapy recognizes that the illogical thinking is so ingrained that the client cannot change it by himself.

A final step goes beyond dealing with the specific illogical ideas of the client and considers the main general irrational ideas, together with a more rational philosophy of living, so that the client can avoid falling victim to other irrational ideas and beliefs.

The result of this process is that the client acquires a rational philosophy of life; he substitutes rational attitudes and beliefs for irrational ones. Once this is accomplished, the negative, disturbing emotions are eliminated, along with self-defeating behavior.

Ellis discusses the six necessary and sufficient conditions of constructive personality change proposed by Rogers[14] and points out exceptions to each of them.[15] He then asks, "Are there, then, any other conditions that are absolutely necessary for constructive personality change to take place?" Although he concludes that the answer is probably No, he nevertheless is inclined to feel that there is one, "and that is that somehow, through some professional or non-professional channel, and through some kind of experience with himself, with others, or with things and events, the afflicted individual must learn to recognize his irrational, inconsistent, and unrealistic perceptions and thoughts, and change these for more logical, more reasonable philosophies of life. Without this kind of fundamental change in his ideologies and philosophic assumptions, I am tempted to say, no deep-seated personality changes will occur." [16] However, he recognizes that some people *seem* to change without meeting this condition, including those who change as a result of modification of environmental conditions. But Ellis notes that it is largely tautological to say that the individual must change his thinking or his value system to change his personality. Thus, he admits that he is not talking about necessary conditions, which would deal with *how* such a change occurs. In this connection, he also admits that it is probably not necessary for the counselor to go beyond the second step described above, although he feels that few clients, or other people, "seem to have significantly improved in spite of their not having a conpetent rational therapist to help them understand how they acquired, how they are currently sustaining, and how they can and should forthrightly attack and annihilate their basic irrational attitudes and assumptions." [17]

Thus, he concludes that there are no necessary conditions for personality change, but only desirable ones, and that it is an either/or situation. Nevertheless, he still feels that rational-emotive therapy is, in his experience at least, the most effective method for achieving basic personality change.

IMPLEMENTATION: TECHNIQUES OF THERAPY

Ellis refers to rational-emotive therapy as "a somewhat unusual technique of therapy." [18] His discussion of technique is not extensive, however. Perhaps it is because there is essentially only one technique, which is illustrated in his book by several excerpts. These excerpts are all apparently edited to bring out clearly the method of therapy.

Pointing out that "all effective psychotherapists, whether or not they realize what they are doing, teach or induce their patients to reperceive or rethink their life events and philosophies and thereby change their unrealistic and illogical thought, emotion, and behavior," [19] Ellis feels that the techniques other therapists use to accomplish this are relatively indirect and inefficient. Techniques such as abreaction, catharsis, dream analysis, free association, interpretation of resistance, and transference analysis are often successful, at least in bringing the client to recognize his illogical thinking. However, Ellis feels that even when most successful, these "emotional" methods are wasteful. The relationship itself and expressive-emotive, supportive, and insight-interpretive methods, although used in rational-emotive therapy, are preliminary techniques to establish rapport, to enable the client to express himself, and to show him he is respected. "If, because the patient is exceptionally upset when he comes to therapy, he must first be approached in a cautious, supportive, permissive, and warm manner, and must sometimes be allowed to ventilate his feeling in free-association, abreaction, role playing, and other expressive techniques, that may be a necessary part of effective therapy. But the rational therapist does not delude himself that these relationship-building and expressive-emotive methods are likely to really get to the core of the patient's illogical thinking and induce him to cogitate more rationally." [20] While occasionally this is sufficient, more often it is not.

The essential technique of rational-emotive therapy is active, directive teaching. After the initial stage the counselor assumes an active teaching role to reeducate the client. He demonstrates the illogical origin of the client's disturbance and the persistence of illogical self-verbalizations that continue the disturbance. Clients are shown "that their internalized sentences are quite illogical and unrealistic in certain respects . . . The effective therapist should continually keep unmasking his patient's past, and, especially, his present illogical thinking or self-defeating verbalizations by (a) bringing them forcefully to his attention or consciousness; (b) showing him how they are causing and maintaining his disturbance and unhappiness; (c) demonstrating exactly what the illogical links in his internalized sentences are; and (d) teaching him how to re-think, challenge, contradict, and re-verbalize these (and other similar) sentences so that his internalized thoughts become more logical and efficient." [21]

"Rational-emotive psychotherapy makes a concerted attack on the disturbed person's illogical positions in two main ways: (1) The therapist serves as a frank counter-propagandist who directly contradicts and denies the self-defeating propaganda and superstitions which the patient has originally learned and which he is now self-instilling. (2) The therapist encourages, persuades, cajoles, and occasionally even insists that the patient engage in some activity (such as doing something he is afraid of doing) which itself will serve as a forceful counter-propaganda agency against the nonsense he believes." [22]

The rational-emotive counselor thus uses logic and reason, teaching, suggestion, persuasion, confrontation, deindoctrination, indoctrination, and prescription of behavior to show the client what his irrational philosophies are, to demonstrate how these lead to his emotionally disturbed behavior, to change his thinking—and thus his emotions—replacing these irrational philosophies with rational, logical ones. In addition, as was indicated earlier, the counselor goes further, to instruct the client, as a protective measure, in the major irrational ideas of our culture and to provide him with more effective rational ones.

Ellis cautions about overexpectations from any method of counseling or psychotherapy.[23] He feels that there are many biological tendencies, which he enumerates, leading to the development and persistence of emotional disturbance and neurotic behavior in human beings. It might be argued, however, that it is more likely that human beings have the potential for developing in many different ways, rather than specific tendencies in one direction or another. Thus, it is likely that the early social environment is more influential than Ellis believes. This appears consistent with the fact that many of his so-called biological tendencies (instincts) are opposites or contradictory. There remains, of course, a biological aspect to behavior.

But whether biologically or biosocially determined, there is no doubt that the factors that Ellis notes are important in limiting the use and effectiveness of counseling or psychotherapy, and should lead to modest expectations on the part of counselors or psychotherapists.

EXAMPLE

The patient with whom the following recorded interview is held is a thirty-one-year-old free-lance copywriter who has been a fixed homosexual since the age of fourteen. He has had only a few heterosexual experiences, when girls have taken the initiative with him; and these did not turn out well, since he has shown himself to be too passive, effeminate, and "campy," and the girls therefore quickly sought other lovers. He has been very promiscuous homosexually; but even in this area has tended to be unaggressive and passive, and never to make the first overtures himself and thereby risk possibly being rejected.

The recorded interview [of which the first half is reproduced below] comprises the fifteenth session with the patient, who had been seen irregularly for individual psychotherapy over a period of seven months at the time it occurs. However, he has more regularly attended group psychotherapy for the past five months. He first came to therapy largely because he wanted to do creative writing but did not have the courage to try, even though he was competent as a copywriter. After a few months of therapy, he did actively try some creative writing, and has been steadily progressing at it ever since. He also considerably improved his general working habits. At first, however, he made no attempt to work on his homosexual problem; and only in the few weeks before the fifteenth session did he show any inclination to do so. Both the therapist and his therapy group had been encouraging him to try going with girls, and he now seemed ready to make a serious attempt to do so—though, as the contents of this interview show, he is resisting heterosexual participation in several subtle and obvious ways.

The recorded session that follows is a fairly typical interview, employing rational-emotive technique, except that the patient, probably because of the previous individual and group sessions he has had, is more accepting than many other patients are, and requires relatively little counterattacking and annihilating of his irrationally held positions. But he does give considerable lip service, as so many patients do, rather than true allegiance, to sane views and actions; and the therapist consequently keeps trying to induce him to question and challenge his lip service, and to think and act in a manner that will lead to truly rational convictions, and hence to thoroughgoing emotional and behavioral changes.[24]

(The first few minutes of the session consist of joking about making the tape recording.)

THERAPIST   How are things?

PATIENT   Oh, pretty good. I'm uh, haven't been too well, I can't say I haven't been too disturbed. I've been keeping pretty busy, but I'm on that going to sleep routine again.

TH   Yeah?

PT   And I don't, you know, I don't, I don't think I really need the sleep but I just sleep.

TH   How much have you been sleeping?

PT   Uh, well, like last . . . I've been making it a point to get home at midnight and usually if I'll go to, you know, if I, if I go to sleep at midnight I feel that I should wake up around eight or nine, you know eight-thirty in the morning . . .

TH   Yeah?

PT   And it's to my advantage to wake up then 'cause I can get a day started. And I'm discovering that I'm waking up at nine-thirty and ten and eleven . . . (laughs while saying this)

TH   Yeah, yeah?

PT   And then in the afternoons, if I get tired . . . Like yesterday afternoon I went in and I thought, "Well I'll flop down." I was sort of, I'd been writing all day; my eyes were tired; and I thought, "I'll sleep for an hour because, um, then I'll go out to dinner." And this was at five and I woke up at eight-thirty. And this is just too much sleep, you know. I'm just wasting too much time sleeping . . . (laughs while saying this)

TH   Yeah?

PT   And I don't, uh . . . You know, if, if I were physically exhausted it might make sense, but I'm not.

TH   Are you sleeping past an alarm, or anything like that? Or are you not bothered with the alarm?

PT   Uh, no, I haven't. I haven't bothered with the alarm, except that I know for a fact last night I slept through a phone call; the phone rang and it didn't wake me up. And the messenger boy from the desk had a package and he came up about, he said about six, and said he knocked and knocked on the door and I didn't wake up. So evidently I'm really going out, you know. I'm not waking up to noises.

TH   Yeah, really sleeping right through them . . .

PT   Yeah, yeah. And you know, and it, like an unexpected noise. I would, I should think I would, wake up, you know, more rapidly. At least I used to be a very light sleeper. Anybody walked through the room, I'd wake up.

TH   Yeah?

PT   And if somebody . . . (last part of sentence inaudible because of T's interruption)

TH   Well, uh, why don't you have an alarm on?

PT   Well, up until just recently . . . oh, the last year . . . I've always been able to flop down and say I'm going to sleep for an hour, and I'd sleep for an hour and wake up.

TH   Yeah.

PT   And now I'm getting, you know, like . . . I don't know, an attitude of "I can sleep." Or, or I don't, I don't respond to what I'm telling myself: that I'm gonna wake up.

TH   You don't have that internal alarm clock going . . .

PT   No, which I used to . . . could count on.

TH   Yeah.

PT   You know, if I'd say, "I gonna wake up at seven," I'd be up at, you know, five minutes till.

TH   But isn't the thing, then: if your internal alarm isn't working, to use the . . .

PT   Yeah.

TH   . . . external until it does work?

PT   But it's uh; it's just that I, you know . . . If, if I have to get up, I suppose I could, you know. I would use an alarm. . . .

TH   Yeah?

PT   But just the. . . . What bothers me is the idea of, of why am I wanting to sleep so darn much (laughs while saying this), you know, when I know it's physically not necessary for me now, because I'm getting more sleep than I ever have . . .

TH   Yeah.

PT   Unless it's, uh, you know, just a hiding kind of habit . . .

TH   And then you think it, it possibly might be that you're trying to evade work, or evade life, or something like that?

PT   I think that probably that's the only thing I can figure. But one thing: since I told you I was, you know, I was quitting with the boys . . .

TH   Yeah?

PT   I've, uh, you know, seen some of the, the, the boys that I've known . . .

TH   Yeah? (barely audible)

PT   They have come to dinner and things like that. But this is where I've made it a point to be home by twelve o'clock. And I haven't, I ain't had no sex at all for two or three weeks, 'cause I haven't made it with any of the girls I've met yet.

TH   Yeah.

PT   And, uh, you know, I have the feeling that maybe I'm sort of hiding behind sleeping, you know. I know, I know I'm not getting the sex I would like, so I go to sleep and sleep it off, you know. (laughs while saying this)

TH   Yeah.

PT   That's the only reason I can, think I can figure. Of course, I don't feel frustrated in any . . . particularly in any other area.

TH   But when you're awake, do you feel sexually frustrated?

PT   No. Now this is also the strange part. I was noticing this morning that since this, you know, since I said I was gonna try really working at getting girl friends and things, I haven't been at all, uh particularly desirous of sex. You know, I haven't, uh, just felt like gee, you know, I've gotta go out and, and, and find something or somebody.

TH   Yeah.

PT   Of course, for one thing, frankly, the times I have felt I want to have some, you know, have sexual relief, it's just too easy to masturbate, you know. I can always take care of myself that way (laughs while saying this), which isn't, you know, doesn't really solve the problem particularly except . . .

TH   Yeah.

PT   . . . it is a relief.

TH   Well, again: do you think that your lack of sex desire is an evasion for . . . ?

PT   Yeah, I do. I think that on one, on one hand, uh, I'm thinking, you know. . . . I say now, you know, I want this and logically this is what I want to do; and still I'm some, you know, more subconsciously then and, and sort of sneaky subconsciously (sort of laughs) I must be fighting it too, dodging it, ducking it, not, you know. . . . Taking the easy way out . . .

TH   All right now. Let's ask ourselves. . . . Let's assume for the moment that this is true, that you are "sneaky subconsciously," as you say, fighting it. Let's ask ourselves exactly what you would be saying to yourself, sneaking subconsciously, in order to fight it. What would you be afraid of with, let us say, the girls, that would induce you (a) to sleep more, which you are doing, and (b) when you're awake, not to have that much of a sex desire?

[Up to this point, the therapist has waited, somewhat more patiently than is often done in the highly active-directive method of rational-emotive psychotherapy, for the patient to bring out some material that would show that he is not yet acting on his resolve to go with girls instead of, as in his whole previous life, with boys; when this material is brought up, the therapist is then able to use it to illustrate to the patient exactly what he is telling himself—consciously or unconsciously—to create his inactivity and his indecision. He now tries to get the patient to see that his lack of sex desire and his greater demands for evasive sleeping do not exist in their own right, but *are* related to concrete, simple exclamatory sentences with which the patient is indoctrinating himself.]

PT   Now that's the . . . that's the hard one, frankly, 'cause I don't think I'm afraid, in the sense of being afraid of girls . . .

TH   Yeah?

PT   . . . I mean, uh, of a sex relationship. I think what I'm afraid of is probably just the going out and the, and the first. . . . I'm really afraid of the first contact, the how to get into it.

TH   Yeah, of the encounter, the meeting . . .

PT   Yeah, yeah.

TH   That you do have to go out first and get to meet and know the girl . . .

PT   Yeah. And, and that's, when I, you know, I get terribly shy and I get all, you know, messed up. And I think probably what I'm doing is, is, you know, well, if you oversleep, then you don't have to go out.

TH   Yes, that's true. And if you don't have the sex desire, you don't have to go out.

PT   Yeah, yeah!

[The therapist solidly nails down the circumlocuting patient, and gets him to admit that his sleepiness and his lack of sex desire are both excuses for his not wanting to go with girls because he is afraid of rejection, especially during the first contacts. But, not being satisfied with this admission or insight on the patient's part, he still tries to get him to see the exact self-sentences he is employing to create his fear so that he can then logically parse and attack these internalized sentences.]

TH   All right, now. Let's assume that, for the moment, that you're afraid of the contact. Now let's get the exact sentence which you're saying to yourself to make yourself afraid of this contact. What are you saying is *dreadful?*

PT   Well, it sounds too simple to say, "They won't like me," you know . . .

TH   In oth . . .

PT   . . . And I'm sure that's the bottom of it.

TH   Yeah. In other words, you're saying, "If I go . . ."

PT   But I'm inventing a lot of crap to say (sort of laughs) "I won't . . . They won't like me," I guess.

TH   Well, let's get that a little more specific. You're saying, "If I go out and meet the girls or a girl," let us say, "then there's a good possibility that she won't like me and that would be *dreadful . . .*"

PT   Yeah.

TH   ". . . if she didn't." Is that the sentence you think you're saying?

PT   I don't, I don't, I can't say that that's just it, though.

TH   Yeah?

PT   It's, it's like, uh, you know. I defeat myself before I go out, because pretty, half the time I just said, "well, I'm gonna go somewhere and I'm. . . ." You know, like, you know. I joined the Museum of Modern Art and I've gone a couple of times and I walk in and I look around and immediately I don't e . . . , I don't even see a girl I, that, that is appealing looking to me.

TH   Yeah.

PT   You know. So already before I, you know, I'm, I'm, I'm cutting myself short before I even start.

TH   Yeah, but again . . .

PT   And I don't know whether . . .

TH   . . . is that just another technique for the fear again? You, you've given two techniques so far: one, you say . . .

PT   (interrupting and answering T's first question) It probably is, it probably is.

TH   . . . asleep; two, you lose the desire. And three is you're saying, "The girl isn't good-looking enough."

PT   Yeah.

TH   But we still get back to the proposition that if you did have the desire, if you did get up early, and if she were good-looking enough, and you did make some kind of a, an overture, that she then wouldn't like you?

PT   Yeah.

TH   And that would be terrible?

PT   Yeah, I guess. Yeah, uh, I, I, I'm, I mean, that, that's, that's right . . .

TH   Uh-huh. (barely audible)

PT   But I don't even think I've got to the stage of finishing it out and saying, "that would be terrible." (laughs while saying this)

TH   But you don't say it . . .

PT   (interrupting) I mean, I'm, I'm, you know, I'm not rationally saying, I mean, I'm not letting, openly saying it to myself . . .

TH   You're not consciously saying that. Right. But doesn't your behavior show *by inference* that you must be saying something like that? Because if you were saying just "If I went out and did these things, didn't sleep, had the sex desire, and liked the girl physically, she might reject me"—just that; if you were saying that, would you then start going into these evasive dives of yours? If you weren't saying that "It would be terrible if she did reject me," because if she rejected you, you'd still get the lovely *experience* of being rejected . . .

PT   Yeah, yeah.

TH   So on some level you must be saying that "It would be terrible, if would be awful! I couldn't take it; look what a crumb I would be if she rejected me!"

PT   Also involved in there is that, uh. . . . As we talk I'm realizing that I think I'm still very, I'm too much on my own terms. Like when I go out to the, to the Modern and I wanna meet a girl and I don't meet her in the first ten minutes . . .

TH   Yeah.

PT   Then, you know, it's a bad deal; and I walk out and go home. (laughs while saying this)

> [Although the patient keeps talking in a slippery, somewhat over-cavalierly accepting and yet evasive manner, the therapist keeps trying to pin him down; and insists that his behavior, if not his words, *show* that he must be telling himself that it would be awful if he were rejected by a girl. Instead of becoming defensive about this persistence on the therapist's part—which according to many psychoanalytic and client-centered theories he is theoretically supposed to do—the patient is partly driven from his lair, and makes an even more incriminating admission: namely, that he not only goes to sleep and downs his own sex desires, but that even when he finally drives himself to the museum to look for girls, he doesn't really give them a chance, but rejects them during the first ten minutes and gives up the search. This often occurs during rational-emotive therapy: the therapist's active persistence brings out more confirming material from the patient, instead of leading to classic resistance.]

TH   Is there a little . . . ?

PT   You know, uh, I'm, I'm sort of making the effort but not really the effort, at least, uh . . .

TH   Yeah. Now is there a little grandiosity here? Really . . .

PT   Yes, unfortunately, I, I, you know, I'm looking for somebody good enough for me, not me good enough for them. (sort of laughs while saying this)

TH   Yes, and is this . . . ?

PT   And I think it is part of the problem . . .

TH   Is there another sentence?—that if John goes out and does these kinds of things . . .

PT   . . . they ought to come flocking and they don't! Yeah.

TH   That's right. "And they don't and this is terrible!"

PT   I think that's even more than the fear . . .

TH   Yeah.

PT   You know, more than the physical fear . . .

TH   The fact that it's so unfair that they're not flock . . .

PT   Yeah, yeah!

TH   And they should!

PT   Yeah. Because, you know, I get, it's, uh, it's a crooked thing. I get all this shit from everybody about, you know, "You're a good-looking guy and . . ." you know . . .

TH   Yeah.

PT   "You shouldn't have any problems about meeting people . . ."

TH   Yeah.

PT   And I do! (sort of laughs) You know, I just flat out do. And I go out with this great feeling of gee, you know, "I'm God's gift to women." And then nothing happens (laughs while saying this), you know . . .

> [Again, the therapist, by his insistent, direct interpretation, has smoked out the patient a little more. Rather than wait for the patient to see that, in addition to being overly fearful, he is also grandiose—which he might or might not finally see—the therapist directly questions him about this, and he admits that there is a grandiose element mixed in with his fear. In fact, as the patient goes on to see, his feelings of grandiosity then lead to his becoming still more fearful; since, when he starts out with the idea that he's God's gift to women and, largely because of his own quick withdrawal or lack of full participation, nothing happens to help him meet suitable girls, he then becomes *more* afraid to make overtures and thereby prove that he is not so great as he assumes he is.]

TH   Yes. But isn't that notion that you're a good-looking guy and you shouldn't have any trouble meeting people, isn't that rather unrealistic? Because, no matter how good-looking you are and how bright you are and how well educated, don't we *all* have trouble meeting people?

PT   Well, I don't know about the rest of the world; but *I* do! (laughs while saying this). No, really, you know, it's . . .

TH   But, but don't you think that most people have some degree of trouble—even though they have relatively less than others who are not good-looking, or are stupid and uneducated? Don't they always have some trouble? And don't they have to do some work to overcome that some degree of trouble?

> [The therapist emphasizes here one of the main ideas of rational-emotive therapy: namely, that insight into one's disturbances is not enough, and that after gaining such insight, one must *work* to counteract one's self-defeating philosophies and to *do* what one is afraid to do.]

PT   Yeah, that's it. I think that really, you know, a lot of the problem is that I, I, it's, it, I finally made up my mind that I would work at it and . . . But I'm not performing.

TH   Yeah.

PT   You know, up here I'm, I said it once. . . . I'm gonna work at it, but then I'm ducking it by going . . .

TH   But, that is, what is it, you're, what is . . . ?

PT   . . . at, at, at meeting people: at, at pushing myself a little more into walking up and saying, you know, "What's your name?" (laughs) Just that simple . . .

TH   That's fine. But isn't that the *second* thing you have to work at? You do have to work at that. But don't you also have to work at that crap you're telling yourself?—"They should . . .

PT   Yeah, yeah.

TH   ". . . they *should* do this for dear old John. And wouldn't it be *awful* if they didn't!"—and so on? Now isn't *that* where the work may *first* be required, before you can secondly get off your ass and go out and actually talk to girls . . .

PT   Yeah.

TH   . . . and meet them and so on? So you're seeing it, number two, as your . . .

PT   The goal, but I'm not seeing the, uh . . .

TH   Yeah. But are you seeing the *more important goal,* which has plagued you all your life in so many other respects, in your work and so on? The number one, that I must work on *me,* on John . . .

PT   Um-hm. (barely audible)

TH   . . . on what *I* tell myself. Now are you seeing *that* very clearly?

PT   Not really. That's where I get bogged down.

TH   Yeah.

[The therapist, again as an integral part of the rational-emotive therapeutic approach, wants to make sure that the patient just doesn't jump in, without any real understanding of the basic issue involved, to approach the girls he wants to meet. Instead, the therapist insists that he must first tackle problem number one—the basic philosophic nonsense that he is telling himself to create his fear of girls—and to create difficulties in his work and other aspects of his life. If he tackles this number-one problem and sees what irrational sentences he is telling himself to create his anxiety and his inertia, then he can more easily and logically tackle problem number two, the actual making of overtures to the girls.]

PT   And that, that was where the other day, I was, uh . . . , I no—, I . . . I noticed after I'd been talking to the whole group (that is, his therapy group) that I kept talking about things; and that in a sense is my thing.

TH   Yeah.

PT   Is, I mean. . . .The, the goal is, I'm substituting the goal as a thing rather than, than working on *me* as a thing . . . (sort of laughs while saying this)

TH   That's right, that's right; you got it with the others in the group . . .

PT   Yeah.

TH   You could see it with Betty the other time in the group—but are you really seeing it with *you?*

> [In his previous group therapy session, the patient pointed out to some of the other members of the group that they were not really working on *themselves,* but on changing certain things about their external lives. He now begins to see that he is doing exactly this himself, trying to change his overt behavior with girls, but not trying to change his own basic catastrophizing philosophies, which create his fearful behavior.]

PT   I mean, now. . . . Like the first date is the thing I'm shooting for; and it really shouldn't be that important to me.

TH   Yes. Oh, it should be important . . .

PT   I mean, it should be important. But it shouldn't be the. . . . It's for *later.* (laughs) That it happened . . .

TH   The main, right. . . . The main thing is changing *John.*

PT   Yeah.

TH   What *he's* telling himself; *his* ideas, *his* philosophies. Which have kept you back, as we just said a minute ago, in lots of other respects, including and especially this one with the girls. Now shouldn't most, or a great deal, of the work, at least, be *there?* Then, finally, you still will have to do the work of . . .

PT   Yeah.

TH   . . . getting up, as I said, off your ass and going out and meeting the girls. But you never quite get to that when you're doing the counterwork, we might say, of falling asleep . . .

PT   Yeah, yeah. (barely audible)

TH   . . . so much; of not having sex desires; of seeing that the girls are ugly; and so on—which is John. That's *John.*

PT   Yeah, yeah. (barely audible)

TH   There: that's what you're telling yourself at what I call point *B* . . .

PT   At the, yeah. At the same time I must, I must, ah, ah, just out of sheer fairness to me and the discussion (sort of laughs) admit that I *have* been noticing pretty girls more lately . . .

TH   Yes?

PT   I mean, uh, occasionally on the subway, I haven't had, haven't had . . . have yet to get the nerve to walk over to a pretty girl I'll see on the subway . . .

TH   Yeah?

PT   . . . and say, you know, you know, "I'd like to call you or something . . ." (sort of laughs)

TH   But the defenses are going down somewhat . . . ?

PT   But I'm seeing a lot prettier girls than, than I have, and . . .

TH   Yeah?

PT   . . . and discovering that I'm no—, that the, the prettier girls I'm seeing are younger . . .

TH   Yeah?

PT   . . . than me. Which is, I never noticed people, girls that were younger than me . . .

TH   You didn't notice all . . . ?

PT   They were always my age, or a little older.

TH   Yeah. Because you edited out . . .

PT   Yeah, yeah.

TH   . . . the most eligible and best-looking ones . . .

PT   Yeah.

TH   . . . so you wouldn't have to do anything about it.

PT   I'm, I'm, I'm sure that's it. But I, I really am noticing that there is an awful lot of younger, prettier girls around . . .

TH   All right. So that, that, that fearful and that grandiose sentence at point B of "Wouldn't it be awful if I failed or they should do this to me!" seems to be going down a bit and giving you leeway.

PT   At least I can look now! (laughs)

TH   That's right. At least you can look. But's it's still there . . .

PT   Yeah.

TH   . . . and it requires more work, apparently; you have done some on it, 'cause you have asked yourself, uh, "*Would* it be so awful?" And in your copywriting work and all, you are doing things now . . .

PT   Yeah.

TH   . . . which you've never done before in your life. Isn't that true?

PT   Um-hm. And I've even, I've even been active enough that I have made a couple of passes at people, and, you know, been refused. But at least I'm, I'm sort of trying even there.

TH   Yeah.

PT   Granted, I, the, that, one, one of the gals I made a pass at is as sick as I am, I think, and this is her problem, too. (laughs) But, uh, you know, at least I tried in some way to make known what I wanted to happen. (sort of laughs while saying this)

TH   And you weren't too afraid?

PT   No.

TH   So you're contemplating the fact that maybe it *isn't* so awful?

PT   No, actu—, and, and it was, uh, as I say. I, I, uh, uh, you know, it was. . . . It's a girl I, I know, Jane Hall; and I know she's, she and I have known each other for a long time and sort of been, you know, just good friends for years. I, I find Jane very appealing.

TH   Yeah.

PT   And, uh. . . . But I don't think I'd ever get anywhere with Jane, 'cause ah, she's, she's just a little too, uh, too hip on being a big businesswoman and one of the editors of *Harper's* and *Vogue*. And her career's gonna come first and all that kind of stuff . . .

TH   Yeah.

PT   . . . so that she sort of builds the wall out, too.

TH   Yes.

PT   And we had dinner the other night and she invited me up for a drink after dinner. And I went, and uh, I made a pass and she said No and that was that. But at least I tried. (laughs) Although granted I was, it was a pretty safe territory, 'cause I must, I, you know I, it was, I, I guess in a way, I felt that I probably would be refused anyway. It was like practice time. (laughs)

TH   I see. Yeah. So you were able to do it easier than with some girl that you wouldn't be sure of . . . ?

PT   Yeah, that I had no idea of.

TH   Yeah. But still it was an advance; and the practice is good, isn't it?

PT   Yeah, yeah, and I found, and I really did find, that I could make a pass without being embarrassed myself . . .

TH   Yeah.

PT   . . . at having, you know, made an improper approach or something.

TH   Sure.

PT   And I didn't get hit, so I guess I came out on top! (laughs while saying this)

TH   And you did get some experiences, too . . .

PT   Yeah, yeah. I mean, I came out more plus than minus, I guess. (still is sort of laughing)

TH   Right. How many girls have you made a pass at in your whole life?

PT   Four or five.

TH   So this was one of the four or five.

PT   Um-hm. I've been very reticent in that area, I will admit it. (laughs)

TH   Yeah.

PT   No. In fact, uh, even carry it further back. I don't think I've even made a pass with a guy, it was always, you know, they chased me . . .

TH   Yeah.

PT   And I'm sure that this has a lot of bearing on it. I want the women to chase me, too.

TH   Yes, that's right, too . . .

PT   You know, it's an old habit pattern as well as, yeah . . .

TH   Yeah, and isn't that one of the main reasons for homosexuality—that boys find that other boys will chase them, while women won't?

PT   Yeah.

TH   And it's much safer; and it wouldn't be so terrible, because they won't get rejected that often . . .

PT   Yeah. You can say Yes without being the villain of the piece.

TH   That's right.

> [As usual, the therapist tries to go a bit beyond the immediate conversation and to make the educational point that the patient is much like many other homosexuals, that he has been afraid to be assertive with girls and to risk rejection thereby; so he has found it easier to be passive with males. Fear of rejection will naturally lead to nonassertive behavior, the therapist is saying; and only by tackling this fear and seeing that it is not terrible to be rejected will the patient become truly nonhomosexual and otherwise more assertive.]

PT   You know . . .

TH   You refuse them, but they're not going to refuse you . . .

PT   Yeah, that's, that's very true, because . . .

TH   Let's get back to changing John. *Would* it be so terrible if you got refused, even by a girl you didn't know that there was a good chance beforehand she was going to refuse you, and you didn't know at all what was going to be? Or *would* it be so terrible if you grandiosely *didn't* get exactly what you wanted without any effort and without their selecting you?

PT   No, it, it, uh, it wouldn't be bad. This I, you know, I, this I can, I can logically believe this.

TH   At *times.*

PT   Yeah, at times.

TH   But *most* of the time, more strongly, you still believe the other things . . .

PT   Yeah. And somehow, I, I don't catch myself saying it to myself.

TH   That's right.

PT   It's, it's an old habit pattern of . . . I, I mean, you know, I don't even really know when I say to myself, you know, "duck and dodge!"

TH   And yet isn't that the value of the symptom, such as the sleeping too much . . .

PT   Yeah.

TH   . . . and so on—that if you track 'em down, you'll find that you must be saying . . .

PT   Yeah.

TH   . . . these things to yourself if the symptom is still there?

> [The therapist points out that even though at times the patient believes that it is not terrible if he gets refused by a girl, most of the time he still believes that it *is,* and he is concretely telling himself that it is. The patient agrees, but points out that he does not clearly see that he is saying catastrophizing sentences to himself. Persistently, however, as is common in this form of psychotherapy, the therapist shows him that his symptoms prove, behaviorally, that he *must* be telling himself something along these catastrophizing lines.]

PT   But the, what I'm saying is that I see it *after* the fact . . .

TH   Right.

PT   After I've gone to sleep (sort of laughs) and wake up, I think, "Oh, oh, it's eight o'clock! You've shot the whole evening, you know . . ."

TH   Yes, but if you . . .

PT   ". . . you goofed!" (laughs) But . . .

TH   All right. But if you clearly see it *after* the fact and keep admitting completely after the fact even, that, "Yes, I still do have this horrifying idea," won't you get it back to *before* the fact, in time?

PT   I guess I will.

TH   We must perceive that we have the negative notions—the fears and the hostilities and the grandiosities—before we can really get to work on them. And if you can perceive and perceive and perceive them through these symptoms—the lack of sex desire, the oversleeping, and so forth—then you can finally get back and clip them, contradict them, challenge them, kick them in the teeth.

SUMMARY AND EVALUATION

Rational-emotive counseling assumes that, although there are powerful biological and social forces leading to irrationality, man has the potential for being rational. In fact, emotional disturbance and neurosis are irrational thinking, and can be remedied by changing such thinking, and consequently emotions and behavior, to a logical, rational kind. The aim of counseling or psychotherapy is to help the disturbed individual achieve this substitution. While other commonly practiced methods of therapy may be used at the beginning of the process, rational-emotive therapy relies mainly on a didactic, or teaching, process wherein the irrational ideas and thinking of the client are pointed out, their relationship to his disturbance or unhappiness is explicated, and his thinking is changed by logic and reasoning, suggestions, persuasion, and prescription of activities.

Ellis does not claim that his approach is effective with all kinds of clients. He admits its limitations and the usefulness of other methods. This method is not claimed to be effective with clients lacking in intelligence, though no exact limits are specified. Clients who are too severely disturbed or confused are also not appropriate subjects. The very young and the very old, the too impressionable and the inflexible, those too prejudiced against logic and reason, and the organically defective are others for whom it is felt to be inappropriate. The cases discussed by Ellis include a homosexual, a schizophrenic, and a psychopath, among others, indicating the wide range of clients for whom his approach apparently is appropriate. Nevertheless, Ellis claims 90 percent success with the method, although by success he does not mean cure, but improvement. As in the case of all therapists, however, there is, no doubt, a selective factor operating in determining the clients whom he sees, so that it might be questioned whether 90 percent of all those who are disturbed and who seek counseling would benefit from this approach. The criteria of success must also be considered.

In this respect, the aims or goals of counseling stated by Ellis appear to be similar to those of most other counselors or psychotherapists. He speaks not only of the elimination of anxiety, depression, fears, inferiority, unhappiness, and other symptoms, but of happiness, effective living, rational behavior, independence, responsibility, and even self-actualization. The question may be raised as to the evidence that all these things are achieved or are achieved as well as by other methods. Because the methods of Ellis are quite different from those of many other counselors who seek the same goals for their clients, it is necessary to determine if the results are the same. Other counselors, as Ellis recognizes, place the responsibility for correcting the client's illogical ideas on the client himself. Ellis, perhaps because of the nature of his personality, does not have confidence in the client's ability to achieve this himself—or perhaps he is too impatient to allow the client to do so in his own slow, plodding way. Ellis admits that clients have the potential for growth and health, but he believes that this potential is so covered by long-standing irrational attitudes, beliefs, and emotions that only an active, direct effort on the part of the counselor can uncover it.

If the arguments of Ellis regarding the helplessness, dependence, and self-discouragement of clients were valid, then it would appear that less directive methods would have little chance of any success, although Ellis himself admits that they are sometimes, if not often, successful, but unnecessarily time-consuming. The less directive counselors would argue that time is necessary for the client to mobilize his growth potential, and that it is better for him to do this himself and reach his own solutions than for the counselor to present him with ready solutions to his problems. They would argue that the obsession of many counselors with efficiency, their emphasis on speeding up the counseling process, their desire to achieve results quickly, may have some disadvantages or possibly some undesirable results. In addition to depriving the client of the satisfaction of achieving his own solutions, it is possible that this active, efficiency-oriented approach may lead to the client's dependency and lack of confidence in himself. Lasting changes in personality and behavior may be achieved better by the slower process in which the individual works through his problems in his own way and at his own pace.

This is, of course, a matter for research, and a not unimportant question should be, better for what? in what way? It may well be true, of course, that the client would not, by himself, reach the same end results as do those clients who are treated by Ellis' methods. This is likely because rational-emotive counseling includes indoctrination in a large number of rather specific concepts, ideas, and philosophies that the average client might not explore and develop by himself. However, it does appear that the irrational ideas that Ellis identifies as being at the basis of emotional disturbance characterize many, if not most, disturbed individuals.

The emphasis upon the importance of perceptions and attitudes toward events in influencing behavior and emotional disturbance suggests that Ellis' approach might be similar to that of those counselors who accept a perceptual or phenomenological theory of human behavior. Ellis does not talk about the self-concept or self-ideal, however, although these concepts are apparent in the individual's self-verbalizations and his shoulds and musts as controlling ideas. There is no direct reference to phenomenology, but it is apparent in the recognition that behavior (C) is not determined by the stimulus (A), but by the individual's perception and definition of it (B).

Ellis agrees that the essence of effective counseling or psychotherapy is the changing of attitudes. While many other therapists believe that since attitudes are emotion-laden, a direct attack on them is ineffective, Ellis believes that since the attitudes of the disturbed person are irrational, a direct attack on their irrationality is best. He states that one of the main methods of changing attitudes is the didactic method and points to the effectiveness of propaganda as evidence for this approach. However, the evidence for the success of direct methods of changing attitudes is probably not as great as Ellis appears to believe. Everyday experience and common sense indicate that direct methods and argument are not effective methods of changing attitudes and behavior, but lead to resistance. Ellis recognizes the existence of resistance. While some resistance may be created by poor technique on the part of the counselor, however, there is also the resistance to change. But this resistance, Ellis notes, is to be expected, and should not prevent the counselor from persisting in his attempts to overcome it. Ellis does not appear to be aware of, or concerned about, the possibility that direct attacks on client resistance constitute a threat to the client, which only increases the resistance and makes change more difficult, if not impossible. There seems to be sufficient evidence that threat results in impairment of learning and reasoning to warrant being cautious in the use of direct, active methods, which might constitute a threat. However, it must be remembered that these methods are used within a therapeutic relationship; again, it would appear that the relationship aspects of rational-emotive therapy are underemphasized.

The fact that these methods are incorporated into a counseling situation, which involves a special kind of relationship, may influence their success. Even the special kind of relationship established in so-called brainwashing may lead to changes in opinions, beliefs, and attitudes, particularly when the indoctrinator genuinely and sincerely believes in what he is indoctrinating the subject in and is concerned about the subject's accepting it.

This leads to a comment on the imparting of values in counseling. There is, of course, no question that values are involved in counseling; that the values of the counselor must be considered; and that all counselors, since they determine the goals of counseling, are, to that extent at least, directive. But there are degrees of indoctrination, or of imposition of values or philosophies of life upon clients. It would appear that rational-emotive counseling is rather extreme in the extent and detail of the values it imposes on its clients. Ellis notes the danger that the counselor "may use his authority to induce his patient to acquire *his*, the therapist's, particular brand of beliefs," [25] yet does not seem to recognize that this is essentially what he does; although, to be sure, he uses reason and logic, together with authority.

There will undoubtedly be much criticism of rational-emotive therapy as being too rational, with neglect of the emotions. The popularity of psychoanalysis and other depth psychologies brought with it acceptance of the belief that disturbed behavior is due to mysterious repressed emotions. It has never been clear just how unexpressed emotions could exist and influence behavior. Nor has it been clear just how psychoanalysis or any other therapy deals with such unexpressed emotions directly. Making the so-called unconscious conscious is nothing more than putting into words unexpressed thoughts and ideas. Ellis has contributed to our understanding of the relation between emotion and thinking and has clarified what goes on in all counseling, since all counseling involves some verbalization.

Ellis also notes that cognition is gaining increasing recognition and attention in psychology. But, just as the emphasis of psychoanalysis and depth psychology, as a corrective against extreme rationalism, went too far, it is possible that the emphasis on cognition may likewise overextend itself. There appears to be much of experience or experiencing that cannot be verbalized. Such experiencing is important, and sometimes the sharing of it by just being in the presence of, or sharing in a relationship with, another understanding person can be clarifying and helpful.

Thus, it may be contended that the role, importance, and effectiveness of logic and reason are overemphasized, while the importance of the relationship is neglected. Things can go on in counseling when there is no overt verbalization, and changes in the client can occur. Now, of course, it can be noted that there are subvocal verbalizations going on in the client, and no doubt this is so at least some of the time. But it is not necessarily so. And when there is internal verbalization on the part of the client, it is the relationship with the counselor that makes this possible.

I would suspect that Ellis' results are more influenced by the relationship he has with his clients than he is willing to admit. His genuine interest in and concern for the client are apparent and must be important factors. In fact, if there are any necessary and sufficient conditions for personality change resulting from a personal relationship, they are probably these characteristics of the relationship. Ellis himself cites a case in which a paranoid client insisted that he did not understand her, yet she accepted and adopted some of his attitudes and values.[26] Ellis feels that it was the force of logic that influenced her. It is also possible that it was the relationship. Of course, it might possibly have been the authority and prestige elements, as these undoubtedly enter into other of his cases. For regardless of how logical and persuasive Dr. Ellis is, it is unlikely that he succeeds by this alone.

It is also true, as Ellis emphasizes, that rational-emotive counseling is not a cold, rational analysis, but does involve emotions. The client's self-verbalizations, which are related to his disturbance, are emotionally charged. Assuming that these thoughts are present—and there is no doubt that there are many unexpressed and relevant emotionally charged thoughts in clients—then it would appear that rational-emotive counseling is essentially an interpretive method, in which the counselor, on the basis of his theory of the nature and causation of emotional disturbance, interprets the client's unexpressed thoughts. While the apparent success of the method might be taken as evidence for the validity of the theory, it must be remembered that other interpretive methods, using other theories—for example, psychoanalysis—claim success and apparently are successful. As in these other systems, the client's acceptance of the interpretation does not validate it. On the other hand, if various interpretive methods are successful, it is possible, and indeed quite likely, that they all are utilizing the same (or some of the same) valid concepts, though they may be using different language.

We may conclude—although Ellis has not presented the evidence—that rational-emotive counseling is probably effective, at least with some clients. But a number of questions must still be raised: (1) Is it effective for the reasons Ellis believes? (2) In what ways is it effective—that is, does it achieve the same kinds of results as other approaches? Does it lead to independence and responsibility in the client, especially when compared with the results of other approaches, which emphasize the activity and responsibility of the client during the counseling process? (3) And finally, does the improvement persist? These, of course, are questions that must be asked of every approach to counseling.

REFERENCES

[1] Ellis, A. *Reason and emotion in psychotherapy.* New York: Lyle Stuart, 1962. P. 7.   [2] Ellis, A. New approaches to psychotherapy techniques. *J. clin. Psychol., Monogr. Suppl.,* No. 11, 1955.   [3] Ellis, A. Psychotherapy techniques for use with psychotics. *Amer. J. Psychother.,* 1955, **9,** 452–476.   [4] Ellis, A. An operational reformulation of some of the basic principles of psychoanalysis. *Psychoanal. Rev.,* 1956, **43,** 163–180.   [5] Ellis, A. Rational psychotherapy and individual psychotherapy. *J. indiv. Psychol.,* 1957, **13,** 38–44. [6] Ellis, A. Outcome of employing three techniques of psychotherapy. *J. clin. Psychol.,* 1957, **13,** 344–350.   [7] Ellis, A. Rational psychotherapy. *J. gen. Psychol.,* 1958, **59,** 35–49.   [8] Ellis, A. Rationalism and its therapeutic applications. In A. Ellis (Ed.), *The place of values in the practice of psychotherapy.* New York: American Academy of Psychotherapists, 1959.   [9] Ellis, A. *Reason and emotion in psychotherapy.* New York: Lyle Stuart, 1962. P. 50.   [10] *Ibid.,* p. 54. [11] *Ibid.,* p. 61.   [12] *Ibid.,* p. 89.   [13] Braaten, L. J. The main theories of "existentialism" from the viewpoint of the psychotherapist. *Ment. Hyg.,*

1961, **45,** 10–17.   **[14]** Rogers, C. R. The necessary and sufficient conditions of therapeutic personality change. *J. consult. Psychol.,* 1957, **21,** 459–461. **[15]** Ellis, A. *Reason and emotion in psychotherapy.* New York: Lyle Stuart, 1962. Chap. 5.   **[16]** *Ibid.,* p. 117.   **[17]** *Ibid.,* pp. 118–119.   **[18]** *Ibid.,* p. 38. **[19]** *Ibid.,* pp. 36–37.   **[20]** *Ibid.,* p. 95.   **[21]** *Ibid,* pp. 58–59.   **[22]** *Ibid.,* pp. 94–95.   **[23]** *Ibid.,* chap. 20.   **[24]** From a typescript provided by Albert Ellis.   **[25]** Ellis, A. *Reason and emotion in psychotherapy.* New York: Lyle Stuart, 1962. P. 367.   **[26]** *Ibid.,* p. 116.

PART TWO

Learning Theory Approaches to Counseling

4

Introduction

Learning may be defined as changes in behavior that are not due to native response tendencies, maturation, or temporary states of the organism (for example, fatigue or drugs).[1] Counseling or psychotherapy is concerned with behavior change and must, therefore, involve learning and be concerned with learning theory. Counseling or psychotherapy would thus be an application of principles of learning or learning theory.

While this reasoning is essentially acceptable to most psychologists and counselors, the actual situation is not as simple as such reasoning may suggest. Most approaches to counseling or psychotherapy have not developed from learning theory. Although it would appear that any approach must be consistent with or explainable by learning theory, most approaches have not been systematically evaluated from this point of view.

Two reasons apparently account for this lack of rapprochement. First, learning theory is still in a stage where it cannot be automatically applied widely to practical situations, particularly to situations involving abnormalities of behavior or deviation from normal behavior. While experimentation and research has recently burgeoned beyond the laboratory, it is limited for the most part to relatively simple behaviors in controlled situations.

Kimble, summarizing the situation regarding conditioning, writes:

79

It may, some day, be known whether the laws of conditioning do or do not explain (say) psychopathological behavior. But that day is still far in the future. For the time being all that is possible is to attempt the explanation of complex phenomena in simpler terms. It is to be expected that the resulting explanations will be incomplete and imperfect. Complex behavior, if it is explainable at all in these terms, certainly involves the simultaneous operation of many principles of conditioning. Unfortunately, these principles are not exactly known, and we know even less about the way in which they combine and function together.[2]

This statement should be kept in mind when reading accounts of therapy based upon learning theory and principles. These accounts usually state or imply that the methods are based upon known and experimentally demonstrated principles of learning.

Second, it is not possible to speak of a learning theory or a theory of learning. There is no single theory, but many theories, usually related, in the case of human beings, to limited areas of behavior, such as paired-associates learning of nonsense syllables or learning a simple psychomotor performance. Thus, when the claim is made that a particular approach or method of psychotherapy or counseling is an application of, or based upon, learning theory or learning principles, one must ask, "What theory?" or "What principle?"

The two major sources, in learning, for the various methods and techniques of learning-based approaches to counseling or psychotherapy, are classical (or respondent) conditioning and operant (or instrumental) conditioning. Classical conditioning derives from the work of Pavlov. Though others before him recognized and studied conditioning, he was the first to study it systematically and intensively. The paradigm for classical conditioning is the presence of an unconditioned stimulus that automatically evokes an unconditioned response, and a conditioned stimulus that evokes a conditioned response—which is similar to, or a part of, the unconditioned response—when paired with (presented shortly before) the unconditioned stimulus. Three aspects of classical conditioning are overlooked or ignored by many of those who apply this model to complex behavior in counseling or psychotherapy. The first is the fact that the conditioned response is not identical with the unconditioned response, sometimes being quite different and constituting an anticipatory response. The second is that (as Pavlov noted in his work with dogs) the specific response is not the only behavior evoked by the unconditioned or conditioned stimulus; the total organism responds, so that there are what might be termed "side effects" in conditioning. The third fact is that in laboratory work on conditioning, the subject is in a situation from which it cannot escape by developing avoidance (or instrumental) responses.

In operant conditioning voluntarily or spontaneously emitted (operant) behavior is strengthened (or discouraged) by positive reinforcement (reward) (or by negative reinforcement, which is a stimulus whose removal increases the probability of the behavior it follows), by lack of reinforcement (failure to reward either positively or negatively), or by punishment. The terms "operant" and "instrumental" derive from the concept that the conditioned behavior operates upon the environment or is instrumental in obtaining the reinforcement or the reward. In this sense the behavior appears to be beyond the control of the experimenter. Behavior, it is emphasized, is controlled by its consequences. Yet since the experimenter controls the consequences, or the application of reinforcers or punishment, he does control the behavior of the subject. There is an implication of cognitive awareness and choice, yet awareness is not necessary for conditioning to occur; in fact, strict behaviorists reject the existence of choice.

Classical and operant conditioning are not distinctly separable. In classical conditioning the unconditioned stimulus follows the conditioned stimulus. Thus the unconditioned stimulus may be seen, in operant conditioning terms, as reinforcing the association between the conditioned stimulus and the response. In operant conditioning the reinforcement follows the response that it is desired to strengthen, and this response may be said to become associated with the action (or stimulus) which preceded it. In operant conditioning the voluntary, spontaneously omitted behavior which is said to "produce" the reinforcement may be seen as the unconditioned stimulus. In classical conditioning the unconditioned stimulus is independent of the subject's behavior, while in operant conditioning it is dependent (contingent) upon his behavior. As Yates points out, if the classical conditioning experiment in which a conditioned stimulus is associated with a shock leading to the dog's involuntarily lifting his paw when the conditioned stimulus is present alone, is changed so that the animal is allowed to escape or avoid the shock by lifting his paw before the unconditioned stimulus has occured, then classical aversive conditioning becomes instrumental or operant aversive conditioning.[3]

Attempts have been made to combine or integrate the two types of conditioning into one model. Pavlov attempted to reduce instrumental conditioning to classical conditioning. Hull's system attempted to reduce classical conditioning to instrumental conditioning. Mowrer, who earlier proposed a two-factor theory of learning based upon their distinction,[4] later attempted to bring them together under the classical position.[5]

Concern about the relationship between learning and counseling or psychotherapy dates back many years.[6-13] The early discussions were mainly concerned with reinforcement theory and were mainly limited to interpretation or translation of methods of counseling or psychotherapy, such as psychoanalysis, into learning theory terms. The work of Dollard and Miller [14] is classical and is, therefore, included in this section. Rotter's social learning theory,[15] involving reinforcement, is an interesting variant and is also included. It is similar to the work of Dollard and Miller in that it is theory-based, deductive in orientation, and related to clinical experience in counseling or psychotherapy. Two other systematic attempts are those of the Pepinskys [16] and Pascal.[17] Phillips' interference theory approach is also a variant of reinforcement theory.[18]

In contrast to these essentially reinforcement theory approaches is Salter's application of classical conditioning.[19] Wolpe's approach,[20] included here, is also based essentially upon classical conditioning. The classical conditioning approach to modifying human behavior dates back to the work of Mary Cover Jones with Peter and the rabbit,[21] under the influence of Watson.[22]

But learning approaches to counseling or psychotherapy are not restricted to either the classical or instrumental paradigm. Salter is probably closest to the classical approach. Wolpe is less restricted to classical conditioning, though his theoretical base derives essentially from this paradigm. Dollard and Miller, deriving their work from Hull's theory, emphasize reinforcement and are thus closer to the operant paradigm.

The recent work in operant conditioning derives from Skinner.[23] Operant conditioning was first considered in relation to counseling or psychotherapy in terms of verbal conditioning in interviews.[24–32] This work has not been developed into an integrated systematic approach to counseling or psychotherapy, which is no doubt because of the atheoretical and operationalistic influence of Skinner.

The use of operant conditioning in modifying the behavior of hospitalized psychiatric patients was apparently first explored by Peters [33] and by Lindsley.[34] Its application in institutional settings, including the school classroom, has burgeoned tremendously since then.

The term "behavior therapy" was apparently first used by Lindsley.[35] (Lazarus [36] and Eysenck [37] later used the term independently of Lindsley and of each other.) It has come into common usage to refer to the application of a wide variety of techniques derived from, or related to, learning principles or theory, to the modification of more or less specific abnormal behaviors, both in the counseling or therapy interview situation and outside. The term "behavior modification" is also widely used, often interchangeably with behavior therapy, but particularly in this country to refer to operant conditioning methods to distinguish this approach from the behavior therapy of Wolpe, or as a more general term to cover application of learning principles in a wide variety of situations outside the therapy interview. Here we are limiting our concern to interview-mediated behavior change; programs or systems for changing behavior in institutions, such as token economies, are not considered.

Research and writing in this area are proliferating rapidly, with new journals being established to accommodate briefer reports of research and case studies (for example, *Journal of the Experimental Analysis of Behavior, Behavior Research and Therapy, Journal of Applied Behavior Analysis*), edited books being published to provide surveys and reviews,[38–47] and case studies, and books being written to include more extensive treatments of the field.[48–51] The extent of the activity and the implications for psychotherapy and behavior change have led to the application of the word "revolution" to the movement [52–53] Levis suggests that behavior therapy constitutes the fourth revolution (following Pinel, Freud, and community mental health).[54]

Unlike earlier approaches to counseling or psychotherapy, and although the term "learning theory" is frequently used, behavior therapy or behavior modification is essentially atheoretical and even nonsystematic. It is empirical, experimental-analytic, and inductive rather than deductive in nature. Ullmann and Krasner note that "while there are many techniques, there are few concepts or general principles involved in behavior therapy." [55] Books on behavior therapy thus become essentially compendiums of techniques and methods. They are not systematic in the sense that an author has adopted a theoretical point of view, developed its philosophy and assumptions, and presented techniques derived from, or consistent with, the assumptions and theory. Behavior therapy, Yates claims, is inductive, rather than deductive, is based upon experiments, and applies the experimental method to the treatment of the individual client. Thus, Yates states that Dollard and Miller were not behavior therapists, and even Wolpe is not considered a behavior therapist in the English usage of the term.[56]

Yates defines behavior therapy as "the attempt to utilize systematically that body of empirical and theoretical knowledge which has resulted from the application of the experimental method in psychology and its closely related disciplines (physiology and neurophysiology) in order to explain the genesis and maintenance of abnormal patterns of behavior; and to apply that knowledge to the treatment or prevention of those abnormalities by means of controlled experimental studies of the single case, both descriptive and remedial." [57] Not all those who call themselves behavior therapists function in this manner or only in this manner, however.

Nor is the atheoretical, empirical limitation accepted by all behavior therapists. Franks, for example, writes: "In the best of all possible worlds, it would seem highly desirable for the therapist to aspire to be a scientist even if this goal were difficult to realize. To function as a scientist, it is necessary to espouse some theoretical framework. . . . How the behavior therapist practices (including his choice of technique, his approach to the problems of general strategy, and his specific relationships with his patient) thus depends both upon his explicit theoretical orientation and upon his implicit philosophical and cultural milieu." [58]

There is evidence that behavior therapists are becoming more diverse and are moving toward so-called traditional counseling or psychotherapy, particularly in recognizing the importance of the counselor-client relationship. (The importance of the experimenter-subject relationship in verbal conditioning has been demonstrated by the research referred to earlier.) Many behavior therapists are recognizing the importance of cognitive and affective variables, including awareness or consciousness.[59] There appears to be a movement away from the application of techniques taken from laboratory research, to a recognition of the complexities of human *in situ* behavior, as compared to the behavior of animals in the laboratory. Franks, for example, asks:

> Can it be assumed, on the basis of a concomitance that is sometimes observed between certain measures of acquisition and extinction in the laboratory, that there must inevitably be a high positive relationship between the rapidity and strength with which new responses are acquired during behavior therapy and the resistance to therapeutic extinction of possibly quite different responses which are already in existence? Similar issues arise with respect to the generalization of conditional responses during therapy. If the basic parameters of laboratory conditioning are still in dispute, it is hardly surprising that the relationships between conditioning in the laboratory and conditioning in the clinical situation remain unclear. Unfortunately, many clinical investigators proceed as if the relationships were clear.[60]

With such diversity among those who call themselves behavior therapists, it may be questioned whether there is *a* behavior therapy or behavior *therapies*. Nevertheless, Franks argues for the term "behavior therapy," even though admitting that "there is a bewildering conglomeration of techniques," on the basis that "all forms of behavior therapy are predicated upon the common, explicit, systematic, and a priori usage of learning principles to achieve well-defined and predetermined goals." [61] He feels that the term "behavior therapies" "implies little more than a grab bag of behaviorally oriented therapeutic techniques." Yates takes the same position.[62] The Association for the Advancement of the Behavioral Therapies changed its name to the singular in 1968, and the singular is used by most writers, even though they include, or refer to, a variety of methods or approaches that are not integrated into any system.

Yet the observer may obtain the strong impression that behavior therapy is essentially little more than a grab bag of techniques, applied to specific problems with little theoretical justification or support. Certainly, no systematic, integrated, theoretically oriented presentation of behavior therapy has appeared. Perhaps this represents the state of the field at the present time, and it is too early to expect an integration of the proliferating techniques and methods into a systematic approach. Certainly, any such attempt at the present time would be exceedingly difficult. It is not the function of this book, nor is it within the capabilities of the author, to present a systematic position, when none exists or has been attempted by proponents of a position.

Krasner notes that "as one plods through the vast literature on behavior therapy, one is reminded of the parable of the blind men who described the elephant solely on the basis of their feeling the animal." Each described a different part of the elephant. Krasner feels that "the

elephant of behavior therapy does indeed exist and can be discriminated from other creatures of the jungle." [63] He proposes to do
so in his review and lists fifteen streams of development of behavior
therapy, including social psychology and social learning, and reviews
the literature of the latter 1960s to give a broad overview of behavior
therapy, but he does not articulate the parts of the elephant into a
whole.

Kanfer and Phillips call for "establishing a well integrated framework from which a practitioner can derive new techniques with clearly
stated rationales with predictable effects and with well defined criteria
and methods for examining their efficacy." [64] So far there is no well-
integrated framework. The earlier works of Dollard and Miller, and
of Wolpe, as well as others that are not included here, while not
comprehensive or all-inclusive, are systematic. Apparently, no one is
interested enough, or feels able, to attempt a current integration. No
doubt this is in part a result of the current reaction against schools
or systems. It is also perhaps rooted in the empirical foundations of
behavior modification.

Wolpe's work, including his 1958 book and its supplementation
in 1969, offers a relatively systematic view of behavior therapy based
mainly upon classical conditioning theory and research. There appears
to be no comparable presentation of therapy based upon operant
conditioning theory and research. Nor is there a systematic attempt
to integrate both these approaches under a broader, more comprehensive learning theory. However, there is a broadly based compendium
of behavior therapy that includes both of these approaches, presenting
them as separate models, and also includes therapeutic procedures
that partake of both models, presenting them as mixed models. This
is the work of Kanfer and Phillips. This section closes with a summary
of this work, which probably presents the best statement of a comprehensive behavior therapy to date.

Space does not permit an adequate evaluation of behavior therapy here. A number of critiques (and rejoinders) have been published.[65] The most comprehensive review and evaluation currently
available is probably the chapter by Murray and Jacobson, in *Handbook
of Psychotherapy and Behavior Change,* referred to above.[66] Behavior therapists in general appear to be becoming less parochial, less narrow and
rigid, less simplistic. As experience and research accumulate, there is
a recognition of the complexities of human behavior and behavior
problems, and a realization that behavior therapy is not a panacea. The
book by Kanfer and Phillips is a case in point.

Lazarus, who has been identified as a behavior therapist and who
was associated with Wolpe for several years, has presented a critical
review of behavior therapy in the first chapter of his recent book. He
writes that "the methods of behavior therapy are extremely effective
when applied to carefully selected cases by informed practitioners. But
when procedures overstep the boundaries of their legitimate terrain,
ridicule and disparagement are most likely to ensue. Far from being

a panacea, the methods are then held to have no merit whatsoever, and the proverbial baby gets thrown out with the bath water." [67] He continues: "The danger lies in a premature elevation of learning principles into unwarranted scientific truths and the ascription of the general term of 'modern learning theory' to what in reality are best described as 'modern learning theories. . . . Thus, Eysenck's insistence that behavior therapy denotes 'methods of treatment which are derived from modern learning theory' amounts to little more than a beguiling slogan." [68] He regards Wolpe's twenty or so behavioral techniques as "a useful *starting point* for increased clinical effectiveness rather than a complete system which can put an end to 90 percent of the world's neurotic suffering." [69] He regards behavior therapy as an objective psychotherapeutic adjunct. He states that "several behavior therapists now acknowledge the fact that more varied and complex interactional processes other than reciprocal inhibition and operant conditioning permeate their interviews and contaminate or facilitate the application of their specific techniques." [70]

REFERENCES

[1.] Hilgard, E. R., & Bower, G. H. *Theories of learning.* (3rd ed.) New York: Appleton-Century-Crofts, 1966. P. 2.   [2] Kimble, G. A. (Ed.), *Foundations of conditioning and learning.* New York: Appleton-Century-Crofts, 1967. P. 436. [3] Yates, A. J. *Behavior therapy.* New York: Wiley, 1970. P. 34.   [4] Mowrer, O. H. On the dual nature of learning: a reinterpretation of "conditioning" and "problem solving." *Harvard educ. Rev.,* 1947, **17,** 102–148.   [5] Mowrer, O. H. *Learning theory and behavior.* New York: Wiley, 1960.   [6] Shaw, F. J. A stimulus response analysis of repression and insight in psychotherapy. *Psychol. Rev.,* 1946, **53,** 36–42.   [7] Shaffer, L. F. The problem of psychotherapy. *Amer. Psychologist,* 1947, **2,** 459–467.   [8] Shoben, E. J., Jr. A learning theory interpretation of psychotherapy. *Harvard educ. Rev.,* 1948, **18,** 129–145. [9] Shoben, E. J., Jr. Psychotherapy as a problem in learning theory. *Psychol. Bull.,* 1949, **46,** 366–392. Reprinted in H. J. Eysenck (Ed.), *Behavior theory and the neuroses.* New York: Pergamon Press, 1960.   [10] Shoben, E. J., Jr. Some observations on psychotherapy and the learning process. In O. H. Mowrer (Ed.), *Psychotherapy: theory and resesearch.* New York: Ronald, 1953.   [11] Magaret, Ann. Generalization in psychotherapy. *J. consult. Psychol.,* 1950, **14,** 64–70.   [12] Kanfer, F. H. Comments on learning in psychotherapy. *Psychol. Rep.,* 1961, **9,** 681–699.   [13] Bandura, A. Psychotherapy as a learning process. *Psychol. Bull.,* 1961, **58,** 143–159.   [14] Dollard, J., & Miller, N. E. *Personality and psychotherapy.* New York: McGraw-Hill, 1950.   [15] Rotter, J. B. *Social learning and clinical psychology.* Englewood Cliffs, N.J.: Prentice-Hall, 1954. [16] Pepinsky, H. B., & Pepinsky, Pauline. *Counseling: theory and practice.* New York: Ronald, 1954.   [17] Pascal, G. R. *Behavioral change in the clinic—a systematic approach.* New York: Grune & Stratton, 1959.   [18] Phillips, E. L. *Psychotherapy: a modern theory and practice.* Englewood Cliffs, N.J.: Prentice-Hall, 1956.   [19] Salter, A. *Conditioned reflex therapy.* New York: Creative Age Press, 1949 (Capricorn Books, 1961).   [20] Wolpe, J. *Psychotherapy by reciprocal inhi-

bition. Stanford: Stanford University Press, 1958.   **[21]** Jones, Mary Cover. A laboratory study of fear: the case of Peter. *Pedogogical Sem.,* 1924, **31,** 308–315.   **[22]** Watson, J. B., & Rayner, R. Conditioned emotional reactions. *J. exper. Psychol.,* 1920, **3,** 1–14.   **[23]** Skinner, B. F. The behavior of organisms. New York: Appleton-Century-Crofts, 1938; Skinner, B. F. *Science and human behavior.* New York: Macmillan, 1953.   **[24]** Greenspoon, J. S. The effect of a verbal stimulus as a reinforcement. *Proc. Iowa Acad. Sci.,* 1950, **59,** 287; Greenspoon, J. S. The reinforcing effect of two spoken sounds on the frequency of two responses. *Amer. J. Psychol.,* 1955, **68,** 409–416.   **[25]** Hildum, D. C., & Brown, R. W. Verbal reinforcement and interviewer bias. *J. abnorm. soc. Psychol.,* 1956, **53,** 108–111.   **[26]** Krasner, L. Studies of the conditioning of verbal behavior. *Psychol. Bull.* 1958, **55,** 148–170.   **[27]** Salzinger, K. Experimental manipulation of verbal behavior: a review. *J. gen. Psychol.,* 1959, **61,** 65–94.   **[28]** Krasner, L. The therapist as a social reinforcement machine. In H. H. Strupp & L. Luborsky (Eds.), *Research in psychotherapy.* Vol. II. Washington, D.C.: American Psychological Association, 1962. P. 62.   **[29]** Krasner, L. Reinforcement, verbal behavior and psychotherapy. *Amer. J. Orthopsychiat.,* 1963, **33,** 601–613.   **[30]** Krasner, L. Verbal conditioning and psychotherapy. In L. Krasner & L. P. Ullmann (Eds.), *Research in behavior modification.* New York: Holt, Rinehart and Winston, 1965.   **[31]** Kanfer, F. H. Implications of conditioning techniques for interview therapy. *J. counsel. Psychol.,* 1966, **13,** 171–177.   **[32]** Salzinger, K. The place of operant conditioning of verbal behavior in psychotherapy. In C. M. Franks (Ed.), *Behavior therapy: appraisal and status.* New York: McGraw-Hill, 1969. Pp. 375–395.   **[33]** Peters, H. N. An experimental evaiuation of learning as therapy in schizophrenia. *Amer. Psychologist,* 1952, **7,** 354 (abstract); Peters, H. N. Learning as a treatment method in chronic schizophrenia. *Amer. J. occup. Ther.,* 1955, **9,** 185–189; Peters, H. N., & Jenkins, R. L. Improvement of chronic schizophrenics with guided problem-solving, motivated by hunger. *Psychiatric Quart. Suppl.,* 1954, **28,** 84–101.   **[34]** Lindsley, O. R., & Skinner, B. F. A method for experimental analysis of the behavior of psychotic patients. *Amer. Psychologist,* 1954, **9,** 419–420; Lindsley, O. R. Operant conditioning methods applied to research in chronic schizophrenia. *Psychiatric Res. Reports,* 1956, **5,** 118–139.   **[35]** Lindsley, O. R., Skinner, B. F., & Solomon, H. C. *Studies in behavior therapy. Status report I.* Waltham, Mass.: Metropolitan State Hospital, 1953.   **[36]** Lazarus, A. A. New methods in psychotherapy: a case study. *So. African Med. J.,* 1958, **33,** 660–664.   **[37]** Eysenck, H. J. Learning theory and behavior therapy. *J. ment. Sci.,* 1959, **195,** 61–75.   **[38]** Eysenck, H. J. (Ed.), *Behavior therapy and the neuroses.* New York: Pergamon Press, 1960.   **[39]** Eysenck, H. J. (Ed.), *Experiments in behavior therapy.* New York: Pergamon Press, 1964.   **[40]** Franks, C. M. (Ed.), *Conditioning techniques in clinical practice and research.* New York: Springer, 1964.   **[41]** Krasner, L., & Ullmann, L. P. (Eds.), *Research in behavior modification.* New York: Holt, Rinehart and Winston, 1965.   **[42]** Ullmann, L. P., & Krasner, L. (Eds.), *Case studies in behavior modification.* New York: Holt, Rinehart and Winston, 1965.   **[43]** Rubin, R. D., & Franks, C. M. (Eds.), *Advances in behavior therapy: 1968.* New York: Academic Press, 1969.   **[44]** Krumboltz, J. D., & Thoresen, C. E. (Eds.), *Behavioral counseling: cases and techniques.* New York: Holt, Rinehart and Winston, 1969.   **[45]** Franks, C. M. (Ed.), *Assessment and status of the behavioral therapies.* New York:

McGraw-Hill, 1970.   [46] Levis, D. J. (Ed.), *Learning approaches to therapeutic behavior change.* Chicago: Aldine, 1970.   [47] Ossipow, S. H., & Walsh, W. B. (Eds), *Behavior change in counseling: readings and cases.* New York: Appleton-Century-Crofts, 1970.   [48] Eysenck, H. J., & Rachman, S. *The causes and cures of neurosis: an introduction to modern behavior therapy based on learning theory and principles of conditioning.* San Diego: Knapp, 1965.   [49] Bandura, A. *Principles of behavior modification.* New York: Holt, Rinehart and Winston, 1969. [50] Kanfer, F. H., & Phillips, Jeanne S. *Learning foundations of behavior therapy.* New York: Wiley, 1970.   [51] Yates, A. J. *Behavior therapy.* New York: Wiley, 1970.   [52] Krasner, L. Review of H. J. Eysenck and S. Rachman, "The causes and cures of neurosis." *Contemp. Psychol.,* 1966, **11**, 341–344. [53] Krumboltz, J. D. (Ed.), *Revolution in counseling.* Boston: Houghton Mifflin, 1966.   [54] Levis, D. J. Behavioral therapy: the fourth therapeutic revolution? In D. J. Levis (Ed.), *op. cit.*   [55] Ullmann, L. P. & Krasner, L. *A psychological approach to abnormal behavior.* Englewood Cliffs, N.J.: Prentice-Hall, 1969. P. 252.   [56] Yates, A. J., *op. cit.,* pp. 15, 18.   [57] *Ibid.,* p. 18.   [58] Franks, C. M. Introduction: behavior therapy and its Pavlovian origins: review and perspectives. In C. M. Franks (Ed.), *Behavior therapy: appraisal and status.* New York: McGraw-Hill, 1969. P. 21.   [59] See, for example, the discussions of Patterson, C. H. Some notes on behavior theory, behavior therapy and behavioral counseling. *Counsel. Psychologist,* 1969, **1** (4), 44–56, and Murray, E. J., & Jacobson, L. I. The nature of learning in traditional and behavioral psychotherapy. In A. E. Bergin & S. L. Garfield (Eds.), *Handbook of psychotherapy and behavior change: an empirical analysis.* New York: Wiley, 1971. Pp. 709–747. See also Lazarus, A. A. In support of a technical eclecticism. *Psychol. Reports,* 1967, **21**, 415–416, and Lazarus, A. A. *Behavior therapy and beyond.* New York: McGraw-Hill, 1971.   [60] Franks, C. M. Introduction: behavior therapy and its Pavlovian origins: review and perspectives. In C. M. Franks (Ed.), *Behavior therapy: appraisal and status.* New York: McGraw-Hill, 1969. P. 22.   [61] *Ibid.,* p. 2.   [62] Yates, A. J., *op. cit.*   [63] Krasner, L. Behavior therapy. *Am. Rev. Psychol.,* 1971, **22**, 483–532.   [64] Kanfer, F. H., & Phillips, Jeanne S. A survey of current behavior therapies and a proposal for classification. In C. M. Franks (Ed.), *Behavior therapy: appraisal and status.* New York: McGraw-Hill, 1969. P. 448.   [65] Grossberg, J. M. Behavior therapy: a review. *Psychol. Bull.,* 1964, **62**, 73–88; Breger, L., & McGaugh, J. L. Critique and reformulation of "learning theory" approaches to psychotherapy and neuroses. *Psychol. Bull.,* 1964, **63**, 338–358; Rachman, S., & Eysenck, H. J. Reply to a "critique and reformulation" of behavior therapy. *Psychol. Bull.,* 1966, **65**, 165–169; Weitzman, B. Behavior therapy and psychotherapy. *Psychol. Rev.,* 1967, **74**, 300–317; Wiest, W. M. Some recent criticisms of behaviorism and learning theory with special reference to Breger and McGaugh and Chomsky. *Psychol. Bull., 1967,* **67**, 214–225; Breger, L., & McGaugh, J. L. Learning theory and behavior therapy: a reply to Rachman and Eysenck. *Psychol. Bull.,* 1968, **65**, 170–173; Patterson, C. H. Some notes on behavior theory, behavior therapy and behavioral counseling. *Counsel. Psychologist,* 1969, **1** (4), 44–56.   [66] Murray, E. J., & Jacobson, L. I., *op. cit.*   [67] Lazarus, A. A. *Behavior therapy and beyond.* New York: McGraw-Hill, 1971. P. 1.   [68] *Ibid.,* pp. 5, 6. [69] *Ibid.,* pp. 6–7.   [70] *Ibid.,* p. 9.

5

Reinforcement theory and psychoanalytic therapy: Dollard and Miller

The learning theory developed by Hull and his students and associates, including Neal Miller, has been applied to psychotherapy by John Dollard and Neal Miller in their *Personality and Psychotherapy: an Analysis in Terms of Learning, Thinking, and Culture.*[1] John Dollard (1900–   ), after taking his Ph.D. at the University of Chicago in 1931, went to the Institute of Human Relations at Yale University, where he has remained since, becoming Professor of Psychology in 1952. He is the author of *Caste and Class in a Southern Town* (1937), among other books.

Neal E. Miller (1909–   ) took his Ph.D. in 1935 at Yale and remained there until 1966, except for a postdoctoral year of training at the Psychoanalytic Institute in Vienna and for the war years, when he was associated with the Air Force selection and classification program. He was James Rowland Angell Professor of Psychology from 1952 to 1966, when he went to Rockefeller University as Professor of Psychology. In addition to being the author of numerous articles in the field of learning and learning theory, he is coauthor with Dollard of *Social Learning and Imitation* (1941), and with Dollard, Doob, Mowrer, and Sears of *Frustration and Aggression* (1939).

89

BACKGROUND AND DEVELOPMENT

Unlike the approaches attempting to apply principles of conditioning to counseling, the approach of Dollard and Miller attempts to integrate learning theory—essentially Hullian behaviorism—the insights of psychoanalysis about human behavior and personality, and the contributions of social science to the social conditions of learning. The result, Dollard and Miller hope, will be a general science of human behavior. The nature of neurosis and its treatment would be included as part of this science. Psychotherapy, particularly psychoanalysis, is thus accepted as a contributor to this general science. Psychotherapy is seen as providing a window that allows one to look into the mental life in a way that cannot usually be done in the study and observation of the normal individual. The laws and theory of learning applied to psychotherapy should provide a rational foundation for psychotherapy.

PHILOSOPHY AND CONCEPTS

Neurosis is a product of experience rather than primarily of instinct or organic damage. Therefore, it must be learned, and learning is governed by laws, some of which are known, and some of which, now unknown, may be discovered through the study of neuroses by means of psychotherapy. Thus, learning theory and psychotherapy supplement each other. In their book, however, Dollard and Miller attempt "to give a systematic analysis of neurosis and psychotherapy in terms of the psychological principles and social conditions of learning." [2]

What Is a Neurosis?

The neurotic is miserable, stupid in handling his emotional problems, and suffers from a variety of symptoms. He is capable of normal activity, but is unable to function normally or to enjoy life. The more common symptoms are sleeplessness, restlessness, irritability, sexual inhibitions, phobias, headaches, irrational fears, distaste for life, and lack of clear personal goals. The neurotic's condition is the result of conflict produced by two or more strong drives leading to incompatible responses. The neurotic is unable to solve his conflicts because he is not clearly aware of them. They are repressed; that is, they are unlabeled, and "he has no language to describe the conflicting forces within him." [3] He appears to be stupid because he is unable to use higher mental processes to deal with his problems, since he doesn't know what they are.

Although the neurotic's symptoms cause him to suffer, they actually reduce his conflict. "When a successful symptom occurs it is reinforced because it reduces neurotic misery. The symptom is thus learned as a habit." [4]

Basic Principles of Learning

The behavior of all human beings, which ranges from the very simple avoidance of a hot radiator by a child to theory construction by a scientist, is learned. There are four fundamental factors that are important for all learning.

The first factor is *drive*, or motivation. Drives are strong stimuli that impel action. Certain classes of stimuli are primary, or innate, drives: pain, thirst, hunger, etc. There are also secondary, or learned, drives, which "are acquired on the basis of primary drives, represent elaborations of them, and serve as a façade behind which the functions of the underlying innate drives are hidden." [5] Many of the most important drives are learned. Fear (or anxiety) is a major learned drive.

The second factor in learning is the *cue*, or stimulus. When a person is impelled by a drive, "cues determine when he will respond, where he will respond, and which response he will make." [6] Both external and internal stimuli may function as cues (as well as being drives) when they serve as distinctive cues for specific responses. Changes, differences, and patterns of stimuli serve as cues. Fear has the properties of a strong external function as a cue. "When fear is learned as a response to a new situation, it serves as a cue to elicit responses that have previously been learned in other frightening situations," [7] such as verbal responses expressing fear, meek muteness, or withdrawal. Fear may also become a cue to avoid an act or response that leads to punishment when it has become attached to cues produced by the thought of performing the prescribed act. After effective punishment for an act, the individual feels afraid when he thinks about or begins to perform the punished act, and is thus led to stop, or withdraw. The fear is reduced, and thus the stopping, or withdrawing, becomes reinforced.

Fear produces, or is associated with, certain innate responses, such as increase in stomach acidity, increase in and irregularity of heartbeat, muscular tension, trembling, startle, freezing (with fear), perspiration, dryness of mouth and throat, feelings of unreality, mutism, and amnesia. Many of these reactions are the symptoms of neurosis or psychosis.

A third factor in learning is *response*. Cues lead to responses. Responses may be arranged in a hierarchy in terms of their probability of occurrence. A dominant response (one high in the hierarchy) is one that has a strong connection with the stimulus. The nature of this causal connection is unknown. The changing of the strength of connections between stimuli and responses (or the changing of the position of responses in the hierarchy) is learning. But a response must occur before it can be connected with a stimulus. Such new responses may occur by trial and error, by imitation, or as the result of verbal direction. All these methods are ways of producing responses that can be rewarded. In conditioning, the response to the unconditioned stimulus is the dominant response. Fear is an innate response to certain stimuli.

The fourth factor is *reinforcement,* or reward. "Any specified event . . . that strengthens the tendency for a response to be repeated is called reinforcement." [8] The reduction or cessation of a painful or noxious stimulus acts as a reinforcement, as does the reduction in the strength of a strong drive or stimulus. There are learned, or secondary, reinforcements, for example, money, as well as innate reinforcements. Learned rewards function in the same way as unlearned rewards. While reinforcement may operate in a situation of awareness on the part of the subject, reinforcement may also operate directly, occurring without awareness.

In addition to these four factors or conditions of learning, there are several other aspects of the learning process that require definition. One of these is *extinction.* When a learned response is repeated without continued reinforcement or reward, it tends to decrease in its occurrence. The tendency for it to occur lessens; that is, it is extinguished. If responses were not subject to extinction, they would persist indefinitely, even responses that were rewarded by chance. Responses are extinguished at different rates, with strong responses persisting longer than weak ones. The strength of the drive during learning, the magnitude of previous reward, and the strength of the drive during extinction influence the rate of extinction. Although the extinction process may be prolonged, all learned habits that have been studied have been found to be extinguished eventually when they are no longer reinforced.[9]

When a response has been extinguished, it may recur after a period of time without reward having occurred in the meantime. This is known as *spontaneous recovery* and indicates that the response or habit has only been inhibited, not destroyed. However, after repeated extinctions the response does disappear.[10]

The reinforcement accompanying a particular stimulus not only increases the tendency of that stimulus to elicit the response but spreads to similar stimuli, so that they tend to elicit the same response. The less similar the stimuli or cues, the less the tendency for the response to occur. This spread or transfer to other stimuli is termed *generalization,* and the variation in tendency for responses to occur is known as the *gradient of generalization.* No two stimuli or stimulus situations are exactly the same, and if there were no generalization, learning could not occur.

On the other hand, if the response occurred with any stimulus, learning would not occur either. Dissimilar stimuli are differentiated and not responded to. Or *discrimination* between responses may be established by not rewarding or by punishing responses to stimuli that differ in some way or degree from the rewarded stimulus.

Reinforcement is more effective the closer the response is to the reinforcement, so that delayed reinforcement is less effective than immediate reinforcement. There is thus a *gradient of reinforcement:* re-

sponses occurring before the final reinforced response are also reinforced, but less so than the final response.

The gradients of generalization and of reinforcement lead to the
principle that "responses near the point of reinforcement tend, whenever physically possible, to occur before their original time in the
response series, that is, to become anticipatory." [11] *Anticipatory responses*
thus crowd out useless acts. Withdrawal from a painful stimulus will
occur prior to touching the object that causes pain. The anticipatory
tendency is involuntary and may lead to errors or nonadaptive responses as well as to adaptive elimination of useless acts. Use of reinforcement, such as punishing or not rewarding responses that are not
preceded by desirable anticipatory responses, may prevent the elimination of these desirable responses.

The importance of fear in behavior becomes apparent when it
is seen that it is one of the most significant of the learned drives. Fear
is easily learned, transfers easily to new stimuli, and can develop into
a powerful drive, thus becoming involved in the production of conflicts
leading to neurotic behavior. When fear becomes attached to a new
situation, it is accompanied by many of the reactions that are a part
of the innate pattern of fear. It serves as a cue to elicit responses that
have been learned in other fearful situations. When drive-reducing
responses are punished, fear is learned and will then motivate responses that prevent reduction of those drives, leading to inhibitions
that result in disturbance and neurotic symptoms. Fear seems to be
a part of many socially learned drives, such as guilt, shame, pride, the
need for social conformity, and the desire for money or power. Fear
of the loss of love or status, of failure, and of poverty seem to be
socially learned. The reduction of fear is reinforcing for the learning
and performance of new responses such as avoidance responses. Fears
are often highly resistant to extinction, and sometimes they appear not
to be extinguished completely. Like other responses, fear can be inhibited by incompatible responses such as eating.

There are many other learned social motives, but some that are
especially important for personality development and psychotherapy
are gregariousness, sociability, dependence and independence, conformity and nonconformity, the need to receive and show affection,
the desire for approval from others, pride, fairness, and honesty.
Learned drives and their reinforcements vary among cultures and
among social classes within a culture. Therapists must be aware of this
variability.

Normal Use of Higher Mental Processes in Solving Emotional Problems

Little is known today about the solution of social and emotional
problems, compared to the solution of problems posed by the physical
environment. Psychotherapy itself, which is concerned with social and
emotional problems, offers an opportunity to learn more about this
area.

Behavior may be divided into two "levels." The first consists of immediate, automatic responses. The second includes behavior that follows, or is mediated by, a series of internal responses, images, or thoughts called higher mental processes. It is this latter kind of behavior with which we are concerned. In the former kind of behavior, responses are instrumental acts in that they influence the individual's relationship to the environment directly and immediately: they are instrumental in changing the environment. In the second kind of behavior, the intervening responses are called cue-producing responses. They may be verbalized or unverbalized. Their main purpose is to produce a cue that functions as a part of the stimulus pattern for another response. Such cues, when verbalized, may serve as substitutes for instrumental responses, stimulating another person to perform the response—as, for example, in asking another person to do something for one. But the important function here is that of serving as cues to the person making the responses. These cue-producing responses are usually in the form of words and sentences. It is assumed that language and other cue-producing responses, rather than thoughts that have not been articulated, are central to the higher mental processes. The laws applying to responses to external cues are assumed to apply to such internal response-produced cues.

The attaching of the same label (cue-producing response) to different objects gives them a certain "learned equivalence" resulting from verbally mediated generalization. Giving different labels to similar objects increases their distinctiveness and facilitates their discrimination. Labeling is important "because language contains those discriminations and equivalences that have been found useful by generations of trial and error in a given society." [12]

Labels or words can arouse drives; that is, learnable drives can be attached to words. Drives elicited by words are called mediated learned drives. Words, spoken or unspoken, can also provide reassurance, thus mediating rewards. Verbal and other cue-producing responses are important in helping one respond to future possibilities and thus in producing foresight. The association of motivational and instrumental responses with verbal cues makes great economy in verbal learning possible, so that much of human learning is in terms of verbal responses or hypotheses that may lead to sudden changes in many other responses (a process often called insight). Verbal learning is often described as logical learning, in contrast to rote learning; in this light it is apparent why logical learning is superior to rote learning.

Verbal cue-producing responses make reasoning and planning possible. Reasoning involves verbal or symbolic trial and error, but is not restricted to this. Verbal cue-producing responses are not limited to a single sequence, as are instrumental responses, but "it is possible for certain cue-producing responses that have been associated with the goal to move forward in the sequence and provide cues that have a selective effect on subsequent responses." [13] These are called *anticipatory goal responses*. It is also possible for a chain of cue-producing responses to begin at the goal and work backward to the correct response in the problem situation. Reasoning and planning require the inhibition of immediate instrumental responses, the occurrence of appropriate cue-producing responses, and the execution of appropriate instrumental responses in place of the direct responses that have been inhibited.

Society has developed solutions to many problems, and passes these solutions on to its new members through education and training. Social training in language is important in leading to problem solving. Words and sentences copied from others can be used in reasoning and planning. Verbal responses are learned in social interaction, but the process is not clearly known. Imitation plays a central role in the process of learning to talk.[14] Training involving listening, following the suggestions of others, stopping to think, matching words correctly to the environment, making oneself understood, being logical, being oriented, and responding to verbal cues with appropriate action and emotion helps to make one's behavior appropriate to the social situation. When such training is not too effective, the individual may appear to have a poor sense of reality or a weak ego. Cue-producing responses that are not socially evident, such as images of various kinds, are not subject to direct social training; they may be less inhibited, but also less orderly and less useful in problem solving.

How Neurosis Is Learned

Neurotic behavior is based upon an unconscious emotional conflict, usually originating in childhood. "Neurotic conflicts are taught by parents and learned by children." [15] The patterns of child training contain inconsistencies and thus inherent conflicts, and parents vary in their consistency, effectiveness, and goodness in conducting child training. The task is a complex and difficult one, and the appropriate rules and conditions are only partly known. There is also the problem of determining what kind of child it is desirable to produce. Although our knowledge is inadequate, we know that the period of childhood is important, and we must attempt to reconstruct childhood in order to understand adult life.

Children are helpless and thus at the mercy of confusing patterns of training. "The young child is necessarily disoriented, confused, deluded, and hallucinated—in short, has just those symptoms that we recognize as psychosis in the adult. Infancy, indeed, may be viewed as a period of transitory psychosis." [16] Rather than being indulged, supported, and gradually trained during infancy, the child is pushed by incompatible and impossible demands, and is expected to control impelling drives and to learn rapidly.

The child is faced with training demands in four critical situations. The ways in which this training is handled lead to the development of learned responses that persist throughout life. The feeding situation may be handled so as to lead to optimism or apathy, to security or apprehension, to sociability or lack of social feeling, to fear of being alone or later compulsive sociability. Premature or rigid cleanliness training, which must proceed without verbal aids, arouses strong emotions—anger, defiance, stubbornness, and fear. Anxiety, conforming behavior, feelings of unworthiness, and guilt may result. Sex training may lead to conflicts generated by taboos, sexual anxieties, and heterosexual fears and conflicts deriving from the Oedipus situation. Finally, the treatment of anger responses in the child may give rise to anger-anxiety conflicts as fear is attached to anger cues. Anger is inevitable because of the many frustrations produced in the child in the process of training and as a result of sibling rivalry and of the helplessness and mental limitations of the child. Repression of anger may go beyond inhibition of aggression to inhibition of feelings of anger and thus lead to an overinhibited personality.

These early conflicts of the child occur before he can verbalize or before he can do so adequately. They are therefore unlabeled, and thus unconscious. They cannot be reported later in life. We cannot learn from the individual (except to some extent in psychotherapy) the nature of these conflicts. Much of what we know about these conditions has come from neurotics in psychotherapy. Normal people may not have as severe conflicts; some individuals may be less able to handle conflicts through higher mental processes; or some people may be more predisposed than others to neurotic reactions.

How Symptoms Are Learned

Phobias are a person's learned fears whose basic origins currently are not understood. The avoidance response reduces the fear and is thus strongly reinforced. Phobias tend to persist because the avoidance of the phobia situation reinforces them through reduction of fear and so prevents extinction. Like phobias, *compulsions* are acts that reduce anxiety of unknown origin. They persist because they reduce the anxiety temporarily. *Hysterical symptoms* are likewise learned responses that avoid or reduce fear. Here the factors determining the specific response, such as an arm paralysis, are unclear, although the origin of the fear, such as active combat in war, may be clear. *Regression* is the occurrence of the next strongest response (usually one learned as a strong habit during childhood) when the dominant (adult) habit is blocked by conflict or extinguished through lack of reward. When the dominant response is replaced by another response that is strong because of generalization, rather than by an earlier response, the process is called *displacement. Rationalizations* occur when, as a result of social training, the individual feels the necessity for logical explanations for his behavior, but cannot accept the true explanation because it would provoke anxiety or guilt. *Delusions* are only quantitatively different from rationalizations; socially acceptable explanations are more difficult to find, and delusions are resorted to—and persist—to reduce the strong anxiety or guilt. *Hallucinations* are a result of wide generalization of strongly motivated perceptual responses. When external cues become highly disturbing, the shifting of attention to internal images (hallucinations) may reduce the fear. *Projection* results from the many factors that lead us to think that others are motivated as we are. When this leads to the imputation of motivation in others that is in error, it is called projection. Often the individual is incorrect in labeling his own motives as well as those of others. Projection is reinforced by the reduction of anxiety when blame is shifted to someone else. *Reaction formations* are thoughts, statements, or behaviors opposite to those that the individual is motivated toward but which he fears or disapproves of. *Alcoholism* results from the reinforcement of the use of alcohol to reduce fear.

Although in the long run many symptoms are maladaptive, they delay the increase in misery, and the immediate results are favorable, thus reinforcing the symptoms. The strengthening effect of an immediate reinforcement may be much greater than the deterring effect of a much stronger but delayed punishment. When there appears to be an immediate increase in misery, the explanation of the persistence of the symptoms presents a problem, but the situation can be accounted for theoretically in various ways consistent with a drive-reduction interpretation of reinforcement theory.

While any strong drive can motivate symptoms, and its reduction reinforce them, certain drives appear to be more likely to do so in our society than others. Fear is perhaps the most common motivating drive. Sex, aggression, and the striving for social mobility are others. The repression of verbal responses to these drives increases the likelihood of the appearance of maladaptive behavior or symptoms. When it is physically possible to perform direct drive-reducing responses, such responses may be prevented by conflict, so that the drive must be reduced by symptomatic behavior. Two strong drives may have incompatible dominant responses, but some of the less dominant responses may be compatible and will tend to occur. Symptoms are often such compromise responses, which are strongly reinforced because they reduce both drives.

The resistance of symptoms to elimination, or extinction, is apparently due to the fact that they have been strengthened by long reinforcement, they continue to be reinforced, and interrupting their occurrence makes the individual feel worse. "If the symptom is reinforced by drive reduction so that interrupting it causes the drive to mount, we would expect this increased drive to motivate the learning and performance of new symptoms. Thus treatment that is aimed only at eliminating specific symptoms by such means as hypnosis or physical punishment should tend to be followed by the appearance of new symptoms. As is well known, this is indeed the case." [17] Elimination or reduction of the drive motivating a symptom leads to the disappearance of the symptom. If the drive reappears, the symptom reappears, particularly if the elimination of the drive did not involve the pitting of incompatible responses against it, as in interpretation.

How Repression Is Learned

In the individual's psyche, the repressed or the unconscious, as Freud pointed out, is the unverbalized. Drives, cues, and responses that have never been labeled will be unconscious. Most of what is repressed originates in childhood before the acquistion of language, but even later in life some aspects of life remain unverbalized or poorly labeled. Suppression is the conscious avoidance of unpleasant thoughts, but repression is automatic; and since it is not under the control of verbal cues, it cannot be revoked by the individual. Repression is reinforced by the reduction of the unpleasant drive. The removal of repression results in an increase of the drive. An innate response to the drive of fear may be to stop thinking. For example, children learn to fear saying certain words, and the fear generalizes to the thoughts represented by those words. Thoughts themselves may become attached directly to fears, as when the thoughts precede acts that are immediately punished. Even delayed punishment may result in attachment of fear to thoughts when the punishment is accompanied by an explanation of the reason for the punishment. And sometimes parents can tell what a child is going to do and warn or reprimand him while he is only thinking about the act, thus attaching fear to the thought.

Repression may intervene in a drive sequence in three different ways: (1) The drive may not be labeled, or it may not be recognized for what it is and may be mislabeled. (2) The drive may be inhibited by stronger competing responses. For example, fear may lead to the inhibiting of the sexual drive. Hunger may even inhibit fear if the hunger is strong and the fear is weak to begin with, as in the experiment of Mary Cover Jones with Peter and the rabbit referred to in Chapter 4. (3) In the case of mediated learned drives, the inhibition of the mediating responses, which produce the cues eliciting the drive-producing responses, will eliminate the drive. Thus, for example, if one stops thinking about another's comments as insults, this can reduce anger. It is the first type of repression, in which the drive is present at full strength but unlabeled, that leads to symptomatic behavior.

Repression may be viewed as the result of an approach-avoidance conflict, that is, a conflict between trying to remember or think about something and trying to avoid the topic because of its fear-producing quality.

The superego, or conscience, is in part unconscious. This may be because the emotional components of the moral sanctions were learned before language developed, or because the responses were so strongly learned that they have become direct responses to nonverbal cues, like strong habits that may function without thought.

The presence of repression generates deficits in the higher mental processes, which involve verbal cue-producing responses. The inability to use labels leads to primary stimulus generalization or inadequate discrimination, and thus to displacement. Inability to attach the same label to similar situations leads to a decrease in learned (secondary) generalization. Absence of verbal responses removes the capacity for responding to remote goals or stimuli or for dealing with the future with foresight. Reasoning and planning will be affected, as well as ability to communicate with others and to obtain their help. Behavior is more childish and thus abnormal compared to that of other adults. The fact that repression is usually limited to certain areas or topics means that not all behavior is affected, of course, or else the individual would not be able to function at all. These expectations drawn from behavior theory are all supported by clinical data and fit Freud's description of the results of repression.

To summarize, the neurotic is one in whom there is a conflict between drives such as sex and aggression, and a strong fear. The satisfaction of his drives is prevented, resulting in a state of chronic high drive described as misery. The strong drives tend to evoke behavior that elicits fear. He responds by avoiding such behavior, thus not approaching the goal, which reduces the fear, thus reinforcing these responses. The state of conflict also results in tension, and the fear, too, is accompanied by unpleasant physiological reactions. In addition, the fear leads to repression of verbal and other cue-producing responses, so that thinking and reasoning are prevented and stupidity results. Symptoms are produced by the strong drives and/or fear, and are reinforced by reduction of these drives or fear.

THE THERAPY PROCESS

The neurotic who comes for counseling or psychotherapy has suffered long, and relatives, friends, and even his physician have given up attempts to help him. He himself is becoming hopeless. He doesn't know what to do; he can't explain himself; he is afraid to express himself or attempt to satisfy his drives; he is confused and can't think adequately. He has failed in many areas of life, senses that others know he is a failure, and thus lacks self-esteem. He cannot solve his own problems and requires new conditions of therapeutic learning to achieve a better adjustment. Counseling or psychotherapy offers these new conditions of learning. The therapy process is essentially a situation in which neurotic responses are extinguished and better, normal, responses are learned.

The Selection of Clients

Since psychotherapy is a learning process, it is desirable to exercise selection of those who can learn under the conditions of psychotherapy. If these conditions and the principles of learning are known, such selection should be possible. The rules of selection based on these principles seem to agree quite well with those developed from clinical experience and psychoanalytic theory.

First, the disorder must be learned, not organic. To be un-learned, the condition must first be a product of learning. Second, there must be motivation for therapy, since motivation is important in learning. A person who is miserable and suffering is more motivated than one who is self-satisfied. One who seeks therapy on his own is better motivated than one who is compelled or forced into therapy. The more disadvantageous the symptoms, the stronger the motivation for therapy. Third, the more strongly the symptoms are reinforced, the poorer the prognosis. Secondary gains, such as pensions or compensation, may reinforce symptoms and reduce motivation for therapy. Fourth, the greater the potential rewards for improvement, the better the prognosis. Good physical health, youth, beauty, intelligence, education, special skills, a good position, a good social-class status, wealth, and a good marital partner or prospects of one increase the possibility of reward. Fifth, a certain minimum achievement in social learning is necessary, since psychotherapy does not provide the basic training that should be received in the family. A minimum ability to use and respond to language is required; this is related to intelligence, of course. Potentiality for higher mental processes, that is, having such processes to restore or the presence of such functioning in some areas, increases the favorability of the prognosis. If age-graded achievements, such as aspects of the conscience or superego, are lacking, psychotherapy will be difficult. Sixth, a history of neurosis going back into childhood is unfavorable. Finally, habits that interfere with psychotherapy, such as inability to listen or to talk reasonably, extreme suspiciousness, excessive passivity and dependence, or extreme independence and pride, are unfavorable signs.

The Elements of Therapeutic Learning

The therapeutic process consists of a number of aspects.

The first is the *lifting of repression* through extinguishing or counterconditioning the fear or anxiety associated with repressed material. "In therapy a new type of social situation is created, the opposite of that responsible for learning repression."[18] That is, the client says the words that have been attached to fear, shame, and guilt in a permissive, warm, accepting atmosphere, and this leads to the extinction of the fear and guilt. This extinction generalizes to thinking, and from painful but not repressed topics to more repressed topics. The drives motivating repression become weakened, and cycles of extinction and generalization occur until "the repression is gradually unlearned under permissive social conditions that are the opposite to the punitive ones under which it was learned."[19] Thus, the therapeutic situation is characterized by permissiveness which leads to the lifting of repression.

The process is a slow and difficult one because fear and anxiety accompany the discussion of repressed ideas. Even though the therapist is permissive and neutral, the fact that he is a human being means that anxiety is generalized to him. But the therapist is also seen as a specialist in whom the client can have trust and confidence, and he thus provides reassurance. The client experiences fear and anxiety while he is talking, which is a necessary condition for extinction. At the same time, he experiences the benign attention of the therapist. Punishment does not occur, and the fear attached to the forbidden sentences is not reinforced. In terms of the approach-avoidance conflict that characterizes repression, the avoidance gradient is reduced by the attitudes and activity of the therapist, so that the client, as a result of the approach drive, can begin to move toward the goal that will satisfy his drive.

In addition to the verbalizations of the client about himself and his past, the *transference relationship* is a second necessary part of therapy. It provides information that the client is not able to give directly. The client reacts to the therapist emotionally—with fear, hate and love—without being aware of it. These emotional reactions are called transference, since they are not elicited by the therapist as he actually is, but are transferred to him as a representative of other figures, to whom they were originally directed.

Transference occurs in all areas of normal life, for emotional reactions occur in many situations that would not be considered adequate stimuli for them. In therapy these transferred reactions are utilized to obtain information useful in helping the client. The therapist stimulates transference reactions by attempting to remain ambiguous, which allows the client to generalize to him more easily. The weakening of repression through permissiveness also facilitates transference —avoidance reactions to the therapist are thus not as strong as they are to others.

The generalization, or transfer, of many previously learned adaptive habits to the therapy situation makes therapy possible to begin with. These include being sensible, logical, and reasonable; being self-critical; speaking in an orderly, intelligible way; listening; being influenced by experts; expressing appropriate emotions; having hope, trust, and confidence in the therapist and in science; and wishing to please the therapist.

These generalizations, or transference reactions, serve to facilitate therapy. Others interfere with therapy. Fear and dependence or helplessness may be immediately transferred to therapy. False hopes of quick or easy cure may transfer from experience with doctors. These generalizations do not facilitate but hinder therapy. The client also brings more specific responses to therapy that obstruct the process. These reactions are his habitual ways of escaping from anxiety situations; when brought into therapy to escape anxiety, they impede progress. They include stopping talking or being silent, obscuring or confusing issues by quibbling, focusing on minor or irrelevant matters, talking in circles, and being repetitious. Fear may be reacted to with anger directed toward the therapist. Or anger may evoke fear responses. A common well-learned response to an anxiety-producing situation is to leave it, and the client may thus break off therapy. These reactions are considered transference reactions because they are not appropriate to the therapy situation. It is, of course, possible that at times the emotional reactions directed toward the therapist are appropriate, as when the therapist is hasty, stupid, or cruel (which are indications of incompetence) or when he makes a mistake (in which case it is best for him honestly to admit it).

While transferred reactions in the client may be considered as resistance on the part of the client, it must be recognized that they are generalized automatically to the therapy situation and are not purposely produced by the client. The transference situation is not a duel, but a real battle. Therapy is not simply a verbal intellectual discussion. The emotions involved in the neurosis must be brought out in therapy, at least to some extent.

The appearance of emotional responses in therapy entails responses that the client cannot talk about because they have never been labeled. They are, therefore, brought out where they can be discussed and labeled.

A third aspect of the counseling process is *learning to label,* or to think about new topics. The feelings arising with the lifting of repression, and those manifested in transference, must be dealt with verbally. "The neurotic is a person who is in need of a stock of sentences that will match the events going on within and without him. The new sentences make possible an immense facilitation of higher mental processes. . . . By labeling a formerly unlabeled response he can represent this response in reasoning." [20] Labeling must not be misunderstood as mere intellectualization. Therapy involves a new emotional experience with the therapist, and this leads to learning that may occur unconsciously. But "the learning is more transferable, and therefore more efficient, when adequate labeling occurs." [21] The client must have his own emotional experience and must correctly label it. It is not sufficient for the client to acquire a collection of sentences that are not related to emotional or instrumental responses.

A fourth aspect of therapy is the *learning of discriminations.* The neurotic "must clearly see that the conflicts and repressions from which he suffers are not justified by the current conditions of reward and punishment. He must further learn that the conditions in the past which produced these conflicts are sharply dissimilar from those of the present . . ." [22] Only then can he have the courage to try new responses, which, when rewarded, can break the neurotic impasse.

Discrimination is useful in reducing the anxiety that prevents the client from making a formerly punished and now inhibited response, by enabling him to recognize that the situation is different now. Simply using the labels "past" to refer to the dangerous situation and "present" to denote the harmless situation may provide a discrimination that can quickly reduce anxiety. Labeling thus facilitates discrimination, and discrimination tends to generalize to similar situations.

The importance of recovering past conditions is in contrasting them with present conditions so that differentiation or discrimination can occur. Describing the past constitutes a kind of reliving of the past with some of its emotions. The past can thus be brought to some extent into the present and compared with it, thereby facilitating discrimination. The realization of the contrast between his present habit of repression and inhibition and the positive opportunities for gratification that exist in his environment helps the client mobilize his drives to be sensible and realistic; with the therapist's help it may inhibit anxiety, making action possible.

Verbal responses are important in discrimination, making possible the recognition of dissimilar stimuli to which similar responses are made, and of similar stimuli to which dissimilar responses are made. Verbal cues can prevent generalization of anxiety from the past to the present. When anxiety is reduced by discrimination, new responses become possible, and as these reduce neurotic drives, they can become the basis for new habits that permanently resolve the neurotic conflict.

Result: Restoration of the Higher Mental Processes

Therapeutic gains can occur without improved labeling, or insight. The permissive attitude of the therapist probably reduces the client's fear, and this should generalize from the therapeutic situation, leading to general improvement. This is usually not sufficient for complete cure, however; the removal of repression, new labeling, and improvement in discrimination and in the higher mental processes must also occur. The higher mental processes require verbal and other cue-producing responses, and thus depend on the removal of repression and on labeling. A number of changes in thinking result.

One of these is the ability to make *adaptive discriminations,* which leads to the reduction of primary stimulus generalization and of irrational fears. Another is the ability to make *adaptive generalizations,* which improves secondary stimulus generalization, leading to adaptive responses to culturally defined similarities. A third change or improvement is anticipating danger and *motivating foresightful behavior.* Verbal and other cue-producing responses can mediate hope, as well as enable the individual to reward himself for subgoal achievement and to wait for delayed rewards. A fourth is improvement in *reasoning and planning* through being aware of the real problem and defining it accurately. A fifth is the better *utilization of the cultural storehouse of tested problem solutions* that are available. A sixth is the *avoidance of the waste of contradictory behavior* through logical thinking. Finally, the verbalization of previously repressed material does not result in uninhibited behavior, but in *behavior that is under better social control.* Such verbal control of behavior requires that the words be attached to proper emotional and instrumental responses and not merely to other words.

Considerable practice or "working through" is needed before appropriate labeling, and thus discrimination and generalization, becomes a habit. Also, thoughts and plans must be translated into action, which is then rewarded, if behavior is to improve. All this takes time, so that therapy is a long process, and improvement may continue after therapy sessions have ended.

Real-World Aspects of Therapy

The therapy sessions are the "talking" phase of therapy. The second phase is the outside or real-world aspect. Real-life problems must be solved with new behavior outside of therapy. An aspect of this is the generalization of responses to the therapist to other persons. This is an important part of cure. These responses will be strengthened or extinguished depending upon whether they are rewarded or punished.

The performing in the real world of responses learned in therapy is not sufficient, however. Responses never performed in therapy will be necessary. Therapy can prepare for these responses by reducing the anxiety associated with them, but they must be made to persons in the client's real world. The extinction of fear of talking about such actions must generalize to fear of performing them. Once this fear is reduced, the drives leading to these actions increase and overcome inhibitory drives or stimuli. As the goal becomes nearer, strong anxiety reactions may arise, but they are overcome by the drive to respond. The approach-avoidance conflict must be resolved. Therapy contributes to this by reducing the avoidance gradient. In the neurotic the attempt to increase the approach gradient only leads to increase in conflict and misery, with possible breaking off of the therapy. Therapy may be a slow process of trying and failing, or of trying and succeeding in part, until success is achieved. Risks must be taken, and sometimes failure results. Therapy is not complete until actions follow verbalization.

Freudian theory seemed to assume that responses outside of therapy would occur automatically, although some analysts do encourage or direct real-life trials. While there is a tendency for such responses to occur without direction, it is not innate. But if therapy is to be successful, verbal cues must be connected to overt responses; the client must act. Some clients are apathetic about doing this, in which case the therapist must "get some 'action' responses following upon the cues of plans, and this connection must be slowly rewarded and strengthened." [23] In the later stages of therapy, when fear (avoidance) has been reduced, increasing motivation (approach) may have a good effect.

Since the major sources of drive reduction are not in the therapeutic situation, the therapist cannot provide the rewards the client needs. They must come in real life. The nature of the life conditions or environment of the client are thus important for the success of therapy, and the therapist has no control over these conditions. Therapists do attempt to select clients whose life conditions are favorable.

Therapy is limited in what it can do. It cannot give all that the client may wish—better speech, social advancement, an advantageous marriage, etc. It cannot remake the person, particularly the older person, nor can it remedy all the deficiencies of early development and training. Solutions must also be within the moral codes of society; otherwise the client exchanges an unconscious mental conflict for an open social conflict, which is likely to be still more maladaptive.

IMPLEMENTATION: TECHNIQUES OF THERAPY

The techniques of counseling are not completely separate, or discrete, but are blended or combined in infinite variety. Nevertheless, they can be identified and discussed separately.

Permissiveness

"From the patient's standpoint, the novelty of the therapeutic situation lies in its permissiveness. He is allowed a good turn to talk. His statements are received by the therapist with an even, warm attention. The therapist is understanding and friendly. He is willing, so far as he can, to look at matters from the patient's side and make the best case for the patient's view of things. The therapist is not shocked by what he hears and does not criticize. The frightened patient learns that here is a person he can really talk to—perhaps the first such person in his life." [24] In the accepting, permissive situation, fears attached to repressed topics are gradually extinguished. Without this, therapy could not occur. By his permissiveness and his lack of criticism and judging, the therapist sets himself apart from those who are not accepting and permissive.

The permissiveness applies to thoughts, but not to actions. Therapy attempts to remove repression of thoughts, but not restraint of antisocial acts. There are also definite restrictions of actions during therapy: the client is asked not to take important steps such as change in his marital status, in his job, or in other significant areas. Such actions are to be suppressed until the client is in a position to take action that is free from neurotic influences. The client may also be asked to limit therapeutic conversation to the therapy hours.

Free Association

While permissiveness allows the client to speak, the rule of free association requires him to speak without the inhibitions and censoring that influence ordinary conversation and without the consistencies and logic of such conversation. He is to report everything that comes to his mind, immediately and without reservations. "The rule is a force which is applied against the force of neurotic fear. Without it, and unless he follows it, the patient will remain fixed in his neurotic habits and cannot recover the free use of his mind." [25] The client must talk; this is his responsibility. The therapist cannot obtain the relevant information by questioning, since he doesn't know the relevant questions. Furthermore, the client must volunteer information in the presence of fear, or extinction cannot occur. Thus, free association is not free and easy.

The client begins with material that is less important, less anxiety-producing, and then, as the anxiety is extinguished by the therapist's responses and attitudes and as the effects generalize, he proceeds to more important, significant, and relevant material. This cycle of fear, extinction, generalization, and then fear again is repeated in a process that appears to be a testing of the therapist. The result of this proces is a gradual lifting of repression—the remembering of forgotten experiences, events, repressed sentences, and emotions. The therapist listens to it all, with no a priori hypotheses, to obtain a complete and rational verbal account of the client's life. As he attempts to make sense of it all, he will see gaps and inconsistencies, and will develop hypotheses about them. His own thoughts may describe what remains repressed in the client's mental life. Blockings in the client's association serve as aids to the therapist, since they point to areas where repression exists. Failure to deal with common important areas, as well as dreams and slips of the tongue, also points to repressed material. The therapist deals with these gaps and indications of repression essentially by following to the letter the rule of free association, urging and encouraging the client to further exploration, and pointing out certain omissions, attitudes, etc. ("permissive interpretation").[26]

Rewards for Talking

The client must be rewarded for talking while fearful and anxious in order to reinforce his talking and to enable him to continue and to progress in uncovering repression. The therapist may reward such talking in various ways. One of these is by listening—giving his full, free, and exclusive attention to what the client is saying. Another reward is his acceptance of what the client says and his avoidance of judging and condemning. The client's talking without acceptance and forgiveness, or catharsis, is not effective. A third reward is the therapist's understanding and his remembering what the client has said in the past. The therapist's calmness in the face of important revelations that the client is ashamed of or anxious about is a fourth reward. The therapist may even reward the client by expressions of sympathy or approval, but this is used sparingly. Finally, the therapist does not cross-question or make definite pronouncements, but speaks tentatively and suggests possible implications or relationships. He is patient and adapts to the pace of the client.

These rewards for forbidden sentences spoken with fear, instead of punishment, lead to the extinction of the fear. However, the fear of real dangers, of punishment for antisocial behavior, is not extinguished. "This discrimination must be made quite clearly by the therapist. The therapist can, so to say, promise nonpunishment for certain activities—those which were once punished but are now no longer forbidden—but the therapist cannot tamper with life's realities." [27]

Handling the Transference

The transference provides the therapist with indirect information about the client, in addition to what is obtained during free association. The therapist can label such data, while the client cannot.

The therapist is in many ways similar to teachers, parents, and age-graded superiors, which facilitates transference of responses learned in interaction with authoritarian figures. The therapist encourages or produces such transference by remaining as ambiguous as possible. In addition, the extinction of anxiety related to speaking about forbidden matters, under the permissiveness of the therapist, generalizes to the fears leading to avoidance and inhibition of emotional responses, so that these responses appear and are directed toward the therapist.

When the client obstructs therapy because of transference-induced reactions, the therapist attempts to overcome the obstruction. If the client falls silent, the therapist may interpret his silence, or assure the client that he can't have a blank mind, or give a clue as to what thoughts the client might have. When obfuscation occurs, he points out that it is an escape and urges the client to resume his work. "The therapist is under stress in accepting, identifying, and using transferred reactions for the ends of therapy. Though informative, transference emotions are often obstinate and difficult to deal with. . . . It is particularly important that the therapist should not imply that the patient is purposely producing these reactions, else he will confuse his patient and possibly give real cause for a feeling of injustice. The therapist's task is to identify these responses as transferred and find out how they arose." [28] While the client feels that his reactions must be real, the therapist must prove to him that they are not. The angry client may criticize obvious defects of the therapist (for example, his foreign accent), but the therapist must not respond with anger or irritation.

The therapist may have to identify the existence of the transferred response, show that it is not objectively justified as directed toward the therapist, and raise questions regarding its origin and the person from whom it is transferred. Since transferred responses are learned responses, they are therefore a source of inference about early conditions in the client's life. When the inappropriateness of the transference response and its obstruction of therapy are pointed out, the acquired drives to be logical and to progress in therapy lead the client to resume work and free association. "If the therapist does not know how to recall the patient to his proper task, such responses may persist and may end therapeutic progress. Failure to understand transference manifestations is one of the commonest sources of failure for the amateur in psychotherapy. The therapist lost many patients in this way, and inexperienced therapists still do." [29]

Labeling

Free association and the transference produce emotional responses that have never been labeled. The therapist must help the client label these responses. In order to do this, the therapist, on the basis of the material provided by free association and the transference, must develop an understanding of the client, so that he can not only empathize with the client (feel his feelings) but also label the client's feelings. Labeling consists of producing new verbal responses by connecting words to the correct emotional or environmental cues. The client may acquire these new verbal responses in at least three ways.

1   He may discover or create the new verbal units himself, under the compulsion of free association. Anxiety associated with them is extinguished by the therapist's permissiveness. Their production increases during therapy, both because anxiety is reduced and because there is increasingly more to build on. "The more of the essential work the patient can perform by himself during therapy, the more certain he is to be able to do what he needs afterward. The therapist should be careful not to deprive the patient of the pleasure of making his own discoveries." [30]

2   The therapist may selectively strengthen client responses that he thinks are important, without contributing his own ideas. The therapist may reward the client in various ways, such as by saying "uh-huh," including the client's ideas in summaries, and repeating what the client has said. Questions that are asked for clarification of material already introduced by the client may also serve this purpose by focusing attention on the client's responses.

3   The client may rehearse responses provided by the therapist as interpretations. Strong anxiety or the failure of the label and the cues produced by the emotion to occur at the same time may prevent the client from being able to label his responses himself. The therapist may provide the labels at the appropriate time. The client's rehearsal may be in paraphrase, using his own words, or may take place in his thoughts rather than out loud. The client is rewarded by the reduction of anxiety, the increase of hope, and the feeling of progress. Sometimes anxiety is increased, however, and the client resists the interpretation. Resistance may be related to the client's strong desire to be independent and do it all himself. Or it may occur when the therapist makes a stupid or awkward interpretation.

An incorrect label may give some temporary relief by reducing anxiety, but because it is not correct, it will not continue to be rewarded and will not persist. Verbal responses may be attached to emotional cues, to environmental cues, to instrumental acts, and to other verbal cues. The last relationship may be termed clarification and often involves ordering responses, linking events in a temporal and causal order.

Interpretation, or "prompting," by the therapist is necessary if therapy is to be efficient and maximally successful, since the client cannot usually do it all by himself, although this is to be preferred. The client who can do this makes rapid progress and is ready for dismissal when he can do it well by himself. The second of the methods described above is necessary when the client makes a number of different and confusing or contradictory hypotheses or statements.

The third method, though sometimes necessary, has some disadvantages. The therapist cannot be as certain that the client uses interpretation when he rehearses it to himself as when he speaks it aloud. Silent responses are probably weaker and less effective. Weakening also occurs through generalization from the therapist's voice to the client. Finally, there is the resistance, or "interpretation shock."

The therapist should not intervene with interpretations until the client ceases to make progress by himself, and then only to the extent that he feels the client can bear. Moreover, "the skillful therapist . . . does not make interpretations on mere hunches. He waits until he has strong evidence for his hypothesis before he supplies a label, points out a transferred response, or teaches a discrimination. If the patient is to be convinced, the evidence must be convincing. The fewer ill-founded notions the therapist utters, the greater his authority when he does speak." [31]

Teaching Discrimination

Discrimination involves attaching different verbal cues to stimulus patterns that are actually different. The therapist teaches the patient to discriminate in various ways. One is to call attention to a problem area in order to evoke new discriminations by failing to understand the client, which stimulates him to reexamine the area. This is similar to the Socratic method of teaching. Applying a word or label to which an elaborate series of responses is already attached transfers these responses to the new situation. The therapist may discourage certain responses by labeling them as false or doubtful. The therapist is thus "an operator in the field of language, exciting learned drives and administering learned rewards, eliciting adequate sentence chains to guide instrumental responses." [32] Generalization to similar sets of stimuli can be facilitated if the therapist points out their similarity.

The therapist may also foster discrimination by pointing out the difference between the past and the present and assuring the client that the present environment is benign.

EXAMPLE

Dollard, Auld, and White have presented an analysis of a case of brief psychotherapy using techniques based on the theories of Dollard and

Miller. The student would benefit from reading the complete presentation and analysis of this case, but only the verbatim transcript of the eleventh interview, which is given under the heading of "Tactics: Examples of Therapeutic Techniques in This Case," is included here, without comment.[33] It is perhaps well to note that the authors felt that the therapist was too active, and thus that this interview does not illustrate free association well, or not as well as other interviews in the case.

The Eleventh Hour of Therapy

PATIENT   . . . We've had a hectic day today. We've been working like slaves, my mother and I, all morning, since seven-thirty. For a big family dinner tonight. And I'm tired. But she's doing all the cooking . . . I haven't that to worry about, but the little things, you know. Do you know I've been thinking about the conversation that we had last week . . . and . . . my life is very boring and dull . . . but it really is my own fault. I really should go out and get a job and work, I think, so that during the day my mind is occupied—my time is taken up at night—I'll be very contented to sit home and do nothing. And . . . and I guess I shouldn't complain about it . . . being so dull. Because it really is my fault.

THERAPIST   How do you mean, it's your fault?

PT   Well, I mean I shouldn't . . . I should be so busy during the day that at night I won't mind staying in and being bored or leading a quiet life. But . . . I don't know what I . . . I'm not qualified to do anything really—I mean to get a job. I used to take those parts in our theater group plays but I could never go into show business professionally. I could only work in a gift shop or as a receptionist or a telephone-answering service, or something like that. I haven't taken any courses in . . . in any secretarial work or anything like that. But I suppose I could do it. Now I could take up bookkeeping or typing and shorthand.

TH   Yes, un huh.

PT   I could get . . . you know, take that course and six easy lessons, is that what they . . . (laugh) You see it advertised. It's a short course. I was thinking about doing that. But, it's funny, I don't know what's the matter with me, I . . . have two lovely children, I have a wonderful husband, I have a lovely home . . . but I'm not happy. That doesn't make sense.

TH   I don't understand, you say is life too easy . . .

PT   Well, I mean is it because I . . . I have things too easy that I'm . . . discontented . . . if I had it harder would I feel that I shouldn't complain about anything?

TH   How does that sound to you?

PT   It seems logical. It seems that my life is too easy for me. That . . . I have no complaints to make at all for . . . I mean as far as . . . having a wonderful husband and a wonderful daughter and son and a lovely home, and I entertain when I want to . . . and it seems as though I'm discontented. I'm not happy and I complain all the time.

TH   Well, there must be some reason, don't you think?

PT   Well, I don't know, that's what I can't understand; why should I feel this way? Why should I feel that I'm discontented, that I'm looking for something all the time? Why shouldn't I be contented to stay home and . . . and have the things I have? I can . . . I don't know. I still can't understand it. Why should I complain about my boring life or monotonous life? I have no right to, really.

TH   How's that?

PT   Well, people . . . many people are worse off than I am, that haven't got the things that I have. Why should I complain? Why should I be unhappy? Does it all have to do with what I went through as a child?

TH   Well, I don't see . . . of course other people have it more difficult and other people have greater problems . . .

PT   Yes.

TH   . . . but I don't think we should judge your problem on the basis of what other people's problems are but should try to understand your problems and see why you should have . . .

PT   What am I looking for? I don't know what I want in life. What am I . . . what's . . . what . . . I don't know what is my aim in life. Shouldn't I be contented—the way it is? But I'm not. I'm unhappy.

TH   Well, isn't that then our problem?

PT   Yes, but . . .

TH   Not the question whether you should or should not be contented, but the fact that you are not and that we want to find out why.

PT   But I'm ashamed to complain about it. Because I have so much. I mean I have a . . . a good husband and a nice house and a wonderful daughter and son. It really makes me ashamed. Am I making a mountain out of a molehill?

TH   Well, there's something in this picture which seems to be missing; I mean you mention all these things that are seemingly satisfying and yet you are not satisfied . . .

PT   But I'm not.

TH   . . . and there must be something that is wrong.

PT   I don't know why—I can't put my finger on it, really. Well, I don't know what I'm striving for. What do I want? What do I expect from life? Why should I get bored all the time? Why should life be so monotonous? Is it because I don't have enough to do? Is it because I have time on my hands? If I went out and worked I probably wouldn't feel this way. I kept asking myself that for the past two days. I don't know what I want out of life, what I'm striving for, but I expect what I want . . . my husband is good to me, my daughter is wonderful, and I have a fine boy. I entertain nicely. People have said that they feel very welcome in . . . and I'm a cordial hostess, and they were comfortable in my home. Doesn't everybody do that? Isn't that everybody's life?

TH   Well, if this were all so, then it would be very amazing that you shouldn't be satisfied. And I wonder whether these things really are so.

PT   But, they are all so, but still I'm unhappy, still I'm unhappy, still I want to run away . . . and . . . get away from my house. But I think it's lack of something to do, lack of interest, lack of . . . working maybe, that's what I need. Paul has gone away to school. Doris is growing up now, she doesn't need me for anything, really . . . except to get her meals and things like that, but that's nothing. And Paul is away at school all winter and at camp in the summer. My husband only needs me for the meals and things like that.

TH   What kind of things?

PT   Dinner, and washing, and cleaning, but outside of that I . . . my time is my own.

TH   Is that really the only thing that your husband needs you for?

PT   Well . . . he's very . . . he seems to be very contented with the life that he lives . . . leads. I don't interfere with his life. He seems to . . . like to come home, and stay home and relax, after putting in a tough day with those law cases of his. I certainly can't . . . interfere with that. It wouldn't do me any good if I tried. We are . . . a . . . two very different personalities completely. He's very placid and reserved and I'm the opposite. I'm happy-go-lu . . . I mean I used to be . . . happy-go-lucky and nothing bothered me too much. I like to have a good time. I like to have fun. I don't feel as though I'm old . . . too old to enjoy life. But he . . . he likes quiet things . . . the quiet life.

TH   But this difference in personality hasn't been bothering you—at least you haven't said so—all through the last sixteen years or so.

PT   Oh, I thought about it . . . yes, I have. I've thought about it a long time . . . how we can be visiting and I'll be having a good time and all of a sudden he'll say, "Come on, let's go home." So, quick like that I have to leave and go home . . . I mean it's been going on for years. It isn't anything new. And as I told you before, if we're invited out and he's tired, we don't go. I mean things like that. But I guess I can't be a playgirl all the time. But I don't feel old . . . really, I mean, where I have to stay home all the time. I feel as though I want to have fun and enjoy myself. Is that wrong?

TH   No. Of course, you are young; you are quite young enough to have an enjoyable life, and I think that you have a right to that kind of thing, but I'm just wondering . . .

PT   You mean it isn't wrong to still feel young in your heart and to want to get fun out of life.

TH   If one considers such a thing as "right" or "wrong," I'm quite sure that it is not wrong.

PT   Do I sound immature, do I sound like a child when I say things like that? Childish?

TH   Do you think you do?

PT   I'm afraid to say I do. I think it is childish just to want to have a good time and enjoy myself. I think now that my children are growing up and I'm getting older I should want to settle down and not do anything—and just lead a very quiet, simple life.

TH   Why do you think you should?

PT   We . . . I don't know, I just feel as though I . . . I can't go out and do the things I used to do, although I still feel as though I could . . . I mean, inside. But it doesn't look right; it isn't right to do it.

TH   With Doris getting older and more independent, do you feel that you are, well let us say, getting old, being an old woman now?

PT   No. It doesn't bother me. I never think of it that way. Is that wrong?

TH   No, what you say, that you feel that you should . . .

PT   Well, I do . . . I mean, I feel I should on account of the people around me, convention's sake, you know what I mean, having people talk about me. I still feel that I can . . . I ought to have fun . . . and . . . and enjoy myself, even though the children are growing up and don't need me as much now. I think I really could have a better time . . . but I'm afraid of what people will say. My friends, my husband.

TH   What do you think they might say?

PT   They'll say that she ought to grow up, she's not . . . she's got growing children, she should act like a mother. (embarrassed laugh) But Bob is very restrained . . . not restrained but placid; he's very quiet. We have been away—as a matter of fact I don't even enjoy going away with Bob, because he likes to go to a place where you can just eat, and sleep, and you know, relax, go to bed early. I do that every night. All the time. I don't even like to go away on vacations with him, or anyplace . . . but I go. He wants to relax all the time; I'm not tired, I don't feel that kind of tired that . . . I want fun, I want life, I want people around. Is that wrong?

TH   Just . . . how do you feel about this? You seem to feel . . .

PT   Well, I don't know . . . I can't understand . . . I mean, this . . . feeling that I've had about Bob being . . . placid. . . . I've always . . . held it in, I mean I've never said anything about it. I've never said, "Oh, I'd like to go someplace where it's fun." I've always kept my mouth shut and not said anything about it . . . because I knew it wouldn't do any good to say it. I mean it's always been in the back of my mind. We went on a vacation once for four days, and all I did was sit on the porch and read. I can do that at home. I . . . and people said, "Oh, you must have had a wonderful time on your vacation." I was bored to death! I hated every minute of it. Of course, I didn't say anything to him. I said it was very nice . . . but I hated it. And I won't go away with him anymore. And I can't go alone, so I'm stuck. (half-laugh) So I . . . so I guess for me the only way I can go . . . I mean get away . . . is to go with him and do what he wants to do. So you see how different we are? Exact—just like night and day. Maybe it's better. Maybe he holds me down. Maybe I need that sort of thing. But I feel that I've missed so much in my younger days. I wasn't allowed to do anything. But I thought being married, and . . . it would be different. But it hasn't changed a bit. I mean as far as . . . pleasure . . . and enjoyment. It sounds crazy, doesn't it? (pause) But he's so good that I can't. . . . I guess I can't be any different with him, I mean I can't . . . I can't go . . . a . . . I can't disagree with him, as far as things like that go. I can't say, "I'm going out to a nightclub tonight and you can stay home." I've never done it.

TH   At the time you were telling me about, when you used to be active in that amateur dramatic group and so on . . .

PT   The rehearsals were sometimes in the afternoon.

TH   Yes, but you were then also going out and having . . . fun. Did that have any relationship to this feeling?

PT   Sure. It made me feel that I could have fun one or two afternoons or evenings a week, and I could sit home the other evenings. At least I had some fun; I got that in. But he . . . I . . . listen . . . I . . . I feel he's entitled to living the kind of life he wants to live. I don't object to it, I mean, as far as he's concerned. He puts in a hard day; he's tired. He really—I'd never deprive him of going to bed at nine o'clock or ten o'clock; I would never say anything to make him feel that . . . that I was unhappy about it, I just don't say anything. Course I feel terrible, but I don't say anything about it. We . . . we refuse a million invitations on account of him. Is it wrong to feel that you still want to have fun in life?

TH   Well, there might be other compensations . . .

PT   Well . . .

TH   . . . for this, and I wonder whether you feel that there are or there are not . . . and, I mean, other compensations in your relationship.

PT   Well, he . . . he's a . . . he's good.

TH   How do you mean?

PT   He's . . . reliable, he's honest, he's a hard worker . . . he's a homebody. (apologetic laugh) He likes to stay home. Maybe I haven't . . . maybe I'm not mature; maybe I'm still a child—I haven't matured enough, maybe I'm not grown-up enough, I don't know.

TH   Well now, the things you mentioned as . . . the good points of your husband. Are those really the only things you would expect from a husband?

PT   No. I think a husband should be . . . as excited to do something as the wife should. I feel that . . . Bob should feel like I feel, about having a good time, about going out and being with people. That he should be as congenial as I am. (pause) Even when we were younger—I mean even before we were married and . . . we were engaged, it was the same way, although I always figured, well, he had a hard day the next day and I wouldn't interfere. I would let him . . . he would . . . we . . . when we used to have dates he left me at ten-thirty or eleven o'clock, early. We never stayed up past midnight, ever. I never remember staying out till twelve or one o'clock. I sound silly, though, to make an issue of it, don't I?

TH   Well, this is a problem which is bothering you, and I don't see why you consider that silly.

PT   Yes, but how . . . I . . . I can't straighten it out. How can I do anything about it? There's no way of . . . of changing it. I certainly couldn't say to Bob, "I'm going out on a date tonight, good-by." (throaty laugh) Or, "I'm going out to have fun." I couldn't do that; I'm not built that way. As much as I would probably love to do it, I wouldn't do it. Is it . . . is it because I feel that I missed so much when I was younger that I feel that now I want to . . . do the things I didn't do before?

TH   Is that what you think it is?

PT   Yes, I do. I think I never really had a chance to . . . really go out and . . . well, I don't know, it sounds silly to even talk about. It's ridiculous. Can't do anything about it anyway. I sound like a child. Once the pattern is made you have to stick to it, I guess. Once you start your life the way you do you can't change. Especially your married life. I've never told Bob how I felt about this . . . because I knew it wouldn't do any good. I'm sure it wouldn't. Because he wouldn't understand, he wouldn't . . . he . . . he'd think I was acting like a baby. So, if I get myself something to do during the day, where I'd get busy and not think about it, maybe it'll be better to a . . . at night I'd be contented to stay home. It's like knocking your head against a stone wall, isn't it? Can you straighten out a problem like that? Is it possible?

TH   Well, I'm still not sure whether we really have the whole problem in front of us.

PT   Well, what do you mean? I don't understand; I've told you how I felt about it.

TH   But you say yourself, again and again, it sounds childish and it doesn't make sense.

PT   But it's because there's no way of solving it. There's no way of solving that problem. How can I go to Bob and say, "I want to go out tonight. I want to have fun. I'm tired of staying home." If I did, he'd say, "I'm sorry, I'm tired." So what am I going to do? Go out by myself? Can I do that?

TH   Well, that's a question you'd have to ask yourself.

PT   Well, I can't, I've never done it, I wouldn't know where to—how to start. So I keep asking myself, well am I str—what do I want out of life? What am I striving for, what am I working for? Where am I getting? I have a nice home, a nice daughter and son, a nice husband, but that's all. It sounds stupid, doesn't it?

TH   No, it doesn't sound stupid; it sounds like an incomplete picture to me.

PT   Well, it isn't incomplete. That's exactly how I feel. I feel that I . . . do what I have to do, but I still want to get some pleasure out of life too. But why am I different from most people? Most people, I guess, don't feel the way I do. They don't complain about not going out. Well, what's wrong with me? Why should I feel like I want to enjoy myself and have fun?

TH   Well, of course, again we can't say what happens to most people, because we are dealing with —appraising—your problem rather than other people . . .

PT   Well, that's what I mean, there's no comparison, I mean I don't understand it. There are . . . there's a friend of mine who . . . who's in worse circumstances than I am, but she never complains. Maybe because she has three kids to take care of during the day and she's probably tickled to death when they go to bed so she can relax at night. Maybe it's because I don't have enough to do during the day. (pause) I don't know. But I've felt like this for a long time. I feel that I'm not getting everything out of life that I would like to.

TH   What would you like to get out of life? That you're not . . .

PT   I don't know. That's what I'd like to know. That's what I wonder. What do I want? What do I? That's where I can't put my finger on it. There's something that I . . . that I . . . I'm hoping for, but I don't know what.

TH   When you were engaged to your husband and this pattern had already been . . . you know, you say this pattern had already been established back then—was there something that you were hoping for that might compensate you for some of the socially unexciting times?

PT   There was nothing. Nothing. I was young, I didn't know, I was madly in love. I thought he was wonderful and I adored him. I thought he was a wonderful guy. I didn't look for anything else. He was sweet, he was . . . oh, I didn't need . . . I didn't want anything else. He was thoughtful and he was considerate. I used to work in a gift shop; I was substituting there one summer. He used to pick me up in the morning and drive me to work, pick me up at five-thirty in the afternoon. I thought he was just marvelous. And Bob is very secure. As far as I can see, he . . . he . . . nothing seems to bother him too much. And he's had a very tough life, too, because he worked his way through college . . . as a salesman . . . in the summertime. And his family were poor. He was really, he's really a terrific guy. Self-made (pause) And I always felt that Bob was the "old reliable," I mean somebody you could depend on all the time. That was the feeling I had, he was always there when you wanted him, when you needed him. He still is, I mean that's the w . . . you know. That's what he is today.

TH   And yet, somehow you sound as if you were disappointed . . . I can't quite put my finger on it.

PT   Disappointed? (pause) No, I don't know. Maybe it's because I . . . that he's older that I'm disappointed. I mean, maybe if I had married somebody younger that . . . that wasn't so . . . set in their ways. Bob is a lot like I remember my father to be. He had a wonderful disposition, easygoing, reliable, I mean, those are the traits.

TH   Well, isn't there something that one expects from a husband that one doesn't expect from one's father?

PT   Love and companionship? Romance? (pause) That's when you're young. When you're older it doesn't mean anything anymore. Or when you're married a long time it changes completely, doesn't it?

TH   How do you mean, it changes completely?

PT   Well, I don't know, when you're young it's kid stuff I guess, but when you get older you don't . . . think about it, or . . . it doesn't mean anything. It's like . . . being married when you're older . . . it's like a habit. I mean it's like brushing your teeth. It's . . . it's . . . your husband is there and you're . . . and that's the way it is.

TH   I wonder whether that is the way it really has to be.

PT   Well, I don't know. I mean I can't answer that question. I don't know.

TH   Well, let me put it this way, could it be that you would rather that it were not that way?

PT   Well, I don't know that either, because I don't under—I don't know. I don't know any different. It's . . . it's . . . it's a different kind, it's . . . a deeper feeling you have than when you're younger. I think.

It's a closer feeling when you get older. But in a different way. I don't know, I can't answer that either, I guess. It's more of a take-it-for-granted feeling. Doesn't that make sense? I mean, does that sound . . . you know he's there. That's all. You know that he's . . . that you have somebody, that you . . . that you feel close to. I can't . . . explain it. All I know is that it isn't the same as when you're young. But, it isn't supposed to be, I don't think. People are not . . . Bob is not a demonstrative person at all.

TH   How do you mean, "demonstrative"?

PT   Well, I mean, he . . . he . . . he doesn't call me pet names, like some husbands call their wives or he doesn't show any affection, like some husbands show their wives . . . from what I've seen. He's never been that way. I guess I'm the aggressive one. Oh, it's so silly to talk about this, because nothing can be done. It's so foolish. I can't go out and get a divorce tomorrow just because I have a husband that likes to stay home all the time. I can't do that.

TH   What made you think of divorce?

PT   Well . . . isn't that what people usually do when they're unhappy? Don't they usually . . . if they're not happy they . . . divorce? They . . . maybe . . . maybe I'm childish, thinking about it this way. Maybe I shouldn't even think about it. As my mother says, "You make your bed; you lie in it." I mean, not that I've even discussed this with her at all, but I mean it's just that she's passed that . . . she has said that about . . . you know.

TH   I wonder why you pick on this particular . . . saying.

PT   "You make your bed; you lie in it?"

TH   Yes.

PT   I don't know, I've heard my mother say it.

TH   Well, there are lots of other sayings. I wonder why you used this particular one.

PT   Well, it's . . . it's something that you do, and you just have to . . . take it. (sigh) There's no way of getting out of it. Oh, I don't know, some days I feel like I just . . . like to go away and . . . just see what the other side of the world looks like. But I'm not—do I sound like I'm complaining?

TH   Do you think you are?

PT   I don't know, is it a complaint? Or is it just unhappiness or is unhappiness a complaint too?

TH   I don't know. If you want to call it something, I think you sound disappointed.

PT   Disappointed. Maybe I am disappointed. I've been disappointed all my life. It's nothing new. (pause) But then I feel guilty about talking about it . . . Because I feel that Bob is good to me . . . that I shouldn't complain, or I shouldn't say it. . . . It sounds crazy. Maybe it's that I'm not matured enough. Maybe I'm still a child. Maybe I . . . I haven't grown up. Maybe I expect too much. I don't know.

TH   What do you mean, expect too much?

PT   Maybe I expected more out of life.

TH   Such as what?

PT   Well, that's it, I don't know. I can't . . . I don't know. Everything isn't perfect. Sometimes I wonder if I had lived by myself, when I first got married, whether it would be any different.

TH   In which respect are you thinking of?

PT   I mean living by myself, alone, maybe our lives would be different?

TH   You say, how do you . . . I don't understand, you say by yourself, alone?

PT   Yes, I mean living in a room by ourselves, without living in . . . in the house with my mother.

TH   Is that "by myself alone" you mean "by ourselves"?

PT   No, I meant by ourselves alone. Maybe we would have lived differently, maybe we . . . I don't know.

TH   How would you have lived differently?

PT   Well, maybe it's because we were restrained when we were home. That we . . . that . . . maybe Bob felt that he didn't want to . . . do anything, I mean go out or anything on account of living at my mother's. I don't know, it's all . . . mixed up. But I keep thinking about that. Maybe our lives would have been different.

TH   In the very beginning, when we first met, you told me that in the years when you lived at your mother's house you felt . . . kind of restrained, or inhibited, about intercourse because you had the feeling that your mother might be coming into the room. If you had lived away, do you think that might have been different?

PT   It might have been. Maybe it would have. I don't know. So many years ago, it might have been different.

TH   Well, but then you moved out of your mother's house, and that restriction or restraint, inhibition, was removed. Did things change then?

PT   Yes and no.

TH   How do you mean?

PT   I don't know, I can't . . . I can't . . . I don't know. Maybe . . . Maybe, I don't know . . . I can under—I can't explain it. Maybe it . . . maybe that feeling stayed with us. (half-apologetic laugh) Is it possible?

TH   Well, you have to tell me whether it did or not.

PT   (laughing) Maybe it got to a point where it didn't matter. (cynical tone)

TH   That what didn't matter?

PT   Anything. That's not very clear, is it? (laughs)

TH   No.

PT   Well, maybe . . . maybe we felt that it wasn't important, because we had been restrained for so many years. Is that possible?

TH   Well, now, you say, "we felt," what did you feel?

PT   Well, both of us, I'm sure. I don't know, maybe it wasn't me, maybe my husband felt that way, I don't know. I've never asked him.

TH   Well, how did you feel about it?

PT   Well, I felt relaxed and relieved when I was in my own home . . . because I felt free. Nothing bothered me. (pause) I still feel free in my own home, as far as that goes. Maybe it isn't my fault. (half-laughing)

TH   What isn't your fault?

PT   What you said.

TH   What did I say?

PT   Maybe . . . maybe he's inhibited.

TH   You see, this whole picture you painted of your married life, and all the things you said about your husband, you said he's hardworking, he's conscientious, he's honest, and so forth. In all these things, there's always been something missing, and this was your sexual relationship and I always wondered why there was this hold, because after all, when one has been married for a number of years, one talks about one's relationship with one's husband. I mean there is the sexual relationship in addition to all the other things, and you have talked about all the other things and I wondered why you have always been leaving this out, and I wonder whether it's very difficult to talk about that and whether it may not be that this is one of the things that you have always been getting away from when we started talking . . . in this direction.

PT   Well, I don't like to talk about personal problems, things like that.

TH   But don't you know that, within the treatment, it's very important . . .

PT   I know . . . but I still think it's none of anybody's business (apologetic laugh)

TH   . . . not to leave anything out? Well, as long as you feel that some parts of your life are none of my business, we can't get very far in our treatment.

PT   I know. (pause) It's very difficult to talk about it because I never talked about it, with any—at all, ever.

TH   I know, and that's what I meant when I said repeatedly that you have to work real hard in order to say some of these unpleasant things that we don't ordinarily talk about, because only when we have all areas of your life clearly before us can we understand what some of your problems are.

PT   Um hum. I never liked to talk about things like that. I never have. I always thought it was something that belonged to me.

TH   But then you again have been holding out, haven't you?

PT   Um huh.

TH   And we can't possibly make any progress in the treatment . . .

PT   I know it.

TH   . . . as long as you have this private understanding . . .

PT   But I . . .

TH   . . . that you will hold out on certain aspects.

PT   To tell you the truth, I didn't think it would enter the picture. I always thought that those things were never talked about. I didn't know you discuss things like that too.

TH   Well, again, there shouldn't be anything that you think doesn't have any relationship, because whatever happens to come into your mind is what you want to say without any restrictions and . . .

PT   Embarassing!

TH   Well, now, it is difficult to say and it's embarrassing and it's sometimes frightening to say, but nevertheless this is the hard work which is involved in the treatment, and you have to understand that there shouldn't be anything that you should keep to yourself, thinking that it has nothing to do with or has nothing . . . is none of my business.

PT   It's very embarrassing to talk about it. Because I always felt that those things, nobody was supposed to talk about. And I didn't know that I had to talk about them. I really didn't, honestly.

TH   Well, it's part of our general understanding . . .

PT   I know.

TH   . . . that you will say anything that comes to your mind, do you see?

PT   Yes, that's what you said. Well, I didn't realize that I had to . . .

TH   That includes everything.

PT   I didn't know I had to talk about those things too. (pause) The time is up. And I still didn't get anything. (sigh)

TH   Well, maybe this is one of the reasons why we haven't gotten very far, because you still . . .

PT   Because I've been holding out.

TH   . . . have some private understanding that there are certain things that are none of my business.

PT   I still don't understand why they're so important, I mean why things like that really . . . a . . . make a problem.

TH   Because it's part of the general picture and in order to understand it we have to get at all parts of it.

PT   Yes, that's what you said. See you on Monday.

SUMMARY AND EVALUATION

Neurosis is learned in early childhood. Although a single drive can be raised to traumatic heights and cause pain and suffering, neurosis is usually the product of the conflict of drives originating in the feeding situation, cleanliness training, sex training, and anger-anxiety situations. These conflicts are repressed; that is, they are unconscious. The unconscious is that which cannot be verbalized, that which is unlabeled. Fear is the most basic and the strongest drive involved in conflict; it inhibits the expression of other drives, thus preventing their satisfaction. Both fear and the conflicting drive produce symptoms that consist of responses—often compromise responses—that lead to some drive reduction. Thus, they are rewarded, or reinforced, and persist. The neurotic is miserable because of his conflicts, which prevent the satisfaction of his drives. He appears stupid because repression prevents him from knowing the nature of his problem.

The therapeutic situation provides the conditions for new learning. Free association leads to the uncovering of repression. The transference further reveals the nature of the conflicting drives. The client and the therapist engage in the process of labeling these drives, experiences, feelings, and conflicts. Such labeling makes possible the discrimination of experiences and situations that are apparently similar but actually different, and the appropriate generalization to situations that are actually similar. Labeling and the resultant insight enable the client to engage in the higher mental activities that make adaptive behavior possible.

Neurosis is essentially an approach-avoidance conflict, that is, a situation in which the individual has strong tendencies to approach and to avoid the same goal. The gradient of avoidance (the increase of the tendency for avoidance, or fear, with closeness to the goal) is stronger than the gradient of approach (the increase of the tendency for approach with closeness to the goal). The neurotic is a person who has strong avoidance tendencies. An attempt to increase his motivation to approach the goal will only increase his fear and conflict. This is often what well-meaning relatives and friends try to do. If the therapist does the same, the client will tend to leave therapy. Therefore, rather than attempt to raise the approach gradient, the therapist attempts to reduce the avoidance gradient. His acceptance, permissiveness, and understanding reduce the client's fears.

In one publication Miller refers to the situation in which the client's fears are realistic, and the achieving of the goal results in punishment. The client is then punished if he reaches the goal, or suffers strong fear or conflict if the punishment keeps him just barely away from the goal. "In such cases, attempting to decrease fear and avoidance will indeed produce a negative therapeutic effect, while conversely, a positive therapeutic effect may be produced by increasing the strength of fear and avoidance to the point where the subject remains far enough away from the forbidden goal that he is no longer strongly punished or even tempted enough to be in conflict." [34] When punishment occurs some time after the achieving of the goal, strong fear (or guilt) is felt after the goal has been reached, but only moderate fear before then. Again, increasing the height of the avoidance gradient might produce therapeutic changes.

Dollard and Miller present a meticulous, systematic, and reasoned approach based on reinforcement learning theory. They have integrated learning theory with the clinical system of psychotherapy developed by psychoanalysis. They have shown essentially that psychoanalysis is consistent with, or can be rationalized to appear consistent with, reinforcement learning theory. The concept of reinforcement is substituted for Freud's pleasure principle. The concept of ego strength has been translated into that of the higher mental processes and of culturally valued learned drives and skills. Repression becomes the inhibition of the cue-producing responses that mediate thinking and reasoning. Transference is a special case of generalization. Conflict is seen in terms of learning theory. Additional concepts and principles, such as inhibition and restraint, are added to extend some of those of psychoanalysis. The concept of reality is extended, or concretized, in terms of the physical and social conditions of learning. The need for responses to be made and reinforced outside of therapy, in real life, is emphasized.

Compared to the rather crude and narrow approaches of Wolpe and Salter, that of Dollard and Miller is broad and comprehensive and carries an impressive authority. Rather than reject psychological and social factors such as the nature of the client-therapist relationship, it incorporates them and indicates their consistency with learning theory. There is a major point of disagreement with the techniques of Salter and Wolpe. On the assumption, supported by empirical evidence, that the avoidance gradient is stronger than the approach gradient in an approach-avoidance conflict, Dollard and Miller base their techniques upon the reduction of the avoidance gradient. (However, they do recognize the need in some cases to motivate the client to go beyond talking and take action, although they do not specify how this is to be done.) In direct contrast to this, the techniques of Salter and Wolpe appear to be directed toward the raising of the approach gradient. Since Dollard and Miller present empirical evidence and suggest clinical evidence for their position, how, then, can Wolpe and Salter achieve success with their techniques? Two possible explanations present themselves. First, as suggested in the discussion of Wolpe's approach, the clients (or many of them) are not clinically neurotic, but possess isolated symptoms or limited disturbances which can be helped by these approaches. That is, they are individuals in whom the approach gradient, though somewhat weak, can easily be made stronger by techniques such as those used by Salter and Wolpe. Second, it is possible that their success is the result, not of the techniques to which they ascribe it, but of other aspects of the treatment, such as their earnest, sincere interest in, concern for, and efforts to help their clients.

The contrasting views of treatment in terms of the approach-avoidance gradient appear to be related to contrasting views regarding whether behavior changes first and then feelings and attitudes or vice versa. Wolpe and Salter appear to accept the former position. Dollard and Miller appear to adhere to the latter. For them fear is an attitude, or feeling, and their approach is to reduce fear through the therapeutic relationship before they expect behavior to change.

There is another related, and somewhat contradictory, aspect of this basic difference. Wolpe emphasizes that the client must be relaxed when engaging in desirable new behavior, such as sex activity, so that behavior is reconditioned by being associated with a pleasant or non-anxious feeling. (Wolpe also describes it as the inhibition of fear by another incompatible response.) Dollard and Miller, on the other hand, advocate that the client make a sex response while he is afraid, so that when it is not followed by punishment, extinction will occur.[35] It is, of course, likely that, in the case of Wolpe's method, some anxiety or fear does exist, even though the client is somewhat relaxed, and, in the case of Dollard and Miller, that fear or anxiety has been reduced sufficiently to permit the client to act when he could not before. Wolpe emphasizes reconditioning, while Dollard and Miller emphasize extinction.

Dollard and Miller also disagree with Salter and Wolpe and

behavior therapists in their belief that symptoms are the neurosis and that removal of the symptoms is equivalent to cure of the neurosis. They state that since "a learned symptom produces a certain amount of reduction of the state of high drive motivating it . . . interfering with the symptom . . . will be expected to throw the patient back into a state of high drive and conflict. This will tend to motivate the learning of new responses. These new responses may be either more adaptive ones or new, and possibly worse, symptoms." [36] Dollard and Miller concede that "after the inhibitions blocking the more adaptive goal responses have been sufficiently reduced, however, we might expect different results." [37] Then the therapist might interfere with a symptom by means of an unfavorable interpretation, which might cause the goal response to become stronger than the weakened inhibition. This may be a factor in the apparent success of Wolpe and Salter's methods. Dollard and Miller also rely more on discrimination than on automatic conditioning. Their approach is thus more verbal and more rational than conditioning approaches. Although they recognize the affective and emotional aspects as essential, the emphasis on verbal labeling, discrimination, and generalization gives a more verbal-rational cast to their approach than traditional psychoanalysis has. It is interesting that at the close of the chapter on labeling, Dollard and Miller feel it necessary to note that they "are not advocating any mere intellectualization of the therapeutic process." [38] But while there is concern with affective elements, there is, nevertheless, emphasis upon rational analysis. The therapist is seen as performing a teaching function to a great extent.

There are some gaps and inconsistencies in the Dollard and Miller approach. For example, what repression *is* receives attention, but the *process* of repression itself is given inadequate treatment. In discussing free association, they claim that speaking is easier, or less anxiety-producing, than thinking, so that "the extinction effects which are first attached to talking out loud generalize swiftly to 'talking without voice' (thinking)." [39] Later, however, discussing client obstructiveness, they suggest that "even though the patient goes on thinking the sentences which produce anxiety, it may be that this anxiety is considerably less than when he makes the same responses out loud." [40] These are minor things, however. A more general criticism is that Dollard and Miller's approach is derived from a learning theory that has been developed mainly from experiments with animals and then extended to human behavior, often by analogy.[41] It suffers also from the limitations of reinforcement theory,[42] which does not appear to account adequately for all learning and behavior change, particularly the complex behavior of human beings. The Dollard and Miller approach is thus oversimplified and restricted to a view of man as a reaction system responding to situational stimuli that reduce his drives. Secondary, or learned, drives, which derive from the primary drives, are recognized; but their nature and their development, or derivation from the primary drives, remain rather vague.

Dollard and Miller present their ideas as hypotheses, not proven principles. They stress that their book is not complete or adequate for the practice of psychotherapy. They contemplated further books to fill in the gaps and deal with unsolved problems. It is a pity that this plan was not realized. But it is also a pity that the presentation in this book has not been given the attention it deserves either by others interested in counseling or psychotherapy or in the education of counselors or psychotherapists. It is one of the few really systematic approaches to counseling. Their integration of so-called insight and psychotherapy with learning theory anticipated current efforts by almost twenty years.

REFERENCES

[1] Dollard, J., & Miller, N. E. *Personality and psychotherapy.* New York: McGraw-Hill, 1950.   [2] *Ibid.,* p. 9.   [3] *Ibid.,* p. 15.   [4] *Ibid.*   [5] *Ibid.,* pp. 31–32. In subsequent publications [Miller, N. E. Liberalization of basic S-R concepts: extensions to conflict behavior, motivation, and social learning. In S. Koch (Ed.), *Psychology: a study of science. Study I: Conceptual and systematic.* Vol. 2. *General systematic formulations, learning, and special processes.* New York: McGraw-Hill, 1959, pp. 196–292; Miller, N. E. Some implications of modern behavior theory for personality change and psychotherapy. In D. Byrne & P. Worchel (Eds.), *Personality change.* New York: Wiley, 1964, pp. 149–179], Miller has modified his views to include the channeling by learning of certain presumably innate drives such as curiosity.   [6] Dollard, J., & Miller, N. E., *op. cit.,* p. 32.   [7] *Ibid.,* p. 77.   [8] *Ibid.,* p. 39.   [9] "This statement is no longer accurate. At present it is not known whether all learned responses would extinguish if given enough unreinforced trials." Miller, N. E. Personal communication. July 8, 1964.   [10] Same comment as above applies to this statement.   [11] Dollard, J., & Miller, N. E., *op. cit.,* p. 57.   [12] *Ibid.,* p. 103.   [13] *Ibid.,* p. 111.   [14] Dollar, J. & Miller, N. E., *Social learning and imitation.* New Haven, Conn.: Yale University Press, 1941   [15] Dollard, J., & Miller, N. E., *op cit.,* p. 127.   [16] *Ibid.,* p. 130.   [17] *Ibid.,* p. 196.   [18] *Ibid.,* p. 240.   [19] *Ibid.*   [20] *Ibid.,* p. 281.   [21] *Ibid.,* p. 303.   [22] *Ibid.,* p. 305.   [23] *Ibid.,* p. 338.   [24] *Ibid.,* pp. 243–244.   [25] *Ibid.,* pp. 241–242.   [26] *Ibid.,* p. 259.   [27] *Ibid.,* p. 250.   [28] *Ibid.,* p. 274.   [29] *Ibid.,* p. 278.   [30] *Ibid.,* p. 287.   [31] *Ibid.,* p. 284.   [32] *Ibid.,* p. 312.   [33] Reprinted with permission of The Macmillan Company from *Steps in psychotherapy* by J. Dollard, F. Auld, Jr., and Alice M. White. Copyright 1953 by The Macmillan Company, pp. 128–143.   [34] Miller, N. E. Some implications of modern behavior theory for personality change and psychotherapy. In D. Byrne & P. Worchel, *op. cit.,* p. 154.   [35] Dollard, J., & Miller, N. E., *op. cit.,* p. 307.   [36] *Ibid.,* p. 385.   [37] *Ibid.,* p. 386.   [38] *Ibid.,* p. 303.   [39] *Ibid.,* p. 250.   [40] *Ibid.,* pp. 270–271.   [41] Miller, J. G., & Butler, J. M. Review of Dollard, J., & Miller, N. E., "Personality and psychotherapy." *Psychol. Bull.,* 1952, **49,** 183–185.   [42] Raimy, V. C. Clinical methods: psychotherapy. *Ann. Rev. Psychol.,* 1952, **3,** 321–350.

6

Psychotherapy by reciprocal inhibition: Wolpe

Joseph Wolpe (1915–   ) was educated in South Africa, receiving his M.B. and B.Ch. in 1939 and his M.D. in 1948 from the University of Witwatersrand, Johannesburg. He was lecturer in psychiatry at Witwatersrand from 1949 to 1959, except for the year 1956–1957, when he was a Fellow at the Center for Advanced Study in the Behavioral Sciences at Stanford. From 1960 to 1965 he was Research and Clinical Professor of Psychiatry at the University of Virginia Medical School, Charlottesville, Virginia. In 1965 he became Professor of Psychiatry in the Department of Behavioral Sciences of the School of Medicine at Temple University and the Eastern Pennsylvania Psychiatric Institute, Philadelphia, Pennsylvania.

Wolpe's M.D. thesis was entitled "An Approach to the Problem of Neurosis Based on the Conditioned Response." Publication of journal articles in 1952, 1954, and 1956 preceded his book *Psychotherapy by Reciprocal Inhibition,* published in 1958. In 1966, with Arnold A. Lazarus, he published *Behavior Therapy Techniques: A Guide to the Treatment of Neuroses.* In 1969 he published *The Practice of Behavior Therapy.*

BACKGROUND AND DEVELOPMENT

Wolpe dates the beginning of his method of psychotherapy to 1944 when his reading, while he was serving as a medical military officer,

125

led him to a questioning of psychoanalysis. He learned that psychoanalysis was not accepted in Russia, and looking into the reason for this, he was led to Pavlov, thence to Hull and to studies of experimental neuroses in animals. This resulted in his conducting experiments with cats in which neurotic reactions were induced by electric shock. These neurotic reactions were removed in every case by getting the animal to eat in the presence of small, and then increasingly larger, doses of anxiety-evoking stimuli. Thus, there occurred a conditioned inhibition of the anxiety responses.[1]

This led to the idea that human neurotic anxieties might be dealt with—as in Mary Cover Jones' experiments with Peter—by counter-conditioning them with eating. Wolpe never actually attempted this, but he used other anxiety-inhibiting responses.

PHILOSOPHY AND CONCEPTS

All behavior conforms to causal laws. There are three classes of processes that lead to lasting changes in an organism's behavior: growth, lesions, and learning. "Learning may be said to have occurred if a response has been evoked in temporal contiguity with a given sensory stimulus and it is subsequently found that the stimulus can evoke the response although it could not have done so before. If the stimulus could have evoked the response before but subsequently evokes it more strongly, then, too, learning may be said to have occurred." [2] The strengthening of the connection between the new stimulus and the response is called reinforcement, and the events that lead to strengthening are reinforcements. A number of factors are related to reinforcement. The new, or conditioned, stimulus must precede the unconditioned stimulus at an optimal interval. The shorter the interval between the response and the reduction of a strong drive (by reward), the greater the reinforcement. The greater the number of reinforcements, the greater the strength of the connection; and spaced reinforcements are more effective than massed reinforcements. In general, the greater the reinforcement, the greater the reduction in drive, although there appear to be instances when increase in drive is reinforcing.

When a conditioned stimulus occurs repeatedly without the unconditioned stimulus or without reinforcement, the response ceases to occur, or is extinguished, although there is partial recovery if the stimulus is not applied for some time and then is reapplied. The disappearance of the response is the result of negative conditioning and of reactive inhibition due to fatigue, which dissipates with time, allowing for recovery.

Reciprocal inhibition is the inhibition, elimination, or weakening of old responses by new ones. "When a response is inhibited by an incompatible response and if a major drive reduction follows, a significant amount of conditioned inhibition of the response will be developed." [3]

Wolpe performed a series of experiments in which neurotic reactions (anxiety and fear with their behavioral and physiological concomitants) were induced in cats by electric shock. These symptoms were generalized, occurring outside the experimental cage. They were intensified by an auditory stimulus that had been presented with the shock. The magnitude of the symptoms varied directly with the similarity of the environment to the room in which the neuroses had been induced.

The neurotic reactions were produced in a feeding situation. This provided the possibility of removing them by reciprocal inhibition. Two methods were used. The first was the addition to the stimulus situation in the experimental cage of a factor to favor or strengthen or induce the feeding response. Since in their living cages the cats were fed by hand, it was expected that the hand had become a conditioned stimulus evoking approach responses to food. Food was therefore presented on a spatula held in the experimenter's hand. Four of the nine cats so treated were induced to eat in this manner and gradually were led to eat from the food box. Three cats were forcibly led to eat from the food box. Over a period of several days the neurotic reactions decreased and finally were eliminated.

A second method consisted of feeding the animals under conditions in which the anxiety-producing stimuli were less potent. The five (out of nine) cats who did not respond to the hand-feeding method were offered food outside the experimental cage, in surroundings arousing decreasing symptoms of anxiety, until they were able to eat the food. When all were able to eat in some situation, they were offered food in situations that had evoked increasing symptoms of anxiety. Eventually, all apparently were brought to the point where they could eat from the food box inside the experimental cage, and symptoms of anxiety disappeared.

However, when the conditioned auditory stimulus was presented, anxiety recurred. Two cats were induced to eat at gradually decreasing distances from the auditory stimulus, until they were able to eat in the cage with no anxiety. The remaining seven cats were given food in the experimental cage, followed by a brief presentation of the auditory stimulus, followed by more food, etc., with the result that the cats' delay in eating the food decreased. Then the duration of the stimulus was increased until the cats were able to eat with no anxiety in the presence of the auditory stimulus. Eventually, the stimulus became a conditioned stimulus for food-seeking movements. To determine whether the neurotic reactions were still present but dormant, the food-seeking response to the auditory stimulus was extinguished by not following the response with food. Then food was offered, and when the cat approached it, the auditory signal was presented continuously, with no effect either in anxiety or in inhibition of eating.

Prior to the removal of the anxiety-evoking effects of the auditory stimulus, two cats were offered food, and then the stimulus was presented as they moved toward it. Neurotic anxiety developed, and eating was inhibited in the situations in which the stimulus was presented.

Are the experimental neuroses in animals and the clinical neuroses in humans the same? The criteria of a clinical neurosis are anxiety, unadaptive behavior, persistence, and acquisition through learning. These criteria appear to be met by the cats in these experiments. The responses of the cats in the experimental environment without the shock were the same responses made in the presence of shock, thus conforming with the definition of learning given above. Learning under shock occurs so rapidly, because of the great reduction in drive upon cessation of the shock and because of the secondary reinforcement of stimuli from the experimental environment that become anxiety-inducing, that removal from the experimental environment reduces anxiety and at the same time reinforces the anxiety responses to the stimuli of this environment.

The question arises as to the persistence of neurotic habits that are not reinforced, that is, their resistance to extinction. Since neurotic responses are unadaptive, they are unrewarded. However, they have an antecedent drive that is reduced when removed from the action of the anxiety-producing stimulus. Thus, responses associated with such removal are reinforced. Responses such as autonomic reactions, which are continually evoked and inevitably present at the time of such drive reductions, are therefore highly persistent, whereas other more variable or intermittent motor responses may be extinguished.

The removal or cure of the experimental neurosis is the result of making possible the feeding response in the presence of stimuli conditioned to anxiety responses that otherwise inhibit feeding. "When stimuli to incompatible responses are present simultaneously, the occurrence of the response that is dominant in the circumstances involves the reciprocal inhibition of the other. As the number of feedings increased, the anxiety responses gradually became weaker, so that to stimuli to which there was initially a response of the anxiety pattern there was finally a feeding response with inhibition of anxiety." [4]

It seems that there are a number of aspects to this process: (1) Neurotic (anxiety) responses are inhibited. (2) There is a positive conditioning of the feeding response by hunger drive reduction. (3) There is a reduction of the drive antecedent to the anxiety responses by the reciprocal inhibition. "With repetition more and more conditioned inhibition was built up, so that the anxiety-evoking potential of the stimuli progressively diminished—eventually to zero." [5] The general principle formulated on the basis of the experiments is as follows: "If a response antagonistic to anxiety can be made to occur in the presence of anxiety-evoking stimuli so that it is accompanied by a complete or partial suppression of the anxiety responses, the bond between these stimuli and the anxiety responses will be weakened." [6]

Neurotic behavior is thus learned behavior. It is "any persistent habit of unadaptive behavior acquired by learning in a physiologically normal organism." [7] Anxiety is a common or central constituent of neurotic behavior. Anxiety, or fear (the two are used synonymously), is unpleasant and may interfere with performance of many activities or lead to behavior that is restrictive, disadvantageous, or unadaptive. Unadaptive behavior usually disappears, since it is unrewarded. Unadaptive behavior that persists and that has been learned rather than being the result of organic pathology (for example, hyperthyroidism or epilepsy) is neurotic behavior.

Unlearned (unconditioned) anxiety, or fear, is the characteristic response of the organism to noxious or threatening stimuli. Neurotic anxiety is anxiety that has been conditioned to intrinsically nonharmful stimuli. The anxiety is the same physiologically—a widespread discharge of the autonomic nervous system, predominantly the sympathetic division. Reactions include tachycardia, raised blood and pulse pressures, hyperpnea, sweating, and dryness of the mouth. Anxiety is the keystone of most neuroses, and the severity is determined by the amount and duration of unadaptive anxiety.

The cause of clinical (human) neuroses is the same as the cause of experimental neuroses in animals, that is, situations that evoke high-intensity anxiety. These include noxious stimuli (analogous to shock)—either a few severe noxious stimuli or a large number of small noxious stimuli—difficult discriminations, or conflict. In humans, however, direct evocation of anxiety by unconditioned stimuli and the conditioning of anxiety to previously neutral stimuli are less frequent than the attachment of new stimuli to previously conditioned stimuli, including ideas. Or anxiety may result from conflict, with neutral stimuli becoming conditioned to it. Analogous to physical confinement with animals is the psychological confinement that operates in humans.

Pervasive (free-floating) anxiety occurs when anxiety is conditioned to many and various aspects of the environment and is only a more general form of specific anxiety. It seems to be the result of an intense anxiety evocation at the time of induction of the neurosis and/or of the lack of clearly defined stimuli at the time of induction.

Hysterical reactions consist of conditioned neurotic responses other than anxiety occurring in persons with a particular personality, that is, extroverted rather than introverted. Obsessions, which reduce anxiety, develop from the conditioning of anxiety-relieving responses. If a real threat in the past is removed by a specific type of behavior, this behavior occurs in conjunction with *any* similar anxiety.

Some kinds of neurotic behavior are not unadaptive, but are secondary neurotic responses that diminish anxiety. These include avoiding anxiety-evoking stimuli, displacing attention by engaging in other activities, and taking drugs. These are not conscious, planned activities, but develop on the basis of conditioning, as a result of anxiety reduction.

Anxiety conditioning is, of course, produced in many situations without the formation of a permanent neurosis, and improvement may occur in a neurosis without treatment. This is because reciprocal inhibition is induced by many experiences in the ordinary course of life.

Patients may raise moral issues regarding the acceptability of behavioral outcomes of behavior therapy. Many question the morality of assertive behavior. Three possible approaches to interpersonal relations may be pointed out to them. The first is to consider oneself only, attempting to get what one wants regardless of the effects on others. The second is submission, unselfishly putting others before oneself. Both of these approaches lead to difficulty. The third approach is the golden mean, in which oneself is placed first but others are considered.

This practical philosophy easily resolves the problem of what behavior is suitable under specific circumstances. A rational approach such as this may lead to treatment that may be questioned by some, particularly in marriage (advising divorce) or religion (questioning religious dogma). The therapist must not confuse technical decisions with moral ones, or his own morals with the requirements of the patient's situation.

The objection is often made that the behavior therapist assumes omnipotence, demanding the acquiescence of the patient to his methods, thus stripping the patient of human dignity. But such acquiescence is required in any other branch of medicine, and patients are ready to do what is prescribed by an expert.

THE THERAPY PROCESS

"Behavior therapy, or conditioning therapy, is the use of experimentally established principles of learning for the purpose of changing unadaptive behavior. Unadaptive habits are weakened and eliminated; adaptive habits are initiated and strengthened." [8] It is an applied science, in contrast to earlier systems of psychological medicine, which were speculative and intuitive. The behavior therapist, when necessary for the welfare of his patients, goes beyond methods derived from principles, using methods that have been empirically shown to be effective.

"A widely prevalent belief is that the quality of the therapeutic relationship is more basic to therapeutic outcome than the therapist's specific methods and techniques, and this is probably true of the conventional therapies." The mobilization of the patient's expectation of help and hope of relief is a powerful therapeutic instrument, present in behavior therapy. Conditioning procedures add to this effect. [9]

The purpose of psychotherapy is to overcome the suffering caused by neurotic symptoms and related disabilities. "One result of realizing that neurotic behavior is learned is to place responsibility for the patient's recovery unequivocally on the therapist. . . ." [10] If the patient does not improve, it must be because of faulty analysis of the problem, because of inappropriate application of techniques, or because no available techniques offer a solution. In the latter case the therapist should admit temporary defeat, though as new methods are developed, they should be applied.

When one method fails to result in change, another is tried

according to appropriate indications, and when a procedure shows signs of effectiveness, it is systematically applied. There are three categories of conditioning operations.

1 *Counterconditioning*   Anxiety is an almost universal part of neurotic reactions. Its elimination is usually achieved by a competing response, developed through reciprocal inhibition. *"If a response inhibitory of anxiety can be made to occur in the presence of anxiety-evoking stimuli it will weaken the bond between these stimuli and the anxiety."* Assertive responses and relaxation responses are encouraged for this purpose. The reciprocal inhibition principle is also the basis for aversion therapy to inhibit obsessional and compulsive habits.

2 *Positive reconditioning*   "In order to establish a new behavior pattern in a particular situation, the desired response has to be elicited and each time rewarded, while the undesired behavior is consistently not rewarded and even punished." [11] Operant conditioning principles are being used increasingly here.

3 *Experimental extinction*   When there is continued nonreinforcement of a habit, it progressively weakens.

Therapy begins with the taking of a careful clinical history. Neurotic reactions are explored in terms of the circumstances of their onset, later contingencies leading to their modification or extension, and the current stimuli maintaining the behavior. When the presenting problem is not anxiety, the exploration is more difficult. However, other conditions are usually consequents of anxiety, and the relationship may be clear.

Following the exploration of the presenting reactions, the patient's life history is obtained, focusing upon family relationships, education, employment, sexual development, and social relationships. The patient is then given the Willoughby Questionnaire, a Fear Survey Schedule developed by Wolpe and P. J. Lang, and sometimes the Bernreuter Self-Sufficiency Scale. A medical examination is obtained if there is any suggestion of organic disease. Anxiety attacks with no constant stimulus antecedents may be caused by hypoglycemia or hypothyroidism or less commonly by other neurological or physiological disturbances.

Therapeutic goals and strategies are discussed with the patient, though the therapist decides, on the basis of the degree to which a neurotic habit is handicapping, to which areas priority is to be given. Therapy is an individual matter, but there are some general rules:

1   The emotional climate is a blend of objectivity and permissiveness with regard to acts and attitudes that the patient may deplore.

2   The patient must be assured that his reactions, having been learned, can be unlearned.

3   Misconceptions about symptoms must be corrected as soon as possible.

4   Unless there are extreme phobic reactions against it, assertive behavior should be instigated early.

The behavior therapist maintains an objective, nonjudgmental attitude. All behavior is subject to causal determination. The patient is therefore not blamed for his behavior. Rather than moralize, the therapist "goes out of his way to dislodge any self-blame that social conditioning may have engendered and that may have been magnified by friends, relations, and previous therapists." The patient is assured that as the unlearning of the experimental neurosis induced in animals is completely in the control of the experimenter, so "the overcoming of a human neurosis is within the control of the therapist through techniques quite similar to those used in the laboratory." [12]

The patient is introduced to the practice of behavior therapy either by short didactic speeches or by discussion. The central role of fear (and anxiety) is brought out in statements such as the following:

> You have realized that fear figures excessively in your life. It is necessary to have some perspective about it. It is an emotion that plays a normal part in everybody's life whenever a situation involving a real threat arises—for example, walking alone and unarmed at night in an unsavoury neighborhood, learning that one's firm is about to retrench its staff, or being confronted by a poisonous snake. Nobody would come for treatment because he experiences fear in such situations. It is a different matter when fear is aroused by experiences that contain no real threat—such as seeing an ambulance, entering a crowded room, or riding in a car—to take examples other than your own. To be fearful in such situations is obviously inappropriate, and can interfere with daily functioning in a most distressing way. It is this that we call neurotic fear; and it is the task of therapy to detach it from the stimuli or situations that provoke it.
>
> Let us consider how neurotic fears originate. The process is really what common sense would lead you to expect. Let me illustrate it by the old-fashioned example of the burnt child. The child places his hand on the big, black, hot coal stove. He quickly withdraws the painful hand, tearful and fearful. His mother comforts him, but later notes that he keeps away from the stove and seems afraid of it. Clearly, the child has developed a beneficial habit of fearing and avoiding an actually harmful object.
>
> But in some cases the experience also has other and less favorable consequences. Suppose in the mother's bedroom there is a large black chest of drawers. The child may have become afraid of this too—purely on the basis of its *physical resemblance* to the stove—a phenomenon known in psychology as generalization. Fear of the chest of drawers is neurotic because there can be no harm in touching it. It can have several undesirable implications. In the first place the very presence of an unpleasant emotion like fear, where it is not appropriate, is objectionable. Secondly, the child is now forced to make a detour if the chest of drawers is in his path; and thirdly, he no longer has easy access to any delectable contents of the drawers, such as candy. In these features of the child's case we have the model of all neurotic fear reactions.
>
> Your own fears were likewise acquired in the course of

unpleasant experiences, some of which we touched upon in your history. The unpleasant emotions you then had became conditioned, or connected, to aspects of the situation that made an imprint on you at the time. This means that subsequent similar experiences led to the arousal of these same unpleasant feelings. Now just because these reactions could then be produced by particular stimulus-triggers as a result of the operation of a process of learning it is possible to eliminate them by the application of the principles of learning.

In animals the treatment of a neurosis is a very straight-forward matter, especially when the experimenter himself has induced the neurosis. In human subjects it can be just as simple but may be complicated by various factors in the more complex organism. However, endowed with language we can unravel most webs and our very complexity gives to human behavior therapy the possibility of a large repertoire of techniques.[13]

In addition to this, the following typify other connective statements that may need to be made and developed:

1   *"You are not mentally ill and there is no chance of your going insane."*
2   "All your reactions are explicable."
3   "There is no virtue in confronting your fears." [14]

IMPLEMENTATION: TECHNIQUES OF THERAPY

Assertive Training

Assertive responses include not only aggressive behavior but affectionate and friendly behavior, indeed practically all feelings except anxiety, which it tends to inhibit. "Assertive training, generally speaking, is required for patients who in interpersonal contexts have unadaptive anxiety responses that prevent them from saying or doing what is reasonable and right." [15] Suppression of feeling resulting from inhibiting actions about which they feel strongly causes inner turmoil and even psychosomatic illnesses. In addition to inhibiting anxiety, assertive behavior is reinforced by its consequences, including reduction of anxiety. Thus, counterconditioning and operant conditioning occur simultaneously.

The need for assertive training becomes apparent in the taking of the clinical history and from answers to the Willoughby Questionnaire, as well as answers to questions asked by the therapist, such as "What do you do if someone pushes in front of you in line?" Most patients recognize their need to be more assertive, but are unable to change.

Simple instruction, or leading the patient toward action, using examples from other cases, is sometimes sufficient. The patient is encouraged to use assertive statements, derived from the individual case. "Hostile" (or negative) statements are more numerous than "commendatory" (or positive) statements because of the nature of the patients' needs. Patients report their progress and are commended and encouraged to continue. One basic rule must be observed: *"Never instigate* an assertive act that is likely to have seriously punishing consequences for the patient."* [16] If there is a phobic reaction toward assertion or fear of aggression from others, systematic desensitization may be necessary.

Behavior rehearsal, in which the patient takes the role of a person toward whom neurotic inhibition exists and practices assertive statements, may be used. Indirect ways of expressing aggression by gaining control of an interpersonal relationship such as those in Stephen Potter's *Lifemanship,* may be encouraged.

Therapeutic Sexual Arousal

THE TREATMENT OF IMPOTENCE   When impaired sexual performance is treated, anxiety must be removed from the sexual encounter. Thus, the cooperation of the wife must be obtained, so that she will avoid making her husband tense or anxious. If the husband cannot obtain the wife's cooperation, the therapist should see her. The process is a slow and gradual one. Male sex hormone and tranquilizing drugs may be used.

If the wife will not cooperate, "it seems entirely reasonable to encourage the husband to seek out another woman who may be more responsive to him." The restoration of potency may improve the marriage, but even if it doesn't, the man is better off.[17]

In thirty-one cases of male sexual inadequacy, twenty-one (67.7 percent) recovered entirely and another six (19.4 percent) satisfactorily.

THE TREATMENT OF FRIGIDITY   Frigidity is a matter of degree, and also either "essential" (general) or "situational" (limited to a particular male, often the husband). Essential frigidity may be organic, or constitutional, but is usually the result of conditioned inhibition.

Reeducation and the removal of misconceptions is often the first step in treatment. Treatment of the remaining negative emotional response and anxiety is usually by systematic desensitization. In situational frigidity the problem may be that the wife no longer cares for her husband. There is nothing that can be done about this, although every effort should be made to change the husband's behavior, when desirable and reasonable, preferably through the wife's asserting herself appropriately.

Systematic Desensitization

Systematic desensitization is the breaking down of neurotic anxiety-response habits step by step. A state that is physiologically inhibitory to anxiety, usually relaxation, is induced, and then the patient is exposed to a weak anxiety-arousing stimulus. Progressively stronger stimuli are introduced as the weaker ones are tolerated, until the strongest stimulus is reacted to with the degree of anxiety that the mildest stimulus evoked, which is then reduced to zero. The method parallels closely the technique of feeding cats in the presence of increasing amounts of anxiety-evoking stimuli. Systematic desensitization is useful in noninterpersonal neuroses where assertive behavior training is not useful, such as phobias, or in situations where the mere presence of another person evokes fear.

Desensitization requires the training of the patient in relaxation, following Jacobson,[18] for about six interviews, interspersed with the patient's practicing at home for two fifteen-minute periods a day. Relaxation of the arm muscles is first, followed by the head (second and third session), the neck and shoulders, the back, abdomen and thorax, and finally the lower limbs.

At the same time that training in relaxation is progressing, anxiety hierarchies are also constructed, but not while the patient is under relaxation. "An anxiety hierarchy is a list of stimuli on a common theme ranked in descending order according to the amount of anxiety they evoke." [19] Hierarchies are constructed from the patient's history, from responses to the Willoughby Questionnaire and to the Fear Survey Schedule, and from probings, including the patient's listing, as homework, all situations, thoughts, or feelings that he finds fearful or disturbing in any way. The various fears are grouped into themes. Stimuli or situations need not have been experienced to be included, but can be imaginary situations. Basically objective fears are not included and are not, of course, treated by desensitization.

These items are general, and must be developed into specific situations that can be placed in a hierarchy. There may be multiple dimensions, such as room size and duration of confinement in claustrophobia. The hierarchy may be constructed by having the patient rate the items according to the amount of anxiety they would evoke, using a scale of 0 to 100. An example of an hierarchy of external stimuli is the following:

1. The sight of a physical deformity.
2. Someone in pain (the greater the evidence of pain the more disturbing).
3. The sight of bleeding.
4. The sight of somebody seriously ill (e.g., heart attack).
5. Automobile accidents.
6. Nurses in uniform.
7. Wheelchairs.
8. Hospitals.
9. Ambulances.[20]

If the patient cannot achieve adequate relaxation, drugs (tranquilizers), carbon dioxide–oxygen mixtures, or hypnotism (in about

10 percent of cases) may be used. The imagining of relaxing scenes may also be used. When adequate relaxation is present, a neutral scene is presented, and the patient is asked to imagine it. Then the procedure itself begins: the patient is asked to imagine the least anxiety-arousing scene and to raise his finger when he sees it clearly; the therapist allows the scene to remain for a few seconds (five–seven), terminating it by saying "Stop the scene," and then asking the patient to rate the degree of induced anxiety felt (using the scale of 0 to 100). Relaxation is then induced again for ten to twenty seconds. This continues for as long as is necessary to reduce the anxiety accompanying each scene to 0 (with repetition for overlearning in some cases) going through all the scenes in the hierarchy. Sessions are usually fifteen to thirty minutes in length, with the number of scenes presented varying with the patient. Sessions are usually two to three times a week.

Systematic desensitization involves the imagination of anxiety-evoking scenes, not in vivo experiencing of them. Yet progress is reflected in improvement in reaction to real situations. Difficulties or failures usually reflect difficulties in relaxing, misleading or irrelevant hierarchies, or inadequate imagery.

In the cases of thirty-nine patients randomly selected from the files, systematic desensitization was judged effective in thirty-five patients, or 90 percent, with the median number of sessions per patient being ten.

Variants of Systematic Desensitization

TECHNICAL VARIATIONS OF CONVENTIONAL CONSULTING-ROOM PRACTICE   Two ways have been used to reduce the amount of time the therapist has to spend with patients.

Mechanical aids to systematic desensitization / A specially modified tape recorder has been used to enable the patient to desensitize himself. Relaxation instructions were taped, and a pause switch enabled the patient to stop the tape while relaxing according to the specific instruction. Before the presentation of the first scene, brief general relaxation instructions were given, followed by an instruction to pause. Then instructions to visualize the first scene were given, followed by the instruction to pause until visualization was clear, and then to continue. After ten seconds of silence the instruction to stop visualizing and, if anxiety was felt, to press the repeat button was given. The repeat button rewound the tape back to the beginning of the general relaxation instructions, where a metal foil stopped it. The process of visualization could then be repeated. If the repeat button was not pressed, the tape continued to the next relaxation instructions (also preceded by a metal foil), followed by scene 2. The tape was recorded by the patient himself, following instructions. A simpler tape recording has also been developed.

Group desensitization / Patients with the same phobia have been treated successfully in groups, not only by Wolpe, but by others also.

ALTERNATIVE COUNTERANXIETY RESPONSES FOR USE WITH IMAGINAL STIMULI
Therapist-evoked counteranxiety emotional responses are an alternative to relaxation.

External inhibition / In this technique mild to moderate electric shocks are administered when imagined scenes are accompanied by anxiety.

Desensitization based upon inhibition of anxiety by a conditioned motor response / Here the patient is asked to imagine a scene. When he signals that the scene is clear, he receives a mild shock in the forearm, causing the flexing of the arm.

Emotive imagery / In this procedure the hierarchical stimuli are presented while the patient places himself in an imaginary situation characterized by aspects that are antagonistic to anxiety. This method is more appropriate to children than to adults.

DESENSITIZATION USING EXTEROCEPTIVE STIMULI TO ANXIETY   Either the actual feared objects or pictorial representations of them are used in these procedures.

In vivo desensitization / Having the patient expose himself to the actual stimulus situation up to which he has been desensitized has been used to consolidate progress and as a means of getting feedback. But it can be the prime method in those 10 to 15 percent of patients who cannot imagine hierarchical scenes or do not respond to them emotionally. Natural stimuli can be used, with graded exposure and the therapist present, as a guide and anxiety inhibitor.

Anxiety-relief conditioning is another method used in vivo. It consists of the direct conditioning of an anxiety-inhibiting response to a neutral stimulus word, such as "calm," by administering an uncomfortable shock that can be stopped when the patient says the word aloud. The relief, in people who experience not only pain but emotional disturbance in response to shock, may be strong, and on repetition often becomes conditioned to the word, which can be used subsequently to reduce anxiety in disturbing situations.

Modeling / Bandura and his associates have demonstrated that observation of filmed or live models engaging in fear-provoking interactions is effective in eliminating or reducing fears, or phobias.

Procedures Involving Strong Anxiety Evocation

EMOTIONAL FLOODING   The first use of this method is attributed to Guthrie. An adolescent girl with a phobia for automobiles was forced into a car and driven for four hours. After she had quickly reached a panic level, her fears gradually subsided, and she became free of her phobia. Frankl's technique of paradoxical intention is essentially the same procedure, though Frankl did not relate it to learning theory. Stampfl's implosive therapy is also an example of this method, although it does not deal with actual behavior. Like desensitization, it utilizes imagination, but starts directly with the top of the hierarchy, although more recently a gradual approach has been used, still, however, maximizing the evocation of anxiety with each scene, and without relaxation techniques.

Flooding techniques are apparently based upon the paradigm of experimental extinction, that is, the repeated presentation of the conditioned stimulus without reinforcement (by an unconditioned stimulus for fear). However, "so far, nobody has cured an experimental neurosis simply by exposing the animal for long periods (hours or days) to the stimuli to which anxiety has been conditioned. This makes it exceeding unlikely that experimental extinction can be the mechanism of the favorable effects of flooding when they do occur. . . . Other processes must be relevant; but as long as we have not identified them, flooding procedures are a gamble we take at the patient's risk." [21]

The method is very successful with some patients; some are unaffected; and some become worse. Thus, it is used as a final recourse after every other method has failed. Research is necessary to determine how to differentiate those individuals who will respond positively from those who will respond negatively.

ABREACTION   Abreaction is "the re-evocation, with strong emotional accompaniment, of a fearful past experience. Some abreactions are followed by therapeutic changes, while others are not, and may even leave the patient worse off than before." [22] The difficulty with this method is thus similar to that with flooding—its results cannot be predicted in the individual case. In addition, its induction is not under the complete control of the therapist. It is thus used when other methods have failed. It may be nearly indispensable with patients whose unadaptive emotional responses were originally conditioned to stimuli not present in current stimulus situations.

Abreaction, to be therapeutic, must take place in a protected setting such as the psychotherapeutic relationship. Thus, the therapeutic effects may be the result of nonspecific factors leading to the inhibition of anxiety by other emotional responses.

Hypnosis and drugs may be useful in eliciting abreaction. Pentobarbital (Pentothal) was introduced for this purpose in 1936 and was used extensively in World War II. Wolpe has found little lasting benefit from drug-induced abreaction. Ether and LSD_{25} have been used with success by some therapists.

Aversion Therapy

Aversion therapy is a mode of application of the reciprocal inhibition principle to deconditioning motor or thinking habits. It is not usually the treatment of first choice, except possibly in drug addiction, but it may be useful in treating obsessions, compulsions, fetishes, and attraction to inappropriate sex objects (for example, homosexuality). If the habit has a basis in neurotic anxiety, this should usually be deconditioned first, in which case the compulsion or other undesirable behavior may disappear. Even after successful aversion therapy, anxiety may remain and need to be deconditioned.

"The essence of aversion therapy is to present, in the context of an undesired response, the stimulus to a strong avoidance response, the most typical stimulus being strong electric shock. In eliciting the strong avoidance response, the shock is likely to inhibit the undesirable response. Whenever it does so, there will be a diminution next time in the evocation of the latter response by the stimulus that evoked it." [23] The stimulus for the undesired response is conditioned to shock, and the stimulus-response bond weakened, so that there is a conditioned inhibition of the response.

Electric stimulation is advantageous because its administration can be precisely controlled in terms of amount and timing. It can be used in relation to actual objects or situations or with imagery. The strength of the shock can be adjusted to the individual patient. Drugs have been used extensively in the aversion treatment of alcoholism. The procedure is difficult, not highly successful, and if successful, does not allow social drinking. Other unpleasant stimuli have been used in aversive treatment of smoking, obesity, and other conditions.

Azrin and Holtz provide practical guidelines for the use of aversion therapy.[24]

Operant Conditioning Methods

"There is no reason to believe that there is more than one *kind* of learning. . . . The distinction between respondent and operant conditioning is not in the nature of conditioning, but in the fact that in the former 'nonvoluntary,' especially autonomic behavior is predominantly involved; whereas in the latter the behavior is either motor or ideomotor. It is because neurotic behavior is usually primarily a matter of autonomic conditioning that operant techniques have not been prominent in the treatment of neuroses." [25] Operant conditioning is more clearly related to reinforcing events, or more clearly under the control of its consequences. However, autonomic behavior can be brought under the control of its consequences. [Recent work in control of brain waves by feedback, as well as of other involuntary responses, has clearly demonstrated this.]

There are six operant techniques: positive reinforcement, extinction, differential reinforcement, response shaping, punishment, and negative reinforcement. The last two were included in the discussion of aversion therapy. The third and fourth are developments of the first two.

POSITIVE REINFORCEMENT   The establishing of a habit by arranging for a reward, or reinforcement, to follow each or many of its performances is a powerful means of changing behavior. Its therapeutic potentialities have been demonstrated mainly with schizophrenics, where it effects changes in behavior but does not "cure" the psychosis, which is probably a matter of biochemistry. Anorexia nervosa is one of the few neurotic conditions in which positive reinforcement has been used successfully as the main method of treatment.

In "thought stopping," the patient is asked to verbalize a disturbing repetitive thought (an obsession, when chronic). During the verbalization the therapist calls "stop," and calls the patient's attention to the fact that the thought did actually stop. This is repeated. Shock may accompany the stop signal. The habit of thought inhibition is apparently reinforced by the anxiety-reducing consequence of each successful effort at inhibition.

EXTINCTION   When a response is made repeatedly without reinforcement, it is extinguished. Extinction may be slow in clinical cases because the responses have been sustained by long periods of intermittent reinforcement. Dunlap's method of "negative practice," which is now mainly used in the treatment of tics, depends upon extinction through massed responses without reinforcement. The undesirable response must be performed to the point of exhaustion, to produce strong reactive inhibition.

The Use of Drugs in Behavior Therapy

SYMPTOMATIC USES   Drugs may be used to reduce strong anxiety or emotional disturbance without preventing the achieving of basic changes through behavior therapy, and they may actually promote such changes. Drugs can sometimes control certain behaviors (such as enuresis) indefinitely when continued.

ADJUVANT USES OF DRUGS   Drugs can be used to facilitate relaxation in systematic desensitization, as noted earlier. In cases of pervasive free-floating anxiety, the most satisfactory measure is one to four, single, full-capacity inhalations of a mixture of 65 percent carbon dioxide and 35 percent oxygen (or a 40 percent–60 percent combination for those for whom the standard mixture is irritating, and 100 percent carbon dioxide for refractory cases). The mechanism of anxiety reduction is not known. It is not simply pharmacological. It may be based upon reciprocal inhibition of anxiety by either the responses produced by the gas, the postinhalation state of relaxation, or both. The effect may last from hours to weeks or months.

Methahexitone sodium (Brietal or Brevital) acts either as a primary anxiety-inhibiting agent or an adjuvant to relaxation.

THE USE OF DRUGS FOR SPECIFIC DECONDITIONING   Chlorpromazine, meprobamate, and codeine (as well as alcohol) have been prescribed for patients to take before exposure to disturbing situations. After usage for a period of weeks or months, it has been found that the drug has not been necessary. Classroom anxiety and phobias have responded to such treatment. Chlordiazepoxide (Librium) and related drugs (Valium and Serax) have been used effectively.

"It is reasonable to assume that reciprocal inhibition was the mechanism of this relearning." [26] Avoidance responses are presumably inhibited by other responses being produced by other stimuli in the environment. If this method is to be effective, high anxiety evocation can never occur; if it does, it may be expected to recondition anxiety.

Evaluation of Behavior Therapy

The nonspecific effects of a therapeutic relationship are common to all therapies, and presumably account for the fact that in all therapies about 40 percent of neurotic patients are reported to be markedly improved by treatment. "It is because there are factual grounds for believing that behavior therapy does exceed the common average in *both* percentage and speed of recoveries that its techniques are confidently offered in this volume. This confidence falls short of the assurance that would be engendered if we could point to impeccably controlled and replicated clinical trials supporting the methods, but it is a considerable confidence, based partly on impressive clinical experience, and partly on a few very well controlled experimental studies." [27]

Of 210 patients treated in private practice, 89 percent either showed at least an 80 percent improvement or apparently recovered, according to criteria suggested by Knight for psychoanalytic therapy. The mean number of sessions was thirty. Lazarus has reported that 78 percent of 408 patients seen by him derived marked benefit, according to "very stringent criteria."

To the claim that behavior therapy deals with simple cases, it may be replied that an analysis of eighty-six cases indicated that sixty-five were complex in nature. Fifty-eight (89 percent) of these were either apparently cured or much improved, which was the same percentage as for the total group. The median and mean number of sessions were greater—29 and 54.8, compared to 11.5 and 14.9 for the noncomplex cases.

It has also been suggested that behavior therapy is superficial, not removing the basic neurosis, but only the symptoms, with symptom substitution to be expected. But "after behavior therapy has been successful, recurrence of symptoms is very unusual. Every instance of it that has been investigated has been clearly found to be due to reconditioning. The only 'relapse' among 45 patients followed up from two to seven years that I reported in 1958 was in a man who was known to be seeing another psychiatrist. Symptom substitution is only found when therapy is carried out without attention to the autonomic core of neurotic reactions." [28]

EXAMPLE

The following material consists of excerpts from two interviews held with a client before a seminar audience, to demonstrate the behavioristic approach. The comments between the two interviews are Wolpe's.

First Interview

THERAPIST   Good morning, Mrs. Schmidt. What's your trouble?

CLIENT   I get very upset sometimes.

TH   What upsets you?

CL   Lately the children.

TH   What, what is there about the children that upsets you?

CL   Uh, before I moved where I am now, I used to . . . they used to listen to me and all that. It disturbs me also that my husband is to—not enough home with them. He is, doesn't spend enough time with the children and I feel like I am raising them by myself.

TH   What does your husband do?

CL   He works as a barber now.

TH   What prevents him from being home enough?

CL   He has long hours.

TH   What are his hours?

CL   He leaves at seven, and he comes home half past eight.

TH   Certainly very long. Well, that's a practical problem. Is there anything else that upsets you?

CL   Yes, many things.

TH   Well, for example?

CL   The things that I read in the paper.

TH   Like what?

CL   Oh, like, uh, I have seen plenty killings in the war and now I feel the same like over here. When I first came here I . . . I just thought there is no place like this, I . . . I thought that you could live in peace and there would never be any trouble. You, you couldn't, you wouldn't hear of anything and now, I . . . I hear more and more things and I get very upset about it.

TH   What year did you come here?

CL   In '47.

TH   In '47. How old were you then?

CL   21.

TH   Now let me get one thing clear. If you had gone on feeling the way you felt during those few years, then you would not be here?

CL   I would not have to come here.

TH   Right. Can you say what happened to make you unhappy again after that?

CL   I don't know. It might be . . . you see, uhm, when I was born my mother died in childbirth and she never wanted to even look at me, my grandmother used to tell me . . . she didn't even want to hold me once and as she was dying she was sorry that she was leaving the house behind. She had a feeling for home but she never said that she was leaving the child behind and my grandmother used to always talk about that, which she shouldn't have. And so hard things, I have so many things to talk about and uh . . .

TH   Was your grandmother with you here?

CL No, my grandmother got killed.

TH Oh, well. . . . But, can you say more or less what year you began to feel that you were not so happy anymore?

CL You see, I was disappointed in the family life. I was always looking for somebody like a mother, you know. A somebody. And they would tell me that they would be like a mother to me. And then I found out different—many things and ever since then and—like if I would find somebody and I would get, I can't get too close to them. When I get too close I am afraid that I get hurt and then I run.

TH Does that mean that at first when you came here you were trusting people and you . . . you felt you could easily form close relationships with them and then . . . and then at some stage you found that these people were disappointing you?

CL Uh, uh, I had a few but one I remember is my aunt. She told me that she wanted to be like a mother to me when I came here and I thought that she would and—well, many things happened but if I remember very closely I was expecting my first one. When I was in the hospital waiting, uh, to give birth, I had the baby at 11:55 and my hus . . . 10:55 and my husband called her to say . . . to tell her the news so she said, "You woke us up and we couldn't go back to sleep." She said, "Couldn't it wait till the morning?" And he shouldn't have even told me that—I was very sad. But there were many, many things I knew happened but this I remember.

TH Are the other things that happened of this kind? Were they always things that somebody who should have been friendly to you was in some way uh . . .

CL I don't get that close. I don't wait to find out.

TH Yes, well, but in that case you did get close.

CL Yes.

TH You mentioned that your children don't obey you properly and you mentioned that your husband works too much; therefore, he doesn't help you with the children. Now, both of these things are things that any person could be expected to be upset by and, well, maybe solutions could be worked out. But, if you come for psychiatric treatment it means that you feel that there is some kind of situation where you're not reacting as you should . . . where you are perhaps more upset than you ought to be.

CL There were many times, days that I just didn't feel like going on living. If I had the courage I would have just killed myself many times and I still feel like that. I used to feel like that when I was a child. If I, uh, where I lived with my grandparents, my uncle and my aunt lived there and they just didn't want me. They used to call me all kinds of names and my grandmother used to tell me it would be good if I run away because they didn't want me and that's the time I started feeling that, I just felt like I didn't want to go on living.

TH Uh-huh. I want to ask you how you react in certain rather common situations. Suppose that you're standing in a line and somebody gets in front of you. What do you do?

CL Sometimes I let—if I, if I feel that there is a reason for it I let them go. But if I, if I have to make time, I just don't like it.

TH   What do you do?

CL   I don't do nothing. I get upset. (laughs)

TH   If you go into a shop and you buy, say, a woolen pullover like that and when you come home you inspect it and you see there is a little moth hole in the sleeve, what do you do?

CL   I take it back. I show it to them.

TH   You don't mind taking it back?

CL   I don't know.

TH   I mean, can you do it quite easily or is it difficult to take it back?

CL   I, I don't like to bother people too much. I don't like to—for that reason I don't like to take it back. I—if something goes wrong in the house—they don't fix things right or they don't make them right, my husband has to force me to talk and he, he tells it often that I can't do it. He says that's why people take advantage of me, because I don't have the courage to speak up.

TH   Well, that is very much a matter of habit. Now, it's a thing that one can learn to change.

CL   So far I haven't succeeded.

TH   Well, but, I . . . I want to tell you how you can succeed. Look, let's, let's take this, uh, little example that we used first where somebody gets in front of you in the line. Suppose you're in a hurry and somebody does that. You get cross. You are annoyed. But when you, when you have any thought of doing anything about it, you're kept back at the same time by feeling you don't want to hurt his feelings, you don't want to distress him, maybe it will make a scene, things like that. Now, what I want you to do in the future in this little situation is express these feelings. Now, of course it's difficult, but if you will express this feeling that you have and say, "Will you kindly get to the back of the line?" then, in the act of doing it, you will sort of push back the fear feelings. You will push them down to some extent. And if you do that, the next time it will be a little easier.

CL   I will try.

TH   Well, the more you try, the easier it will become, and of course there are many situations like this. But it requires action.

CL   But if somebody asks me for a favor and I know I can't do it, I just can't tell them *no*. I go out of my way and I do it. There has to be a *no* which I am trying to learn.

TH   That's right. You can only learn to make the *no* a part of action if you say the *no* and it's usually easier if you start by saying *no* in a small situation.

CL   Maybe at home to the children?

TH   Yes, that kind of thing. Now, oddly enough, last month I had a patient who has exactly this problem but probably much worse than you—this is a man who works in a university and the situation has been that if his secretary says to him, "Will you go to the post . . . to the post office and register this letter?" he can't say *no*. He has to do it for his secretary. And you see how ridiculous this is. The first—I, I said to him, "Will you please crawl across the room for me?" (patient laughs) And it was very hard for him to say *no*, but he said *no* and after a little while it became easy. So, anyway, there are many many things of this kind where it is reasonable and right for you to express your feelings, to do according to your feelings and you must learn to be able to—of course that does not mean that you are becoming rude or nasty. There is one general thing I want to tell you that if you get into the habit of saying *no* correctly at the right time, then you don't have to become violent about it. But if you, if you don't exert your authority immediately, and the other person goes on doing what you don't want, then you become more and more annoyed and eventually you can't control yourself and it comes out in violence. I would like to consider for a moment some of these situations where you feel that, that people are rejecting you.

CL   I don't try to get that close to them to find out. I don't want to find it out.

TH   Yes, but there are other kinds of rejection and, which are a smaller kind, and I would also like to know about those. For example, suppose you walk in the street and there is an acquaintance, a person you don't know well, and you expect that person to greet you and she just walks past. Does that worry you?

CL   Yeah, I don't like it. Because I say hello to everybody that I know.

TH   Now, what about this kind of situation. Suppose you are having afternoon coffee with two friends and you notice that one of the friends is speaking more to the other one than to you. Does that bother you at all?

CL   I don't know.

TH   Can you think of any other situations that happen nowadays between you and other people that upset you?

CL   My aunt came up last time and, uh, she, she was complaining that I don't invite the family for dinner and I just, I just thought that I wasn't up to invite them because I always get upset with them.

TH   What upsets you?

CL   They always, you know, uh, they always think you don't, you don't do enough for them. And every time I have them over, there's always something, she likes to boss me around—set the table this way—feed this one like that—she always tries to tell me what to do and I, I think I'm capable of taking care of the people myself and if she, I don't do what she wants me, she gets very angry.

TH   What do you do or say when she tries to boss you around?

CL   Sometimes I take it and sometimes I just tell her that—"Don't worry about it, I'll do it, I'll take care of it myself." Things like that. Sometimes I just don't answer but then I get upset inside.

TH   Yes. Well this is another example of what we were talking about a few minutes ago. That here, also, where she is, where she is taking unreasonable advantage of you and it's your home and your right to control the matter, you should say to her, "Please keep out of this. I will organize it my way."

CL   I don't want to hurt her feelings, to say that.

TH   Well, it won't hurt her feelings and if you don't do it, you're hurting yourself. In a way that is much more important than anything you can be doing to your aunt. Well, these are the things you have to learn. You have to learn to express your personality because in doing that you will gradually weaken these fears.

CL   But when I think of telling her that or something then I think of myself, I mean, I don't have to expect really anything of her, why should I expect those things of her?

TH   But all you're expecting is justice. Is justice too much to expect? Well, Mrs. Schmidt, that's about all I want to do with you today.

Comments

From the contents of the first interview it was clear that the patient acceded too readily to the wishes of others and required training in assertive behavior to overcome this and related anxieties. Systematic desensitization was indicated for her gross fear of rejection. In the second interview details are found of her training in muscle relaxation, which was done in a much more skimpy way than is usual in clinical practice.

The later part of the second interview demonstrates systematic desensitization. In this technique, progressively more disturbing scenes on a particular theme are presented to the imagination of the deeply relaxed patient. Each scene is presented until it ceases to evoke any anxiety. The particular scenes used here came from a list set up with the patient's help between the interviews on the basis of information that had been obtained during the first interview. The list consisted of people known to her, ranked according to the degree to which rejection by them would disturb her. Of the two individuals named, Mrs. Benning and Selma, Mrs. Benning aroused very little anxiety as a rejecting figure, Selma substantially more. The image of Selma was introduced only after it had been ascertained that Mrs. Benning did not arouse anxiety when imagined as ignoring the patient. Imagining of rejection by Selma did disturb her, and when presentations of this were repeated, disturbance decreased progressively. The presentations were repeated until the patient ceased to have any disturbance at all. In later sessions, increasingly anxiety-arousing items from this and other relevant lists of stimulus situations would have been subjected to desensitization.

A didactically fortunate coincidence occurred that afternoon. When the patient was on her way home, she encountered Selma outside the subway station, and Selma was preoccupied and did not respond to her. The patient telephoned her clinical psychologist in gleeful excitement that evening to tell him that she had been quite unconcerned at not being greeted by Selma.

Second Interview

TH   We are now going to go on to the demonstration of the technique of relaxation training and also a small demonstration of desensitization which we've worked out rather hastily; and it will be tentative. If there are therapeutic effects, we will regard ourselves as fortunate. Altogether, this is going to be a very condensed session because the training in relaxation ordinarily takes anything between five and seven sessions to accomplish. I will of course show you my own standard way of doing this. There is nothing absolute about this; other people use a different order of training in relaxation and there are all sorts of little details of technique which can be varied.

Well, now, Mrs. Schmidt, I'm going to show you how to relax your muscles.[29] As you know, when you relax you become more comfortable, and if you're anxious you feel less anxious. Now, I'm going to show you how to bring about a deep relaxation so that you can fight the anxiety more effectively than you have been able to in the past. Now, what I want you to do is, with your left hand, hold the arm of your chair quite tight. I want you to observe certain things that are a result of your holding this chair tight. First of all, there are certain sensations. To begin with, you have sensations in your . . . in your hand and you may have other sensations. With your right hand, point out to me all the places where you get any kind of feeling which seems to be a result of holding the chair tightly.

CL   (Points to left hand and top of forearm. Points to left biceps.)

TH   Now, I want to show you the main idea of the action that you take if you want to relax deeply. When you relax ordinarily, you let go. Now, I want to show you how to let go more than the usual way, and what I'm going to do is this—I'm going to hold your wrist again and ask you to pull against it. When you pull, you will notice that the muscle becomes tight again. Then I will say to you, "Let go gradually." Now, when you let go, I want you to notice two things. The tight feeling will become less, and I want you also to notice that the letting go is something that you do—something active that you put in the muscle. Well, your forearm will eventually come down to rest on the arm of the chair and ordinarily that would seem to you as though that's the end of the matter. You have let go. But it will not really be quite the end, because some of the muscle fibers will still be contracted, so that when your forearm has come down to the chair I will say to you, "Keep on letting go. Go on doing that in the muscle, that activity which you were doing while it was coming down." Now, pull against me. Now, do you get the feeling up there in the muscle? Tight feeling? OK now, let go gradually. Come on, let go. And notice how the feeling changes. Try and make it go further and further. Now, you see, this is difficult. It takes quite a lot of practice, really, to do it properly. You just have to keep on trying to let your muscle go in a negative direction. At this time, when you have never done it before, it could easily take you twenty or thirty minutes to make any important change in the muscle, but you'll find later on, when you've been practicing, that you can relax the whole body quite well in a few seconds. Meanwhile, you just have to keep on trying and you have to practice. You should try and practice for fifteen minutes twice a day. Now, do you get the idea of what I'm trying to do?

CL   Yes. I feel much more relaxed already. (she laughs)

TH   Good. Keep on relaxing. Let's try and make it go further and further. We're going to rush ahead today. So we are going now to do the muscles of the face. So here are these very tense muscles and now I'm going to start relaxing, so I relax a little . . . more . . . more. . .

more. Now, from about this point onwards there is very little that you can see, but relaxation continues; and this part that you can't see is the important part because this is what takes us beyond the normal point of relaxation, and this is the part that brings about the calm feeling that we are trying to get. You can contract them to be sure where they are and then just spend a few minutes relaxing. If you find it's easier to close your eyes, then close your eyes.

Next we do the muscles of the neck. The muscles of the neck that we are mainly concerned with are those at the back of the neck, the muscles that hold the head up. Well, if you let them go, then of course your head will fall forward. Now, let that happen. Do you feel anything in the back of your neck when you do this?

CL   It's the pressure over here.

TH   You'll find that if you do this as I suggested twice a day, that in about a week or two your chin will come right down onto your chest and you won't feel this pulling in the back of your neck at all. Well, we'll go on to the muscles of the back. Try and arch your back backwards. You should feel two columns of muscles on either side of the spine. OK. Now, we do the muscles of the abdomen; now, that means, make your stomach tight, as though you were expecting somebody to punch you in the stomach. Can you feel it? All right, so we've now done all of the usual muscles, certainly rather skimpily toward the end.

Well, let's go on now to the next step. I want you to close your eyes. Now, with your eyes closed I want you to try and make use of all the information I have just given you and get as relaxed as possible. So, let's go through these muscles in a systematic order. OK, now, you are quite nice and relaxed. Now, keep your eyes closed and I'm going to ask you to imagine some scenes. Now, you will imagine these scenes very clearly, and generally speaking they will not affect your state of relaxation. But if by any chance anything does affect your state of calm, you'll be able to signal that to me by raising your right forefinger about an inch. So now, I want you to imagine just that you're standing on a street corner and you're watching the traffic. Just a nice, pleasant, peaceful day, and you're watching the cars, and the taxis and trucks, and people all passing at this corner. OK, now, stop imagining this scene. Now, if the scene didn't worry you at all, do nothing. If that scene disturbed you, raise your finger now. (no finger movement) OK, that's fine, now just keep on relaxing.

Now, I want you to imagine that you're walking along the sidewalk and you see, walking toward you from the other side, Mrs. Benning. Now, as you pass Mrs. Benning, you see she is looking toward you and you get ready to greet her, and she just walks past as though she didn't recognize you. Now, stop imagining that. Now, if that, if imagining that disturbed you even a very small bit, I want you to raise your right index finger now. If it didn't worry you, don't do anything. (no finger movement)

Now, I want you to imagine again that you're walking on the sidewalk and you see, moving toward you, Selma and you get ready to greet her, and she seems to see you but she walks right on—she doesn't greet you. Now, stop imagining this. If you felt any disturbance at that . . . (right forefinger rises)

OK. Thank you. Now, just keep relaxed. Now, don't think of

anything except muscles. Let yourself sink more and more deeply into this calm, relaxed state. Now, again imagine that you're walking along the sidewalk and you see Selma approaching and she seems to see you, and you expect her to make some response but she just walks right on. Stop imagining this scene—just relax. Again, think only of your muscles. Just be calm and comfortable.

Again imagine that you're walking along the sidewalk and you see Selma coming toward you, but there are also other people on the sidewalk, and you think she sees you but she walks right past without greeting you. Now, stop imagining. Now, if you felt any disturbance when you imagined it this last time, raise your finger now. (finger rises) OK. Now, if the amount of the disturbance that you have been feeling, if the amount is getting less, do nothing. If it is not getting less, raise your finger again. (finger does not rise) OK, now, just keep relaxing as well as you can.

Again imagine that you are walking along the sidewalk and Selma approaches and passes you without recognition or greeting. Stop the scene. Only relax.

Now, again imgine that you're walking along the sidewalk and you see Selma coming and she seems to see you, and then you pass each other without her greeting you. Stop imagining. If there was any disturbance this last time, raise your finger. (finger rises) OK. If the amount of disturbance is still getting less, do nothing. If it is not getting less, raise your finger. (finger does not rise) All right. Keep on relaxing. Think only of relaxing.

You're walking along the sidewalk and you see Selma approaching. You expect her to recognize and greet you but she just walks straight past. Stop the scene. Just relax.

Again imagine that you are walking on that sidewalk and you see Selma approaching and she seems to see you, and you are ready to greet her but she just walks past without any recognition. Stop the scene. If there was any disturbance, raise your finger. (finger does not rise) OK, now. Just relax. Now, I'm going to count up to 5 and then you will open your eyes and feel calm and refreshed. 1–2–3–4–5. How do you feel?

CL   I feel like, I wouldn't feel like doing any work today anymore. The last time when I seen her I just didn't care whether she said hello or not.

TH   How did you feel the first time?

CL   I was very mad. At least, the least she could do is say hello when I live just across the way from her. The last time it was, if she didn't think enough of me to say hello, then let her just go.

TH   Very good. Thank you very much. You've been a great help to us.[30]

SUMMARY AND EVALUATION

Emotional disturbance, or neurosis, is characterized by unadaptive behavior, usually accompanied by anxiety, which has been learned through conditioning. Emotional disturbance originates when the individual is punished for behavior motivated by a bodily need or drive, with the result that he experiences anxiety and becomes inhibited when the need again arises. Fear, or anxiety, has been aroused by some noxious stimulus or an idea conditioned to such a stimulus, or as the result of a conflict situation, and has become associated, through conditioning and generalization, with other neutral stimuli.

Treatment consists of eliminating the association, thus removing the inhibition, mainly by the technique of reciprocal inhibition, which is essentially counterconditioning or experimental extinction. This is accomplished by means of the performance and practice, in the anxiety-evoking situation, of responses that are antagonistic to anxiety, which results in the suppression of the anxiety responses. Therapy involves motivating and enabling the client to perform responses antagonistic to anxiety. Techniques of motivating the client include explanation and instruction concerning the nature and origin of his condition, the prescription of specific activities, reasoning and assurance that the prescribed activities will remedy the situation, and encouragement, support, and pressure to engage in the activities.

The claim of success (90 percent apparently cured or much improved) must be viewed with some skepticism. As Wolpe recognizes, in order for his figures to be comparable with data from other methods, which usually report much lower rates of success, two assumptions must be made. The first is that the clients are similar, and that they are not selected in any way that would bias the results. While this assumption cannot be disproved, neither is there any evidence to support it. Wolpe does limit his clients to those diagnosed as neurotic. The case examples that he uses indicate that some were severe cases; on the other hand, many, if not most, would appear to present rather minor or limited problems. The behaviors treated are certainly specific, and while sometimes seriously disabling, are not usually part of a complex disturbance. They certainly do not appear to be similar to the run of cases treated by practitioners of other methods of psychotherapy. According to Wolpe, the common rate of improvement in other methods of psychotherapy is 40 percent markedly improved. Some improvement occurs in about two-thirds of those treated, according to other estimates. Wolpe attributes this common rate of improvement from diverse methods to "nonspecific" factors common to all methods or relationship factors. This could be interpreted as indicating that about two-thirds of the patients accepted for therapy by other practitioners have problems for which relationship therapy is effective. Such therapists (except for those practicing orthodox psychoanalysis) do little selection of their patients. Thus, the remainder, who do not improve, probably have other kinds of problems—many of them, perhaps, problems suitable for various techniques of behavior therapy. That behavior therapists have a higher rate of success could well be because of their selection of patients or problems appropriate for their methods. Behavior therapy, therefore, could not be claimed to be more effective for the kinds of patients, or problems, seen by therapists utilizing other methods.

As in the case of other behavior therapy approaches, Wolpe's greater rate of success may be explained in terms of the selection of clients who present only rather isolated, even if severe, symptoms. Since these symptoms are not part of a deeper and/or general personality disturbance, their removal is not followed by the development of other symptoms. The value of symptom removal as a goal of therapy may be questioned. It may not be sufficient or adequate in comparison with other goals. And it may have some undesirable accompaniments or consequences. As London says, "the relief from symptomatic pain in Action therapy may encourage its parties to disregard the cost or consequences of that relief." [31] Mowrer suggests that the method may remove symptoms at the expense of character.[32]

The second assumption is that the criteria for success are similar to those applied by others. There is no evidence for this assumption. The evaluations were made by Wolpe only. Some of his clients were not included in his tabulations; clients were included "only if they have had an 'adequate' amount of therapy. Therapy is naturally regarded as adequate in every patient who is either apparently cured or much improved. In those who have benefitted less, it is regarded as adequate if a reasonable trial has been given to each of the reciprocal inhibition techniques that seem applicable to the case." [33] Such selection of clients must be considered in any evaluation, both in terms of the kinds of problems for which an approach is applicable and in terms of the results with clients who are accepted. Stevenson notes that if we were to take the entire series of 295 cases that Wolpe reports having seen for at least an intake interview, the success rate would drop to 65 percent.[34]

The main criterion for success is symptom improvement. Wolpe appears to agree with Eysenck that "there is no neurosis underlying the symptom, but merely the symptom itself. Get rid of the symptom and you have eliminated the neurosis." [35] It does appear that many of the clients treated by Wolpe presented rather circumscribed symptoms. On the other hand, it also appears that more general changes occurred than symptom disappearance, including general improvement in functioning, increased confidence, and development of a more favorable self-concept.

It probably cannot be denied that results are achieved by Wolpe's method, even if they may be more limited in extent than his claims suggest. The question arises as to how and why they occur, and if they occur in the way and for the reasons Wolpe indicates. There are a number of questions that may be raised.

A first question has to do with the nature and origin of neuroses, or unadaptive behavior. The analogy between experimental neuroses in animals and human neuroses is only an analogy and one whose validity has been questioned. Wolpe's arguments are not highly convincing. He agrees that noxious stimuli usually do not operate in the production of human neuroses. Nor are the conflicts that give rise to anxieties in humans the same kinds of ambivalent stimuli that result in animal neuroses. Conflicts of needs, desires, etc., are equated with discriminatory ambivalence, though they would not appear to be the same. Wolpe seems to recognize a weakness in the analogy when he writes: *"Apparently,* simultaneous, strong, conflicting action tendencies *somehow* generate high degrees of anxiety within the nervous system."[36] This kind of reasoning and evidence is characteristic of the application of the animal analogy to human neuroses.

Wolpe seems to imply that second-order conditioning is involved in human neuroses.[37] Since second-order conditioning is not as stable or as persistent as first-order conditioning, the problem of the persistence of unadaptive neurotic anxiety and other behavior must be faced. As Mowrer points out, in ordinary life, as in the laboratory, fears that are not reinforced spontaneously are extinguished, contrary to the assumption of behavior theory as well as of psychoanalysis.[38] Here again, Wolpe's arguments are not impressive, even in terms of the animal neuroses that are the bases for his argument.[39]

As for the concept of reciprocal inhibition, taken from Sherrington, who used it in reference to reflex behavior, it may be questioned whether what Wolpe includes under this term is anything more than what is already covered by the concepts of extinction or counterconditioning. Extinction consists of the disappearance of anxiety and nonadaptive behavior, and is made possible by the inhibition of the neurotic (or anxiety) responses by any means. Essentially, the stimulus for anxiety is allowed to occur in a situation where it is not reinforced. If the neurotic responses are inhibited, the activity causing them to be inhibited becomes (positively) conditioned to the former anxiety-arousing stimulus. Thus, in addition to experimental extinction, Wolpe instigates other behavior in the presence of the anxiety-evoking stimulus. It would appear that the main aspect of his approach, and the reason for his success, is the inducement of such behavior. He does this by encouragement, support, suggestion, command, and, in the interview, suggestion and hypnosis. His method can thus be viewed as reconditioning.

In the therapy situation the client faces anxiety-evoking situations in his imagination and learns that they are not to be feared. Outside of therapy the client is led or forced to face such situations and finds that they are not to be feared. In effect, the client is put into the anxiety-producing situation and learns that there is no reason to fear it; that is, the unconditioned stimulus receives no reinforcement. The methods and techniques for inducing or forcing the client to enter and stay in the anxiety-producing situation are devices to create a situation in which extinction can take place. The client cannot do it himself because of his fear. An alternative approach, the one used by most counselors and therapists, is to work on reducing the fear, so that the client will voluntarily approach and face the anxiety-producing situation. In effect, Wolpe's approach consists of changing attitudes or feelings by first changing behavior. The client is forced to act so that he can learn that he need not fear the results of his behavior. As

London says, "In effect, by his own admission then, a large part of reciprocal inhibition therapy consists simply of getting people to do the very things they fear." [40]

There does not appear to be anything new or different about Wolpe's methods. Mowrer, in his critique, refers to Dunlap, Burnham, Ewen Cameron, and Dollard and Miller as others who used Wolpe's methods before he did.[41] Mary Cover Jones used counterconditioning almost half a century ago.[42]

Like Eysenck, Wolpe appears to believe that the relationship between therapist and client is not important in counseling or psychotherapy. He does note, however, that since all approaches in counseling or psychotherapy involve an interview relationship, this is a common element. The aspect of the relationship that is important, and that he feels accounts for the common level of success of all approaches, is the reciprocal inhibition of anxiety responses by the antagonistic emotional responses evoked in the interview. However, although the counselor undoubtedly does produce some deconditioning, reconditioning, or extinction of anxiety, the relationship may go beyond this. Wolpe, as indicated above, does not achieve his results only by the use of conditioning in the interview. Suggestion appears to be a major aspect of his approach, and this and other methods of inducing the client to act appear to be responsible for much of the success of the method, even though they do not constitute conditioning. Klein, Dittman, Parloff, and Gill, after closely observing Wolpe and Lazarus, wrote: "Perhaps the most striking impression we came away with was of how much use behavior therapists make of suggestion and of how much the patient's expectations and attitudes are manipulated." [43] Lazarus, who at that time was associated with Wolpe, commented in the Klein, Dittman, Parloff, and Gill article on this statement: "Both Wolpe and I have explicitly stated that relationship variables are often extremely important in behavior therapy. Factors such as warmth, empathy, and authenticity are considered necessary but often insufficient." He continues later: "If suggestion enables the person to attempt new responses, these may have positive effects. One thus endeavors quite deliberately to maximize the 'placebo' effect." And he agrees that "even the results of a specific technique like systematic desensitization cannot be accounted for solely in terms of graded hierarchies and muscle relaxation." [44] Wolpe does not seem to go as far as Lazarus. Yet it would appear that the effects of behavior therapy are the result, to a much greater extent than Wolpe acknowledges, of the nonspecific effects of the therapy relationship, of the placebo effect of suggestion, of therapist confidence in the techniques, and of client belief in the therapist and his techniques.

Behavior therapy may be more limited than is now apparent, since it does not seem to be applicable to problems of meanings or goals and the fears and aspirations related to them. Not all the problems that people seek help with are symptoms or limitations of function; many involve systems of meaning. The behavior therapist must, as London notes, "drastically curtail the range of persons and problems he attacks. Courting specificity, the Actionist risks wedding triviality." [45] If he widens the concept of symptom, as many do, until it includes meaning, his position becomes scientifically tenuous, according to London. One might ask the behavior therapist how he would decondition the pain or suffering of the client who suffers from a realization that he is not functioning up to his potential or up to his aspiration level, who has a concept of himself as a failure, or who experiences a lack of meaning in his life. Then the therapist's method of treatment, or the effective ingredient, may be the counseling relationship rather than the specific techniques of behavior therapy. As London suggests, "there must be men who, freed of all their symptomatic woes, discover then a truer misery, until now buried underneath a lot of petty ills. Preoccupied no more with pedantries, with headaches, phobias, or vile thoughts, a nauseating emptiness appears to them ahead, a nameless terror of a nameless end. Can this still be a symptom, and if so, still violable by some concrete act, by formulation of a habit or association with some pleasantness-arousing stimulus pulled from a bag of therapeutic tricks?" [46]

Rotter, in his review of Wolpe's book, makes some comments that may serve to summarize this evaluation:

> The description of how human beings learn or what they learn that Wolpe presents seems . . . inadequate and highly oversimplified. It does not explain satisfactorily how human beings learn in more simple situations and it is far from explaining the therapeutic changes which Wolpe himself obtains with his methods. It appears . . . that all of Wolpe's theorizing regarding the neural locus of learning, the nature of the autonomic responses and of the conditioning process are not only controversial at best but are also more or less superfluous to what he actually does. One could say, after a careful reading of the wide variety of methods and the great variety of behaviors which he attempts to substitute for the patient, that he has one basic principle: when the patient presents certain unadaptive behaviors or symptoms, then other behavior, which the therapist considers to be more adaptive and possible to substitute in specific situations, should be taught directly to the patient by whatever method is possible. Apparently, what has frequently been referred to in the past as prestige-suggestion is the method he relies on most heavily. The patient is led to expect that his problems will be solved if he will do as the therapist suggests, and at least in many cases the patient is willing to try out these behaviors, finds them successful, and so maintains them.[47]

Again, it appears that, though minimized by Wolpe, the relationship is important—a relationship in which the counselor wants to help the client, using methods that he strongly believes in and is able to lead the client to believe in.

Lazarus, who as indicated above was associated with Wolpe for several years, has voiced several criticisms of his approach. Responding to Wolpe's definition of behavior therapy as "the use of experimentally established principles of learning for the purpose of changing unadaptive behavior," [48] he asks: "Just what are these so-called 'experimentally established principles of learning'? Do they apply to human beings as well as to animals? . . . Some established principles of learning may exist in animal laboratories, but insofar as their relevance for human behavior is concerned, there are, to say the least, many debatable points of issue." [49] Again, he points out that although there is considerable evidence that neurotic behavior is learned, it is still a hypothesis, while Wolpe treats it as an established fact. Finally, he criticizes the narrowness of Wolpe's approach, which treats man as an animal, without a cerebral cortex, a "hypothalamic, subcortical creature dominated by a primitive autonomic nervous system," whose neuroses are in all essential respects like those experimentally induced in animals. But, Lazarus continues, "when confronted by people intent on self-destruction, torn asunder by conflicting loyalties, crippled by too high a level of aspiration, unhappily married because of false romantic ideals, or beset by feelings of guilt and inferiority on the basis of complex theological beliefs, I fail to appreciate the clinical significance of Wolpe's neurotic cats and sometimes wish that life were really as simple as he would have us believe." [50]

REFERENCES

[1] Wolpe, J. *Psychotherapy by reciprocal inhibition.* Stanford: Stanford University Press, 1958. Pp. ix–xi.   [2] *Ibid.,* p. 19.   [3] *Ibid.,* p. 30.   [4] *Ibid.,* p. 67.   [5] *Ibid.,* p. 71.   [6] *Ibid.*   [7] *Ibid.,* p. 32. Wolpe now states, referring to the last phrase: "I no longer include this. Schizophrenics and other abnormal organisms can develop neurotic reactions." (Personal communication. August 6, 1964.)   [8] Wolpe, J. *The practice of behavior therapy.* New York: Pergamon Press, 1969. P. vii.   [9] *Ibid.,* p. 13.   [10] *Ibid.,* p. 18.   [11] *Ibid.,* p. 16.   [12] *Ibid.,* p. 56.   [13] *Ibid.,* pp. 57–58.   [14] *Ibid.,* pp. 59–60.   [15] *Ibid.,* p. 61.   [16] *Ibid.,* p. 67.   [17] *Ibid.,* p. 77.   [18] Jacobson, E. *Progressive relaxation.* Chicago: University of Chicago Press, 1938.   [19] Wolpe, J. *The practice of behavior therapy.* New York: Pergamon Press, 1969. P. 107.   [20] *Ibid.,* p. 120.   [21] *Ibid.,* p. 190.   [22] *Ibid.,* p. 193.   [23] *Ibid.,* p. 201.   [24] Azrin, N. H., & Holtz, W. C. Punishment. In W. K. Honig (Ed.), *Operant behavior.* New York: Appleton-Century-Crofts, 1966.   [25] Wolpe, J. *The practice of behavior therapy.* New York: Pergamon Press, 1969. P. 219.   [26] *Ibid.,* p. 180.   [27] *Ibid.,* p. 267.   [28] *Ibid.,* p. 277.   [29] "It is important at this point to recognize the condensed nature of the passages dealing with relaxation. In the total interview the patient's attention was drawn to a number of muscle systems, and she was instructed in the relaxation of these systems. The passages must thus be regarded only as illustrative of the total relaxation method." (Wolpe)   [30] Wolpe, J. *The Case of Mrs. Schmidt.* Typescript and record published by Counselor Recordings and Tests, Box 6184,

Acklen Sta., Nashville, Tennessee. Typescript reproduced by permission. [31] London, P. *The modes and morals of psychotherapy.* New York: Holt, Rinehart and Winston, 1964. P. 119.   [32] Mowrer, O. H. Freudianism, behavior therapy and "self disclosure." In O. H. Mowrer (Ed.), *The new group psychotherapy.* New York: Van Nostrand Reinhold, 1964. P. 221.   [33] Wolpe, J. *Psychotherapy by reciprocal inhibition.* Stanford: Stanford University Press, 1958. P. 205.   [34] Stevenson, I. Discussion. In J. Wolpe, A. Salter, & L. J. Reyna (Eds.), *The conditioning therapies.* New York: Holt, Rinehart and Winston, 1964. P. 17.   [35] Eysenck, H. J. Learning theory and behavior therapy. In H. J. Eysenck (Ed.), *Behavior therapy and the neuroses.* New York: Pergamon Press, 1960. P. 9.   [36] Wolpe, J. *Psychotherapy by reciprocal inhibition.* Stanford: Stanford University Press, 1958. P. 79. (Italics added.)   [37] *Ibid.,* pp. 78–79. [38] Mowrer, O. H., *op. cit.,* p. 217.   [39] Wolpe, J. *Psychotherapy by reciprocal inhibition.* Stanford: Stanford University Press, 1958. P. 66.   [40] London, P., *op. cit.,* p. 91.   [41] Mowrer, O. H., *op. cit.,* pp. 219–221.   [42] Jones, Mary Cover. A laboratory study of fear: the case of Peter. *Pedagogical Sem.,* 1924, **31,** 308–315. Reprinted in H. J. Eysenck (Ed.), *Behavior therapy and the neuroses.* New York: Pergamon Press, 1960.   [43] Klein, Marjorie, Dittman, A. J., Parloff, M. B., & Gill, M. M. Behavior therapy: observations and reflections. *J. consult. clin. psychol.,* 1969, **33,** 259–266.   [44] *Ibid.*   [45] London, P., *op. cit.,* p. 122.   [46] *Ibid.,* p. 38.   [47] Rotter, J. B. Substituting good behavior for bad. Review of J. Wolpe, "Psychotherapy by reciprocal inhibition." *Contemp. Psychol.,* 1959, **4,** 176–178.   [48] Wolpe, J. *The practice of behavior therapy.* New York: Pergamon Press, 1969, P. vii.   [49] Lazarus, A. A. *Behavior therapy and beyond.* New York: McGraw-Hill, 1971.   [50] *Ibid.,* p. 6.

7

Rotter's social learning approach

A theory of personality and behavior and of its application to counseling or psychotherapy that has been derived from behavior theory is presented by Julian B. Rotter in his *Social Learning and Clinical Psychology.*[1] Rotter (1916–   ) took his Ph.D. in 1941 at Indiana University. After a brief period working in a state mental hospital, he spent four years in the service as a personnel consultant and aviation psychologist. In 1946 he became Professor of Psychology and Director of the Psychological Clinic at Ohio State University. In 1963 he moved to the University of Connecticut, where he is Professor of Psychology. He is a Diplomate in Clinical Psychology of the American Board of Professional Psychology.

BACKGROUND AND DEVELOPMENT

Rotter describes his approach as "an attempt to apply a learning theory to complex social behavior of human beings. It is, consequently, a more molar theory than other learning theories . . ."[2] He refers to it as an expectancy-reinforcement theory. Expectancy is treated in a Hullian manner, but Rotter's reinforcement principle is empirical in nature, rather than being a drive reduction principle. His theory is presented as tentative—an unfinished system. Its objective is not to present the true nature of reality, but to develop a system of constructs that will provide maximum prediction and control of behavior.

PHILOSOPHY AND CONCEPTS

General Principles

Personality is a construct referring to the stable, characteristic modes of behaving, or of interpreting the world, of a unified, complexly organized person. *Behavior* (or experience) is an event in which a living organism is one of the referents. A *construct* is a term representing an attempt to abstract the nature of an event or events. *Mode of description* refers to a set of constructs describing events from a consistent orientation.

POSTULATE 1   The unit of investigation for the study of personality is the interaction of the individual and his meaningful environment.

COROLLARY 1   Personality study is the study of learned behavior or of behavior that is modifiable, changing with experience.

COROLLARY 2   Personality study is the historical investigation of experience or sequences of events.

POSTULATE 2   Personality constructs, while consistent with constructs in fields such as physiology, biology, or neurology, are not dependent upon these other constructs for explanation.

POSTULATE 3   Behavior as described by personality constructs occurs in space and time, and is one way of describing events.

COROLLARY 1   Any conception of behavior in which "physiological behavior" is conceived as causing "psychological behavior," or vice versa, is rejected as dualistic.

POSTULATE 4   Only behavior at a particular level or stage of complexity may be usefully described by personality constructs.

COROLLARY 1   Physiological or other constructs may be used in describing some of the conditions present at the time of the acquisition of personality characteristics.

COROLLARY 2   Such constructs may be used by psychologists for practical purposes.

COROLLARY 3   Learned meanings (or symbols) describing physiological states may be used by the human organism in reacting with itself.

POSTULATE 5   A person's experiences influence each other, so that the personality has unity.

COROLLARY 1   Behavior as described by personality constructs can be spoken of only in terms of the conditions necessary for its occurrence, not in terms of causality.

POSTULATE 6   Behavior has a directional aspect; that is, it is goal-directed (motivated). This is inferred from the effect of reinforcing conditions. Reinforcement is broader than drive reduction, which is inadequate to explain all motivated behavior. It is "any action, condition, or state that affects movement toward a goal." [3]

COROLLARY 1   Needs or goals are learned or acquired, early needs arising from association with physiological homeostatic conditions, and later ones arising as means of satisfying earlier learned goals. We speak of needs when our attention is on the individual, and goals when we are looking at the environmental conditions.

COROLLARY 2   Early acquired goals are the result of satisfactions and frustrations controlled by other people; this is the basis for a social learning theory.

COROLLARY 3   To occur regularly in a given situation or situations, a particular mode of behavior must have been made available to an individual by having led to reinforcement during previous learning experience.

COROLLARY 4   Behaviors, needs, and goals are related in systems in ways determined by previous experience.

POSTULATE 7   Behavior is determined not only by the nature or importance of goals or reinforcement but also by anticipation or expectancy, based on previous experience, that these reinforcements will occur. In human beings, at least, "it seems extremely difficult even to attempt an explanation of human learning in complex social situations without some construct that deals with the effect on behavior of the anticipation of future reinforcements." [4]

Basic Concepts

There are three basic constructs utilized in the measurement and prediction of behavior: (1) *Behavior potential* is the potentiality of the occurrence of specific behavior in any given situation (or situations) as measured (relatively) in relation to a single reinforcement or a set of reinforcements. Implicit behavior is recognized and accepted, that is, "behavior that is not readily observed directly," but "must frequently be determined by the presence of the behavior with which [it is] associated either invariably or with high frequency." [5] Examples would be the clenching of one's fist when frustrated, or looking for alternative solutions, which may be measured by the time taken by subjects for the solution of problems. (2) *Expectancy* is the probability held by the individual that a particular reinforcement will occur follow-ing specific behavior in a specific situation or situations. In a given situation expectancy may be formulated as a function of probability of occurrence as based upon past experience in situations perceived as the same, and upon the generalization of expectancies for the same or similar reinforcements to occur in other situations for the same or functionally related behaviors (that is, behaviors leading to the accom-plishment of the same or similar reinforcements or goals). Objective probability is only one of several factors entering into internal proba-bility. (3) *Reinforcement value* is the degree of preference for any one of several reinforcements to occur when the possibilities of occurrence are equal. Such preferences are independent of expectancy.

The relationships among these three concepts are expressed in several formulas, which may be translated as follows:

1   The potential for a particular behavior to occur in a particular situation in relation to a particular reinforcement is a function of the expectancy of the occurrence of the reinforcement following the behavior in the situation and the value of the reinforcement.

2   The potential for a particular behavior to occur in a particular situation in relation to all potential reinforcements for which the in-dividual has expectancies is a function of the expectancies of the occur-rence of all these reinforcements in the situation and the values of these reinforcements.

3   The potential for a particular behavior to occur in relation to all potential reinforcements in all situations is a function of the expectancies of the occurrence of these reinforcements in these situa-tions and the values of these reinforcements.

4   The potential for a group of functionally related behaviors to occur in all situations is a function of the expectancies of these behaviors leading to particular reinforcements in these situations and the values of these reinforcements.

5   From these formulations the constructs of need potential, freedom of movement, and need value (to be defined later) may be derived, and may be used to reduce formulation 4 to a more general prediction: the potentiality of occurrence of a functionally related set of behaviors that leads to the satisfaction of some need (need poten-tial) is a function of the expectancies that these behaviors will lead to these reinforcements (freedom of movement), and the strength or value of these reinforcements (need value); or need potential is a function of freedom of movement and need value.

The Nature of Reinforcement

When the occurrence of some observable event changes the potentiality of occurrence of a behavior that has preceded that event with regularity, such an event is by definition a reinforcement. This definition avoids the difficulties of postulating drives to be reduced and makes a measurable criterion of reinforcement possible. Internal reinforcement is the subject's experience of an event that has value for him. External reinforcement is the occurrence of an event known to be reinforcing for a group to which the subject belongs. The two are not necessarily related in a one-to-one manner, although when it is known that an occurrence has resulted in internal reinforcement for a particular person, it may also be considered an external reinforcement for him.

The value of any reinforcement is a function of the reinforcements it has previously been paired with, or has led to, or is perceived as leading to. Stated in terms of expectancy and reinforcement value, this may be formulated as follows: the value of a particular reinforcement in a particular situation is a function of the expectancies that this reinforcement will lead to other reinforcements in the same situation and of the values of these other reinforcements in the situation.

Psychological Directionality

Need refers to the potentiality of occurrence of a set of functionally related behaviors directed toward a group of functionally related reinforcements. Psychological needs arise through learning, although their source is the drives described in physiological terms. They are activated more by the correct cues or stimuli than by some cyclical internal condition on a physiological level. Psychological goals need not be explained in terms of their satisfaction or reduction of a physiological drive. "Behavior directed toward the attainment of a learned goal or external reinforcement may be predicted through knowledge of the situation the organism is in and from a knowledge of his past experience." [6] In other words, psychological needs can become independent of their origin in physiological drives, and their strength is determined by learned or acquired goals or satisfactions.

Relationships Among External Reinforcements

Values of various reinforcements may be predicted on the basis of functional relationships among them, which may be described by concepts of generalization. Primary stimulus generalization occurs on the basis of original functional similarity among external reinforcements or goals. Mediated stimulus generalization gives rise to functional equivalence of behaviors that lead to (are mediated by) the same reinforcement. Generalization of expectancy changes is a function of the similarity of reinforcements; the occurrence (or nonoccurrence) of a given reinforcement changes the expectancy for the occurrence of other reinforcements, following a gradient.

Reinforcements may be grouped as similar, and the classification may be broadened until a single overall concept of directionality, or need, is reached. This single need may be called security or psychological homeostasis. The broader the classification, the greater the variety of behaviors about which predictions can be made, but the less the accuracy in any particular case. The development of a classification system for categorizing needs has not been accomplished, but is necessary. It is an endless task, however, since new problems will require new abstractions. Six broad categories are suggested: (1) recognition-status, (2) protection-dependency, (3) dominance, (4) independence, (5) love and affection, and (6) physical comfort.

Broader Conceptions

The preceding concepts are more relevant for the testing of theoretical principles than for clinical use. The four descriptive concepts that follow are more useful in the clinical situation.

1 *Need potential* is defined as the mean potentiality of a group of functionally related behaviors occurring in any segment of an individual's lifetime. The classification of behaviors into need groups was considered above. A practical estimate of need potential may be arrived at by sampling behaviors in a variety of situations. Individual deviations from the cultural definitions of the nature of external reinforcements must be considered. To estimate a person's need potential, one should have a thorough knowledge of the individual's prior learning background, his own description of his needs and the significance of his behavior, and a broad general knowledge of all of his behavior. Need potential must be separated from expectancy.

2 *Need value* is the mean preference for a set of functionally related reinforcements. It involves the selection of one set of reinforcements over another, with expectancy held constant, and it is determined, like need potential, by preferences for alternatives. Here also, individual differences from cultural values must be considered. Need values may be classified as goals, using the same system that is used to classify need potential.

3 *Freedom of movement* is the mean expectancy of obtaining positive satisfactions as a result of a set of related behaviors directed toward the attainment of a group of functionally related reinforcements. High freedom of movement consists of expectancies of success for many behaviors, while low freedom of movement implies expectancies of failure or punishment. Freedom of movement is perhaps related to concepts such as anxiety and feelings of inadequacy. Behaviors known as defense mechanisms or escape mechanisms may be an indirect measure of freedom of movement or of the lack of it.

4 *The psychological situation* refers to the fact that behavior is related to the situation as perceived by the person who is performing the behavior. Although this has been recognized, little attention has been paid to the categorizing of psychological situations. It is proposed that situations be categorized in terms of their characteristic reinforcements, that is, in a manner parallel to the categorizing of psychological needs. An individual's classification of situations may differ from the cultural classification. Expectancies are dependent upon the characterization of the situation. The values of reinforce-

ments also vary with the situation. Social roles consist of learned behaviors appropriate to (or reinforced in) particular situations. The same situation may with experience (or new reinforcements) be categorized differently, thus resulting in changes in behavior (or expectation for future reinforcements) in the same situation. Categorization of people or events on the basis of some common objective characteristic of the stimulus or situation constitutes a social attitude.

Minimum Goal Levels

Potential outcomes may be placed on a continuum—for example, from failure to success—in terms of preference. The minimum goal level is the lowest goal or outcome perceived as a satisfaction. Levels vary widely among individuals. Maladjustment or dissatisfaction occurs when the minimum goal level is consistently above the reinforcements that follow behavior. Minimal goals may change with experience, although this usually occurs as a result of the changing standards of others—actual or anticipated—rather than as a direct or automatic result of success or failure. Some minimal goals are set by the culture and represent relatively inflexible standards.

Language in Social Learning

Verbalization appears to speed up both learning and extinction of behavior, including conditioned responses. Language as a stimulus may represent objects and events of both the past and the future through a process of symbolizing or abstracting. Words are thus cues, or they direct attention to specific cues in a complex situation, applying previous experience to a current situation, so that it can be dealt with on the basis of past learning rather than as a new situation to be handled by trial-and-error behavior. Language thus serves to enhance generalization. Words are also reinforcers, and even though their values are acquired, they are frequently more powerful as satisfiers than the original nonverbal stimuli.

Implicit language is difficult to define, but it seems to be a very important factor in changing behavior through changing expectancies by recategorization of situations. Language can be used to change other persons' expectancies and thus to change their behavior. The fostering of generalization may also be stimulated in others, with resultant behavior changes.

Social Learning Theory and Maladjustive Behavior

In social learning theory many of the concepts used in other systems to describe behavior are avoided. These include terms such as "maladjusted," "anxious," "neurotic," "conflicted," "abnormal," "repressed," and "unconscious," all of which refer to behavior that is felt to be in need of change through counseling or psychotherapy.

From the point of view of social learning theory, individuals who are candidates for therapy are those whose behavior is not satisfying and/or does not contribute to the welfare or satisfaction of others. In terms of this theory such persons have either low expectancies for gratification or low freedom of movement with high need value. They have minimum goals that are too high to allow for reinforcement or satisfaction.

Thus, anticipating punishment, they avoid situations either physically or by repression. They may attempt instead to reach goals by rationalization, fantasy, or symbolic means. Such behaviors are unreal. Other implicit behaviors, including awareness of disturbed body states, fixation, or punishment, narrowing the field of attention, and preoccupation with obsessive thoughts, may be present and may interfere with constructive problem-solving behavior.

Social reinforcement theory "attempts only to describe *how* social behavior is developed and changed—which behavior, if any, the clinical psychologist should accept as his responsibility to change, he must decide on some basis that goes beyond a systematic psychological theory." [7]

THE THERAPY PROCESS [8]

Psychotherapy is a learning process. The changes that take place both in and outside of the therapy room follow the same laws and principles. "The therapist himself has no special characteristic." [9] While the therapist may have some advantages over relatives in attempting to change behavior, he also has some disadvantages. For example, a change of attitude on the part of a child's parents may be more effective than hours of play therapy.

Social learning theory, like any other theory applied to psychotherapy, may be used in different ways or lead to different methods, depending upon the goals of the therapist, which are not a part of the theory or derivable from it. The goals of therapy accepted by Rotter are "helping the patient to lead a more constructive life, to contribute to society, to maximize his potential for achievement, to maximize his feeling of affection or contribution to others," and "to help the patient reach a state of greater happiness or comfort or pleasure." [10] The following value commitments are made: (1) The therapist expects his behavior to influence the client's behavior, as well as his goals and ethical judgments, and accepts some responsibility for these changes. (2) The therapist seeks to direct the client's behavior to goals that the client values or that will provide him with satisfaction. (3) However, the therapist avoids, or seeks to eliminate, goals that he feels are clearly detrimental to others in society. (4) The therapist believes that the client should make some contribution to society in return for the satisfactions he receives.

In an expectancy-reinforcement theory of social learning, such as this one, the therapist's function is to increase freedom of movement and to reduce need value. This is accomplished by changing expectancies and reinforcements, which results in changes in unrealistic minimum goal levels.

Changing Expectancies

In agreement with Mowrer [11] and Dollard and Miller,[12] the maladjusted person is seen as an individual who does not learn adjustive behavior automatically because he engages in persistent avoidance behavior that keeps him out of situations where he could learn more adjustive behavior. Although in the long run such behavior is not satisfying and is eventually punished, it is immediately satisfying and thus persists. Not only is punishment delayed, but it may not be as great as the anticipated punishment that is being avoided. In addition, maladjustive behavior may bring attention, sympathy, protection, or other desirable reactions.

Thus, the individual's high expectancy of punishment or failure causes him to continue avoiding situations, and he fails to learn that his fears are no longer realistic. Or he may have an expectancy that his avoidance behavior will lead to greater satisfaction (or less punishment) than would behavior seen by others as more desirable or adjustive. A major problem of therapy is thus "lowering the expectancy that a particular behavior or behaviors will lead to gratifications or increasing the expectancy that alternate or new behaviors would lead to greater gratification in the same situation or situations. In general learning terms we might say we have the choice of either weakening the inadequate response, strengthening the correct or adequate response, or doing both." [13] Research indicates that reward for the correct response is more effective than punishment for the incorrect response. Most approaches to therapy operate on the assumption that elimination of the bad response is more effective, and little attention is given to acquisition of adjustive responses. But it is difficult to eliminate maladaptive responses when the client has nothing better to substitute. Therapy, then, consists primarily of increasing the expectancy for gratification for alternative or new behaviors, and secondarily of reducing the potential for maladaptive behavior.

Changing Reinforcement Values

Changing the value of external reinforcements or goals requires changing the expectancy that immediate reinforcement will lead to specific subsequent reinforcements. The problem is essentially the same as that of changing expectancies for the occurrence of reinforcement, but with added practical difficulties.

The values of goals may be maintained over a long period of time with relatively stable expectancies for subsequent rewards if the relationships have not been verbalized and the individual is unaware of them. Thus, a delayed negative reinforcement may follow an earlier reward, but the individual may fail to see the relationship and may persist in seeking the goal. The values of goals can therefore be changed sometimes by analyzing earlier rewards, which may no longer be operating, and by recognizing present and future consequences that have not been associated with the goal. Insight into the acquisition of particular goals and into the delayed consequences of present behaviors and goals may lead to the changing of the values of goals.

Goals are usually firmly established and are often still being reinforced; they are thus difficult to change. In some cases it may not be the goal, but the way of reaching it, that is unacceptable, inadequate, or ineffective. "It seems a great deal easier to change the behavior that a person uses to reach a goal than to change the importance of the goal for him." [14] This may be regarded as a pedagogical problem; the client may be taught to search for alternative ways of reaching goals as a general method of dealing with his problems and of finding ways of achieving more satisfaction in his life. "The assumption that once the patient is free from some kind of internal disorganization, conflict, repression, etc., he will automatically be able to find adequate ways to reach his goals, does not appear useful to this writer. It is often precisely because the patient does not have alternate pathways that he frequently holds on to his less effective behavior in spite of insight into his situation." [15]

Low freedom of movement may be a result of using inappropriate behaviors, as well as a result of using ineffective behaviors. Inappropriate behaviors indicate a failure to make discriminations among social situations. Analysis, with the therapist, of the nature of different situations may help the client make these discriminations. Insight into others, including their thoughts, feelings, and expectations, is as necessary as insight into oneself.

The therapist's behavior varies, depending on the nature of the problem, the nature of the resources available outside of therapy, and the kind of client he is working with. Social learning theory implies that the therapist must show great flexibility in adjusting to the specific needs of the client. Since therapists are inherently limited in flexibility, perhaps there should be more concern with matching clients to therapists or with changing therapists early in therapy when this is indicated.

IMPLEMENTATION: TECHNIQUES OF COUNSELING

Structuring

Structuring is discussion concerned with the purpose and goals of therapy, the plans of the therapist, the respective roles of the therapist and the client, and the attitudes of each. It continues throughout therapy. It is minimal in therapy consisting of direct reinforcement, but of great importance in therapy involving rational techniques, verbal communications, and insight. The purpose of structuring is to get the client to attend to, react to, or concern himself with the appropriate things, instead of leaving the situation ambiguous or leaving what the client learns almost to chance.

In structuring, the therapist makes it clear to the client that while therapy includes understanding his attitudes and reactions and discovering alternatives to them, this is not sufficient for "cure": the client must have motivation to change and be willing to try out new behaviors. The practice of requiring the client to avoid important decisions is not acceptable, since it places him in a passive role; it should be made clear that the therapist is not going to make decisions or prescribe actions for him.

Limitations of therapy are also made clear to the client. "The objective is not to produce a perfectly adjusted person who has acquired some power to avoid frustration, but for the patient to learn to handle problems as they arise, to enjoy many aspects of his life more, and to deal with frustrations without allowing them to lead to self-defeating and socially unconstructive defenses." [16] The client's conceptions should be discussed, and any misconceptions corrected.

Structuring should be continued as necessary during therapy to explain what is occurring when improvement is followed by losses, when progress is not as rapid as the client expects, or when encouragement that therapy will be helpful is needed. "In other words, the patient's behavior of seeking help and coming for therapy must be reinforced so that the expectancy that it will lead to satisfaction is maintained at a high enough level to insure continuation of his efforts." [17]

Continued structuring is necessary to keep the client aware of why he is doing what he is doing and what the ultimate purpose of therapy is. Fixation on means, such as uncovering unconscious repressions, dreaming more interesting dreams, and achieving a less inhibited form of expression, must be avoided.

Relationship and Transference

The client must feel that the therapist is concerned with him, interested in him, wants to help him, and likes him; others who have attempted to change him may not have shown these attributes. On the other hand, the therapist must avoid the kind of personal involvement that others have with the client and that frequently interferes with attempts to change his behavior. The counseling relationship, as a result of its atmosphere of acceptance and reassurance, leads to the client's developing expectations for direct reinforcement from the therapist.

While the psychoanalytic conception of transference may be supported to some extent by the concept of generalization, it is actually contrary to the evidence regarding generalization. The therapist is quite different from other figures in the client's life; he is not a plastic medium onto which the client's attitude toward his parents or others can be projected; rather, the client sees him as an individual. Transference also relates to the degree of involvement the client has with the therapist. From a social learning point of view, it is a direct function of the amount of reinforcement the client receives or expects to receive from the therapist. The client becomes dependent upon the therapist for future satisfactions, and the relationship may involve affectional goals. This dependence upon the therapist for acceptance, warmth, and liking is not to be confused with dependence upon the therapist to solve the client's problems. While the therapist does not foster dependence, he must be able to accept the dependency needs of those clients who bring them to therapy.

The therapist's *acceptance* of the client as he is, without judgments of moral inadequacy, is apparently necessary for successful therapy. "If the therapist is able to accept the patient's problems as real, as problems that do not call for scorn or criticism but require understanding and help, the patient not only finds a comfort and satisfaction in the therapy situation but tends to generalize his expectations that the therapist will not react with criticism or punishment for his other behaviors." [18] Thus, he is able to speak openly and frankly about his attitudes and past experiences. The therapist must avoid any indication of sympathy or approval, which would reinforce existing attitudes such as projection of blame.

Certain kinds of *reassurance* seem to be required or are beneficial in therapy. These include reassurance that the client's problems are real and that seeking therapy is justified and not an indication of weakness. A second kind of reassurance involves fostering the expectation that therapy can be successful and can lead to satisfying alternatives in behavior. Of course, no guarantee of cure can be given by the therapist. A third kind of reassurance involves giving direct reassurance that the client is capable of achieving specific goals in order to increase his expectancy of success. Caution must be used, so that the client does not interpret this reassurance to mean that he does not need therapy, or so that he does not use reassurance as a substitute for actual accomplishments. From the social learning point of view, reassurance is a direct reinforcement, the occurrence of which increases the expectancy for future reinforcement for some behavior.

The therapist must limit the kind and frequency of direct reinforcement, as well as the direct satisfactions the client obtains from him, by interpretation of their relationship and of the client's defenses, in order to avoid the development of an extreme relationship in which the therapist becomes more satisfying as a person than anyone in the client's environment. He also uses his reinforcement value to develop independent behavior in the client, even encouraging the client to conclude therapy and try to get along on his own.

The therapist may obtain reinforcement from the client, becoming attached to him in a countertransference relationship. Such a relationship is not detrimental, but natural and helpful, as long as the therapist is aware of it and its influence.

Catharsis

Catharsis as the recall and reliving of earlier painful (and now repressed) experiences without the original punishment, resulting in extinction, only weakens an inadequate response pattern; it does not provide new responses. It is thus useful only in *some* cases and only as a part of therapy.

Catharsis as ventilation of feelings to a warm, sympathetic, accepting therapist reinforces the client's defenses, even though he may feel better as a result and become attached to the therapist. Catharsis as encouragement of the release of pent-up feelings, in play therapy or through expressive arts, may result in some extinction, but generalization may be limited. Catharsis through physical exercise and activities is similarly limited. Catharsis as discussion of past history and experiences, without dramatic recall or emotional reliving, may result in insight; but this is more the result of the therapist's direction and help than of the so-called carthartic process.

Thus, catharsis may be either harmful or useful, depending upon its nature and the activities of the therapist. Positive effects are the result of guided new learnings and the direct reinforcement provided by the therapist.

Insight

Insight is defined in many ways, often with a distinction between intellectual and emotional insights, the former usually being verbalization of understandings without any influence on behavior. Intellectual insight may not affect behavior, because the client is only repeating what the therapist has said or what he thinks the therapist will approve of. There may be stronger competing responses, strengthened over the years, which prevent the development of new responses. Or motivation to change may be low.

Verbalizing or understanding the underlying bases for behavior may lead to the development of new expectancies through the recategorization of previous experiences. In general, however, it has only the effect of reducing the expectancy for satisfaction from present maladaptive behavior, and thus reducing the behavior potential of such behavior.

New understanding and new learning may occur without the therapist's assistance or interpretation. "However, the patient's unguided discussions of past or present are usually not enough to effect substantial changes, nor are they efficient in any sense." [19]

Interpretation

The therapist may aid the client by guiding him, through interpretation, in the process of verbalizing his experiences, that is, by focusing the client's attention on particular aspects of his experiences or by directly suggesting explanations of relationships.

Almost all the verbal responses of the therapist may be considered as interpretations of some kind. Thus, the question of how much the therapist should interpret is essentially the question of how active the therapist should be. The social learning therapist would be fairly active in order to provide new experiences, ideas, and relationships. He would first need to develop an understanding of the client; although since many interpretations are in the form of questions, he would not need to have a complete knowledge of the client. As the client progresses, he has less need for the therapist's interpretations. Thus, the therapist is relatively inactive in the early part of therapy, becomes more active as therapy progresses, and then becomes less active again toward the end.

Interpretations may be ordered on a continuum in terms of the degree to which they may be threatening or provoke defensive behavior. The least threatening kind of interpretation is perhaps the directing of the client's attention to a particular aspect of his experience or his statements. This might be termed reflection of content. Reflection of feeling would be a little farther along the continuum. The leading question would represent a second stage of interpretation. The next stage might be the interpretative question: "Have you ever thought . . . ?" Direct statements are at the farthest end of the continuum and may vary considerably in their conditionality, from "Sometimes this means . . ." or "I wonder if . . ." to "It seems to me . . ." or "I think . . ." Stronger statements could, but probably should not, be made in therapy. It is desirable that the client achieve new meanings and relationships himself to as great an extent as possible, but it is often inefficient to wait for him to do so. The therapist faces the dilemma of wanting therapy to be as brief and efficient as possible and yet not wanting to push or hurry the process too much.

So-called deep interpretations may be dangerous in that they may result in new defense or avoidance behaviors more serious than the old ones. Some resistance to interpretation must be expected, however, and sometimes progress cannot be made without the occurrence of resistance and its subsequent interpretation. Deep interpretation of unacceptable motivations may result in changes in expectancies or reinforcement values and thus in behavior, but the importance of such interpretations may be overemphasized in comparison with the development of alternative new behaviors.

Interpretations need not be correct or "true" to be effective, but only plausible and acceptable to the client. They are more easily accepted when they are phrased in commonsense language than when they use theoretical concepts or complex terms such as psychoanalytical jargon.

Premature interpretation may lead to the client's leaving therapy, but progress may be delayed if interpretations are avoided because they meet with resistance. "In fact, the interpretation that is readily accepted is probably not necessary. *The interpretation that is in itself helpful and provides something new for the patient may have to be presented many times in many different forms before the patient accepts it, and it needs to be supported by different evidences or experiences of the patient himself.*"[20]

Threatening interpretations should be avoided when the relationship is not strong or if the patient is likely to react with increased maladjustment. Interpretations implying that the therapist has a good understanding of the client should not be made early in therapy, since the client may justifiably question the competence of the therapist.

The content of interpretation is not limited to a particular area, such as underlying motivation and childhood influences, but includes all areas. If there is any place of emphasis, it would be on the relationships between client behavior and the behavior of other people in his present situation.

This discussion has dealt with the utilization of common techniques in therapy within a social learning framework. It might be well to summarize or integrate them in terms of how they are used to achieve the changes in expectancies and in reinforcement values to which therapy is directed.

Techniques of Changing Expectancies

Five ways are suggested to increase the expectancy for gratification for new behaviors: (1) Direct reinforcement is the most direct and simple way. Adjustive behaviors are used in some situations by maladjusted persons. The therapist can teach parents to reinforce these behaviors when they occur in children. With adults this is more difficult to do; therapists don't leave their therapy rooms to work with relatives, associates, and bosses. The therapist can, and does, reinforce adjustive behavior—chiefly verbal behavior—in therapy. (2) The therapist can place the client in, or help him find and enter, situations where he may observe alternative behaviors and their consequences in others, or as in group therapy, where he can try to understand the behavior of others retrospectively. (3) The therapist may deal with the client's history of alternative behaviors, reducing his expectancy that they will now result in the negative reinforcements as they did in the past, and verbally increasing his expectancy that these alternative behaviors will now lead to gratification. (4) The therapist may discuss new possible alternatives, showing how the behaviors are carried out and creating an expectancy that they may lead to gratifications. (5) The therapist can create and reinforce an expectancy that the client may solve his problems more effectively by looking for and trying out alternative solutions or behaviors.

In lowering expectancies for reinforcement the therapist may also use direct reinforcement or a verbal technique. By failing to react with concern, sympathy, protection, or attention, the therapist may reduce the potentiality of previously rewarded behavior. Failing to reinforce such behavior may place a strain on the relationship, and such a technique should be balanced by positive rewards for desired behavior. Verbal methods may contrast the client's past situation with the present to point out the carryover of inappropriate expectations. In his discussion the client may discover that the punishments or failures he has been avoiding are not likely to occur now. Reduced expectancy for punishment will lead to reduced expectancy that he is achieving any goal by his avoidance. By himself or through the therapist's interpretation, he may also discover that punishment is not avoided in this way, but only delayed.

Techniques for Changing Reinforcement Values

Often direct reinforcement is not effective in changing expectancies for subsequent reinforcements, since these are further removed from behavior directed toward the initial reinforcement and the client may not associate them with the problem behavior. Verbal interpretation seems necessary and desirable in attempts to change goal or need values. Such verbal interpretations may be used with children. Reinforcement of goal values may also be changed by verbal analysis of past experience and of present experiences, as well as of future experience. Such analysis frequently concerns the relationships between goals and past, present, and future dissatisfactions.

The reduction of minimum goal levels may be achieved by reinforcing lesser accomplishments with praise instead of punishment, criticism, or exhortations to do better. Direct reinforcement by the therapist, through acceptance and understanding rather than criticism and condemnation of transgressions, errors, and inadequacies, is effective here. Discussion of the inadequate bases on which, or inappropriate manner in which, high standards or minimum goal levels were established is possible.

Therapy must be flexible rather than technique-centered. Different people learn most effectively under different conditions. One may need little interpretation, while another may benefit from relatively threatening interpretations. One may change more quickly through verbal analysis of the origins of his behavior, while another may respond more to the therapist's direct reactions to his behavior. But in every case the therapist is guided by the same set of logical principles based upon social learning theory.

Reinforcement is a principal method in therapy. The warmth, understanding, and acceptance expressed by the therapist make him an important source of reinforcement to the client. At the beginning of therapy reinforcement leads to the development of a relationship in which the client learns to desire and expect reinforcement.

The experience of success early in therapy provides reinforcement of the client's interest in continuing therapy and reduces resistance to change. Such success can be assured by dealing first with problems that are of minor significance or of recent origin and thus are most amenable to change.

Generalization of changes in behavior from the therapist in the therapeutic situation to other people in situations outside of therapy does not occur simply or automatically. The therapy situation and the therapist's behavior are quite different from what the client experiences elsewhere. It is necessary for the therapist to deal with these other situations, at least on a verbal level, in therapy.

The effectiveness of reinforcement appears to be related to "the degree to which an individual feels that what happens to him is a function of his own characteristics, skills, behavior, etc., or, instead, depends on events external to himself over which he has no control." [21] Those who have a high degree of belief in external control, and who see reinforcements as being lucky or the results of others' actions, appear, on the basis of research studies, to be less susceptible to the influence of positive reinforcement and to persist in behavior that is not reinforced. With such clients an analysis of this attitude may be required before change can take place.

The implications of social learning theory for therapeutic practice may be summarized as follows:

1   Psychotherapy is a learning situation in which the function of the therapist is to assist the client to achieve planned changes in his behavior and thinking. Since clients have different motives, values, goals, expectancies, and skills, conditions of optimal learning will vary, so that the therapist must be flexible and willing to experiment. Thus, there is no technique that is applicable to all clients.

2   Client difficulties are frequently seen as problems that can be solved through the application of problem-solving skills such as searching for alternative approaches to goals, seeing differences or making discriminations, and recognizing the needs and attitudes of others.

3   The therapist generally sees his role as partly one of guiding a learning process and thus actively engages in interpretation, suggestion, and direct reinforcement. "The therapist, however, does not consider himself merely a mechanical verbal conditioner, but rather a person whose special reinforcement value for the particular patient can be used to help the patient try out new behaviors and ways of thinking. The patient ultimately determines for himself the value of new conceptualizations and alternate ways of behaving in his experiences outside of therapy." [22]

4   While an understanding of the origins of behaviors and expectancies is important and is an aspect of insight, of greater importance is insight into the future consequences of behaviors and the influence of expectancies on present behavior.

5   In social learning emphasis is placed upon the client's understanding of others. "It is usually believed that what the patient lacks most is insight into himself, but it is likely that in general what characterizes patients even more consistently is lack of insight into the reactions and motivations of others." [23]

6   Important insights and new experiences occur in the life situation, not in the therapy room. Thus, there must be discussion in

therapy of the client's current experiences, and when possible, the client's environment must be controlled and manipulated.

7   Psychotherapy is a social interaction in which the laws and principles that obtain in other interpersonal situations apply. The therapist is an active partner in the process, applying learning principles to help the client achieve a better way of dealing with the problems of life.

SUMMARY AND EVALUATION

Rotter outlines a reinforcement-expectancy theory of social learning. Seven postulates and their corollaries are presented. These define the theory in terms of underlying assumptions. Personality is the interaction of the individual and his meaningful environment. The area for study is psychological behavior, which is not dependent upon any other field such as physiology or neurology; these are different ways of describing the same events. Experiences interact in a unified personality. Behavior has a directional aspect—it is goal-directed. Behavior is determined not only by goals or reinforcements but by the anticipation or expectancy that these goals will be achieved.

Three basic constructs are proposed to describe and predict behavior. *Behavior potential* is a function of *expectancy* and *reinforcement value;* or in broader terms, *need potential* is a function of *freedom of movement* and *need value.* Maladjustive behavior is behavior that is unsatisfying. Maladjusted individuals have low freedom of movement with high need value; that is, they have low expectancies for gratification and high goals. Often they are individuals who have minimum goal values that are too high to allow for satisfaction or reinforcement.

Counseling or therapy is directed toward changing expectancies and reinforcement values to allow for satisfaction and reinforcement. Inadequate responses must be weakened and adequate responses strengthened. Social learning theory emphasizes the acquisition of new, adjustive responses, rather than, as in the case of most other approaches, the elimination of bad responses. Therapy is concerned not merely with assisting the client in obtaining a better understanding of himself but with changing his behavior. The therapist is active, using both direct and verbal reinforcement, including interpretation. Therapy is concerned not only with what happens in the interview situation but with the changes resulting from new experiences that occur as the result of trying out new or alternative behaviors.

Rotter's theory not only utilizes the reinforcement theory of Hull and the expectancy concept of Tolman but includes aspects of the theories of Lewin, Adler, and others. Phenomenology is implicit in Lewin's concept that the individual interacts, not with any real or objective world, but with a meaningful world, or the world as perceived (or organized or constructed) by the individual. It is thus a comprehensive theory, and as a social learning theory, goes beyond learning theories that are simply transplanted from animals to man. Its empirical concept of reinforcement is not subject to the criticisms made of a drive reduction theory of reinforcement. The addition of expectancy to reinforcement gives the theory an advantage over a single-variable drive or need theory. It goes beyond orthodox behaviorism in recognizing and accepting implicit or internal behavior. The theory is supported by a number of research studies that were derived from the theory and conducted to test deductions from it.

Comprehensiveness is associated with complexity, a characteristic recognized by Rotter. But his theory also tends to be abstract, with relatively little content. Its concepts (accompanied by symbols and formulas) are sometimes difficult to comprehend, and the argument difficult to follow, partly as a result of the use of a terminology that must be learned. Although the basic concepts are few, they represent complexes or classes of variables, which tend to be confusing at times and difficult to keep in mind. Rotter feels that a complex theory is necessary in view of the infinite complexity of human behavior. This may be true, but even a complex theory must, and can, be organized and presented clearly, systematically, and simply. Rotter is fairly successful in doing this, although not as successful as Dollard and Miller. The theory is difficult to understand in terms of, or to transfer to, clinical and everyday behavior, whereas Dollard and Miller have successfully done this for the reader. Concepts are not always phrased in the simplest form for communicating understanding, and there are instances of poor grammatical construction which impede understanding.

In spite of its comprehensiveness and complexity, the theory is probably oversimplified or incomplete, as Rotter would no doubt be ready to admit. While incorporating many of the concepts in general use in other personality and behavior theories, Rotter excludes others, such as maladjustment, neurotic behavior, the unconscious, psychosomatic illness, anxiety, the self, and conflict, and discusses his reasons for doing so. In some cases, however, it would appear that the rejected concepts are, to some extent at least, included in his system. The self and anxiety are two such concepts. The psychological unit of the person is similar to the self, and Rotter notes that the expectancies that a person has regarding the outcome of his behavior might be considered as the self-concept. Anxiety is felt to be an ambiguous concept with varying connotations and definitions, and behaviors commonly included under it are felt to be accounted for in other ways. But as Rotter recognizes, anxiety may be an expectancy—the expectancy of punishment. It would appear that concepts that have such general acceptance and apparent usefulness should be included in the system, refined if necessary, or redefined in terms of the variables of the system.

The approach to counseling or therapy is not greatly different from many, if not most, other approaches. It shares with the other conditioning and learning theory approaches the concern for behavior outside of the therapy situation. It utilizes most of the techniques that other approaches commonly use and in much the same way. It tends to be an active approach. Yet it recognizes the importance of the relationship between the counselor and client, and the importance of the participation of the client in learning—including the desirability of the discovery method of problem solving, in which the client achieves his own solutions. On the other hand, it is concerned with efficiency, being unable always to wait for the client to reach his own solutions, lacking confidence that all clients can do so, at least within acceptable time limits. Although not emphasized or specifically identified as such, one reason that clients cannot be expected to achieve solutions alone, without active interpretation, is discussed. This is the concept of secondary gain, which suggests that a client is not likely to give up easily, or without resistance—without some pressure, coercion, or support from the therapist—behaviors that may be providing him with considerable satisfaction.

The theory as a whole is coherent, consistently developed, and consistently applied to counseling, although not as rigorously developed as Hull's theory. Undefined terms are used at times, along with implicit assumptions. Causality is denied, yet there appears to be at least implicit acceptance of causality in the relationship between reinforcement and expectancy and behavior potential. Details, particularly in techniques of application, are lacking. There are no verbatim illustrations of the counseling process. Nevertheless, the theory stands as one of the better attempts at a systematic approach to behavior and its change through counseling or psychotherapy.

The emphasis upon learning leads to emphasis upon a rational, problem-solving approach to counseling, with neglect of feelings and emotions. However, Rotter's approach is an advance over traditional learning theory approaches in at least two respects. One is the concept of expectancies, which makes this a theory looking toward the future rather than the past. The second is the concern with the social aspects of learning and behavior. These two concepts generate a counseling situation concerned with present behavior and with its future consequences, as well as with expectations of the future, and with the current experiences of the client in his social interactions with others.

REFERENCES

[1] Rotter, J. B. *Social learning and clinical psychology.* Englewood Cliffs, N.J.: Prentice-Hall, 1954.   [2] *Ibid.,* p. 80.   [3] *Ibid.,* p. 98.   [4] *Ibid.,* p. 103.   [5] *Ibid.,* p. 136.   [6] *Ibid.,* p. 116.   [7] *Ibid.,* p. 226.   [8] This and the following section, "Implementation: Techniques of Counseling," incorporate material from Rotter, J. B. Some implications of a social learning theory for the practice of psychotherapy. In D. J. Levis (Ed.), *Learning approaches to behavior change.* Chicago: Aldine, 1970. Pp. 200–241.   [9] Rotter, J. B. *Social learning and clinical psychology.* Englewood Cliffs, N.J.: Prentice-Hall, 1954. P. 335. [10] Rotter, J. B. Some implications of a social learning theory for the practice

of psychotherapy, *op. cit.*   [11] Mowrer, O. H. Learning theory and the neurotic paradox. *Amer. J. Orthopsychiat.,* 1948, **18,** 571–610. (Also in O. H. Mowrer, *Learning theory and personality dynamics.* New York: Ronald, 1950. Pp. 483–530.)   [12] Dollard, J., & Miller, N. E. *Personality and psychotherapy.* New York: McGraw-Hill, 1950.   [13] Rotter, J. B. *Social learning and clinical psychology.* Englewood Cliffs, N.J.: Prentice-Hall, 1954. P. 338.   [14] *Ibid.,* p. 346. [15] Rotter, J. B. Some implications of a social learning theory for the practice of psychotherapy, *op. cit.*   [16] Rotter, J. B. *Social learning and clinical psychology.* Englewood Cliffs, N.J.: Prentice-Hall, 1954. P. 354.   [17] *Ibid.,* p. 356.   [18] *Ibid.,* p. 361.   [19] *Ibid.,* p. 380.   [20] *Ibid.,* p. 391.   [21] Rotter, J. B. Unpublished paper, 1962.   [22] Rotter, J. B. Some implications of a social learning theory for the practice of psychotherapy, *op. cit.* [23] *Ibid.*

8

Learning foundations of behavior therapy: Kanfer and Phillips

Frederick H. Kanfer (1925–   ) obtained his B.S. in 1948 from Long Island University, and his M.A. in 1952 and his Ph.D. in 1953 from Indiana University. From 1953 to 1957 he was Assistant Professor of Psychology at Washington University; from 1957 to 1962 he was Associate Professor of Psychology at Purdue University; and from 1962 to 1969 he was Professor of Medical Psychology and Psychiatry at the University of Oregon Medical School (Portland). He is now Professor of Psychology at the University of Cincinnati. He is a Diplomate in Clinical Psychology of the American Board of Professional Psychology. Since 1954 he has been writing extensively in professional journals on learning and psychotherapy.

Jeanne S. Phillips (1929–   ) received her B.A. in 1951 and her Ph.D. in 1957 from Washington University, where she was an Assistant in 1951–1952, Teaching Assistant in 1952–1953, and a Fellow in Medical Psychology in the Medical School from 1953 to 1955. From 1955 to 1957 she was a Research Fellow at Massachusetts General Hospital. In 1957 she went to the University of Oregon Medical School (Portland), where she was Instructor of Medical Psychology from 1957 to 1959, Assistant Professor of Medical Psychology from 1959 to 1965, and Associate Professor from 1965 to 1969, when she became Professor of Psychology at the University of Massachusetts. She is now

Professor of Psychology at the University of Denver. She is also a Diplomate in Clinical Psychology of the American Board of Professional Psychology.

BACKGROUND AND DEVELOPMENT

Kanfer and Phillips developed their interest in presenting their integration of behaviorally oriented therapeutic practices from their experiences with graduate students in clinical psychology, interns, and residents as well as experienced clinicians in the Department of Psychiatry at the University of Oregon Medical School. They "became aware of the clinician's great need for a storehouse of behavioral psychological principles" as a basis for clinical practice. They felt that the student needed more than an understanding of the technology of the specific behavioral techniques that were attracting attention in the early 1960s. Armed with these principles, "any professional should be able to judge for himself the appropriateness of a given technique for his own cases or research. He should be able to construct idiosyncratic treatment programs to suit the circumstances of a particular clinical situation. He should be able to adapt to the changes and innovations that are inevitable and necessary in a new and often unproven field. By his grasp of the ties between theory, laboratory investigation, and application, the professional should understand the utility and limitations of various techniques." [1]

PHILOSOPHY AND CONCEPTS

Kanfer and Phillips refer to their work as "an integrated storehouse" of behavioral psychological principles and methods, or a "cohesive framework" for a general understanding of these methods.[2] It is not "a manual for clinicians, however. Its main purpose is to present the research and theory underlying the current application of learning principles and techniques to therapeutic change, as well as to point out the problems involved in practical usage." [3] It is thus research-based, rather than clinically based. Basic behavior theory is covered "as it applies to the treatment of behavioral problems, rather than dwelling on the causes of human maladjustment or the significance of the person's behavioral adjustment in his own life," though these are recognized as important.[4] Similarly, biological and cultural variables, though significant, are only touched upon.

Profiting from the advancement of other fields of psychology, the learning principles approach to clinical behavior change provides a broader, more flexible frame of reference than other approaches, and thus places clinical psychology in the position of an applied science that can contribute both to human welfare and to the understanding of human behavior. This approach rejects the medical disease concept and the current psychiatric diagnostic system. The locus of psychological problems is not in people's mental apparatus, but in the integration of people with their social environment.

The behavioral learning model based upon neobehaviorist methodology and experimental learning data, with the methods of behavior modification derived from it, is primarily a content-free model. Its methodology focuses upon the systematic analysis of behavior, in order to specify functional relationships between independent variables and response classes. No theory can encompass all the details of human behavior, but this is not necessary for effective therapeutic intervention. The clinician must exercise skill and judgment in applying the general principles of psychology to the individual case. Although incomplete, the learning model, which includes perceptual, motivational, and biological phenomena, integrates the results of research on behavior change, and has led to the development of the clinical techniques comprising behavior therapy.

The theoretical orientation adopted tends toward Skinner's point of view, but includes elements from social learning, cognition, and other pertinent areas. The theory attempts to utilize all the findings of experimental psychology, not those of learning and conditioning alone. Thus, it draws upon research in perception, cognition, emotion, and social psychology and interpersonal relations, going far beyond the stimulus response model. "A simple conditioning model may be a basic beginning for a learning approach to behavior change, but it does not reflect the limitations of this approach in taking advantage of man's manifold potentialities." [5] The scientific methodology and a few basic principles are the foundations for the clinical researcher to build on or to use in developing progressively better approximations to a model of human behavior.

The Behavioral Learning Model

The behavioral learning model of psychopathology and therapy has only recently received widespread attention in competition with the psychodynamic model. The latter model developed from clinical experience, philosophical considerations of the nature of man, and conceptualizations concentrating on subjective experiences. Learning models have developed out of laboratory studies, with emphasis on observation and manipulation of objective events, and reduction of complex variables into simpler components.

No single learning theory exists today, nor is there any theory, as yet, capable of handling social, perceptual, verbal, and intrapersonal processes, although progress is being made. Skinner's approach, particularly, has stimulated research in the analysis of complex behaviors. This approach serves as a basis for organizing the methodological characteristics and assumptions about human behavior that are common to most learning approaches.

COMMON ASSUMPTIONS OF BEHAVIORAL LEARNING MODELS

1   The learning-based model focuses on *behavior*. A person's activity is described in objective terms without resort to theoretical

constructs or concepts. The person's verbalizations and self-descriptions are behaviors.

2   In the learning model, an attempt is made to change deviant behavior or symptoms directly, not to modify traits, impulses, or other hypothesized personality structures. A symptom is "any target response selected for change," and "does not imply a surface indicant of underlying causes or a disease state. Recognition that the environment plays a crucial role in determining behavior implies that the appearance of symptoms may be restricted to an identifiable range of situations and is not invariantly characteristic of the person's behavior." [6]

3   All behaviors, including social response patterns, responses to emotional stimuli, and the learning of skills, result from the operation of the same principles of learning that (together with biological and social conditions) shape any class of behavior.

4   The common methods of inquiry of all other sciences are accepted in the learning model.

5   "Although training is necessary to enable any observer to recognize and reliably report the incidence of a specified behavior, no greater skill or theoretical knowledge is needed for learning approaches than for observation of any behavior—in man or animal, in naturalistic settings or in the laboratory. . . . Precise definition of the observed (or treated) behavior, and the underlying requirement for dealing only with publicly observable responses, therefore permit use of observers with limited knowledge of psychological theory." [7] Additional training and talent is required, however, for the formulation of a behavioral analysis and a treatment program and its evaluation.

6   While the importance of past events in the *formation* of learned behaviors is recognized, programs for behavior modification deal with *current* behaviors, which constitute the problem.

In contrast to the psychodynamic approaches to assessment and treatment, the behavior modification approach emphasizes empirical data and experimental techniques.

THE BEHAVIORAL EQUATION AS A UNIT OF ANALYSIS   Behavior is continuous, but for purposes of study it must be partitioned into segments. The formula for the behavioral equation may be written as:

←——Antecedent ←——Consequent
　S　　O　　R　　K　　C

where
　　S = prior stimulation
　　O = biological state of the organism
　　R = response repertoire
　　K = contingency relationship
　　C = consequence

The behavioral equation summarizes *all* the relevant conditions acting at the time of the response, thus indicating that all behavior is considered a function of specific and limited determinants, which are fully represented by the elements in the equation.

The response, R / Responses have been classified as *respondents,* when they are elicited by a specific stimulus without training, and as *operants,* or *instrumental responses,* when the eliciting stimuli are not known and the responses are conditioned by their consequences. The value of the distinction has been questioned. The most significant difference is that respondents are modified by variations in prior stimulus conditions, while operants are modified by changes in subsequent reinforcing consequences. Simple operants are rare; most responses are under the control of some signal, cue, or discriminative stimulus and, therefore, can be brought under stimulus as well as reinforcement controls.

Emotional behaviors, involving autonomic activity, are considered to be respondents and are controlled by stimulus control. Behaviors involving the skeletal system, motor movements, and verbal responses are operants and are controlled by the manipulation of consequences. Clinical behavior modification deals mainly with operants. Most specific behavior patterns are learned and can be modified. Man is highly pliable.

Responses are not limited to body movements, but include social and verbal responses. The latter are responses and are not to be taken as substitutes for mental events, internal states, or other inferred processes. Covert processes—thinking, perceiving, controlling oneself, or deciding—can be dealt with "only when they can be directly measured, observed, or defined in such a way that there need be no recourse to hypothetical intervening events that are not demonstrable. Whether the behaviors examined are ordinarily overt or covert, responses are defined by the experimental operations performed to measure or manipulate them." [8] It is often difficult in clinical work to achieve clarity of response specification. Most target responses, such as enuresis, phobia, and depression are very general classes without operations for precise identification and measurement.

Responses are usually treated as dependent variables, and their "causes" sought. But in behavior therapy they are also treated as independent variables, in terms of their consequences for others as well as for the person.

External and Internal Environments, S / While the unconditioned stimulus in respondent behavior is inherently related to the response that it elicits, in operant conditioning control is built up by discrimination through differential reinforcement. Although free operant behavior does not involve the S of the behavioral equation, operants encountered in the clinic are not randomly emitted; they are emitted and reinforced only in the presence of some environmental signal or discriminative stimulus (SD). Thus, the stimulus is a *discriminated operant.* Discriminative stimuli include stimuli produced by the person himself as well as by others. Behavior is composed of series, or chains, of responses in which one response becomes a discriminative stimulus for the next response, each response being affected by the terminal consequences.

The stimulus components must be defined from the viewpoint of the behaving organism, not from that of the observer.

Social influences are mediated by discriminative stimuli provided by persons in the environment. Such influences vary with different social and cultural environments.

The Organism, O / There is disagreement about the influence of biological or genetic factors in behavioral disturbances. Whatever the degree of influence, biological characteristics, both permanent and temporary, must always be included in the behavioral equation. Since attitudes toward biologically deficient conditions differ, the social milieu must be taken into account in the definition of biological adequacy.

The Consequence, C / Thorndike's *law of effect,* Hull's *drive reduction* principle, and Skinner's *reinforcement* are all recognitions that the consequences of a response influence the subsequent probability of the occurrence of the response. "The effectiveness of a reinforcing stimulus for a given response varies as a function of all the components in the behavioral equation. . . . Even a reinforcing stimulus that appears to have a fairly constant physical relationship to an organism's activity may produce opposing effects under changing conditions. . . . In fact, in application of operant learning methods to behavior modification it must constantly be remembered that a particular event selected as a potential reinforcing stimulus can be so defined with certainty only *after* it succeeds in changing the probability of the preceding response." [9]

Conjugate reinforcement requires continuous behavior to maintain the reinforcing event. In *episodic reinforcement* a long sequence of events is required before reinforcement occurs. Much complex social behavior represents conjugate or episodic reinforcement.

The Response-Consequence Contingency Relationship, K / There are many different relationships between behavior and its consequences. Many behaviors have inevitable consequences because of the nature of our physical world. Social behaviors have few such inevitable consequences. Contingencies may be deliberately withheld and presented on schedules.

In schedules of reinforcement the *proportion (ratio)* of reinforced responses, or the time *interval* after which reinforcement is given may vary. Ratios or intervals may be *fixed* or *variable. Multiple,* or combination, schedules often characterize human behavior.

The speed with which a response is acquired, its strength, and its decay or extinction are determined not only by its consequences but also by the schedule of reinforcement. Intermittent schedules (with less than 100 percent reinforcement) predominate. [Intermittent reinforcement is ineffective in learning, but when used following continuous reinforcement, it leads to resistance to extinction.]

In *shaping,* the experimenter at first reinforces behavior that is only similar to the behavior that is ultimately desired but does not exist at present. Responses that are more similar to the desired ones are gradually reinforced, and less similar ones left unreinforced, leading eventually to the performance of the desired behavior.

IMPLICATIONS OF THE BEHAVIORAL EQUATION IN CLINICAL USE   The behavioral equation is related to the assumptions of the behavior therapies.

Stress on current influences / Knowledge of the original controlling variables, which may be obtained from the patient's history, seldom indicates how the current behavior can be controlled. Current behavior is controlled by variables acting in the present. The clinician must locate these variables, whether they are S (stimulus), O (organism), or K (contingency) variables.

Symptoms are learned / If problem behavior is learned, then (1) it may be unlearned, or (2) the environment may be modified to eliminate the antecedent conditions that control it.

Subjective experiences / Clinical complaints often involve subjective reactions and feelings, which cannot be dealt with directly, since they cannot be brought under the therapist's control. However, "subjective experiences are assumed to have their origin in some earlier social experience and can be influenced through therapeutic operations." [10] Analysis of the patient's verbal reports of such behaviors can bring some of his self-reactions under control by his altering the behaviors leading to them.

Continuity of behavior across species / The behavioral model is derived from laboratory research with animals. Although the behavior of higher species is more complex, "the basic principles of learning are expected to remain unchanged for all living organisms and no special psychological principles are required for the understanding of human behavior. It is necessary to supplement the more general principles with special relationships due to the unique features of human life." [11] But the same methodological approach is appropriate for the analysis of these relationships.

The Clinician As Researcher

Behavior modifiers function as therapists and researchers. The clinician is bound by certain practical considerations, however: (1) His task is to observe and treat the single individual, whose behavior is subject to simultaneous influences from many uncontrolled variables. (2) The patient's condition requires immediate action, even though scientifically validated methods may not exist. Therefore, the clinician acts upon objective data and "educated guesses." (3) Scientific knowledge is blended with personal experience and information. (4) The clinician, since his decisions may have immediate and far-reaching impact on several people, must constantly evaluate his goals and methods for their effectiveness and social consequences. These practical considerations limit the solutions available to the therapist, leading to compromise solutions.

Scientific laboratory research requires systematic, empirical study involving control of all variables. There must be (1) focus on a preselected class of events (dependent variables), defined objectively so as to be publicly observable and measurable, (2) planned manipulation of one or more similarly defined other classes of events (independent variables), to assess their effects on the dependent variables, (3) avoidance of other sources of influence, and (4) attention to sampling of subjects, events, definitions, measures, and manipulations to allow for generalization.

The two models differ, yet they are similar and overlap. The behavioral clinician's plan of conduct should follow the steps followed by the experimental psychologist: (1) the formulation of the problem, (2) design of operational procedures to test hypotheses derived from the problem, (3) execution of the treatment (independent variables), (4) analysis of the data (dependent variables), and (5) evaluation of the implication of the results for the problem. In clinical procedures the steps are not as discrete, and there is more shifting back to the formulation, or reformulation, of the problem, as well as changes in treatment. Also, the direction of change is predicted, not simply an effect. The clinician cannot eliminate or control extraneous variables; he may use them therapeutically, however, since he is not mainly concerned with understanding but with control. Favorable outcome supports his assessment of the problem and choice of procedures, as accurate prediction supports the hypothesis of the experimenter. The clinician discontinues the process when favorable effects are produced, even though he is not clear about how it was achieved. Since extraneous circumstances affect outcomes, outcome alone is not validation —or lack of validation—of his hypotheses. "Behavior change, not understanding, is the clinician's main goal." [12] And it is limited to the specific problem presented rather than change in the total life pattern of the patient.

The clinician deals with the individual case. Objective, reliable behavior records, comparable to the scientist's laboratory data, are the goal of the behaviorist. However, his observations are limited for practical reasons, though he often goes beyond the office interview and subject report to direct observation. Even here, however, the clinician cannot, as in a laboratory experiment, control situational variables.

The individual case approach can be subjected to research analysis. Skinner and other operant conditioning researchers utilize the single case for a functional analysis of behavior. General statements of relationships are derived from replication with other individual cases. The procedure for such research involves (1) a baseline, or free-operant, measure of the dependent variable (A); (2) introduction of a treatment condition, with a second measure of the variable, or response (B); and (3) removal or cessation of the treatment condition, or a return to the baseline condition, with a third measure of the dependent variable (A). The therapist, of course, does not, or cannot, leave the patient in this condition, but reinstates the treatment. The fact that the condition is reversible with cessation of treatment constitutes a problem, of course, since the patient may revert again following treatment. The ideal clinical method would change behavior from A to B so that it is not easily reversible.

The clinician is a participant observer, which introduces bias in a number of ways, including his expectations of the patient. While some of these factors, such as the "demand characteristics" of the situation, are present in the laboratory as well as in the clinic, they are more prominent in the clinic.

Even though they recognize that their main responsibility is improving the patient's behavior, behavior therapists are aware of their potential for contributing to general psychological knowledge. Research, however, is limited by the restrictions of the clinical setting. Nevertheless, more than other therapists, the behavior therapist applies the scientific method to his actual practice in the clinic.

Behavior Therapy and Other Approaches

"Behavior therapists tend to select specific symptoms or behaviors as targets for change, to employ concrete, planned interventions to manipulate these behaviors, and to monitor progress continuously and quantitatively. A patient's early life history is largely ignored, except as it may provide clues about such factors as currently active events which maintain symptoms, or hierarchies of reinforcers. Behavior therapists tend to concentrate on an analysis of particular symptoms. They devote far less attention than other clinicians to subjective experiences, attitudes, insights and dreams." [13] They are more concerned with evidence from observations of behavior than from empathy. A planned, carefully outlined procedure is carried out with the monitoring of its effects.

The following behavioral assumptions underlie differences between the procedures of traditional therapy and those of behavior therapy:

1 Psychological problems are not viewed as diseases rooted in early faulty personality development.

2 The behavior to be changed is not a symptom of an underlying disease process, but is itself the problem. It is a learned response that is detrimental to the patient.

3 Treatment is directed toward changing the problem behavior.

4 Treatment methods are tailored to the individual's specific problems, not to a diagnostic label attached to him or his condition.

Relationship Variables

Behavior therapy is "only one area of application of knowledge from the broader field of behavior influence and interpersonal communication." [14] The variables of interpersonal influence are not technique-specific, and they are involved in any personal contact with a clinician, including behavior therapy. The quality of the interpersonal relationship influences the process and outcome of therapy, whatever the theory of behavior change or the techniques used. Thus, in behavior therapy the effectiveness of behavioral techniques may be enhanced or hindered by the therapist's personal and interactional characteristics. These characteristics may be used for deliberate enhancement of the therapeutic effect. However, the number and nature of specific variables, their interrelationships and the basic factors involved, and the mechanisms responsible for their effects are not well enough known for effective use of these variables. Two broad factors under which interactional variables may be classified appear to be positive social reinforcement and expectancy congruence between the therapist and the client.

The diverse variables, functional relationships and variables in laboratory and clinical studies of effective models, and social reinforcers must be clarified and integrated before they can be useful. Beyond this, the results must be translated into stimulus-response language and given demonstrable behavioral referents.

Relationship variables, such as "mutality of role expectations," are complex, and involve cognitions and expectancies that are often excluded from behavior therapy models. But a learning theory approach is not incompatible with such constructs if the behavioral events to which they refer are clearly defined, operational, and repeatable. Expectancies, attitudes, and "meanings" can be put into behavioral terms and incorporated into behavioral or learning methods of therapy.

Although relationship variables are viewed by some as the major effective variables in behavior change, they are viewed in behavior therapy as nonspecific effects.

The Humanistic Issue

The humanists' criticism of behavior therapy is that "the emphasis on behavior may run the risk of disregarding the value and dignity of human life itself." This questions the adequacy of the scientific method for the study of man. The objectivity and detachment of the method seem to involve the danger of reducing man to "nothing but" a set of relationships, leaving out the richness of feelings, ambitions, dreams, and agonies. "The implicit assumption appears to be that knowledge of laws that govern behavior is incompatible with sensitivity to the variations in the expression of these lawful relationships. This assumption is parallel to the assumption that a knowledge of chemistry or natural processes reduces the aesthetic and utilitarian values of products, such as stained glass windows, or natural processes, such as the bloom of flowers." [15] The high degree of control involved, with deprivation and restrictions to enhance the utility of incentives and the use of aversive stimuli, have led to fears of dehumanization, or the reduction of human beings to the status of animals.

But the success of behavior modification, even on a simplistic level, as in work with psychotic patients, increases the human dignity of the patients as they regain an ability for independent living.

Behavior modification is a technology that can be used for whatever purposes society wants to accomplish. It is nonhumanistic rather than antihumanistic, and nonethical in that it does not set standards or values, as do some other psychotherapeutic schools. It is pragmatic, and can be applied to achieve humanistic values and goals. These values originate in society and its institutions, not in the therapist. In modifying behavior, the therapist acts as an instrument representing the goals of others, either the patient or a social agency. However, as a citizen and humanist, the psychologist, with his knowledge of human behavior, is in a position to participate in the shaping or changing of value systems, particularly in providing methods of studying the consequences of different value systems.

The Issue of Control

"Each therapist must ask himself questions such as: To what extent do techniques of behavior control violate the individual's freedoms? Does *failing* to apply a potential technology for behavior change represent ultimate loss of freedom for the individual and society and an unjustified waste, or a necessary caution against manipulation?" Behavior therapy may be viewed as threatening humanistic values and respect for human dignity and choice. "Social prescription of behavior may ignore experiential and emotional needs, which are perhaps more basic to human fulfillment." [16] The therapeutic community of a mental hospital ward differs little from Chinese thought reform, both having the same assumption of social control "for your own good" and depending on the same procedures. "Whatever the setting, the danger is that a therapist may assume the right to decide how the patient and environment *should* act, using his own criteria of desired social effectiveness instead of the criteria offered by the therapeutic influence or society." [17]

The problem of social control applies to traditional psychotherapies, to the extent that they are effective, as well as to behavior therapy. Scientific progress leads inevitably to the ability to control behavior. The issue becomes that of "who controls whom, by what methods, in respect to which behaviors, and according to whose set of values." [18]

The picture of the behavior therapist as a cold automaton controlling the client is inconsistent with the knowledge of the importance of warmth, spontaneity, and genuineness in therapeutic effectiveness. The specific goals achieved by planned and subtle methods are compared unfavorably to the more fluid process of self-actualization as a goal, a goal also selected or prescribed by the therapist, and achieved by subtle, covert operations of the therapist. The abstract process goals reduce to the goals of the behavior therapist when they are operationalized.

Some object to the use of positive reinforcement as a method of control, since it is not easily detectable by the recipient or is characterized as a bribe. It is seen as more dangerous, more potentially threatening, and of lesser moral value than control by aversive stimuli; yet punishment is questionable as a method of control, both psychologically, and ethically and morally.

The behavior therapist is in a difficult position because he does not view the patient as sick. Therapy is sanctioned by society for sick people, and punishment for illegal acts. But society is not so clear about other behaviors. "Despite conflicting social values, the behavior therapist must decide which behaviors require change and which can be overlooked. By the nature of his work, the behavior therapist not only has to accept the onus of behavior control. Often he must also assume the burden of siding as an accomplice either on the side of the patient or on the side of society in determining what behaviors should be controlled. This issue is not easily resolved." [19]

The problem of the individual's rights and civil liberties is also present. However, it must be recognized that the patient is actually being controlled by his social environment, and the ethical problem is not simply one of control or no control. To leave the patient under the control of an unfavorable environment is an ethical decision.

While control in the acquisition of motor skills is valued, control of interpersonal skills and of complex functions is resisted. Some deny that behavior methods can control such complex functions as creativity, self-control, empathy, or value formation. Yet such control is sought in traditional therapy and by other means.

Behavior therapists are concerned about the ethics of control. They openly state their goals and operations, which may be rejected by the client or society. Behavior therapy "is doing in a planned and efficient way what other procedures strive for but approach with less efficiency or clarity; and the therapeutic goals are defined by society, its agents, or the patient and not by the theory underlying the modification process itself." [20] The problem of what social agency should establish acceptable goals for manipulation is an unsolved social issue for discussion.

BEHAVIOR THERAPY

Behavioral Diagnosis and Assessment

The process of assessment, or diagnosis, has been given inadequate attention by behavior therapists, although models and techniques for behavioral diagnosis are beginning to be suggested. Thus, rather than being based upon laboratory or clinical research, this area must deal with trends, tentative directions, and future potentials.

The goal of behavior therapy is the development of a complete set of psychological principles to apply to an individual patient from the initial presentation of his complaint to his discharge. This requires systematic methods of collecting information to appraise the patient's difficulties and to reach decisions about a treatment program. The behavioristic framework requires that the therapist (1) locate the problem and (2) translate the initial complaint into a language and a set of questions appropriate for available behavioral technology.

BEHAVIORAL MODELS OF PATHOLOGY   "The behavioral model of abnormal psychology has no place at all for traditional diagnostic labels in the formulation of treatment strategies." [21] Such nonspecific and unreliable labels are appropriate only for a therapy whose goals are vague, nonspecific, and subjective.

The medical model of psychopathology is rejected, as noted above. Two other, related, learning theory models have been proposed. One, accepted by the stimulus control therapies (the Pavlovian, classical conditioning therapies represented by Eysenck and Rachman), accepts the classification of neurosis, psychosis, and sociopathic and homosexual behaviors. Neurotic behaviors are viewed as classically conditioned respondents (anxiety) and behaviors reinforced by a reduction of the anxiety drive, and are "cured" by Pavlovian procedures. Psychotic behaviors are endogenous; operant conditioning of psychotic symptoms is referred to as "rehabilitation." Sociopathic behaviors represent a failure of conditioning, or an appetitive conditioning leading to unlawful behaviors.

Operant behavior modifiers tend to view all deviant behaviors as the result of untoward reinforcement processes, past and present; the behavior is deviant because it is discrepant from the behavior desired by the society or culture. Since behavior is a result of a multitude of interactions, it is difficult to obtain evidence of the reinforcement history of problematic behavior. Animal research and longitudinal studies may establish that various behaviors can be produced by various reinforcement patterns, but it may not be possible to specify this for the individual patient.

The traditional psychological tests of the clinical psychologist, including projective tests and questionnaires are of little use to the behavior therapist. "Behavioral assessment is aimed neither at personality description nor patient assignment to particular personality types. . . . Behavioral diagnosis attempts to provide information that permits the clinician to define targets for change, to identify conditions maintaining the undesirable behavior, and to select the most practical means for producing the desired changes." [22] Such a diagnosis requires a wide range of data, including historical, social, cognitive, and biological factors as well as directly observable behavior. These data may be organized under the following components: (1) analysis of the problem situation, (2) clarification of the problem situation, (3) motivational analysis, (4) developmental analysis, (5) analysis of self-control, (6) analysis of social relationships, and (7) analysis of the sociocultural-physical environment. The specificity of the data may be seen by the description of the first component: "The patient's major complaints are categorized into classes of behavioral excesses and deficits. For each excess or deficit the dimensions of frequency, intensity, duration, appropriateness of form, and stimulus conditions are described. In content, the response classes represent the major targets of the therapeutic intervention. As an additional indispensable feature, the behavioral assets of the patient are listed for utilization in a therapy program." [23] Data included are often direct samples of behavior, reports of past behavior, and patient self-ratings. Assessment is a continuing part of behavior therapy, with quantitative evaluation of change in target behavior and in therapeutic tactics on the basis of continuing monitoring.

The assessment of factors maintaining problem behaviors and of effective or potent reinforcers is particularly difficult at present, and is based on little more than hunches. The construction of behavioral assessment procedures is a difficult but feasible task, utilizing extensions of laboratory-analogue and response-sampling techniques.

Until such procedures are developed, the behavior therapist must operate upon the basis of clinical lore and judgment in evaluating patients and deciding where to intervene. "As yet the decision making processes of the behavioral clinician are poorly understood. There is little scientific basis for the selection of the best course of treatment for particular patient-target-environment combinations. The clinician tries to sort and match variables on the basis of a functional analysis to achieve the optimal solutions of the problems presented by an individual patient, with only the crudest rules to guide him. Many of the factors that influence the chosen treatment approach are not specific to the behavior therapies, although they are described in behavioral terms." [24]

Behavior Modification by Control of Stimulus-Response Arrangements

The classical conditioning paradigm controls an undesirable response by controlling the stimuli that elicit it. Emphasis is upon the S, O, and R, rather than the C, of the behavior equation. Aversion therapy parallels the classical conditioning model most closely. (Counterconditioning under Wolpe's reciprocal inhibition principle, using a positive new stimulus, includes other elements besides classical conditioning and is an example of a mixed model, to be discussed later.)

In *aversive therapy* a noxious unconditioned stimulus (UCS) (producing an unpleasant event) is paired with a stimulus associated with the undesirable behavior (CS). "It is assumed that the stimulus function of the CS becomes predominantly one of signaling the onset of an unpleasant, fear arousing event." The CS now evokes an unpleasant response that is incompatible with the original pleasurable consequence. "Its effects may serve to interrupt the objectionable behavior sequence. New and more appropriate responses can then be developed." [25]

Aversion therapy has been used extensively with sexual deviations, alcoholism, and enuresis. Its use in alcoholism may be taken as illustrative. The cues that are associated with alcohol and elicit drinking, including the sight, smell, taste, and thought of alcohol, are the conditioned stimuli; they are paired with unconditioned stimuli for pain or unpleasant reactions until they take on a similar stimulus function.

In early studies, in the 1920s, drugs were used as the unconditioned stimulus, and these studies were not too successful because of factors related to this (for example, impairment of conditioning because of sedation) and other factors. Thus, the method of treatment was abandoned for about twenty years. Antibuse, a drug that operates not through conditioning but by causing nausea and vomiting when followed by ingestion of alcohol, came into use. Emetic drugs (for example, emetine) have been used as unconditioned stimuli. Following injected and/or oral emetine, patients are given alcohol to smell or taste just before the expected onset of nausea and vomiting. In an early study of 4,000 patients, 60 percent remained abstinent for at least one year, 51 percent for at least two years, and 38 percent for at least five years. Electric shock has been used more recently as the unconditioned stimulus.

Alcoholism is difficult to treat because of the wide variability of the external and internal stimuli and their surroundings. In addition, there is difficulty in finding a competing alternative response. "Neither classically conditioned cues nor universal operant reinforcers present appropriate alternatives for the response of drinking alcohol. Hence, arriving at a substitute for drinking is difficult or impossible until one can state for *which* aspect of the chain of behaviors and consequences in alcohol consumption the substitution is made." [26] The same problem is present in treating overeating, use of narcotics, or cigarette smoking by conditioning. A punishment model may be more effective than aversion therapy. Therapy should include behavioral treatment of anxiety symptoms, development of social and vocational skills, and provision of necessary environmental reinforcers as well as aversion conditioning.

Imagined aversive events have been used, instead of drugs or shock, as the unconditional stimulus. The terms "covert sensitization" or "aversive imagery" have been used to designate this technique. The conditioned stimulus may also be imagined.

When the symptom itself is used as the conditioned stimulus, the assumption that classical conditioning is the basic mechanism is doubtful. When such behaviors are followed by aversive stimuli, the situation becomes one in which the aversive stimuli serve as punishing consequences for the symptom. In other cases, such as the treatment of alcoholism by aversive conditioning of the smell and taste of alcohol, the unconditioned stimulus has aversive reinforcing characteristics for other behaviors occurring immediately prior to its onset, such as raising the glass, taking a sip, and tasting. Thus, operant conditioning of these instrumental acts takes place.

The operant conditioning paradigm is likewise not pure. A reinforcing stimulus can become associated through classical conditioning to other cues in the situation that function as conditioned stimuli. "In our alcoholism example, if only the sight or smell of alcohol is used as the CS, and if preceding approach responses are ignored, then shock (UCS) is controlled by the experimenter and is delivered in a noncontingent fashion. If the subject's response of raising the glass and sipping from it is the critical response for shock delivery, and if spitting out the alcohol is immediately followed by termination of the shock, then the reinforcing stimulus is contingent and controlled by the subject's own behavior. He can avoid the UCS by not engaging in the target response." Effective treatment, as does the everyday behavior of alcohol consumption, may depend on both conditioning processes, "thereby changing the discriminative (or eliciting) and secondary reinforcing values of the CS (by classical conditioning) and suppressing the target response (R) while reinforcing an alternative response (by operant conditioning)." [27]

It is apparent that learning situations cannot be classified into classical or operant conditioning, even in the laboratory. Aversive stimulation in therapy includes three practices: (1) punishment, or use of an aversive stimulus to suppress undesirable behavior, (2) escape and avoidance learning, where the aversive stimulus serves to establish new responses that prevent or terminate the noxious stimulation, and (3) classical conditioning, where the aversive stimulus leads to unpleasant results that become associated with, and thus inhibit, the undesirable behavior. The distinction between aversive conditioning and punishment often depends upon whether the therapist identifies with classical or operant learning theory.

Combinations of classical and operant conditioning thus occur in most behavior therapy, with or without the intention of the therapist. Some therapists deliberately combine the procedures, particularly in the treatment of homosexuality.

Mixed Models of Stimulus and Response Control

The combination of classical and operant methods is particularly applicable to complex situations where emotional responses surround the target instrumental response, and where covert and overt verbal responses serve as controlling stimuli for behavior. The latter are cognitive mediating responses.

The major emotional response present in behavior disorders is anxiety. Since there are various, and unrelated, measures of anxiety, the selection of the therapeutic target presents a problem. The unconditioning of physiological-emotional responses may or may not result in changes in other behaviors. Many symptomatic responses are considered as adjustive reactions that avoid or terminate anxiety. When such actions successfully avoid the anxiety, there is the puzzling question of why they are continued, and are so resistant to extinction, since, because anxiety is never experienced, they are not reinforced by its relief or cessation. The problem has not been adequately resolved. The avoidance responses, rather than the anxiety responses themselves, often constitute the target for modification.

Awareness and instructions, operating through verbal structuring, influence the acquisition and extinction of responses in humans. Many behavior therapy techniques are based almost entirely on manipulation of verbal responses believed to affect other behaviors. Although a person cannot stop being anxious by simply telling himself not to be, labeling emotional states can affect behavior. Thus, cognitive factors are important in the person's regulation of his own behavior, and cognitive set (expectations) can influence anxiety and the effects of aversive stimuli.

Wolpe's method of reciprocal inhibition is a widely used method for treatment of neurotic anxiety. The subject is exposed to a weaker form of the conditioned stimulus presumed to have been originally conditioned to anxiety through association with some potent unconditional stimulus (desensitization), followed by the introduction of a response that is antagonistic to the anxiety response (reciprocal inhibition), which conditions a more probable competing response to the conditioned stimulus (counterconditioning). [See preceding chapter for more detail.]

Wolpe's method has usually been classified as classical conditioning. But it demands that an antagonistic response, toned with positive affect, be elicited and maintained, and such responses are usually operants. Thus, the method is a "mixed model." Assertive responses are such operants, and are usually rewarding when made by the patient. Relaxation, sexual behaviors, eating, etc., are also operant responses maintained by reinforcement.

Research involving controlled experiments on systematic desensitization support its effectiveness, but are not clear regarding the bases for its effectiveness. Relaxation alone and the relationship alone are not effective. And, apparently, desensitization alone is not usually effective, but desensitization with relaxation is effective. These results suggest that inhibition is more effective than extinction. Extinction is, however, effective, or more effective than counterconditioning in elementary avoidance responses.

"Flooding" rather than gradual desensitization appears to be effective in many situations. Stampfl's *implosion therapy* utilizes "flooding," without the counterconditioning or relaxation. The method is successful, and its *modus operandi* is assumed to be extinction. However, investigators other than Stampfl and his co-workers have not had as much success [see chapter on Wolpe], suggesting that other factors in the situation are important.

The influence of the reinforcing effects of the therapist's words and actions must not be overlooked in the classical or mixed model of behavior therapy. In the latter, as well as in operant conditioning, the fact that response-contingent reinforcement may serve as information may lead to behavior change through cognitive verbal control. The patient's evaluation of his own behavior may affect his subsequent behavior through a new set of controlling verbal stimuli that arises during the treatment process. Suggestion and verbal operant conditioning would also appear to function in desensitization therapy. It is apparent, then, that behavior therapy is not a simple matter of conditioning.

> Once the desensitization procedure is modified to suit the particular problems encountered with other behavior disorders [besides emotional arousal and phobic avoidance behavior], the very elegance and clarity of the systematic desensitization operations are lost. The restricted applicability of the desensitization paradigm to particular problems and the success obtained when this technique is fitted into the patient's total therapeutic program remind us once again to guard against the false hope that all the richness and complexity of human behavior may be encompassed by one single model. We must also keep in mind that it is naive to expect a single standardized procedure to be effective for all instances of a particular class of problems or to believe that only one therapeutic procedure may be applicable to each class of behavior problems.[28]

Moreover, the effectiveness of a therapeutic method does not necessarily substantiate the theoretical explanation of why it works. Although the mixed models discussed above have been demonstrated to be effective, the specific effective variables and necessary elements of the methods have not been clearly established, even though considerable research has been done. The models have been adopted widely, however, on pragmatic grounds.

Social Learning and Behavior Rehearsal

Social learning, through observation, imitation, or modeling, broadens behavioral learning principles, extending them to the characteristically human aspects of persons and their environments. Its recent development reflects dissatisfaction with the conditioning models and is an attempt to deal with more complex social phenomena and human capacities within the learning theory model. The acquisition of most adult behaviors is not easily explained in learning terms, particularly S-R learning.

Living organisms are not passive, but engage in exploratory behavior that changes their environment. Many species (including rats, monkeys, and humans) engage in behavior that results in the imitation of the behavior of peer models. They learn vicariously by observation.

The higher the level of the necessary behavioral repertoire for survival, the greater is the role of observational learning. Language, or the ability to verbalize observations, enhances such learning. Such learning can be used to change behavior in psychotherapy.

Five classes of observational learning can be differentiated:

1   *Matched-dependent learning,* or learning to imitate. The subject learns to follow the example of a leader, with reward for success.

2   *Identification.* The subject acquires noninstrumental (nonessential) idiosyncratic behaviors (style) of a model by observation and is not rewarded for specific instrumental responses but for imitation of the style.

3   *No-trial learning.* Following observation of a model, the subject is given opportunity to perform the same task without apparent practice or contingent reinforcement for his performance.

4   *Co-learning.* The model and the observer are engaged in the same learning task, with alternate opportunities for watching and doing.

5   *Vicarious classical conditioning.* The subject witnesses the administration of an unconditioned stimulus for an emotional response or the response itself, and its impact on the subject's observation, learning, and performance is measured. The arousal of emoional responses by observation of another person occurs frequently in the dramatic arts. The observer's vicariously elicited response becomes connected, through temporal contiguity, to formerly neutral stimuli.

Although there has been considerable research on observational learning, the theoretical aspects are vague and incomplete. Several different theories have been proposed, including Dollard and Miller's and Skinner's theories of matched-dependent behavior, Mowrer's and Bandura's theories of imitation, Gewirtz's model of conditioned discrimination learning, and Berger's vicarious instigation hypothesis. This lack of a clear conceptualization of the process may be related to the fact that therapists make little use of the methods.

Social learning, or modeling, has been utilized in behavior modification mainly in three forms. In the *modeling treatment of phobias,* subjects are exposed to live models or films depicting models who engage in activities related to the phobic object, for example, children playing with dogs, or adolescents and adults handling snakes. Live demonstrations appear to be more effective than films, unless films depict a broader range of models and aversive stimuli. Modeling has been shown to be more effective than desensitization in snake phobias in research done by Bandura and his associates.[29] Live modeling plus guided experience was most effective. Subjects who had failed to lose their phobias under symbolic modeling, desensitization, and control conditions all lost their snake-phobic behavior in a few sessions of live modeling with guided experience. Modeling of approach responses, according to Bandura, reduces the arousal potential of the aversive stimulus to a level that does not activate avoidance responses, allowing the observer to make approach responses, which do not result in aversive consequences.

Modeling approaches to interview behavior include exposing clients, prior to the counseling process, to interviews (either live, taped, or in typescript form) in which desirable client behaviors are modeled. Such behaviors can include problem statements and self-exploration. Discussion following the pretherapy exposure to modeling can reinforce the desirable behaviors. Whether such modeling is superior to simple instructions is not known.

In interview therapy the therapist serves as a model for the client. "In fact, the skillful therapist has often been described as a person who is able to model, by his comments and his actions, the way in which a patient ought to view himself, consider his problems, and arrive at an effective plan for action." [30]

Replication techniques do not clearly involve vicarious learning, but include the therapist's use of information input as stimulus control for therapeutic ends. These techniques replicate, or simulate, relevant parts of the patient's environment. The patient can then evaluate his problem behaviors and try out new behaviors in a protected environment. Such situations thus reduce anxiety and foster the elimination of problem behaviors by rehearsal or observational learning. Audio or video tapes of the patient's behavior enable him to discover improved behaviors. Role enactment, with reinforcement for new behaviors, can be used. Role playing, including psychodrama, provides feedback and practice in new behaviors. Kelly's fixed-role therapy enables the patient to practice new behaviors in an "as if" situation, which allows him to practice new behaviors and gain new perceptions and feedback. Behavior rehearsal is used as an adjunct to desensitization.

Neither the underlying process involved in vicarious learning nor the effectiveness of role rehearsal techniques has been established. The procedures are usually inadvertently or loosely used in therapy, rather than being deliberately applied.

Behavior Modification by Manipulation of Consequences

While classical conditioning focuses upon the S and O of the S-O-R-K-C equation and their relationships to the following responses, operant conditioning concentrates on the relationship of the response (R) to the subsequent elements, K and C. "Therapeutic interventions based on the operant model primarily rearrange contingent behavioral consequences, including rewards and punishments, in order to alter undesired behaviors or to remedy behavioral deficiencies. The operant paradigm, since it does not require specification of antecedent conditions, is more convenient for conceptualizing and manipulating a wide range of responses in natural settings that do not permit clear identification of eliciting stimuli." [31] The relation or interaction between the behaving organism and the environment is the focus of attention.

CHARACTERISTICS OF THE OPERANT PARADIGM   There are four aspects of the operant approach that are particularly relevant to therapeutic behavior change:

1   It is empirical, and there is no need for internal variables or mediational constructs. The existence of inner states or variables is not denied, but they are not considered necessary or relevant.

2   It is a practical engineering approach. While atheoretical, it is capable of testing hypotheses through variation of consequences. It focuses upon observable and easily measured behaviors, such as frequency of specific responses. Interest is in experimental control of behavior, and discovery of the independent variables that provide such control is sufficient, without further conceptual explanations.

3   Analysis of the single case is emphasized. The single individual is studied, and the effects of the consequences (C) or schedules (K) on the individual, rather than statistical analysis of group data, are of concern. Replication of effects on different individuals provides a basis for generalization.

4   The emphasis on present determinants does not deny the importance of historical variables. Problematic behaviors may have originated and have been maintained by determinants that no longer function. It is important to know the determinants for cases where they may be operating in the establishment of problem behavior, but when one is dealing with a current problem situation, it is sufficient if the present disturbing behavior can be modified by dealing with its current reinforcers without regard to its original determinants.

The response that is of concern in therapeutic behavior change may consist of a large response class such as "disruptive behavior." Positive reinforcement, negative reinforcement (removal of aversive stimuli), punishment, extinction, response differentiation or shaping, and discrimination are operations involved in treatment. The choice of procedures used in modifying a particular response class depends upon (1) availability of controlling stimuli, (2) the limits of the individual's repertoire for acquiring new patterns of simpler response components, and (3) the availability of reinforcing stimuli for therapeutic purposes.

Reinforcement Operations / "Reinforcement basically involves an environmental event or stimulus consequence (C) that is contingent upon the particular response (R) and whose occurrence increases the probability that the response will occur again." [32] It is not necessary to be concerned with how reinforcements work (through expectancy mechanisms, positive feedback mechanisms, contiguity mechanisms?) or what they have in common that determines their reinforcing power (drive reduction, change in hedonic state, production of central arousal?). It is sufficient that they work.

Reinforcement operations are of four kinds: positive stimuli can be presented (positive reinforcement) or removed (response cost) contingently, or negative stimuli can be presented (punishment) or removed (negative reinforcement), contingently. In addition, positive stimuli can be withheld after a period of presentation (extinction), and negative stimuli can be similarly withheld (avoidance). Complexity is introduced, since stimuli may be manipulated noncontingently as well as contingently. Further complications are present, since reinforcers cannot be defined in advance, being dependent upon the individual and the circumstances. Thus, "in any experimental design or clinical application, the effectiveness of a particular stimulus or reinforcer must first be demonstrated for the given situation and a given subject. In the clinical situation, in which conditioning may proceed over a long period of time, it is even necessary to reevaluate the effectiveness of a reinforcing stimulus a few days or weeks after its general introduction." [33] In addition, the effectiveness of a stimulus varies with the reinforcement schedule (K).

Reinforcement and Motivation / Motivational constructs are unnecessary in operant conditioning. Differing probabilities of response can be accounted for by variables such as degree of deprivation or satiation. Some stimuli, called primary reinforcers, are reinforcing to most members of a species regardless of prior conditioning history. These include food, water, stimuli that reduce pain or discomfort, and sexual stimuli.

Conditioned Reinforcement and Social Reinforcers / Most reinforcers have acquired their potency from repeated association with other reinforcing events, and are thus *conditioned reinforcers.* They are resistant to extinction, presumably because they have been acquired on an intermittent schedule of reinforcement. Conditioned reinforcers that have been conditioned to many different primary and secondary reinforcers are called *generalized reinforcers.* Money and attention are examples. Tokens are another example.

Social Reinforcement / The verbal and nonverbal actions of other people constitute powerful reinforcers for human behavior. Many patients' complaints relate to interpersonal interactions and social evaluations. Social reinforcement is probably significant in conformity, imitation, and social evaluation, as well as self-evaluations.

Chaining of Responses / Complex response chains can be built up, in which component responses become discriminative stimuli for the following response. The final chain may be seen as a single operant in which all the components are related to the final reinforcing event. Analysis of the chain is often necessary in therapeutic situations, where "the behavior modifier's task is often that of slowly building up appropriate response chains through positive reinforcement." Chains involving alternative reinforced elements, or "branching," appear to represent much of normal behavior. "With few other procedures are we as strongly reminded of the applied technological nature of therapeutic operant behavior modification; success in building repertoires of response chains in behavior-deficient patients is mainly a matter of careful engineering." [34]

Schedules of Reinforcement, K / Reinforcement may be given not only continuously (following each response) but intermittently on var-

ious schedules, in terms of *time intervals* that must elapse before reinforcement or in terms of the number of responses per reinforcer, or
ratio schedules. Time intervals or ratio schedules may be fixed or variable. Behavior established by intermittent schedules is more resistant
to extinction. Programs of behavior modification begin with continuous reinforcement which is gradually thinned out on a schedule. Too
rapid thinning out and changes in schedules can disrupt behavior.

THERAPEUTIC USE OF REINFORCEMENT OPERATIONS   Positive reinforcement
is most useful in treating behavioral deficits, that is, in dealing with
responses that fail to occur with sufficient frequency or intensity, in
appropriate form, or under appropriate conditions. Thus, it builds
new responses, rather than removing pathological responses, though
the latter may be removed by extinction when they are replaced by
desirable responses or desirable competing responses.

Strengthening Incompatible Responses / When there is an undesirable
response, treatment may consist in strengthening a different, desirable
response. "If the two response classes are competitive and cannot
occur at the same time, strengthening the more desirable class should
reduce the probability of the symptomatic one. This tactic, often
termed 'counter-conditioning,' is a parallel within instrumental conditioning of Wolpe's substitution of relaxation for anxiety as classically
conditioned responses to particular stimuli." [35] This method has the
advantage over punishment or extinction of filling the gap and thus
avoiding symptom return or substitution. It can be used when the
reinforcers of the undesirable response are unknown or cannot be
controlled.

The withholding of positive reinforcement, or extinction, is useful when behavioral excesses are the target. It may be a necessary
preliminary to positive reinforcement of weak but desired behaviors.
Extinction involves several problems. Removing all reinforcers of the
behavior, including self-reinforcement, may be difficult. Complete
control of the environment is required. The rate of response and its
intensity rise briefly immediately following nonreinforcement, and
subsequent reduction is not smooth but is highly variable, which may
lead environmental reinforcers (such as teachers or parents) to abandon the procedure. Less-than-perfect withholding of reinforcement
constitutes intermittent reinforcement and increases the response. Resistance to extinction may be great for a response that has developed
under intermittent reinforcement. Extinction has aversive characteristics, thus producing undesirable side effects.

Response Differentiation or Shaping / When new and complex responses are desired, shaping, or the use of successive approximation,
may be used. This method combines reinforcement and extinction
into a technology "which reorganizes elements of available behaviors
into what appear to be new responses, either by molding complex new
behaviors from simple elements or by building complex chains of
simpler responses." [36] Shaping is important in remedying behavior

deficits, since the rewarding of small steps ensures adequate reinforcement throughout the treatment. Waiting for the complex behavior to occur before reinforcement would be impossible. Even so, the shaping process may be a long and slow one. Shaping enters into therapies involving vicarious and imitation learning paradigms, as well as in replication techniques, such as role playing and psychodrama.

Discrimination and Stimulus Control / The function of the discriminative stimulus is to set the stage for responding, indicating when a particular response is appropriate. Most behavior involves discriminated operants; thus, stimulus control plays a vital role in behavior modification, and therapy may be described as being primarily a matter of discrimination training.

A problem in therapy arises when stimulus control is limited to the therapy situation, without generalization outside.

ENVIRONMENTAL ENGINEERING   Operant technology is particularly applicable to natural environments and to use by persons without extensive training in psychology or therapy. Technicians can be easily trained to use the techniques. Instrumentation of procedures by mechanical devices extends their applications. Patients can be trained in self-regulatory behaviors.

Behavioral engineering can be applied in families, school classrooms, and institutions for the mentally retarded, delinquent, and emotionally disturbed. Tokens, which become general reinforcers, can be used systematically and on a large scale; such systems are often called token economies. The operant model is well suited to the construction of special therapeutic-educational, or "prosthetic," environments in hospitals, schools, penal institutions, etc.

BEHAVIOR CONTROL BY AVERSIVE CONSEQUENCES   Aversive stimuli in the operant model, where they are contingent upon the behavior of the subject, differ from their use in the classical model, where they are not consequences of the behavior of the subject. Much everyday behavior is controlled by aversive consequences, and society relies heavily upon punishment or threats of punishment. "Discipline" usually consists of punishment rather than positive reinforcement. Yet many psychologists see the origin of personality disorders in aversive social control.

Paradigms for Aversive Control of Behavior / The presentation of an aversive stimulus that cannot be avoided or escaped following an act is *punishment.* The contingent removal of an aversive stimulus following a response is *negative reinforcement* (in the language of instrumental conditioning, it fits the escape paradigm). It is often termed *aversion relief.*

Positive stimuli can be manipulated aversively. Forced consumption of excessive stimuli, or *satiation,* can be aversive. *Extinction,* involving the omission of reward, can be considered aversive. *Time-out,* that is, removal from all positive reinforcement, is similar. *Response cost,* or the removal of positive reinforcers by fines, for example, or increasing the requirements for reward, is also aversive. Finally, neutral stimuli that are associated with removal of positive reinforcement (by classical conditioning) may become secondary aversive stimuli.

Noncontingent delivery of aversive stimuli usually leads to *arousal.* They may become adventitiously connected to a preceding response, resulting in *superstitious* conditioning, or when noncontingently removed, they can produce *superstitious negative reinforcement. Punishment* is the contingent dinglivery of an aversive stimulus. Acts that are successful in leading to *escape* or *avoidance* of an aversive stimulus are reinforced. When aversive stimuli are removed in the presence of a neutral stimulus, the latter may come to function as a positive reinforcer (a "relief" stimulus) through classical conditioning.

A difficulty arising in work with aversive stimuli is the lack of a universal definition of the term "aversive."

Respondent and Operant Elements in Aversive Control / As was indicated earlier in the discussion of mixed models, the separation of classical and operant models using aversive stimuli is arbitrary. "At the level of theoretical description, the distinction between the stimulus-building function of classical conditioning and the response-contingency function of the operant conditioning model seems clear. In actual practice, however, the two models cannot be made mutually exclusive. Observed effects can usually be ascribed to either model only by arbitrary decision, or by attending only to certain elements in the behavioral equation." [37]

Inescapable Aversive Stimulation / Sudden, intense aversive stimulation is the unconditioned stimulus for emotional reactions, including anxiety. Noncontingent aversive stimulation has been used therapeutically to arouse anxiety that may lead to learning. However, aversive stimuli, whether contingent or not, can produce unexpected effects, because of the (unknown) past history of the individual with such stimuli.

Escape and Avoidance Training / In escape learning, onset of the aversive stimulus becomes a discriminative cue for the response (escape) that terminates it, and the termination acts as a positive reinforcer. In avoidance, however, since the occurrence of the aversive stimulus is prevented, there is a dilemma in explaining what is reinforcing. Yet avoidance behaviors are extremely resistant to extinction.

Many behavioral deviations represent avoidance or defensive reactions. But escape-avoidance training has therapeutic uses. Examples of aversion therapy include many examples of escape and avoidance training. Autistic children have been rapidly taught to approach the experimenter when such approach behavior resulted in the avoidance of shock.

Generalization in aversion therapy is more difficult to obtain, since the patient's everyday environment cannot be relied upon to support the treatment. Also, the necessary special equipment and procedures separate the situation from everyday life. The influencing of the patient's verbal and thought processes through interviews is used as an ancillary procedure to bridge this gap. The use of multiple-paradigm procedures also helps.

Punishment / "While avoidance teaches the individual 'what to do,' punishment teaches him 'what not to do.' In both cases the training goal is achieved when aversive stimulation is no longer suffered. The practical difference is that passive 'not responding' is sufficient for evasion of punishment. No new behaviors are substituted unless they are positively reinforced." [38]

Punishment is often the procedure chosen in situations where the reinforcement history and the reinforcers for the current maintenance of the undesired behavior are unknown. If the latter were known, extinction could be used. The use of punishment can be complicated by the patient's previous experience with the punishing stimulus, including adaptation to it, or its association with positive reinforcement, when it becomes a signal of a reward. The availability of alternative responses leading to positive reinforcement without punishment enhances the effects of punishment. On the other hand, the effectiveness of punishment is weakened when there is opportunity for escape or avoidance responses.

Removing the subject from positive reinforcers, or time-out, is aversive. It is useful when punishment is impractical, when extinction may not be possible, and when the interaction, as of teacher and pupil or parent and child, can escalate to explosive levels. To be effective, the situation from which the subject is banished must be relatively rewarding, and the time-out period or situation must not offer the opportunity for escape or avoidance responses. Physical isolation as time-out may be aversive in itself, in addition to removing positive reinforcement.

Punishment has long been unpopular because of presumed undesirable or harmful effects, as well as the apparent greater effectiveness of positive reinforcement. Recent research and clinical experience have reduced the fears of harmful effects. The effectiveness of punishment is limited by the difficulty of achieving generalization, since subjects discriminate so highly that therapeutic goals may be thwarted. "Application of the aversive event in a range of naturalistic settings, by a variety of persons, for a variety of examples of the target response class, and rapid and complete suppression of the naturally occurring behaviors are suggested as safeguards." [39] Other problems may arise, including the patient modeling the therapist's punishing or aggressive behaviors, the development of substitute responses, or other side effects. Side effects may be positive. "By breaking up an old behavior pattern, punishment can provide the occasion for the positive reinforcement of new operants that are of greater value to the person. The combination of positive reinforcement with punishment appears most effective." [40]

The influence of punishment on the punisher is an important factor from a social point of view. Punishment of a child's obnoxious behavior, for example, terminates this behavior, thus giving the parent relief. There is thus a danger that punishment may be used, by therapists as well as by parents, more extensively than might be desirable, because of the satisfaction received by the person administering it.

Verbal Mediation and Self-Regulation

VERBAL BEHAVIOR AND THE INTERVIEW   The complete control of the individual's environment is impossible, in part because man can create his own subjective environment, enabling him to become to some extent independent of his physical environment. In many cases, verbal and thought processes, interposed between stimulus and action, constitute the problematic behavioral process.

> Although unwanted in the studies that emphasize the input-output relationships in behavior (because of the methodological problems they present and their great individual variations), these private experiences constitute the core of what is often regarded as the source of man's most magnificent experiences. A behavioral viewpoint cannot disregard the importance of these subjective experiences and their influence in modifying the role of the physical environment. The distinction between the achievement of behavioral change by an externally controlled program and by self-initiated changes parallels a major distinction made by many writers in contrasting behavior therapy methods and traditional psychodynamic approaches. . . . The use of verbal methods of behavior control underlies most traditional dynamic psychotherapies and all procedures that use interview methods.[41]

The processes of thinking, problem solving, imagining, dreaming, fantasizing, speaking, and similar activities are involved in interpersonal clinical interactions and must be accounted for in a psychology of human behavior. Yet little is known about these processes. They are not directly observable. But both stimulus and response components can occur in the internal, or private, psychological space, which is not observable by another person. Nevertheless, Skinner has proposed that these private events, including language, be treated by the same method of experimental analysis as are overt behaviors.

Mediational models for private behaviors as intervening events have been proposed. Osgood's mediation hypothesis, derived from Hull's learning theory, is closest to a behavioral approach. Dollard and Miller also propose a mediational model. These models rely essentially on the simple association of internal events, including words, with objective external stimuli through conditioning. *Psycholinguistic models* are more complex and attempt to account for facts of language acquisition that are not explained by simple associationist or environmental interpretations.

Verbal Therapy: The Interview / Verbal processes are basic to interview therapy, in which the therapist hopes to influence the patient's thoughts and speech, his attitudes, and his perceptions of himself and his environment, thereby leading him to change his behavior. Since it is behavior outside the office that is usually the target, and not the verbal interaction of therapist and patient, interview therapy is an indirect approach to behavior modification. But even in direct manipulation of environmental contingencies, or in desensitization and classical conditioning, verbal control over behavior is evident and used. The verbal interview is also used for diagnosis or obtaining information about the patient's behavior. Verbal behavior, as in delusional speech, may be the target of therapy.

There is a voluminous literature on verbal therapy techniques and their effectiveness, but it is still the least understood method of behavior change. In behavior therapy the interview has been given only a secondary role. Only some common problems of interview methods, which are present when these methods are used in behavior therapy, are considered here.

The meaning of the verbal report, or self-report, for actual experience is important. The subject's response to a stimulus and his report about it are not the same. Reports thus may be influenced, in varying degrees, by the stimulus object or by the patient's history and experiences, and thus reports have varying degrees of validity in terms of the actual events. Verbal utterances may be studied as responses in themselves, rather than as reports of an event. The lack of correlation between verbal reports and behavior does not mean that verbal reports are useless. The verbal behavior may be studied in terms of its determinants and its effects on the social environment and on the person himself. "For some situations it may be as important to know what the patient says as to know how he 'feels' or responds physiologically." [42]

Verbal reports are influenced by the nature of the situation. Social desirability influences questionnaire responses. Results of experiments are influenced by the subject's perception of the purpose of the experiment (its demand characteristics) and by the tendency of subjects to support the expectations of the experimenter. Clinical interviews would be expected to be affected by the same biasing factors. Research indicates that a variety of factors associated with the personality of the therapist and of the patient and the nature of the relationship influence the patient's responses.

Although social intercourse is based on the congruence between verbal statements and motor acts, this relationship has not been widely studied. A number of studies demonstrate close correlation, but others do not. "Insight" does not necessarily lead to behavior change and indeed may follow rather than precede such change. Patients often "know" or can verbally describe desirable behaviors but are unable to perform them. The self-regulatory function of verbal responses, necessary for the execution of behaviors indicated verbally to others, apparently can be developed by training.

The influence of the therapist on patients' verbal productions through *verbal conditioning* has been studied extensively in the past twenty years. "The results of verbal conditioning studies clearly make it necessary to reexamine the assumption that a patient's interview behavior is mainly determined by his thought content, personality, or past experience. It. is also necessary to pay careful attention to the interviewer's behavior and the clinical setting as determinants of the obtained interview material. The conditionability of verbal responses in laboratory situations similar to the clinical interview also suggests that the process of behavior modification by interview may be partially described by the verbal operant conditioning paradigm." [43] Studies in the actual interview situation have also demonstrated the effectiveness of operant verbal conditioning.

The generalization of successful changes in verbalization has not been conclusively demonstrated, though a number of studies have shown continuing changes in noninterview verbal behaviors such as responses on self-report questionnaires. Cognitive theorists have questioned whether the mechanism operating is simple operant conditioning, suggesting that what is learned is the correct response-reinforcement contingency. Awareness thus would be an important factor, and studies have shown that the presence of awareness is associated with better learning, though the awareness may follow improvement in performance.

In addition to the influence of the therapist on specific responses and their content, there are influences on structural aspects of speech such as duration of utterances, the frequency of interruptions, silence, and speech disturbances. In spite of the considerable amount of research on interviewer-interviewee influence, "the data on learning processes and the mutual influence of interviewers and interviewees seem to be useful mainly as a conceptual guide for the clinician rather than to offer a set of rules for interview conduct." [44]

A learning view of interview therapy differs from the traditional approach. It stresses reportable or observable behavior rather than hypothetical states or dynamics. Nor is the interview "employed primarily to permit the patient to develop his own insights and understanding of his unconscious motivation, of his feelings, and of the events in his past history that have resulted in his maladaptive behavior. However, the importance of the therapeutic relationship in interview therapy is not denied. The relationship between therapist and patient can serve to promote behavioral change through the therapist's efforts to establish himself as a potential source of reinforcement during each interview. Therapeutic tactics in later interviews consist in selectively reinforcing verbal behaviors that promise to serve as controlling stimuli for more effective action on the part of the patient." [45]

Behavior modification techniques have been developed for cases where interview therapy is neither feasible nor efficient. Behavior modification can be obtained by direct control of the environment. Conditioning is not to be substituted for all interviewing therapy; rather both are to be used so as to be most effective for the particular patient. The use of conditioning methods, however, "is not merely a minor revision of interview methods but a drastic change in the relative importance of interviews as therapeutic instruments. Improvement in conditioning techniques may eventually relegate interview therapy to the status of an *adjunct* for behavior modification techniques. . . . When the focal symptoms consist of public behaviors, understanding the patient's thinking becomes less important and treatment requires fewer interviews and a less intimate personal relationship if direct modification techniques can be applied." The close personal relationship, however, is "an ideal vehicle for modifying directly those problems that consist of a patient's difficulties in relating to another person and in using appropriate interactional behaviors," though it is not necessarily always *the* ideal method.[46] Interview therapy is also useful for patients who require information, attitude changes, or the development of verbal behaviors for efficient assessment of life situations, evaluation of feelings, or decision making. The principles of behavior modification can be applied in the interview by the therapist. "This view differs from the assumptions that change is due to spontaneous growth for which the therapist serves only as a catalyst, or that *internal* processes are simply directed or set free by the therapist." [47]

SELF-REGULATION AND ITS CLINICAL APPLICATION   Procedures that bring about behavior changes by environmental control and reinforcement require the presence of the therapist (or of other behavior modifiers) and give little responsibility for change to the patient. Self-regulation and patient regulation of his environment go beyond this. The interpersonal relationship through which this is accomplished consists essentially of a training or tutoring relationship to help the patient learn skills that enlarge his repertoire in the control and regulation of his own behavior. The term "instigation therapy" may be applied to this approach, since the relationship is used for joint planning and for instigating actions by encouraging and supporting the patient. The patient's active role and perception of himself as the major agent of change increases his predisposition toward further change and personal development.

The Self Construct / The self is not a process entity or mental structure, but the system of attitudes and responses toward the self. These self-reactions are learned, as responses to external objects and events are learned. Since the social environment provides inadequate feedback regarding the individual's effects on it, self-knowledge is often incorrect. Yet self-knowledge is an important motivational factor in behavior.

Self-Control / Instigation therapy requires that the patient have the capacity to put behavior under his own control. Self-control involves the same components (S, R, K, and C) as in external control, but all are in the person (O). Self-control requires the subject's manipulation of controlling responses that make the undesirable response less probable or impossible . Application of a time lock to a refrigerator or cigarette case are examples. Self-reinforcement and

self-punishment can be used, but the conceptualization of these processes is not clear. The role of reinforcement in self-control is not yet
well defined, since no data are available on how critical it is or on
whether it is, indeed, required. The response to be controlled always
has conflicting consequences; either the response has immediate, positive, and long-range aversive consequences, or immediate aversive but
long-range positive effects. "Generalized social reinforcement and
self-descriptive statements with reinforcing properties can be made
contingent on the execution of self-control. Thereby some behaviors
may be strengthened that, at first look, appear detrimental to the
organism." [48] Self-control involves the abandonment of immediate or
close reinforcers for later and more important ones, or the delay of
gratification. Training in delayed gratification is affected by the organism's experience with postponed rewards. The internalization of
social norms, or socialization, is an example of the inculcation of
self-control, by various learning mechanisms, especially aversive methods creating guilt. Modeling and positive reinforcement are also
equally important in the genesis of conscience.

Clinical Use of Self-Control Procedures / Patients can be trained
through instruction to bring their behavior under control by *setting up
behaviors that change the environment, or rearranging behavioral sequences.*

In the method of *covert sensitization,* the patient is taught to relax,
then to visualize the undesirable behavior, and to follow this by imagining aversive stimuli. Following successful avoidance or escape, the
patient is told to imagine a positive reinforcement, such as a feeling
of relief. The technique is used increasingly by the patient on his own
in his daily life. It has been successful in obesity and homosexuality.

Contingency management teaches the patient covert verbal responses (coverants) that serve as controlling cues for desirable behaviors. He may be helped to relax and then taught to associate this state
with the word "relax." He may be taught to make positive coverant
statements, such as "I am master of my own fate," prior to engaging
in desirable behaviors.

In *contract management* the therapist and the patient agree upon
specific behaviors that the patient will engage in, which will be followed by a predetermined therapist reinforcement.

Patients can be taught to apply either positive reinforcement or
an aversive stimulus according to a planned treatment program. Patients can also be given behavioral analysis training, which enables
them to recognize functional relationships between their actions and
antecedent and subsequent environmental events. "Use of this technique is limited to persons with sufficient educational background,
strong motivation, and interest to undertake a program that at first
seems to have only distant relevancy to his current behavioral problems." [49]

With the introduction of self-regulatory techniques, the behavior
therapies have moved beyond techniques using only external or environmental controls, into the area of "mental" events, which were

earlier excluded from behaviorist systems. However, numerous problems are involved, stemming from limited knowledge of behaviors in which the person is both subject and object.

EXAMPLES

Kanfer and Phillips present no clinical examples of the methods that they consider. This is consistent with their purpose, which was not to write a manual for clinicians or to present a series of illustrative case studies, but to "present the research and theory underlying the current application of learning principles and techniques to therapeutic change, as well as to point out the problems involved in practical usage." [50] Clinical examples are given in the research summaries.

SUMMARY AND EVALUATION

Kanfer and Phillips have presented the most comprehensive survey of the methods and techniques of the behaviorists currently available. They have covered the usual techniques developed from the classical model of conditioning, which have been available to some extent in other sources, including Wolpe, and the methods derived from the operant conditioning paradigm, which have not heretofore been collected. In addition, they consider the mixed model of methods and techniques that are complex and overlap both models. Finally, they go beyond most other behavior therapists in discussing the self-regulation of behavior from the point of view of behavioral models. They go beyond most treatments of behavior therapy also in including cognitive behavior.

The presentation is not clinically oriented, but is research-based. For the practitioner this is a weakness as well as a strength. But it was not the intention of the authors to provide a textbook of clinical practice. They succeed in presenting the learning foundations of behavior therapy.

Kanfer and Phillips have not presented a systematic theory or approach to behavior therapy. They have instead, as was indicated at the beginning of this chapter, presented a storehouse of behavioral psychological principles. Their failure to present a systematic approach lies not in themselves, but in the nature of the material that they set out to integrate. There appears to be no single systematic behavior therapy. The authors at least implicitly recognize this in their preference for the term "behavior therapies" rather than "behavior therapy."

Because no (over) simplified system is presented, the book is very difficult reading, as is no doubt its condensation here. Indeed, it is impossible to do it justice in a condensation, because of the comprehensive detail it contains. It is in effect a (selective) review of the experimental and research literature on the major methods or techniques of the behavior therapies. It is difficult to digest and summarize, because the results of the research are contradictory and confusing, so that few conclusions or generalizations can be made. The major conclusion that forces itself upon the reader is that the methods and techniques of the behavior therapies are much more complex and involve more variables and factors than most practitioners realize or are aware of; certainly behavior therapy is not as simple as the writings of Wolpe and others imply.

The fact that the results of research are not clear or always in agreement surely means that the field is not in a state where the results of laboratory research can be directly applied in practice. Kanfer and Phillips, in introducing their discussion of those techniques styled as Pavlovian, note that this "will serve to plunge us into some of the complexities involved when theoretical models, or even controlled laboratory procedures, are used to provide, describe, or explain procedures for modifying naturally occurring symptom behaviors. It can raise questions not only about the extent and manner in which therapies have actually been deduced from learning principles, but also about the interaction of incomplete principles and impure techniques to produce the uncertainty still remaining as to which techniques are more effective and why." [51] The same statement could be made about methods and techniques supposedly based upon the other models besides the Pavlovian.

Certainly, the reading of Kanfer and Phillips does not support the repeated claim that behavior therapy is based upon the results of laboratory experiments. The repetition of this claim, without supporting evidence, by so many behavior therapists suggests that its very repetition is being used as a method of conditioning the reader (and perhaps the writer as well) to accept behavior therapy as more scientific than other methods. Such terms as "scientific research," "laboratory-based," "experimentally derived," "modern learning theory," "experimentally established" appear to be used for their prestige value by many behavior therapists. As a matter of fact, it seems clear that the methods and techniques are more clearly empirical than based upon experimental (or nonexperimental) research results. Many behavior therapists seem to be unaware that (1) other methods are supported by research; (2) the procedures used by behaviorists are not always based upon prior research demonstrating their effectiveness (not that this should necessarily be the case) but are often developed on the basis of clinical experience; (3) the research evidence for the validity of their method is far from conclusive, and in fact, as more research data have accumulated, the more complex the apparently simple methods appear to be; and (4) the methods are not necessarily explainable only by so-called modern learning theory (whatever that is) but can be rationalized in other ways.

Behavior therapists do operate from a more experimental approach than other therapists. Their model is inductive, developing from a context of discovery, rather than deductive, developing from assumptions or hypotheses. Thus, they operate with a different image of man, an image derived from empirical investigation rather than from theory or philosophy.

Contrary to the impression often given that the methods are simple and clear-cut, and that their modes of operation are clearly understood, it is becoming evident that they are highly complex and not clearly understood, as some behaviorists are willing to admit. Moreover, there is no integrating theory to tie together the many methods or techniques. "While there are many techniques, there are few concepts or general principles involved in behavior therapy." [52] Weitzman suggests that behavior therapy is actually "a nontheoretical amalgam of pragmatic principles." [53] The behaviorists make a virtue out of necessity in expressing their willingness to try anything that seems to work or that might work. Behaviorists will try anything and, of course, sometimes, with some clients, anything will work. Thus, specific techniques are being tried and recommended and accepted on a superstitious basis until extinguished after enough failures.

Kanfer and Phillips, however, are not extremists. They make no unsupported claims. They are laboratory- and research-oriented, and perhaps it is just because of this that they are cautious in their statements. This lack of conclusiveness can be frustrating to the practitioner. But it is a good, and necessary, antidote to the oversimplified conclusiveness of writers such as Wolpe.

One might well ask if Kanfer and Phillips provide us with a picture of the elephant of behavior therapy referred to by Krasner. As presented by Kanfer and Phillips, the outline is certainly blurred, since there is no clear distinction between the behavior therapy elephant and the cognitive therapy rhinoceros. (Kanfer believes that "liberalized behavioral approaches, even when using mediational constructs, can be differentiated from cognitive theory on two broad bases: (1) they presume the same processes to operate in overt and covert events; and (2) they attempt to organize models inductively, with minimal use of constructs that are not anchored in data." [54]) Within the skin of the elephant there is some question about how the bones of classical and operant conditioning articulate; perhaps they mesh in an amorphous soft structure rather than a bony skeleton. The question can well be raised: can all the methods and techniques be brought together under a general systematic learning or behavior theory? If they can, and it is assumed that eventually they will be, the resulting theory will be a behavior theory in a much broader sense than the term is currently being used.

REFERENCES

[1] Kanfer, F. H., & Phillips, Jeanne S. *Learning foundations of behavior therapy.* New York: Wiley, 1970. P. vii.   [2] *Ibid.,* pp. viii, 2.   [3] *Ibid.,* p. 1. [4] *Ibid.,* p. 2.   [5] *Ibid.,* p. 20.   [6]. *Ibid.,* p. 52.   [7] *Ibid.,* p. 53. [8] *Ibid.,* p. 60.   [9] *Ibid.,* p. 70.   [10] *Ibid.,* p. 75.   [11] *Ibid.,* p. 76.

[12] *Ibid.*, p. 29.   [13] *Ibid.*, p. 17.   [14] *Ibid.*, p. 460.   [15] *Ibid.*, p. 21.
[16] *Ibid.*, p. 532.   [17] *Ibid.*, p. 533.   [18] *Ibid.*, p. 535.   [19] *Ibid.*, p. 35.
[20] *Ibid.*, p. 538.   [21] *Ibid.*, p. 520.   [22] *Ibid.*, pp. 504–505.   [23] *Ibid.*,
p. 508.   [24] *Ibid.*, p. 461.   [25] *Ibid.*, p. 109.   [26] *Ibid.*, p. 122.
[27] *Ibid.*, pp. 97–99.   [28] *Ibid.*, p. 183.   [29] Reported in Bandura, A.
Principles of behavior modification. New York: Holt, Rinehart and Winston, 1969.
[30] Kanfer, F. H., and Phillips, Jeanne S., *op. cit.*, p. 231.   [31] *Ibid.*, p. 241.
[32] *Ibid.*, p. 250.   [33] *Ibid.*, p. 254.   [34] *Ibid.*, pp. 266, 267.   [35] *Ibid.*,
pp. 279–280.   [36] *Ibid.*, p. 287.   [37] *Ibid.*, p. 331.   [38] *Ibid.*, p. 351.
[39] *Ibid.*, p. 365.   [40] *Ibid.*, p. 359.   [41] *Ibid.*, p. 373.   [42] *Ibid.*, p.
384.   [43] *Ibid.*, p. 391.   [44] *Ibid.*, p. 399.   [45] *Ibid.*, p. 401.   [46]
Ibid., p. 402.   [47] *Ibid.*, p. 403.   [48] *Ibid.*, p. 416.   [49] *Ibid.*, pp. 439–
440.   [50] *Ibid.*, p. 1.   [51] *Ibid.*, p. 95.   [52] Ullmann, L. P., & Krasner,
L. *A psychological approach to abnormal behavior.* Englewood Cliffs, N.J: Prentice-
Hall, 1969. P. 252.   [53] Weitzman, B. Behavior therapy and psychotherapy.
Psychol. Rev., 1967, **74**, 300–317.   [54] Kanfer, F. H. Personal communica-
tion. February 11, 1972.

PART THREE

Psychoanalytic Approaches to Counseling

9

Introduction

The selection of psychoanalytically oriented approaches to counseling or psychotherapy for inclusion in a book such as this poses a difficult problem. In addition to orthodox Freudian psychoanalysis,[1] there are a good half-dozen or more systematic approaches bearing a significant relationship to the orthodox approach, but different enough to warrant separate consideration. These would include the theories of Adler,[2] Fromm,[3] Horney,[4] Jung,[5] Rank,[6] and Sullivan.[7]

To include all of these would require more space than could be justified in a book of this kind. The purpose of this book is to provide the student with synopses of various points of view with which he should be familiar, but which are not easily available or accessible to him. There can be no question that the student should be familiar with Freudian psychoanalysis and its major variants. However, synopses of most of these are now available.

The survey by Harper [8] is comprehensive, but the treatments are too brief to be of much value to the serious student. Somewhat more intensive is the survey by Clara Thompson.[9] However, it is not adequate for the student who wants a fairly complete, though relatively brief, account of the major variations on the orthodox Freudian approach. This need is met by Ruth Munroe's book.[10] Her chapter "Basic Concepts of Psychoanalysis" provides an excellent presentation of those concepts held in common by all schools of psychoanalysis. Later chapters deal with the approaches of Adler, Fromm, Horney, Jung,

215

Sullivan, and Rank. In addition to this standard reference, the volume by Ford and Urban [11] contains chapters on the systems of Adler, Horney, Rank, and Sullivan, as well as the so-called ego analysts. Stein's book [12] also includes a chapter by Dreikurs on the Adlerian approach.

In view of the availability of these sources, it was decided not to discuss any of the systems of psychoanalysis in this book, but rather to include a presentation of one psychoanalytic approach to therapy and of an approach to psychological counseling that, while perhaps not warranting the designation of psychoanalytic, is probably better included here than in any of the other sections into which this book is divided.

The psychoanalytic approach is that of Alexander and French.[13] Alexander and French adhere essentially to orthodox Freudian theory. However, they adapt it, as well as its techniques, to a briefer therapy than orthodox psychoanalysis. They differentiate between psychoanalysis and psychoanalytic therapy. The latter is not only shorter, it is less intensive, being on a once- or twice-a-week basis instead of daily. It is conducted in a face-to-face setting instead of with the client on the couch. And it is more active, directive, or manipulative than orthodox analysis.

Bordin's [14] psychological counseling, while somewhat eclectic in nature, is probably the only presentation of a point of view in general counseling that utilizes psychoanalytic theory and principles.

It is interesting that these approaches tend to be quite rational in nature. It is with psychoanalysis that the study of the role of feelings and emotions in psychological experience originated, as a reaction against the rationalism and intellectual emphasis of the then current psychology and psychiatry. Yet, as a method of therapy, psychoanalysis, and even more so some of its variants—particularly psychoanalytically oriented therapy—has become quite rational in its approach. Thompson notes that one of the dissatisfactions of Rank and Ferenczi with psychoanalysis in the 1920s was that it had become too much of an intellectual process.[15] Although Rank and others moved away from this rationality, it has persisted. Hobbs, reviewing Sullivan's *The Psychiatric Interview*, notes that while psychoanalysis "helped the world see the forces of unreason operating in all of us . . . it is in the psychoanalytic prescription for this state of affairs that the great paradox occurs: the cure for unreason is reason; the antidote for hurtful experience is rationality." [16] Hobbs sees Sullivan as stressing man's unreason, with the therapist unraveling the truth against the opposition of the client. Then the therapist presents his findings to the client and prescribes a reasonable course of action. Alexander's psychoanalytic therapy, although rational in its general approach, emphasizes "corrective emotional experience" rather than intellectual insight.

It should be noted that it is not rational behavior as the goal of counseling or psychotherapy that is at issue here, but the use of reason as the method for meeting and resolving emotional situations and problems. Here psychoanalysis and psychoanalytically oriented approaches differ perhaps relatively little from other approaches presented earlier, except perhaps in the greater complexity of the reasoning, or interpretation, that is utilized.

The student who is interested in more extensive accounts of the various psychoanalytic approaches may begin with the references that have been cited above.

REFERENCES

[1] Freud, S. *Introductory lectures on psychoanalysis.* London: Allen and Unwin, 1929; Freud, S. *New introductory lectures on psychoanalysis.* New York: Norton, 1933; Freud, S. *A general introduction to psychoanalysis.* New York: Liveright, 1935.   [2] Adler, A. *The neurotic constitution.* New York: Moffatt, 1917; Adler, A. *The practice and theory of individual psychology.* New York: Harcourt, Brace & World, 1927; Adler, A. *Understanding human nature.* New York: Greenberg, 1927; Ansbacher, H. L., & Ansbacher, Rowena R. *The individual psychology of Alfred Adler.* New York: Basic Books, 1956; Dreikurs, R. *Fundamentals of Adlerian psychology.* New York: Greenberg, 1950; Dreikurs, R. *Adlerian family counseling; a method for counseling centers.* Eugene, Oregon: University of Oregon, 1959. [3] Fromm, E. *Escape from freedom.* New York: Farrar and Rinehart, 1941; Fromm, E. *Man for himself.* New York: Rinehart, 1947; Fromm, E. *The sane society.* New York: Rinehart, 1955.   [4] Horney, Karen. *The neurotic personality of our time.* New York: Norton, 1937; Horney, Karen. *New ways in psychoanalysis.* New York: Norton, 1939; Horney, Karen. *Our inner conflicts.* New York: Norton, 1945; Horney, Karen. *Neurosis and human growth.* New York: Norton, 1950. [5] Jung, C. G. *Collected works,* Vol. 16, *The practice of psychotherapy.* New York: Pantheon, 1954; Dry, Avis M. *The psychology of Jung: a critical interpretation.* New York: Wiley, 1961.   [6] Rank, O. *Will therapy and truth and reality.* New York: Knopf, 1947.   [7] Sullivan, H. S. *Conceptions of modern psychiatry.* Washington: William Alanson White Psychiatric Foundation, 1947; Sullivan, H. S. *The interpersonal theory of psychiatry.* New York: Norton, 1953; Sullivan, H. S. *The psychiatric interview.* New York: Norton, 1954.   [8] Harper, R. A. *Psychoanalysis and psychotherapy: 36 systems.* Englewood Cliffs, N.J.: Prentice-Hall, 1959.   [9] Thompson, Clara. *Psychoanalysis: evolution and development.* New York: Hermitage, 1950 (Grove Press, 1957).   [10] Munroe, Ruth. *Schools of psychoanalytic thought: an exposition, critique, and attempt at integration.* New York: Holt, Rinehart and Winston, 1955.   [11] Ford, D. H., & Urban, H. B. *Systems of psychotherapy.* New York: Wiley, 1963.   [12] Stein, M. I. (Ed.), *Contemporary psychotherapies.* New York: Free Press, 1961.   [13] Alexander, F. *Psychoanalysis and psychotherapy.* New York: Norton, 1956; Alexander, F., & French, T. M. *Psychoanalytic therapy.* New York: Ronald, 1946; Alexander, F. *Fundamentals of psychoanalysis.* New York: Norton, 1963.   [14] Bordin, E. S. *Psychological counseling.* (2nd ed.) New York: Appleton-Century-Crofts, 1968.   [15] Thompson, *op. cit.,* p. 14.   [16] Hobbs, N. Curing unreason by reason. Review of H. S. Sullivan, "The Psychiatric Interview." *Contemp. Psychol.,* 1956, **1,** 44–45.

10

Bordin's psychological counseling

Edward S. Bordin (1913–) received his Ph.D. from Ohio State University in 1942. From 1942 to 1946 he was associated with the counseling bureau at the University of Minnesota (except for a year as a civilian consultant to the Adjutant General's Office) and was acting director of the bureau during 1945–1946. From 1946 to 1948 he was Associate Professor of Psychology at Washington State College, moving to the University of Michigan in 1948 as Associate Professor and Chief of the Counseling Division of the Bureau of Psychological Services; he became Professor of Psychology there in 1955. His book *Psychological Counseling* was published in 1955, and a second edition appeared in 1968. The second edition incorporates a consideration of community psychology, behavior therapy, and a new chapter on vocational counseling, as well as changes in his concept of the therapeutic relationship. He is a Diplomate in Counseling of the American Board of Professional Psychology.

BACKGROUND AND DEVELOPMENT

In his *Psychological Counseling* [1] Bordin attempts to draw upon psychiatry, education, and social work to provide a description of counseling as a process based upon psychological foundations. The book is

218

directed to graduate students who are planning to become counseling or clinical psychologists.

PHILOSOPHY AND CONCEPTS

In the course of personality development the individual meets difficulties in his interpersonal and intrapersonal life. In the extreme these difficulties take the form of neurotic and psychotic states. Concern about meeting the mental health needs of large numbers of people, with limited manpower, has led to attempts to identify and provide assistance to individuals in the early stage of emotional disturbance. Further, attention is being turned to modifying or eliminating social conditions conducive to the development of psychological problems. There is still, however, a place for professional help for the individual at critical points in his development. "Intrapsychic conditions . . . have an important influence on how effectively and constructively the individual responds to his physical and social environment. Increasingly, the individual is able to select and modify that environment as well as to adapt to it." [2]

Psychological counseling is offered "to persons who are at some critical point in their development," but whose discomforts are not severe enough for them to seek psychotherapy.[3] These critical points may occur at transitional points in the life cycle, such as between the eight stages defined by Erikson. The child's leaving the family to enter school, the onset of puberty, becoming economically independent, marriage, parenthood, and retirement with the prospect of death may become a crisis. The tension and discomfort, while not sufficient to lead the individual to seek psychotherapy, nevertheless make him receptive to psychological help that is clearly linked with the disturbing situation. "Entering into such a process need not be construed as an admission of helplessness or as a step committing oneself to a thorough examination of all of the details of one's life," [4] though this may be necessary. Although without help the crisis will probably wane, it may leave a residue that will continue to interfere with fully effective functioning.

"*Counseling, as well as psychotherapy, are terms which have been used to apply to interactions where one person, referred to as the counselor or the therapist, has taken the responsibility for making his role in the interaction process contribute positively to the other person's personality development.*" [5] For counseling services to be utilized by persons when they become aware of a disturbance manifested by a specific problem or situational difficulty, it must be available at the appropriate time and place. A variety of persons offer counseling services in different settings, including psychologists, social workers, and psychiatrists. While there is a great deal of overlap between these groups and their training, *Psychological Counseling* was written for psychologists.

While a person usually comes to a counselor with a specific problem, situational difficulty, or a decision to make, the counselor's *primary* goal is not to contribute to the resolution of these immediate situations. That major goal lies further ahead. The primary goal requires understanding of the obstacles to further personality growth and development that are typified by this person's rather specific and temporarily limited difficulty. The counselor aims to contribute to the removal of these deeper lying personal obstacles and to bring about the reactivation of the psychological growth processes in that person. Thus, the solution of the immediate problem is one desired outcome, of course, but it alone is not a sufficient measure of the psychological counselor's usefulness to his client.[6]

This is similar to the distinction in psychotherapy between removing symptoms and changing personality.

Counseling differs from psychotherapy, though attempts at making a distinction have not led to elimination of confusion or to general agreement. Bordin does not succeed in clarifying the presumed difference, concluding that the difference is more quantitative than qualitative. As indicated above, while the counselor is presented with specific or situational problems, he does not deal only or specifically with these. "Psychological counseling has as its aim influencing the individual's maturation at the profoundest level possible. How general and far-reaching the effect of a particular counseling relationship will be will depend, assuming fully competent counseling, upon the particular needs of the client and his readiness for growth." [7] Yet, "the counseling relationship is characterized by much less intensity of emotional expression and relatively more emphasis upon cognitive and rational factors than is the relationship in psychotherapy." [8]

Psychological counseling includes educational and remedial counseling that does not consist simply of information giving or teaching, but that involves emotional and motivational aspects. The same applies to marriage counseling. Religious counseling is a more complex situation, but if a religious counselor is concerned primarily with the personality development of a client and secondarily with his religious beliefs, then he is engaged in psychological counseling.

Counseling is closely related to education, since both share the same general goal; also, counseling can make its great contribution to individuals during the age range when they are engaged in obtaining an education. Thus, many counselors function in educational settings. Counselors and teachers must work together, each contributing according to his specialized training and experience. Both must deal with the total individual, who cannot be divided into intellectual and emotional components. The counselor sometimes acts as a teacher, and the teacher, by providing a good relationship, may contribute to the student's maturation and personality development.

Various positions with respect to counseling and psychotherapy can be reconciled and integrated, at least in part, for the therapeutic character of interpersonal relationships is multiply determined. The personality theory and therapeutic hypotheses of psychological counseling draw upon several sources.

Personality Theory

Therapeutic theory is best conceived as one application of personality theory. There are a number of assumptions about personality theory underlying psychological counseling.

CENTRALISM   Behavior is organized in a network of interdependent systems that includes nuclear attitudes, emotions, and impulse systems. While certain aspects of behavior may include only the periphery of the network, most of the behavior involved in problem situations taps far-reaching systems of motives and emotions. Lasting and significant modifications in behavior must thus comprehend the system as a whole, including its nucleus. The larger the system involved, the more extensive the behavior change that occurs.

PSYCHOANALYSIS   The development and form of the systems of motives that comprise personality structure and control its growth are based upon psychoanalytic theory, "because it seems to offer a basis for explaining more of human behavior. Unlike other theories which emphasize personality dynamics and the centralist hypothesis, psychoanalytic theory goes beyond broad propositions about the effects of interpersonal relations on personality." [9] These effects are analyzed in terms of the stage of development of the individual and the nature and purpose of parental pressures. Defense mechanisms are differentiated and related to the genetic process. "Most decidedly we do not hold that all psychoanalytic hypotheses have been fully and generally confirmed. But as we see it, accumulating evidence supports more and more aspects of this conceptual system and we are encouraged to believe that it has distinct value as a preliminary to the more tightly reasoned and more thoroughly validated system of some future day. Pragmatically, right now its breadth and depth provide a perspective adapted to the subtlety and complexity of human behavioral phenomena." [10]

A RANKIAN TREND   The Rankian concept of the conflict between independence and dependence can be incorporated into an essentially orthodox psychoanalytic view. The pressures of individuals to actualize themselves and the concept of differentiation also seem significant. However, the opposed tendency toward regression must be recognized as well.

A DEVELOPMENTAL EMPHASIS   Erikson has modified the psychoanalytic emphasis on the first six years by elaborating on the psychosocial (as opposed to the psychosexual) stages of development throughout the entire life cycle. "Each phase is described in terms of the extremes of successful and unsuccessful solutions which can be arrived at in it, though in reality the outcome is usually somewhere between the extremes: (1) basic trust vs. mistrust; (2) autonomy vs. shame and doubt; (3) initiative vs. guilt; (4) industry vs. inferiority; (5) identity vs. identity diffusion; (6) intimacy vs. isolation; (7) generativity vs. stagnation; (8) integrity vs. despair." [11] This conceptualization provides a basis for psychological counseling with its goal of furthering personal development rather than only remedying maldevelopment.

RESISTANCE AND TRANSFERENCE IN PSYCHOTHERAPY   Defense and resistance are important aspects of the counseling and therapeutic process. In addition to arising as a reaction to inappropriate interpretation, resistance also occurs in response to internally determined anxiety concerning the recognition of impulses of which the client is afraid. This resistance is an unavoidable aspect of successful therapy. "If this second type of resistance does not appear, the therapist must examine his own behavior to see whether he has unconsciously allied himself with his patient to prevent expression of the impulses which underly the difficulty." [12] The client may also resist giving up his autonomy; the counselor must avoid encroachment upon his client's feeling of independence.

"While accepting the analytic position on transference in general," it is assumed that "it is possible for people to hurdle the barrier of repression without an intense use of transference." [13] The essentially mature person can be expected to utilize the therapeutic relationship in such a way that the defensive process will give way readily.

Diagnosis and Understanding

There is no set of diagnostic categories useful for counseling and psychotherapy. However, it is important to understand the client in terms of basic impulses and satisfactions. A well-differentiated personality theory provides the basis for such understanding. The greater the total knowledge the counselor has about the client, the deeper the understanding he can have about what the client is feeling. Care must be taken that interest in the client's history and his potential feelings doesn't lead to neglect of the significance of his current behavior. Limiting understanding to what can be obtained through the internal frame of reference may result in a superficial understanding of the client and his feelings. Diagnostic classification is, nevertheless, useful in determining goals and therapeutic methods, and in selecting or referring applicants coming to an agency.

Dimensions of Therapeutic Relationships

THE AMBIGUITY DIMENSION   Ambiguity is the lack of structure, or the presence of incompleteness or vagueness, in a stimulus situation, so that the situation does not elicit or demand the same response from all persons. Ambiguity is a characteristic of projective tests. Such stimulus situations maximize the influence of individual needs or motives on perception, so that the person's responses reflect his personality. The counselor defines himself and the situation for the client by his verbalizations and his actions. Three areas of definition are (a) the topic he considers appropriate for the client to talk about, (b) the characteristics, including the closeness, of the relationship, and (c) the counselor's values in general and in terms of the goal of counseling. The definitions provided by the counselor may vary in their degree of clarity; some areas may be quite clearly defined, while others are left vague. The rule of free association, for example, is an ambiguous definition of the topics for discussion. There are other aspects of the psychoanalytical situation that can maximize ambiguity. The counselor structures the situation to varying degrees, whether deliberately or inadvertently. Nondirective techniques, for example, tend to be ambiguous. Talking decreases ambiguity; silence increases it.

Ambiguity in therapy has three major functions: (1) It elicits responses that represent unique aspects of the client's motivational and emotional life, thus making it possible for him to bring his major conflicts into the therapeutic relationship. Ambiguity facilitates the appearance and development of transference phenomena through the projection that it encourages. (2) Transference enables the therapist to understand more fully and more deeply the motivational sources of the client's actions. The client's reactions in the ambiguous situation reveal his conflicts, his defenses, and the kinds of relationships he has with people involved in the conflicts. (3) The ambiguous situation provides a background against which the client's irrational feelings are contrasted. It thus contributes to the effectiveness of interpretation.

Maximum ambiguity is not necessarily desirable in therapy. The degree of ambiguity desirable in each of the three areas of definition listed above is determined by the needs of the particular client. The goal is to maintain the optimum level of anxiety, since ambiguity arouses anxiety. High ambiguity is not indicated in therapy with psychotics. Likewise, in counseling a schizoid client about his vocational plans, ambiguity may not be helpful in encouraging maintenance of his contact with reality. Neither should the relatively adequate person who comes to a counselor for help with a specific problem be faced with the ambiguity appropriate to the extended, intimate relationship of therapy.

The counselor himself may be threatened by ambiguity, since it encourages anxiety in the client and the expression of feelings that may be directed toward the counselor. The counselor may increase ambiguity as an expression of his need to avoid revealing himself to the client, or as an expression of his uncertainty or fear of making a wrong move, rather than to meet the client's needs. Ambiguity is a powerful tool requiring training and knowledge of human behavior and personality for its use. The untrained counselor who attempts to be nondirective with clients may become involved in an intense relationship that he is not competent to handle. Relatively untrained counselors and personnel workers should maintain a structured relationship limited to rational, factual discussions of problems. Most counseling relationships, since they involve relatively well-integrated clients who are reasonably free of intense conflicts, are not characterized by transference phenomena. However, all counselors are likely to encounter some clients who need therapy and who are ready to accept and utilize an ambiguously defined therapeutic relationship.

THE COGNITIVE AND CONATIVE DIMENSIONS   Cognitive, or instrumental, behavior is a part of all purposive, or goal-directed, behavior. Cognitive behavior refers to the conceptual, perceptual, and motor processes. Behavior also has another aspect, the conative, or affective, which includes strivings, feelings, and emotions. Cognition organizes and directs need-dictated behavior. The conative aspect of behavior corresponds to the id, and the cognitive aspect to the superego, of psychoanalytic theory. When external conditions would punish the disorganized expression of affect, however, the cognitive and motor processes minimize it, dividing it up and keeping some of it from expression except as tension, while draining some of it indirectly as defense mechanisms. Thus, the cognitive aspects of behavior may promote the fullest possible expression of affect or, as in neurosis, may control and repress affect. The goal of therapy is not the uncontrolled expression of affect, however, but organized expression.

The conflicted person cannot benefit from cognitive emphasis through interpretation until there is a loosening of the grip of the defensive processes on the experiencing and expression of affect. Thus, interpretation is not indicated early in therapy, since it will be used in the service of these defenses through intellectualization and isolation. A second principle in the use of interpretation is that the more intense the affect, the more cognitive the therapist can be in his communication without leading the client to revert to cognitive processes as a means of repression. Sometimes, however, cognitively dominated communication may be encouraged as a respite from tension related to the expression of affect. Accurately stated and appropriately timed interpretations are experienced by the client as an awareness of his own feelings, rather than as a perception of what the therapist thinks about him.

Assuming that a client will not discover something for himself, and so interpreting for him, is not an expression of lack of respect for his integrity or learning ability. We do not expect children to rediscover all the principles of science by themselves. This would prevent the accumulation of knowledge and learning from the experiences of others.

Counseling is more cognitively dominated than psychotherapy. The client's problems are less severe, more specific, and tend to be external rather than of his own making, and there is less distortion of reality. The client will be more cognitively oriented and will overlook or minimize the affective aspects of his behavior. On the other hand, the counselor may neglect the realistic and cognitive aspects of the client's life in his interest in affective elements. Circumstances sometimes require attention to an immediate problem or decision even though emotional problems may be present.

The counselor must understand as fully as possible both the

cognitive and conative aspects of the client's communications. Focusing exclusively on one or the other may give a distorted picture of the client. Understanding the conative aspect requires that the counselor be grounded in personality theory, so that he can recognize the nature of the client's major conflicts and his ways of dealing with them. In addition to cognitive understanding, empathy—or conative understanding—is important.

The needs of the counselor influence his understanding and interpretations through the distorting effects of countertransference. When the client's conflicts are related to those of the counselor, the latter may impose interpretations on the client that arise from his own defenses. Also, the counselor may be unable to bear the intensity of a close emotional relationship with the client and so may encourage cognitive interchange with him. There seems to be an element in the natural selective process for counselors that results in the selection of counselors and psychotherapists who tend toward intellectualization, and who thus make great use of cognitive interpretation.

"Whether one assumes that the processes of therapy are solely those of understanding and acceptance of the client or one assumes that therapy involves understanding plus some form of appropriate interaction with the client, achieving the deepest possible understanding will remain as one of the prerequisites of effective counseling or psychotherapeutic process." [14]

PERSONAL DIMENSIONS IN THE RELATIONSHIP   Knowledge of the nature of therapeutic relationships cannot be applied mechanically. The counselor must function in a spontaneous manner. The aspects of the counseling relationship that are least under conscious control are those involving its emotional tone. The emotional tone is thus influenced by the counselor's natural ways of interacting with others and by his personality. Earlier in psychoanalytic and client-centered therapy the neutrality of the therapist was emphasized. Now there is an emphasis upon the kind of person the therapist is. "A person cannot learn to be, or function as, a therapist without being wholly involved. He cannot approach psychotherapy as he would a purely intellectual exercise—antiseptically free of any contact with personal reactions." [15]

WARMTH AS A THERAPEUTIC INGREDIENT   Warmth refers to a complex of qualities including liking and caring, expressing and giving, and being genuine and human. Three specific characteristics of warmth are considered.

Commitment / Commitment on the part of the therapist is a matter of degree, and indicates the extent to which he is willing to substitute his own resources for those that the patient lacks or cannot use at the moment. The degree of commitment that is beneficial is related to the patient's dependency state. The patient who is overtly dependent demands excessive help. The counterdependent patient denies his dependency and attempts to control the therapy situation by assuming an active, leading, even competitive role. The truly independent client is ready to rely on his own resources but can rely on others when necessary. There appear to be two opposing forces, one pushing the person toward separation and self-reliance and the other toward intimacy and mutuality. The ambivalence has its source in a drive toward mastery and the anxiety accompanying its exercise.

In addition to commiting his time, energy, and skill, the therapist adapts the nature and depth of his commitment to the characteristics of the patient. While with the overtly dependent patient "he will take pains to spell out clearly his willingness to step in with aid of all varieties," with the counterdependent patient he will avoid this as anxiety-arousing and will emphasize "his recognition of the resources the patient possesses and his readiness to allow their fullest use. . . . Ultimately, of course, the therapist's aim is to facilitate the maximum use by every patient of his own resources. But, how the therapist reacts in particular situations will be conditioned by his understanding of the patient's dependency anxiety." [16]

"Commitments . . . are a way of communicating and establishing a relationship." [17] The patient must also make commitments: to honor appointments, to pay fees regularly when they are involved, and to work toward the mutually agreed upon goal. "A therapist's offers of commitment have little power to activate change unless they are met by his patient's giving the corresponding commitment of which he is capable." [18] Sometimes the therapist must make active commitments to gratify intense need states—panic, intense mourning, overwhelming elation. These states require immediate, direct help, such as drugs, restraint, or setting prohibitions, as a preliminary to establishing a relationship in which the sources of the need states are dealt with.

Effort to Understand / The line between commitment and understanding is tenuous. But "all psychotherapy involves an effort for the therapist to understand another person. . . . Certainly, it is the therapist's effort to understand which produces the first major emotional tie between patient and therapist in most forms of psychotherapy." [19] It is the effort to understand rather than the acuteness of the understanding that is emphasized. This effort is manifested by intent listening, questions expressing interest, and questions designed to check one's understanding. The effort to understand communicates warmth.

The effort to understand is not related to theoretical or intellectual formulations of the patient's communication, but involves an attempt to enter his world, to perceive how he is experiencing his world.

Spontaneity in Therapeutic Relations / Spontaneity is difficult to define. Lack of spontaneity is evidenced by tension or inhibition. While spontaneous behavior is free, it is not unorganized or undirected. Spontaneous behavior is human, expressive, and not the neutrality or "blank screen" of early psychoanalysis and client-centered therapy.

"Commitment and effort to understand will appear cold, impersonal, and stereotyped when not accompanied by spontaneity." [20] Thus, it is a necessary component of warmth, though by itself it does not communicate warmth. It must be combined with commitment and effort to understand.

Support and reassurance / There is considerable difference of opinion concerning the value of reassurance and support, and it does not seem possible to take a stand on the controversy. The utility of these methods varies with the situation. When the client complains about his difficulties, it will probably be annoying to him to be told that his situation is not unusual. Similarly, minimizing the importance of his conflicts and emotional reactions may be frustrating and lead to the client's questioning the counselor's ability to understand. On the other hand, the reassurance of the counselor's commitment may be helpful to some clients. In addition, the encouragement to talk about his impulses in a rational manner may be supportive for the client who is having difficulty controlling his impulses. The setting of limits may also help such clients.

THE COUNSELING PROCESS

A number of aspects of the counseling process were considered in the discussion of the dimensions of therapeutic relationships.

Counseling is initiated when a client faces a problem that he feels inadequate to handle without assistance from a professional person. Most clients consider coming to a counselor as a reflection upon their own adequacy. Thus, while the client needs the counselor's commitment to help him, he may resist any implication that the counselor feels the client can't get along without his aid.

The client frequently sees his problems as pretty much outside himself. Before counseling can progress, he must recognize and accept the fact that his own feelings have been an important factor in his problems, and he must take responsibility for himself and his problems. In addition, clients often see the solutions to their problems as coming from outside themselves, in the form of advice or information. Again, for a counseling relationship to develop, the client must accept some responsibility for the solution of his problems.

Counseling, then, is not an abstract, rational discussion of external problems, but a relationship that includes some emotional commitment and involvement on the part of both the client and the counselor. However, as has been noted earlier, in counseling there is more emphasis on cognitive and rational factors than there is in psychotherapy. Nevertheless, "the heart of the therapeutic process is the ability to be sensitive in the fullest possible way to the reactions of the client and one's own reactions to them." [21]

Psychological counseling is a more limited form of therapeutic treatment than psychoanalysis. It does not attempt to bring unconscious infantile conflicts into consciousness and resolve them.

It is concerned rather with the ways in which these conflicts appear in conscious and preconscious actions. Psychological counseling attempts to bring to awareness those aspects of infantile conflicts which are already close to awareness and are not deeply threatening to the ego. In counseling, increased insight into ego defenses is won through the counselor's interpretation of omissions, contradictions, denials, forgetfulness, and so on, as these appear in the client's story. In such a process the client is enabled to approach his situation more realistically, to abate some of his tendencies toward self-defense, and to become more effective in controlling the distorting effects of his infantile conflicts. Although the counselor makes use of transference elements in his client's reactions, unlike the analyst he does not encourage an intense, consuming, transference reaction. He may make use of positive transference, but does relatively little interpreting of it.[22]

Since psychological counseling is limited to contributing to a fuller development of relatively mature and integrated persons, the counseling relationship is relatively brief. An average of four or five counseling contacts per client for about 20 percent of its students is about all that a college or university can be expected to provide for in its budget. Even if economic resources were available, the kinds of clients dealt with do not need a more extended process of counseling. "We are assuming that a relatively well-integrated person can make use of a brief counseling experience to set in motion a learning process that carries far beyond the relationship itself." [23] The client will want to continue counseling as long as he has confidence in the counselor and feels that he has not yet achieved the results he desires from counseling. However, the client's wish to continue may reflect regressive desires to retain the relationship as a source of satisfaction. Pressure for a long-term intensive counseling relationship may also arise from the counselor, who finds satisfaction and enhancement of his personal worth in influencing a client's personality structure and development. The typical counseling client comes for help on a limited problem, but the counselor, who wants to help the client psychologically rather than concretely by providing information, interacts with the client in a way that encourages him to look at himself. This may lead to an intense and extended relationship that may not be appropriate to the wishes of the client or the limited goals of counseling.

Counseling differs from psychotherapy in the role played by psychological tests. When tests are used in a psychotherapeutic clinic, they are administered as part of the intake process, and the client is given little explanation of the purposes of testing and no report of the results. "He remains in the dark, feeling that testing is a somewhat unfathomable process." [24]

The client comes to counseling oriented toward getting information, which he expects will be provided by tests. Tests become an integral part of the educational-vocational counseling process. Their use presents problems, however. The client may see the counselor as an expert who uses tests as a scientific version of the crystal ball to provide answers to all his problems. Tests may be an escape from dealing with his feelings and from the responsibility of making his own decisions. Thus, the client's concentration on tests can pose an obstacle to the counseling process. The counselor may need to remove this obstacle by discussing the place of tests in counseling. Tests contribute to counseling by providing the client with the opportunity to become aware of gaps, or deficiencies, in his life experience and of his capacities. Thus, they often provide information about himself that he has been aware of and supply a stimulus for self-exploration, which can lead to clarification of his attitudes toward himself.

The relatively superficial and transitory nature of the counseling relationship frequently leads to interruptions, which often constitute termination, leaving a sense of incompleteness about the counseling. The counselor faces a problem in handling interruptions—whether to contact the client in some way or to wait patiently for the client to make the move to return. The client may react to a follow-up by the counselor with irritation if he feels the counselor is overprotective or with fright if he thinks the counselor feels his problems are serious.

Counselors often tend to prolong counseling, feeling, perhaps as a result of their own perfectionism or insecurity, that not enough has been done for the client. Forced endings are frequent in situations such as college counseling, where the end of a semester or year results in the departure of clients or counselors. Counselors must prepare for such endings or arrange for the transfer of a client to another counselor. The forced ending may have a value as a limit, resulting in the acceleration of progress. Other clients, however, may hesitate to open up new problems with an ending imminent.

The counselor must be aware of the possibility of giving the client the impression that he can expect further trouble and should consider further counseling or psychotherapy in the future. It would appear to be more desirable to leave the client with the feeling that he will be able to handle future situations adequately. When a client's problems have only been dealt with partially, so that there is a basis for apprehension about the future, leaving him with such an impression will not be helpful, of course. Rather, such clients should be helped to plan for future difficulties.

IMPLEMENTATION: TECHNIQUES OF COUNSELING

Initiating the Counseling Relationship

Child guidance and mental hygiene clinics commonly subject prospective clients to interviews with a social worker and a psychiatrist, and interviewing and diagnostic testing by a psychologist. Counseling agencies may require an intake interview by a relatively untrained staff member, which includes a history taking and is followed by psychological testing, before the client sees a counselor.

The procedure by which the client sees the counselor without any contact other than his making an appointment with the receptionist is preferable to the clinic method. It simplifies the process by which the client enters counseling. Elaborate intake procedures may discourage the client from persisting in implementing his decision, perhaps hesitantly made, to seek counseling. The disturbed person may see the intake procedure as red tape, indicating more interest in procedures than in him as a person.

Since many disturbed people, some of whom may need other services, come for counseling, the counselor needs information before committing himself to any specific course of action. He may obtain this in the initial interviews. The response of the client to the ambiguous characteristics of the therapeutic situation is an indication of his flexibility and spontaneity. The aspects of his problems that he takes up and the order in which he relates material, together with the accompanying affect, are meaningful. The counselor is alert to the implications of the sequence of the client's communications, the relationships between topics, and the connections between persons discussed under succeeding topics. He may use psychological tests to aid in obtaining a diagnostic understanding as a basis for decisions about acceptance for counseling and about the conduct of the counseling process.

In opening the initial interview, many counselors seek to establish rapport by small talk, attempting to find a common ground. This is usually a relatively artificial process. The client may be anxious to begin "really" talking and be impatient with the counselor's waste of time. The fact that the client had a purpose in coming provides the basis for an immediate relationship. The counselor should thus neither initiate nor encourage social interaction. The general rule is that the counselor should wait for the client's lead to indicate the direction of discussion. Client silences may be of different kinds. When silence indicates a waiting for the counselor to begin or to tell the client where to begin, the counselor responds in such a way that he orients the client to the idea that counseling requires the client's acceptance of initiative in the communication process.

The beginnings of subsequent interviews, particularly early in the counseling process, may pose problems similar to the initial interview, and should be handled in the same way. If the counselor makes long structuring statements, the client may feel they are criticism for not learning what he should do or for not being a good client.

If the client moves into significant material toward the end of the hour, the counselor may be tempted to suggest he think about it, and may open the next interview by suggesting the client continue. When the aim is to limit the counseling relationship this may be appropriate. But it is usually not effective. The client may become defensive and resist the counselor's pressure.

If the client presents an urgent, immediate problem that is

beyond his present capacity to handle, the counselor cannot ask him to postpone it until he has acquired the capacity to meet it. In providing a solution, however, the counselor must be aware of the possibility of underestimating the client's resources and must not provide more help than is necessary.

The counselor must be sensitive to the client's capacity for interacting in the counseling relationship. The degree of ambiguity and the closeness or the distance between the client and the counselor must be judged by the counselor, so that he can help the client adapt to the counseling relationship.

In the beginning of a counseling relationship, the counselor feels the need to understand the client. The inexperienced counselor often becomes impatient with the slow process of acquiring understanding by attentive listening and may not be sensitized to the client's communications through his tone of voice, pose, bodily position, facial expression, and other signs. He may push ahead, feeling he can accumulate information more efficiently by questioning or by guiding the conversation.

The task of the client is to reveal himself to the counselor. The counselor does little defining of this task. He may only have to pause expectantly after the client is seated for the client to begin. If the client does not begin, a simple question such as, "Would you like to tell me what brings you to see me?" may accomplish the definition of the task. Following this initial free communication, the counselor must decide how close to free association he wants the client's task to be. Then he defines the task, both in words and through indirect verbal and nonverbal cues. By his verbal and nonverbal responses he lets the client see what he is interested in and what he expects the client to do. The typical client is not prepared for the task of free association, but he should be able to talk about his feelings.

Interpretation

Two principles in the timing of interpretation have already been suggested in the discussion of the cognitive-conative dimensions of counseling. Interpretation is ineffective in early interaction, since it will be used as a defense through intellectualization. But when the client is able to express affect and feelings, interpretation can lead to effective integration of feelings and conceptual, perceptual, and motor processes.

The form in which interpretations are delivered depends more upon art than upon theory. Useful definitions of three types of interpretation have been given by Colby.[25] *Clarification* interpretations attempt to crystallize the client's thought and feelings, to focus his attention, to pick out a theme, or to summarize. These interpretations are in the form of questions or simplified restatements. *Comparison* interpretations are those that place two things side by side to show similarity or contrast. Thus, past behavior may be compared with present behavior to emphasize similarities or differences. *Wish-defense* interpretations are those that refer to the two components of a neurotic conflict. Following psychoanalytic theory, the defense aspects are interpreted first.

Introduction of new cognitions through interpretation is not effective when the client is defensive and fearful, or when the client is rapidly making discoveries for himself. In the former situation it is best to allow his fearful and defensive feelings to build up more strongly, until their implications of avoidance are close to awareness, at which point the significant interpretation of resistance can be made. In the latter case interpretations may be perceived as efforts to rob the client of his initiative and his feeling of having accomplished something himself. When he is involved in active self-exploration, "it is the client who makes the final interpretation. The counselor's role is that of making partial interpretations which lead up to but do not themselves state the important ones." [26]

Awareness of relationships resulting from interpretation does not automatically change reactions or behavior. The various contexts of the impulse-defense conflict must be brought to awareness in order to achieve the generalized awareness that can lead to less distorted action on the impulse. Thus, not only an intellectual and rational grasp of a single interpretation but also an integrated understanding, which may be termed "insight," is required. The process of achieving this is termed "working through." In counseling this is usually not the extended process that it is in psychotherapy.

Maintaining a Cognitive-Conative Balance

The counselor can encourage either the cognitive or the conative aspects of the client's communications by his reactions. Focusing upon a feeling leads to its disappearance. Interpretation thus may be used to increase the cognitive aspect and may lead to intellectualization. When a client intellectualizes, thereby repressing feelings and emotions, he needs to be encouraged, paradoxically, to pay less *attention* to his feelings and to express them more freely, relaxing efforts to control or analyze them. If the relationship becomes too emotionally oriented, cognitively oriented communication can be encouraged by the counselor.

Cognition, in the form of information or reasoning, is more characteristic of counseling than of psychotherapy. Clients who are relatively well integrated emotionally can make fuller use of a cognitive approach. Counselors, however, often overemphasize cognition, conducting purely intellectual discussions without any real feeling being involved.

Testing in Counseling

A THEORY OF THE FUNCTION OF TEST INFORMATION   "Psychological testing is one medium through which the client can carry on a reality-testing process. It is a resort to instruments by which one can test the accuracy of his perceptions of his capacities, his interests and other personality traits, and the reasonableness of the goals he has set or might set for himself." [27] Reality testing that relates to the individual's expectations of accomplishment—his wishes or aspirations—involves emotional and motivational dynamics. These stimulate exploration of attitudes toward himself and activities in which he might engage.

APPLICATION TO TEST SELECTION   When there is concern or conflict over a decision, the client is not an unbiased observer, ready to know the facts. Reality testing is influenced by the pulls of conflicting feelings, sometimes to such an extent that the client cannot admit certain factual information.

When the client is unprepared for reality testing, the introduction of testing by a procedure that requires at best the passive concurrence of the client may lead to the termination of counseling. Another possible reason for the client's failure to continue is the failure of the counselor to establish a relationship between the tests assigned and the client's needs and problems. The counselor should give the client the opportunity to become emotionally ready to subject himself to a realistic scrutiny by dealing with his feelings and fears.

Too many counselors approach testing from the standpoint of their own need for information of a certain sort. But if tests are to contribute to the major aims of the counseling process, the client must participate actively in the selection of the tests. The client must see the information supplied by the test as relevant to the plan that he himself must work out. When this is the case, the client can participate more fully and enthusiastically in testing.

In having the client share in test selection, certain procedures are useful. The client does not select a specific test, but is given a nontechnical description of the psychological characteristics evaluated by the tests, with their relationships to his problem. This is not a mere recital, but a real effort to help the client understand the nature of the test and its relevance to him. In the process the client may reveal a good deal about himself, which may become a part of counseling.

APPLICATION TO TEST INTERPRETATION   The counselor must give the client an accurate interpretation of test results. This means that the range of probable outcomes associated with his score is presented to him. The lack of certainty as to the outcome for him as an individual is presented as well. Adequate interpretation requires a thorough knowledge of tests by the counselor. The interpretation should be nonevaluative, avoiding terms such as "very high" or "very well." "What *is* important in this situation is not the counselor's valuation of various abilities and characteristics of the client but rather the values which the client attaches to each of them. When the counselor introduces his own values for social or other reasons, it may interfere with the client's freedom to express his own preference." [28]

Test interpretation is more than an information-giving process.

The emotional and motivation reactions arising from ego involvement must be considered. High test scores, as well as low test scores, may threaten some clients. The counselor must proceed slowly, according to the client's willingness and readiness to digest the information, taking time out to deal with reactions and problems that arise. Pausing for the client to react is not sufficient; the counselor should invite a reaction from the client, perhaps asking him how the result fits in with his impressions and expectations.

Personality tests present a special problem in interpretation. The counselor may use clinical tests of personality for his own information; if this is the case, he should indicate this to the client at the time tests are being selected. However, the client may be disturbed by the test and concerned about the results. He may feel he has revealed some mysterious, deep attitudes and feelings. An interpretation emphasizing some of his surface attitudes and feelings, probably those that have already appeared in counseling, will quiet his anxiety and allow him to explore these feelings further.

Controlling the Intensity and Duration of Counseling

Counseling, as has been indicated, is less intensive and less extended than psychotherapy. There are factors in the client and in the counselor which may lead to intensive extended relationships. These must be controlled if the counselor's functions are to be distinct from those of the psychotherapist. Psychological counseling is concerned with the personality of the client, not only with a specific decision or situational problem. But personality is complex, and counseling cannot explore it in all its breadth and depth. Thus, the client's "personality is dealt with only as it bears on the decision or problem situation and the client is not encouraged to go much farther afield." [29]

The counselor controls or limits the relationship, then, by keeping close to the reality problem. Clients often have no specific or concrete problem, however, but give evidence of long-standing diffuse conflicts. In such cases the counselor selects certain critical aspects of the conflict for attention. "The counselor does this by selective responsiveness and by helping the client to establish greater intellectual control over other conflicting impulses." [30] This task of the counselor is one that cannot be carried out mechanically but requires a testing out and the modifying of a general orientation.

The relationship may also be kept within limits by the counselor's avoiding the fostering of a vague and ambiguous conception of the trend of the relationship. This can be done "by giving more direction and a clearer shape to the client's interaction with him." [31] This may include summarizing toward the end of each hour and discussing possible new directions.

Giving more cognitive emphasis to the interaction, as indicated earlier, also limits the relationship. Rational analysis, rather than communication of feelings, can be encouraged. There is a danger that this may reinforce the client's neurotic efforts to dam up his feelings. The counselor must be alert to the expression of inappropriate affect, which suggests that the cognitive processes are not progressing toward greater integration.

A Model for Vocational Counseling

While the consideration of the counseling process has dealt with vocational problems, the nature of career development has implications for counseling that must be considered.

Early conceptions of vocational counseling, still reflected in many situations, centered on a vocational choice made at a particular time in terms of environmental opportunities and occupational requirements. A later stage introduced the adolescent's tested characteristics, which were to be matched with the requirements of occupations. In a third phase, problems of occupational choice were viewed as symptoms of an emotional or neurotic problem, and attempts were made to transform vocational counseling into personal counseling.

Initiated by Super, a developmental conception of vocational choice has been emerging. Roe has attempted to relate early childhood experiences and personality to later occupational choices. Bordin and his associates (Barbara Nachmann and S. J. Segal) have incorporated aspects of psychoanalytic theory into a framework whose "pivotal assumption is that insofar as he has freedom of choice an individual tends to gravitate toward those occupations whose activities permit him to express his preferred ways of seeking gratification and of protecting himself from anxiety." [32]

This framework consists of modes of gratification and methods of seeking them or of reducing anxiety induced by their frustration. The physiologically based sources of gratification consist of (1) nurturant activities (feeding and fostering), (2) aggressive activities (cutting, biting, devouring), (3) manipulative (power) activities, (4) sensual (pleasurable) activities, (5) anal-derived activities (acquiring, time ordering, hoarding and smearing), (6) phallic and genital-derived activities (erecting, penetrating, impregnating, producing), (7) exploratory activities (seeing, touching, hearing), and (8) activities of flowing-quenching, exhibiting, and rhythmic movement. Five different ways in which these activities may be expressed in an occupation are given.

Vocational counseling is seen as a self-confrontation under conditions of minimal anxiety. The process includes three stages: an exploratory, contract-setting stage, a stage of critical decision, which merges into the third stage of working through problems inherent in the client's current stage of development or that have been of long standing.

In the first stage the counselor must avoid the pitfalls of acquiescing to a client's request for tests and information, on the one hand, and, on the other, of inappropriately directing the process into long-term psychotherapy. "Somehow he must strive to disclose to his client that the question of his vocational choice deserves a closer, more painstaking look at the kind of person he is, his ways of seeking gratification and protecting himself from anxiety, and the images of self that go along with it." [33] He does this by staying with the client's focus on vocational choice and encouraging him to examine "thoughts and feelings about occupations which are intimately related to his reactions to and observations of himself." [34] The counselor applies the views of occupations in terms of modes of gratification in his reactions to the client's reactions.

In the stage of critical decision the client, recognizing a struggle for growth and change, and his views of himself as he is and as he would like to be, "also begins to see the counseling process not only as a means for effecting a decision, but also, if he desires it, as a part of a process of personality change. He then begins to struggle with the question of whether he should retain his more limited original objective or seek broader goals in counseling. The counselor must be alert to the appropriate time for offering explicit statements of his choice." [35] The counselor must also avoid pushing the client either way in terms of his own motivations, and if the client elects to work for personality change, the counselor must decide whether he is competent to continue with the client or to refer him elsewhere.

In the working-for-change stage the relevance to vocational identity is retained as the central theme, even though the total scope of the client's experiencing and functioning is included, and secondary attention may be given to personality problems or conflicts in general. During the more general consideration of problems, the counselor relates them to the problem of vocational choice. Thus, this model "provides a basis for eliminating the spurious dichotomy between vocational and personal counseling without reducing one to the other. It permits us to relate a person's difficulties with his vocational choices to the vicissitudes of his personality development and, through helping with these choices, to influence the fullness of that development." [36]

EXAMPLE

One of the areas of concern of psychological counseling is vocational counseling, which involves the use of tests. Most other approaches to counseling have neglected this area. It is therefore appropriate that an example of such counseling be provided here.[37]

Case of Ril

As one example of this interpretative process [with interest and personality inventories] we choose a portion of a second interview with a freshman student who was trying to establish a vocational goal. In his first interview, the student, Mr. Ril, mentioned as fields he was considering law, medicine, and the ministry, but said that he was now fairly sure that he would exclude the last alternative. During the first interview he also indicated that he was responding to his family's expectation that he would get a professional education. Although Mr. Ril seemed to be accepting this pressure rather passively, the counselor noted some evidence that there was an underlying unconscious rebellion against this authority. Mainly, it became evident through his critical reactions to his professors. Most of the first hour was devoted to a discussion of tests in which he participated quite actively.

At the very start of the second interview, Mr. Ril was ready to plunge right into the results of tests. Almost as soon as the counselor greeted him, he was asking whether the tests had shown that he was inconsistent. However, the counselor did not turn immediately to test results. Instead, he asked whether there had been any change in Mr. Ril's thinking. When he replied that the issue of the ministry was reopened, they discussed briefly what could account for the shift. During this discussion, Mr. Ril indicated that his father disapproved of the choice because he did not think that he had sufficient religious faith to become a minister. Mr. Ril showed that he shared his father's doubts on this score and confessed to the feeling that the ministry's main attraction was its central role in a dramatic religious service. It is at this point that the counselor begins to introduce the interest and personality inventory results.

COUNSELOR   These things that we're talking about here are all ideas about yourself that are pretty well supported by the tests that you took. That is, you were consistent in that sense that the things we're talking about here also showed on the tests and that you seemed to have quite a lot of reaction to the whole idea of having contact with people.

STUDENT   Uh-huh.

CO   Of having influence or putting on some kind of a . . . (ST: show) well, I don't want to say a demonstration or a show either, but at least it adds up to putting something across.

ST   Uh-huh.

CO   I think that's the main idea.

ST   Uh-huh.

CO   That seems to be one of the most important pictures of yourself that seems to come out from these tests that you took. Does that help you feel more sure that . . .

ST   Well, I'm positive of that.

CO   Uh-huh. There isn't—wasn't any doubt in your mind.

ST   Uh-huh.

ST   But there is just about the end of my own picture of myself.

CO   I guess you're saying that really isn't definite enough— that you want something of which you can be (ST: yes, [with little laugh]) sure.

ST   If there is any possibility of getting something like that.

CO   (short pause) Well, perhaps it would be of some value if, instead of unraveling the thing in such a general way, that we try looking at it more specifically and see what we can come across. A little while ago you suggested that I begin at the beginning, but I've never been able to figure out where the beginning is. (ST: oh, I see) I just wander along into it. This measure here gives some indication of your feelings about yourself in relation to differents kinds of activity—as what you prefer to do and what you prefer not to do, that kind of thing. For instance, it suggests that you have a very strong negative feeling toward anything along mechanical lines. Is that so?

ST   Uh-huh.

CO   So that pretty much excludes a number of occupations. For instance, dentistry (ST: uh-huh) might be excluded on that basis, since there is quite a lot of mechanical work involved there. But I guess you never included that as a possibility anyway.

ST   No.

CO   It might conceivably apply to medicine too, but more indirectly. There is an awful lot of laboratory work involved in a medical training program. That might be something to (ST: uh-huh) stop and think about.

ST   I was hoping to go into psychiatry when I got through Med. School.

CO   That still would include the necessity of going . . .

ST   Going through it.

CO   . . . training, and this indicates that it might be something pretty unpleasant.

ST   Uh-huh.

CO   Not for sure, but just points. That's a question that you have to answer (ST: uh-huh), whether you want to put up with that much practical work, lab work.

ST   Well, it's funny. I have a funny attitude about that now. I don't mind working in a laboratory or something like that. But when it gets out to making something, I don't want to do it unless it's something that I actually want myself. I mean, if I'm working on a photographic project or something and I want a gadget, I'll go ahead and try to make it. I can't make it very well. But I'll make it. I'll enjoy making it. If I have to make something for somebody else, I wouldn't enjoy it at all.

CO   You sort of use it as a way of . . .

ST   A means to an end.

CO   Uh-huh. Well, I guess there's no point making too big an issue, as you seem to understand the idea. You don't seem to have any—well, you—it's kind of a mild feeling of liking for dealing with numbers. Apparently you don't have any great ambitions along those lines, but you also don't seem to mind computing or working with figures.

ST   Uh-huh.

CO   That kind of thing I think we talked about that last time. Didn't we?

ST   Uh-huh.

co I've already mentioned one here that seems to stand out as the strongest feeling about yourself as somebody who is a persuader, somebody who influences other people. (ST: uh-huh) That kind of preference seems to be the strongest with you, that you like to make an impression. (pause) The other one point that seems to indicate some preference is a musical one, that hasn't fitted in with anything except perhaps just for fun.

ST Uh-huh.

co But at least you seem to think of yourself as a person who likes music and enjoys it, maybe knows something about it. I don't know about that last part. At least you have a positive feeling about music is the most this can tell. (pause) You also seem to have some positive reactions to the idea of being in sort of a helping position, a welfare role or having some concern for—for helping other people, doing some good for other people. Does that fit in at all or . . .

ST Well, it depends. It's very hard for me to analyze that. Because I want to help some people and yet there are other people I don't want to help. I don't know. It's very peculiar. I think what it actually amounts to is that if I get into contact with somebody that needs help I want to help them. People I don't know about and the general class I don't want to help.

co Uh-huh.

ST I don't know where it comes about. It just seems to be that way.

co You mean it's sort of a limited conception of yourself as a helping person. (ST: uh-huh) It's not so much a feeling of wanting to help humanity as of wanting to help specific . . .

ST Individual people.

co Uh-huh. But at least we can say that you don't want to think of yourself as a person who doesn't care about anybody. That is an issue with you.

ST Uh-huh.

co Apparently, though, you might like to help somebody. (pause) This scale here is one that gives some indication of how your patterns of interests are similar to those of people who are already doing different kinds of jobs. And I've already presented generally the ideas, the same ones, that you seem to be the kind of person who is like men who are doing promoting kinds of work. In this particular test, it seems to come out as a combination between people who do personal contact work along welfare lines. Do those (ST: uh-huh) two ideas fit together? It seems as if they still are describing you as the same kind of person we were talking about all along.

ST Do they have individual professions running down this column?

co Well, it just has the names of the ones that they use as (ST: I see) a criterion, but they don't mean anything specifically.

ST I see what you mean.

co We think of them more as groups rather than individuals.

ST Uh-huh.

co It doesn't seem to indicate that there's much similarity between your patterns of interest and those of people who are successful doc-

tors or who have taken any kind of training along the specific professional group of that kind. That particular kind of profession—at the
present time you don't seem to be like those people. (pause) There
seems to be some similarity between your patterns and those of people
who are in intellectual work, something more like lawyers and writers,
that (ST: uh-huh) kind of dealing with words. I'm inclined to feel that
perhaps some of the work of a minister fits into that area too, as well
as the field of law. (pause) That to me seems to be saying the same
thing we've been saying right along.

ST   Yes.

CO   Does this make you think of anything?

ST   Well, no. It doesn't make me think of anything. It just makes me
feel a little bit, oh, not very much more certain, but I'm pretty well
decided I want to limit to those three, but—there was always the
possibility at the back of my mind for teaching but (sounding doubtful)
I don't know.

CO   Well, that would still . . .

ST   Still, it would be all contained with the same group. I want to find
out how to isolate that group.

CO   You seem to be having a little difficulty really deciding for yourself
which one. (ST: uh-huh) As if you kind of would like some outside . . .

ST   (breaking in) I'd like to have two jobs. Yeah, sort of, I'd like to
have . . . outside pressure and also I'd like to have two. I'd like to
have—be trained for two jobs. (lower) It's kind of foolish but I would
like to be trained that way.

CO   Would you care to say more about what it is that makes you want
to do that?

ST   Well, I don't know. I'd like to do two things. That sounds rather
ridiculous, but I've always had the idea in back of my head to run a
restaurant. I've always had little projects of trying to make money out
of something, and they've always more or less failed, but I've enjoyed
doing them, and I was at one time thinking of teaching and then trying
to run a restaurant too. But I always like to be dabbling in something
different. That's why I'd sort of like the ministry because I would be—I
wouldn't be able to have a private business or anything, but I would
always be able to start some new projects somewhere. Usually you can
have—ministers have notorious kinds of gardens that they can putter
around with, things like that. I'd have a chance, in my opinion, to get
some of my music worked out. I'd get an access to an organ. I'd like
to take organ lessons. I don't know. Maybe I'm basing my opinions
on just one particular minister. I don't know. But he seems to have
enough time to do those things that I'd like to do. He can, if he wanted
to, take organ lessons. But he doesn't particularly care about that. But
he has enough time to read. He has organized a book club within his
church and he does a lot of reading for himself. He has organized a
book club. He has organized a lot of other things for the church. He
sponsored a lot of clubs. He's active on the Labor-Citizens Committee,
which is supposed to settle labor disputes in the home town, and he
gets time to do a lot of different things. And that's what I'd like to do.

I always want to do a lot of different things. I don't want to be confined just to one little narrow field where I can operate. I want something new and different coming up all the time. I sort of like to organize things, get them started, and pull out and let somebody else take over.

co   There isn't anything still that changes the picture. (st: no) It's almost as if we still have this picture of you as a person who likes to promote things, who likes to have a variety of things going on, who likes to contact people, make things run, things of that sort. It seems almost as if it's pretty much up to you what particular area that you decide to do it in. The—the business area is indicated here. The intellectual area is indicated. That would include the ministry, and that would also include this helping kind of thing, promoting for the benefit of others. Starting a book club is an example. I think there may be some questions about the field of law. That is, it tends to suggest that it might become pretty busy in one kind of thing, but that would be a matter of individual planning. That is, it's still a pretty confining and demanding profession. It would be contrary to this (st: uh-huh) minister who has time to putter. It's more a matter of the size of church and things of that sort that you got into. Does that seem like a . . .

st   Uh-huh.

co   . . . realistic consideration? There's also the matter of the training. That is, the training for a lawyer is a tough grind for several years, whereas the training either as a business type of promoter or a minister—a religious type of promoter, or even a teacher, includes a kind of liberal education, allowing chances for (st: uh-huh) extracurricular activities and side interest (short pause). I'm doing a lot of talking. Maybe you have some . . .

st   No.

co   . . . reflections on all this?

co   You understand, of course, that most of this during the last few minutes has been speculative (st: uh-huh) stuff. We really can't get much more definite with the tests than this general picture of you; we'll keep coming back to you.

st   Uh-huh. (pause)

> In the discussion that follows this section of the interview, Mr. Ril goes on to indicate that there is some home pressure to go into law, and that with regard to medicine, he would be primarily interested in psychiatry. Then he reveals that his father is a psychiatrist. He has wanted to be a lawyer for a good many years, whereas the idea of psychiatry is of relatively recent origin. The counselor and the client go on to discuss the fact that among the ministry, teaching, and law it isn't absolutely necessary to make a specific choice at this point, since all three curricula are rather broad in the first two years; whereas medicine does require a much more restricted curriculum. In the process of this discussion Mr. Ril decides that the restrictive nature of the premedical curriculum makes it a less desirable choice. This seems to give him considerable relief.

SUMMARY AND EVALUATION

Psychological counseling is a means of helping essentially mature and minimally anxious people to overcome obstacles to personality growth and development that are reflected in difficulties in dealing with specific problems or situations. It thus differs from psychotherapy in that it is more cognitively oriented. Nevertheless, it is not simply a rational, problem-solving process. It is concerned with, and deals with, affect, motivations, and personality. It does so, however, only as these are involved in, or related to, the specific problem situation. The personality theory accepted as the basis for understanding and helping the client is that developed by psychoanalysis.

Three dimensions of therapeutic relationships are identified and analyzed. These are the ambiguity dimension, the cognitive-conative dimension, and the personal dimension of the relationship. The counseling process and counseling techniques are dealt with essentially in terms of these dimensions. Compared to psychotherapy the counseling situation is less ambiguous, more cognitive, and involves less intensity of feeling.

The counseling process involves a relationship in which the client, with the help of the counselor, is able to analyze his problems, reach solutions or decisions, and—to the extent that they are involved in the problem—understand and modify personality characteristics. The counselor's major techniques include acceptance, understanding, and interpretation. Since clients frequently come to counseling with educational and vocational problems, the use of tests constitutes an important technique in psychological counseling. The counseling process is relatively brief, both because of the nature of the problems the clients bring to the counselor and because the counselor discourages and avoids intensive, long-term relationships.

Bordin's treatment of his approach, in terms of the nature of normal and disturbed behavior, the counseling process, and the techniques of counseling, is neither systematic nor detailed. Even the presentation of the dimensions of the counseling process is hardly a thorough, systematic exploration and development of the concepts, although this discussion represents one of the main contributions of the approach.

The attempt to distinguish between counseling and psychotherapy does not result in any convincing or clear-cut bases or criteria for separating them. It would appear that they fall on a continuum, and that the differences between them are quantitative rather than qualitative. Counseling is brief; but sometimes psychotherapy is also brief, so there is certainly a great overlap in this characteristic. Psychotherapy, according to Alexander, may be limited to a single interview, and counseling can hardly be briefer than that. The attempt to determine when counseling becomes psychotherapy, in terms of Bordin's dimensions, or in terms of differentiating between dealing with personality factors related to a specific problem and dealing with basic personality conflicts, is doomed to failure, since no adequate criteria are available. Nor is it any easier to determine which conflicts are close to awareness, so that they may be pulled into consciousness and dealt with by counseling, and which conflicts are not close (how close?) to awareness and are thus left alone in counseling. Bordin uses the terms "counseling" and "psychotherapy" throughout his book, and there appears to be no consistency in the way in which the two terms are used.

The cognitive-conative dichotomy presents a problem also. The counselor, it would appear, is in a constant conflict, or choice, situation in which he must determine if the relationship is too cognitively, or intellectually, oriented, on the one hand, or too affect-oriented, on the other. He constantly adjusts his methods and techniques to maintain the proper balance. And, of course, what is the proper balance is something for which there are at best only vague criteria. Actually, the counselors described by Bordin (through his brief transcripts) do not seem to be involved in such a process of adjustment, and it is only in retrospect that Bordin can praise or criticize their handling of the balance.

A major value of Bordin's *Psychological Counseling* is that it deals with vocational counseling and the use of tests. This is a real contribution, which the student will not find duplicated in any of the other approaches to counseling considered in this book. Here, in all too brief a form, is a major source for the student interested in a systematic approach to the use of tests in the counseling process. The book has a number of typescripts of interviews, and those that deal with the discussion of test selection and test results are especially useful to the student. This contribution alone makes Bordin's approach a significant source for the counselor interested in vocational counseling.

The model for vocational counseling, which is an addition in the second edition of the book, is interesting but less likely to be useful because of its psychoanalytic orientation. However, the case illustration is not closely tied to the psychoanalytic theory, but is a good example of incorporating consideration of personality factors into discussion of vocational choice.

REFERENCES

[1] Bordin, E. S. *Psychological counseling.* (2nd ed.) New York: Appleton-Century-Crofts, 1968.   [2] *Ibid.,* p. 6.   [3] *Ibid.,* p. 7.   [4] *Ibid.,* p. 9.   [5] *Ibid.,* p. 10.   [6] *Ibid.,* p. 13.   [7] *Ibid.,* p. 17.   [8] *Ibid.,* p. 19.   [9] *Ibid.,* p. 137.   [10] *Ibid.,* p. 138.   [11] *Ibid.,* p. 139.   [12] *Ibid.,* p. 141.   [13] *Ibid.,* p. 142.   [14] *Ibid.,* p. 177.   [15] *Ibid.,* p. 185.   [16] *Ibid.,* p. 195.   [17] *Ibid.,* p. 199.   [18] *Ibid.,* p. 200.   [19] *Ibid.,* p. 201.   [20] *Ibid.,* p. 204.   [21] *Ibid.,* p. 105.   [22] *Ibid.,* p. 120.   [23] *Ibid.,* p. 368.   [24] *Ibid.,* p. 295.   [25] Colby, K. M. *A primer for psychotherapists.* New York: Ronald, 1951. Pp. 82–106.   [26] Bordin, E. S., *op. cit.,* p. 179.   [27] *Ibid.,* p.

299.   [28] *Ibid.,* p. 309.   [29] *Ibid.,* p. 370.   [30] *Ibid.,* p. 374.   [31] *Ibid.,* p. 381.   [32] *Ibid.,* p. 427.   [33] *Ibid.,* p. 430.   [34] *Ibid.,* p. 431. [35] *Ibid.,* p. 440.   [36] *Ibid.,* p. 444.   [37] From *Psychological Counseling,* 2nd Edition, Edward S. Bordin, Copyright © 1968. By permission of Appleton-Century-Crofts, Educational Division, Meredith Corporation. Pp. 356, 358–363, 364.

11

Psychoanalytic therapy: Alexander

Franz Alexander (1891–1963) was born in Budapest, Hungary, and received his M.D. degree in 1913 from the University of Budapest. After several years of research in medicine (bacteriology), he did graduate work in psychiatry at the University of Berlin in 1920–1921. He was the first student to matriculate (1921) at the first psychoanalytic institute, the Berlin Psychoanalytic Institute, founded in 1920; and a few years later he was appointed to its staff, where he continued as a lecturer until 1930. In 1930 he came to the United States. After a year at the University of Chicago as visiting professor of psychoanalysis and a year at the Judge Baker Foundation in Boston as research associate in criminology, he became the first director of the Chicago Institute for Psychoanalysis, where he remained until 1955. During 1955–1956 he was a Ford Foundation Fellow at the Center for Advanced Study in the Behavioral Sciences at Stanford. In 1956 he became Chief of Staff of the Psychiatric Department and Director of the Psychiatric and Psychosomatic Research Institute at Mt. Sinai Hospital, Los Angeles, California. He was continuously engaged in private practice and held appointments at various universities; at his death he was associated with the University of Southern California. He was the author of numerous articles in psychoanalytic journals and of a number of books, some of which are *The Psychoanalysis of the Total Personality* (1929), *Mental*

245

Hygiene and Criminology (1930), *The Medical Value of Psychoanalysis* (1936), *Our Age of Unreason* (1942), *Psychoanalytic Therapy* (with T. M. French and others, 1946), *Fundamentals of Psychoanalysis* (1948, revised in 1963), and *Psychoanalysis and Psychotherapy* (1956).

BACKGROUND AND DEVELOPMENT

In the 1930s Alexander, and other staff members of the Chicago Institute for Psychoanalysis, began questioning some of the traditional psychoanalytic beliefs. Among these were the beliefs that (1) the depth of therapy is necessarily proportionate to the duration of treatment and the frequency of interviews, (2) results achieved in a small number of interviews are necessarily superficial and temporary, (3) prolongation of an analysis is justified on the basis that the client's resistance will eventually be overcome and success achieved. As a result of this questioning an attempt was begun to define principles and to develop methods and techniques that would make a shorter and more efficient psychotherapy possible.

When little was known about the genesis and pathology of neurosis, and each case was the subject of research, the extensive and standard form of treatment was necessary and desirable. "With the advance of knowledge in this field, however, we can now use generalizations and principles tested by our extended experience to develop a more flexible and economical procedure adjusted to the individual nature of the great variety of neurotic patients."[1] This approach is not to be considered a shortcut to therapy. While at first a sharp differentiation was made between the more flexible methods and "standard" psychoanalysis, it was later recognized that there was no essential difference between the two sets of procedures, but only a difference in the extent to which various procedures were used. The same theories, as well as techniques, were involved. The induction of emotional discharge to facilitate insight and the exposing of the ego to the unresolved emotional constellations that it must master were present in both methods. The approach was therefore designated as psychoanalytic psychotherapy, as distinguished from psychoanalysis.

"Perhaps the most significant development in psychiatry consists in the emergence of what is commonly called 'psychoanalytically-oriented psychotherapy.' Psychoanalytically-oriented psychotherapy consists in the flexible application of the fundamental principles of psychodynamics. . . . It applies these principles in various technical procedures which are precisely adjusted to the individual nature of each case. The routine application of the same standardized procedure (the standard psychoanalysis) gradually is becoming enriched by more individualized and more economical treatment."[2]

The standard approach is applicable to a limited and relatively small number of psychiatric patients, and few of these require strict adherence to the standard technique during the entire treatment. This approach is not as suitable for severely disturbed individuals whose basic deficiency in ego functions makes them unable to face their conflicts nor for those with milder acute incipient disturbances. It is with the second group that the modified procedures of psychoanalytic therapy can be useful. Early skillful treatment of these cases can prevent the development of chronic conditions, which often resist the most intensive therapy.

The modifications characterizing psychoanalytic therapy are not new; it is the clarification of their usefulness and their systematic use that constitute the contribution of Alexander's approach. The application of the approach to the milder chronic and acute neuroses is an important social contribution because of their prevalence. The postulation of the etiology of neurosis in childhood, based on the observation of this etiology in those cases selected as suitable for psychoanalysis, is not valid for acute neurotic breakdown or mild chronic cases. Latent neurotic tendencies, present in everyone, may develop into acute neurotic states under stress or exposure to difficulties beyond the power of adaptation of the individual.

The utilization of psychoanalytic psychotherapy rather than psychoanalysis does not imply that any different or lesser qualifications or training are required. Not only those practicing psychoanalytic therapy but all psychotherapists should be trained in psychoanalytic theory and should undergo a personal analysis.[3]

PHILOSOPHY AND CONCEPTS

The basic principles of psychoanalytic theory underlying psychoanalytic therapy are presented in *Fundamentals of Psychoanalysis,* first published in 1948 and revised in 1963.[4]

Principles of Psychodynamics

FUNDAMENTAL POSTULATES There are two underlying assumptions of psychology as a science. The first is that minds can study minds. The second assumption is that the process of life can be studied by two approaches, the somatic and the psychological. The functions of the mind are biological and will eventually be described in terms of physics and chemistry. At present, however, the psychological approach, in which man describes his sensations to others, affords insight into the complex biological functions.

THE PRINCIPLE OF STABILITY Life is a dynamic equilibrium. Disturbances are manifested as needs and wishes that motivate behavior. The organism seeks to keep these tensions at a constant level; this is the principle of stability, which Freud borrowed from Fechner, and whose physiological aspect, first recognized by Claude Bernard, was labeled homeostasis by Cannon. The function of the ego is to implement this principle through the recognition of internal needs and external conditions, and to integrate these needs and conditions in such a way as to gratify the needs as much as possible. The principle of stability is a more precise and useful formulation of the instinct of self-preservation.

THE PRINCIPLE OF ECONOMY, OR INERTIA In addition to innate, automatic functions, there are other functions that the organism must learn through trial and error and repetition. The principle of stability requires that the organism find ways of reducing internal tensions. The economy principle, or the principle of inertia, refers to the tendency of the organism to perform the functions necessary for the maintenance of equilibrium with the minimum expenditure of energy. It overlaps partly with the so-called repetition compulsion. The principle of inertia interferes with new learning, leading to *fixation* on behavior that was satisfactory in the past but is not adequate under changed conditions. Under new, difficult, or threatening conditions, the individual reverts, or *regresses,* to earlier patterns of behavior. Changing conditions require flexible behavior, but the organism clings to old patterns, thus causing a continuous struggle.

THE PRINCIPLE OF SURPLUS ENERGY Growth and propagation require a principle in addition to those of stability and inertia. Growth is biologically predetermined. Activity is spontaneous and pleasurable. Playful activity belongs to the "erotic" category. Erotic phenomena expend rather than conserve energy; they are creative and progressive. The energy expended is surplus energy.

THE VECTOR ANALYSIS OF THE LIFE PROCESS Life is a relationship among three vectors: the intake of energy (food, air), its partial retention for use in growth, and the expenditure of energy to maintain existence —its loss in waste, in heat, and in erotic playful activity. Surplus energy is the source of all playful erotic activity in the child and of sexual activity and sublimated creative activity in the adult.

THE DIFFERENT FORMS OF EROTIC BEHAVIOR

Oral Eroticism / The oral phase of growth and development includes both the pleasure sensation in the oral zone from sucking and thumb-sucking as a form of oral play; these can be exercised for their own sake, without self-preservative aspects, but constitute the expenditure of surplus excitation. Security, dependence, and passive, receptive, and demanding attitudes toward the mother become linked with the relief of hunger and the receiving of oral pleasure. This complex of emotions is referred to as oral-receptive or oral-incorporative. When the flow of milk is inadequate, the child bites; this represents an oral-aggressive attitude and is linked with envy and possessiveness.

Anal Eroticism / Anal retention is pleasurable, interfering with training. Anal retentiveness is related to stubbornness, independence, and possessiveness. Expulsion is also pleasurable and is associated with pride. After weaning, toilet training is the second serious interference with the child's basic biological functions, and results in frustration, leading to sadistic aggression. Sadism is aggression or hurting for its own sake, or for the sake of the pleasure achieved, and is thus like all erotic phenomena.

Other Early Types of Eroticism / A great many functions of the body, including the use of the limbs and eyes, may be sources of erotic pleasure.

Phallic Eroticism / Phallic eroticism includes urination and masturbation, and their emotional complements are competitiveness, assertiveness, pleasure in achievement, and ambition. This stage usually reaches its peak in the fifth or sixth year. The Oedipus complex is the typical emotional constellation of this age. It is a "mixture of love, jealousy, inferiority, and guilt occasioned by the child's possessive sexual attraction to the parent of the opposite sex." [5] Like the earlier periods, this period is later obscured by infantile amnesia due to repression. The child's conflicts are the result of the uneven development of instinct, intellect, and genitality, which makes childhood the most vulnerable period of human development. Traumatic experiences increase the conflict, leading to pathogenic influences in later life. The repression of the conflicts of the Oedipal period begins the period of latency, which lasts to puberty.

Genital impulses / In puberty endocrinological changes lead to a more adult form of sexual impulses. Sexual maturity is reached, and the adolescent struggles to adjust himself to his new biological status. Competitiveness, showing off, and other forms of defensive behavior are ways of overcoming inferiority and achieving security. With maturity and security, genital sexuality is possible, that is, "love assumes for the first time a generous, giving quality, the evidence of strength and energy which the mature organism no longer requires for its own maintenance." [6] Pregenital love is based on identification with its objects; it is narcissistic. In adult love the impulse to give of oneself is added.

The Concept of Sexuality

EARLY FREUDIAN VIEWS   Freud first accepted the distinction between self-preservation and racial preservation, or the sexual instinct; but with the recognition of sexual libido in infancy, sexuality was extended beyond the concept of race preservation. All early pleasurable excitations that did not aid self-preservation were labeled sexual. Although Freud persisted in his dualism, this distinction between self-preservation and sexuality could not be maintained, since early eroticism is related to self-preservative functions.

THE THEORY OF LIFE AND DEATH INSTINCTS   To overcome the difficulties of this dualism, Freud proposed another in the theory of life and death instincts. According to this, the erotic drive is constructive, anabolic, while the death instinct is destructive, or catabolic. This distinction is basic.

The description of life as a process of anabolic construction and catabolic destruction is supported by biology, but there is a difficulty with the philosophical concept of the disintegrating factor as a death instinct. Death is an inevitable result of the disruptive tendency, but not necessarily its aim. Contrary to Freud's theory, the death instinct is not necessary to explain social disintegration. In both the individual and the social situation the disintegrating factor is the individualistic tendency of each biological unit. The death instinct has been assumed to be a component of every neurosis, but the analysis of masochistic manifestations indicates that they are aimed at eliminating guilt and gaining love.

Thus, there are two dynamic opposing vectors in life, one constructive and one destructive, but they are not manifestations of opposing instincts. Biological units organize to survive under pressure of external danger, but when the need for cooperation diminishes, the individualistic tendencies of the units result in disintegration. In the multicellular organism the units cannot exist alone, so that disintegration leads to the death of the cells. The integration of functions in the organism is adaptive and promotes survival. The so-called death instinct is the disintegration of mature behavior, leading to regression, in situations beyond the organism's adaptive capacity. "What Freud called the death instinct is a tendency not toward death, but toward old and worn patterns of life." [7]

A PSYCHOSOMATIC VIEW OF SEXUALITY   The erotic pleasures of the infant are varied, involving many functions and many parts of the body, but they are sexual in nature. The sexual impulse is not specific; any emotion can become sexualized. Sexuality represents the discharge of any surplus excitation, in both infants and adults. In the course of maturation the genito-urinary tract assumes the function of draining surplus excitation. The persistence of other ways of discharge leads to the adult perversions. "Propagation results from surplus energy generated by growth. The psychological equivalent of propagation is love." [8]

The Functions of the Ego and Its Failures

THE STRUCTURAL THEORY OF THE MENTAL APPARATUS   Freud divided the mind into three structurally different parts: (1) the id, or reservoir of chaotic instinctual impulses, (2) the ego, or integrating part, which coordinates the id impulses with external reality, and (3) the superego, which embodies the code of society. It is difficult to maintain this structural division. Although it is justifiable to distinguish different functions, the boundaries are fluid. The unconscious superego cannot be sharply separated from the ego, and the latter merges with the id developmentally. For various reasons, including the emphasis in psychoanalysis upon irrational behavior, we know relatively little about the integrative functions of the ego. We do know that it has two perceptive surfaces, one directed inward toward the instinctive impulses and the other directed outward toward external reality through sense perception, and that its integrative function is to harmonize the conflicting demands of these two sorts of perceptions. It also has an executive function in controlling voluntary motor behavior, adaptively maintaining homeostasis within the organism. The ego is the most flexible part of the mind, engaged in a continual reconciliation between the demands of external conditions and desires incompatible with such demands. Under strong or continued stress, the adaptive functioning of the ego may break down, resulting in neurosis or psychosis. Behavior then reverts to the use of defense mechanisms that had been utilized earlier to cope with impulses that the child could not equilibrate.

DEVELOPMENT OF THE EGO FUNCTIONS   The ego is the agent of the stability principle, concerned with maintaining constant conditions. It must ward off or reduce external and internal stimuli. Before these functions have developed, the child's impulses seek gratification without regard to the needs of the total organism; he is dominated by what Freud calls the pleasure-pain principle. He learns to coordinate his impulses and to relate them to the environment according to the reality principle. In addition to learning from trial and error, the ego can learn from experiences with others, such as parents, through identification.

The early stages of ego development are not well known, since not only have they not been observed, they cannot be communicated during the prespeech period of childhood. An early phase is the gradual differentiation between the internal and external worlds, the ego and nonego. Fantasy gratification, probably present at the beginning, is given up and replaced by real satisfaction, which is learned when uncoordinated activity deriving from tension leads to behavior that results in relief from tension. Impulses are controlled primarily by repression, until better methods of control are gradually developed.

DEFENSE MECHANISMS OF THE EGO

Repression / This is the ego's fundamental defense measure. It consists of excluding impulses and their ideational representations from consciousness, and occurs when the impulse would cause unbearable conflict and anxiety if it were to become conscious. It is an unconscious inhibition that thus "presupposes an unconscious inner perception which leads to automatic reflex inhibition." [9] The censorship, or unconscious judgment, is unable to make subtle differentiations and thus may repress impulses that might be acceptable later. Thus, all sexual impulses may be repressed along with early incestuous impulses. This broad and oversevere repression is one of the causes of psychoneuroses. Impulses that cannot be integrated within the (weak) ego, by sublimation or other means, are excluded in order to maintain the ego's integrity. Conscious manifestations in the form of countercathexis (for example, pity against tendencies toward cruelty) and anxiety appear. The repressed psychological forces continue to exist, requiring the ego to drain its resources in defensive measures, so that it loses the surplus energy that is the source of sexual and socially creative activities.

Anxiety / Anxiety is internalized fear. Fear is aroused by the memory of painful past experiences, that is, experiences associated with punishment for the gratification of an impulse, and thus becomes connected with the impulse. Anxiety, then, is aroused by a dangerous impulse, and it serves as a signal to the ego of the breaking through of the impulse. As an unconscious reaction to repressed tendencies, it is rationalized, or it may appear as free-floating anxiety. In male neurotics the unconscious anxiety is the fear of castration; this fear appears openly in children, compulsive-obsessive neurotics, and schizophrenics. The Oedipus complex leads to the castration wish (to replace the father) and thence to fear of retaliation, or castration fear. Freud regarded this fear as the primary factor in the resolution of the Oedipus complex, in which the boy relinquishes his sexual attachment to the mother and develops identification with the father. This process is not smooth even in normal individuals and may involve complications leading to neuroses. The process in girls is different, but there is little agreement on it.

Overcompensation (Reaction Formation) / The development of attitudes or character traits exactly opposite to those that have been repressed is the most common defensive measure against repressed tendencies. Persistent overcompensatory measures that become character traits are termed "reaction formations." The principle of polarity, or opposites, was one of Freud's most fundamental principles in personality. Philosophical assumptions about opposing forces are not necessary to explain this apparent polarity, however. As the child becomes a member of various groups, his surplus energy is expressed in libidinous, or erotic, attachments to others. The only genuine polarity is that between self-love and love of others. What Bleuler described as ambivalence—love and hatred directed toward the same person at the same time—is a universal polar phenomenon and is a result of the fact that man is both an individual and a member of society. The antithesis of love of self and love of others arises because the more one loves another, the more love one takes away from oneself, so that all love objects are enemies of the narcissistic core of personality, and thus objects of hate under certain conditions. Normally, one of these attitudes is buried, but in abnormal conditions both parts may be conscious.

Rationalization / All human acts are overdetermined, that is, impelled by a number of conflicting motives. Rationalization consists of selecting the most favorable motives to explain behavior. Other, unacceptable, motives are repressed.

Substitution and Displacement / Displacement consists of the replacement of the object of an emotional attitude by another, with the attitude remaining the same. Substitution, often used synonymously with displacement, is the changing of the act but not the object, as when anger toward a person is replaced by destructive, but energy-consuming, and useful acts, such as chopping wood. Displacement and substitution may result from frustration as well as from repression, and if successful as a compromise, they may make repression unnecessary.

Sublimation / The modification of unacceptable urges so that they become socially acceptable is sublimation. It is a form of substitution. Aggressive sports are sublimations of destructive, hostile impulses. Creative activities are sublimations of sexuality.

Provocative Behavior / The provocation of hostility toward oneself justifies the release of one's hostility in retaliation.

Projection / Projection is the attributing of characteristics in oneself to others. It occurs when the ego can no longer repress objectionable tendencies that are unacceptable to the individual, who must deny them by projecting them onto the external world. The differentiation between the ego and the external world is thus obliterated.

Turning Feelings Toward Oneself / When repression fails, alien impulses may be directed toward the self instead of projected onto others. Hostility toward others is unacceptable and so becomes hostility toward the self. Directing hostility toward oneself releases it and relieves guilt feelings.

Identification As a Defense / In traumatic situations the ego may compensate for an unbearable loss by identifying with the lost love. This introjection incorporates the ambivalent attitudes toward the love object, which may lead to hostile and destructive attitudes toward the self. Identification with a threatening person may be a means of allaying anxiety.

Guilt Feelings and Masochistic Defense / The sense of guilt is the fear of one's conscience, which demands punishment to relieve anxiety and remorse. Thus, the individual must punish himself or induce others to punish him. Suffering relieves guilt or is atonement for his misbehavior. Expressed allegorically, "the ego bribes the superego through suffering to lessen its dependence upon the latter." [10] When the need for punishment is eroticized, and its discharge results in erotic gratification, the term "masochism" is used. Suffering becomes an erotic aim rather than serving merely to relieve guilt.

Defenses Against Inferiority Feelings and Their Relationship to Guilt Feelings / In inferiority feelings self-condemnation is the result of feelings of weakness or inadequacy, rather than the result of recognition of wrongdoing, as in the case of guilt. Inferiority feelings stimulate competition and aggression; showing superiority in competition eradicates the inferiority feelings. Guilt feelings lead to the opposite, to self-debasement and punishment. The coexistence of guilt and inferiority feelings thus results in a conflict that characterizes many neuroses. Inferiority feelings represent a deeper conflict than guilt feelings, stemming from earlier childhood conflicts between the wish to grow up and become an adult and the regressive longing for dependence. The regressive wish is reacted to by the ego, which identifies itself with the progressive attitude, with the resultant development of a sense of inferiority.

Conversion / In conversion the unacceptable impulses are converted into innervations or inhibitions of the voluntary neuromuscular and sensory systems, resulting in symptoms such as hysterical paralysis, contracture, anesthesia, blindness, deafness, etc.

Regression / Regression is a tendency of the organism to reestablish an earlier situation, and thus is essentially Freud's repetition compulsion. It has been referred to earlier as a common manifestation of the inertia principle. Under stress more recently acquired adaptive mechanisms may break down, and the organism may revert to earlier, more automatic behavior patterns. Regression is present in all psychopathological manifestations, although it is one of the most ineffective defenses of the ego against demands that cannot be met on a mature, acceptable level.

Psychopathology

DEFINITION OF NEUROSIS   A neurosis is a disease rooted in disturbances in the functioning of the organism, centered in the ego, and resulting in discomfort and suffering. It is characterized by the failure of the ego in its coordinating or integrative function, with the development instead of defense mechanisms, repression, and regression to deal with the rebellious impulses. It originates in excessive repression of impulses in childhood, with repression becoming the method of dealing with impulses, so that they remain in the unconscious to cause trouble later, rather than being allowed into consciousness to be dealt with by the ego and to contribute to its healthy development. Early traumatic experiences of an overwhelming, intimidating nature favor repression. Parental attitudes are the most important sources of such experiences. Children, of course, vary in their susceptibility to traumatic experiences. While these early experiences are basic, they result essentially in vulnerability to strain later in life, so that neuroses then develop. The relative contributions of childhood experiences and later environmental stress vary. Thus, heredity, childhood experiences, and current difficulties all contribute in varying degrees in different cases. Neurosis is a breakdown of the ego in a given situation.

There are two types of regression: regression to fixation points that represent earlier successful adaptations and regression to unresolved traumatic situations. The first represents a seeking for gratification in the face of a situation that the ego cannot master, and the second is a return to a traumatic event in the attempt to master it. Both types of regression occur in the transference situation, probably equally frequently, and usually they are combined or occur together. The first type of regression is a form of resistance, being an evasion of a conflict centered in a later stage of development, as well as an attraction to a fixation point. The second type is an ally of therapeutic aims. The estimation of the balance between the two is difficult or impossible to assess.

PSYCHONEUROTIC AND PSYCHOTIC SYMPTOMS The nature of a neurosis and psychosis is to a large extent determined by the kinds of defenses adopted by the ego for its protection against emancipated impulses. There are also certain general characteristics of symptoms.

Psychoneurotic Symptoms / Neurotic symptoms appear to be irrational, both to the neurotic and to observers. They are dissociated from the conscious psychic life and are regressive in nature.

DYNAMIC STRUCTURE AND DEVELOPMENT OF A PSYCHONEUROSIS The failure to satisfy emotional needs in human relations, occupational activities, or sexual life, accompanied by internal conflict, leads to neurosis. After a struggle recourse is taken to regressive neurotic gratifications. This revives earlier anxieties and frustrations, which have been repressed. Neurotic behavior is the ego's defense against these early emotions; anxiety keeps the regressive tendencies repressed. Different methods of defense result in different forms of neurosis. Substitute gratifications, for example, consist of various types: conversion symptoms, phobias, obsessive-compulsive states, depressions and delusions of grandeur, paranoid projections, hallucinations and delusions, the impulsive behavior of character neuroses (psychopathic personalities), and the manic phase of manic-depressive psychosis. The defenses are also varied, including those listed earlier. Symbolic gratification by means of symptoms is a form of defense, but it is not sufficient to allay anxiety, so that specific defenses are aimed at relieving the sense of guilt.

The development of a neurosis consists, then, of (1) precipitating factors, with (2) failure in the solution of actual problems, leading to (3) regression, which (4) revives primary conflicts, followed by a futile struggle to resolve them with (5) substitute gratifications and self-punishment expressed in symptoms, resulting (6) in secondary conflict and the impoverishment of the ego. Symptoms absorb energies, which impairs effectiveness in dealing with actual life situations, resulting in a vicious circle.

SECONDARY GAIN In addition to the primary suffering, illness has secondary consequences that are advantages. Financial compensation, avoidance of unpleasant duties and responsibilities, sympathy, and attention are some of these secondary gains. Dependent longings may lead to exploitation of the illness. The existence of the infantile trait of dependence is, however, a significant factor in the neurosis. The point to note is that secondary gains prolong the illness and therefore should be reduced wherever possible.

REVIEW OF PSYCHOPATHOLOGICAL PHENOMENA

Anxiety neurosis / This form of neurosis is characterized by free-floating anxiety. Failure in important social or sexual relations is the precipitating factor, which results in regression to hostile and destructive impulses that threaten to become conscious. Anxiety, the fear of conscience, appears in consciousness. The ego develops defenses against the anxiety, which subsides but may recur. Other forms of neurosis or psychosis develop, depending on the defenses employed.

Phobias / Phobias are fears of specific situations; they replace early anxiety-laden situations. The situations avoided have an unconscious symbolic meaning, which is often sexual. Failure and regression lead to dependence; the phobia localizes anxiety and conceals the real problem from the ego.

Obsessive-Compulsive States / Such states consist of obsessive (asocial) ideas and compulsive rituals. Character traits of rigidity, doubt, indecisiveness, and dependence are typical. Obsessions are breaches in the repressive defenses that are separated from normal thinking in order to disown them as one's own thoughts. Compulsions represent overdoing the good to allay anxiety. There is a struggle to maintain a balance. These states exhibit the "magic of ideas" or the "omnipotence of thought" of the child, in which need is gratified in fantasy, but anxiety results.

Depressions / These are marked by the symptoms of melancholy, hopelessness, retardation of psychic processes, self-criticism, and sometimes suicidal impulses. Hostile impulses are directed inward, arousing guilt. The depressive individual is dependent in love relations, and the loss of a love object is a common precipitating cause of depression. The hostility that is part of his ambivalent relationship to the love object is turned against himself; this is aided by introjection of the love object.

The Manic-Depressive Reactions / It is improbable that manic-depressive psychosis is a metabolic or endocrine disturbance, if only because it responds to psychotherapy. The depressive phase of the psychosis is similar to a reactive depression. The manic phase includes elation, self-confidence, flight of ideas, aggression, irritability, and unrestrained sexuality. The change in behavior corresponds to a change in the ego's handling of rejected impulses, from guilt and punishment to uninhibited expression. Each form of behavior is a reaction to the other. In the depressive phase the individual pays—or overpays—for the guilt incurred in the manic phase, and is then able to recoup this overpayment in a return to the manic phase. The first phase, which may be either manic or depressive, is precipitated by an event that disturbs the equilibrium between the repressed and repressing forces in the personality.

The Hypochondriac Syndrome / This is not a disease entity but a syndrome that appears in different conditions, such as depressions and schizophrenia. It consists of an anxious preoccupation with the body or a part of the body that is believed to be diseased. It represents a narcissistic withdrawal of interest from objects and focusing of interest on the self caused by the frustration of the wish to be loved, a need for punishment because of guilt feelings resulting from hostile impulses, and a displacement of anxiety to another organ as a defense against castration fears.

Neurotic Character (Psychopathic Personality) / These individuals act out their neurotic impulses. They were long considered to be asocial, lacking in conscience, or constitutionally defective and untreatable. Actually, they are more like normal persons than are neurotics; they require realistic activity, not fantasy, to satisfy their needs. Their adjustment to the social environment is based on faulty principles, established by early parent-child relations. Such individuals include psychopathic criminals and eccentrics. They are characterized by the irrationality and stereotyped behavior patterns arising from the dominance of unconscious factors, and by self-destructiveness arising from unconscious guilt. The guilt, stemming from repressed conflicts (usually from the Oedipal situation), is displaced to criminal behavior, which is less objectionable than the forbidden desire in the unconscious. The punishment for the former relieves the guilt for the latter. Psychopathic personalities thus unconsciously seek apprehension. "After severe punishment for a relatively minor offense the conscience is relieved and the neurotic offender is emotionally ready for recidivism. The psychiatric superstition that these patients are incurable stems from this psychodynamic phenomenon. They remain incurable as long as society conforms to their neurosis by punishing them." [11]

Alcoholism and Drug Addiction / These habits are usually secondary to depression and character neuroses. Alcohol is an escape from depression, a means of overcoming inhibitions, and its adverse consequences replace other forms of self-punishment.

Traumatic Neurosis / Traumatic neurosis cannot be separated, psychodynamically, from other neuroses. Emotional experiences are more traumatic than physical experiences. Trauma is present to some degree in all neurosis; in the so-called traumatic neurosis it is more dramatic. The varied symptoms manifest regressive responses to extreme stress and anxiety.

Conversion Symptoms / Repressed wishes can be expressed and rejected at the same time. Freud used the term "conversion" to indicate the replacement of an emotionally charged idea by a physical symptom. There is no mysterious conversion or transformation of a psychological to a physical quality; the process is no different physiologically from the normal expression of emotions in expressive movements such as laughter or weeping. In neurosis the conversion is motivated by unconscious, repressed impulses, which are expressed without passing through the ego. The inactive symptom is an inadequate expression of the impulse, which requires action for adequate release, so the symptom becomes chronic. But because the symptoms provide emotional release, the individual appears impassive and unemotional (*la belle indifférence*).

The Schizophrenias / The psychoneuroses involve a conflict among the different structural parts of the mental apparatus rather than, as in the psychoses, a disturbance of the personality in its relation to the outside world. But the psychotic relinquishes his contact with reality or alters it in order to mold reality to his subjective demands. The psychoses present two kinds of conflict. In one, the conflict between the world as it is and as the psychotic desires it to be is solved by developing a world of fantasy. The other, identical with neurotic conflicts, arises from unacceptable hostile and sexual impulses. But whereas the neurotic represses these impulses and develops symptoms, the psychotic projects them instead. The paranoid, however, both represses impulses (usually of a homosexual nature), transforming them into hostile attitudes, and projects these attitudes onto others. The paranoid schizophrenias are thus different from those not characterized by paranoid hallucinations and delusions. They are more like the neuroses, but with a less deteriorated ego structure. Yet they resemble the other schizophrenias in their abandonment of contact with reality. Psychotics have never firmly established the first step in development, the differentiation between the ego and the external world, while in the neurotic the later social adjustments have been disturbed.

The precipitating causes in psychoses and neuroses are the same, emerging in adolescence or adult life. The psychotic regresses further, however. Because the foundations are laid in infancy, inherited constitutions play a more important role, although the constitutional theory is not established. The contribution of psychoanalysis to the schizophrenias is more explanatory than therapeutic.

Psychological Factors in Organic Brain Disease / "The contribution of psychoanalysis to the organic psychoses consists mainly in the dynamic understanding of the psychological content of the symptoms. It has little to contribute to their etiology and therapy. . . . The symptoms can be understood as reactions of the personality to these organic changes. The best known example is the explanation of the grandiose ideas of general paretics as compensatory defenses of the ego against the perception of waning mental faculties (Ferenczi-Hollos)." [12]

Perversions / These are of two kinds: (1) those consisting in the distortion of the quality of sexual strivings—sadism, masochism, exhibitionism, voyeurism, transvestism—and (2) those in which the object of the sexual striving is abnormal—homosexuality, pedophilia, zoophilia. In fetishism both kinds are involved. Perversions are the result of interrupted sexual development, which prevents the integration of the pregenital components of sexuality into a mature form. Fixation on the early immature forms of sexuality occurs. The interruption of sexual development is related to emotional involvements in the family arising from the Oedipus situation. The various forms of perversion are related to the components of the complex that are disturbed.

THE THERAPY PROCESS

The goal of psychoanalytic therapy is to restore mental health. There are two aspects of mental health. One is adaptation to the external environment; the other is adaptation to the internal environment. The environment includes "the possible environments which the patient

can choose to enhance his satisfaction and efficiency as a human being.
. . . Psychoanalytic treatment may enhance to a very great extent the
adaptability and the flexibility of a person and by eliminating inhibitions may free the way to fuller utilization of the patient's talents and
abilities." [13] In terms of the view of neurosis as the failure of the ego
to harmonize impulses with each other, and with internal standards
and external demands, psychoanalytic therapy enables the individual
to extend the integrative capacity of the ego over impulses that have
been repressed.

Therapy reverses the process of repression. This is possible in
the emotional atmosphere of the therapeutic situation. The therapist
reacts differently from the way the patient's parents did—he does not
evaluate or judge. The patient learns that the therapist does not con-
demn him, and he becomes able to express his thoughts and desires
freely. The unconscious thus becomes conscious. "Helping unconscious material to become conscious is an indispensable part of the
therapy." [14]

The repressed attitudes of the patient are directed toward the
therapist in the transference neurosis; that is, attitudes originally directed toward the parents are transferred to the therapist. This emotional experience is an important aspect of the curative process. The
patient's ego has an opportunity to face situations that it could not
handle in childhood (when the ego was weak) in a new setting, with
a person who does not react as the parents did. The patient recognizes
that his reactions are no longer suited to the present. Along with his
increasing freedom to react to the therapist, there is a similar change
in behavior in everyday life.

The recognition of the inappropriateness of his behavior is not
only an intellectual insight but a "corrective emotional experience."
This experience is the central therapeutic agent in the process of
change, which consists of a series of corrective emotional experiences.
These must take place under the special conditions of psychoanalytic
treatment.

The three factors of emotional abreaction, intellectual insight,
and appearance of repressed memories are interrelated and interdependent, although different writers emphasize one or another.
Without emotional abreaction, intellectual insight is ineffective. Recollection of repressed events is a part of insight. "The recovery of memories is a sign of improvement rather than its cause." [15] Treatment is
not complete after the analysis of the transference neurosis. The "lifting of the infantile amnesia" is a necessary part of treatment. The
"working through" of the transference manifestations in terms of
former experiences and the actual life situation also must be accomplished. Although there have been developments that have overemphasized either the emotional or the intellectual factors, it has generally been recognized that the two are indivisible. The therapeutic
process consists of the insight that accompanies emotional experience.

The emphasis upon ego analysis is an emphasis upon the process of working through. In the course of treatment there is a breaking up of the primitive emotional patterns of the unconscious material, and a building up of new and more complex relationships. Freud long considered the emergence of preconscious material into consciousness as the establishing of a new connection. The ego performs a synthesizing function in the establishment of new connections. The new synthesis makes possible more flexible behavior in place of the rigid, automatic behavior produced by the unconscious synthetic patterns. "According to this concept, the process by which an unconscious content becomes conscious corresponds to a recapitulation of ego development, which also consists in a gradual building up of more and more complex and flexible systems of connections between different instinctual needs and sense perceptions. In this light the therapeutic process appears as the continuation of the learning process, which has been interrupted by repressions." [16]

As a result of interpretation, the neurotic patient learns to differentiate; therapy is thus a type of discriminatory learning. Interpretation serves the function of breaking up primitive connections and establishing new, more differentiated ones. Emotional experience and insight are synchronized in *the integrative principle of interpretation.*

Every new synthesis increases the ability of the ego to face new unconscious material and thus facilitates the appearance of such material. "In analytic therapy our main allies are the *striving of the unconscious forces for expression and the integrating tendency of the conscious ego.* Even if we do nothing else but not interfere with these two dynamic forces, we will be able to help many patients." [17]

To understand the process of therapy we must consider the emotional involvement of the therapist as well as that of the patient. In 1910 Freud introduced the term "countertransference" to refer to this involvement. It was not until thirty years later that the analyst's reactions and their significance for the treatment were explored. There are differences of opinion as to the nature of this phenomenon. Most writers define countertransference as those reactions of the therapist that are inappropriate to the patient-therapist relationship, being determined by the therapist's own characteristic performed reaction pattern. All interpersonal attitudes, however, are a composite of realistic and unrealistic reactions to the relationship.

While the patient's transference is a complication in therapy, it is necessary and is the most important aspect of therapy. The countertransference, though, is a disturbing factor, an unavoidable impurity. The therapist must be aware of and control his own emotional reactions; one of the major objectives of the training analysis is to make this possible. The minimizing of the therapist's personality reactions in the therapy makes it possible for him to approach the ideal of being the blank screen on which the patient can reflect his own reaction pattern; that is, it encourages the transference situation. The therapist cannot be entirely neutral, however, and remains a real person; after the transference relationship is established, his own spontaneous responses are important in therapy.

But the therapist does have emotional reactions that are not appropriate, that cannot be concealed, and that do enter into the therapy and interfere with progress. The therapist must recognize and control these reactions. Control usually means not expressing his reactions, or behaving differently than he would if he did not know or understand his reactions. This will lead to an impersonal attitude, which, while best in the opening phase of treatment, is not necessarily best in later phases. The modification of this approach in psychoanalytically oriented psychotherapy will be considered below.

IMPLEMENTATION: TECHNIQUES OF THERAPY

"Psychoanalytic principles lend themselves to different therapeutic procedures which vary according to the nature of the case and may be variably applied during the treatment of the same patient." [18] The traditional method of psychoanalysis, with daily interviews continued for months or years, is only one technique, and not necessarily the most efficient and effective method in every case. It is suited best to severe chronic psychoneuroses and character disturbances, but even in these cases therapy will be more effective if the procedure is modified to meet the varying needs of the individual patient and the phases of treatment.

Psychoanalytic therapy emphasizes the value of developing "*a plan of treatment,* based on a dynamic-diagnostic appraisal of the patient's personality and the actual problems he has to solve in his given life conditions. In devising such a plan of therapy, the analyst must decide in each case whether a primarily supportive or uncovering type of treatment is indicated, or whether the therapeutic task is mainly a question of changing the external conditions of the patient's life." [19]

Whereas the traditional method has been passively to let the treatment take its own course, in psychoanalytic therapy the analyst is more active, and systematic planning becomes necessary. "In addition to the original decision as to the particular sort of strategy to be employed in the treatment of any case, we recommend the *conscious use of various techniques in a flexible manner,* shifting tactics to fit the particular needs of the moment." [20] It is not possible to decide in advance just what course a treatment will take. The goal is to develop a more economical procedure in terms of time and effort by adapting the technique to the individual case.

Universal Factors in Psychotherapy

In all forms of psychotherapy the therapist, by the mere fact of offering help, gives emotional support. This opportunity for the patient to gratify some of his regressive need for dependence may be therapeutic by reducing his need for gratification through symptoms.

In addition to emotional support, the therapist also provides intellectual support by giving the patient the opportunity to discuss his problems objectively, which allows him to use his own intellectual capacities to handle his practical problems. All forms of psychotherapy provide an opportunity for the patient to express his emotions, which relieves tension and prepares the way for insight. These supportive measures grow out of the therapeutic situation and require only the techniques of instilling confidence and listening to the patient with benevolent understanding. These measures are based on common sense, although they have been recognized and improved by psychiatry.

Such supportive measures, in some cases with the additional support of the ego's defenses and manipulation of the life situation, constitute supportive treatment, and may be sufficient as treatment in cases where the functional impairment of the ego is of a temporary nature, resulting from acute emotional stress. The use of these techniques, however, should be based upon an understanding of the underlying psychopathology. If improperly applied, they may lead to aggravation rather than relief. Moreover, it is not possible at the beginning to determine the amount and type of therapy that a patient needs, and thus to determine that supportive treatment rather than uncovering treatment is all that will be necessary. "All forms of psychotherapy must, therefore, be based on a knowledge of personality development and psychodynamics."[21] All therapists, then, should know psychoanalytic theory.

The Techniques of Psychoanalysis

FREE ASSOCIATION   The rule of free association requires the patient to tell whatever comes into his mind without conscious selection or the application of logic to his train of thought. Freud developed this method of reaching unconscious material after the failure of hypnosis and waking suggestion. Fantasies and dreams, as well as feelings and thoughts, are sources of unconscious material, and thus are subjects of free association. Free association is a method of recalling the past and also of discharging the emotions connected with the traumatic events of the past. As a technique to obtain self-evaluation on the part of the patient, it is facilitated by the objective, understanding attitude of the therapist. The rule of free association eliminates conscious suppression as a factor in keeping material in the unconscious, leaving only repression as a factor, and repression is not strong enough by itself to prevent some material from entering consciousness. Over a period of time, more and more of the repressed materials of the past, as well as impulses, are revealed. Until repressed tendencies become conscious, they cannot undergo modification and sublimation under the control of the ego.

THE TRANSFERENCE   The transference consists, as was indicated earlier, of the emotional reaction of the patient to the therapist in which he directs his impulses and attitudes toward the therapist. The word is used here in the strict sense, in which it is identical with the transference neurosis except that it includes transient neurotic reactions. It is thus "an irrational repetition of stereotyped reaction patterns which have not been adjusted to conform to the present situation." [22] In the transference the patient reenacts his pathogenetic past, which therefore becomes accessible to the therapist. Psychoanalysis, in fact, consists essentially in the development of the transference neurosis and its resolution.

The patient naturally develops a transference to the therapist, who, in turn, does not discourage but encourages its development by his attitudes and techniques. The core of the transference is a dependent attitude, which is inherent in the manner in which the patient comes to the therapist for help.

The resolution of the transference neurosis is a major part of the therapy. The fact that it is only in the mind of the patient that the therapist becomes his father or another important early figure provides the opportunity for the patient to become aware of his reactions. He can discriminate between the old conflicts and the transference conflicts that, without adequate reason, he has directed toward the therapist. The therapist facilitates the differentiation by reacting differently from those early figures in the patient's life. He does not retaliate or intimidate or threaten. It is because the therapist does not react like the father that the transference reaction is unrealistic, and so can be contrasted with the original situation.

INTERPRETATION   The patient experiences the fact that the transference situation is not the same as the original situation. But the therapist also points out, or interprets, the fact that the patient's attitude is rooted in his childhood and is not an adequate reaction to the therapist. This leads to insight, or "intellectual cognition." Interpretation thus aids differentiation. "The analyst's interpretations help the patient to replace the older automatic superego functions with conscious judgment, or, in other words, superego functions are replaced by ego functions." [23]

Although some analysts (for example, Reich) have distinguished between the interpretation of resistance and the interpretation of content, the two cannot be separated. There is no free-floating resistance; it is always directed against something. Therefore, "every resistance should preferably be interpreted in connection with what it is directed against, provided of course that the content interpretation is timely." [24] It is true, of course, that in the interpretation of content the therapist can go only slightly beyond what the patient is able to see alone at any given moment.

Interpretation facilitates therapy. "The longer the patient is exposed to material which puzzles him, which seems strange, and appears to him as a foreign body, the longer the analysis will be retarded and the appearance of new unconscious material blocked." [25] Interpretations connect unconscious material to what is already understood by the patient, so they should refer to previous insights. Interpretations point out connections formed by the mind in infancy so that the patient can see the faulty identifications and generalizations. "It is perhaps too much to expect that the patient will be able without help to recognize the infantile generalizations as something self-evident. I do not doubt, however, that after the old primitive connections are broken up, the patient, because of the integrating power of his ego, would in time establish the new synthesis alone." [26] The therapist can accelerate this integrating process by interpretation and thus become an active participant in the process. "Through our interpretation we do help the synthetic functions of the ego. How much such active help each patient needs is one of the most timely issues." [27] A general principle of interpretation is that it should always start from the surface and go only as deep as the patient is able to go while experiencing the situation emotionally.

Interpretations that connect actual life situations with past experiences and with the transference situation are *total interpretations.* They best fulfill the double purpose of interpretation—the acceleration of the assimilation of new material by the ego and the mobilization of further unconscious material.

Modifications in Psychoanalytic Therapy

INDICATIONS FOR THERAPY Both internal and external factors must be considered in estimating treatability. The individual's adaptability may be estimated by a study of the life history, considering the severity of breakdowns, their frequency, the amount of provocation, and the degree of mental health during intermissions. External factors such as physical defects, intelligence, age, and the life situation may facilitate or impede treatment. Sometimes a neurosis may be the only solution to the patient's problems. Responses to trial interpretations are helpful in gauging treatability.

Although both approaches are used in most therapy, a choice must be made between two general types of therapy. Supportive therapy, in which no attempt is made to effect permanent ego changes, is indicated in cases of acute neurotic disturbances in previously well-adjusted persons, and with severe chronic patients where there is little hope of achieving permanent change. In the former instance support is all that is necessary for recovery; in the latter it is all that is possible. Uncovering therapy, aimed at achieving permanent change through insight and emotional experiences, is applicable in a wide variety of cases, both acute and chronic.

PLANNING PSYCHOTHERAPY Persistence and good intentions are no substitutes for consciously directed effort. Treatment can be more pertinent, efficient, and economical when it is planned. Goals and the general approach, anticipated problems, and solutions enter into the plan. The ground strategy may remain the same, but the tactics should be considered "subject to change." A comprehensive plan is a *sine qua non* for any properly handled psychotherapy.

Adequate dynamic formulations should be arrived at early. A clear perspective can be gained in the first few hours, before the patient has become deeply involved emotionally. The preliminary investigative period varies with the emotional attitude of the patient. The history may be easy or difficult to obtain. It is important to determine the motive for treatment. This avoids later problems, such as those caused by the patient who does not consider his problem psychological, but who expects medical treatment for a physical illness. Physical complaints must be investigated. A comprehensive therapeutic plan can then be mapped out. With this plan in mind, the therapist is less likely to be taken by surprise and become discouraged by disturbing complications.

Exploring psychosomatic complaints and external difficulties constitutes a first psychotherapeutic attack on the patient's problem and enables the therapist to observe how he approaches his problem. It also provides an evaluation of the patient's ego strength, which is important especially when uncovering therapy is being used, with infrequent interviews. How the patient feels about things is more important for tentative formulations than a large amount of merely factual data. The therapist also draws upon his experience with similar cases in formulating his plan.

Since emotional readjustment, not insight, is the goal of therapy, the first question in the formulation of a therapeutic plan is what emotional readjustments are necessary to relieve the patient. These are the goals of therapy, and insight is only one method for achieving them. Some patients cannot tolerate insights into their conflicts. In many cases emotional readjustment is necessary before insight is possible. The forcing of insight may lead to disturbing complications.

THE PRINCIPLE OF FLEXIBILITY   In psychoanalytic therapy, techniques are selected and varied to suit the patient, rather than the patient being selected to fit the procedure, as in psychoanalysis. "As we now practice psychoanalytic therapy, we seldom use one and the same method of approach from the first day to the last day of treatment." [28] Either the couch or sitting face-to-face may be used, with free association or direct conversations; the full-fledged transference neurosis may be developed or it may be avoided. Drugs and environmental manipulation may be used. An approach of this sort may be called psychoanalytic because it is based on psychodynamic principles. The so-called standard approach also varies in its techniques.

Choice of technique is determined by many factors, including the psychodynamics of the case, the actual circumstances of the patient's life, and the therapist's experience and skills. Therapists emphasize or specialize in certain techniques. Nevertheless, the therapist selects the techniques that seem most appropriate in the light of the total situation. The ability to choose appropriately is the result of training and long experience.

FREQUENCY OF INTERVIEW Daily interviews tend to gratify the patient's dependency needs more than is desirable. The expectation of daily interviews for an indefinite period of time fosters regression and procrastination. The amount and remoteness in time of the regressive material is not a measure of the depth of the analysis, but may represent neurotic withdrawal, resistance, and escape. Long, deep regressions can and should be avoided. Daily interviews often reduce the patient's emotional participation, becoming routine. Lessening the frequency of interviews allows the intensity of impulses to be built up to the point at which the patient can become aware of them. The optimum level of emotional intensity varies from case to case; the analysis should maintain as high a level as the patient's ego can stand without losing its capacity for insight. After the relationship has become well established, therefore, the frequency of interviews can be varied to maintain this level and also to prevent the treatment from becoming a withdrawal from participation in life. The same results as those obtained with the standard procedure may be achieved with fewer interviews and less time by changing the frequency of interviews according to the needs of the patient. Psychotherapy is thus more economical.

INTERRUPTIONS AND TERMINATION OF TREATMENT Patients may continue treatment indefinitely because of inertia as long as there are no excessive inconveniences associated with it. The number of interviews may be reduced in order to lead up to an interruption to test the patient's capacity to function without therapy. The patient has the assurance he can return to therapy. Interruptions pave the way for termination. Length of treatment cannot be predicted, and the patient's capacity to function without treatment must be tested by blocking neurotic retreat to fantasy and pressing him toward the difficulties of his life situation.

The transference neurosis offers gratification of dependent needs and is not as unpleasant as either the original conflicts or the ones that the patient faced when he entered therapy. Therefore, he may settle comfortably into the transference and tend to continue indefinitely. Interruption may test whether the patient is dependent on the transference relationship, in which case he will regress.

EXTRATHERAPEUTIC EXPERIENCES The neurotic has given up efforts to deal with his problems. Therapy is only preparation for facing and dealing with these difficulties. The therapist must thus influence experiences in real life. This is in contradiction to the accepted attitude that the therapist should not interfere with the patient's life and that no important changes should be made in the patient's life during therapy. Changes may be necessary for progress in therapy. The rule should be: no changes unless both therapist and patient agree. Successes and accomplishments in life are more reassuring than any emotional discharge, recollection, or insight in therapy. The transference relationship is a rehearsal, which must be followed by an actual performance. The fostering of favorable life experiences at the right time shortens therapy. The therapist should encourage and even require the patient to experiment in life activities. "As a scientifically trained therapist, the physician feels he should center his whole attention on the interviews; as a man of common sense he knows he must guide the patient's daily activities to some degree. The common failure lies in not making this guidance an integral part of the whole treatment." [29]

MANIPULATION OF THE TRANSFERENCE RELATIONSHIP In standard psychoanalysis the transference neurosis is considered to be unavoidable and the *sine qua non* of psychoanalytic therapy. The analysis of the transference neurosis accounts for the length of psychoanalysis. It is "handled," not controlled. Gradually, as they have learned more about the "types" of transference relationships associated with various conflicts, psychoanalysts have made efforts to control the transference neurosis. It has become recognized that a transference neurosis is not always necessary or desirable, and that it sometimes is impossible for it to develop, since not all neurotic conflicts can be transferred to a therapist, who may not be a suitable object.

In psychoanalytic therapy the emphasis is on the transference relationship rather than the transference neurosis, which may not be allowed to develop. The intensity and content of the transference relationship are controlled. The initial positive transference relationship is utilized, and a negative transference, or a hostile attitude toward the therapist, which often complicates and prolongs therapy, may not be allowed to develop. In cases in which the transference relationship is controlled and directed, and in which the therapist has become involved in extratherapeutic situations, progress tends to be more rapid, with fewer interviews required.

The use of interpretations (through choice, timing, and manner of presentation) is the most powerful means of regulating the transference relationship, and thus of controlling the intensity of treatment. Interpretation of the infantile neurosis encourages a dependent transference relationship, while restricting interpretations to the present situation avoids this relationship. The variations in conducting treatment, such as use of the couch, and whether the therapist sits behind a desk, or in a lounge chair, or on the couch beside the patient, all influence the transference relationship. The therapist's attitudes toward the patient also have a great deal of influence.

The technique of free association, which prescribes that the therapist follow the trend chosen by the patient, allows the patient to take the line of least resistance and avoid facing the major conflict by regressing to a relatively conflict-free period of adjustment. The regressive material is of significance and should not be disregarded, but the later conflicts that are being evaded should not be lost sight of. Interpretation is one method of making the patient aware that this regression is a form of resistance and an evasion.

In some cases a patient may utilize the therapist in a rational manner, without developing any transference relationship. Improvement in such cases may be permanent and cannot be denied by labeling it a "transference cure." Such a rational use of therapy may be blocked by the development of a transference neurosis in supportive therapy. In supportive therapy, when the patient reacts with guilt or shame, he may be unable to benefit from the permissive and supportive situation. The therapist may have to interpret the motives of guilt underlying the transference neurosis. But by decreasing the patient's sense of dependency—by allowing him to perform a service for the therapist, for example—the guilt feelings may be relieved and the transference neurosis blocked or diminished. Or the therapist may encourage the development of healthy outside interests to lessen the patient's absorption in the therapeutic relationship.

Resistances to disturbing interpretations are not necessarily transference reactions, but may be frank opposition to unwelcome interpretations as a normal reaction in defense of the neurosis; such resistances are irrational only in the sense that the neurosis itself is irrational. They may lead to a transference neurosis, however. Interpretations that are too disturbing are resisted by distorting the understanding of the nature of the therapeutic relationship, that is, by a transference reaction. Resistance of this sort is a sign that the patient is unable to assimilate the interpretation, and is to be expected in the case of important interpretations. The experienced therapist will follow up such interpretations.

In insight therapy, too strong a transference relationship may impair the patient's judgment and interfere with his understanding of the motives for his irrational impulses and of the differences between the earlier situations in which the impulses arose and the present situation. The transference neurosis impairs reality testing, and it may be necessary to damp down the tendency to develop a transference neurosis in order to facilitate the process of reality testing.

Thus, the ideal of impersonal behavior on the part of the therapist must be modified. The therapist should not aim to be a blank screen, but should behave in the way patients would expect of one to whom they have come for help. "We also tentatively treat the patient as a normal and rational human being and we continue to do so except when the patient himself proves the contrary." [30] The patient can then behave as a normal human being, and any irrational tendencies are thrown into sharper contrast. The transference neurosis is allowed to develop, and encouraged, only when and to the extent deemed desirable by the therapist. Concentration on the infantile neurosis encourages more than is necessary the tendency of the patient to interpret present situations as though they were identical with traumatic situations in the past. "Accordingly, insofar as it is our purpose to strengthen the reality testing function of the ego, our policy should be just the opposite; we should center the patient's attention rather on his real problems and should turn his attention to disturbing events in the past only for the purpose of throwing light upon the motives for irrational reactions in the present." [31] Similarly, the patient's attention should be focused upon his problems in the external world rather than upon his reactions to the therapist. The focusing of attention upon present problems follows Freud's concept of therapy as a process of reeducation, a resumption of an interrupted learning process. The primary concern in therapy is not the recovery of the past, but the discovery of solutions for present problems.

CONTROLLING THE COUNTERTRANSFERENCE The standard approach emphasizes that the countertransference reactions of the therapist must be understood and controlled. However, it has been recognized that occasionally spontaneous countertransference reactions may by chance be helpful. If the countertransference attitude happens to be the same as the original parental attitude, the original conflict will easily repeat itself in the transference situation, but it will be difficult for the patient to modify it. However, if the therapist has, and unwittingly expresses, a different attitude, a novel situation is created which may contribute to the therapy. It is suggested that the therapist "should attempt to replace his spontaneous countertransference reactions with attitudes which are consciously planned and adopted according to the dynamic exigencies of the therapeutic situation." [32] Knowledge of the early interpersonal attitudes that contributed to the patient's neurosis can help the therapist to assume an attitude that will provoke the kind of emotional experience that will be conducive to the undoing of the pathogenic effect of the original attitude. The therapist must be aware of his countertransference attitudes, be able to control them, and must also substitute the appropriate attitudes. While the intuitive therapist often functions in this way, it is desirable to replace intuition with conscious understanding. Thus, it is possible that, as transference was first considered to be an impurity and later became the axis of therapy, so the impurity of countertransference may become an important instrument of therapy.

The creation of a suitable interpersonal atmosphere through the expression of appropriate attitudes does not mean that the therapist plays a role or assumes the role of a significant person in the patient's past. Nor does it mean that the therapist's personality does not enter into the relationship. Nor does it deny the importance of the therapist's objective interest and permissiveness in the therapeutic process.

DREAM INTERPRETATION Dreams express in a disguised form the alien impulses and desires of the patient. They are distorted by the resistance aroused by the impulses. The manifest (open) content of the dream is a compression or condensation of the latent (repressed) elements. Details often express hidden personal allusions. Causality is replaced by temporal sequences. Many things are represented by their opposites. The dream is the result of a compromise between two opposing forces—the wish to express a desire or relieve tension and the tendency to reject the desire. Painful dreams, from which the dreamer awakes in terror, represent the failure of the dream work to disguise the objectionable content sufficiently, or are the result of a guilty conscience.

Dreams are analyzed by having the patient engage in free association with regard to the manifest content. With the assistance of the therapist, the latent elements are discovered. The free association and the therapeutic situation lessen the patient's unconscious censorship, so that the pressure of the repressed wish breaks through. Certain dream elements are common symbols of universal human experience.

Resistance to the therapist's interpretation of a dream may lead to another dream rejecting the interpretation. The second dream may yield clues as to the nature of the resistance. Dreams provide an excellent estimate of the psychodynamic situation as the treatment progresses. Dream sequences reveal progressive integrative accomplishments of the ego.

THE PRINCIPLE OF CORRECTIVE EMOTIONAL EXPERIENCE   In all psychotherapy the patient must undergo a corrective emotional experience to repair the traumatic influence of previous experiences. This experience may occur during treatment in the transference relationship, or in the patient's daily life. Narcosynthesis is the simplest example of a situation in which an experience is relived, and with the help of the narcotic and the presence of the therapist to reduce anxiety, the outcome is different from that which originally occurred. The mastery of an unresolved conflict becomes possible in the transference relationship because it is experienced less intensely than it was originally and because the therapist's attitude differs from that of the parent in the original situation.

Intellectual insight is not sufficient for such resolution of conflict; the patient must *feel* the irrationality of his emotional reactions, and this will lead to dealing differently with them. The difference between the old conflict situation and the therapeutic situation constitutes the value of the latter. The resulting relationship between the patient and the therapist is thus different, leading to a new experience for the patient. The therapist must understand the genetic development of the patient's conflicts, so that he may revive them in order to enable the patient to reexperience them. The control of the countertransference in the ways discussed above facilitates the development of corrective emotional experiences.

MANIPULATION OF THE ENVIRONMENT   In addition to supportive therapy and uncovering therapy, which attempts to modify the patient's personality structure to harmonize it with environmental requirements, therapy includes making the patient's situation easier by adapting his environment to his needs. In actual therapy with a particular individual, these methods are used in various combinations.

Supportive therapy itself may be considered environmental treatment, since the therapist is part of the patient's environment and his control of his own behavior constitutes manipulation of the environment. "Transference cures," in which the patient obtains great relief on beginning treatment without the development of any insight, may be considered environmental treatment.

Putting the patient in a different environment and changing the behavior and attitudes of people in the patient's environment are the main methods in what is usually considered manipulation of the environment.

Conclusion

In order to be relieved of his neurotic ways of feeling and acting, the patient must undergo new emotional experiences suited to undo the morbid effects of the emotional experiences of his earlier life. Other therapeutic factors—such as intellectual insight, abreaction, recollection of the past, etc.—are all subordinated to this central therapeutic principle. Re-experiencing the old, unsettled conflict *but with a new ending* is the secret of every penetrating therapeutic result. . . . In the patient-physician relationship, the therapist has a unique opportunity to provide the patient with precisely that type of corrective experience which he needs for recovery. It is a secondary question what technique is employed to bring it about. The *standard* psychoanalytic technique is only one—and not in every case the most suitable one—of the many possible applications of fundamental psychodynamic principles that can be utilized for this kind of emotional training." [33]

There are disadvantages in any routine procedure. Treatment must be flexible, allowing for the use of those techniques best suited to the nature of the case.

EXAMPLES

Alexander's writings do not include typescripts of interviews. The 1946 publication by Alexander and French contains many presentations and discussions of cases, however. Any single case may be atypical, and any one is limited in presenting a point of view as comprehensive as psychoanalytically oriented psychotherapy. Space does not allow the inclusion of several cases or even a long single case. A single brief case is presented here. The interested reader may refer to *Psychoanalytic Therapy* for others.

Reactive Depression

A physician, a German refugee 45 years old, came for psychotherapy because of an intense depression resulting from extreme irritation with his son. He was seen for a single consultation with excellent results. The therapist (a man) was also a recent immigrant.

The patient had had no serious neurotic difficulties before. He had been in this country for ten months, and his wife and only child, a nine-year-old boy, had only recently joined him. His chief complaint was that he felt extremely irritated by his son, that he could not concentrate on his work in the boy's presence, that he was annoyed by his demanding attitude and his constant need for attention. He was now so discouraged over his inability to adjust himself to the child that he had become exceedingly depressed and decided to consult a psychiatrist.

In the course of the discussion, the patient's attention was distracted from his complaints about his son with a few questions about the way he had lived before his family joined him. He then talked freely about the circumstances of his immigration and about his first attempts to reconstruct his life in the new environment. Although he had had a hard time in the beginning, he had been fairly successful in getting established in his profession.

As he talked it became clear to him that his son and wife had joined him "too soon," that they had come before he was ready to offer them the security they needed. With considerable emotion—at first hesitantly, then with conviction—he said he realized that life would be easier now if his son and wife were not with him. He saw that the demands of his son were really not exaggerated but seemed so because he himself felt insecure—not only within himself but also in his economic adjustment. He felt guilty and responsible, and even saw some justification for his son's behavior, since his own difficulties in the new environment did not allow him to be the ideal father his standards demanded. As he talked the whole situation over, he gained more and more insight into these feelings (which were not far under the surface) and with this insight he experienced marked relief.

But insight alone was not enough. It was necessary also to help this patient make some practical arrangement whereby he could adjust his way of working to the American style of life—chiefly through having an office outside the home. This made it possible for him to divide his energies; he could be a hardworking doctor part of the time, and an attentive father and husband the rest of the time.

When he was seen by the therapist two years later, the patient referred to himself as a "week-end father." He expressed his gratitude for the insight he had gained in this one interview, and added that not only his relationship to his son but his relationship to other aspects of his family life and to the American scene in general had greatly improved.

Comments. It might be argued that a confidential talk with a friend would have helped this patient as much as the psychiatric interview. The evidence, however, is against this assumption, since the patient had often talked over his difficulties with his refugee friends, many of whom had had difficulty in adjusting themselves to new ways and conditions.

The therapeutic success in this case consisted mainly in bringing into consciousness conflicting emotions which were preconscious but still suppressed. This man had become rebellious against too much responsibility in a trying situation and was depressed as a result. Insight into his unconscious reaction to immigration in general, and to his family situation in particular, facilitated his emotional readjustment. He had a strong, efficient ego and its powers of integration were readily mobilized and set to work.

The fact that the patient was seen in only one interview precludes any analysis of the transference situation. We surmise, however, that the patient saw in this analyst who, he knew, had also gone through the trying experience of immigration a few years before, a good object for identification. This in itself speeded the rapport necessary for any successful therapy and served as a support of the patient's ego, which had begun to fail under the heavy load of responsibility.

Another reason for this therapist's being especially suitable for this patient was the fact that he had already learned the ways of American doctors and could give the patient concrete advice and help in establishing himself in the medical profession.[34]

SUMMARY AND EVALUATION

Psychoanalytically oriented psychotherapy is psychotherapy utilizing psychoanalytic principles and methods, but modified or adapted to the needs of the individual case. Modifications include varying the frequency of interviews, encouraging the patient to take actions with regard to his life situation, interrupting therapy on a trial basis, and manipulating the patient's environment. Therapy may vary from a supportive type—involving only listening, acceptance, and catharsis or confession—to deep uncovering therapy. The transference may not exist or may not be allowed to develop, or it may be developed in a full-fledged transference neurosis. Its development is controlled through the frequency of interviews and the nature of the interpretations given. Emphasis is placed upon the "corrective emotional experience" of the patient rather than upon intellectual insight. Insight is not necessary for change in behavior, and often follows such change rather than preceding it.

The therapist is active in controlling the therapeutic process in the ways just indicated, and also in his use of countertransference attitudes. Rather than merely understanding and controlling his countertransference feelings and attitudes, he may express certain attitudes that seem desirable in order to provide a situation that varies from that in which the patient's conflicts developed.

Such an approach to therapy involves planning in advance. Early in therapy the therapist develops a psychodynamic formulation, forms a general plan for the treatment, and attempts to anticipate problems or difficulties that might arise, as well as methods of meeting them. Details of tactics may change, as has been indicated, during the process of therapy. Such therapy differs from orthodox psychoanalysis, which French characterizes as drifting into therapeutic relationships. It requires more skill than the orthodox method. When therapy is not on a daily basis, "an even greater alertness and an even greater agility are required of the therapist." [35]

Psychoanalytic therapy, it is claimed, is more widely applicable than psychoanalysis and is more efficient and economical. It adapts the method to the needs of the patient, rather than selecting patients to fit the method. Results are obtained in a shorter period of time. In their 1946 publication Alexander and French report that their brief psychotherapy required from one to a total of sixty-five interviews over a period of seventeen months in the cases on which it had been used (approximately 600 patients).

> Following the principle of adapting psychodynamic therapy to the structure of the individual case, we find that we can, in a relatively brief period, produce therapeutic changes previously considered possible only when the time-consuming technique of standard psychoanalysis was used. . . . It is not claimed that this abbreviated form of psychoanalysis is possible in all cases. Certain patients need prolonged treatment with frequent interviews. But, as this book shows, there are many instances in which more intensive but less frequent interviews—or even a less intensive treatment—than would have been prescribed in the past, will produce the desired therapeutic changes in an equally dependable but accelerated fashion.[36]

Psychoanalytic therapy, while incorporating modifications in methods and techniques, essentially accepts the orthodox psychoanalytic theory of psychodynamics. The modifications in psychodynamics are small compared to those made by Adler, Rank, or neoanalysts such as Horney and Sullivan. However, Alexander does not accept the association of various kinds of neuroses and psychoses with the psychoanalytic levels of sexual development. He writes that "the attempt to explain the inclination for certain types of symptom formation from fixations to definite phases of development needs further investigation. This theory seems most applicable to schizophrenics and compulsion neuroses." [37] In addition, Alexander's approach does not limit itself to assuming a sexual etiology for all conflicts. Recognition is given to the role of other impulses, particularly hostility, in etiology.

The modifications in techniques have raised disputes as to whether Alexander's approach should be called psychoanalytic. There are those who maintain that the presence of a full-fledged transference neurosis is essential for psychoanalysis or any treatment bearing the title psychoanalytic. Others feel that the other modifications, such as

interviews on less than a daily basis and the changing of their frequency, and the minimizing of insight are basic deviations from the
theory of psychoanalytic treatment.

Alexander, however, defends the use of the term "psychoanalytic" on the basis that he accepts and utilizes the psychodynamic principles of psychoanalysis, and that he uses the techniques of
standard analysis, introducing only conscious and planned application
of them on a quantitative basis. No fundamentally new techniques are
proposed, but just the flexible application of accepted methods.
"Moreover, every therapy which increases the integrative functions of
the ego (through re-exposing the patient under more favorable conditions to those conflicts which have before been met with neurotic
defense mechanisms) should be called psychoanalytic, no matter
whether its duration is for one or two interviews, for several weeks or
months, or for several years." [38]

Psychoanalytically oriented psychotherapy is certainly less rigid
and more flexible than standard psychoanalysis. In the controversy
concerning insight and emotional experiencing, which has been going
on outside psychoanalytic circles as well as within them, psychoanalytically oriented psychotherapists place the emphasis upon the latter.
French, in his contributions to the 1946 publication, appears to favor
insight more than does Alexander. In some respects the approach
fosters less dependence of the patient on the therapist, as is evident
in the control and manipulation of the transference relationship. In
other respects, however, as in guiding and advising the patient, in
encouraging his extratherapy behavior, and in manipulating his environment, it appears to foster greater dependence. This approach is
apparently more manipulative of the therapy relationship and of the
patient's total behavior than orthodox psychoanalysis.

It is claimed that psychoanalytically oriented psychotherapy is a
"rational dynamic psychotherapy." [39] Presumably, this claim is based
upon its adaptation to the individual, following the development of
a plan based upon a diagnostic study of the patient, and its flexibility
in adapting to the changing situation as therapy progresses. This departure from the standard method of utilizing the same techniques or
procedures with every patient introduces the problem of choice of
techniques for the individual case. This requires the identification of
the patient's needs, on the one hand, and of appropriate techniques
to meet these needs, on the other. Alexander and French make some
attempt to do this, but it is hardly adequate. The discrimination of
different needs or classes of needs, or of diagnostic formulations, is
not systematically dealt with. And there is no evidence of the reliability
of the diagnostic formulations that are necessary as a basis for planning the treatment. It is generally recognized that agreement of psychiatrists or psychologists upon such formulations is not high. On the
treatment side, also, the consideration of techniques, with the indications for their differential use, is not systematically approached. It
appears that this whole area is to be the province of the clinical judg-

ment of the individual therapist, based upon training and experience, factors that are stressed by Alexander. He writes: "Because of the variables involved in every treatment, techniques are best demonstrated on the material itself. We shall make no attempt, therefore, to consider the indications for each specific technique but shall try to show in the case presentations of later chapters how interlocked are the psychodynamics and circumstances with the method of procedure necessary for each case, and how we have learned from experience to choose, modify, and combine techniques as the therapeutic process demands." [40] Alexander recognizes that although there are indications pointing to the desirability of interruption of treatment on a trial basis, and of termination, there are no quantifiable criteria. The patient's own intimation is not acceptable.

While the analyses of the cases presented in *Psychoanalytic Therapy* may be impressive, there is no evidence for their reliability or validity. Many of the methods and techniques, and their justifications, appear reasonable and would be accepted by many psychotherapists. They are essentially not new departures or innovations, as Alexander clearly notes, but methods that have been used by psychoanalysts, as well as by other therapists, for many years.

In some respects these methods, or their flexible use, are an improvement upon the rigid insistence of orthodox psychoanalysis on an inflexible, standard procedure. In other respects, however, flexibility creates problems. These include problems of the bases for choosing among techniques and for changing them. Problems relating to the reactions of the patients are also unsolved, although these are not recognized by Alexander. While the avoidance of the full-fledged transference neurosis reduces one kind of dependence and may shorten therapy, the use of active guidance and direct influence on the patient through suggestions, advice, encouragement, etc., while also apparently speeding up therapy, may lead to another kind of dependence. Finally, the possibility that changing techniques may appear as inconsistent to the patient, confusing him and thus slowing up therapy, must be considered.

Before his death Alexander moved still further from orthodox psychoanalysis, apparently as a result of the findings from a long-term study supported by the Ford Foundation and conducted at Mt. Sinai Hospital in Los Angeles. This study involved the observation and tape recording of psychoanalytic therapy sessions. His concept of psychotherapy moved toward learning theory; some of the intimations of this move can be seen in the summary in this chapter. He wrote that the most important conclusion from his research "is the fact that the traditional descriptions of the therapeutic process do not adequately reflect the immensely complex interaction between therapist and patient. The patient's reactions cannot be described fully as transference reactions. The patient reacts to the therapist as to a concrete person and not only as a representative of parental figures. The therapist's reactions also far exceed what is usually called countertransference.

They include in addition to this, interventions based on conscious deliberations and also his spontaneous idiosyncratic attitudes. Moreover, his own values are conveyed to the patient even if he consistently tries to protect his incognito." [41] Alexander's revised learning theory view appears to be closely related to that of Dollard and Miller.

REFERENCES

[1] Franz Alexander and Thomas Morton French, *Psychoanalytic therapy. Copyright 1946. The Ronald Press Company,* New York. P. vii.   [2] Alexander, F. M. *Fundamentals of psychoanalysis.* New York: Norton, 1963. P. 3.   [3] Alexander, F. M. *Psychoanalysis and psychotherapy.* New York: Norton, 1956. P. 172.   [4] Alexander, F. M. *Fundamentals of psychoanalysis.* New York: Norton, 1963. [5] *Ibid.,* p. 53.   [6] *Ibid.,* p. 55.   [7] *Ibid.,* p. 75.   [8] *Ibid.,* p. 76.   [9] *Ibid.,* p. 96.   [10] *Ibid.,* p. 119.   [11] *Ibid.,* p. 239.   [12] *Ibid.,* p. 259. [13] Alexander, F. M. *Psychoanalysis and psychotherapy.* New York: Norton, 1956. P. 11.   [14] *Ibid.,* p. 39.   [15] *Ibid.,* p. 55.   [16] *Ibid.,* p. 67.   [17] *Ibid.,* p. 69.   [18] Alexander, F. M. *Fundamentals of psychoanalysis.* New York: Norton, 1963. P. 273.   [19] Alexander, F. M., & French, T. M. *Psychoanalytic therapy.* New York: Ronald, 1946. P. 5.   [20] *Ibid.,* p. 6.   [21] Alexander, F. M. *Fundamentals of psychoanalysis.* New York: Norton, 1963. P. 157.   [22] Alexander, F. M., & French, T. M. *Psychoanalytic therapy.* New York: Ronald, 1946. P. 72.   [23] Alexander, F. M. *Psychoanalysis and psychotherapy.* New York: Norton, 1956. P. 45.   [24] *Ibid.,* p. 57.   [25] *Ibid.,* p. 67.   [26] *Ibid.,* p. 68.   [27] *Ibid.,* p. 70.   [28] Alexander, F. M., & French, T. M. *Psychoanalytic therapy.* New York: Ronald, 1946, P. 25.   [29] *Ibid.,* p. 19.   [30] *Ibid.,* p. 87. [31] *Ibid.,* p. 88.   [32] Alexander, F. M. *Psychoanalysis and psychotherapy.* New York: Norton, 1956. P. 93.   [33] Alexander, F. M., & French, T. M. *Psychoanalytic therapy.* New York: Ronald, 1946. P. 338.   [34] Franz Alexander and Thomas Morton French, *Psychoanalytic therapy.* Copyright 1946. The Ronald Press Company, New York. Pp. 155–157.   [35] *Ibid.,* p. 140.   [36] *Ibid.,* p. 207.   [37] Alexander, F. M. *Fundamentals of psychoanalysis.* New York: Norton, 1963. P. 250.   [38] Alexander, F. M., & French, T. M. *Psychoanalytic therapy.* New York: Ronald, 1946. Pp. 338–339.   [39] *Ibid.,* p. 341.   [40] *Ibid.,* p. 106.   [41] Alexander, F. M. The dynamics of psychotherapy in the light of learning theory. *Amer. J. Psychiat.,* 1963, **120,** 440–448.

PART FOUR

Perceptual-Phenomenological Approaches to Counseling

12

Introduction

There are a number of approaches to counseling or psychotherapy that, though differing in many significant respects, have in common a major concern with the perceptions or perceptual field of the individual client. Client-centered therapy is perhaps the first major approach to represent a concern with the way things appear to the individual, with his phenomenal world. The general development of the phenomenological theory of personality underlying client-centered therapy will be found in Combs and Snygg.[1] Although a number of writers have adopted the client-centered approach to counseling, the formulation devised by the originator of the approach, Carl Rogers,[2] has been selected for presentation here.

A second approach selected for inclusion, which is quite different from the client-centered approach, is the method of therapy developed by Kelly[3] on the basis of his psychology of personal constructs. Although the theory is a cognitive theory of personality and the therapy a highly rational one, both are perceptually oriented, as well as essentially phenomenological in nature.

A relatively recently developed perceptual approach to psychology has been given the label "transactional" by those closely associated with its evolution.[4] The term "transaction" has been taken from Dewey and Bentley.[5] It applies to the treatment of events as processes in space and time and environment. A segment of time in this process is labeled a transaction and includes, in the case of man,

281

the organism, or the individual, and his environment. Man's activities cannot be treated as his alone, or even as primarily his, but must be seen as processes of the organism-environment. That is, neither one exists or can be understood without the other. Transaction is defined by English and English as "a psychological event in which all the parts or aspects of the concrete event derive their existence and nature from active-participation in the event." [6] In this respect the transactional view is different from the concept of interaction, with which it is sometimes confused.[7] The concept of interaction implies two separate or independently existing objects that interact with each other. It appears that the transactional point of view has been adopted and utilized, at least to some extent, by many who have not adopted the term itself, and who have perhaps sometimes been thought of as concerned with interactions between the individual and his environment. These would include George H. Mead, Kurt Goldstein, the Allports, Gardner Murphy, Prescott Lecky, and Rogers. Thus, there is perhaps some point to Levitt's comment that "transactionalism is a somewhat fancy label applied to a viewpoint which is far from new." [8] It is a point of view that is implicit in much of the recent thinking about perception and in phenomenological psychology.

Two recent publications in counseling or psychotherapy have adopted the term "transactional." One is Berne's *Transactional Analysis in Psychotherapy.*[9] The second is *Psychiatric Social Work: A Transactional Case Book* by Grinker and his co-workers.[10] Neither is a theoretically systematic attempt to apply the transactional viewpoint to counseling or psychotherapy, however. Both are related to psychoanalysis. Berne makes no reference at all to the origin of the term "transactional," and it may be that his use of the term is unrelated to its use in psychology. He uses it to apply to group therapy, which may be preceded by a type of individual therapy that he calls structural analysis, and may be followed by psychoanalysis. Although his theory is a very interesting one, it did not seem as though it would be particularly useful or meaningful to the audience to which this book is directed, and it is therefore not included. The approach of Grinker and his associates was felt to be more pertinent and was therefore selected for inclusion.

An approach to psychotherapy that is perceptual in nature, and that is receiving increasing attention currently, is gestalt therapy. Its development has been associated with Frederick W. Perls, whose 1947 book [11] (republished in 1969) was followed by a book in collaboration with Ralph Hefferline and Paul Goodman in 1951,[12] and by another book in 1969,[13] based almost entirely on audio tapes of weekend seminars and an intensive four-week workshop. The presentation of gestalt therapy included here is based upon these books.

REFERENCES

[1] Combs, A. W., & Snygg, D. *Individual behavior: a perceptual approach to behavior.* (Rev. ed.) New York: Harper & Row, 1959.   [2] Rogers, C. R. *Client-*

centered therapy. Boston: Houghton Mifflin, 1951.   [3] Kelly, G. A. *The psychology of personal constructs.* Vol. I. *A theory of personality.* Vol. II. *Clinical diagnosis and psychotherapy.* New York: Norton, 1955.   [4] Cantril, H., Ames, A., Jr., Hastorf, A. H., & Ittelson, W. H. Psychology and scientific research. *Science.* 1949, **110,** 461–464; Ittelson, W. H. *The Ames demonstrations in perception.* Princeton, N.J.: Princeton University Press, 1952; Kilpatrick, F. P. (ed.), *Human behavior from the transactional point of view.* Hanover, N.H.: Institute for Associated Research, 1952; Kilpatrick, F. P. *Explorations in transactional psychology.* New York: New York University Press, 1961.   [5] Dewey, J., & Bentley, A. F. *Knowing and the known.* Boston: Beacon Press, 1949.   [6] English, H. B., & English, Ava C. *A comprehensive dictionary of psychological and psychoanalytical terms.* New York: Longmans, Green, 1958. P. 561.   [7] Kanfer, F. H. Review of R. Grinker and others, "Psychiatric social work: a transactional case book." *Contemp. Psychol.,* 1962, **7,** 295–296.   [8] Levitt, E. L. Review of W. H. Ittleson & S. B. Kutash (Eds.), "Perceptual changes in psychopathology." *Contemp. Psychol.,* 1962, **7,** 255–256.   [9] Berne, E. *Transactional analysis in psychotherapy.* New York: Grove Press, 1961.   [10] Grinker, R. R., Sr., MacGregor, Helen, Selan, Kate, Klein, Annette, & Kohrman, Janet. *Psychiatric social work: a transactional case book.* New York: Basic Books, 1961.   [11] Perls, F. S. *Ego, hunger and aggression.* New York: Random House, 1969.   [12] Perls, F. S., Hefferline, R. F., & Goodman, P. *Gestalt therapy.* New York: Julian Press, 1951.   [13] Perls, F. S. *Gestalt therapy verbatim.* Moab, Utah: Real People Press, 1969.

13

Kelly's psychology of personal constructs and counseling

One of the most systematic approaches to counseling or psychotherapy is that developed by George A. Kelly on the basis of his psychology of personal constructs. Kelly (1905–1967) received his B.A. in 1926 at Park College, his M.A. at the University of Kansas in 1928, a B.Ed. in 1930 from the University of Edinburgh, and his Ph.D. from the State University of Iowa in 1931. Although his Ph.D. was in psychology, his earlier work included study in education, sociology, economics, labor relations, speech pathology, biometrics, and cultural anthropology. In 1931 he became an Instructor at Fort Hays State College, Kansas, and was an Associate Professor when he entered the Navy for two years in 1943. He was an Associate Professor at the University of Maryland during 1945–1946. In 1946 he became Professor of Psychology at Ohio State University and served as Director of the Psychological Clinic from 1946 to 1951 and also in 1963, while continuing as Professor of Psychology until 1965. He then became Professor of Psychology at Brandeis University and remained there until his death in March of 1967. He was a Diplomate in Clinical Psychology of the American Board of Professional Psychology. In 1969 Brendan Maher published a collection of his papers under the title *Clinical Psychology and Personality*. One of the papers in this book, entitled "The Autobiography of a Theory," is a personal account of the development of personal construct theory, beginning with Kelly's repudiation of stimulus-response determinism, through a Freudian period, to the present- and future-oriented view of constructive alternatism.

BACKGROUND AND DEVELOPMENT

The Psychology of Personal Constructs,[1] in two volumes, began, Kelly reports, twenty years before its publication, as a handbook of clinical procedures. But the "how to" approach was not satisfying, and he began to explore the "why." It was then discovered that the result he obtained was far different from traditional psychology. Many implicit assumptions were recognized, and this led to a third approach, that of system building, which required the development of explicit assumptions and the expression of convictions that had been taken for granted in clinical practice. The first task, then, was the construction of a theory of personality, followed by the development of its implications for psychological practice.

The resultant system differs from the familiar psychological systems. Far from occupying the central place, as it does in most contemporary systems, the term "learning" hardly appears. Concepts such as ego, emotion, motivation, reinforcement, drive, need, and unconscious do not appear. Instead such concepts as foci of convenience, preemption, propositionality, fixed-role therapy, creativity cycle, transitive diagnosis, and the credulous approach are met with. Other common concepts, such as anxiety, guilt, and hostility, carry new definitions. The result is an unorthodox theory of personality and of therapy.

PHILOSOPHY AND CONCEPTS

The Philosophy of Constructive Alternativism

POINTS OF DEPARTURE   Two simple notions underlie Kelly's theory of personality. One is that man is better understood when viewed in the perspective of centuries; the other is "that each man contemplates in his own personal way the stream of events upon which he finds himself so swiftly borne." [2] Within these notions there is the possibility of discovering ways in which the individual can restructure his life. The long-range view focuses attention upon man's progress and upon *man the scientist,* seeking to predict and control the causes of events in which he is involved. Thus, human motivation is seen in a new light, instead of in terms of appetites, needs, and impulses.

Man exists in a real universe, which he is gradually coming to understand. Thoughts also really exist; but the correspondence between what people think exists and what really exists is imperfect, although in a constant state of change. The universe is integral, with all its parts having exact relationships to each other. But it is a constantly changing universe, so that there is a dimension of time, which must be considered. While some aspects of the universe make sense without the time dimension, life makes sense only when viewed in the perspective of time.

Life has the capacity to represent other forms of reality or to represent its environment, and can place alternative constructions upon the environment; thus, it does more than respond to its environment. The individual may misrepresent the real phenomenon, but the misrepresentation will itself be real; "what he perceives may not exist, but his perception does." [3] Man looks at the world through patterns, which are ways of construing the world, or *constructs*. Though man seeks to improve his constructs by increasing his repertory, in order to provide a better fit between his perceptions and the real environment, the larger system that his constructs are a part of may resist change because of his personal investment in or dependence upon it.

Construction systems that can be communicated can be shared, and progress in such communication has been great. Systems may be designed to fit special fields or realms, for example, the realms of psychology and physiology. But realms may overlap or may give rise to alternative systems or ways of representing or viewing the same facts, as is the case with psychology and physiology. There is no universal system of constructs. All our systems are miniature systems with limited ranges. The system of personal constructs is limited to human personality and problems of interpersonal relationships. Systems have centers, or points where they work best. The theory of personal constructs tends to focus on the area of human readjustment to stress and thus to prove most useful to the psychotherapist.

Constructs are used to predict events. They are thus tested in terms of their predictive efficiency. A construct may appear to be validated by events that are misrepresented because of the need to validate it. Constructs are more susceptible to revision when they are immediately tested on an experimental basis. The continuing course of events reveals constructs either as usefully valid or as misleading, and thus provides the basis for revision of constructs and construction systems. Some people are afraid to express and test their constructs; this is a problem in psychotherapy.

THE PHILOSOPHICAL POSITION   The world may be construed in various ways. Interpretations constitute successive approximations of an absolute construction. Constructive alternativism assumes "that all of our present interpretations of the universe are subject to revision or replacement. . . . We take the stand that there are always some alternative constructions available to choose among in dealing with the world. No one needs to paint himself into a corner; no one needs to be completely hemmed in by circumstances, no one needs to be the victim of his biography." [4] Some alternatives are better than others; some lead to difficulty. The criterion is the specific predictive efficiency of each and of the system it could become a part of.

Constructs are not necessarily symbolized by words, nor are they capable of being verbalized; and the concept as such may seem to be psychological rather than philosophical. Constructive alternativism is a philosophical point of view rather than a philosophical system. It bears some relation to various philosophical systems, however, falling within the area of epistemology called *gnoseology*. It also relies upon *empiricism* and *pragmatic* logic, although it is in a measure *rationalistic* and stands apart from traditional realism, which makes man a victim of circumstances. Ontologically, it is a *monistic* position.

The notion of an integral universe implies determinism. But since there is no repetition, and each sequence of events is unique, "there is not much point in singling it out and saying that it was determined. It was a consequent—but only once!" [5] The sort of determinism that is important here is the control exercised by a superordinate construct over its elements. The elements do not determine the construct, which is thus free from or independent of them. "Determinism and freedom are then inseparable, for that which determines another is, by the same token, free of the other. Determinism and freedom are opposite sides of the same coin—two aspects of the same relationship." [6] Thus, man, "to the extent that he is able to construe his circumstances, can find for himself freedom from their domination. . . . Theories are the thinking of men who seek freedom amid swirling events. The theories comprise prior assumptions about certain realms of these events. To the extent that the events may, from these prior assumptions, be construed, predicted, and their relative courses charted, men may exercise control, and gain freedom for themselves in the process." [7] For those individuals whose constructs limit and restrict them, the theory of personal constructs is concerned with finding ways to help the person reconstrue his life in order to keep himself from being a victim of his past.

Basic Theory

FUNDAMENTAL POSTULATE   A person's processes are psychologically channelized by the ways in which he anticipates events. As a postulate, this assumption is not subject to question. It is accepted as a presupposition. The term "processes" indicates that the person is a behaving organism, so that it is not necessary to account for or establish the existence of some sort of mental energy. "Channelized" refers to a network of pathways, flexible but structured, which both facilitates and restricts a person's range of action. "Anticipates" indicates the predictive and motivational features, which point toward the future. "Anticipation is both the push and pull of personal constructs." [8] The psychology of personal constructs develops from this postulate through corollaries that in part follow from and in part elaborate it.

CONSTRUCTION COROLLARY   A person anticipates events by construing their replications. This means that events are predicted by placing an interpretation upon or structuring the recurring aspects of events. Construing is not identical with verbal formulation; it may not necessarily be symbolized.

INDIVIDUALITY COROLLARY   Persons differ from each other in their construction of events. This is because no two persons participate in the same event in the same way.

ORGANIZATION COROLLARY   Each person characteristically evolves, for his convenience in anticipating events, a construction system embracing ordinal relationships between constructs. A system of constructs minimizes incompatibilities and inconsistencies, and involves a hierarchy of constructs, with some being superordinal and others subordinal. An individual's system sometimes needs revision, but he may choose to conserve its integrity. While this appears to be similar to Lecky's concept of the need for self-consistency, it is not for consistency itself that the individual is seeking to preserve the system, but because the system is essential for his anticipation of events.

DICHOTOMY COROLLARY   A person's construction system is composed of a finite number of dichotomous constructs. Similarities and contrasts, which constitute replication, are in terms of the same aspect; that is, if we select an aspect in which A and B are similar but in contrast to C, this same aspect is the basis of the construct. "In its minimum context a construct is a way in which at least two elements are similar and contrast with a third." [9] Concepts are meaningless except in relation to or comparison with their contrasts, opposites, or complements; for example, good has no meaning except in comparison with bad.

CHOICE COROLLARY   A person chooses for himself that alternative in a dichotomized construct through which he anticipates the greater possibility for extension and definition of his system. Choice consists of placing relative values upon the alternatives of the dichotomies. Extension and definition include both elaboration, or comprehensiveness, and explicitness, or clarity. While the choices might be said to constitute "a seeking of self-protection," or "acting in defense of the self," or "the preservation of one's integrity . . . from our point of view a person's construction system is for the anticipation of events. If it were for something else, it would probably shape up into something quite different." [10] The individual does not seek pleasure, satisfactions, or rewards to satisfy needs or reduce tensions, but seeks to anticipate events; "there is a continuing movement toward the anticipation of events, rather than a series of barters for temporal satisfactions, and this movement is the essence of human life itself." [11]

RANGE COROLLARY   A construct is convenient for the anticipation of a finite range of events only. Constructs are limited and are applicable only within a restricted range of the perceptual field. Some persons use a construct more comprehensively than others.

EXPERIENCE COROLLARY   A person's construction system varies as he successively construes the replications of events. Events subject a person's construction system to a validation process, which leads to revision of the system or to a reconstruing of events and a reconstruction of one's life through experience. Learning is inherent in this corollary and is thus a part of the assumptive structure of the theory; it is not a special class of psychological processes, but synonymous with any and all processes.

MODULATION COROLLARY   The variation in a person's construction system is limited by the permeability of the constructs within whose range of convenience the variants lie. Permeability is the admitting of new, as yet unconstrued, elements. Variants are the old and the new constructs. Change thus occurs within a system in which superordinate constructs admit new constructs to its context.

FRAGMENTATION COROLLARY   A person may successively employ a variety of construction subsystems that are inferentially incompatible with each other. Successive inconsistency between subsystems may be tolerated within a larger system. Successive formulations may not be derivable from each other; new constructs are not necessarily direct derivatives of one's old constructs, but rather are derivatives of the larger system.

COMMONALITY COROLLARY   To the extent that one person employs a construction of experience that is similar to that employed by another, his psychological processes are similar to those of the other person. It is not the experiencing of the same events, or stimuli, but the placing of the same construction on events (which may be phenomenally dissimilar) that results in similar psychological processes. Identity of construction or processes is impossible, phenomenologically speaking.

SOCIALITY COROLLARY   To the extent that one person construes the construction process of another, he may play a role in a social process involving the other person. This is more than seeing things as another does; it is also seeing his way of seeing, or outlook, for some measure of acceptance of him and his way of seeing things is a basis for playing a constructive role in relation to him. Construing what others are thinking enables us to predict what they will do. While commonality may make the understanding of another's construction system more likely, it is not essential.

The Nature of Personal Constructs

PERSONAL USAGE OF CONSTRUCTS   "A construct is a way in which some things are construed as being alike and yet different from others." [12] The contrast is included in the construct, rather than being considered to be irrelevant or to be another concept, as it is in conventional logic. It differs in this respect from a concept. It includes the abstraction element of a concept, but it also includes percepts. The dichotomy represents an aspect of all human thinking.

The individual is unable to express the whole of his construction system. He may misconstrue what his construction of a situation will be in the future. He may not be able to express certain constructs in a way in which others can understand them or subsume them under their own systems without predicting his behavior incorrectly. He may express his constructs incompletely, omitting the contrast, saying, for example, "Mary is gentle." But to say that Mary is gentle implies that at least one other person is gentle and one other is not gentle, or that at least two other persons are not gentle, since the minimum context for a construct is three things. Any other statement is illogical and unpsychological. To say that everyone is gentle, for example, has no meaning. Since constructs are primarily personal, they may not be easily understood by others. Thus, there are a number of conditions that may make it appear that a person does not mean what he says.

Constructs abstract repeated properties of events and imply that the replicated properties may all reappear in another event. Prediction is therefore implicit in construing. It is not a specific event that is predicted, but its properties, intersecting in a prescribed way. The prediction is validated only when an event occurs that can be construed like the intersect.

Constructs provide the means of binding or grouping events so that they become predictable, manageable, and controllable. Man controls his own destiny "to the extent that he can develop a construction system with which he identifies himself and which is sufficiently comprehensive to subsume the world around him. . . . According to this view, mankind is slowly learning to control his destiny, although it is a long and tedious process." [13]

The individual has a choice between the two ends, or dichotomies, of his constructs, but he is controlled by the network of his construction system. He can, however, develop new constructs to expand his system. A construct, in effect, represents rival hypotheses upon either of which he can act.

The self is a construct. The use of the self as a datum in forming constructs leads to constructs that operate as rigorous controls on behavior, particularly behavior in relation to, or in comparison with, other people. These comparisons, as the individual construes them, control his social life. "As one construes other people, he formulates the construction system which governs his own behavior," [14]—that is, he defines his own role. His own construct system is revealed when he talks about others.

FORMAL ASPECTS OF CONSTRUCTS   Symbolism allows one of the elements of a construct to represent the construct itself. Communication is, then, the reproduction of the symbolic element to elicit a parallel construct in another person. Words are useful as symbols but are not always effective. Figures, such as the mother or father, may symbolize constructs. This sort of symbolization is characteristic of children. Such figures give clarity and stability or rigidity to the construct.

Dimensions against which the constructs of others can be evaluated may be set up. A commonly used dimension is abstract versus concrete, but this does not seem to be particularly useful; permeability versus impermeability, already referred to, is a more useful dimension. A *preemptive construct* is one that preempts its elements exclusively for its own realm—a ball can be nothing but a ball. It is a pigeonholing, or nothing-but, approach. A *constellatory construct* permits its elements to belong to other specified realms concurrently. A *propositional construct* leaves its elements open to construction, not specifying all the other realms to which it may belong. It is at the other end of the continuum from preemptive and constellatory constructs. There are other dimensions, also, such as *anxiety, hostility, transference* and *dependence,* to be mentioned later.

CHANGING CONSTRUCTION   Validation is the payoff of an anticipation or prediction. Validation is not reinforcement; it is much broader, for it may include such things as the breaking of one's leg after it has been anticipated. Failure of validation leads not only to changes of prediction but to a turning to another construct upon which to base a prediction, or to a revision of the construct system. The formation of new constructs is favored by certain conditions. These conditions include approaching the constructs in contexts that do not involve the self or family members and providing a fresh set of elements as a context. This is what therapy does. Another condition is an atmosphere of experimentation, in which propositional constructs are "tried on for size." Still another condition is the availability of validating data— knowledge of the results. Results must be seen from the subject's, not the experimenter's, point of view, however.

The most important condition unfavorable for the formation of new constructs is threat. "A construct is threatening when it is itself an element in a next-higher-order construct which is, in turn, incompatible with other higher-order constructs upon which the person is dependent for his living." [15] Such elements have been excluded from the person's construct system because they are incompatible and are seen as threats when they are presented as elements of a new construct, and thus cannot be utilized easily. "The effect of threat is to compel the client to claw frantically for his basic construct. Threat arouses the necessity for mobilizing one's resources. It should be borne in mind that the resources which are mobilized may not always be mature and effective. Therefore a threatened person may often behave in childish ways. Another effect of introducing threatening elements, and frequently an undesirable one, is the tendency for the traumatic experience to act as further subjective documentation or proof of the client's own maladaptive conceptual framework." [16]

A second unfavorable condition for the formation of new constructs is preoccupation with old material or old impermeable constructs or old habits. A third condition is the lack of a laboratory in which to try out new constructs in a relatively controlled or protected situation.

THE MEANING OF EXPERIENCE   Our experience is the portion of the world's happenings that happens to us. But things happen to us personally only when we behave in relation to them, when we construe them—not when we just react to them. People do not learn *from* experience; learning constitutes experience. Successive construing or reconstruing of happenings increases experience.

The psychology of personal constructs accepts the individual's experience as phenomenological, but attempts "to lift our data from the individual at a relatively high level of abstraction. This is a little like saying that we deal concretely with a person's abstractions rather than abstractly with his concretisms. Behaviorism, for example, did it the other way, it created elaborate public abstractions out of minute personal concretisms." [17] The personal-construct psychologist observes the client's constructs or abstractions of behavior. He takes what he sees and hears at face value, including what he sees and hears about his subject's constructs. This is commonly called acceptance; it is the *credulous attitude.* The abstractions in the subject's system are the concrete elements awaiting construction in the psychologist's system. "All of this means that we cannot consider the psychology of personal constructs a phenomenological theory, if that means ignoring the personal construction of the psychologist who does the observing." [18]

Personal-construct theory, like perceptual theories, takes an ahistorical approach, which is the view that since one's activity at a given moment is determined by one's outlook at that moment, the past influences behavior only through current perceptions. The basis of perception includes "nonconscious" as well as conscious processes. The historical method of study may be used to help reveal the successive patterning of the elements entering into a person's personal constructs.

Other people are important in the validation of a person's constructs. Their opinions may be validators of constructs about nonhuman events. In the case of constructs involving other people as elements, when another person fails to perform according to expectations, he becomes threatening. The individual is affected in turn, and even though he may reject the expectancies of others, he construes himself in relation to those expectancies. Another aspect of validation by group expectancies involves his construction of his role. The term "role" applies to a course of activity played out in the light of one's construction of one or more other persons' construct systems. Thus, in playing a role, the individual acts according to what he believes others think, so that his construction of his role must be validated in terms of the expectancies of these others. This last situation illustrates the characteristic approach of the personal-construct psychologist, who seeks to establish a role in relation to other people. Personal-construct theory is essentially "role theory."

The culture influences the personal constructs of the individual, the same culture resulting in similarities among those in it. The psychologist or therapist must understand these cultural influences, seeing the group constructs as elements upon which the individual builds his personal constructs. Thus, both the similarities and the differences among persons in a culture must be recognized.

Diagnostic Constructs

The purpose of diagnostic constructs is to give the clinician a set of professional constructs under which he can subsume the personal constructs of his clients, so that he can assume a professionally useful role relation with them. These constructs are not disease entities, types of people, or traits; they consist rather of a set of universal coordinate axes with respect to which it is possible to plot any person's behavior and the changes occurring in his psychological processes. They are not used to pigeonhole clients, but to represent different lines of movement open to them. The tentative structuring of the client's experience record by the clinician is termed "structuralization." "Construction" refers to the better-organized formulation that arranges the client's behavior under his inferred personal constructs and then in turn arranges them, or subsumes them, under the clinician's own system. The phenomenologist's approach is used to arrive at the individual's personal constructs, and then the normative approach is used to put these together with what is known about other persons, thus bringing each client's system into the public domain.

A good diagnostic construct should have the characteristics of other good constructs, which include propositionality (relative independence), dichotomy, permeability, definability (operational), temporality, futurity (prognostic), sociality, and the ability to generate hypotheses, particularly treatment hypotheses.

GENERAL DIAGNOSTIC CONSTRUCTS

Preverbal Constructs / A preverbal construct is one that the client continues to use even though it has no consistent word symbol. Words facilitate the utilization and modification of constructs, while other symbols are more cumbersome, impeding communication and discussion. Preverbal constructs usually originate in infancy and often relate to the client's dependency. They may represent a kind of core of his construction system. They may be overlaid by misleading verbalized constructs. Signs of preverbal constructs are confusion in verbalization, greater ability to illustrate the construct than to verbalize it, the appearance of the construct in dreams that are not remembered clearly, and the remembering of events that the client is not sure actually happened. Preverbal constructs cover in part the concept of the unconscious. Other aspects of this concept are included in the constructs described below. The failure of the client to construe things in the same way as the clinician should not be interpreted to mean that he really does construe things in this way but is unaware of it. His later ability to construe things as the clinician does constitutes a new construction for him, not a revelation of the unconscious.

Submergence / Submergence refers to the omission or avoidance of one of the ends of the dichotomous construct, usually the contrast end. Constructs that have one end submerged cannot be tested.

Suspension / As constructs are revised, some elements drop out and others become more prominent. "When a structure is rejected, because at the moment it is incompatible with the over-all system which the person is using, we may say that it has undergone *suspension.*"[19] This is similar to forgetting, dissociation, and repression. What is unstructured is "forgotten" or "repressed."

Level of Cognitive Awareness / The preceding three constructs involve low levels of cognitive awareness. A high-level construct is one that is readily expressible in socially effective symbols, has alternatives that are both readily accessible, falls well within the range of convenience of the client's major constructions, and is not suspended by its superordinating constructs.

Dilation and Constriction / Dilation is the broadening of the perceptual field to organize it more comprehensively, following a series of alternating uses of incompatible systems. Constriction occurs when the individual narrows his field to minimize apparent incompatibilities in his system.

Comprehensive Constructs and Incidental Constructs / Comprehensive constructs subsume a wide variety of events; they are not necessarily superordinate constructs, however. Incidental constructs subsume a small variety of events.

Superordinate Constructs and Subordinate Constructs / A superordinate construct utilizes another construct as its contextual element; the construct so utilized is a subordinate construct.

Regnancy / A superordinate construct that assigns each of its elements to a category on an all-or-none basis is a regnant construct. For example, if one were to say that all spades are implements, then implement would be a regnant superordinate construct. This is an example of classical logic and simplifies one's personal construct system.

Core Constructs and Peripheral Constructs / Core constructs are those that the individual uses to maintain his identity and existence. In the healthy person they are comprehensive and permeable. Peripheral constructs may be altered without serious modification of the core structure. Their reformulation is a much less complicated affair than the reformulation of a core construct.

Tight Constructs and Loose Constructs / Tight constructs lead to unvarying predictions, while loose constructs lead to varying predictions. Loose constructs are like preliminary sketches of a design.

TRANSITIONAL CONSTRUCTS   Constructs provide a stable element in experience. Yet constructs change, and the transitions present problems.

Transitional constructs concern this process of change and include the following.

Threat / "Threat is the awareness of imminent comprehensive change in one's core structures." [20] The therapist, who expects the client to change, is thus threatening, especially when the client is on the verge of a major change.

Fear / Fear is the awareness of an imminent change in an incidental core construct rather than a comprehensive construct.

Anxiety / Anxiety is the recognition on the part of the individual that the events confronting him lie outside the range of convenience of his construct system. Since his constructs do not apply, an inability to construe the events meaningfully, or an ambiguity, results. Loosening the superordinate constructs may increase tolerance for ambiguity, and may be sufficient to reduce anxiety; if loosening proceeds too far, however, it may lead to schizophrenia. Redefinition and increase in the permeability of the superordinate system is also effective against anxiety. Tightening is another defense against anxiety.

Guilt / Within the individual's core structure is the core role, which involves that part of the role structure by which he maintains himself as an integral being. Guilt is the experience resulting from the person's perception of his apparent loss of his core role structure. The core role is not a superficial role, but "a part one plays as if his life depended upon it. Indeed, his life actually does depend upon it." [21] When the individual discovers he has not been acting in accordance with this role, he feels guilt. Punishment is not the result of guilt, but vice versa. We punish those who threaten us, to protect ourselves from the threat of being like them and to make them feel guilty.

Aggressiveness / Aggressiveness is the active elaboration of one's perceptual field. The aggressive individual has a greater than average tendency to set up choice points, precipitating himself into situations that require decision and action. Areas of anxiety tend to be areas of aggressiveness. The aggressive person is seen as threatening.

Hostility / Hostility is the effort to force another person to validate a prediction that is invalid. "The other person is the victim, not so much of the hostile person's fiendlishly destructive impulses, as of his frantic and unrealistic efforts to collect on a wager he has already lost." [22] Recurring evidence that he is wrong leads the hostile person to feel guilty.

SEQUENTIAL CHANGES IN CONSTRUCTS   There are typical sequences of changes in constructs which people employ in order to function in everyday situations. Two of these follow.

The C-P-C Cycle / This cycle is a sequence of construction from circumspection to preemption to control, resulting in a choice involving the self. Circumspect construction employs a series of propositional constructs. Thus, there is a process that goes from looking at elements in a multidimensional manner to focusing on one element, and results in a choice, or the control of the construct through superordination. To understand choice, one must understand the alternatives facing a person, from his point of view. *Impulsivity* is a form of control in which the period of circumspection preceding the choice or decision is shortened. It is an attempt at a quick solution.

The Creativity Cycle / This cycle begins with loosened construction, involving exploration and experiment, followed by tightened and validated construction.

The constructs are chosen as consistent with personal-construct theory and as useful to the clinical psychologist. They represent primarily lines along which a person may change in reconstruing his life, and secondarily ways in which individuals vary among themselves, as well as from each other, at different times. They are not categories for classifying people.

THE TYPES OF PSYCHOLOGICAL DISORDERS   To illustrate the use of the dimensions of diagnosis, or the diagnostic constructs, the constructs are included in a multidimensional system that illustrates representative types of psychological disorders. The diagnostic constructs themselves do not necessarily refer to disorders, but they are designed to be relevant to various personal construct systems. A disorder usually involves more than one dimension. Disorders are not nosologic categories or disease entities.

A disorder is any personal construction that is used repeatedly in spite of consistent invalidation. There may be other bases of explanation for psychological disorders, such as past events. But the past cannot be changed and treatment on this basis is a tedious cancelling out of each old experience with a new one, or a turning back of the clock. One can do something, however, about a person's personal construct system. Repentance is substituted for atonement, reconstruction for compensation, the future for the past.

There are two major groupings of disorders—disorders of construction and disorders of transition.

Disorders of Construction / [Disorders of Dilation] Dilation is a disordering process that occurs when the individual has no superordinate constructs to order his dilated field. He may have lost or abandoned governing constructs and then reverted to inappropriate preverbal constructs of dependency, which are comprehensive and permeable. Dilation may occur with loose construction, which is an effort to span or embrace the dilated field. The so-called manic client is usually dilated. In the depressive phase, he makes an effort to constrict his field. Dilation is also seen in cases diagnosed as paranoid.

Disorders Involving Tightening and Loosening of Constructs. The individual with tight constructions makes precise, exact predictions. His superordinate structure lacks permeability. But his anticipations fail to materialize, and constructs must be discarded. He becomes anxious and must resort to constriction or preverbal comprehensive structures. Suicide or psychosis may be the result. The person with loose constructs is variable, adapts to experiences by stretching his constructions, and seldom misses in his predictions because they are so broad. Extreme looseness of construing is difficult to follow and may lead to avoidance on the part of others, and thus to social withdrawal. Such persons are often labeled schizophrenic. With the loss of a social role, guilt may develop if the individual is aware of the loss and does not deny it by constriction.

Disorders Involving Core Constructs. Physical complaints often involve core constructs and also imply that dependency is involved. "Psychosomatic symptoms" are required, just as sustenance and safety are required. In "conversion reactions" the client is thinking dualistically and translates his problem from a psychological to a physiological problem. In this preemptive construction his problem is wholly physical.

Disorders of Transition / Aggression and Hostility. Aggression is often a solution for hostility, giving rise to activities that relieve the hostility. Hostility requires solution by reconstruing, not drainage by catharsis. Aggression may lead to ignoring one's role or failing to elaborate one's role, dealing with others as objects to be manipulated rather than as people to be understood. Coping with others as people rather than objects requires time, which the impatient aggressive person is often not willing to spend. He has "authority problems" for this reason. Aggression may lead to guilt in various ways when the individual feels his role is jeopardized. Hostility is unrealistic, yet it may achieve results if it obliges others to provide the outcomes the hostile person wants to order to placate him or indulge his whims.

Disorders of Anxiety, Constriction, and Guilt / The anxious person has a construction system that is failing him, and he has no better or new system available. In a sense all disorders of construction involve anxiety. Anxiety cannot be observed, but it can be inferred from the measures undertaken to control or avoid it, such as weeping, impulsivity, dilation, or constriction. All behavior may be seen as directed toward the avoidance of anxiety or of the perception of anxiety. But this would lead to nirvana; usually people seek to master rather than avoid anxiety.

Constriction may be viewed as an avoidance of anxiety. It is a way of shrinking one's world until it becomes manageable. Constriction and preemption often go together. The individual becomes narrow, limited, restricted. Issues accumulate that lead to insurmountable anxiety. Involutional melancholia is an example of what results.

Life is difficult in the face of extreme guilt, which involves the person's core role. Guilt may lead to hostility or to physical illness, if not to death. Paranoid homosexuality represents a disorder of guilt.

Disorders Involving Undispersed Dependency / Dependency is not considered a principal axis of the diagnostic construct system, but it does constitute the basis for disorders. Everyone is dependent on others. The normal person dispenses his dependencies widely and in a discriminative fashion; the disordered person is indiscriminate in his dependencies and seeks someone on whom he can unload all his dependency at once. Hostility frequently results when his search does not turn out well.

"Psychosomatic" and "organic" Problems / Somatic symptoms in a person with a psychological conflict are difficult to reach because they are perceived as physical in the client's dualistic way of thinking. Many psychological disorders involve "psychosomatic" symptoms. But the term has no precise meaning in the system of personal constructs.

The characteristics of the organically deteriorated person stem from his attempt to reconstrue himself in a constricted world. Deteriorated constructs, or constructs that have become relatively impermeable, may be used. The "organic" picture may also be found in a person with a deep-seated feeling of inadequacy who finds himself beyond his depth.

Disorders Involving Control / Disorders of control reflect faulty superordinate construction systems. The superordinate construct may be such that it subsumes, or controls, all new experiences, with no change in itself. Disorders involving impulsivity represent difficulties with the phases of the circumspection-preemption-control cycle resulting in foreshortening of the cycle.

Not all disorders are disorders of the *form* of personal constructs, although these forms constitute the elements of the diagnostic dimensions. Some difficulties arise from the *content* of the constructs. In addition, some therapy can take place without concern for diagnostic constructs. Not all the important learning takes place on the couch.

THE THERAPY PROCESS

Counseling or psychotherapy is a psychological process that changes one's outlook on some aspect of life. It involves reconstruing, usually of the client's life role or the role he envisions for himself. Psychological disorders can be traced to the characteristics of a person's construction system. They manifest themselves in complaints—complaints of the person about himself and others, and complaints of others about him. At the phenomenal level, then, the goal of psychotherapy is to alleviate complaints.

The Client's Conceptions and Expectations

The client's widely varying conceptions of psychotherapy must be accepted by the therapist at the outset. He must be able to subsume the client's construction of psychotherapy in order to utilize it within his own more comprehensive perspective. As therapy progresses, the client's concept changes. His view becomes more comprehensive. He discovers that the outcome of psychotherapy is not a fixed state of affairs, but a vantage point for viewing a life plan, and the opening phase of a continuing process.

The client also conceptualizes the therapist and his role in relation to his (the client's) conceptualization of psychotherapy. His perceptions may be stretched to construe the therapist to meet his expectations. The client may construe the therapist in various ways—as a parent, a protector, an absolver of guilt, an authority figure, a prestige figure, a possession, a stabilizer against change, a temporary respite from stress, a threat, an ideal person or companion, a stooge or foil, or a representative of reality. The last is best suited to achieve therapeutic goals, since it leads to a relationship in which the client tests out his constructs in an experimental or laboratory situation. The therapist is expected to play the parts of many figures, to make himself articulate, and to serve as a validator. Any but the most inept therapist can help a client who construes him in such a way. Yet some fail, usually because they insist upon an authoritarian rather than a cooperative relationship, or because they are afraid of the outcome of such an experimental relationship.

The Therapist's Conceptualization of His Role

Clinicians assist in the reconstruction, or continuous shifting, of the client's construct system, a process that should continue throughout the client's lifetime. All change or movement, great or small, takes place as a function of change in constructs.

The role of the clinician is broad. It includes producing superficial change by creating an atmosphere of threat or anxiety, by consistently invalidating the client's devices, by precipitating the client into a situation in which he perceives a contrasting role that is expected of him, and by exhorting the client. Less superficial approaches include controlled elaboration or helping the client "work through" his construct system to bring certain minor constructs in line with the system.

But the major or most fundamental role of the therapist is to help the client revise his constructs. He begins, however, by accepting the client's construction system as it is. Such acceptance does not mean approval, but the readiness to use the client's system, to attempt to anticipate events the way the client anticipates them. Acceptance alone is not sufficient for therapeutic progress, except in simple cases. The therapist, while putting himself in the client's place, maintains his professional overview of the client's problems. He subsumes the client's construction system under a comprehensive frame which he provides.

Basic Approaches to the Revision of Constructs

The therapist helps the client develop new constructs or make major revisions of his constructs in several ways.

1. The therapist selectively adds new conceptual elements. These experiential elements must not fit too neatly into the client's present system, or they will not challenge it and will lead only to superficial movement. On the other hand, if the new element leads the

client to attempt a sweeping revision of his constructs, there is danger of his becoming deeply disturbed. The therapist must be keenly aware of how the client is handling the new elements. The role of the therapist "includes the skillful introduction of new conceptual elements which challenge the client's construction system but which are carefully chosen so as not to precipitate a catastrophic revolution in it." [23]

2.   The therapist accelerates the tempo of the client's experience. Life experience accelerates during therapy, both within and outside the interviews, with the therapist confronting the client with problems intended to pull him through the normal succession of life experiences at an accelerated pace.

3.   The therapist imposes recent structures upon old elements. Although the emphasis of the approach is upon the present, the way in which the adult sees the past influences the way he sees the present. Thus, if the past is seen through the eyes of his childhood, new events that are similar to those of the past may be dealt with in a childish way. The therapist helps the client apply his adult constructs in dealing with childhood recollections. Thus, the client is better prepared to handle present and future events that may appear to be repetitions of the past.

4.   The therapist helps the client reduce certain obsolete constructs to a state of impermeability. When it is not possible to get the client to reconstrue certain events or figures of the past, the therapist "may get the client to define the limits of the construct, to tie it firmly to past events and figures which are so unusual that there is little likelihood that their counterparts need be perceived in the future, and finally to wrap the construct up tightly with a word symbol by means of which it can be kept under control." [24]

5.   The therapist helps design and implement experiments. Therapy is a laboratory for testing ideas, and the therapist helps the client survey new data and develop hypotheses for testing that do not involve too much risk at one time. He may also participate in the experiment by enacting required parts.

6.   The therapist serves as validator. By his reactions to the client's constructs the therapist serves as a validator. The therapist should be a sample of the social world, being a reasonably faithful example of the natural human reactions that the client will meet outside therapy.

The therapist does not try to pass on his own constructs to the client. If he should do so, the client will try to translate them into his own construct system. Thus, a client told to be self-confident may respond with behavior that the therapist feels is conceited. Nevertheless, the therapist does shape the client's system by the elements he introduces, by the constructs he validates or invalidates, and by the hypotheses of the client that he selects for experimentation. "His very choice of points at which to clear his throat, nod his head, or murmur acceptance reflects his bias as to what is inconsequential, what is transitional, or what is understandable." [25]

Psychotherapy according to the psychology of personal constructs is an experimental process, since the system is built upon the model of science. Constructs are hypotheses, with prediction the goal. The therapist helps the client to define hypotheses and to design and implement experiments, using the psychotherapy room as a laboratory. The therapist participates in the experiment, serving as a part of the validating evidence. "Psychotherapeutic movement may mean (1) that the client has reconstrued himself and certain other features of the world within his original system, (2) that he has organized his old system more precisely, or (3) that he has replaced some of the constructs in his old system with new ones." [26] The last is the most significant type of movement.

IMPLEMENTATION: PROCEDURES AND TECHNIQUES

The Appraisal of Experiences

The case history is elicited by the use of schedules and outlines. The material is structured in the light of the client's deep-seated personal outlook. The case history is important, not in terms of what happened in the past, nor even just in terms of what the client thinks now, but in terms of what it reveals about the outlook of the client. The chronicle of events is also important in providing validational evidence and checkpoints against which the client's constructs may be understood.

CULTURE AND EXPERIENCE   The clinician must be aware of cultural variations, since the culture provides the client with evidence of what is "true" and with much of the data used in his personal construct system. Culture controls in that it limits the data and evidence at the client's disposal, but there is a tremendous variety in the ways in which clients handle the data within their construct systems.

The client's culture must be seen critically through his eyes. Cultural group memberships throw light on his constructs. These include, or are expressed in, socioeconomic class, racial and national extraction, family migration history, retirement plans, complaints, and church membership. Although the client cannot describe his own culture as a culture, the clinician can assess cultural-experiential determinants by inquiry along appropriate lines.

PERSONAL EXPERIENCE   The assessment of cultural influence can be made indirectly through the study of the client's community experiences. Information is first sought at a popular level of abstraction, with the psychological and sociological levels attempted later, after the data have been obtained. The inquiry regarding the community, and the neighborhood as well, covers descriptions of the population, community economics, transitions through which the community is going, religious organizations and mores, schools and educational patterns, and recreational resources.

An appraisal of the school will help in dealing with children from the school. Such an appraisal would include observation of the building, the playground, the classrooms, and classroom behavior, as well as interviews with teachers and the principal. In the interviews the constructs of the teachers and principal indicate the directions along with the children can move. The teachers' attitudes toward tests and records are revealing of constructs.

The individual's community interrelationships should be studied through the eyes of the person himself. Groups and organizations, and individuals in the person's life, reveal the influences on him. His educational experiences are analyzed. In the case of a child, the teacher is interviewed to determine what she considers to be the problem, or how she construes the situation. The person's home relationships constitute important social expectancies and should therefore be explored. Although man is not the slave of his biography, the family history is important as seen through the client's eyes.

The Appraisal of Activities

SPONTANEOUS ACTIVITY   All activity is spontaneous, yet controlled in the sense that it is lawful and predictable. Interests direct activities along particular lines. Areas of spontaneous activity indicate areas of permeable constructs, and thus areas where optimal conditions for evolution exist. Inactivity, or "laziness," is the result of impermeable thinking. The analysis of the client's spontaneous activities is thus a basic task of the clinician. The discovery of permeable constructs provides leads to the client's capacity for psychotherapeutic change.

Spontaneous activities may be studied through verbal inquiry or by time-sampling observation. The way in which the individual interprets his experiences is important, however. Activities include not only physical movements but conversation and reading. The observation of a child in a group is difficult but profitable. Observation of the child in the family is also revealing.

Vocational choice exercises a selective effect upon experience. The vocation is usually an area of permeable constructs and thus gives an indication of the kinds of changes the individual may be prepared to make. A vocation or a course of study often represents the seeking of a compromise between what is challenging and what is safe. The vocation provides the system of validating evidence to which the individual's daily expectations are subject. It is also one of the principal means by which his life role is given clarity and meaning.

STRUCTURAL INTERPRETATION OF EXPERIENCE   The biographical record is appraised by viewing it in five ways. The client must make sense from this. It reveals something of the person's past construction system, and thus suggests behavior to which he may have recourse if his present constructs fail and become invalidated. It indicates the kinds of validators against which he has to check his construct system. It throws light on his present construct system. And, finally, it is something that will have to be rationalized by the client in any therapeutic reformulation of his role. It is in these ways that birth, maturation, and physical care are evaluated, as well as behavior problems, interpersonal relations, and education and occupation.

The health of the client is a concern of the psychologist, since it has a bearing upon psychological evaluation. The individual's physical being constitutes both part of the facts against which he must validate his constructs and the implements with which he must explore his world. Illness and disability limit activity and interests and require psychological adjustment. Old dependency patterns are reactivated; there may be regression to earlier modes of conceptualization.

The clinician must interpret the client's structurizations. In this way the clinician subsumes the client's structure and establishes a role relationship with him. He is then in a position to anticipate the client's perceptions and behavior. The clinician's construction of a case develops by successive approximations. Structurization, then, refers to the preliminary formulations, while construction is the final organization of the record into a well-subsumed system. The former is descriptive, limited to the past and present; the latter is dynamic, relating to the future.

The structurization of a case, utilizing the client's experience record, may make use of the terms that follow. These are not constructs, but collecting terms. They represent section headings that may be used in case presentations and case records. Since they refer to the kinds of events the client has had to anticipate, they are validators.

1 *Figure matrix*   This includes information regarding the kinds of people the client has known intimately. The individuals are *figure constructs,* which are assembled into the figure matrix.

2 *Cooperative relationships*   This section would consist of information regarding the client's participation in socially constructive processes.

3 *Characterizations of the client*   This heading includes the ways in which the client is described by people with whom he must live.

4 *Externally imposed group identifications*   This topic refers to how the client is seen by others in terms of his group memberships.

5 *Areas in which the client is incorporated or alienated*   Incorporation refers to the willingness to see others as like oneself; alienation is unwillingness to do this. This heading includes the groups who see the client as like themselves, and the ways in which they see him like this.

6 *External patterns of conflict and solution*   This area is concerned with the social issues and conflicts in the client's milieu that he must experience and construe.

7 *Thematic repertory*   Thema are the themes and patterns of the social world surrounding the client, against which he plays his part.

8 *Symbolic system*   The symbolic system includes the language, religious, nationalistic, institutional, proverbial, epigrammatic, etc., background of the client.

9 *Climate of opinion out of which complaints arise*   What are the conventionalized complaints in the client's social setting?

10 *Versatility*   This includes the range or breadth of the client's activities or thinking, indicating his freedom to experiment.

11 *Biographical turning points*   Are there points of change in the experience record? The presence and nature of such changes suggest the client's capacity for change and the manner in which future changes may be expected to take place.

12 *Physical resources*   These include not only personal resources of property but the resources of the community.

13 *Social resources*   Who are the people who can help the client with his problems?

14 *Dependencies*   Are there resources upon which the client has become so dependent that their loss would interrupt his whole pattern of life?

15 *Supportive status*   This section consists of items indicating how and in what manner the client is seen as necessary to other people.

The clinical constructs used to bring together or structuralize the client's experiences are of intermediate rather than salient significance, from the point of view of the psychology of personal constructs.

Steps in Diagnosis

Diagnosis is the planning stage of client management. Client management is broader than therapy or treatment: it includes all actions directed toward the client's welfare.

There are many ways in which the same facts may be construed. Since the psychologist is interested in helping his clients, clinical diagnosis construes the facts in terms of their relevance to a solution of the client's problem, or client reconstruction. The term "transitive diagnosis" is used to indicate the concern with transitions in the client's life, or bridges between his present and his future. "Moreover, we expect to take an active part in helping the client select or build the bridges to be used and in helping him cross them safely. . . . If the psychologist expects to help him he must get up off his chair and start moving along with him." [27]

The diagnostic constructs or dimensions presented earlier represent avenues of movement as seen by the therapist, and are the bases of transitive diagnosis. The psychology of personal constructs is directed against the tendency to impose preemptive constructs upon human behavior, a tendency in which "diagnosis is all too frequently an attempt to cram a whole live struggling client into a nosological category." [28] The question in transitive diagnosis is not, In what category should this client be classified? but, What is to become of this client? A temporary preemptive construction is necessary for deciding the immediate disposition of the client, including whether to accept him for treatment or not.

There are six practical issues that arise in the making of a transitive diagnosis. In outline form they are as follows:

I.   NORMATIVE FORMULATIONS OF THE CLIENT'S PROBLEM.
      1. Description of the manifest deviant behavior patterns (symptoms).
         a. The clinician's behavior norms.
         b. Deviation from the ways of the primary group.
         c. Incompatibility with own norms.
         d. Inconsistency with common interpretations or expectations.
         e. Frequent abandonment of adjustment patterns.
         f. Distinction between deviations and transparency.
         g. Deviation in the manner of complaining.
         h. Data for description of the manifest deviant behavior.
         i. Elicitation and description of the complaint.
         j. Temporal patterns in the deviant behavior.
      2. Description of the correlates of the manifest deviant behavior patterns.
         a. The cultural context.
         b. The personal-social context.
         c. Threat or stress concomitants.
         d. The occupational pattern.
         e. The domestic pattern.
      3. Descriptions of the gains and losses accruing to the client through his symptoms (description of validational experience).

II.   PSYCHOLOGICAL DESCRIPTION OF THE CLIENT'S PERSONAL CONSTRUCTIONS.
      1. The client's construction of what he believes to be the problem area.
      2. The client's construction of his life roles.

III. PSYCHOLOGICAL EVALUATION OF THE CLIENT'S CONSTRUCTION SYSTEM.
      1. Location of the client's areas of anxiety, aggressiveness (or spontaneous elaboration), and constriction.
      2. Sampling the types of construction the client uses in different areas.
      3. Sampling the modes of approach.
      4. Determination of the client's accessibility and his levels of communication.

IV.   ANALYSES OF THE MILIEU IN WHICH ADJUSTMENT IS TO BE SOUGHT.
      1. Analyses of the expectancy system within which the client must make his life role function.
      2. Assessment of the socioeconomic assets in the case.

      3. Preparation of information to be utilized as contextual material in helping the client reconstrue life.

V.   DETERMINATION OF IMMEDIATE PROCEDURAL STEPS.
      1. Physiological construction of the available data.
      2. Other professional constructions of the available data.
      3. Evaluation of the urgency of the case.

VI. PLANNING MANAGEMENT AND TREATMENT.
      1. Selection of the central psychotherapeutic approach.
         a. Size of the client's investment.
         b. Accessibility and level of communication.
         c. Type of transference.
         d. Threat implications.
         e. Fear implications.
         f. Anxiety.
         g. Guilt.
         h. Loosening.
         i. Elaboration of the complaint.
         j. Finding validation of new constructs.
         k. Areas to be opened to elaboration.
         l. Dealing with submerged ends of constructs.
      2. Designation of the principally responsible clinician.
      3. Selection of adjunctive resources to be utilized.
         a. Dealing with other minor problems (for example, medical).
         b. Occupational therapy.
         c. Recreation.
         d. Dilation.
         e. Community participation.
         f. Resources for the nonhospitalized client.
      4. Designation of the responsible clinician's advisory staff.
      5. Determination of the ad interim status of the client.
      6. Setting of dates or conditions under which progress will be reviewed by the advisory staff.

The issues at the beginning of the outline are essentially descriptive. Those in the middle require more scientific sophistication to handle, while those at the end require therapeutic training for their resolution.

"Effective diagnosis is a matter of making some reasonable predictions as to what a client will do under different circumstances and then proposing to create a set of circumstances which will lead to the client's doing what we think he generally ought to do." [29]

Psychological Testing in Diagnosis and Psychotherapy

One direct approach to the client's personal constructs is by means of psychological tests, which involve a formal assigned task. So-called objective tests are considered *dimensional measures* of personal constructs, for example, cultural commonality, rather than direct revelations of the constructs themselves. Other tests elicit the constructs themselves; these are the tests under consideration here. There are five functions of a test in a clinical setting:

1 To define the client's problem in usable terms.

2 To reveal the pathways or channels along which the client is free to move.

3 To provide clinical hypotheses that may subsequently be checked and put to use.

4 To reveal those resources of the client that might otherwise be overlooked by the therapist.

5 To reveal those problems of the client that might otherwise be overlooked by the therapist.

The clinical utility of a test from the standpoint of the psychology of personal constructs can be appraised by considering the following questions:

1 Whose yardstick does the test represent? "Objective" tests utilize the clinician's axes, not the client's. Projective tests recognize the client's yardsticks. The clinician cannot use the client's yardsticks, however; he must use his own, but he should use them to attempt to measure the client's yardsticks.

2 Does the test elicit permeable constructs? Is it one that can embrace the future as well as pigeonhole the past? Does it measure constructs that are likely to be used again and that are not only of historical interest?

3 Are the test elements representative of life's events? Can one infer from the client's reactions to the test elements how he will react to other elements, such as people? "It might be easier to predict what a subject would do on a Rorschach Test, for example, from a knowledge of how he deals with people in his world than it would be to predict what he would do with the people in his world from a knowledge of how he deals with ink blots." [30]

4 Does the test elicit role constructs; that is, does it relate to how the client manages his life in a social setting?

5 What is the balance between stability and sensitivity? A test should show consistency on a day-by-day basis, but should also reflect changes over longer periods of time. Moreover, the test should measure constructs that continue in operation over long periods of time, but that are expected to change or be revised during psychotherapy.

6 Will the test reveal constructs that are communicable to other clinicians?

7 Will the test serve its basic functions?

A good clinical test should fulfill the functions listed above. A diagnostic instrument that attempts to fulfill these functions and meets the above requirements has been developed to elicit personal constructs. It is the Role Construct Repertory Test (Rep Test). It is aimed at eliciting role constructs and is thus concerned with those persons with whom the subject has had to deal in his daily life. The subject is given a Role Title List and asked to designate persons in his own realm of experience who fit the role titles. Then groups of three of the persons named are selected, and the subject is asked to tell in what important way two of them are alike but different from the third. There are various forms of the test, including tests for both group and individual administration.

The test has been developed on the basis of personal-construct theory. There are six assumptions in interpreting the results:

1   The constructs elicited are permeable.

2   Preexisting constructs are elicited by the test.

3   The figures are representative of the people to whom the subject must relate his self-construed role.

4   Constructs will be elicited that subsume, in part, the construction systems of the element figures.

5   The constructs elicited are regnant over the subject's own role.

6   The constructs elicited are adequate to communicate to the examiner some understanding of how the client organizes the elements in the test.

The test can be subjected to both formal and clinical analyses. Clinical analysis considers the number and overlap of the constructs elicited, their permeability or impermeability, fields of permeability, contrasting constructs, unique figures, linkage of constructs through contrasts and figures, preemptive constructs, superficial constructs, dependency constructs, etc. The test contributes to diagnosis in the area of the client's construction of his life role.

During therapy, tests may contribute to the understanding of the client's personal-construct system, thus broadening the therapist's perspective. They may also dispel some of the bias of the therapist or point to content related to one of his "blind spots."

Tests also affect the outlook of the client, bringing him face-to-face with issues he might otherwise ignore or reject as being the therapist's incorrect perceptions. Test material may be used as "entry material" or as a point of departure for beginning a therapy hour, although such material is probably not as useful as other entries devised by the therapist.

Tests may pose a threat to the psychotherapeutic relationship, more so later on in the relationship than at the start. Threat may be reduced by reassuring the client that there is no passing or failing involved, and by structuring the use of the test as a help to the therapist in understanding him better. Projective tests, particularly sentence-completion tests, are likely to be less damaging than objective tests. The word-association test seems to be most damaging.

The Psychotherapeutic Approach

BASIC TECHNIQUES

Setting Up the Relationship / The therapist does not allow himself to become an intimately known and sharply delineated personality for the client; instead he maintains a personal ambiguity. This makes it more likely that the client will develop a secondary rather than a primary transference, and allows the therapist to play the versatile roles required of him. This ambiguity enables the client to cast the therapist in the parts necessary in his reconstructive experiments. The therapist therefore avoids social relationships with his client, as well as contacts with members of the client's family. Nor should he treat two members of the same family.

The Client's Relationships to Others / There is no prohibition on the relationships of the client with others. The purpose of therapy is to foster good relationships between the client and others, and this cannot be done if the client is limited to his relationship with the therapist. Therapy may even include helping others through the client.

Multiple Approach / Sometimes several individuals may act as therapists with one client in *multiple therapy*. However, a versatile and flexible therapist should be able to provide a variety of relationships for the client without the confusion introduced by several therapists. Total-push therapy in an institution is another form of multiple approach.

Physical Arrangements / Privacy or the sense of privacy is essential. Recording of interviews is done with the client's knowledge and consent, but inconspicuously. Both the room and the therapist's desk should be uncluttered, and the room should be as quiet as possible. The interviews are conducted with a desk or table between the participants; this tends to focus the attention of each on the face of the other, where it should be. Chairs should be comfortable, six to eight feet apart, and both placed at right angles to the line between the therapist and the client in order to permit the client either to face or to turn away from the therapist. Group therapy and play therapy require special rooms and equipment.

Controlling Interviews / Because of the different ways a client may have of construing his world, the therapist must maintain a flexible relationship with a client. Each interview, nevertheless, requires some planning, although the plan can be altered as necessary, within prescribed limits. As therapy proceeds, the therapist becomes aware of danger areas to be avoided and develops the ability to predict what the client will say. Special activities of the client may call for special interviewing plans. Interviews may be spaced to meet the client's needs for contact. For most purposes a forty-five-minute interview is adequate. Notes or summaries of interviews should be kept to assist the therapist's memory from interview to interview. They should include predictions of what the client will do before the next interview. This is an important point because "if the therapist is able to 'call the shots' on his client, he can be reassured that he is developing a fairly adequate construction of the case." [31]

Since he has prepared a plan, the therapist initiates the interview with that plan in mind. Interviews should be terminated on time and not continue on out the door in "threshold therapy." The tempo of the interview is controlled by the therapist as necessary to broaden or narrow the scope of the client's immediate perceptual field and for other purposes. The therapist should avoid a guilt-laden dependency on the part of the client by not listening to outpourings of wrongdoings, unless he is prepared to assume continuing responsibility for the client's welfare.

The Psychotherapist's Manner / Communication is not limited to words. The therapist should appear to be physically relaxed and mentally receptive during interviews. Gestures should be of the accepting type. His voice should be responsive, and his speech clear yet colorful and adapted to the client's vocabulary. While the therapist should appear to be "shockproof," he should not be so impassive that the client cannot observe the results of his experiments.

Teaching the Client How to be a "Patient" / The client should be taught how to respond in the therapeutic relationship. In long-term relationships this may take months. Such structuring may include formal verbal structuring as well as intermittent instructions and orientation.

PALLIATIVE TECHNIQUES

Reassurance / Reassurance is never more than a temporary expedient to give the client the impression that his behavior and ideas are consistent, acceptable, and organized. It helps to hold the client's construction system together until it can be rebuilt. Reassurance can backfire if things turn out badly after the therapist has assured the client they would not. It tends to support existing maladjustive mechanisms. Too much reassurance leads to dependency.

Some ways of providing reassurance are less likely to produce unfavorable results than others. Predictions made as reassurance should not be sweeping. Acceptance of anxiety-laden material as not unexpected is reassuring. Both the process of structuring and the therapist's manner can be reassuring. On the other hand, value labels used as reassurance can be hazardous, preventing the client from changing his evaluation. Comfort as reassurance may create "resistance" in a client who is ambivalent about his complaints. It may lead the client to feel that there is no solution, that the therapist feels this way also, and that all he can do is "grin and bear it."

Since reassurance slows therapeutic movement, it should be used only when retardation is desired. For example, it may be used as a temporary preventive of fragmentation of constructs. It may be used to encourage loosening of conceptualization, with less danger of fragmentation. Reassurance controls anxiety. It may also be used to keep an important chain of associations temporarily from being broken. It should always be used in minimal and calculated amounts.

Support / Support is provided by acceptance without agreement or by understanding the client's communication without telling him he is right before he has had a chance to experiment. It is a response that allows the client to experiment widely and successfully. Support recognizes and accepts the client's dependency patterns of behavior;

it thus may be threatening to the client and may arouse guilt feelings.

The therapist shows support by being on time for his appointments, by remembering what the client has said in the past, and by construing things as the client does. This last is one of the therapist's main functions and is sometimes enough. Support includes adapting to changes in the client's thinking and helping him verbalize his new rationale. It also includes doing things for the client outside the interview situation.

Support may be used in certain anxiety cases, or as an approach to helping a client understand his dependency striving, or to stabilize a situation temporarily. Support, like reassurance, should be used sparingly and be limited to situations in which the client cannot take everything in his stride.

Transference / Transference is a construct. In its broad sense transference is lifting a construct from one's repertory and transferring it, or applying it, to a particular situation. When facing a therapist, the client takes a construct from his repertory and uses it in looking at, and dealing with, the therapist. In psychotherapy transference is concerned with role constructs and refers to the way in which a person attempts to subsume the constructs of others. In reference to the client, it represents the effort of the client to construe the therapist by transferring role constructs onto him. The therapist is constantly extricating himself from the client's constructions, both those that are useful and those that are not useful. The client tends to cast the therapist into the form of a highly elaborated prejudicial stereotype, such as the father or father figure, which becomes fixed.

Transference Dependency / Transference sometimes involves dependency constructs, which may be immature and may not lend themselves to verbalization. The client responds to the therapist as if his life depended upon him. Sometimes therapists invite dependency transferences by the attitude that he knows what is best for the client.

Counterdependency Tranference / If the therapist cannot adequately construe the client within a set of professional constructs, he runs the risk of transferring his own dependencies to the client. Prevention of this requires an organized and meaningful set of diagnostic constructs, acquired through thorough professional training, and the use of the client's own personal constructs within the subsuming system. The therapist who finds himself overly concerned with and preoccupied by the client's relationships to himself and others, in almost a jealous manner, should be alerted to the possibility that he has developed counterdependency tranference.

Primary and Secondary Transference / The application of a varying sequence of constructs from a variety of figures of the past is secondary transference. The therapist can utilize this tranference to reorient the client's constructions of other persons by playing various parts. When the client construes the therapist preemptively, as a unique person, a type, and develops a personal identification with him, a primary transference exists. This kind of relationship limits the experiments that the client can perform with the therapist. The client focuses upon the therapist as a unique figure and is unable to generalize the lessons learned in the therapy situation to other persons outside therapy.

Control of Transference / Transference should be allowed only to the extent that it appears to be safe and useful. Transference seems to go in cycles. The therapist must determine at the end of each whether to begin another or to terminate therapy. A transference cycle can be shortened by abandoning concept-loosening techniques, shifting to current material, dealing with lower levels of abstraction, and in general engaging in a more structured, superficial form of therapy. Primary transference, once it occurs, should be resolved immediately. Two methods may be used. In one the therapist assumes a rigid, preservative, repetitive, and stereotyped role. In the other, less drastic, the therapist uses free roles, forcing the client to play opposite various other persons, whose parts the therapist enacts.

ELABORATING THE COMPLAINT

Uncontrolled Elaboration / Most therapeutic elaboration starts with an elaboration of the complaint. The elaboration may be uncontrolled, with the therapist being "nondirective." There are contraindications for this undirected elaboration. One is if the therapist is going to make a referral. Another is if there are excessive guilt feelings. A third is excessive repetition by the client. A fourth is in cases of loose construction.

Controlled Elaboration / Controlled elaboration avoids the hazards of undirected elaboration, but not the serious hazard that the therapist may not be able to know precisely how the client managed to incapacitate himself, and thus may not be able to make contact with the client's personal-construct system so as to establish a meaningful role in relation to him.

Questions should be used to get the client to place his problems, if possible, on a time line, to see them as fluid and transient, and to interpret them as being responsive to treatment, the passage of time, and varying conditions. These procedures lead to construing the problems in ways in which they can be solved. Pressuring the client to explain why he has certain difficulties may be profitable, but may lead to verbal rationalization. Questions about other people who have or have had the same problems put the complaint into a social framework. Sometimes it is advisable to confront the client with complaints or aspects of his problems that he has not mentioned. This may clarify the diagnostic picture as well as the therapeutic relationship. Most frequently, such confrontation is used to broaden the client's field as he is formulating new constructs. Reflection of key terms or ideas may lead to elaboration by the client. Selected elements may be reflected to force the client to elaborate a theme. Review of previous sessions is a form of reflection, and may be used to assure the client that the therapist was listening and to integrate or organize details on a higher level of superordination. It can also be used to draw contrasts between the past and the present. Review may threaten the client, however; it may block development by going back to the old material. Or it may betray the therapist's prejudices. "The more the therapist talks or tries to place verbal structure on what the client has produced, the greater is the likelihood that the sensitive ear of the client will detect harsh notes of criticism and inflexibility." [32]

ELABORATING THE PERSONAL SYSTEM   The basic task of the therapist is the elaboration of the construct system in which the client's difficulties are anchored.

Approach to the Construction System / The turning from the complaint as a reference point to the client's system as a system broadens the picture, raises the issues to a higher level of abstraction, and places the emphasis on seeing alternatives.

Tests, as already mentioned, are one approach to an elaboration of the client's construction system. Another is self-description through the self-characterization sketch used in fixed-role therapy, to be mentioned later. Broad, general questions rather than an outline should be used to help the client produce a self-characterization. The client may be asked to elaborate his life-role structure, including earlier plans and goals as well as a projection into the future—what he wants to be like after therapy. Progressive confrontation with alternatives through use of the C-P-C cycle is another way to maintain the process of elaboration. Elaboration may take place in activities outside the therapy room, such as prescribed occupational, recreational, and social activities. The sorts of play and creative production in which the therapist can participate may also be used to encourage elaboration.

Elaboration of the construct system must be done systematically and with caution. Limits are ordinarily set on the areas to be elaborated in any one phase of the therapy. Elaboration may lead to loosening of the system and thus must be controlled to prevent too much or too general loosening.

Elaboration of Material Arising During the Course of Therapy / The concern here is with the elaboration of bits of material to see where they fit into the total construction system and to determine their relationship to the sequence of developments in therapy.

Since not all clues can be followed up, material must be selected for elaboration. What is selected is determined only partly by its suspected significance; the readiness of the client to deal with it must also be considered. Some of the kinds of material that should be chosen for elaboration are the following: strange or unexpected material, material possibly indicative of an expected therapeutic movement or revision of the construct system, material apparently related to an area under intensive study, material lending itself to psychotherapeutic experimentation, material useful in validation of new constructs, material related to a construct taking shape, and material representing an extended range of convenience of an existing construct.

Recapitulation by the therapist or the client may point up the need for, and lead to, elaboration. Procedures used in recapitulation include client diaries and written summaries, playback of recordings, and discussions by the client, in a therapy group, of his experiences in individual therapy.

Probing is a method of controlling the client's participation in the interview. It can be misused, becoming an inquisition. Probing is used to get the client to explore an area. It may be immediate, done as soon as a cue has been given; but it is preferable to delay probing, so that it may represent a well-thought-out procedure for helping the client elaborate constructs that are meaningful to him. Probing can be used to elicit details about an important incident that may tie in with other incidents. Asking for the antecedents or consequents of an incident is also a means of elaboration. The therapist may ask the client to think of similar or contrasting incidents or experiences, which may lead to elaboration of the construct. Or he may try to relate experiences, which also may lead to elaboration of the construct. In addition, he may relate experiences by asking the client how two are alike and different from a third.

Enactment, in which the therapist plays a role in an incident described by the client, may be an effective way of helping the client to elaborate. Four principles are important in the use of enactment. First, there should be no long preliminary discussions or preparation. Second, the enactment should be brief. Third, there should be exchange of parts, with the therapist taking various parts, including that of the client. Thus, the client may be led to think, This therapist is both sympathetic and versatile; with him here, this room can become a well-equipped laboratory for experimenting with life's perplexing social relations, provided, of course, that I dare experiment at all. The client, in taking the part of another, begins to know a little of how another person might be construing the situation and can begin to adapt himself to what the construction is. Fourth, portrayal of a caricature of the client must be avoided. Enactment should be introduced with a relatively innocuous incident.

LOOSENING AND TIGHTENING

Loosening / The axis of loosened versus tightened construction is an important one, and one with which the therapist deals early in therapy. Loosening is characteristic of those constructs that lead to varying predictions, those whose elements may vary in their classification from one pole to the other. Dreaming is an illustration of loose thinking. It allows for resilience, inconsistencies, and a shifty defense. It is a necessary phase of creative thinking. It frees facts, so that they can be seen in new aspects. Loosening prepares the ground for the changing development of constructs and the developing of new constructs. It is produced in psychotherapy in four principal ways:

1 *Relaxation* The couch or chair, the surroundings, the relaxed manner of the therapist, and his systematic methods of eliciting physical relaxation induce relaxation in the client.

2 *Chain association*   This is the free association of psychoanalysis. Sometimes the client needs to be helped by being given a starting point, being allowed to think without speaking, being instructed to let his mind wander without being concerned about the importance of the content, etc.

3 *Reporting dreams*   Dreams are so loose that it is difficult to report them. It is not the content of the dream, however, but the use of loosened construction in reporting it that is useful, even if the client can remember and verbalize little about the dream itself. In loosening, verbalization is slow. The manic flight of ideas is not loosening; the schizoid's thinking is. Interpretation of dreams tightens construction; therefore, the interpretation should not follow immediately upon the reporting of dreams, but should take place when the therapist wants to move in the direction of tightening. Dreams are often preverbal in nature and thus throw light upon preverbal constructs. They also often involve submerged contrast poles of constructs. This accounts for the fact that dream elements often appear to represent their opposites.

4 *Uncritical acceptance.*   Acceptance is the attempt by the therapist to employ the client's construct system. It is uncritical when the client's thinking is not questioned by the therapist. "Essentially the technique of uncritical acceptance provides the client with a passive validation for his loosened construing which is elastic and nonexperimental." [33]

There are difficulties involved in producing loosened constructions. The client has a tendency to move toward tightening of constructs; he has difficulty in finding symbols, or words, to deal with his ideas. Premature interpretation tightens up the client's construing. Distractions and interference from similar but tightly construed elements interfere with loosening.

Resistance to loosening may be dealt with not only by continuing to use the techniques to produce loosening already mentioned but by the use of other special techniques. Enactment, or role playing, is one. The use of a context in which loosening is possible, followed by a gradual shifting to the desired area or context, is another. Reducing threat or increasing acceptance is a third technique.

Loosening has some hazards. Since it reduces anxiety, it may become like an addiction or an escape. Tight constructions may be a defense, and the loss of this defense may precipitate a severe anxiety state. The skillful use of loosening requires comprehensiveness and flexibility in the therapist's viewpoint.

Tightening / The functions of tightening are to define what is predicted, to stabilize construction, to facilitate organization of the construction system, to reduce certain constructs to a state of impermeability, and to facilitate experimentation. Tightening is a form of elaboration, and techniques of elaboration apply to it also. Other techniques include the following:

1 *Judging or superordinating*   This consists of urging the client to cease free associating, to judge rather than to experience, to put a

superordinate construction on a group of constructs that have been expressed unsystematically.

2 *Summarization* Asking the client to summarize what he has been saying leads to systematization, which involves the tightening of subordinated constructs. Written summaries between interviews may be assigned to the client.

3 *Historical explanation* of his thoughts by the client.

4 *Relating the client's thinking* to that of others.

5 *Direct approach* This involves asking the client to be explicit—to explain or clarify what he means.

6 *Challenging the construction* The therapist may ask the client to repeat what he has said, may express confusion, misinterpret, question, or even label what the client is saying as nonsense.

7 *Enactment* The demands of extemporaneous role playing may at times lead to the tightening up of certain minor constructions.

8 *Concept formation* This involves having the client tell how two things are alike but different from a third.

9 *Asking for validating evidence*

10 *Word binding* The client is asked to name each construct and to stick with the name.

11 *Time binding* The client is asked to date his constructs, restricting them in time.

Difficulties occur in getting the client to tighten up certain constructions. The client may use a symbol consistently, but the construct itself may be vague and inconsistently applied. Tightness may be achieved at the expense of permeability, comprehensiveness, or superordination. The impulsive client, who can hold himself together only with a loose construction of himself, may cause difficulty. The client who wants to limit his world to the therapy room and the therapy relationship, and the client who is unwilling to test his constructs, can also cause difficulty. Loose constructs that are preverbal are difficult to tighten.

There are hazards involved in tightening too. One is the danger of premature tightening, which may bring the client face-to-face with the implications of his construing and force him to test his hypothesis before he has any appropriate alternative construction. Hostility may result if the construct is invalidated, and since the therapist is also involved in the experiment, he too may become hostile at the failure. A second principal hazard in tightening is the possible loss of comprehensiveness, permeability, and propositionality.

Therapy involves alternation in the weaving back and forth between tightening and loosening, essentially in the repetition of the creativity cycle. Therapy proceeds by successive approximations. In the process the client learns a way of developing better modes of adjustment.

PRODUCING PSYCHOTHERAPEUTIC MOVEMENT The techniques considered below are those employed in the stages of therapy in which the therapist is urging the client to experiment with new ideas and behaviors.

Interpretation, Movement, and Rapport / The client's constructs are personal, and the therapist must deal with them on an individual basis rather than in terms of general meanings. There is one basic principle in interpretation: *"All interpretations understood by the client are perceived in terms of his own system.* Another way of expressing the same thing is to say that it is always the client who interprets, not the therapist." [34] Again, the therapist's job "is to help the client make discoveries of his own; it is not to shower him with blessed insights." [35] The basic interpretive formats are those that invite the client to conceptualize in some new or generalized way what he has been talking about. In addition to interpretation, extending the range of convenience of the client's constructs and the use of elaboration are methods of increasing the permeability of the client's constructs.

Movement in psychotherapy is indicated by the client in various ways. One is the surprise of the client when things seem to fall into place; this is the Aha! experience. Another is the client's spontaneous documentation of the usefulness of a new construct. A third is the evidence of permeability when the client incorporates current experiences into a construct. A fourth is a positive change in mood or feeling. The perception of contrast between present and past behavior is a fifth indication. A sixth is the dropping of certain complaints or even the substitution of new for old ones. Client summaries of previous interviews also indicate changes. Finally, the change in content, with the introduction of new content into the therapy, indicates movement.

There are also cues that indicate inadequate new construction. These include loose construction or erratic verbalization of a new construct, bizarre documentation, oversimplification, contrast behavior or "flight into health," and legalistic application of the new "insight."

How does the therapist know when the client's role relationship to him will support a certain type of inquiry into forbidden areas? There are several useful criteria, including relaxation, spontaneity, the ability to control loosening, and the dropping of guards. A fifth criterion is the contrasting of the client's present outlook with his outlook in the immediate past, and a sixth is the contrasting of the present with the future outlook. Optimism, flexibility, and the dropping of defensiveness constitute additional criteria. The ability to enact an aggressive role with the therapist is also a criterion. Another is the ability to construe the task of the therapist. Related to this is the individual's ability to relate attitudes and constructs to his role as a patient or client. Finally, lack of impulsivity and lack of obliqueness in approaching a topic are useful criteria of readiness for new ventures.

Control of Anxiety and Guilt / Anxiety and guilt are not necessarily all bad. "The task of the therapist is to assess them, take account of their functioning in his client, and deal with them in the light of the welfare of the particular personality." [36] Anxiety is detected in various ways. The criteria for the client's readiness for movement listed above are related to anxiety. Knowledge of common anxieties and of the experiences of the client, observation of the client's behavior, and the client's communications are other sources for detecting client anxiety. Restriction of discussion, use of self-reassuring devices, and weeping may indicate anxiety.

One of the outcomes of therapy is to diminish or increase anxiety, as necessary. There are, however, temporary devices to keep anxiety under control. Support and reassurance techniques may be used to reduce anxiety as well as guilt. Acceptance, leading the interview into structured areas, allowing sufficient time for reconstruction before proceeding into another problem area, the use of binding, differentiation, introspection, anticipation of hurdles, encouraging dependency, structuration of the interview, and control of the tempo of the interview are additional methods of controlling anxiety.

Guilt may be controlled by similar techniques. In addition, reconstruction of the core role—the awareness of the loss of this role being the cause of guilt—is an important method. Or alternative roles may be sought with the client. Interpretation of the persons whom the client uses to delineate his role is useful. Broadening the base of the role relation to the therapist also temporarily replaces the lost role.

Psychotherapeutic Experimentation / Psychotherapy and scientific research are similar. The client uses the scientific method in working out his problems. He first elaborates his problems. Then, in loosening, he becomes creative in developing new ideas. Third, by tightening he formulates testable hypotheses. Finally, he engages in experiments to test, or validate, his hypotheses.

Psychotherapeutic experimentation serves several functions. First, it provides a framework in which the client can anticipate alternative outcomes. Second, it places the client in touch with reality and tests his construction system. It also serves as a check on the therapist's construction of the case. In addition, experimentation opens up new vistas of experience. Finally, it puts the client in touch with other people, enabling him to see how others view their worlds, so that he may play a role in relation to them.

The therapist encourages experimentation, both inside and outside the interviewing room, by various techniques. Enactment, discussed earlier, is one of the most useful of these. Permissiveness, responsiveness, projecting the client into a novel situation, and seeing that the client has the necessary tools are methods that encourage and set the stage for actual experimentation. The therapist also gets the client to develop hypotheses or make specific predictions. He asks the client to make interpretations of others' outlooks, to portray how another person views himself, and to portray how another person views the client. Negative predictions may be encouraged. Or the client may be encouraged to elaborate the biographical conditions under which he thinks he would behave differently than he believes he can; this often leads to his behaving differently. The therapist may directly encourage the client to take certain actions. Finally, the client may be placed in a social situation where others are enthusiastically attempting what he could do well if he wanted to.

Obstacles to experimentation include client hostility, anxiety, guilt, dependence, threat of outcomes, and the nonelaborative choice —that is, the client's belief that no matter what the outcome, he is trapped. Some of these difficulties also constitute hazards in experimentation. Other hazards are present too. The client may constrict as a result of being "burned"; excessive loosening may result; or the therapist may urge the client to experiment in an inappropriate setting, with disastrous results.

Fixed-Role Therapy

Fixed-role therapy is a type of psychotherapy specifically derived from the psychology of personal constructs and based upon observations of the effects of dramatic experience.

Fixed-role therapy begins by requesting the client to write a sketch of himself. He does so in the third person, with no detailed outline, but only the following instructions:

"I want you to write a character sketch of Harry Brown, just as if he were the principal character in a play. Write it as it might be written by a friend who knows him very *intimately* and very *sympathetically*, perhaps better than anyone even really could know him. Be sure to write it in the third person. For example, start out by saying, Harry Brown is. . . ." [37]

The self-characterization is the basis for writing the fixed-role sketch. The sketch is designed to invite the client to explore certain sharply contrasting behaviors. It develops a major theme rather than correcting minor faults. It is intended to set the stage for the resumption of growth and movement rather than to attempt a major psychotherapeutic relocation. It sets up hypotheses that can be tested quickly. There is emphasis on role perceptions and role relationships with other people. It is desirable that the sketch be developed by a group of experienced clinicians if possible.

The procedure involved in fixed-role therapy is introduced to the client following the diagnostic phase of therapy, as preparatory to going into his problems. The character sketch is presented with another name than the client's. Following the reading of the sketch, the *acceptance check* determines whether the client understands and accepts the sketch as representing someone he would like to know, not someone he would like to be. If the sketch is accepted as plausible and not threatening, the rehearsal sequence begins. This is initiated with the request that the client, for the next two weeks, act as if he were the person in the sketch, with the therapist's help, in interviews scheduled every other day. The client keeps the copy of the sketch, reads it at least three times a day, and tries to act, think, talk, and be like the person in the sketch.

Clients are skeptical and report failure during the greater part of the two weeks; if the process were easy, it would be ineffective. The client is given help in enacting the role in work situations, social relationships, the family, and situations involving life orientation and plan. Rehearsal takes place through role playing. The therapist treats the client as if he were the person in the sketch. As interviews continue, the client contributes more and begins to feel like the person whose role he is playing. In the final interview the role is withdrawn. The client is more active, while the therapist listens. He does not resort to urging the client to adopt the new role. If the client has found it effective, he will accept it. The therapist decides whether therapy should be continued by some other method; he may, if the client requests it, continue the rehearsals for another predetermined period.

The experience is kept realistic by creating a role that has many day-to-day implications and by keeping the interviews geared to practical situations. Although not generally helpful to schizoid individuals, in some cases it has helped put them in contact with reality. The hazard of unreality is thus not a great one. A greater hazard is that by pressuring the client to act, the therapist will force him to act within his present construct system and push him to the opposite extreme of his dichotomous constructs.

The client's insistance that although the role is working out, he is only acting is not undesirable. It indicates that he has not been threatened. If this attitude persists to the end, however, with the role being too easily accepted, the sketch may not be adequate to lead the client to face crucial issues. The development of spontaneous behavior in which the client forgets he is acting is a good sign as long as the client doesn't look back on it with embarrassment. The reactions of other people to the client as being different indicate progress in fixed-role therapy and lead to further progress by reducing threat. The best evidence of progress is when the client says, "I feel as if this were the *real* me." This is always accompanied by a marked shift in the client's formulation of his problem.

While difficulty with the role and criticism of it are not bad signs, the failure of the client to accept the method or to see the role and its implications in contrast to his old constructs indicates that the method cannot be used as a vehicle for readjustment. Indications for fixed-role therapy include limited time for treatment, desirability of avoiding strong dependent transference, unavoidable client-therapist relationships outside of therapy, inexperienced clinicians, the presence of obvious social and situational components in the case, need for termination of another type of therapy sequence, need for establishment of contact with everyday reality, uncertainty of the client's readiness for change, and defensiveness on the part of the client with respect to therapy. The method is relatively safe, even though it substitutes a new, prefabricated construction system rather than reworking parts of the old one, because the new system is enacted, or playacted, with an artificial identity alongside the old structure, and there are no implications at the outset that the new structure may eventually replace the old one.

SUMMARY AND EVALUATION

The psychology of personal constructs is based upon the philosophical position of constructive alternativism, which is the position that there are many workable ways for a person to construe his world. The system is developed on the basis of a single postulate and its elaboration by means of eleven corollaries. The basic assumption is that "a person's processes are psychologically channelized by the ways in which he anticipates events." [38] The individual's system of personal constructs determines the way he construes the world. Constructs are dichotomous in nature, and the individual chooses the alternative through which he anticipates the greater possibility for extension and definition of his system. Constructs have certain formal characteristics and are organized into a hierarchy of subsystems. The characteristics of constructs form the basis for setting up a system of diagnostic constructs, which are used by the clinician to analyze, understand, and subsume the construct system of the client. Changes in behavior involve changes in the personal-construct system.

Therapy is thus directed toward the reconstruction of the client's system of personal constructs. In therapy based on the psychology of personal constructs the therapist is active, responding to the client in a great variety of ways. Enactment, or role playing, plays a large part in therapy, and in one specific approach to therapy—fixed-role therapy—the playing of an assigned role by the client constitutes the major aspect of the therapy.

The process of therapy is conceived as being similar to the process of scientific experimentation. The task of the therapist is to help the client develop hypotheses and test them experimentally, both within and outside the interview situation. Science is thus the model clients use in reconstructing their lives. The therapist participates in the process as a helper and collaborator, using a wide variety of methods and techniques.

Kelly's approach to counseling and psychotherapy is one of the most systematic, if not the most systematic, which has appeared. It is developed elaborately and in considerable detail, which makes it perhaps the most difficult approach to summarize of any of those included in this volume. Its detail makes it both fascinating and, at the same time, frustrating to read. Although the basic postulate and its corollaries are amazingly simple, their elaboration is amazingly complex. There are probably almost as many concepts as there are in psychoanalysis. Many common concepts or terms are used in somewhat different ways than is common in psychology or psychoanalysis. These include anxiety, guilt, threat, hostility, aggressiveness, and fear. There are also many new terms, such as "preemptive constructs," "constellatory constructs," "propositional constructs," "submergence," "suspension," and "permeability." It becomes difficult to keep all these in mind when reading about the development and application of the theory in therapy. The reader needs to have a system of constructs that is comprehensive, propositional, and permeable to be able to absorb the material.

Few will probably be attracted to this approach, because of the formidability of the new concepts and the detail. Apparently few have become attracted to it since its publication. To master it to the point of being able to practice it would require extensive study, training, and experience. And in spite of its detail, the published material is not sufficient, as Kelly notes, for the application of the approach in therapy. While there is considerable discussion of method and technique, there are no actual therapy protocols to illustrate application.

Nevertheless, for the counselor or therapist who may not want to master this particular approach, there are an amazing number of details relating to problems and techniques in therapy—discussions of what the therapist should do when. For example, ten different kinds of weeping are distinguished. There is a detailed discussion of what to look for in a school classroom in appraising the school environment. The reader will also benefit from many other discussions, apart from the particular theoretical approach. There is a fresh, new way of looking at things, divorced from the usual clinical terminology or jargon. The approach is not diagnostically or externally oriented.

This lack of diagnostic orientation leads to a consideration of the phenomenological nature of the approach. One of its basic concepts is that "each man contemplates in his own personal way the stream of events upon which he finds himself so swiftly borne." [39] But Kelly feels that the phenomenological approach leaves the individual's personal constructs locked up in privacy,[40] whereas they must be brought out for public view. At least the psychologist or psychotherapist must be able to construe the personal constructs of the client, and this to Kelly goes beyond phenomenology. It is difficult not to see this as an expression of the basic impossibility of avoiding a phenomenological approach, since the constructions of the psychologist, while external or public or objective from the client's point of view, are nonetheless phenomenological from the psychologist's viewpoint. Here is one place where Kelly apparently is inconsistent in applying the basic concept noted above. The same difficulty appears later when he says: "We attempt to use the phenomenologist's approach to arrive at personalized constructs which have a wide range of meaning for the given individual; then we attempt to piece together this high-level type of data with what we know about other persons." [41] But how do we obtain this knowledge of other people, except phenomenologically? In most instances, however, Kelly is consistently phenomenological in his approach, although he does not feel that his system is neophenomenological in nature.[42] His basic conception of a role relationship is that the therapist, for example, subsumes the construct system of the client by his acceptance (defined as willingness to see the world through the client's eyes) and thus is able to construe things as the client does, which enables him to predict, or anticipate, the client's behavior. This is exactly the approach taken by Combs and Snygg in their phenomenological system.[43]

It is interesting to consider Kelly's approach as an alternative to client-centered therapy, which also develops from phenomenology. Nothing in phenomenology leads only to the client-centered approach to counseling or psychotherapy. Perceptions or the personal constructs related to perceptions may be changed in various ways. Whereas in the client-centered approach the therapist operates in one way to facilitate change, in therapy based on the psychology of personal constructs the therapist functions in another way. In the latter approach the therapist appears to be a highly active, manipulative individual, constantly prodding, pushing, and stimulating the client.

It is this continually active nature of therapy that creates the need for the therapist to be constantly engaged in evaluation and judgment of the client and his needs, in order to make decisions about what to do next. This places a tremendous responsibility on the therapist. After reading Kelly's books one is left with the feeling that there are few therapists who would want to accept this responsibility. One is led again to the conclusion that it is not so much what you do as the way in which you do it that is important in therapy; the danger of damage is apparently minimized when the therapist is obviously interested and concerned. The client responds to the relationship rather than to the methods. The personal-construct counselor—or at least Dr. Kelly—gives the client the impression that the therapist is in control, that he knows just what he is doing and what he is going to do. While it appears to be close to the "doctor knows best" approach, Kelly recognizes the dangers of this method and disavows it. He mentions several cases in which suicide attempts were precipitated and points out the errors of the therapists in terms of this theory. However, it may be that the error was not so much due to a failure to apply the theory as to a failure to understand the client, together with excessive activity and manipulation, apparently in the effort to play the active, pushing role demanded by the approach. Kelly warns against the therapist playing God, but a therapist using this approach almost has to be God.

The fixed-role therapy is a method of instigating client activity that has some similarities to the prescriptions of client activity in other approaches, such as those of Salter and Wolpe. It is a much more systematic and individually adapted approach, however, than those of Salter and Wolpe; the prescription is not a blanket one, but varies with the client. It also appears to differ in that through the fixed-role sketch, the client's attitudes and perceptions are changed prior to the change in activity, rather than the client's being forced into actions that, it is presumed, will generate changes in attitudes and feelings, following reinforcement.

In addition to its active, manipulative aspects, Kelly's approach is also apparently highly rational and intellectual in nature. "Psychotherapy is the intelligent manipulation of various psychological processes." [44] Psychotherapy is likened to a scientific experiment. Rogers, in his review of Kelly, emphasizes this aspect, noting, "He is continually thinking about the client, and about his own procedures, in ways so complex that there seems no room for entering into an emotional relationship with the client." [45] Nevertheless, it may be that Kelly's description of the way he practices psychotherapy is not quite the way he actually practices it. While he no doubt is highly active, manipulative, and cognitively oriented, there is evidence that he is sensitive to the various possible meanings a client's behavior (such as weeping) or his statements may have.

The approach is highly provocative and stimulating. The theory of behavior and personality is probably more significant than the application of the approach in psychotherapy; the theory can be useful in connection with other methods, since there seems to be nothing inherent in it that would lead to these particular methods of therapy. Many of the methods are those commonly used in other approaches to psychotherapy, including psychoanalysis. The unique approach developed in fixed-role therapy is limited, since, as Rogers points out, [46] it is useful only with clients who are not familiar with the method. Many of the concepts, or constructs, are similar to those of other theorists, but there are unique aspects, which are more than the coining of new words for old concepts. The forward-looking aspect manifested in the basic postulate, involving anticipation, is unique; but it is similar to the concepts of Rotter and Phillips, although Kelly develops it much more extensively. There is also some similarity between the concept of self-actualization and the concept of elaborative choice (that a person choses for himself the alternative in a dichotomized construct through which he anticipates the greater possibility for extension and definition of his system).

Perhaps one of the major unique concepts is the notion of the dichotomous nature of constructs. The notion of contrast is, of course, nothing new, but it is one that has never been given the place it appears to deserve in psychological theory. It is easily recognized that satisfaction exists only in contrast to, or in relation to, lack of satisfaction, or dissatisfaction. This relativity relationship has recently been elevated by Garan into the basic psychological causal law. [47] While perhaps not warranting such elevation, it does deserve more attention than it has received, and Kelly has made a real contribution here, which does not seem to have been recognized as yet. The relativity relationship contributes, for example, to the dilemma of determinism versus free will, which Kelly considers.

Finally, Kelly's handling of motivation is provocative. There is no concept of motivation, nor any need for such a concept, since he begins by postulating a process rather than an inert substance that must be put into movement. There is thus no consideration of the aspects of motivation that are central to so-called dynamic psychology.

However, Kelly's basic postulate has a motivational aspect, including a goal or direction of all behavior. This postulate is not too different from the motivational theory of the phenomenology of Combs and Snygg, that man's basic motivation is the maintenance and enhancement of the phenomenal self. [48] Similarly, there is no place for the concepts of reward or reinforcement in Kelly's theory. Events are validated by perception of correct anticipation. The scientist is not controlled by reward. "The scientist who attempts only to accumulate a backlog of reinforcements is likely to become rigid, timid, opinionated, and generally inert. The scientist who is inventive, curious, receptive, and progressive is the one who is as happy over negative results and the enlightenment they offer as he is about the positive ones." [49] One might quibble over definitions of reward here, but the general point is clear. The concept of validation is much broader and thus more useful than the concept of reinforcement.

The psychology of personal constructs presents a view of human behavior that is significant. Bruner has called it "the single greatest contribution of the past decade to the theory of personality functioning." [50] In a review of *Clinical Psychology and Personality: The Selected Papers of George Kelly*, Appelbaum,[51] while recognizing that Kelly "has been a significant figure in recent psychology," contends that he has given us little that is new, but simply reiterates the phenomenological and humanistic point of view. "His eminence [was] an accident of his time. . . . His point of view will fade away into the limbo of [the history of ideas], and even now its main interest lies more in what it tells us about our professional culture than in its substance." It may be true that Kelly has contributed little beyond what other phenomenologists and humanists have given us, but he has integrated it and systematized it. Perhaps his particular integration, his concepts and terminology, will not persist, but the basic substance, the point of view, undoubtedly will, since it appears to be necessary for an adequate understanding of, and therapy with, human beings. In addition, Kelly has stimulated a reexamination of some traditional and current views of human behavior and therapy. He has succeeded in a wish stated in 1963: "If I had to end my life on some final note, I think I would like it to be a question, preferably a basic one, well posed and challenging, and beckoning me to where only others after me may go, rather than a terminal conclusion—no matter how well documented." [52]

REFERENCES

[1] Kelly, G. A. *The psychology of personal constructs.* Vol. I. *A theory of personality.* Vol. II. *Clinical diagnosis and psychotherapy.* New York: Norton, 1955.   [2] *Ibid.,* Vol. I, p. 3.   [3] *Ibid.,* p. 8.   [4] *Ibid.,* p. 15.   [5] *Ibid.,* p. 21.   [6] *Ibid.* [7] *Ibid.,* pp. 21–22.   [8] *Ibid.,* p. 49.   [9] *Ibid.,* p. 61.   [10] *Ibid.,* p. 67. [11] *Ibid.,* p. 69.   [12] *Ibid.,* p. 105.   [13] *Ibid.,* p. 127.   [14] *Ibid.,* p. 133. [15] *Ibid.,* p. 166.   [16] *Ibid.,* pp. 167–168.   [17] *Ibid.,* p. 173.   [18] *Ibid.,* p. 174.   [19] *Ibid.,* p. 472.   [20] *Ibid.,* p. 489.   [21] *Ibid.,* p. 503.   [22] *Ibid.,* p. 511.   [23] *Ibid.,* Vol. II, p. 590.   [24] *Ibid.,* p. 592.   [25] *Ibid.,* p. 594.   [26] *Ibid.,* p. 941.   [27] *Ibid.,* p. 775.   [28] *Ibid.*   [29] *Ibid.,* p. 829.   [30] *Ibid.,* Vol. I, p. 209.   [31] *Ibid.,* Vol. II, p. 635.   [32] *Ibid.,* p. 975.   [33] *Ibid.,* p. 1049.   [34] *Ibid.,* p. 1090.   [35] *Ibid.,* p. 1053. [36] *Ibid.,* p. 1111.   [37] *Ibid.,* Vol. I, p. 323.   [38] *Ibid.,* p. 46.   [39]

Ibid., p. 3.   **[40]** *Ibid.,* p. 173.   **[41]** *Ibid.,* p. 455.   **[42]** *Ibid.,* p. 517.
[43] Combs, A. W., & Snygg, D. *Individual behavior: a perceptual approach to human behavior.* (Rev. ed.) New York: Harper & Row, 1959. P. 35.   **[44]** Kelly, G. A., *op. cit.,* Vol. II, p. 1071.   **[45]** Rogers, C. R. Intellectualized psychotherapy. Review of G. A. Kelly, "The psychology of personal constructs." *Contemp. Psychol.,* 1956, **1,** 357–358.   **[46]** *Ibid.*   **[47]** Garan, D. G. *The paradox of pleasure and relativity: the psychological causal law.* New York: Philosophical Library, 1963; Patterson, C. H. Review of D. G. Garan, "The paradox of pleasure and relativity." *Personnel guid. J.,* 1964, **43,** 82–84.   **[48]** Combs, A. W., & Snygg, D., *op. cit.,* pp. 44–46.   **[49]** Kelly, G. A., *op. cit.,* Vol. II, p. 1166.
[50] Bruner, J. Review of G. A. Kelly, "The psychology of personal constructs," *Contemp. Psychol.,* 1956, **1,** 355–357.   **[51]** Appelbaum, S. A. Review of B. Maher (Ed.), "Clinical psychology and personality: the selected papers of George Kelly." (New York: Wiley, 1969.) *Psychiat. soc. sci. Rev.,* 1970, **3** (12), 20–25.   **[52]** Kelly, G. A. The autobiography of a theory. In B. Maher (Ed.), *Clinical psychology and personality: the selected papers of George Kelly.* New York: Wiley, 1969. Pp. 46–65.

14

Grinker's transactional approach

In their book *Psychiatric Social Work: A Transactional Case Book,* [1] Roy R. Grinker, Sr., Helen MacGregor, Kate Selan, Annette Klein, and Janet Kohrman present an approach to social casework that has relevance for counseling and psychotherapy. The senior author, Roy R. Grinker (1900–   ), is a psychiatrist who received his M.D. degree in 1921 from Rush Medical College. Following residencies at Cook County Hospital in Illinois and in Vienna, Zurich, Hamburg, and London, he became an Instructor in Neurology at Northwestern University in 1925. In 1927 he went to the University of Chicago, where he remained until 1936, when he became Chairman of the Department of Neuropsychiatry at Michael Reese Hospital. In 1946 he became Director of its Institute for Psychosomatic and Psychiatric Research and Training. From 1942 to 1945 he was a Colonel in the Medical Corps. U.S.A.F. He has long been engaged in private practice and is Clinical Professor of Psychiatry at the University of Illinois College of Medicine. He is the author of many articles and books, including *Psychosomatic Research* (1953) and, with J. P. Spiegel, *War Neuroses* (1945) and *Men Under Stress* (1945). The junior authors of *Psychiatric Social Work: A Transactional Case Book* have been members of the psychiatric social work staff of Michael Reese Hospital.

BACKGROUND AND DEVELOPMENT

The approach developed in *Psychiatric Social Work: A Transactional Case Book* originated in a seminar, organized in 1950 by Dr. John P. Spiegel with a group of social workers at Michael Reese Hospital, which was concerned with the question, What are the functions of the psychiatric social worker? Dr. Grinker continued the seminar for another four years after Dr. Spiegel left at the end of a two-year period. Both Dr. Spiegel and Dr. Grinker had become interested in the transactional approach of Dewey and Bentley [2] and applied it in the study of the psychiatric functions of the social worker. Transactional theory is concerned with a process that requires a definition of the setting, the participants (in this case the patients and the social work staff), and the goals.

The setting in which the approach was developed was the eighty-bed Institute for Psychosomatic and Psychiatric Research and Training, a multidisciplinary training and research facility, and its psychiatric outpatient clinic. The institute's orientation was psychoanalytic. Patients in the clinic cover the entire range of psychiatric diagnoses and differ little from patients of private psychiatrists. Fees are charged depending upon ability to pay. Sessions are on a weekly basis.

The social work staff participates in admissions of psychiatric emergencies, in regular intake, and in providing information and referral when the applicant is not accepted. The social worker also acts as either primary or adjunctive therapist for accepted cases. Cases in which he is primary therapist do not include suicidal cases, panic reactions, or acute disturbances. In addition, he serves as consultant on social service matters and as liaison with the community social agencies, and sees relatives in collaborative treatment.

It was in the formulation of the social worker's goals of action that dissatisfaction developed, which led to the abandonment of psychoanalytic terminology and the application of transactional theory. The result was a statement of patient roles and clinic roles, with the transactional system connecting them, indicating "the reciprocal, reverberating cyclic processes going on between patient and the therapist and several possible resolutions." [3] The approach was applied to the intake interview or exploration, the communication of information or recommendations to the patient, supportive therapy, and psychotherapy. For the purposes of the present exposition we have omitted consideration of the first two areas of application.

PHILOSOPHY AND CONCEPTS

The relationship between the patient and the therapist is transactional within the current life situation; that is, it is "a relationship of two . . . individuals within a specified environment which includes both of them, not as distinct and separate entities or as individuals, but only as they are in relatedness with each other within a specific system." [4]

Each acts on the other in a reciprocal and cyclic process of action, response, and feedback, which is influenced by the setting and includes the life situations of the patient and the therapist as well as the therapeutic setting.

This approach differs from traditional concepts in social work and psychotherapy. Adjustment theory, for example, assumes that the social worker does something *to* or *for* the patient to help him. This help is directed toward an a priori goal of "mental health," "adaptive behavior," or "adjustment." Needs theory assumes that the worker determines the needs of the patient and provides services to meet them. This is an interaction theory in which each person acts in a stereotyped and fairly steady, explicit role, with the therapist influencing the patient after determining his needs. The total fields of the participants and the changing implicit roles of each are ignored.

Transactional theory emphasizes "the changing mutual and reciprocal system of communications, between the two participants of the transaction. Within the context of communications expressed verbally, nonverbally by gestures and expressions, and paralingually by grunts, ahs, ughs, and pauses, meanings are expressed and concealed." [5] In addition to the explicit roles of therapist-patient, there are a variety of implicit roles involved, related to past transactions of the participants. The relationship is enacted within and influenced by the field or setting, including the life field or social matrix of the patient, which relates to his implicit roles.

The transactional approach makes use of the contributions of other theories, among which is *field theory*, which emphasizes the interrelationships of all systems within the total field, so that change in one affects all the others. The total field cannot be fractionated except artificially for analysis. Field theory stresses the importance of the past and present social, cultural, economic, and ethnic environments of the patient and the therapist.

Communications and information theory is relevant, since it is through communication—verbal or nonverbal—that the patient and therapist relate to each other. Disturbed communication is a part of psychopathology. The therapist must be an expert in understanding language; his own background, including his age and social class, is thus related to his facility in understanding his patients. Language is often lacking in necessary appropriate symbols, such as those required for psychological contact through space without physical contact, and we must resort to terms of physical description, such as "warmth" and "coolness."

Role theory provides a method of describing and studying the interactions of persons in a social system. A role is a pattern of acts, goal-directed and defined by the cultural process, by which the person carries out his social transactions. In a small social group the roles allocated to the individuals are related to each other, or are complementary, which results in stability or equilibrium. Speaker-listener, parent-child, teacher-pupil are some examples of complementary roles. Disequilibrium occurs when role complementarity is disturbed, and the disappointment of expectations leads to tension, anxiety, and self-consciousness in the individual, and disruption of interpersonal relations. This is in essence the definition of neurosis. [6] Following disequilibrium there are attempts at reequilibrium, which is achieved by inducing others to alter their roles, by mutual modification of roles, and by role reversal, in which each person attempts to put himself in the other's place.

Social roles are largely explicit; that is, they are conscious, describable in general terms, and communicable by rational verbalizations and standard behaviors. They refer to consciously motivated behavior and are instrumental when they contribute to solving problems.

There are also implicit roles, which are usually unconscious. These express complicated aspects of personality—characteristics of a wide variety of shifting internalizations and identifications. Implicit roles may express identifications representing early mother-child transactions and their conflicts. Both explicit and implicit roles are brought to psychotherapy by the patient. For example, while he enters psychotherapy explicitly to get well, his implicit behavior may be that of a child seeking a dependency relationship.

Psychoanalytic theory constitutes the most fruitful theory in modern psychiatry, although it is not readily applicable to psychotherapy. Psychoanalytic psychodynamics contributes the structure for the understanding of the two-person transactions in psychotherapy. Such concepts as defenses, regression, narcissism, etc,. are indispensable and have become a part of the public domain of psychiatry. "Psychoanalytic theory serves as the best conceptual system for the functional interplay *within* the mental apparatus." [7]

The transactional approach involves communications through role relationships within a designated and defined field. But the field is not an unchanging or a separate entity; it is in part determined by the persons acting within it.

THE THERAPY PROCESS

"Therapy as a system consists of the behavior of a patient in terms of his roles in transaction with the therapist as a role partner." [8] The relationship of the therapist and the patient constitutes a system of transactions. The transactional approach exposes or evokes implicit roles and the repetition of old unadaptive patterns. This leads to noncomplementarity in the patient-therapist relationship, resulting in disequilibrium, which makes reequilibrium possible. The old repetitive processes are disrupted and a new system established.

It is from behavior within the therapeutic transaction that understanding and change arise, not from so-called insight. Implicit roles are made explicit, thus being brought into awareness, so that they may be modified and controlled. Behavior in the two-person transaction underlies progressive changes in relationships with other people in other environments.

In the here-and-now transaction of psychotherapy, the patient and therapist share common experiences. The quality of the behaviors of the patient are observed by the therapist and communicated by interpretation to the patient, so that the patient's distortions become meaningless and must be abandoned in favor of reality. Learning, growth, and change are thus effected, and neurotic behaviors are diminished.

Transactional therapy differs from psychoanalysis in that (1) it avoids conditions favorable for regression and the development of a transference neurosis; (2) the development of a transference neurosis is also avoided by the limited frequency of interviews (weekly), by the face-to-face position of patient and therapist, and by the focus on the here-and-now rather than the past, as well as on rapid generalization from an interpretation of an implicit transactional role, with no interpretation of latent dream content apart from the current role relationships; (3) there is no concern with "primary conflicts," "working through," or lifting of "infantile amnesia"; and (4) there is avoidance of the "delusion that 'complete personality reorganization' and 'cure' could be achieved by any psychotherapy." [9]

On the other hand, transference manifestations are dealt with, as is resistance, and countertransference is exploited as the process whereby the therapist "understands and appreciates the patient's implicit communications by observing his own emotional reactions to them." [10]

The goals of psychotherapy cannot be predetermined; rather they depend upon, and develop out of, the transactional experiences in therapy. As the patient's motivation, degree of disturbance, capacity to endure the suffering of therapy, and ability to learn become clear, as well as the efficacy of the therapist in the particular case, goals crystallize.

The following tables summarize the transactional approach in supportive therapy and insight therapy.[11]

IMPLEMENTATION: TECHNIQUES OF PSYCHOTHERAPY

Supportive Psychotherapy: Complementary Relationships

In the complementary relationship the aim is to attempt to satisfy the patient's current needs rather than to uncover psychodynamics and reconstruct the personality. It is thus what is usually called supportive or superficial psychotherapy.

The relationship is begun with the patient and the therapist having clearly defined explicit roles: the patient needs help with a problem, and the therapist assumes the role of the helper. The patient, however, implicitly assumes the role of a child and assigns a comple-

EXPERIENCING COMPLEMENTARY RELATIONSHIPS
(Supportive Psychotherapy)

patient roles	*transactional system*	*clinic (worker) roles*
a Explicitly Assigned Role Patient, client, mother with problem.	Complementarity (and therefore equilibrium) in patient-clinic system is maintained through acceptance by clinic of implicitly assigned roles.	*a* Explicitly Assigned Role Instrumental or expressive sharing of problem.
b Implicitly Assigned Role Unknown.	Clinic is then instrumentally concerned with explicitly defined area of problem presented by patient. The system in this area may take three main forms: 1 Self-stabilizing transaction—where the equilibrium is so delicately balanced that system cannot change, i.e., may persist for years. 2 Self-limiting transaction through: *a* Patient spontaneously finding another relationship for implicit role needs.	*b* Implicitly Assigned Roles An array of parental roles such as: 1 Teacher—reality interpreter. 2 Moral authority and standard setter. 3 Emotional communicator—absorption and reflection of affect (safety valve). 4 Appreciator and identifier—primary interpersonal relationship.
c Explicitly Assumed Role Person in trouble needing help with problem.	*b* Gentle verbalization of implicit role by therapist resulting in withdrawal of patient.	*c* Explicitly Assumed Role Complementary to both explicitly and implicitly assigned roles.
d Implicitly Assumed Roles An array of child roles such as: 1 Learner—needing help with understanding and interpretation of reality. 2 Guidance seeker—especially in standards and normative judgments. 3 Emotional communicator. 4 Identity seeker.	3 Self-developing transaction: Beginning definition of implicit role by patient or therapist results in patient's realization of responsibility in therapy, and system moves to Area 5 (see under Techniques).	*d* Implicitly Assumed Role Unknown.

mentary role to the therapist. The therapist accepts both the patient's explicit and implicit roles and his own role assignment, becoming a teacher and interpreter of reality, an authoritative setter of standards, a listener, or an appreciator of the patient's self and attributes, depending on the implicit childish role of the patient.

This assumption of a complementary role requires that the therapist accurately ascertain the implicit role of the patient and the implicit role-complementarity, which involves considerable skill.

MODIFYING COMPLEMENTARY RELATIONSHIPS
(Intensive or Insight Psychotherapy)

patient roles	*transactional system*	*clinic (worker) roles*
a Explicitly Assigned Role Patient able and willing to enter cooperative working relationship with professional helper.	1 Explicit complementary roles develop, spiral, and close when information becomes repetitive. Patient's implicit role made explicit and new focus developed.	a Explicitly Assigned Role Therapist who cures by magic, words, advice, etc.

b Implicitly Assigned Role
Unknown—varies with problem.
	2 Control of acting out.
	
	3 Anxiety held to workable quantity.
	  a System may move slowly and certainly, with increasing insight by patient, improved behavior in social roles, and more stable and lighter affect.
	
	  b System may be disrupted by premature implicit role interpretation, etc., and patient leaves transaction.
		b Implicitly Assigned Roles
		Vary with focus of transaction, needs of patient, regression, and insight.

c Explicitly Assumed Role Patient a tester, expects miraculous cure.		c Explicitly Assumed Role Complementary to explicitly assigned role until transaction becomes complete, obtains closure, then interpretation of patient's implicitly assumed roles.
d Implicitly Assumed Roles Vary with focus of transaction, depth of regression and insight obtained.		d Implicitly Assumed Role Unknown—depends on own unresolved problem.

The transaction may take several forms: (1) An equilibrium is established and persists unaltered for considerable time; (2) the equilibrium is sufficiently satisfying for the length of time the real problem requires for solution; (3) the patient finds another person with whom complementarity may be achieved naturally in a real-life situation; (4) when the patient becomes aware of the nature of his implicit role, he takes flight from the transaction; (5) definition of the patient's implicit role results in his realization of the need for his own responsibility and efforts in therapy, and he moves into an area of intensive psychotherapy.[12]

The role relationships in supportive therapy tend to persist once they are stabilized, which may lead to interminable therapy. There are few reliable criteria for determining when a patient is ready to continue on his own. "The therapist should help the patient test his strength by gradually becoming less active and asking the patient to make more of his own decisions, to endure less frequent interviews, and to experience interruptions in therapy for weeks or months at a time. Sometimes a termination date may be set well in advance or a crucial decision may be demanded of the patient by the therapist." [13]

Intensive Psychotherapy: Modifying Complementary Relationships

The modification of complementary relationships is what is usually called intensive, deep, uncovering, insight, dynamic, or modified psychoanalytic therapy. Its goal is considerable internal change in the patient and modification of his behavior, although questions about how deep or intensive such psychotherapy is and how much personality reorganization it achieves, as well as what its relation to psychoanalysis is, are unanswered.

In the supportive, or role-complementarity, relationship, the therapist may tentatively begin to make explicit the patient's implicit roles as a test of his ego strength or of his capacity for learning. If the result is favorable, the transaction can be oriented toward modifying the complementary relationship.

Transactional therapy takes a middle ground between a bland, neutral passivity on the part of the therapist, on the one hand, and highly active, premature, deep interpretations, on the other. In this middle ground the therapist continuously and patiently interprets the implicit roles of the patient while attempting to understand his own implict roles in the transaction.

THE PLAN AND GOALS OF THERAPY   Patients should be selected for psychotherapy in terms of suitability and motivation. Determining these factors is the function of the intake exploration. Following the intake exploration are the diagnostic evaluation and diagnostic staffing, which are concerned not only with classification but with a preliminary formulation of psychodynamics on which a tentative treatment plan is based. Since these psychodynamics may be inaccurate, the plan for therapy should be flexible, and "the goals of therapy cannot be set without constantly testing the patient's capacities to learn, grow, endure anxiety, and experiment with new behavior." [14] To avoid rigidity resulting from bias produced by the psychodynamic formulations, a focus is delineated; decisions to stop, continue, or change the focus are based on the transactional process. The focus is set by the therapist, and not by the patient in "free associations." "In this sense our therapy is directive, but only in effecting concentration and in avoiding defensive flight from a significant therapeutic focus." [15] The therapist may have to refuse to develop complementarity of explicit roles in order to get the patient to reveal his implicit role relationships so that the therapeutic focus can become clear.

THE FIELD   Too often therapy is separated from the patient's total field. But what goes on in the interview is influenced by this field. Pretherapy study gives the therapist some knowledge of the patient's life and background, but the field is constantly changing. The therapist must know about the patient's current life outside of therapy if he is to help the patient to the fullest extent. If there are questions about shifts in the patient's attitudes or communications, the therapist should inquire about what has been happening between interviews.

THE EXPLICIT ROLES The explicit roles of patient and therapist are highly structured. The patient must participate as a patient, although as his implicit roles are recognized, he may resist help, clarification and insight, or change. But psychotherapy requires that the patient be basically willing to cooperate with the therapist and that he abandon his expectations of being given material help or told what to do. The therapist, in his role, respects the patient as a worthwhile human being, and hopes and believes that he will change as a result of his inherent capacity for growth. Overenthusiasm, however, creates expectations in the therapist and patient that may lead to disappointment.

THE BEGINNING OF THE TRANSACTION At the beginning the therapist and the patient may be "represented as convex arcs of two incomplete circles across which distorted, misunderstood, and incomplete messages traverse in both directions." [16] As communication is achieved, complementarity of explicit roles results, and the two convex arcs become concave, forming a small temporary circle. Communication about the particular topic or problem then becomes repetitive.

Therapy starts with the here and now of the patient-therapist relationship. Of course, there is no time restriction on the immediate relationship, so that material from the recent or distant past may be brought in, but neither is there an exploration of the past or of early memories. The patient will recognize the way in which past experiences conform to the current transaction.

DEALING WITH ANXIETY Since anxiety is the basis of many of the patient's defensive or security operations and the resulting symptoms, it enters into every therapy relationship. The old concept that emotional expression is therapeutic leads to a tendency to permit or encourage excessive anxiety, which disturbs cognitive and conative functions, throwing the therapeutic transaction out of therapeutic equilibrium. Some anxiety is necessary for progress. The therapist, however, must maintain an optimum level of anxiety. He must be prepared to reduce anxiety by supportive and reassuring statements or by removing anxiety-producing pressures. But "the goal is to determine what implicit roles are associated with anxiety and communicate this fact within the current situation before the patient becomes involved in panic or defensive maneuvers. The most effective way to gain relief from anxiety is to know its cognitive correlations, and that is the principle of interpretations at the right time." [17]

ACTIVITY In transactional therapy the therapist is active, narrowing the transaction to a specific focus and shifting to another when desirable. Long silences are avoided. Maintaining the focus is one of the responsibilities of the therapist, even under pressure from the patient who wants to leave the field and talk about something else or who insists there is nothing more to say.

UNDERSTANDING AND INTERPRETING IMPLICIT ROLES Following the achievement of mutual understanding within explicit roles, the therapist communicates his understanding of the patient's implicit role and of the role the patient is attempting to ascribe to him. He rejects the ascribed role, thus avoiding role-complementarity. The patient must then turn to the reality of the transaction, and with pressure from the therapist, new solutions are sought and reached. The implicit roles carry the emotional, expressive, and neurotic behavior. The therapist becomes aware of these implicit roles and responds to them. He does not assume complementarity with the patient's implicit roles, but makes explicit in his communication with the patient what these implicit roles are. "Thus the therapist primarily searches for information, and the interventions consist of making clear to the patient the information he has obtained about his implicit roles." [18] He attempts to get the patient to see how his implicit roles lead him to seek out or even create stimuli that elicit the neurotic patterns he has learned, thus perpetuating them.

Transference neurosis is avoided, and with it, regression and highly infantile dependent relationships. If a transference neurosis seems to be developing, it is counteracted by as broad a generalization from the patient's personal communication as possible. Transference phenomena are present in the patient's implicit communications, which are colored by the past, and in the dependent-helping relationship of patient and therapist.

The therapist is honest in admitting his positive and negative feelings within the therapeutic transaction. Annoyances and irritations are felt by the patient, and if the therapist denies them, communication is blocked. Communication is also disturbed by misunderstandings on the part of the therapist related to his distorted implicit responses, or what are called countertransference difficulties in analytic therapy. The therapist's honesty is not inconsistent with the permissiveness that is necessary if the patient is to bring up feelings and memories.

DIRECTIVE TACTICS Transactional therapy is more directive than psychoanalysis. Permissiveness does not extend to behavior. The patient must learn about reality in life. The therapist prohibits "acting out," expresses value judgments regarding past and future behavior, and expresses approval and disapproval. The patient is not permitted to become anonymous, to intellectualize, or to talk persistently about others. He is encouraged to experiment in relationships outside therapy.

THE THERAPIST AS AN INSTRUMENT The personality of the therapist is the only tool of therapy. "The therapist's feelings are the only sensitive instrument that he has available. This tool needs great care, frequent calibration and many practive readings. Eventually it can become a trustworthy instrument." [19] Personal therapy or psychoanalysis may help free the therapist from compulsive rigidities and restrictions. Imagination, capacity for empathy and identification, and freedom of personality are necessary. These are learned emotionally, not by rote.

EXAMPLE

The patient is a twenty-eight-year-old single woman who comes to the clinic because she has been told by a number of people that she needs psychiatric help. She is only aware now that she is attracted to men who have no wish to get married and is not attracted to those who are good possibilities for marriage. The patient was processed through an intake interview, the intake staff, a diagnostic interview, and the diagnostic staff.

First Session

The patient arrived, on time, dressed informally in sweater and skirt, short sport jacket, and low heels. She began the interview by asking if this was still "part of the diagnostic." *She was told that her diagnosis had been completed and therapy had been recommended on a once-a-week basis. I was her therapist and would be seeing her weekly.* "Then I can start?" *She was told that she could start where she wished.* "Then I'd like to talk about something that happened to me last week." She then began a long detailed account in logical sequence with no demonstrable affect. Throughout *I asked for her emotional reactions and for her role in these recent experiences.* It was only late in the interview that I began to get some affective responses.

Two weeks previous the patient arrived in California to stay with her friend Paul for a vacation. On arrival she learned from his roommate, who did not know of Paul's homosexuality, that he was out with a man. She stayed at Paul's apartment all night, and when he came home in the morning she was "building up to a big scene" and confronted him with his being out all night in spite of her expected arrival. She asked where he had been and he stated directly he had been having an affair with a homosexual friend that night—a man he had met once. She has a funny feeling in her stomach and cannot look him in the eye when he talks to her of his homosexuality, but steadfastly denies other feelings about it. Paul then pulled out her letter and proved that she had not stated that she was to arrive Friday night. This always happens—he makes her feel "small and insignificant" when she tries to argue with him. She is always wrong and he is right, but she reveals no further affect about this.

They then had three wonderful days together—until Monday night when Paul again had a date with his homosexual friend. At this point she was very stirred up, could not stand to see this man, and kept out of the way until he and Paul left. She became very upset, paced up and down and was afraid of what she might do to him. She awakened his roommate to ask for two sleeping pills, slept for three hours to stop thinking, and then "knew what she had to do"—leave Paul. She wrote him a note that she was sorry and was leaving. She called Kay (a platonic friend of Paul's who had slept with him only once, but whom she likes better than any girl she has met for a long time) and went to stay with her. The next day was spent with Kay and Paul's roommate. After a day spent with the two people most closely involved with Paul, with precautions not to meet him, and advice from both that Paul was in need of treatment, she returned to Chicago.

She denies disappointment at not having heard from Paul; says that she has felt numb, but knew she had to leave him. *Finally I state directly that she is personally involved and must have some reaction to the ending of the relationship.* She asks, "Why did he do this to me? Why did he go out with this man the night I was there?" She brings out that it is only when she sees him that she gets so involved. She expects him to be with others when she is not there.

She gives me a history of their relationship. She met him at the "lowest point of my life"—when she was twenty and was compelled to live with her father. "I finally pulled myself away from that." She then brings up her father's past psychiatric treatment and the fact that three people have told her to seek psychiatric treatment. She was pushed for her reaction to each one of these and was finally able to admit that she felt each recommendation arose out of some hostile feeling toward her: (1) The girl who thought Paul was a "nice, normal young man" and that patient should get herself straightened out to marry him. (2) A man friend who insisted that she needed psychiatric treatment because she did not love him. (3) A male friend who broke down, was hospitalized, and who insisted that she, too, needed treatment. *I commented that one did not have to seek treatment on this basis.* With some relief she agreed—she wants treatment for herself, she knows. She is freer in the interview after this.

She returns to discuss Paul. When she asks me, *I state that this is an involved personal relationship.* She knows she loves Paul, has to be close to him, has to be demanding of him—"I want to get married." I ask if she means to Paul and she replies, "No." She knows that when she is ready she will be able to fall in love with some other man. *I ask if she has ever felt that Paul had some "fatal fascination" for her.* She does not answer directly but tells in great detail of Paul's many homosexual and heterosexual affairs, ending with "Paul is promiscuous." *I ask for a reaction to this.* She indicates that for the first time she questioned him about his standards when he picks up a man in a bar and goes home and sleeps with him. He told her, "It's different with men like this." *How does this make her feel about her role with him?* "I failed him." How? "He just wanted me for a friend and I wanted more than that." *I point out that she has her own stake in this* and she tells how she had advised Paul to break off with a girl who had fallen in love with him and whom he did not want. He had taken her advice. She tries to deny any feeling about it and then says it was strange but she had been conscious of watching the girl. There follows praise of Paul, of his taste in art, his intelligence, his absolute integrity—patient repeats the latter twice as if she is beginning to doubt it herself, and a little later makes a fleeting reference to these "sordid affairs." At another point in the interview she tells me that she and Paul are much alike—they think alike, feel alike, have the same tastes and interests.

She asks me again why Paul did this to her. *I tell her I do not know, but that he may have a need to hurt and depreciate women now. This is something she can react to, but all we know now is that her relationship with Paul is complicated and I am not clear where she stands.*

Comments on First Session

The patient, in her first transaction with her therapist, assumes the explicit role of a dependent, uninformed individual needing reassurance or help on when and how to begin her therapy. The therapist, in response, rejects the assigned role of the controlling and all-knowing authority, reassigns to the patient the task of assuming responsibility for starting wherever the patient wishes. Here immediately we are able to see a transaction in which the patient and therapist do not enter into role-complementarity, since the patient is attempting to assign to the therapist a role that is inappropriate and unrealistic. The therapist's rejection of the assigned authoritarian role results, then, in the patient's reassigning to the therapist the role of listener, while she assumes the role of a logical discussant. Because this "listener role" is an appropriate one at this point for the therapist, it is accepted and complementarity is achieved, resulting in the patient's disclosure of pathological sexual experiences during the vacation which immediately preceded her entering treatment. The worker let the patient go on spontaneously in order to get an understanding of the form and content of her communications. She realized that the patient reveled in telling dramatic stories and wondered if the patient would have new ones to relate at each session. Apparently, in telling these stories, episodes are revealed in an exhibitionistic manner without any concern for confidentiality. The worker wondered whether the vacation before the start of treatment was not really a last-ditch flight away from therapy. It was as if this were structured in an effort to terminate the affair with Paul prior to treatment. This period consisted of a vigorous acting-out experience, which probably was intended to be her last fling before therapy, although this behavior is her defense against emotional learning. Implicit in her story is the indication that she somehow or other managed to arrange that Paul should not know she was coming to visit and that he be caught acting out the anticipated hostility toward her. There was obviously some contriving to bring the situation to a head. Inasmuch as the patient's account of the vacation activities contained little regarding her own emotional responsibility and involvement, the worker experimentally tried to evoke some emotional reactions and to question her statement in an effort to mobilize her curiosity. Here again in a new, modified way we see the patient slipping back obediently on one level while she maintains two conflicting roles; namely, that of the dependent and needful child or the intellectually adequate and competitive woman. The patient partially rejects the worker's attempts to fathom the underlying emotional attitudes and struggles to maintain the defensive position of having no personal emotional identity. Since the therapist cannot realistically accept this, role-complementarity is not achieved. The patient and therapist continue in the treatment process with movement necessitated by patient's having received partial gratification from the therapist's rejection of her unsatisfying defensive maneuvers (which part of the patient wishes to give up) and her need to cling to these familiar childhood patterns.

The patient is aware of the fact that the people who have urged her to go into therapy have all been sick themselves and she also knows that her father's treatment was a failure because he recovered only from the acute episode. She lives in a social system of pseudo-intellectuals who trade anecdotes about their own psychopathology. They are mildly delinquent without external guilt, and even proud of their deviations. Within their group they are able to revolt against authorities and need no other relationships as long as the group enables them to create a fantasy of closeness and warmth. Individuals who break away from the group usually become depressed and isolated, for this type of personality seems to be involved in a struggle against remembering deprivations which, if exposed, result in depression. This leads us to predict that in the relationship with the therapist there will develop, if treatment moves, a strong, dependent, and demanding hostile relationship within which the patient may be precipitated into a depression. It can also be predicted, however, that there will be a terrific struggle against the exposure of her dependent needs, and its consequences will be flight into further affairs with other members of the group.[20]

SUMMARY AND EVALUATION

The transactional approach to psychotherapy attempts to view psychotherapy as a transaction between patient and therapist in which both are part of a larger process in which their past and present experiences and environments are represented. In this process neither exists as a separate individual, and each acts upon the other reciprocally.

Therapy focuses upon the roles of the patient in his current, here-and-now experiences. The roles that the patient plays in therapy are emphasized as representative of his role behaviors outside the therapy situation. The transactions of the patient in therapy represent his transactions in real life. Roles are of two kinds—explicit and implicit. The implicit roles are those of which the patient is not aware. The purpose of therapy is to discover these recurrent implicit roles and to make the patient aware of them so that he can change his self-defeating behavior patterns.

The therapist also has explicit and implict roles. It is his explicit role to help the patient. Sometimes his implicit roles, such as countertransference, interfere. The patient, in addition to recognizing the therapist's explicit role, attempts to ascribe or assign other roles to him. While not designated as such, this would appear to be similar to psychoanalytic transference, which, however, has no place in transactional therapy. The therapist refuses to accept the ascribed roles, thus breaking up the complementarity of the relationship. This stimulates the patient to examine and analyze his own implicit roles, which are complementary to those he attempts to ascribe to the therapist. The disequilibrium created makes the development of a new equilibrium possible.

The transactional approach is presented in a very general and sketchy way. There is no reference to transactional psychology as developed in the study of perception. The theory is general and rather vague. In brief, the approach is not systematically developed. However, the authors do not present the approach as a "system of therapy." [21] They are not even sure that it is therapy, since they have no answers to questions about the kind of patients or therapists for which it is applicable, or the therapeutic results, if any, that it achieves. They present it as an approach to communication and understanding between patients and therapists, and a frame of reference for understanding the nature of the therapeutic relationship.

The question can be raised as to whether there is anything new or different about this approach which does not appear in other approaches. Is it anything more than a psychoanalytically oriented approach? The authors accept psychoanalytic theory as the basis for understanding individual psychodynamics. They are, however, concerned with the present rather than with the past; but so are other neoanalysts, such as Horney and, as we have seen, Alexander. The summaries of cases differ very little from many in the social work literature, although perhaps they are not so heavily loaded with psychoanalytic terminology.

Does the approach, then, only represent an attempted substitution of terminology? To some extent, at least, this appears to be so. In many instances the word "transaction" seems to be used where "relationship" is commonly used. In many respects the approach seems to consist of the adding of a number of concepts onto a psychoanalytic approach. The case summaries, however, may be misleading, since the authors point out that the therapists had been trained in the psychoanalytic approach, and it was difficult for them to change to the new concepts as well as the new terminology. There is also, however, some feeling that traditional purposes and procedures have been forced into the transactional framework.

Again, although the transactional approach emphasizes the importance of the social environment, other approaches in social psychiatry, as well as Sullivan's interpersonal approach, do also. The authors note that

The social worker today seems to be the only professional person concerned with the extended field within which the disturbed or troubled person operates. Psychiatrists have become more and more myopic as their interest in psychodynamics and individual psychotherapy has increased. Imitating the psychoanalytic model even in clinic practice, they not only neglect the immediate social matrix of their patients (family, work, recreation, etc.) but often refuse to see, interview, receive information from, or enlighten close members of the family. Actually, the modern generation of psychiatrists is not really neglectful but has never been taught the importance of environmental influences.[22]

This is perhaps not an accurate reflection of the state of psychiatry or psychotherapy today.[23]

Nevertheless, the focus upon the present, upon the role relationships within the therapy process, and upon the implicit as well as the explicit roles of the patient—both in therapy and in his real life—provide a combined emphasis that differs from many current approaches to psychotherapy.

A major difficulty with the presentation of the approach is the lack of detail in the discussion of the theory and the failure to make explicit the implications of the theory for specific practice. In discussing methods of psychotherapy, the authors write: "Few authors state their specific operations in sufficient detail to enable the reader to grasp what is done. Very few case presentations are published in full; either they are summarized or the patient's verbalizations alone are reported, without those of the therapist; the elements from which the nature of the transaction may be understood are rarely presented. Often the contents of the case presentation are in contradiction to the theoretical framework within which the therapist says he operates." [24] This is a good description of the case summaries presented by Grinker and his associates.

It is difficult to determine just what techniques, if any, are consistent with or unique to the transactional approach. The major technique appears to be interpretation, but it is interpretation of the current feelings and attitudes of the patient, both in and outside of therapy, and of the implicit roles he is playing. The major part of the book consists of interview-by-interview summaries of a single case and comments on them. But the summaries are based upon notes that were made by the therapist from memory following the interview. They were to include as many verbatim quotes as possible. The authors recognize, in discussing the learning of therapy under supervision, that forgetting, distortions, omissions, and discounting of nonverbal communications occur with students and that "even the experienced psychiatrist cannot or does not remember or reveal many facets of the patient-therapist transactions, especially the nuances and subtle connotations of the relationship." [25] Yet apparently there was no thought given to tape-recording therapy sessions. It is puzzling why tape recording has never been accepted and used in social work settings.

The lack of use of transactional psychology restricts the approach. Transactional psychology emphasizes the importance of assumptions and expectancies in determining perception and behavior. These are concepts that are present in other approaches discussed in this book. Thus, the transactional approach, as presented by Grinker and his associates, is a limited one. It is presented as an operational theory of psychotherapy deriving, not from a theory of personality or psychodynamics, but from the empirical operations involved in psychotherapy itself. Nevertheless, it is included here because it is the first attempt to introduce some transactional concepts into psychotherapy. It is to be hoped that the authors or others will develop a truly transactional approach, an approach that might well incorporate many of the significant concepts of other approaches into a unified system.

REFERENCES

[1] Grinker, R. R., Sr., MacGregor, Helen, Selan, Kate, Klein, Annette, & Kohrman, Janet. *Psychiatric social work: a transactional case book.* New York: Basic Books, 1961.   [2] Dewey, J., & Bentley, A. F. *Knowing and the known.* Boston: Beacon Press, 1949.   [3] Grinker, R. R., Sr., et al., *op. cit.,* p. 291.   [4] *Ibid.,* p. 20.   [5] *Ibid.,* p. 293.   [6] Grinker, R. R., Sr. A transactional model for psychotherapy. In M. I. Stein (Ed.), *Contemporary psychotherapies.* New York: Free Press, 1961. P. 197.   [7] Grinker, R. R., Sr., et al., *op. cit.,* p. 297.   [8] *Ibid.,* p. 18.   [9] *Ibid.,* p. 299.   [10] *Ibid.,* p. 294.   [11] *Ibid.,* pp. 24-25. [12] *Ibid.,* p. 95.   [13] *Ibid.,* p. 105.   [14] *Ibid.,* p. 307.   [15] *Ibid.,* p. 308. [16] *Ibid.,* p. 311.   [17] *Ibid.,* p. 313.   [18] *Ibid.,* p. 323.   [19] *Ibid.,* p. 326.   [20] From *Psychiatric social work: a transactional case book,* by Roy Grinker, et al., © 1961 by Basic Books, Inc. New York. Pp. 139–143.   [21] *Ibid.,* p. 329.   [22] *Ibid.,* p. 8.   [23] See, for example, Patterson, C. H. *Counseling and psychotherapy: theory and practice.* Chap. 5. Cultural factors in psychotherapy. New York: Harper & Row, 1959.   [24] Grinker, R. R., Sr., et al., *op. cit.,* p. 119.   [25] *Ibid.,* p. 302.

15

Gestalt therapy

Friedrich (Frederick or Fritz) S. Perls (1893–1970) is credited with being the founder and developer of gestalt therapy. He was born in Berlin. He was educated in Germany, obtaining the M.D. degree. He served as an assistant to Paul Schilder and Kurt Goldstein, and studied at the Vienna and Berlin Institutes of Psychoanalysis. With the advent of Hitler he went to South Africa in 1934, establishing the South African Institute for Psychoanalysis in Johannesburg. Following the death of Jan Smuts and the rise of apartheid, he came to the United States in 1946. With his wife he founded the New York Institute for Gestalt Therapy and was briefly at the Cleveland Institute for Gestalt Therapy. For several years before his death he was associated with the Esalen Institute at Big Sur, California, as Associate Psychiatrist. When he died, he was living in Vancouver, British Columbia, where he had established an Institute for Gestalt Therapy.

While in South Africa in the early forties he wrote *Ego, Hunger and Aggression: A Revision of Freud's Theory and Method,* which was published in England in 1947, and republished in America, with the subtitle changed to *The Beginning of Gestalt Therapy,* in 1969.[1] His books *Gestalt Therapy Verbatim* [2] and *In and Out of the Garbage Pail* [3] were also published in 1969.

In 1951 *Gestalt Therapy: Excitement and Growth in Personality* [4] was published in collaboration with Ralph F. Hefferline (1910–   ) and Paul

344

Goodman (1911–1972). Hefferline has spent his entire student and professional career at Columbia University, where he became Chairman of the Department of Psychology. Goodman, with a Ph.D. in humanities from the University of Chicago, taught at Chicago, New York University, Black Mountain College, and the University of Wisconsin, as well as the Institutes for Gestalt Therapy in New York and Cleveland. He was perhaps best known for his more popular books, including *Growing Up Absurd* (1956) and *Compulsory Mis-education* (1964).

BACKGROUND AND DEVELOPMENT

In the Introduction to *gestalt Therapy* the authors note that while gestalt psychology has influenced art and education, and is recognized in academic psychology (especially in perception) through the work of Wertheimer, Koehler, and Lewin, "the full application of Gestaltism in psychotherapy as the only theory that adequately and consistently covers both normal and abnormal psychology has not yet been undertaken. The present work is an attempt to lay the foundation for that." [5]

While based upon gestalt psychology, gestalt therapy also draws upon psychoanalytic theory, semantics, and philosophy. Thus, it utilizes, or adapts, concepts such as superego, repression, introjection, and projection. In addition, gestalt therapy is an existential therapy. Perls includes it with Frankl's logotherapy and Binswanger's daseinsanalysis as one of the three existential therapies.

PHILOSOPHY AND CONCEPTS

In gestalt therapy Perls has built upon Freudian psychoanalysis, retaining what he considered valid and rejecting what he considered in error. Added to this was the gestalt approach with its emphasis upon the organism as a whole and, beyond this, the organism in its environment.

The Nature of the Organism

Perls quotes Wertheimer's formulation of gestalt theory: "There are wholes, the behavior of which is not determined by that of their individual elements, but where the part-processes are themselves determined by the intrinsic nature of the whole." [6] The organism is a whole and normally functions as a whole. Body, mind, and soul are not separate; there is not an *I*, which *has* a body, or a mind, or a soul, but we exist *as* organisms. The healthy organism is thus a feeling, thinking, and acting being. Emotions, for example, have thinking and action (physiological) as well as feeling aspects. Body, mind, and soul are all aspects of the whole organism.

THE TWO INSTINCTS Freud rightly emphasized the importance of the sex instinct. But he overlooked the existence of another instinct which is necessary for the understanding of behavior. This is the hunger instinct. The sex instinct is aimed at the preservation of the species. The hunger instinct is aimed at self-preservation. The numerous specific instincts may all be classified under these two basic instincts.

The stages of the hunger instinct are the prenatal, the predental (suckling), the incisor (biting), and the molar (biting and chewing). These stages are related to psychological characteristics—impatience to the predental, destruction and aggression to the incisor, assimilation to the molar. The understanding of these stages in their normal and abnormal aspects leads to an understanding of behavior that the sex instinct does not clearly or easily explain.

THE STRIVING FOR BALANCE   The basic tendency of every organism is to strive for balance. The organism is being faced at every moment with a disturbing factor, either external (a demand from the environment) or internal (a need), so that balance is never maintained. The striving for a balance, or equilibrium, is aimed at the reduction of tension, which is pleasurable. The process of restoring balance constitutes "organismic self-regulation." [7] Consciousness is not the searching for, or the finding of, the problem or imbalance; it is identical with the problem or disequilibrium, the development into figure (or focus) of the dominant need and its organization of the functions of contact with the environment to achieve reduction of tension.

In relation to the external environment, the individual may adjust his behavior to the environment (autoplastic behavior), or he may adjust the environment to himself (alloplastic behavior).

The concept of organismic balance, with a balance (or rest) point which is disturbed by a lack (or surplus)—plus or minus, thus setting in motion the achievement of the opposite—a surplus (or lack), is a specific case of the general concept of opposites (dialectics). "Differentiation into opposites is an essential quality of our mentality and of life itself." [8] Good and bad (or right and wrong) are opposites whose origin lies in judgments made, by individuals or collective institutions, on the basis of the frustration or fulfillment of demands or needs. In *Gestalt Therapy Verbatim* Perls states that he is "doing away with the whole instinct theory" and simply considers the organism as a system striving for balance. He also, however, says that "every individual, every plant, every animal, has only one unborn goal—to actualize itself as it is." [9] The two opposing functions in human relationships are affection and defense (destruction). In time, there is the past and the future, centering about the present.

AGGRESSION AND DEFENSE   Aggression is not an energy, similar to Freud's concept, but a meeting of resistance to the satisfaction of the organism's needs. Its function is not destruction but overcoming the resistance, leaving as intact as possible the object required for satisfaction. It is similar or analogous to the biting and chewing of food to satisfy hunger: "the use of the teeth is the foremost biological representation of aggression." [10] (Destruction does not actually leave the object intact, but de-structures it—as in biting and chewing—so that a new structure or intactness develops.) "Mankind suffers from suppressed individual aggression and has become the executor and victim of tremendous amounts of released collective aggression. . . . *The re-establishment of the biological function of aggression* is, and remains, the solution to the *aggression problem*." Sublimation (letting off steam in aggressive sports and in physical work) provides helpful outlets. "But they will never equal dental aggression, the application of which will serve several purposes: one rids oneself of irritability and does not punish oneself by sulking and starving—one develops intelligence, and has a good conscience, because one has done something 'good for one's health.'" [11]

Defense is an instinctive self-preservative activity. Defenses are mechanical (shells in animals, character-armor [Reich] in humans) and dynamic, either motoric (flight), secretoric (snake poison), or sensoric (scenting).

REALITY Since the organism is not self-sufficient, it is continually interacting with its environment. In the process of striving for a balance in relation to environmental demands, the organism is not a passive receptor or reactor, but an active perceiver and organizer of its perceptions. "For our purposes we assume that there is an objective world from which the individual creates his subjective world: parts of the absolute world are selected according to our interest, but this selection is limited by the range of our tools of perception, and by social and neurotic inhibitions. . . . The reality which matters is the reality of interests—the *internal* and not the *external* reality." [12]

Reality thus changes with the changing interests and needs of the organism. Interests and needs organize the environment into figure and ground (background or setting). The most relevant need organizes the field (the environment) and behavior; when that need is met, the field changes, and the next most relevant need emerges. In terms of the individual's behavior, the need is figure and organizes behavior in relation to the environment, and when the need is met, it is succeeded by another need. An important aspect of this organization of the environment is that the individual cannot perceive and respond to his entire environment at the same time, but only to one aspect of it, the figure.

THE EGO "The ego is neither an instinct, nor has it instincts; it is an organismic function." [13] It is not a substance with boundaries, even changing boundaries. Rather the boundaries, the places of contact, constitute the ego. "Only where the self meets the 'foreign' does the Ego start functioning, come into existence, determine the boundary between the personal and impersonal 'field.'" [14] It appears that the awareness of two opposites, the self and the not-self, constitutes the ego.

The ego performs an integrative or administrative function in relating the actions of the organism to its needs: "it calls, so to speak, upon those functions of the whole organism which are necessary for the gratification of the *most urgent* need." [15] It identifies with the organism and its needs, and alienates itself from other needs or demands, to which it is hostile. It then structures the environment (the field) in terms of the organism's need. If the organism is hungry, food becomes gestalt. But if the food can only be obtained by stealing, and the person would rather die than steal, the ego alienates the taking of the food.

GROWTH AND MATURITY   Growth occurs through assimilation from the environment, both physically and mentally. Psychological growth is not an unconscious process, but occurs through awareness, which is characterized by *contact, sensing, excitement,* and *gestalt formation.* "Contact as such is possible without awareness, but for awareness contact is indispensable. . . . Sensing determines the nature of awareness, whether distant (e.g., acoustic), close (e.g., tactile) or within the skin (proprioceptive). . . . Excitement . . . covers the physiological excitation as well as the indifferentiated emotions. . . . Gestalt formation always accompanies awareness. . . . The formation of complete and comprehensive Gestalten is the condition for mental health and growth." [16]

Frustration, rather than preventing growth, fosters it. Frustration enables the individual to discover his possibilities and potentials, and to learn to cope with the world. "Without frustrations there is no need, no reason, to mobilize your resources, to discover that you might be able to do something on your own, and in order not to be frustrated, which is a pretty painful experience, the child learns to manipulate the environment." [17]

Through growth the child matures, which means that he makes the transformation from environmental support to self-support. He becomes independent rather than being dependent on others.

Anxiety accompanies learning. It is "the gap between the now and the later. Whenever you leave the sure basis of the now and become preoccupied with the future, you experience anxiety." [18] It is like stage fright, which, when the action begins, becomes the excitement that stimulates a good performance.

PROBLEMS IN DEVELOPMENT   The process of development, even in normal individuals, presents problems related to the expression of the hunger instinct. Instead of the process of assimilation proceeding smoothly, it is characterized by certain kinds of difficulty. There is a similarity of mental and physical functions. "Our attitude towards food has a tremendous influence upon intelligence, upon the ability to understand things, to get a grip on life and to put one's teeth into the tasks at hand. Anyone not using his teeth will cripple his ability to use his destructive functions for his own benefit." [19] Such people are excessively modest and lack backbone, but there is greed behind the apparent lack of interest in food. Another character type of a similar parasitic nature is the person who lives in permanent unconscious fear of starvation and seeks financial security in life.

Resistances related to oral development occur. One is the hunger strike, in the form of lack of appetite: "I just can't swallow a bite." Another is the inability to swallow unpalatable information. *Disgust*, the nonacceptance or emotional refusal of food, is a resistance. Disgust at an object is a reaction to it as if it were in the stomach.

"Retroflection means that some function which originally is directed from the individual towards the world, changes its direction and is bent back towards the orginator."[20] Narcissism is an example. Suicide, a substitute for murder, is another. Aggression and hatred are reversed and directed toward the self. Such behavior is a reaction against meeting hostility and frustration. Inhibiting or suppressing emotions and behavior is sometimes necessary, but it can become habitual. Neurotic repression may result. There is a resulting split in the personality between the self as doer and the self as receiver.

"Introjection means preserving the structure of things taken in, whilst the organism requires their destruction"[21] for assimilation to occur. The introject, not having been "chewed," but rather having been "gulped down," remains intact as a foreign body in the system. Introjection is the natural form of eating in the suckling stage. Its persistence relates to disturbances in the development of the biting and chewing stages. Oral aggression (biting) has been blocked, but food is forced into the child. The oral aggression becomes displaced, in part against other persons. Forced feeding also leads to disgust with food, which is repressed and the food swallowed whole or in chunks. In introjection the organism reacts to an object or situations, as it does to food, by "swallowing it whole," but then being unable to "stomach it."

Projection is placing in the outside world those parts of one's personality with which one refuses (or is unable) to identify oneself (or to express). "The projecting person cannot satisfactorily distinguish between the inside and outside world."[22] Feelings of guilt lead to the projection of blame onto someone or something else. Projections are usually onto the outside world, but can take place within the personality, for example, onto the conscience. Projection gives temporary relief, but prevents contact, identification, and responsibility.

Retroflection, introjection, and projection function "to interrupt mounting excitement of a kind and degree with which the person cannot cope. . . . These mechanisms constitute neurosis only when inappropriate and chronic. All of them are useful and healthy when employed temporarily in particular circumstances."[23]

Neurosis

Neurosis is an interruption or a stagnation of growth. The neurotic, instead of interacting with and assimilating his environment, reacts by manipulating it by playing certain roles.[24] The child manipulates the parents by playing roles such as crybaby, stupid, the good boy, the helpless dependent child, the bully. Energy is invested in the role playing instead of in growth and development. In accordance with the gestalt principle that the organism cannot concentrate on more than one thing at a time, this focus on playing a role prevents concentration on behavior that leads to growth and development. Neuroses are not always related to disturbances or fixations in the development of the sex instinct, as in psychoanalytic theory, but are also disturbances in the development and functioning of the hunger (oral) instinct.

In terms of the self-regulation principle, the neurotic's self-regulation is characterized by deliberateness rather than spontaneity. He is in a constant emergency state. The chronic emergency state disturbs the natural hierarchy of needs relevant to the actual situation. Thus, natural impulses are prevented from emerging into foreground or figure (or are repressed), and behavior is rigid and compulsive rather than flexible. The repetition compulsion of Freud is the presence of an unfinished situation seeking completion.

The neurotic is also caught in the conflict between the biological needs of man and the social (ethical and moralistic) demands made upon him by society. These demands may be against the biological laws of self-regulation. "Often enough, however, the socially required self-control can only be achieved at the cost of devitalizing and impairing the functions of large parts of the human personality—at the cost of creating collective and individual neurosis." [25]

Man develops devices to protect himself from conflict. Defensive dynamics and avoidance are individual devices. These devices impair the holistic function by limiting contact and thus restricting assimilation. The means of avoidance may be classified into joining (additive or plus) functions, disjoining (subtractive) functions, and changes or distortions. Among the first are overcompensation, obsessions, projections, hallucinations, complaints, and intellectualism. Examples of the second are scotoma, inhibition, repression, and flight. The third includes displacement, sublimation, neurotic symtoms, feelings of guilt and anxiety, projection, fixation, and retroflection. The use of these devices to avoid conflict with the environment not only inhibits contact with the environment and assimilation, but leads to the alienation of "those parts of the personality which would lead to conflicts with the environment. *The avoidance of external conflicts,* however, results in the creation of internal ones." [26] This is a manifestation of the alienation function of the ego.

Neurosis does not consist of the conflicts, either between the individual and the environment or within the individual, but in the way in which they are dealt with, which prevents integration and growth of the self.

Neurotic anxiety is the basic, common symptom of all neuroses. It is exemplified in anxiety attacks, and in cases where it may not be felt, it is manifested by excitement or restlessness and difficulty in breathing. The physiological concomitants of excitement are increased metabolism, increased heart activity, quickened pulse, and increased breathing. If the excitement is inhibited, or its expression suppressed by the restricting of breathing, the insufficiency of oxygen leads to difficulty in breathing. "In a state of anxiety an acute conflict takes place between the urge to breathe (to overcome the feeling of choking), and the opposing self-control. . . . *Anxiety equals excitement plus inadequate supply of oxygen.*" [27] The neurotic inhibits or suppresses excitement and suffers anxiety.

Guilt develops when, instead of contacts with others by means of interacting at the boundaries, there is a confluence between persons, "with no appreciation of a boundary between them," and "no discrimination of the points of difference or otherness that distinguishes them." [28] There is then no figure-ground, no awareness, and no contact. Confluence as a result of contact is healthy. It is unhealthy when it prevents contact. A healthy confluence can exist between persons who are close, as in marriage and old friendships. When a confluence is interrupted, guilt or resentment arises—guilt if one feels he is responsible for the interruption, resentment if he feels the other is responsible.[29] Guilt is also aroused when one feels unable to question what one is told he should believe, what he feels compelled to accept as what he ought to do, but is unable to assimilate and accept as his own. Guilt is thus projected resentment.[30]

Psychosis

Neurosis is a disturbance in the self function or the ego, while psychosis is a disturbance of the id functions.[31] In neurosis there is conflict within the self or between individual needs and social demands; in psychosis the individual is out of touch with reality. He is incapable of distinguishing fantasy from reality and thus hallucinates or is deluded. Little consideration is given to the nature of psychosis in the gestalt approach, except for paranoid conditions.

The manic-depressive cycle involves aggression. "In the manic period the unsublimated, but dentally inhibited aggression is not retroflected as in melancholia but is directed in all its greediness and with most violent outbursts against the world. A frequent symptom of cyclothymia is dipsomania which is on the one hand a sticking to the 'bottle' and on the other a means of self-destruction." [32]

In the paranoiac character "*repressed disgust plays an essential part.*" [33] In *paranoiac aggression* there is "an attempt to re-digest projections," which is experienced "not as dental aggression, as belonging to the alimentary sphere, but is directed as personal aggression against another person, or against a collection of individuals, acting as screens for the projections." [34] Introjection is a part of a *paranoiac pseudo-metabolism.*

"*The healthy character expresses* his emotions and ideas, the *paranoid character projects them.*" [35] "The paranoiac character exhibits what is called 'pseudo-metabolism.' " Material is introjected rather than assimilated, is felt as something strange to the self (as indeed it is), and then projected. The introjection represents the "swallowing" without tasting to avoid disgust. The material cannot be brought up to be rechewed because this would involve vomiting (disgust). It is therefore ejected (projected). The paranoiac thus treats as outside material, with attack and aggression, what is really a part of himself. Reintrojection may occur, and the total process repeat itself.

Every paranoid exhibits the megalomania-outcast, or the superiority-inferiority complex. "In the period of introjection—of identification with the faeces—the paranoid character feels himself as dirt; in times of projection—of alienation—he thinks himself superior and looks upon the world as dirt." [36] The obsessional neurosis has a psychotic or paranoid nucleus. The continual washing attempts to undo the feeling of being dirty.

THE THERAPY PROCESS

If pathology is the disturbance of the organismic balance, then "the object of every treatment, psychotherapeutic or otherwise, is to facilitate organismic balance, to reestablish optimal functions." [37] Persisting imbalance is characterized by avoidance of various kinds, including avoidance of emotions and excitement, often under the inhibiting influence of shame. Therapy thus must deal with these avoidances, bringing them to awareness. "*The awareness of, and the ability to endure, unwanted emotions are the conditio sine qua non for a successful cure.*"[38]

In terms of the relationship of the organism to its environment, the purpose of therapy is to reestablish contact and normal interaction, replacing abnormal retroflection, introjection, and projection by assimilation. "Only by re-establishing the destructive tendency towards food as well as towards anything that represents an obstacle to the individual's wholeness, by re-instating a successful aggression, the re-integration of an obsessional, and even of a paranoid, personality takes place." [39]

From the point of view of pathology as a disturbance in the ego function, then restoration of the integrative function of the ego is the object of therapy. "So what we are trying to do in therapy is step-by-step to re-own the disowned parts of the personality until the person becomes strong enough to facilitate his own growth. . . ." [40] The wholeness of the organism must be restored.

As neurosis is an arrest or stagnation of growth, so therapy fosters growth. The focus on organismic control makes it possible for the individual to actualize *himself* rather than attempting to actualize a self-*image*.

Basic to all these objectives is the attaining of awareness: "*awareness per se—by and of itself—can be curative.*" [41] The healthy person "is completely in touch with himself and with reality." [42] Awareness leads to organismic self-regulation, based upon "the wisdom of the organism" in contrast to "the whole pathology of self-manipulation, environmental control and so on, that interferes with this subtle organismic control." [43] When awareness is present, "the organism can work on the healthy gestalt principle: that the most important unfinished situation will always emerge and can be dealt with." [44] This occurs in therapy, so that the therapist doesn't have to dig, since unfinished situations will come to the surface.

Therapy, like living, is in the here and now. "Nothing exists except in the here and now." [45] The past exists only as it is represented in present memory, and the future exists only in present expectation and anticipation. The past affects us and persists as unfinished situations.

IMPLEMENTATION AND TECHNIQUES

There is no systematic presentation of the methods and techniques of gestalt therapy. Specific exercises are presented in *Ego, Hunger and Aggression,*[46] and more systematically in *Gestalt Therapy.*[47] But since neurosis is a symptom of growth stagnation, the remedy is not therapy, but a method of reinstating growth. This is what the exercises accomplish. The object is to discover the self, and this is achieved not through introspection but through action.

Even the average person is lacking in awareness. The first half of *Gestalt Therapy* consists of exercises in developing awareness of the person's functioning as an organism and as a person. The first set of exercises is for everyone and is directed toward (1) contacting the environment through becoming aware of present feelings, sensing opposed forces, attending and concentrating, and differentiating and unifying, (2) developing awareness of self through remembering, sharpening the body sense, experiencing the continuity of emotion, listening to one's verbalizing, and integrating awareness, and (3) directing awareness by converting confluence into contact, and changing anxiety into excitement. Another set of exercises deals with processes that are chronic in organismic malfunctioning and is directed toward changing malfunctioning processes through (1) retroflection, by investigating misdirected behavior, mobilizing the muscles, and executing the re-reversed act, (2) introjection, by introjecting and eating, and dislodging and digesting introjects, and (3) projection, by discovering projections and assimilating projections. These exercises are aspects of therapy.

Here and Now

It is not a function of gestalt therapy to recover the past through remembering. The past influences behavior only as it is represented in the present. "*There is no other reality than the present.* . . . Here the only existing reality is the analytical interview. Whatever we experience there, we experience in the present. This must be the basis for every attempt at 'organismic reorganization.' When we remember, we remember at that very second and to certain purposes; when we think of the future we anticipate things to come, but we do so at the present moment and from various causes. Predilection for either historical or futuristic thinking always destroys contact with reality." [48] Much time can be wasted in digging up the past with a patient, since this is collaborating with the patient's resistance.

This does not mean that the recovery of childhood memories is not important. But it is not the content, but the impulse, feeling, or attitude representing the unfinished situation that is important. These "childish" impulses are not only usually safe to express and satisfy—in a different way than in childhood—but the feelings and attitudes of spontaneity, imagination, directness of awareness and manipulation are desirable in adult life.

The here-and-now orientation is fostered by the therapist's comments and questions. The therapist never asks "Why?" but only "How?" or "What?"—for example, "What is your right hand doing now?" or "How does your voice sound now?"

Frustrating the Patient

"The neurotic is a person who does not see the obvious." [49] He is phobic, full of avoidances, or resistance to awareness. "In contrast to Freud who placed the greatest emphasis on resistances, I have placed the greatest emphasis on the *phobic attitude, avoidance, flight from.*" [50] The neurotic is at an impasse and doesn't want to go through it. "Very few people go into therapy to be cured, but rather to improve their neurosis." [51]

The therapist must get the patient through his impasse, so that he can grow and develop his own potential. This is accomplished through providing situations in which the patient can experience the impasse, and then frustrating the patient. "This is what we are again and again trying to do, to frustrate the person until he is face to face with his blocks, with his inhibitions, with his way of avoiding having eyes, having ears, having muscles, having authority, having security in himself. . . . We apply enough skillful frustration so that the patient is forced to find his own way, discover his own possibilities, his own potential, and discover that *what he expects from the therapist, he can do just as well himself.*" [52] Frustration leads to the discovery that the impasse doesn't exist in reality, but in fantasy; the patient only believes that his resources are not at his disposal, and prevents himself from using them because of his fears and catastrophic expectations. Neurotic anxiety becomes positive excitement when the underlying basis is faced and overcome, since neurotic anxiety is blocking excitement.

Frustrating the patient is not the same as "attacking" or hammering at resistances. "By realizing the resistances experimentally [experientially, through exercises] and letting them [the resistances] act and come to grips with what is being resisted in himself or in the therapy, there is a possibility for resolution rather than annihilation." [53] To attack resistances directly leads to their repression.

Concentration and Awareness

In contrast to the free-association method of psychoanalysis, gestalt therapy emphasizes concentration. The aim is to bring to awareness the conflict between impulses and resistances. Thus, the patient is asked to concentrate on resistances, not to free associate. Free association leads to avoidance, a flight of ideas—to "dissocia-tion." The function of the exercises is not to serve as tasks to be performed but as a means of becoming aware of interferences and resistances.

Concentration involves focusing on the figure, rather than the ground. Since unfinished situations (or problems) will emerge and become figure, in therapy "we don't have to dig. It is all there." [54] Thus, gestalt therapy is not concerned with the "unconscious," but with the obvious, the surface. "In Gestalt Therapy we start with *what* is, and see which context, which situation is there to be found and relate the figure, the foreground experience to the background, to the content, to the perspective, to the situation, and together they form the gestalt. Meaning is the relationship of the foreground figure to its background." [55]

Integration

Dissolution of resistances is not enough, and may be dangerous, since patients may have few if any other ego functions than resistance. "If one deprives them of these resisting and domineering functions, there is nothing left. . . . They have never learned how to enjoy them-selves, how to be aggressive, or how to love, and while their resistances are being analysed, they become completely confused. . . . Moreover, the resisting energies of such people are very valuable, and if they have good domineering and resisting qualities, they will find ample oppor-tunity of using them beneficially." [56] It is necessary to integrate these qualities into the total personality.

In gestalt therapy the focus is integrating rather than, as in psy-choanalysis, analyzing. Those things that are projected, and resisted, must be reowned, reassimilated. "Everything the person disowns can be recovered, and the means of this recovery is understanding, play-ing, becoming these disowned parts. And by letting him play and discover that he already has all this (which he thinks only others can give him) we increase his potential. . . . So what we are trying to do in therapy is step-by-step to *re-own* the disowned parts of the personal-ity until the person becomes strong enough to facilitate his own growth." [57]

The achievement of integration can be fostered by dealing with any of the parts of the total person—his body, emotion, thinking, speech—and his physical and social environment, since all are related and exist in a functional unity. However, if any one is dealt with exclusively, "the effects will not spread sufficiently to those areas which the particular method neglects. If any partial approach is pursued, in isolation from the others, the unaware resistances in other components of the functioning will increase to such a degree as either to make further progress in the selected approach impossible unless or until other kinds of material are admitted, or else to achieve a 'cure' in terms of a new, arbitrary pattern." [58]

The basic rule of psychoanalysis, that the patient should say everything that comes to his mind, is broadened. In addition to expressing his thoughts and emotions, he is expected to express everything he feels in his body, including not only major physical symptoms, but the unobtrusive sensations. Also, since when the patient forces himself to say everything, he suppresses his embarrassment by "either wording the embarrassing material in a non-committal manner, or [by] bracing himself and deadening his emotions. . . . we have to impress upon the patient that he must neither suppress nor force anything, and that he must not forget to convey to the analyst every bit of conscious resistance such as embarrassment, shame, etc." [59] Shame and embarrassment "are the primary tools of repressions. . . . Endurance of embarrassment brings the repressed material to the surface . . . and helps the patient to accept previously refused material via the amazingly relieving discovery that the fact behind the embarrassment may not be so incriminating after all, and may even be accepted with interest by the analyst. . . . *The awareness of, and the ability to endure, unwanted emotions are the sine qua non for a successful cure;* these emotions will be discharged once they have become Ego-functions. This process, and not the process of remembering, forms the *via regia* to health." [60]

Thus, therapy is not a pleasant or an easy experience for the patient. The facing and dealing with avoidances is not painless. As a result, most of those who begin therapy do not continue or complete it. The patient who persists, however, "learns that the hard work is not mere drudgery. However far removed it may at first seem from what he thinks is urgent and therefore the place to start, he gradually gains orientation and perspective. He comes to see particular symptoms as merely surface manifestations of a more general and complicated system of malfunctioning which underlies and supports them. Though now, in a way, the job looks bigger and will obviously take longer than originally supposed, it does begin to make sense." [61]

The therapist is more considerate than relatives or friends in leading the patient to face what he wishes to avoid. Nevertheless, the patient, usually following a "honeymoon" period at the beginning of therapy, becomes critical of therapy and the therapist or enters what the Freudians call a "negative transference" period. If the patient can openly express and discuss this resentment, therapy continues and is accelerated; if he can't or doesn't, it slows down and is likely to be terminated by the patient.

The development of awareness is directed toward repression. However, unlike psychoanalysis, which focuses on recovering what is repressed, gestalt therapy emphasizes awareness of the existence of repression or avoidance, and how it is being done. The blocked impulse will come out by itself. In retroflection the impulse whose expression is being directed against the self, instead of toward the environment, is expressed toward its natural object in the environment. This is not easy or rapid. There is a long process of first becoming aware of the retroflection, the repression, the impulse repressed, its acceptance, its redirection, possibly after modification, and its appropriate expression. The reintegration of dissociated parts is painful; "it always involves conflict, destroying and suffering." [62]

In contrast to the treatment of retroflection, which involves the acceptance and integration of dissociated parts of the self, the treatment of introjection involves becoming "aware of what is not truly yours, to acquire a selective and critical attitude towards what is offered you, and, above all, to develop the ability to 'bite off' and 'chew' experience so as to extract its healthy nourishment." [63]

The chronic drinker, or alcoholic, is anchored in the suckling stage. He wants to drink in his environment, to enter into confluence with others without real contact. He accepts social reproaches uncritically as coming from himself. He may then silence his self-aggressive conscience in alcohol, but afterward its vindictiveness is redoubled. "Since his aggression is not used in attacking his food or his problems, the surplus which is not invested in his conscience often turns outward in surly, irrelevant fights." [64] The sexually promiscuous person is also an introjector seeking immediate sexual satisfaction without the development of a relationship through real contact. Introjection leads to the formation of an ego that is a collection of unassimilated traits and qualities taken over from authorities without understanding. Becoming aware of eating habits of gulping, swallowing whole, greed, and disgust is the first step. The next step is to remobilize or reinstate the experience of disgust in eating by chewing a bite of food until it is fully liquefied; then a bit of reading matter, a difficult sentence is thoroughly analyzed and "chewed up." In therapy, that which has been swallowed whole must be brought back up to be rejected, or chewed, so it can be assimilated. Catharsis is not enough; the patient must learn not to introject. The "working through" of psychoanalysis does this, but only with limited aspects of behavior.

If projections are to be dealt with, they must be discovered or recognized. Projections are encouraged by our language, which attributes our behavior to external causes. The process of alienation must be reversed by changing our language and thinking from "it" (or id) language to the responsible "I." "The aim is to come to realize again that you are creative in your environment and are responsible for your reality—not to blame, but responsible in the sense that it is you who lets it stand or changes it." [65] Once projections are recognized, they must be accepted as aspects of oneself, and assimilated or modified.

The Use of Dreams in Therapy

Freud called the dream the royal road to the unconscious. Perls states that it is the royal road to integration. Whereas the psychoanalyst works with associations to the individual elements of the dream, and interprets it, the gestalt therapist attempts to have the patient relive the dream in the present, in the therapy situation, including acting it out. Interpretation is avoided, as leading only to intellectual insight. The interpretation is left to the patient. "The more you refrain from interfering and telling the patient what he is like or what he feels like, the more chance you give him to discover himself and not to be misled by your concepts and projections." [66]

The dream represents or contains, in some form, an unfinished, unassimilated situation. "The dream is an existential message. It is more than an unfinished situation; it is more than an unfulfilled wish, it is more than a prophecy. It is a message of yourself to yourself, to whatever part of you is listening. The dream is possibly the most spontaneous expression of the human being." [67] The different parts are projections of the self, of different and conflicting sides. In principle, the dream contains all that is essential for the cure, if all its parts are understood and assimilated. "Everything is there. . . . We find all we need in the dream. . . . Understanding the dream means realizing when you are avoiding the obvious." [68] The forms change, but everything is in every dream. "A dream is a condensed reflection of our existence." [69]

Dreams reveal missing personality parts and the methods of avoidance used by the patient. Patients who don't remember dreams —everyone dreams—are refusing to face what is wrong with their existence; they "*think* that they have come to terms with life." [70] Such patients are asked to talk to the missing dreams—"Dreams, where are you?"

In dreamwork the patient is asked to play the part of the various persons and objects. In doing so, the patient identifies with the alienated parts of himself and integrates them. Difficulty in, or resistance to, playing the alienated parts indicates that the patient does not want to reown or take back rejected parts of himself. The use of the empty-chair technique in which the patient changes his seat as he interacts with a dream person or object, or a part of himself, facilitates the process.

RULES AND GAMES The rules and games of gestalt therapy have been collected by Levitsky and Perls and are summarized here.[71]

The rules include the *principle of the now* (using the present tense), the *I and thou* (addressing the other person directly rather than talking about him to the therapist), *using "I" language* (substituting "I" for "it" in talking about the body and its acts and behaviors, the *use of the awareness continuum* (focusing on the *how* and *what* of experience rather than the *why*), *no gossiping* (addressing the person directly when he is present rather than making statements about him), and *asking the patient to convert questions into statements.*

The games are defined briefly as follows:

1 *Games of dialogue* The patient takes the parts of aspects of the split personality and carries on a dialogue between them. These parts include the top dog (superego or shoulds) versus the underdog (passive resistant), aggressive versus passive, nice guy versus scoundrel, masculine versus feminine, etc.

2 *Making the rounds* Extending a general statement or theme (for example, "I can't stand anyone in this room") to each person individually, with additions pertinent to each.

3 *"I take responsibility"* The patient is asked to follow each statement about himself or his feelings with ". . . and I take responsibility for it."

4 *"I have a secret"* Each person thinks of a personal secret involving guilt or shame and, without sharing it, imagines how he feels others would react to it.

5 *Playing the projection* When a patient expresses a perception that is a projection, he is asked to play the role of the person involved in the projection to discover his conflict in this area.

6 *Reversals* The patient is asked to play a role opposite to his overt or expressed behavior (for example, to be aggressive rather than passive), to recognize and make contact with the submerged or latent aspect of himself.

7 *The rhythm of contact and withdrawal* The natural inclination toward withdrawal is recognized and accepted, and the patient is permitted to experience the security of withdrawing temporarily.

8 *Rehearsal* Since much of thinking is rehearsal to prepare for playing a social role, group members share rehearsals with each other.

9 *Exaggeration* or the repetition game. When the patient makes an important statement in a casual way, indicating that he doesn't recognize its importance, he is required to repeat it again and again with increasing loudness and emphasis.

10 *"May I feed you a sentence?"* The therapist suggests a sentence for the patient to repeat, which he feels represents something significant to the patient, trying it on for size. This often involves interpretation.

EXAMPLES

These examples are from workshops, which were Perls' major activity in therapy. These workshops were not therapy groups; rather participants volunteered to "work with" Perls on an individual basis, and the group was not involved except that when a volunteer came to a therapeutic realization, he was sometimes asked to express it in interaction with other participants, in the procedure, or game, called making the rounds.

Linda

LINDA I dreamed that I watch . . . a lake . . . drying up, and there is a small island in the middle of the lake, and a circle of . . . porpoises—they're like porpoises except that they can stand up, so they're like porpoises that are like people, and they're in a circle, sort of like a religious ceremony, and it's very sad—I feel very sad because they can breathe, they are sort of dancing around the circle, but the water, their element, is drying up. So it's like a dying—like watching a race of people, or a race of creatures, dying. And they are mostly females, but a few of them have a small male organ, so there are a few males there, but they won't live long enough to reproduce, and their element is drying up. And there is one that is sitting over here near me and I'm talking to this porpoise and he has prickles on his tummy, sort of like a porcupine, and they don't seem to be a part of him. And I think that there's one good point about the water drying up, I think—well, at least at the bottom, when all the water dries up, there will probably be some sort of treasure there, because at the bottom of the lake there should be things that have fallen in, like coins or something, but I look carefully and all that I can find is an old license plate. . . . That's the dream.

FRITZ Will you please play the license plate?

L I am an old license plate, thrown in the bottom of a lake. I have no use because I'm no value—although I'm not rusted—I'm outdated, so I can't be used as a license plate . . . and I'm just thrown on the rubbish heap. That's what I did with a license plate, I threw it on a rubbish heap.

F Well, how do you feel about this?

L (quietly) I don't like it. I don't like being a license plate—useless.

F Could you talk about this? That was such a long dream until you come to find a license plate; I'm sure this must be of great importance.

L (sighs) Useless. Outdated . . . The use of a license plate is to allow—give a car permission to go . . . and I can't give anyone permission to do anything because I'm outdated . . . In California, they just paste a little—you buy a sticker—and stick it on the car, on the old license plate. (faint attempt at humor) So maybe someone could put me on their car and stick this sticker on me, I don't know. . .

F Okeh, now play the lake.

L I'm a lake . . . I'm drying up, and disappearing, soaking into the earth . . . (with a touch of surprise) *dying* . . . But when I soak into the earth, I become a part of the earth—so maybe I water the surrounding area, so . . . even in the lake, even in my bed, flowers can grow (sighs). New life can grow . . . from me (cries) . . .

F You get the existential message?

L Yes. (sadly, but with conviction) I can paint—I can create—I can create beauty. I can no longer reproduce, I'm like the porpoise . . . but I . . . I'm . . . I . . . keep wanting to say I'm food . . . I . . . as water becomes . . . I water the earth, and give life—growing things, the water—they need both the earth and water, and the . . . and the air and the sun, but as the water from the lake, I can play a part in something, and producing—feeding.

F   You see the contrast: On the surface, you find something, some artifact—the license plate, the artificial you—but then when you go deeper, you find the apparent death of the lake is actually fertility. . .

L   And I don't need a license plate, or a permission, a license in order to . . .

F   (gently) Nature doesn't need a license plate to grow. You don't have to be useless, if you are organismically creative, which means if you are involved.

L   And I don't need permission to be creative . . . Thank you.[72]

Jean

JEAN   It's a long time ago I dreamed this. I'm not sure how it started. I think it first started in the—sort of like the New York subway, and kind of paying—putting a token in, and going to the turnstile, and walking a little way down the corridors, and then kind of turning a corner and I realize that some way or other in here, uh . . . instead of being a subway, it seemed like there were sort of like inclines that started going down into the earth. And it seemed to turn and I realized what was going on, and some way or another just about this point as I discovered this incline, my mother was with me, or maybe she was when I started—I can't remember.

At any rate, it was this incline—it was sort of muddy, sort of slippery, and I thought, Oh! we can go down this! and well, sort of on the side, I picked up a left-over carton—or maybe it was just flattened out or I flattened it out. At any rate, I said, "Let's sit down on this." I sat down on the edge, kind of made a toboggan out of it and I said, "Mom, you sit down behind me," and we started going down. And it sort of went around and around (quickly) and there were other people it seemed like, waiting in line, but then they kind of disappeared, and we were (happily) just going down and around and it just kept on going down and down and down, and I was sort of realizing that I was going down kind of into the bowels of the earth.

And every once in a while I'd turn around and say, "Isn't this fun?"—it seems, although maybe I'll discover I didn't have that attitude either. But it seemed like fun. And yet I wondered what would be down at the bottom of this—going, turn and turn, and then finally it leveled out and we got up and I was just astounded, because here I thought, "Oh my God, the bowels of the earth!" And yet, instead of being dark, it was like there was sunlight coming from somewhere, and a beautiful . . . oh, kind of like a . . . I've never been to Florida, but seemed like a Florida kind of everglades, with lagoons, and tall reeds, and beautiful long-legged birds—herons—and things like that. And I don't remember saying anything particularly, except maybe something like, "Who would ever have expected this!"—or something.

FRITZ   Yes. Now, when the dreamer tells a story like this, you can take it just as an incident or unfinished situation, or wish fulfillment, but if we tell it in the present, as mirroring our existence, it immediately gets a different aspect. It's not just an occasional happening. You see, a dream is a condensed reflection of our existence. What we don't realize enough is that we devote our lives to a dream: a dream of glory, usefulness, do-gooder, gangster, or whatever we dream of. And in many people's lives, through self-frustration, our dream turns into a nightmare. The task of all deep religions—especially Zen Buddhism —or of really good therapy, is the *satori*, the great awakening, the coming to one's senses, waking up from one's dream—especially from one's nightmare. We can start already on this by realizing that we are playing roles in the theater of life, by understanding that we are always in a trance. We decide "This is an enemy," "This is a friend," and we play all these games until we come to our *senses*.

When we come to our senses, we start to *see*, to *feel*, to *experience* our needs and satisfactions, instead of playing roles and needing such a lot of props for that—houses, motor cars, dozens and dozens of costumes, though, when it comes to it, a woman never has anything to wear, so she needs still another costume. Or the man has to get a new costume when he goes to work and when he goes to see his sweetheart—all the millions of unnecessary ballast with which we burden ourselves, not realizing that all property is given to us only for the duration anyhow. You can't take it with you, and if we have money, then we have additional worry what to do with the money. You shouldn't lose it, or should increase it, and so on and so on—all these dreams, all these nightmares, which are so typical of our civilization. Now the idea of *waking up* and becoming real means to exist with what we have, the real full potential, a rich life, deep experiences, joy, anger—being *real* not *zombies!* This is the meaning of real therapy, the real maturation, the real waking up, instead of this continual self-deception and fantasizing impossible goals, feeling sorry for ourselves because we can't play that part we want to play, and so on.

So, let's switch back to Jean. Jean, would you talk again, tell again the dream, live it through as if this was your existence, as if you live it now, see if you can understand more about your life. . . .

J   I don't—it doesn't really seem clear until I find myself—the place has become kind of a top of the chute. I don't remember whether at first I was afraid or not, possibly—oh, I should say this is now?

F   You are now on the chute. Are you afraid to go down?

J   (laughs) I guess I am a little afraid to go down. But then it seems like. . .

F   So the existential message is, "You've got to go down."

J   I guess I'm afraid to find out what's there.

F   This points to false ambitions, that you're too high up.

J   That's true.

F   So the existential message says, "Go down." Again our mentality says, "High up is better than down." You must always be somewhere higher.

J   Anyway, I seem a little afraid to go down.

F   Talk to the chute.

J   Why are you muddy? You're slippery and slidy and I might fall on you and slip.

F   Now play the chute. "I'm slippery and . . ."

J   I'm slippery and muddy, the better to slide and faster to get down on. (laughs)

F   Ahah, well, what's the joke?

J   (continues laughing) I'm just laughing.

F   Can you accept yourself as slippery?

J   Hm. I guess so. Yes. I can never seem to. . . . Yeah, you know, always just when I think I'm about to, you know, say, "Aha! I've caught you now!" it slips away—you know, rationalization. I'm slippery and slidy. Hm. Anyway, I'm going to go down because it looks like it would be fun, and I want to find out where this goes and what's going to be at the end of it. And it seems, perhaps only now, I'm turning around and looking to see what I could use to kind of protect my clothes (laughs) or maybe make a better slide. I discover the cardboard—

F   Can you play this cardboard? If you were this cardboard. . . . what's your function?

J   I'm just—to make things easier. I'm just kind of lying around and left-over, and aha, I have a use for it.

F   Oh—you can be useful.

J   I can be useful. I'm not just left-over and lying around, and we can make it easier to get down.

F   Is it important for you to be useful?

J   (quietly) Yes. I want to be an advantage to somebody . . . Is that enough for being the cardboard? . . . Maybe I also want to be sat upon. (laughter) [F: Oh!] What is that part in the book about who wants to kick who? I want to be pitied, I want to be scrunched down. [F: Say this again.]

    (laughing) I want to be sat upon and scrunched down.

F   Say this to the group.

J   Well, that's hard to do. (loudly) I want to be sat upon and scrunched down . . . Hm. (loudly) I want to be *sat upon* and *scrunched down*. (pounds her thigh with fist)

F   Who are you hitting? [J: Me.] Besides you?

F   I think my mother, who's turning, who's behind me and I look around and see her.

F   Good. Now hit her.

J   (loudly) Mother, I'm scrunching down upon—(hits thigh) ouch! —you (laughs) and I am going to take *you* for a ride (laughter) instead of your telling me to go, and taking *me* wherever *you* want to, *I'm* taking *you* along for a ride with *me*.

F   Did you notice anything in your behavior with your mother?

J   Just now? (laughs)

F   I had the impression it was too *much* to be convincing . . . It was spoken with anger, not with firmness.

J   Mmm. I think I'm still a little afraid of her.

F   That's it. You tell her that.

J   Mom, I'm still afraid of you . . . but I'm gonna take you for a ride anyway.

F   Okeh. Let's put momma on the sled. (laughter)

J   (laughs) You sit behind me. You have to sit behind this time . . .
Are you ready? O.K.

F   You're taking the lead.

J   I'm in the lead. I'm in control. (laughs)

F   You are the driver.

J   (sadly) The only driving I'm doing is with, you know—down. (sighs)

F   Do you ride a bobsled?

J   I've never ridden a bobsled . . . but I've skied. O.K., here we go.
I don't know where we're going—at this point. We're just going off
because it's some place to go and we're there.

F   Well, you said that this is a journey into the bowels of the earth.

J   Yes. But I'm not really sure of that now, I think. I don't really—it
doesn't really dawn on me until I realize just how far we keep going.

F   So, start out.

J   We're going down now. We're sliding down, and then we come to
a turn, and now we go round . . . around . . . around . . . and I see
if she's still there. (laughs) She's still there.

F   Always make it an encounter. This is the *most* important thing, to
change everything into an encounter, instead of gossiping *about*. Talk
to her. If you don't talk *to* someone, you are giving a performance.

J   Are you still there?

F   What does she answer?

J   Yes. I'm still here, but it's kind of scary.
      Don't worry. I've got it all taken care of. (decisively) We're having
fun. I don't know where this is going, but we're going to find out.
I'm scared!
      I think I—don't be scared. It's going down and down and DOWN
and DOWN. . . . (softly) I wonder what's going to be down there.
It'll just be black . . . I don't know what she says.

F   What's your left hand doing?

J   Right this instant?

F   Yah. *Always* right this instant.

J   Holding my head. I'm,—

F   As if? . . .

J   Not to see?

F   Ahah. You don't want to see where you are going, don't want to
see the danger.

J   Umhmm. (softly) I'm really afraid—of what will be down there . . .
It could be terrible or just blackness or just maybe even oblivion.

F   I would like you to go now into this blackness. This is nothingness,
the blankness, the sterile void. What does it feel like to be in this
nothingness?

J   Suddenly, nothingness is I'm going down, now . . . So I still have
a feeling that I'm going down, and so it's kind of exciting and exhilarating . . . because I'm moving, and I'm very much alive . . . I'm not
really afraid. It's more—kind of terribly exciting and . . . the anticipation—what I will discover at the end of this. It's not really black—it's

sort of going down, somehow there's some light, where it's from, I don't. . . .

F   Yah. I want to make a little bit of a shortcut here, to say something. Are you aware of what you are avoiding in this dream?

J   Am I aware of what I am avoiding? . . .

F   Having legs.

J   Having legs?

F   Yah.

J   Legs to carry me some place.

F   Yah. Instead of standing on your legs, you rely on the support of the cardboard, and you rely on gravitation to carry you.

J   Passively . . . passively through the tunnel—through life.

F   What's your objection to having legs?

J   The first thing that comes into my head is that somebody—the first thing was that somebody might knock me down, then I realized that I was afraid my mother would knock me down. She doesn't want me to have legs.

F   Now, have another encounter with her. Is it true she doesn't want you to stand on your own legs—on your own feet?

J   (complaining) Why don't you want me to stand on my own legs? 'Cause you're helpless. You need me.
     I don't need you. I can go through life all by myself . . . I can! She must have said, "You can't."

F   There you notice the same anger [J: Yeah, I did.] and lack of firmness, lack of support.

J   Yeah.

F   You see this is very peculiar how we are built. The lower carriage is for support and the upper carriage is for contact, but without firm support and good support, of course, the contact is wobbly too.

J   I shouldn't be angry.

F   I didn't say you shouldn't be angry, but the anger is still [J: It's too wobbly.] too wobbly, yah.

J   I'm afraid to stand on my own two legs and be angry . . . at her.

F   And *face* her, really. Stand on your legs now, and encounter your mother, and see whether you can talk to her.

J   (softly) I'm afraid to look at her.

F   Say this to her.

J   (loudly) I'm afraid to look at you, mother! (exhales)

F   What would you see?

J   What do I see? I see I hate her. (loudly) I hate you for holding me back every time I wanted to even go across the aisle of the damn department store.
     (high-pitched) Come back here! Don't go on the other side of the aisle.
     I can't even walk across the damned aisle. Can't go to Flushing when I want to go on the bus. Can't go to New York—not until I go to college. Damn you! . . .

F   How old are you when you play this now?

J   Well, I'm . . . in the department store, I'm only anywhere from six to ten or twelve. . . .

F   How old are you really?

J   Really? Thirty-one. [F   Thirty-one.] She's even dead.

F   Okeh, can you talk as a thirty-one-year-old to your mother? Can you be your age?

J   (quietly and firmly) Mother, I am thirty-one years old. I'm quite capable of walking on my own.

F   Notice the difference. Much less noise, and much more substance.

J   I can stand on my own legs. I can do anything I want to do, and I can know what I want to do. I don't need you. In fact, you're not even here if I *did* need you. So why do you hang around?

F   Yah. Can you say goodbye to her? Can you bury her?

J   Well, I can now, because I'm at the bottom of the slope, and when I come to the bottom I stand up. I stand up and I walk around and it's a beautiful place.

F   Can you say to your mother, "Goodbye Mother, rest in peace"?

J   I think I did tell her . . . Goodbye, Mother. (like a cry) Goodbye! . . .

F   (gently) Talk to her. Go to her grave and talk to her about it.

J   (crying) Goodbye, Mom. You couldn't help what you did. It wasn't your fault that you had three boys first, and then you thought it would be another boy and you didn't want me and you felt so bad after you found out I was a girl. (still crying) You just tried to make it up to me that's all. You didn't have to smother me . . . I forgive you, Mom . . . You worked awful hard. I can go, now . . . Sure, I can go.

F   You are still holding your breath, Jean . . .

J   (to herself) Are you really sure, Jean? . . . (softly) Momma, let me go.

F   What would she say?

J   I can't let you go.

F   Now *you* say this to your mother.

J   I can't let you go?

F   Yah. You keep her. You're holding on to her.

J   Mom, I can't let you go. I need you. Mom, I don't need you.

F   But you still miss her . . . don't you?

J   (very softly) A little. Just somebody there . . . what if nobody was there? . . . what if it was all empty, and dark. It's not all empty and dark—it's beautiful . . . I'll let you go . . . (sighs, almost inaudible) I'll let you go, Mom . . .

F   I'm very glad that we have this last experience—we can learn such a lot from this. You notice this was no play-acting. This was no crying for sympathy, it was no crying to get control, this was one of the four explosions I mentioned—the ability to explode into grief—and this mourning labor, as Freud called it, is necessary to grow up, to say goodbye to the image of the child. This is very essential. Very few people can really visualize, conceive themselves as adults. They always still have to have a mother or father image around. This is where Freud went completely astray. One of the few things where he was *completely* wrong. He thought a person does not mature *because* he has childhood traumata. It is the other way around. A person doesn't want to take the responsibility of the adult person, and thereby rationalizes, hangs on to the childhood memories, to the image that they are a child, and so on. Because to grow up means to be *alone,* and to be alone is the prerequisite for maturity and contact. Loneliness, isolation, is still longing for support. Jean has made a big step toward growing, to-night.[73]

Jane

JANE   The dream I started on, the last time I worked, I never finished it, and I think the last part is as important as the first part. Where I left off, I was in the Tunnel of Love—

FRITZ   What are you picking on? (Jane has been scratching her leg)

J   Hmmm. (clears throat) . . . I'm just sitting here, for a minute, so I can really be here. It's hard to stay with this feeling, and talk at the same time . . . Now I'm in the intermediate zone, and I'm—I'm think-ing about two things: Should I work on the dream, or should I work on the picking thing, because that's something that I do a lot. I pick my face, and . . . I'll go back to the dream. I'm in the Tunnel of Love, and my brother's gone in the—somewhere—and to the left of me, there's a big room and it's painted the color of—the color that my schoolrooms used to be painted, kind of a drab green, and to the left of me there are bleachers. I look over and there are all people sitting there. It looks as though they are waiting to get on the ride. There's a big crowd around one person, Raymond. (fiancé) He's talking to them and he's explaining something to them and they're all listening to him. And he's moving his finger like this, and making gestures. I'm surprised to see him. I go up to him, and it's very obvious that he doesn't want to talk to me. He's interested in being with all these people, entertaining all these people. So I tell him that I'll wait for him. I sit three bleachers up and look down, and watch this going on. I get irritated and I'm—pissed off, so I say, "Raymond, I'm leaving. I'm not gonna wait for you any more." I walk outside the door—I stand outside the door for awhile—I get anxious. I can feel anxious in my dream. I feel anxious now, because I don't really want to be out here. I want to be inside, with Raymond. So I'm going inside. I go back through the door—

F   Are you telling us a dream, or are you doing a job?

J   Am I telling a dream—

F   Or are you doing a job?

J   I'm telling a dream, but it's still—I'm not telling a dream.

F   Hm. Definitely not.

J   I'm doing a job.

F   I gave you only the two alternatives.

J   I can't say that I'm really aware of what I'm doing. Except physically. I'm aware of what's happening physically to me but—I don't really know what I'm doing. I'm not asking you to tell me what I'm doing . . . Just saying I don't know.

F   I noticed one thing: When you come up to the hot seat, you stop playing the silly goose.

J   Hm. I get frightened when I'm up here.

F   You get dead.

J   Whew . . . If I close my eyes and go into my body, I know I'm not dead. If I open my eyes and "do that job," then I'm dead . . . I'm in the intermediate zone now, I'm wondering whether or not I'm dead. I notice that my legs are cold and my feet are cold. My hands are cold. I feel—I feel strange . . . I'm in the middle, now. I'm—I'm neither with my body nor with the group. I notice that my attention is concentrated on that little matchbook on the floor.

F   Okeh. Have an encounter with the matchbox.

J   Right now, I'm taking a break from looking at you, 'cause it's—it's a—'cause I don't know what's going on, and I don't know what I'm doing. I don't even know if I'm telling the truth.

F   What does the matchbook answer?

J   I don't care if you tell the truth or not. It doesn't matter to me. I'm just a matchbox.

F   Let's try this for size. Tell us, "I'm just a matchbox."

J   I'm just a matchbox. And I feel silly saying that. I feel, kind of dumb, being a matchbox.

F   Uhhm.

J   A little bit useful, but not very useful. There's a million like me. And you can look at me, and you can like me, and then when I'm all used up, you can throw me away. I never liked being a matchbox . . . I don't—I don't know if that's the truth, when I say I don't know what I'm doing. I know there's one part of me that knows what I'm doing. And I feel suspended, I feel—steady. I don't feel relaxed. Now I'm trying to understand why in the two seconds it takes me to move from the group to the hot seat, my whole—my whole *person* changes . . . Maybe because of—I want to talk to the Jane in *that* chair.

She would be saying, (with authority) well, *you* know where you're at. You're playing dumb. You're playing stupid. You're doing this, and you're doing that, and you're sucking people in, and you're—(louder) not telling the truth! and you're stuck, and you're dead . . .

And when I'm *here,* I immediately—the Jane here would say, (small, quavery voice) well, that's—I feel on the defensive in this chair right now. I feel defensive. I feel like for some reason I have to defend myself. And I know it's not true. So who's picking on you? It's *that* Jane over there that's picking on me.

F   Yah.

J   She's saying . . . She's saying, (briskly) now when you get in the chair, you have to be in the here and now, you have to do it *right,* you have to be turned on, you have to know everything—

F   "You have to do your job."

J   You have to do your job, and you have to do it *right.* And you have to—become totally self-actualized, and you have to get rid of all your hangups, and along with that—it's not—it's not mandatory that you do this, but it's nice if you can be entertaining along the way, while you're doing all that. Try to spice it up a little bit, so that people won't get bored and go to sleep, because that makes you anxious. And you have to *know* why you're in the chair. You can't just go there and not know why you're there. You have to know *everything,* Jane.

You really make it hard for me. You really make it hard. You're really putting a lot of demands on me . . . I don't know everything. And that's hard to say. I don't know everything, and on top of that, I don't know what I'm doing half the time . . . I don't know—I don't know if that's the truth or not. I don't even know if that's a lie.

F   So be your topdog again.

J   Is that—

F   Your topdog. That's the famous topdog. The righteous topdog. This is where your power is.

J   Yeah. Well—uh—I'm your topdog. You can't live without me. I'm the one that—I keep you noticed, Jane. I keep you noticed. If it weren't for me, nobody would notice you. So you'd better be a little more grateful that I exist.

Well, I don't want to be noticed, *you* do. You want to be noticed. I don't want to be noticed. I don't want . . . I don't really want to be noticed, as much as you do.

F   I would like you to attack the righteous side of that topdog.

J   Attack—the righteous side.

F   The topdog is always righteous. Topdog *knows* what you've got to do, has all the right to criticize, and so on. The topdog nags, picks, puts you on the defensive.

J   Yeah. . . . You're a bitch! like my mother. You know what's good for me. You—you make life *hard* for me. You tell me to do things. You tell me to be—*real.* You tell me to be self-actualized. You tell me to—uh, tell the truth.

F   Now please don't change what your hands are doing, but tell us what's going on in your hands.

J   My left hand . . .

F   Let them talk to each other.

J   My left hand. I'm shaking, and I'm in a fist, straining forward, and (voice begins to break) that's kind of—the fist is very tight, pushing —pushing my fingernails into my hand. It doesn't feel good, but I do it all the time. I feel tight.

F   And the right hand?

J   I'm holding you back around the wrist.

F   Tell it why you hold it back.

J   If I let you go you're gonna hit something. I don't know what you're gonna hit, but I have to—I have to hold you back 'cause you can't do that. Can't go around hitting things.

F   Now hit your topdog.

J   (short harsh yell) Aaaarkh! Aarkkh!

F   Now talk to your topdog. "Stop nagging—"

J   (loud, pained) Leave me alone! [F   Yah, again.] Leave me alone [F   Again.]

(screaming it and crying) *Leave me alone!* [F   Again.]

(she screams it, a real blast) LEAVE ME ALONE! I DON'T HAVE TO DO WHAT YOU SAY! (still crying) I don't have to be that good! . . . I don't have to be in this chair! I don't have to. You make me. You make me come here! (screams) Aarkkh! You make me pick my face, (crying) that's what you do. (screams and cries) Aarkkh! I'd like to kill you.

F   Say this again.

J   I'd like to kill you. [F   Again.] I'd like to *kill* you.

F   Can you squash it in your left hand?

J   It's as big as me . . . I'm strangling it.

F   Okeh. Say this, "I'm strangling—"

J   (quietly) I'm gonna strangle you . . . take your neck. Grrrummmn. (Fritz gives her a pillow which she strangles while making noises) Arrghh. Unghhh. How do you like *that!* (sounds of choked-off cries and screams)

F   Make more noises.

J   Hrugghhh! Aachh! Arrgrughhh! (she continues to pound the pillow, cry and scream)

F   Okeh. Relax, close your eyes . . . (long silence) (softly) Okeh. Come back to us. Are you ready? . . . Now be that topdog again . . .

J   (faintly) You shouldn't have done that. I'm gonna punish you for that . . . I'm gonna punish you for that, Jane. You'll be sorry you did that. Better watch out.

F   Now talk like this to each one of us . . . Be vindictive with each one of us. Pick out something we have done . . . Start with me. As this topdog, for what are you going to punish me?

J   I'm gonna punish you for making me feel so stupid.

F   How are you going to punish me?

J   (promptly) By being stupid. Even stupider than I am.

F   Okeh. Do this some more.

J   Raymond, I'm gonna punish you for being so dumb. I'll make you feel like an ass . . . I'll make you think I'm smarter than you are, and you'll feel dumber and I'll feel smart . . . I'm really scared. I shouldn't be doing this. (cries) It isn't nice.

R   Say this to him. Turn it around, "You should not—"

J   You sh—you shouldn't—you shouldn't—you shouldn't be doing —hooo—you shouldn't be doing—you shouldn't be so dumb. You shouldn't play so dumb. Because it isn't nice.

F   You're doing a job again.

J   Yeah, I know. I don't wanna do it. (crying) I—I know how I punish you. (sigh) I'll punish you by being helpless.

RAYMOND   What are you punishing me for?

J   I'll punish you for loving me. That's what I'll punish you for. I'll make it *hard* for you to love me. I won't let you know if I'm coming or going.

F   "How can you be so low as to love somebody like me?" Yah?

J   *I* do that.

F   I know. How can you love a matchbox? . . .

J   Fergus, I'm gonna punish you for being so slow—in your body, but so quick in your mind. The way I'm gonna do that—I'm gonna excite you, try to excite you, and it's the truth. I'll punish you for being sexually inhibited. I'll make you think I'm very sexy. I'll make you feel bad around me . . . And I'll punish you for pretending to know more than you do.

F   What do you experience when you are meting out the punishment?

J   (more alert, alive) It's a very strange experience. I don't know that I've ever had it before, for such a long time. It's kind of—it's a feeling I used to get when I—when I got back at my brothers for being mean to me. I'd just grit my teeth and think of the *worst* thing I could do—and kind of enjoy it.

F   Yah. This is my impression; you didn't enjoy this here.

J   Mm.

F   Okeh. Go back and be the topdog again, and enjoy punishing Jane—pick on her, torture her.

J   You're the only one I enjoy punishing . . . When you're too loud—when you're too loud, I'll punish you for being too loud. (no sound of enjoyment) When you're not loud enough, I'll tell you that you're too inhibited. When you dance too much—when you dance too much, I'll tell you that you're trying to sexually arouse people, When you don't dance enough, I'll tell you that you're dead.

F   Can you tell Jane, "I'm driving you crazy"?

J   (cries) I'm driving you crazy. [F   Again.] I'm driving you crazy. [F   Again.]
       I'm driving you *crazy*. . . . I used to drive everybody else crazy, and now I'm driving *you* crazy . . . (voice drops, becomes very faint) But it's for your own good. That's what my mother would say. "For your own good." I'll make you feel *guilty* when you've done bad things, so you won't do it again. And I'll—I'll pat you on the back when you do something good, so you'll remember to do it again. And I'll keep you out of the moment. I'll—I'll keep you planning—and I'll keep you programmed, and I won't let you live—in the moment. I won't let you enjoy your life.

F   I would like you to use this: "I am relentless."

J   I—I am relentless. [F   Again.]
       I *am* relentless. I'll do anything—especially if somebody dares me to do something. Then I've gotta tell you to do it, Jane, so you can prove it, so you can prove yourself. You've *gotta* prove yourself—in this world.

F   Let's try this. "You've got a job to do."

J   (laughs) You've gotta job to do. You're gonna quit fuckin' around, and—you've been doin' nothin' for a long time—

F   Yah. Now, don't change your posture. The right arm goes to the left and the left arm goes to the right. Say the same thing again and stay aware of this.

J   You've been doing nothing for a long time. You gotta do something, Jane. You've gotta be something . . . You've gotta make people proud of you. You've got to grow up, you have to be a woman, and you gotta keep everything that's bad about you hidden away so nobody can see it, so they'll think you're perfect, just perfect . . . You have to lie. I make you lie.

F   Now take Jane's place again.

J   You're—you're (cries) you are driving me crazy. You're picking on me. I'd really like to strangle you—uh—then you'll punish me more. You'll come back—and give me hell for that. So, why don't you just go away? I won't—I won't cross you up any more. Just go away and leave me alone—and I'm not begging you!! Just go away! [F: Again.]
Just go away! [F: Again.]
Go away! [F: Change seats.]
You'll be just a half if I go away! You'll be half a person if I leave. Then you'll really be fucked up. You can't send me away, you'll have to figure out something to *do* with me, you'll have to *use* me.
Well then—then I—I would change your mind about a lot of things if I had to.

F   Ah!

J   And tell you that there's nothing I could do that's bad . . . I mean, if you'd leave me alone, I wouldn't do anything bad . . .

F   Okeh. Take another rest.

J   (closes eyes) . . . I can't rest.

F   So come back to us. Tell us about your restlessness.

J   I keep wondering what to do with that. When I had my eyes closed, I was saying, "Tell her to just relax."

F   Okeh. Play *her* topdog, now.

J   Just relax.

F   Make her the underdog and you're the topdog.

J   And you don't have to do anything, you don't have to prove anything. (cries) You're only twenty years old! You don't have to be the queen . . .
She says, O.K. I understand that. I know that. I'm just in a *hurry*. I'm in a *big* hurry. We've got so many things to do—and now, I know, when I'm in a hurry you can't be now, you can't—when I'm in a hurry, you can't stay in the minute you're in. You have to keep—you have to keep hurrying, and the days slip by and you think you're losing time, or something. I'm *much* too hard on you. I have to—I have to leave you alone.

F   Well, I would like to interfere. Let your topdog say, "I'll be a bit more patient with you."

J   Uh. I'll be—I'll be a bit more patient with you.

F   Say this again.

J   (softly) It's very hard for me to be patient. You know that. You know how impatient I am. But I'll—I'll try to be a bit more patient with you.

I'll try"—I'll *be* a bit more patient with you. As I say that, I'm stomping my foot, and shaking my head.

F   Okeh. Say, "I *won't* be patient with you—"

J   (easily) I won't be patient with you, Jane! I won't be patient with you. [F: Again.] I won't be patient with you. [F: Again.] I won't be patient with you.

F   Now say this to us . . . Pick a few.

J   Jan, I won't be patient with you. Claire, I won't be patient with you. Dick, I won't be patient with you. Muriel, I won't be patient with you. Ginny, I won't be patient with you . . . And June, I won't be patient with you, either.

F   Okeh. How do you feel, now?

J   O.K.

F   You understand, topdog and underdog are not yet together. But at least the conflict is clear, in the open, maybe a *little* bit less violent.

J   I felt, when I worked before, on the dream, and the dream thing, that I worked this out. I felt good. I keep—I keep—it keeps—I keep going back to it.

F   Yah. This is the famous self-torture game.

J   I do it so *well.*

F   Everybody does it. You don't do it better than the rest of us. Everybody thinks, "I am the worst." [74]

SUMMARY AND EVALUATION

This chapter is based mainly on Perls' *Ego, Hunger and Aggression* and *Gestalt Therapy Verbatim.* The book by Perls, Hefferline, and Goodman (*Gestalt Therapy*) is a more detailed, more intellectually rigorous development of the theory. It is complex, and while the authors attempt to be systematic, it is difficult to read and to follow. As one of the participants in the dream seminar included in *Gestalt Therapy Verbatim* expressed it: "I tried reading your book, *Gestalt Therapy,* but I wish somebody in this group of leading thinkers . . . would write a book in very simple language, if they could, explaining these same theories so that the average person without technical education, etc., could maybe really get something more out of it." [75]

Nowhere in the writing of the gestalt therapists is there a systematic discussion of therapy. In part this is perhaps because therapy consists essentially of exercises, which are systematically presented in *Gestalt Therapy,* and because therapy is considered to be the resumption of normal growth, and thus not therapy in the corrective sense. The developing of awareness of oneself and of one's various parts or aspects, through exercises and role playing of the various aspects of the self, apparently is assumed to free the individual to resume normal growth.

The gestalt approach offers a provocative theory. It overcomes the restrictions of psychoanalysis, with its limitation to the individual and the intrapersonal, and of Sullivan's interpersonal theory, with its neglect of the individual (or psychosomatic unity). The organism-in-the-environment position goes beyond both and can incorporate both. Its concept of the self as the system of, and the awareness of, the contact boundary of the self and its environment is a major addition to the psychoanalytic concept of the ego. The gestalt concept of motivation is a unitary one, almost identical with that of Combs and Snygg [76] and Rogers.[77] It overcomes the problem posed by Maslow's hierarchy [78] in the same way as that proposed by the present writer.[79] Also like the client-centered approach, gestalt therapy is phenomenological in its orientation. The individual creates his subjective (and effectively real) world according to his interests and needs. Internal reality, not external reality, is the only reality that matters.

A further similarity to client-centered theory is the parallel between organismic self-regulation and the concept of the organism as a whole reacting to the phenomenal field developed by Rogers.[80] There is also a parallel with Rogers' concept of the fully functioning person as one who is open to all his experiences, able to accurately symbolize these in awareness, and able to experience himself as the locus of evaluation, with the valuing process being organismically based rather than environmentally based.

Finally, there appears to be close similarity, if not identity, in the goals of gestalt therapy and client-centered therapy. Both strive for awareness in the client, an awareness that leads to a fully functioning or self-actualizing person.

The means by which the goal is achieved appear to differ. Gestalt therapy is a corrective for purely verbal approaches. It directs attention to the body, including feelings and emotions expressed nonverbally, as well as (and perhaps to a great extent instead of) to the verbal expressions of experience. The method of role playing persons and objects in dreams, as well as parts of oneself, through the empty chair technique, serves to get away from talking *about* oneself, often in the past tense, to expressing conflicting and contradictory feelings in a here-and-now context.

In the absence of a systematic discussion of the therapy process, one must depend upon the examples presented, including typescripts and films. These are almost entirely limited to situations in which Perls is the therapist and are demonstrations and parts of workshops and seminars. It is almost impossible to separate the method from the man. Perls was, as he admitted, a showman. In his autobiographical book he writes: "I feel best when I can be a prima donna and can show off my skill of getting rapidly in touch with the essence of a person and his plight." [81] He eschews "gimmicks" and games, yet his demonstrations come dangerously close to these. In a review of *Gestalt Therapy Now*, a collection of papers, Stone notes that "the most unappealing aspect of Perls' therapy is that he and his followers sometimes seem to be playing games on people rather than with them." [82] While the present reviewer would hesitate to go as far as that, it does appear that in many cases the therapist is playing games—often a guessing game—with the patient. The therapist refuses to let the patient play his own games, but insists that he play the therapist's game. Is therapy a game to be played *with* patients? Perls denies interpreting, but if he doesn't do so in an outright way, he comes very close to it. Though he recognizes that nonverbal behavior does not always have the same meaning in different people, he appears to assign general and specific meanings to much nonverbal behavior and makes diagnoses, in terms of his system, on the basis of such behavior.

Perls was superbly egotistical: "I believe that I am the best therapist for any type of neurosis in the States, maybe in the world. How is this for megalomania. The fact is that I am wishing and willing to put my work to any research test." Yet he continues: "At the same time I have to admit that I cannot cure anybody. . . . I can work with anybody. I cannot work successfully with everybody." [83]

What is the source of the success of gestalt therapy? The prior question, of course, is, is it effective? Other than Perls' statement of his personal skill, there is no explicit claim for the effectiveness of the method. And Perls' skill was never evaluated by research. There is thus no evidence for the effectiveness of the approach. Yet when one reads the theory, and the many verbatim typescripts of the demonstrations, there is an impression of validity to the theory and effectiveness of the method, at least for immediate results of awareness and insight.

The brief demonstrations are impressive. But it must be remembered that these "patients" or subjects were often professional people. They perhaps represent the kind of persons for whom gestalt therapy is claimed to be most effective: "overly socialized, restrained, constricted individuals—often described as neurotic, phobic, perfectionistic, ineffective, depressed, etc.—whose functioning is limited or inconsistent, primarily due to their internal restrictions, and whose enjoyment of living is minimal," [84] in other words, essentially "normal" but inhibited, intellectually controlled individuals.

Shepherd cautions against assuming that gestalt therapy offers "instant cure" on the basis of the dramatic results observed in the short time of the demonstrations.[85] Real progress may require a long process of advancing and retreating. The flashes of insight and of good feeling following the brief treatment in a demonstration may fade overnight, leaving no permanent change or improvement.

The demonstrations have in them the elements of the fallacy of personal validation.[86] In one of Perls' seminars one of the participants raised this question: "Dr. Perls, will you—as you've been formulating and experiencing what has come out as Gestalt Therapy, I want to be reassured, I want to hear you say it, it seems like a process of discovery. Yet I think that people can arrange themselves to fit the expectations of the therapist, like, I sit here and watch person after person have a polarity, a conflict of forces, and I think I can do it too. But I don't know how spontaneous it would be, although I think I would feel spontaneous. You've experienced people over a long time; are we fitting you or have you discovered us?"

To which Perls replied: "I don't know." [87]

REFERENCES

[1] Perls, F. S. *Ego, hunger and aggression.* New York: Random House,1969.
[2] Perls, F. S. *Gestalt therapy verbatim.* Moab, Utah: Real People Press, 1969.
[3] Perls, F. S. *In and out of the garbage pail.* Moab, Utah: Real People Press, 1969.   [4] Perls, F. S., Hefferline, R. F., & Goodman, P. *Gestalt therapy.* New York: Julian Press, 1951.   [5] *Ibid.,* p. vii.   [6] Perls, F. S. *Ego, hunger and aggression.* New York: Random House, 1969. P. 27.   [7] *Ibid.,* p. 45.   [8] *Ibid.,* p. 18.   [9] Perls, F. S. *Gestalt therapy verbatim.* Moab, Utah: Real People Press, 1969. Pp. 16, 31.   [10] Perls, F. S. *Ego, hunger and aggression.* New York: Random House, 1969. P. 114.   [11] *Ibid.,* pp. 116, 117.   [12] *Ibid.,* pp. 38, 40.   [13] *Ibid.,* p. 36.   [14] *Ibid.,* p. 143.   [15] *Ibid.,* p. 146.   [16] Perls, F. S., Hefferline, R. F., & Goodman, P. *Gestalt therapy.* New York: Julian Press, 1951. Pp. viii–ix.   [17] Perls, F. S. *Gestalt therapy verbatim.* Moab, Utah: Real People Press, 1969. P. 32.   [18] *Ibid.,* p. 30.   [19] Perls, F. S. *Ego, hunger and aggression.* New York: Random House, 1969. Pp. 114–115.   [20] *Ibid.,* pp. 119–120.   [21] *Ibid.,* p. 129.   [22] *Ibid.,* p. 157.   [23] Perls, F. S., Hefferline, R. F., & Goodman, P. *Gestalt therapy.* New York: Julian Press, 1951. Pp. 211, 212.   [24] Perls, F. S. *Gestalt therapy verbatim.* Moab, Utah: Real People Press, 1969. P. 35.   [25] Perls, F. S. *Ego, hunger and aggression.* New York: Random House, 1961. P. 61.   [26] *Ibid.,* p. 149.   [27] *Ibid.,* p. 77.   [28] Perls, F. S., Hefferline, R. F., & Goodman, P. *Gestalt therapy.* New York: Julian Press, 1951. P. 118.   [29] *Ibid.,* pp. 118–123.   [30] Perls, F. S. *Gestalt therapy verbatim.* Moab, Utah: Real People Press, 1969. P. 48.   [31] Perls, F. S., Hefferline, R. F., & Goodman, P. *Gestalt therapy.* New York: Julian Press, 1951. P. 432.   [32] Perls, F. S. *Ego, hunger and aggression.* New York: Random House, 1969. P. 133.   [33] *Ibid.,* p. 113.   [34] *Ibid.,* p. 116.   [35] *Ibid.,* p. 157.   [36] *Ibid.,* p. 170.   [37] *Ibid.,* p. 69.   [38] *Ibid.,* p. 179.   [39] *Ibid.,* p. 136.   [40] Perls, F. S. *Gestalt therapy verbatim.* Moab, Utah: Real People Press, 1969. P. 38.   [41] *Ibid.,* p. 16.   [42] *Ibid.,* p. 46.   [43] *Ibid.,* p. 17.   [44] *Ibid.,* p. 51.   [45] *Ibid.,* p. 41.   [46] Perls, F. S. *Ego, hunger and aggression.* New York: Random House, 1969. Pp. 192–252.   [47] Perls, F. S., Hefferline, R. F., & Goodman, P. *Gestalt therapy.* New York: Julian Press, 1951. Pp. 30–224.   [48] Perls, F. S. *Ego, hunger and aggression.* New York: Random House, 1969. P. 92.   [49] Perls, F. S. *Gestalt therapy verbatim.* Moab, Utah: Real People Press, 1969. P. 38.   [50] Perls, F. S. *Ego, hunger and aggression.* New York: Random House, 1969. P. 92.   [51] Perls, F. S. *Gestalt therapy verbatim.* Moab, Utah: Real People Press, 1969. P. 39.   [52] *Ibid.,* pp. 38–39.   [53] Perls, F. S., Hefferline, R. F., & Goodman, P. *Gestalt therapy.* New York: Julian Press, 1951. P. 249.   [54] Perls, F. S. *Gestalt therapy verbatim.* Moab, Utah: Real People Press, 1969. P. 21.   [55] *Ibid.,* p. 60.   [56] Perls, F. S. *Ego, hunger and aggression.* New York: Random House, 1969. P. 154.   [57] Perls, F. S. *Gestalt therapy verbatim.* Moab, Utah: Real People Press, 1969. Pp.

37, 38.   [58] Perls, F. S., Hefferline, R. F., & Goodman, P. *Gestalt therapy.* New York: Julian Press, 1951. Pp. 112–113.   [59] Perls, F. S. *Ego, hunger and aggression.* New York: Random House, 1961. P. 74.   [60] *Ibid.,* pp. 178, 179. [61] Perls, F. S., Hefferline, R. F., & Goodman, P. *Gestalt therapy.* New York: Julian Press, 1951. P. 141.   [62] *Ibid.,* p. 166.   [63] *Ibid.,* p. 191.   [64] *Ibid.,* p. 194.   [65] *Ibid.,* p. 216.   [66] Perls, F. S. Four lectures. In Joen Fagan & Irma L. Sheperd. (Eds.), *Gestalt therapy now.* Palo Alto, Calif.: Science and Behavior Books, 1970. P. 29.   [67] *Ibid.,* p. 27.   [68] Perls, F. S. *Gestalt therapy verbatim.* Moab, Utah: Real People Press, 1969. P. 70.   [69] *Ibid.,* p. 147.   [70] *Ibid.,* p. 120.   [71] Levitsky, A., & Perls, F. S. The rules and games of gestalt therapy. In Joen Fagan, & Irma L. Shepherd (Eds.), *op. cit.,* pp. 140–149.   [72] Perls, F. S. *Gestalt therapy verbatim.* Moab, Utah: Real People Press, 1969. Pp. 81–82.   [73] *Ibid.,* pp. 146–154.   [74] *Ibid.,* pp. 264–272.   [75] *Ibid.,* p. 214.   [76] Combs, A. W., & Snygg, D. *Individual behavior: a perceptual approach to behavior.* New York: Harper and Row, 1959.   [77] Rogers, C. R. *Client-centered therapy.* Boston: Houghton Mifflin, 1951.   [78] Maslow, A. H. *Motivation and personality.* (2nd ed.) New York: Harper & Row, 1969.   [79] Patterson, C. H. A unitary theory of motivation and its counseling implications. *J. indiv. Psychol.,* 1964, **20,** 17–31.   [80] Rogers, C. R. *Client-centered therapy.* Boston: Houghton Mifflin, 1951. Pp. 484–492.   [81] Perls, F. S. *In and out of the garbage pail.* Moab, Utah: Real People Press, 1969. (no paging.)   [82] Stone, A. A. Play: the "now" therapy (Review of "Gestalt therapy now"). *Psychiat. soc. Sci. Rev.,* 1971, **5** (2), 12–16.   [83] Perls, F. S. *In and out of the garbage pail.* Moab, Utah: Real People Press, 1969. (no paging). [84] Shepherd, Irma L. Limitations and cautions in the gestalt approach. In Joen Fagan and Irma L. Shepherd (Eds.), *op. cit.,* p. 235.   [85] *Ibid.,* p. 236. [86] Forer, B. R. The fallacy of personal validation: a classroom demonstration of gullibility. *J. abnorm. soc. psychol.,* 1949, **44,** 118–123.   [87] Perls, F. S. *Gestalt therapy verbatim.* Moab, Utah: Real People Press, 1969. Pp. 214–215.

16

Client-centered therapy: Rogers

The approach to counseling that was at first called nondirective, but is now called client-centered, is still best represented by the writing of its originator, or first expositor, Carl Ransom Rogers (1902–). Rogers received his B.A. degree from the University of Wisconsin in 1924, and his M.A. and Ph.D. from Columbia University in 1928 and 1931, respectively. From 1928 to 1938 he was a psychologist at the Child Study Department of the Society for the Prevention of Cruelty to Children in Rochester, N.Y., and from 1931 on, he was the department's director. The department became the Rochester Guidance Center in 1939; Rogers remained as Director for a year, then went to Ohio State University, where he was Professor of Clinical Psychology from 1940 to 1945. During 1944–1945 he served as Director of Counseling Services of the USO. In 1945 he became Professor of Psychology and Executive Secretary of the Counseling Center at the University of Chicago, leaving in 1957 to become Professor of Psychology and Psychiatry at the University of Wisconsin. In 1962–1963 he was a Fellow at the Center for Advanced Study in the Behavioral Sciences at Stanford, and in 1963 he joined the staff of the Western Behavioral Sciences Institute at La Jolla, California, as a Resident Fellow. In 1968 he joined with others in forming the Center for Studies of the Person in La Jolla.

He is the author of *The Clinical Treatment of the Problem Child*

378

(1939), *Counseling and Psychotherapy* (1942), *Client-Centered Therapy* (1951), *On Becoming a Person* (1961), and *Freedom to Learn* (1969), and, with Barry Stevens, *Person to Person* (1967). He has edited *Psychotherapy and Personality Change* (1954, with Rosalind Dymond), *The Therapeutic Relationship and Its Impact* (1967, with E. T. Gendlin, D. Kiessler, and C. B. Truax), and *Man and the Science of Man* (1968, with W. R. Coulson).

In the last several years he has been devoting himself to group procedures. He is a Diplomate in Clinical Psychology of the American Board of Professional Psychology.

BACKGROUND AND DEVELOPMENT

During the period spent in Rochester, Rogers became dissatisfied with the commonly accepted approaches to psychotherapy and began to develop an approach of his own. The traditional highly diagnostically oriented, probing, and interpretive methods did not appear to be very effective. His own experience in practicing therapy led to a recognition of an orderliness in the experience. The views of Rank, brought into the Rochester group by individuals whose training was influenced by them, had an impact on the development of Rogers' therapeutic methods.

The emerging principles of therapy were subjected to critically minded graduate students in clinical psychology at Ohio State University, and it was recognized that rather than being a distillation of generally accepted principles, as Rogers at first considered them, they constituted a new development. *Counseling and Psychotherapy*[1] represented the attempt to present the new approach.

The stimulation of teaching and research at Ohio State and the University of Chicago, and the continuing experience in practicing psychotherapy, resulted in the development of Rogers' approach and in theoretical formulations of the nature of therapy, as well as in a tentative theory of personality. In 1951, in *Client-Centered Therapy*,[2] a current view was presented, together with its application in play therapy (by Elaine Dorfman), group-centered psychotherapy (by Nicholas Hobbs), group-centered leadership and administration (by Thomas Gordon), and student-centered teaching. Also included was a theory of personality and behavior. The point of view continued to be developed in many papers and articles, some of which were brought together in *On Becoming a Person*.[3] The theory of personality was revised and expanded, and presented in *Psychology: A Study of Science* in 1959.[4]

Certain basic convictions and attitudes underlie the theoretical formulation:[5] (1) Research and theory are directed toward the satisfaction of the need to order significant experience. (2) Science is acute observation and careful and creative thinking on the basis of such observation, not simply laboratory research involving instruments and computing machines. (3) Science begins with gross observations, crude measurements, and speculative hypotheses, and progresses toward more refined hypotheses and measurements. (4) The language of independent-intervening-dependent variables, while applicable to advanced stages of scientific endeavor, is not adapted to the beginning and developing stages. (5) In the early stages of investigation and theory construction, inductive rather than hypothetico-deductive methods are more appropriate. (6) Every theory has a greater or lesser degree of error; a theory only approaches the truth, and it requires constant change and modification. (7) Truth is unitary, so that "any theory, derived from almost any segment of experience, if it were complete and completely accurate, could be extended indefinitely to provide meaning for other very remote areas of experience." [6] However, any error in a theory, if projected in a remote area, may lead to completely false inferences. (8) Although there may be such a thing as objective truth, man lives in his own personal and subjective world. "Thus there is no such thing as Scientific Knowledge, there are only individual perceptions of what appears to each person to be such knowledge." [7]

PHILOSOPHY AND CONCEPTS

The Nature of Man and of the Individual

The common concept of man is that he is by nature irrational, unsocialized, and destructive of himself and others. The client-centered point of view sees man, on the contrary, as basically rational, socialized, forward-moving, and realistic.[8] This is a point of view developing out of experience in therapy rather than preceding it. Antisocial emotions exist—jealousy, hostility, etc.—and are evident in therapy. But these are not spontaneous impulses that must be controlled. Rather they are reactions to the frustration of more basic impulses—love, belonging, security, etc. Man is basically cooperative, constructive, and trustworthy, and when he is free from defensiveness, his reactions are positive, forward-moving, and constructive. There is, then, no need to be concerned about controlling his aggressive, antisocial impulses; he will become self-regulatory, balancing his needs against each other. His need for affection or companionship, for example, will balance any aggressive reaction or extreme need for sex, or other needs that would interfere with the satisfactions of other persons.

As an individual, man possesses the capacity to experience, in awareness, the factors in his psychological maladjustment and has the capacity and the tendency to move away from a state of maladjustment and toward a state of psychological adjustment. These capacities and this tendency will be released in a relationship that has the characteristics of a therapeutic relationship. The tendency toward adjustment is the tendency toward self-actualization. Psychotherapy is thus the liberating of an already existing capacity in the individual. Philosophically, the individual "has the capacity to guide, regulate, and control himself, providing only that certain definable conditions exist. Only in the absence of these conditions, and not in any basic sense, is it necessary to provide external control and regulation of the individual." [9] When the individual is provided with reasonable conditions for growth, he will develop his potential constructively, as a seed grows and becomes its potential.

The Philosophical Orientation of the Counselor

The basic philosophy of the counselor is represented by his attitude of respect for the individual, for the individual's capacity and right to self-direction, and for the worth and significance of each individual.[10] The orientation is one that follows from these concepts of the nature of man.

Definitions of Constructs

The theory of therapy and personality makes use of a number of concepts, or constructs. These are briefly defined prior to their use in the theory.[11]

ACTUALIZING TENDENCY: "the inherent tendency of the organism to develop all its capacities in ways which serve to maintain or enhance the organism."

TENDENCY TOWARD SELF-ACTUALIZATION: the expression of the general tendency toward actualization in "that portion of experience of the organism which is symbolized in the self."

EXPERIENCE (NOUN): all that is going on in the organism at a given time, whether in awareness or potentially available to awareness, of a psychological nature; the "experiential field," or the "phenomenal field" of Combs and Snygg.

EXPERIENCE (VERB): the receiving "in the organism of the impact of sensory or physiological events which are happening at the moment."

FEELING, EXPERIENCING A FEELING: "an emotionally tinged experience, together with its personal meaning."

AWARENESS, SYMBOLIZATION, CONSCIOUSNESS: the representation of some portion of experience.

AVAILABILITY TO AWARENESS: capability of being symbolized freely, without denial or distortion.

ACCURATE SYMBOLIZATION: the potential correspondence of symbolization in awareness to the results of the testing of the transitional hypothesis that it represents.

PERCEIVE, PERCEPTION: "A hypothesis or prognosis for action which comes into awareness when stimuli impinge on the organism." Perception and awareness are synonymous, the former emphasizing the stimulus in the process.

SUBCEIVE, SUBCEPTION: "discrimination without awareness."

SELF-EXPERIENCE: "any event or entity in the phenomenal field discriminated by the individual as 'self,' 'me,' 'I,' or related thereto."

SELF, CONCEPT OF SELF, SELF-STRUCTURE: "the organized, consistent conceptual gestalt composed of perceptions of the characteristics of the 'I' or 'me' and the perceptions of the relationships of the 'I' or 'me' to others and the various aspects of life, together with the values attached to these perceptions."

IDEAL SELF: "the self-concept which the individual would most like to possess."

INCONGRUENCE BETWEEN SELF AND EXPERIENCE: a discrepancy between the perceived self and actual experience, accompanied by tension, internal confusion, and discordant or incomprehensible (that is, neurotic) behavior resulting from conflict between the actualizing and self-actualizing tendencies.

VULNERABILITY: "the state of incongruence between self and experience," with emphasis on "the potentialities of this state for creating psychological disorganization."

ANXIETY: "phenomenologically a state of uneasiness or tension whose cause is unknown. From an external frame of reference, anxiety is a state in which the incongruence between the concept of the self and the total experience of the individual is approaching symbolization in awareness."

THREAT: "the state which exists when an experience is perceived or anticipated (subceived) as incongruent with the structure of the self"; and external view of what is, phenomenologically, anxiety.

PSYCHOLOGICAL MALADJUSTMENT: the state that exists when the organism denies significant experience or distorts it in awareness, resulting in incongruence between self and experience; incongruence viewed from a social standpoint.

DEFENSE, DEFENSIVENESS: "the behavioral response of the organism to threat, the goal of which is the maintenance of the current structure of the self."

DISTORTION IN AWARENESS, DENIAL TO AWARENESS: Denial or distortion of experience that is inconsistent with the self-concept, by means of which the goal of defense is achieved; the mechanisms of defense.

INTENSIONALITY: the characteristics of the behavior of the individual who is in a defensive state—rigidity, overgeneralization, abstraction from reality, absolute and unconditional evaluation of experience, etc.

CONGRUENCE, CONGRUENCE OF SELF AND EXPERIENCE: the state in which self-experiences are accurately symbolized in the self-concept—integrated, whole, genuine.

OPENNESS TO EXPERIENCE: absence of threat; the opposite of defensiveness.

PSYCHOLOGICAL ADJUSTMENT: complete congruence, complete openness to experience.

EXTENSIONALITY: perception that is differentiated, dominated by facts rather than concepts, with awareness both of the space-time anchorage of facts and of different levels of abstraction.

MATURE, MATURITY: an individual is mature "when he perceives realistically and in an extensional manner, is not defensive, accepts the responsibility of being different from others, accepts the responsibility for his own behavior, evaluates experience in terms of the evidence coming from his own senses, changes his evaluation of experience only on the basis of new experience, accepts others as unique individuals different from himself, prizes himself, and prizes others"; the behavior exhibited by an individual who is congruent.

CONTACT: the minimal essential of a relationship, in which each of two individuals "makes a perceived or subceived difference in the experiential field of the other."

POSITIVE REGARD: perception of some self-experience of another that makes a positive difference in one's experiential field; warmth, liking, respect, sympathy, acceptance.

NEED FOR POSITIVE REGARD: a secondary or learned need for love, affection, etc.

UNCONDITIONAL POSITIVE REGARD: perception of the self-experiences of another without discrimination as to greater or lesser worthiness; prizing, acceptance.

REGARD COMPLEX: "all those self-experiences, together with their interrelationships, which the individual discriminates as being related to the positive regard of a particular social other."

POSITIVE SELF-REGARD: "a positive attitude toward the self which is no longer directly dependent on the attitudes of others."

NEED FOR SELF-REGARD: a secondary or learned need for positive self-regard.

UNCONDITIONAL SELF-REGARD: perception of the self "in such a way that no self-experience can be discriminated as more or less worthy of positive regard than any other."

CONDITIONS OF WORTH: the valuing of an experience by an individual positively or negatively "solely because of . . . conditions of worth which he has taken over from others, not because the experience enhances or fails to enhance his organism."

LOCUS OF EVALUATION: the source of evidence as to values—internal or external.

ORGANISMIC VALUING PROCESS: "an on-going process in which values are never fixed or rigid, but experiences are being accurately symbolized and continually and freshly valued in terms of the satisfactions organismically experienced"; the actualizing tendency is the criterion.

INTERNAL FRAME OF REFERENCE: "all of the realm of experience which is available to the awareness of the individual at a given moment"; the subjective world of the individual.

EMPATHY: the state of perceiving "the internal frame of reference of another with accuracy, and with the emotional components and meanings which pertain thereto, as if one were the other person, but without ever losing the 'as if' condition."

EXTERNAL FRAME OF REFERENCE: perceiving "solely from one's own subjective frame of reference without empathizing with the observed person or object."

A Theory of Personality

CHARACTERISTICS OF THE HUMAN INFANT   The infant perceives his experience as reality; for him, his experience is reality. He is endowed with an inherent tendency toward actualizing his organism. His behavior is goal-directed, directed toward satisfying the need for actualization in interaction with his perceived reality. In this interaction he behaves as an organized whole. Experiences are valued positively or negatively, in an organismic valuing process, in terms of whether they do or do not maintain his actualizing tendency. The infant is adient toward positively valued experiences and avoids those that are negatively valued.

THE DEVELOPMENT OF THE SELF   As a result of the tendency toward differentiation (which is an aspect of the actualizing tendency), part of the individual's experience becomes symbolized in awareness as self-experience. Through interaction with significant others in the environment this self-experience leads to a concept of self, a perceptual object in the experiential field.

THE NEED FOR POSITIVE REGARD   With awareness of the self the need for positive regard from others develops. The satisfaction of this need is dependent upon inferences regarding the experiential fields of others. It is reciprocal in human beings in that the individual's positive regard is satisfied when he perceives himself as satisfying another's need. The positive regard of a significant social other can be more powerful than the individual's organismic valuing process.

THE DEVELOPMENT OF THE NEED FOR SELF-REGARD A need for self-regard develops from the association of the satisfaction or frustration of the need for positive regard with self-experiences. The experience or loss of positive regard thus becomes independent of transactions with any social other.

DEVELOPMENT OF CONDITIONS OF WORTH Self-regard becomes selective as significant others distinguish the self-experiences of the individual as more or less worthy of positive regard. The evaluation of a self-experience as more or less worthy of self-regard constitutes a condition of worth. The experience only of unconditional positive regard would eliminate the development of conditions of worth and lead to unconditional self-regard, to congruence of the needs for positive regard and self-regard with organismic evaluation, and to the maintenance of psychological adjustment.

THE DEVELOPMENT OF INCONGRUENCE BETWEEN SELF AND EXPERIENCE The need for self-regard leads to selective perception of experiences in terms of conditions of worth, so that experiences in accord with one's conditions of worth are perceived and symbolized accurately in awareness, but experiences contrary to the conditions of worth are perceived selectively or distortedly, or denied to awareness. This presence of self-experiences that are not organized into the self-structure in accurately symbolized form results in the existence of some degree of incongruence between self and experience, in vulnerability, and in psychological maladjustment.

THE DEVELOPMENT OF DISCREPANCIES IN BEHAVIOR Incongruence between self and experience leads to incongruence in behavior, so that some behaviors are consistent with the self-concept and are accurately symbolized in awareness, while other behaviors actualize those experiences of the organism that are not assimilated into the self-structure and have thus not been recognized, or have been distorted to make them congruent with the self.

THE EXPERIENCE OF THREAT AND PROCESS OF DEFENSE An experience that is incongruent with the self-structure is subceived as threatening. If this experience were accurately symbolized in awareness, it would introduce inconsistency, and a state of anxiety would exist. The process of defense prevents this, keeping the total perception of the experience consistent with the self-structure and the conditions of worth. The consequences of defense are rigidity in perception, an inaccurate perception of reality, and intensionality.

THE PROCESS OF BREAKDOWN AND DISORGANIZATION In a situation in which a significant experience demonstrates the presence of a large or significant incongruence between self and experience, the process of defense is unable to operate successfully. Anxiety is then experienced, to a degree depending upon the extent of the self-structure that is threatened. The experience becomes accurately symbolized in awareness, and a state of disorganization results. The organism behaves at times in ways consistent with the experiences that have been distorted or denied and at times in ways consistent with the concept of the self, with its distorted or denied experiences.

THE PROCESS OF REINTEGRATION   For an increase in congruence to occur, there must be a decrease in conditions of worth and an increase in unconditional self-regard. The communicated unconditional positive regard of a significant other is one way of meeting these conditions. In order to be communicated, unconditional positive regard must exist in a context of empathic understanding. When this regard is perceived by the individual, it leads to the weakening or dissolving of existing conditions of worth. The individual's own unconditional positive regard is then increased, while threat is reduced and congruence develops. The individual is then less susceptible to perceiving threat, less defensive, more congruent, with increased self-regard and positive regard for others, and is more psychologically adjusted. The organismic valuing process becomes increasingly the basis of regulating behavior, and the individual becomes more nearly fully functioning. The occurrence of these conditions and results constitutes psychotherapy.

A Theory of Interpersonal Relationships [12]

THE CONDITIONS OF A DETERIORATING RELATIONSHIP   "A person, Y, is willing to be in contact with person X, and to receive communications from him. Person X desires (at least to a minimal degree) to communicate to and be in contact with Y. Marked incongruence exists in X among the following three elements: his experience of the subject of communication with Y; the symbolization of this experience in his awareness, in its relation to his self-concept; his conscious communicated expression (verbal and/or motor) of this experience."

THE PROCESS OF A DETERIORATING RELATIONSHIP   Under the above conditions the following process occurs: "The communication of X to Y is contradictory and/or ambiguous, containing expressive behaviors which are consistent with X's awareness of the experience to be communicated [and] expressive behaviors which are consistent with those aspects of the experience not accurately symbolized in X's awareness. Y experiences these contradictions and ambiguities. He tends to be aware only of X's conscious communication. Hence this experience of X's communication tends also to be incongruent with his awareness of same [and] . . . his response tends also to be contradictory and/or ambiguous. . . . Since X is vulnerable, he tends to perceive Y's responses as potentially threatening." Thus, he tends to perceive Y's responses in a distorted way, congruent to his own self-structure. He also perceives Y's internal frame of reference inaccurately and therefore is not empathic. As a result, he cannot and does not experience unconditional positive regard for Y. Y thus experiences the receipt of, at most, a selective positive regard, and a lack of understanding and empathy. He is thus less free to express his feelings, to be extensional, to express incongruencies between self and experience, and to reorganize his self-concept. X is, in turn, even less likely to empathize and more likely to have defensive reactions. "Those aspects of experience which are not accurately symbolized by X in his awareness tend, by defensive distortion of perception, to be perceived in Y." Y then tends to be threatened and to show defensive behaviors.

THE OUTCOME OF A DETERIORATING RELATIONSHIP The process of deterioration leads to increased defensiveness on the parts of X and Y. Communication becomes increasingly superficial. Perceptions of self and others become organized more tightly. Thus, the incongruence of self and experience remains in status quo or is increased. Psychological maladjustment is to some degree facilitated in both X and Y.

THE CONDITIONS OF AN IMPROVING RELATIONSHIP "A person, Y', is willing to be in contact with Person X', and to receive communication from him. Person X' desires to communicate to and be in contact with Y'. A high degree of congruence exists in X' between the three following elements: (a) his experience of the subject of communication with Y'; (b) the symbolization of this experience in awareness in its relation to his self-concept; [and] (c) his communicative expression of this experience."

THE PROCESS OF AN IMPROVING RELATIONSHIP The communication of X' to Y' is characterized by congruence of experience, awareness, and communication. Y' experiences this congruence as a clear communication. Hence his response is more likely to express a congruence of his own experience and awareness." X', being congruent and not vulnerable, is able to perceive the response of Y' accurately and extensionally, with empathy. Y' feels understood and experiences satisfaction of his need for positive regard. "X' experiences himself as having made a positive difference in the experiential field of Y'." X' reciprocally tends to increase in feeling of positive regard for Y', and this positive regard tends to be unconditional. The relationship Y' experiences has the characteristics of the process of therapy. "Hence communication in both directions becomes increasingly congruent, is increasingly accurately perceived, and contains more reciprocal positive regard."

OUTCOMES OF IMPROVING RELATIONSHIP An improving relationship may result in all the outcomes of therapy, within the limitations of the area of the relationship.

A TENTATIVE LAW OF INTERPERSONAL RELATIONSHIPS "Assuming a minimum mutual willingness to be in contact and to receive communications, we may say that the greater the communicated congruence of experience, awareness, and behavior on the part of the individual, the more the ensuing relationship will involve a tendency toward reciprocal communication with the same qualities, mutually accurate understanding of the communications, improved psychological adjustment and functioning in both parties, and mutual satisfaction in the relationship."

A Theory of Therapy and Personality Change [13]

CONDITIONS OF THE THERAPEUTIC PROCESS For therapy to occur, the following conditions must be present:

1 Two persons are in contact.

2 One, the client, is in a state of incongruence, being vulnerable, or anxious.

3 The other, the therapist, is congruent in the relationship.

4 The therapist experiences unconditional positive regard toward the client.

5 The therapist experiences an empathic understanding of the client's internal frame of reference.

6 The client perceives, at least to a minimal degree, conditions (4) and (5).

THE PROCESS OF THERAPY The existence of the conditions listed above results in a process with the following characteristics:

1 The client is increasingly free in expressing his feelings, through verbal and/or motor channels.

2 His expressed feelings increasingly have reference to the self, rather than nonself.

3 He increasingly differentiates and discriminates the objects of his feelings and perceptions . . . his experiences are more accurately symbolized.

4 His expressed feelings increasingly have reference to the incongruity between certain of his experiences and his concept of self.

5 He comes to experience in awareness the threat of such incongruence . . . because of the continued unconditional positive regard of the therapist. . . .

6 He experiences fully, in awareness, feelings which have in the past been denied to awareness, or distorted in awareness.

7 His concept of self becomes reorganized to assimilate and include these experiences which have previously been distorted or denied in awareness.

8 As reorganization of the self-structure continues, his concept of self becomes increasingly congruent with his experiences . . . defensiveness is decreased.

9 He becomes increasingly able to experience, without a feeling of threat, the therapist's unconditional positive regard.

10 He increasingly feels an unconditional positive self-regard.

11 He increasingly experiences himself as the locus of evaluation.

12 He reacts to experience less in terms of his conditions of worth and more in terms of an organismic valuing process.[14]

OUTCOMES IN PERSONALITY AND BEHAVIOR The process of therapy leads to the following results:

1 The client is more congruent, more open to his experiences, less defensive.

2 He is consequently more realistic, objective, extensional in his perceptions.

3 He is consequently more effective in problem-solving.

4 His psychological adjustment is improved, being closer to the optimum. . . .

5 As a result of the increased congruence of self and experience . . . his vulnerability to threat is reduced.

6 As a consequence of (2) above, his perception of his ideal self is more realistic, more achievable.

7 As a consequence of the changes in (4) and (5) his self is more congruent with his idealized self.

8 As a consequence of [this and (4)], tension of all types is reduced. . . .

9 He has an increased degree of positive self-regard.

10 He perceives the locus of evaluation and the locus of choice as residing with himself . . . he feels more confident and more self-directing . . . his values are determined by an organismic valuing process.

11 As a consequence of (1) and (2), he perceives others more realistically and accurately.

12 He experiences more acceptance of others, as a consequence of less need for distortion of his perceptions of them.

13 His behavior changes in various ways:
    a . . . the proportion of behaviors which can be "owned" as belonging to self is increased.
    b . . . the proportion of behaviors . . . felt to be "not myself" is decreased.
    c . . . Hence his behavior is perceived as being more within his control.

14 As a consequence of (1), (2), (3), his behavior is more creative, more uniquely adaptive . . . more fully expressive of his own purposes and values.[15]

This theory of therapy is an if-then theory, involving no intervening variables. Although there are speculations as to why the relationships between the conditions and the events that follow them occur, the why is not a part of the theory.

A Theory of the Fully Functioning Person

Each individual possesses an inherent tendency toward actualizing his organism. He has the capacity and tendency to symbolize his experiences accurately in awareness. He has a need for positive regard from others and for positive self-regard. When these needs are met, his tendencies toward actualizing his organism and accurately symbolizing his experiences are most fully realized. When these conditions are met to a maximum degree, the individual will be a fully functioning person who is open to his experience, with no defensiveness, and with all experiences available to awareness and symbolized as accurately as the experiential data will permit. His self-structure will be congruent with his experience and will constitute a fluid gestalt, changing flexibly in the process of assimilation of new experiences. He will experience himself as the locus of evaluation, and the valuing process will be a continuing organismic one. He will have no conditions of worth and will experience unconditional self-regard. Each situation will be met with behavior that is a unique and creative adaptation to the newness of that moment. His organismic valuing will be a trustworthy guide to the most satisfying behaviors, because all available experiential data will be available to awareness and will be used, and no datum of experience will be distorted in, or denied to, awareness. The outcomes of behavior in experience will be available to awareness; thus, any failure, because of lack of data, to achieve the maximum possible satisfaction will be corrected by this effective reality testing. The individual "will live with others in the maximum possible harmony, because of the rewarding character of reciprocal positive regard." [16]

The full functioning of a person is synonymous with optimal psychological adjustment, optimal psychological maturity, complete congruence, complete openness to experience, and complete extensionality. It is the goal, or end point, of optimal psychotherapy.

THE COUNSELING PROCESS

The counseling process is outlined in the theory of therapy discussed above. More detailed consideration of the process may be approached from two frames of reference: the phenomenological point of view, or the client's frame of reference, and the external frame of reference, or the frame of reference of an observer.

The Process as Experienced by the Client

In Chapter 3 of *Client-Centered Therapy* [17] there is a description of the therapeutic relationship as experienced by the client. A somewhat more recent description appears in Chapters 5 and 6 of *On Becoming a Person*.[18]

The client's perception of the process is important, since it is upon his perception of the experience and of the counselor's personality, attitudes, and techniques that therapeutic change depends.

THE CLIENT'S EXPERIENCE OF THE COUNSELOR AND THE COUNSELING SITUATION

The client's perceptions are initially influenced by what he expects of the counselor and the counseling situation. These expectations vary and include feelings ranging from fear to eager anticipation, but an ambivalent, fearful feeling seems most characteristic. Progress is facilitated when both client and counselor perceive the relationship in the same way. Verbal structuring of the relationship by the counselor, which was earlier considered desirable, does not necessarily lead to a common perception of the relationship, however.

When the counselor is perceived favorably, as helpful, it is as someone with warmth, interest, and understanding. At first, client-centered methods often appear frustrating to the client, but they are later perceived as leading to self-exploration and understanding. The therapy hour becomes a stable, accepting experience in an otherwise unstable life and is thus experienced as supporting, although the counselor is not supportive in the usual sense of the term.

HOW THERAPY IS EXPERIENCED BY THE CLIENT

The Experiencing of Responsibility / The client soon discovers that he is responsible for himself in the relationship, and this may lead to various feelings, including a sense of being alone, annoyance, or anger, and a growing sense and acceptance of responsibility.

The Experience of Exploration / As therapy develops, the client explores his attitudes and feelings. He reacts with both fear and positive interest as inconsistencies and contradictions are discovered in his self. Honesty in facing himself develops in the nonthreatening counseling relationship. The verbal exploration that takes place in the interview is less than the unverbalized exploration that goes on during and outside the interviews.

The Discovery of Denied Attitudes / As a result of the exploration, attitudes that have been experienced but denied to awareness are discovered. Both positive and negative attitudes arise. Experiences inconsistent with the self-concept, formerly denied or distorted, become symbolized in awareness.

The Experience of Reorganizing the Self / The bringing of denied experiences into awareness necessitates the reorganization of the self. The reorganization of the self begins with a change in perception of, and attitude toward, the self. The client views himself more positively, as a more adequate person; his acceptance of himself increases. This changed perception of the self must begin before he can become aware of and accept denied experiences. The permitting of more experiential data in awareness leads to a more realistic appraisal of himself, his relationships, and his environment, and to placing the basis of standards within himself. The change in the self may be great or small, with more or less accompanying pain and confusion. More or less disorganization may precede the final organization, and the process may fluctuate up or down. The emotions accompanying the process, though fluctuating, appear to be mainly those of fearfulness, unhappiness, and depression; they are not consistent with actual progress, so that a deep insight may be followed by strong despair.

The process of reorganizing the self, of becoming oneself, or becoming a person, includes various aspects.[19] One may be termed "getting behind the mask." In the atmosphere of freedom of the counseling relationship, the client begins to drop his false fronts, roles, or masks and tries to discover something more truly himself. He is able to explore himself and his experience, facing the contradictions he discovers and the facades and fronts behind which he has been hiding. He may discover that he seems to have no self of his own, but exists only in relation to the values and demands of others. There is, however, a compelling need to search for and become himself.

A part of being one's real self is the experiencing of feelings to their limits, so that the person *is* his fear, anger, love, etc. There is a "free experiencing of the actual sensory and visceral reactions of the organism without too much of an attempt to relate these experiences to the self. This is usually accompanied by the conviction that this material does not belong to, and cannot be organized into, the self. The end point of the process is that the client discovers that he can *be* his experience with all of its variety and surface contradiction; that he can formulate himself out of his experience instead of trying to impose a formulation of self upon his experience, denying to awareness these elements which do not fit." [20] In the experiencing of these elements of himself, a unit, harmony, or pattern emerges. All of these experiences are a part of the potential self, which is being discovered.

The result of the reorganization of the self is not only or merely acceptance of the self but a liking of oneself. It is not a bragging, self-assertive liking, but a "quiet joy in being one's self, together with the apologetic attitude which, in our culture, one feels it is necessary to take toward such an experience." [21] It is a satisfying, enjoyable appreciation of oneself as a whole and functioning person.

The process of therapy is not the solving of problems; it is the experiencing of feelings, leading to the being of oneself. It "is a process whereby man becomes his organism—without self-deception, without distortion." [22] Rather than acting in terms of the expectations of others, he acts in terms of his own experiences. It is the full awareness of these experiences, achieved in therapy, which makes it possible for him to come to *be* (in awareness) what he *is* (in experience)—a complete and fully functioning human organism.

The Experiencing of Progress / Almost from the beginning the client feels that progress is being made. This progress is felt even when confusion and depression are present. The facing and resolving of some issues, and the reconstruction of a segment of personality, represent progress and give the client confidence in continuing to explore himself, even though the exploration continues to be upsetting.

The Experience of Ending / The client determines when to end the counseling. Sometimes the end is preceded by a period during which the time between interviews is lengthened. Often it is accompanied by feelings of fear, a sense of loss, or a reluctance to give up counseling, so that the ending may be postponed for an interview or two.

A PROCESS CONCEPTION OF PSYCHOTHERAPY On the basis of listening to many therapy interviews, abstractions of the therapy process were made.[23] A continuum emerged, not from fixity to changingness, but from stasis to process. Seven stages of the process were discriminated. At any one time the client, taken as a whole, falls within a relatively narrow range on this continuum of personality change, although in given areas of personal meaning he may be at different stages. However, for any specific area, there is a regularity of progression through the stages, although there are some retreats along with the general advance.

First Stage / At this stage there is "an unwillingness to communicate self. Communication is only about externals. Feelings and personal meanings are neither recognized nor owned. . . . Close and communicative relationships are construed as dangerous. No problems are recognized or perceived at this stage. There is no desire to change." [24] Individuals at this stage do not come voluntarily for therapy.

Second Stage / If the individual in the first stage can be reached through the providing of optimal conditions for facilitating change, then "expression begins to flow in regard to non-self topics." [25] However, problems are seen as external, with the client accepting no personal responsibility. Feelings may be shown, but they are not recognized or owned. Experiencing is of the past. There is little differentiation of personal meanings and little recognition of contradictions. Clients may come for therapy voluntarily at this stage, but often do not continue or make progress.

Third Stage / Loosening continues, with freer expression about the self, about self-related experiences as objects, and "about the self as a reflected object existing primarily in others." [26] Past feelings and personal meanings—usually negative—are expressed, with little acceptance of them. Differentiation of feelings is less global, and there is recognition of contradictions in experience. Many clients begin therapy at this stage.

Fourth Stage / Acceptance, understanding, and empathy in stage three enable the client to move to the next stage, where feelings that are more intense, though not current, are expressed, as well as some present feelings and experiences, but with some reluctance, fear, or distrust. Some acceptance of feeling is present. "There is a loosening of the way experience is construed. There are some discoveries of personal constructs [see chapter on Kelly's psychology of personal constructs]; there is the definite recognition of these as constructs; and there is a beginning questioning of their validity." [27] Differentiation of feelings is increased, and contradictions are of concern. Feelings of self-responsibility in problems occur. There is the beginning of a relationship with the therapist on a feeling basis. These characteristics are very common in much of psychotherapy, as are those of the next stage.

Fifth Stage / Here present feelings are freely expressed, but with surprise and fright. They are close to being fully experienced, though fear, distrust, and lack of clarity are still present. Feelings and meanings are differentiated with more exactness. Self-feelings are increasingly owned and accepted. Experiencing is loosened and current, and contradictions are clearly faced. Responsibility for problems is accepted. In this stage the client is close to his organismic being, to the flow of his feelings. Experience is differentiated.

Sixth Stage / This stage tends to be distinctive and dramatic. A feeling that has been "stuck" previously is experienced with immediacy, or a feeling is directly experienced with richness or flows to its full result. An experience and its accompanying feeling are accepted as something that *is*, not something to be feared or denied or resisted. An experience is lived, not felt about. The self as an object disappears. Incongruence becomes congruence. "Differentiation of experiencing is sharp and basic. In this stage, there are no longer 'problems,' external or internal. The client is living, subjectively, a phase of his problem. It is not an object." [28] Physiological concomitants of a loosening, relaxing nature are present—tears, sighs, muscular relaxation, and, it is hypothesized, improved circulation and improved conduction of nervous impulses. This stage is a highly crucial one and seems to be irreversible.

Seventh Stage / In this stage the client seems to continue on his own momentum; this stage may occur outside the therapy hour and be reported in therapy. The client experiences new feelings with immediacy and richness and uses them as referents for knowing who he is, what he wants, and what his attitudes are. Changing feelings are accepted and owned; there is a trust in the total organismic process. Experiencing is spontaneous, with an emerging process aspect, and "the self becomes increasingly simply the subjective and reflexive awareness of experiencing. The self is much less frequently a perceived object and much more frequently something confidently felt in process." [29] Since all the elements of experience are available to awareness, there is the experiencing of real and effective choice. This stage, which relatively few clients reach, is characterized by an openness to experience that leads to a quality of flow, motion, and changingness. Internal and external communication is free.

To summarize, the process involves:

1   A loosening of feelings.

2   A change in the manner of experiencing.

3   A shift from incongruence to congruence.

4   A change in the manner in which and the extent to which the individual is willing and able to communicate himself in a receptive climate.

5   A loosening of the cognitive maps of experience.

6 A change in the individual's relationship to his problems.
7 A change in the individual's manner of relating.

IMPLEMENTATION: TECHNIQUES OF COUNSELING

While early presentations of client-centered counseling stressed techniques, the emphasis is now upon the counselor's philosophy and attitudes rather than techniques, upon the counseling relationship rather than what the counselor says or does. "Our concern has shifted from counselor technique to counselor attitude and philosophy, with a new recognition of the importance of technique from a more sophisticated level." [30] Techniques represent implementations of the philosophy and attitudes, and thus must be consistent with them. With the development of this emphasis on philosophy and attitudes, there have been some changes in the relative frequency of use of various techniques. Questioning, reassuring, encouraging, interpreting, and suggesting, though never widely used, have decreased in frequency. On the other hand, there has been a search for a wider variety of techniques, with the goal of better implementing the basic philosophy and attitudes.

Techniques, then, are ways of expressing and communicating acceptance, respect, and understanding and of letting the client know that the counselor is attempting to develop the internal frame of reference by thinking, feeling, and exploring with the client. They are ways of establishing and maintaining a therapeutic relationship. Techniques cannot be used self-consciously, since the result will be that the counselor is not genuine, not himself.

Whereas the process of psychotherapy was viewed from the standpoint of the client—his perceptions and the changes occurring in him—the technique or implementation aspect may be this process viewed from the counselor's standpoint, in terms of his behavior and his participation in the relationship. Thus, the therapy process may be regarded as the facilitation of personal growth in the client,[31] as the characteristics of the helping relationships,[32] or as the necessary and sufficient conditions of therapeutic personality change as provided by the counselor.[33]

The Counseling Relationship

The relationship that the counselor provides for the client is not an intellectual relationship. The counselor cannot help the client by his knowledge. Explaining the client's personality and behavior to him and prescribing actions that he should take are of little lasting value. The relationship that is helpful to the client, that enables him to discover within himself the capacity to use that relationship to change and grow, is not a cognitive, intellectual one.

The counselor in the therapy relationship has, or should have, a number of characteristics. No counselor has these characteristics to their ultimate degree, of course. Thus, they are stated essentially as desirable goals or ideal characteristics.

ACCEPTANCE The counselor should be accepting of the client as an individual, as he is, with his conflicts and inconsistencies, his good and bad points. Such an attitude is more than a neutral acceptance; it is a positive respect for the client as a person of worth. It also involves a liking for and warmth toward him, a "prizing" of him. There is no evaluation or judgment, either positive or negative. The client is accepted unconditionally, that is, without any conditions attached to the acceptance. The counselor manifests unconditional positive regard for the client.

CONGRUENCE The ideal counselor is characterized by congruence in the counseling relationship. He is unified, integrated, consistent; there is no contradiction between what he is and what he says. He is aware of and accepts his own feelings, with a willingness to be and express these feelings and attitudes when appropriate, in words or behavior. He is real, genuine; he is not playing a role.

UNDERSTANDING Understanding means that the counselor experiences "an accurate, empathic understanding of the client's world as seen from the inside. To sense the client's private world as if it were your own, but without losing the 'as if' quality—this is empathy and this seems essential to therapy." [34] Such understanding enables the client to explore freely and deeply, and thus to develop a better comprehension of himself. This understanding does not involve diagnosis or evaluation, which are external in nature. Complete understanding is, of course, impossible, and fortunately is unnecessary. The *desire* of the counselor to understand is accepted by the client as understanding and enables him to make progress.

COMMUNICATING THESE CHARACTERISTICS It is of no value for the counselor to be accepting, congruent, and understanding if the client does not perceive or experience the counselor as such. It is thus important that acceptance, congruence, and understanding be communicated to the client. The counselor who has these attitudes or characteristics will express them naturally and spontaneously in many ways, both verbally and nonverbally. The ways in which he does so may be considered techniques in a narrow sense. Such techniques are not artificial, forced, or studied, but are genuine and spontaneous expressions of the counselor's attitudes.

THE RESULTING RELATIONSHIP If the counselor has these characteristics and attitudes, at least to a minimum degree, and if they are communicated to the client, then a relationship develops that is experienced by the client as safe, secure, free from threat, and supporting but not supportive. The counselor is perceived as dependable, trustworthy, consistent. This is a relationship in which change can occur. "When I hold in myself the kind of attitudes I have described, and when the other person can to some degree experience these attitudes, then I believe that change and constructive personal development will *invariably* occur. . . ." [35]

This presentation of the counseling process and its implementation is rather abstract and impersonal. Rogers, after reading this, suggested (in personal correspondence) that a section of his article " 'The Process Equation of Psychotherapy' would give the reader a better notion of the process as one dealing with warm living people who are dealt with by warm living counselors." [36] Therefore, with his permission the following material from this article is included:

> So then what is the process of counseling and therapy? I have spoken of it objectively, marshaling the facts we have, writing it as a crude equation in which we can at least tentatively put down the specific terms. But let me now try to approach it from the inside, and without ignoring this factual knowledge, present this equation as it occurs subjectively in both therapist and client.
>
> To the therapist, it is a new venture in relating. He feels, "Here is this other person, my client. I'm a little afraid of him, afraid of the depths in him as I am a little afraid of the depths of myself. Yet as he speaks, I begin to feel a respect for him, to feel my kinship to him. I sense how frightening his world is for him, how tightly he tries to hold it in place. I would like to sense his feelings, and I would like him to know that I understand his feelings. I would like him to know that I stand with him in his tight, constricted little world, and that I can look upon it unafraid. Perhaps I can make it a safer world for him. I would like my feelings in this relationship with him to be as clear and transparent as possible, so that they are a discernible reality for him, to which he can return again. I would like to go with him on the fearful journey into himself, into the buried fear, and hate, and love which he has never been able to let flow in him. I recognize that this is a very human and unpredictable journey for me, as well as for him, and that I may, without even knowing my fear, shrink away within myself from some of the feelings he discovers. To this extent I know I will be limited in my ability to help him. I realize that at times his own fears may make him perceive me as uncaring, as rejecting, as an intruder, as one who does not understand. I want fully to accept these feelings in him, and yet I hope also that my own real feelings will show through so clearly that in time he cannot fail to perceive them. Most of all I want him to encounter in me a real person. I do not need to be uneasy as to whether my own feelings are 'therapeutic.' What I am and what I feel are good enough to be a basis for therapy, if I can transparently be what I am and what I feel in relationship to him. Then perhaps he can be what he is, openly and without fear."
>
> And the client, for his part, goes through far more complex sequences, which can only be suggested. Perhaps schematically his feelings change in some of these ways. "I'm afraid of him. I want help, but I don't know whether to trust him. He might see things which I don't know in myself—frightening and bad

elements. He seems not to be judging me, but I'm sure he is. I can't tell him what really concerns me, but I can tell him about some past experiences which are related to my concern. He seems to understand those, so I can reveal a bit more of myself.

"But now that I've shared with him some of this bad side of me, he despises me. I'm sure of it, but it's strange I can find little evidence of it. Do you suppose that what I've told him isn't so bad? Is it possible that I need not be ashamed of it as a part of me? I no longer feel that he despises me. It makes me feel that I want to go further, exploring *me*, perhaps expressing more of myself. I find him a sort of companion as I do this—he seems really to understand.

But now I'm getting frightened again, and this time deeply frightened. I didn't realize that exploring the unknown recesses of myself would make me feel feelings I've never experienced before. It's very strange because in one way these aren't new feelings. I sense that they've always been there. But they seem so bad and disturbing I've never dared to let them flow in me. And now as I live these feelings in the hours with him, I feel terribly shaky, as though my world is falling apart. It used to be sure and firm. Now it is loose, permeable, and vulnerable. It isn't pleasant to feel things I've always been frightened of before. It's his fault. Yet curiously I'm eager to see him and I feel more safe when I'm with him.

"I don't know who I am anymore, but sometimes when I *feel* things I seem solid and real for a moment. I'm troubled by the contradictions I find in myself—I act one way and feel another—I think one thing and feel another. It is very disconcerting. It's also sometimes adventurous and exhilarating to be trying to discover who I am. Sometimes I catch myself feeling that perhaps the person I am is worth being, whatever that means.

"I'm beginning to find it very satisfying, though often painful, to share just what it is I'm feeling at this moment. You know, it is really helpful to try to listen to myself, to hear what is going on in me. I'm not so frightened anymore of what *is* going on in me. It seems pretty trustworthy. I use some of my hours with him to dig deep into myself to know what I *am* feeling. It's scary work, but I want to *know*. And I do trust him most of the time, and that helps. I feel pretty vulnerable and raw, but I know he doesn't want to hurt me, and I even believe he cares. It occurs to me as I try to let myself down and down, deep into myself, that maybe if I could sense what is going on in me, and could realize its meaning, I would know who I am, and I would also know what to do. At least I feel this knowing sometimes with him.

"I can even tell him just how I'm feeling toward him at any given moment and instead of this killing the relationship, as I used to fear, it seems to deepen it. Do you suppose I could be sharing my feelings with other people also? Perhaps that wouldn't be too dangerous either.

"You know, I feel as if I'm floating along on the current of life, very adventurously, being me. I get defeated sometimes, I get hurt sometimes, but I'm learning that those experiences are not fatal. I don't know exactly *who* I am, but I can feel my reactions at any given moment, and they seem to work out pretty well as a basis for my behavior from moment to moment. Maybe this is what it *means* to be *me*. But of course I can only do this because I feel safe in the relationship with my therapist. Or could I be myself this way outside of this relationship? I wonder. I wonder. Perhaps I could."

What I have just presented does not happen rapidly. It may take years. It may not, for reasons we do not understand very well, happen at all. But at least this may suggest an inside view of the factual picture I have tried to present of the process of psychotherapy as it occurs in both the therapist and his client.[37]

EXAMPLES

Experiencing the Potential Self

CLIENT   It all comes pretty vague. But you know I keep, keep having the thought occur to me that this whole process for me is kind of like examining pieces of a jigsaw puzzle. It seems to me I, I'm in the process now of examining the individual pieces which really don't have too much meaning. Probably handling them, not even beginning to think of a pattern. That keeps coming to me. And it's interesting to me because I, I really don't like jigsaw puzzles. They've always irritated me. But that's my feeling. And I mean I pick up little pieces *(she gestures throughout this conversation to illustrate her statements)* with absolutely no meaning except, I mean, the, the feeling that you get from simply handling them without seeing them as a pattern, but just from the touch, I probably feel, well, it is going to fit someplace here.

THERAPIST   And that at the moment that that's the process, just getting the feel and the shape and the configuration of the different pieces with a little bit of background feeling of, yeah, they'll probably fit somewhere, but most of the attention's focused right on, "What does this feel like? And what's its texture?"

CL   That's right. There's almost something physical in it. A, a . . .

TH   You can't quite describe it without using your hands. A real, almost a sensuous sense in . . .

CL   That's right. Again it's, it's a feeling of being very objective, and yet I've never been quite so close to myself.

TH   Almost at one and the same time standing off and looking at yourself and yet somehow being closer to yourself that way than . . .

CL   Um-hum. And yet for the first time in months I am not thinking about my problems. I'm not actually, I'm not working on them.

TH   I get the impression you don't sort of sit down to work on "my problems." It isn't that feeling at all.

CL   That's right. That's right. I suppose what I, I mean actually is that I'm not sitting down to put this puzzle together as, as something, I've got to see the picture. It, it may be that, it may be that I am actually enjoying this feeling process. Or I'm certainly learning something.

TH   At least there's a sense of the immediate goal of getting that feel as being the thing, not that you're doing this in order to see a picture, but that it's a, a satisfaction of really getting acquainted with each piece. Is that . . .

CL   That's it. That's it. And it still becomes that sort of sensuousness, that touching. It's quite interesting. Sometimes not entirely pleasant, I'm sure, but . . .

TH   A rather different sort of experience.

CL   Yes. Quite.[38]

Experiencing an Affectional Relationship

CL   Well, I made a very remarkable discovery. I know it's . . . *(laughs)* I found out that you actually care how this thing goes. *(Both laugh)* It gave me the feeling, it's sort of well . . . "maybe I'll let you get in the act," sort of thing. It's . . . again, you see, on an examination sheet, I would have had the correct answer, I mean . . . but it suddenly dawned on me that in the . . . client-counselor kind of thing you *actually care* what happens to this thing. And it was a revelation, a . . . not that. That doesn't describe it. It was a . . . well, the closest I can come to it is a kind of relaxation, a . . . not a letting down, but a . . . *(pause)* more of a straightening out without tension, if that means anything. I don't know.

TH   Sounds as though it isn't as though this was a new idea, but it was a new experience of really feeling that I did care, and if I get the rest of that, sort of a willingness on your part to let me care.

CL   Yes.

CL   The next thing that occurred to me that I found myself thinking and still thinking, is somehow—and I'm not clear why—the same kind of a caring that I get when I say "I don't love humanity." Which has always sort of . . . I mean I was always convinced of it. So I mean, it doesn't . . . I knew that it was a good thing, see. And I think I clarified it within myself . . . what it has to do with this situation, I don't know. But I found out, no, I don't love, but I do *care* terribly.

TH   Um-hum. Um-hum. I see . . .

CL   It might be expressed better in saying I care terribly what happens. But the caring is a . . . takes form . . . its structure is in understanding and not wanting to be taken in, or to contribute to those things which I feel are false and . . . it seems to me that in . . . in loving, there's a kind of *final* factor. If you do that, you've sort of done *enough*. It's a . . .

TH   That's *it*, sort of.

CL   Yeah. It seems to me this other thing, this caring, which isn't a good term . . . I mean, probably we need something else to describe this kind of thing. To say it's an impersonal thing doesn't mean anything, because it isn't impersonal. I mean, I feel it's very much a part of a whole. But it's something that somehow doesn't stop. . . . It seems to me you could have this feeling of loving humanity, loving people, and at the same time . . . go on contributing to the factors that make people neurotic, make them ill . . . where, what I feel is a resistance to those things.

TH   You care enough to want to understand and to want to avoid contributing to anything that would make for more neuroticism, or more of that aspect in human life.

CL   Yes. And it's . . . *(pause)* Yes, it's something along those lines. . . . Well, again I have to go back to how I feel about this other thing. It's . . . I'm not really called upon to give of myself in a . . . sort of on the auction block. There's nothing final. . . . It sometimes bothered me when I . . . I would have to say to myself, "I don't love humanity," and yet, I always knew that there was something positive. That I was probably right. And . . . I may be all off the beam now, but it seems to me that, that is somehow tied up in the . . . this feeling that I . . . I have now, into how the therapeutic value can carry through. Now, I couldn't tie it up, I couldn't tie it in, but it's as close as I can come to explaining to myself, my . . . well, shall I say the learning process, the follow-through on my realization that . . . yes, you *do care* in a given situation. It's just that simple. And I hadn't been aware of it before. I might have closed this door and walked out, and in discussing therapy, said, yes, the counselor must feel thus and so, but, I mean, I hadn't had the dynamic experience.

CL   I have a feeling . . . that you have to do it pretty much yourself, but that somehow you ought to be able to do that with other people. *(She mentions that there have been "countless" times when she might have accepted personal warmth and kindness from others.)* I get the feeling that I just was afraid I would be devastated. *(She returns to talking about the counseling itself and her feeling toward it.)* I mean there's been this tearing through the thing myself. Almost to . . . I felt it . . . I mean I tried to verbalize it on occasion . . . a kind of . . . at times almost not wanting you to restate, nor wanting you to reflect, the thing is *mine.* Course all right, I can say resistance. But that doesn't mean a damn thing to me now. . . . The . . . I think in . . . relationship to this particular thing, I mean, the . . . probably at times, the strongest feeling was, it's *mine.* I've got to cut it down myself. See?

TH   It's an experience that's awfully hard to put down accurately into words, and yet I get a sense of difference here in this relationship, that from the feeling that "this is mine," "I've got to do it," "I am doing it," and so on, to a somewhat different feeling that . . . "I could let you in."

CL   Yeah. Now. I mean, that's . . . that's that it's . . . well, it's sort of, shall we say, volume two. It's . . . it's a . . . well, sort of, well, I'm still in the thing alone, but I'm *not* . . . see . . . I'm . . .

TH   Um-hum. Yes, that paradox sort of sums it up, doesn't it?

CL   Yeah.

TH   In all of this, there is a feeling, it's still—every aspect of my experience is mine and that's kind of inevitable and necessary and so on. And yet that isn't the whole picture either. Somehow it can be shared or another's interest can come in and in some ways it is new.

CL   Yeah. And it's . . . it's as though, that's how it should be. I mean, that's how it . . . has to be. There's a . . . there's a feeling, "and this is good." I mean, it expresses, it clarifies it for me. There's a feeling . . . in caring, as though . . . you were sort of standing back . . . standing off, and if I want to sort of cut through to the thing, it's a

. . . a slashing of . . . oh, tall weeds, that I can do it, and you can . . . I mean, you're not going to be disturbed by having to walk through it, too. I don't know. And it doesn't make sense. I mean . . .

TH   Except there's a very real sense of rightness about this feeling that you have, hm?

CL   Um-hum.

CL   I'm experiencing a new type, a . . . probably the only worthwhile kind of learning, a . . . I know I've . . . I've often said what I know doesn't help me here. What I meant is, my acquired knowledge doesn't help me. But it seems to me that the learning process here has been . . . so dynamic, I mean, so much a part of the . . . of everything, I mean, of me, that if I just get that out of it, it's something, which, I mean . . . I'm wondering if I'll ever be able to straighten out into a sort of acquired knowledge what I have experienced here.

TH   In other words, the kind of learning that has gone on here has been something of quite a different sort and quite a different depth; very vital, very real. And quite worthwhile to you in and of itself, but the question you're asking is: Will I ever have a clear intellectual picture of what has gone on at this somehow deeper kind of learning level?

CL   Um-hum. Something like that.[39]

Liking Oneself

CL   One thing worries me—and I'll hurry because I can always go back to it—a feeling that occasionally I can't turn out. Feeling of being quite pleased with myself. Again the Q technique. I walked out of here one time, and impulsively I threw my first card, "I am an attractive personality"; looked at it sort of aghast but left it there, I mean, because honestly, I mean, that is exactly how it felt . . . a—well, that bothered me and I catch that now. Every once in a while a sort of pleased feeling, nothing superior, but just . . . I don't know, sort of pleased. A neatly turned way. And it bothered me. And yet—I wonder—I rarely remember things I say here, I mean I wondered why it was that I was convinced, and something about what I've felt about being hurt that I suspected in . . . my feelings when I would hear someone say to a child, "Don't cry." I mean, I always felt, but it isn't right; I mean, if he's hurt, let him cry. Well, then, now this pleased feeling that I have. I've recently come to feel, it's . . . there's something almost the same there. It's . . . We don't object when *children* feel pleased with themselves. It's . . . I mean, there really isn't anything vain. It's maybe that's how people *should* feel.

TH   You've been inclined almost to look askance at yourself for this feeling, and yet as you think about it more, maybe it comes close to the two sides of the picture, that if a child wants to cry, why shouldn't he cry? And if he wants to feel pleased with himself, doesn't he have a perfect right to feel pleased with himself? And that sort of ties in with this, what I would see as an appreciation of yourself that you've experienced every now and again.

CL   Yes. Yes.

TH   "I'm really a pretty rich and interesting person."

CL   Something like that. And then I say to myself, "Our society pushes us around and we've lost it." And I keep going back to my feeings about children. Well, maybe they're richer than we are. Maybe we . . . it's something we've lost in the process of growing.

TH   Could be that they have a wisdom about that that we've lost.

CL   That's right. My time's up.[40]

The Discovery That the Core of Personality Is Positive

CL   I think I'm awfully glad I found myself or brought myself or wanted to talk about self. I mean, it's a very personal, private kind of thing that you just don't talk about. I mean, I can understand my feeling of, oh, probably slight apprehension now. It's . . . well, sort of as though I was just rejecting, I mean, all of the things that western civilization stands for, you see. And wondering whether I was right, I mean, whether it was quite the right path, and still of course, feeling how right the thing was, you see. And so there's bound to be a conflict. And then this, and I mean, now I'm feeling, well, of course that's how I feel. I mean, there's a . . . this thing that I term a kind of a lack of hate, I mean, is very real. It carried over into the things I do, I believe in . . . I think it's all right. It's sort of maybe my saying to myself, well, you've been bashing me all over the head, I mean, sort of from the beginning, with superstititions and taboos and misinterpreted doctrines and laws and your science, your refrigerators, your atomic bombs. But I'm just not buying, you see, I'm just, you just haven't quite succeeded. I think what I'm saying is that, well, I mean, just not conforming, and it's . . . well, it's just that way.

TH   Your feeling at the present time is that you have been very much aware of all the cultural pressures—not always very much aware, but "there have been so many of those in my life—and now I'm going down more deeply into myself to find out what I really feel"—and it seems very much at the present time as though that somehow separates you a long ways from your culture, and that's a little frightening, but feels basically good. Is that . . .

CL   Yeah. Well, I have the feeling now that it's okay, really . . . Then there's something else—a feeling that's starting to grow, well, to be almost formed, as I say. This kind of conclusion, that I'm going to stop looking for something terribly wrong. Now I don't know why. But I mean, just . . . it's this kind of thing. I'm sort of saying to myself now, well, in view of what I know, what I've found . . . I'm pretty sure I've ruled out fear, and I'm positive I'm not afraid of shock . . . I mean, I sort of would have welcomed it. But . . . in view of the places I've been, what I learned there, then also kind of, well, taking into consideration what I don't know, sort of, maybe this is one of the things that I'll have to date and say, well, now, I've just . . . I can't find it. See? And now without any, without, I should say, any sense of apology or covering up, just sort of simple statement that I can't find what at this time appears to be bad.

TH   Does this catch it? That as you've gone more and more deeply into yourself, and as you think about the kind of things that you've discovered and learned and so on, the conviction grows very, very strong that no matter how far you go, the things that you're going to find are not dire and awful. They have a very different character.

CL   Yes, something like that.[41]

Openness to Experience

CL   It doesn't seem to me that it would be possible for anybody to relate all the changes that you feel. But I certainly have felt recently that I have more respect for, more objectivity toward my physical makeup. I mean, I don't expect too much of myself. This is how it works out: It feels to me that in the past I used to fight a certain tiredness that I felt after supper. Well, now I feel pretty sure that I really *am tired*—that I am not making myself tired—that I am just physiologically lower. It seemed that I was just constantly criticizing my tiredness.

TH   So you can let yourself *be* tired, instead of feeling along with it a kind of criticism of it.

CL   Yes, that I shouldn't be tired or something. And it seems in a way to be pretty profound that I can just not fight this tiredness, and along with it goes a real feeling of I've got to slow down, too, so that being tired isn't such an awful thing. I think I can also kind of pick up a thread here of why I should be that way in the way my father is and the way he looks at some of these things. For instance, say that I was sick, and I would report this, and it would seem that overtly he would want to do something about it, but he would also communicate, "Oh, my gosh, more trouble." You know, something like that.

TH   As though there were something quite annoying really about being physically ill.

CL   Yeah, I'm sure that my father has the same disrespect for his own physiology that I have had. Now, last summer I twisted my back, I wrenched it, I heard it snap and everything. There was real pain there all the time at first, real sharp. And I had the doctor look at it and he said it wasn't serious, it should heal by itself as long as I didn't bend too much. Well this was months ago . . . and I have been noticing recently that . . . hell, this is a real pain and it's still there—and it's not my fault.

TH   It doesn't prove something bad about you . . .

CL   No—and one of the reasons I seem to get more tired than I should maybe is because of this constant strain, and so . . . I have already made an appointment with one of the doctors at the hospital that he would look at it and take an X ray or something. In a way I guess you could say that I am just more accurately sensitive—or objectively sensitive to this kind of thing. . . . And this is really a profound change, as I say, and of course my relationship with my wife and two children is . . . well, you just wouldn't recognize it if you could see me inside—as you have—I mean . . . there just doesn't seem to be anything more wonderful than really and genuinely . . . really *feeling* love for your own children and at the same time receiving it. I don't know how to put this. We have such an increased respect—both of us—for Judy and we've noticed just—as we participated in this—we have noticed such a tremendous change in her . . . it seems to be a pretty deep kind of thing.

TH   It seems to me you are saying that you can listen more accurately to yourself. If your body says it's tired, you listen to it and believe it, instead of criticizing it; if it's in pain, you can listen to that; if the feeling is really loving your wife and children, you can feel that, and it seems to show up in the differences in them too.[42]

An Internal Locus of Evaluation

CL   Well, now, I wonder if I've been going around doing that, getting smatterings of things, and not getting hold, not really getting down to things.

TH   Maybe you've been getting just spoonfuls here and there rather than really digging in somewhere rather deeply.

CL   Um-hum. That's why I say . . . *(slowly and very thoughtfully)* well, with that sort of a foundation, well, it's really up to me. I mean, it seems to be really apparent to me that I can't depend on someone else to give me an education. *(very softly)* I'll really have to get it myself.

TH   It really begins to come home—there's only one person that can educate you—a realization that perhaps nobody else can give you an education.

CL   Um-hum. *(long pause—while she sits thinking)* I have all the symptoms of fright. *(laughs softly)*

TH   Fright: That this is a scary thing, is that what you mean?

CL   Um-hum. *(very long pause—obviously struggling with feelings in herself)*

TH   Do you want to say any more about what you mean by that? That it really does give you the symptoms of fright?

CL   *(laughs)* I, uh . . . I don't know whether I quite know. I mean . . . well, it really seems like I'm cut loose *(pause)*, and it seems that I'm very—I don't know—in a vulnerable position, but I, uh, I brought this up and it, uh, somehow it almost came out without saying it. It seems to be . . . it's something I let out.

TH   Hardly a part of you.

CL   Well, I felt surprised.

TH   As though, "Well for goodness sake, did I say that?" (both chuckle)

CL   Really, I don't think I've had that feeling before. I've . . . uh, well, this really feels like I'm saying something that, uh, is a part of me really. *(pause)* Or, uh, *(quite perplexed)* it feels like I sort of have, uh, I don't know. I have a feeling of *strength*, and yet I have a feeling of . . . realizing it's so sort of fearful, of fright.

TH   That is, do you mean that saying something of that sort gives you at the same time a feeling of, of strength in saying it, and yet at the same time a frightened feeling of what you have said, is that it?

CL   Um-hum. I am feeling that. For instance, I'm feeling it internally now—a sort of surging up, or force, or outlet. As if that's something really big and strong. And yet, uh, well, at first it was almost a physical feeling of just being out alone, and sort of cut off from a . . . a support I had been carrying around.

TH   You feel that it's something deep and strong, and surging forth, and at the same time, you just feel as though you'd cut yourself loose from any support when you say it.

CL   Um-hum. Maybe that's . . . I don't know . . . it's a disturbance of a kind of pattern I've been carrying around, I think.

TH   It sort of shakes a rather significant pattern, jars it loose.

CL   Um-hum. (pause, then cautiously, but with conviction) I, I think . . . I don't know, but I have the feeling that then I am going to begin to do more things that I know I should do. . . . There are so many things that I need to do. It seems in so many avenues of my living I have to work out new ways of behavior, but—maybe—I can see myself doing a little better in some things.[43]

SUMMARY AND EVALUATION

Client-centered counseling hypothesizes that man is rational, socialized, constructive, and forward-moving, and that each individual has the potential for growth and self-actualization. Counseling or psychotherapy releases the potentials and capacities of the individual.

The maladjusted, or disturbed, individual is characterized by incongruence between his self and his experiences, which are threatening. He reacts defensively, denying or distorting experiences that are inconsistent with the self-concept. Counseling offers a relationship in which incongruous experiences can be recognized, expressed, differentiated, and assimilated, or integrated into the self. The individual becomes more congruent, less defensive, more realistic and objective in his perceptions, more effective in problem solving, more accepting of others—in short, his psychological adjustment is closer to the optimum.

This process and these outcomes are facilitated when the counselor manifests unconditional positive regard for the client, evidences empathic understanding of him, and is successful in communicating these attitudes to him. The resulting relationship is one in which threat is reduced, thereby freeing the client for experiencing, expressing, and exploring his feelings.

Client-centered counseling developed out of Rogers' experience as he engaged in counseling or psychotherapy with many clients over a period of more than thirty years. The theory grew out of experience, the results of which were not anticipated; in fact, experience led to radical changes in the theoretical point of view held early in his professional life.

Rogers' development of a theory of therapy preceded the development of a theory of personality. The theory of therapy emerged as a way of giving order to the phenomena experienced in therapy. This theory involved personality change, which led to the evolution of a theory of personality, dealing with the nature of normal and abnormal personality and its development.

The theory of personality has been called self theory because of the central importance of the self, or self-concept, in it. More broadly, however, both the theory of therapy and the theory of personality constitute a perceptual theory, or more specifically, a phenomenological theory. The phenomenological nature of this theory is clearly represented by Combs and Snygg in their *Individual Behavior: A Perceptual Approach to Behavior.*[44]

Phenomenology assumes that although a real world may exist, its existence cannot be known or experienced directly. Its existence is inferred on the basis of perceptions of the world. These perceptions constitute the phenomenal field, or the phenomenal world, of the individual. Man can know only his phenomenal world, never any real world. Therefore, he can only behave in terms of how he perceives things, or how they appear to him.

Rogers thus accepts or adopts a phenomenological point of view when he utilizes the internal frame of reference, or the subjective world of the individual, as a basis for empathizing with and understanding him. It is also apparent in his theory of personality when he postulates that the individual perceives his experience as reality—that in fact his experience is his reality—and when he defines experience as the phenomenal field of the individual. In counseling or therapy, it is the *perception* that the client has of the therapist that is important, not what the therapist actually is or may be trying to be. The process of therapy is seen as a reorganization of the client's perceptions about himself and his world. "The essential point about therapy . . . is that the way the client perceives the objects in his phenomenal field—his experiences, his feelings, his self, other persons, his environment—undergoes change. . . ."[45] Rogers quotes, with approval, Snygg and Combs: "we might, therefore, define psychotherapy from a phenomenological point of view as: the provision of experience whereby the individual is enabled to make more adequate differentiation of the phenomenal self and its relationship to external reality."[46]

The outcomes of therapy also include self-direction and the perception of the locus of evaluation and of choice as in the self. The individual is conceived as a free agent, capable of making his own choices and decisions and with the right to do so. "There is the experiencing of effective choice of new ways of being."[47] There is the assumption that the individual is capable of changing, an assumption common to most other theories of counseling or psychotherapy. The client-centered view, however, assumes that the individual is able to change by himself, in ways that he chooses, without the direction or manipulation of the therapist.

Yet phenomenology is deterministic. Combs and Snygg state: "All behavior, without exception is completely determined by, and pertinent to, the perceptual field of the behaving organism."[48] If all behavior is completely determined, then freedom and choice cannot exist. Beck quotes Snygg and Combs as saying that choice does not exist (first edition, 1949).[49] This passage has apparently been deleted from the second edition, and there appears to be no reference to choice or freedom; neither word appears in the appendix. Nevertheless, as Beck notes, phenomenology is deterministic, and thus it appears to be inconsistent with the assumptions of client-centered therapy and the theory of personality on which client-centered therapy is based.

It might be argued that the self influences the phenomenal field, but it could also be argued that the self is itself determined. It therefore would not be possible to contend that the client, by restructuring his phenomenal field, controls his behavior. The behavior leading to the restructuring is itself determined by the phenomenal field at that moment, and so on, with infinite regress. There seems to be no way, philosophically, to reconcile freedom and determinism. Malcolm, a philosopher, states that "freedom and determinism really are incompatible and will remain so." [50]

How, then, does Rogers deal with the apparent deterministic requirement of science and the assumption of freedom and choice underlying his system? He apparently has not recognized the conflict between the assumptions of phenomenology and his system as regards individual freedom and choice, but he does recognize the difference between the determinism of science and the assumption of his system. In research Rogers accepts the world as a determined world, since the assumption of a cause-effect sequence is necessary. "There would be nothing to study scientifically if that were not a part of your assumption." [51]

However, he states that this "is not the whole of the truth about life. . . . The experiencing of choice, of freedom of choice . . . is not only a profound truth, but is a very important element in therapy." [52] The two assumptions seem to be irreconcilable, but they exist in different dimensions, analogous to the wave and particle theories of light. They constitute a paradox that Rogers accepts as insoluble. However, he attempts to see the dilemma in a new perspective:

> We could say that in the optimum of therapy, the person rightfully experiences the most complete and absolute freedom. He wills or chooses to follow the course of action which is the most economical vector in relationship to all the internal and external stimuli, because it is that behavior which will be most deeply satisfying. But this is the same course of action which from another vantage point may be said to be determined by all the factors in the existential situation. Let us contrast this with the picture of the person who is defensively organized. He wills or chooses to follow a given course of action, but finds that he *cannot* behave in the fashion he chooses. He is determined by the factors in the existential situation, but these factors include his defensiveness, his denial or distortion of some of the relevant data. Hence it is certain that his behavior will be less than fully satisfy-

ing. His behavior is determined, but he is not free to make an effective choice. The fully functioning person, on the other hand, not only experiences, but utilizes, the most absolute freedom when he spontaneously, freely, and voluntarily chooses and wills that which is absolutely determined.[53]

Rogers does not claim that this resolves the issue. Certainly, it is not very satisfying or convincing. That what is determined is what is willed or chosen in the case of the fully functioning person, but not in the case of the defensively organized person, seems a little forced, if not moralistic. One might also note that what constitutes determinism is determined by the nature of the person, and inquire as to what produced this nature. However, it does appear that during therapy a defensively organized person may become a fully functioning person. But one might contend that the change was also determined in the particular case.

This difficulty seems to inhere in the assumptions. What one assumes to exist or to be true does exist or is true by virtue of its being assumed. Determinism is assumed by science and by phenomenology. This assumption is accepted by Rogers in the former instance, but not in the latter. Perhaps one need not assume it in either case in order to allow for the existence of science or phenomenology. Paradoxically, man chooses to accept determinism; there is little convincing proof for it. Indeterminism and probability are accepted in many areas of science itself. Rogers points out the paradox of the behaviorist, committed to determinism and the denial of the existence of choice, making choices as to the goals and methods of science and of human life.[54] Choice seems to be as much of a "fact" as determinism.

It might also be noted that Rogers' position is not entirely inconsistent with phenomenology. Although he seems to imply at times that freedom and choice exist in some reality, in most instances he speaks of the *experiencing* or *perceiving* of freedom and choice. This experiencing or perception is clearly phenomenological. And, phenomenologically, what is experienced or perceived is reality for the individual. The recognition that what is important is the client's perception of the counselor, rather than the counselor's personality or techniques as seen by others, is also clearly phenomenological. Studies of this phenomenological variable have demonstrated its significance.

It may also be worth noting that the situation is not necessarily an either-or dilemma. Freedom could not exist without determinism and vice versa. Either concept is meaningless without the other, and both constitute a construct (as contrasts), in Kelly's terms.

While Rogers does not introduce as many new concepts or new definitions of old terms as does Kelly, for example, there are a number of rather abstract concepts in his work. Ford and Urban point to the level of abstraction of concepts, such as organismic experience, as a difficulty in the theory.[55] They also criticize the inclusion of subjective concepts, such as unconditional positive regard. They point out that operational definitions of these concepts have been developed for research and suggest that such definitions are needed for the counselor or therapist as well.

This point appears to be well taken. The concepts of unconditional positive regard, empathic understanding, and congruence have been developed into measurable variables, and their relationship to client progress and change demonstrated. However, the descriptions of these concepts are broad and general, with little if any consideration of how they are manifested by the counselor in the counseling process. This lack of specification is an example of the increasing emphasis upon attitudes, with consequent de-emphasis on, or neglect of, techniques. Rogers states: "I believe the quality of my encounter is more important in the long run than is my scholarly knowledge, my professional training, my counseling orientation, the techniques I use in the interview." [56] While this may be so, the quality of the relationship is not independent of the other factors, including techniques. The beginning counselor especially needs some help in going about the process of implementing the basic attitudes. But the impression is sometimes given that techniques are entirely incidental. Gendlin, for example, states that "many different orientations, techniques, and modes of therapist response could manifest these attitudes. . . . An unlimited range of therapist *behavior* might implement and communicate these *attitudes.*" [57] This, of course, cannot literally be true; there are some limits—some techniques are inconsistent with the attitudes. There are other client-centered writers who give more attention to techniques, however, including Porter [58] and Patterson. [59]

An important question concerning the client-centered approach is whether the conditions presented by Rogers are the necessary and sufficient conditions for counseling or psychotherapy. Rogers states that when these conditions are present, therapeutic personality change invariably and inevitably occurs. However, the conditions are presented, not as final, but as a theory, a "series of hypotheses which are open to proof or disproof, thereby clarifying and extending our knowledge of the field." [60]

Ellis challenges these conditions, questioning whether they are necessary and sufficient, though conceding that they may be desirable.[61] He notes that personality change does occur without psychological contact with another through experiences of reading or listening. It may be questioned, of course, whether, although there is no direct *personal* contact, there is not *psychological* contact, even though certain experiences may not involve any individual. Ellis also notes that individuals who were not incongruent, but basically congruent and unanxious, have improved their personalities significantly through life experiences and reading. He points out that he has seen clients helped by therapists who were emotionally disturbed and incongruent. Whether such therapists were congruent in the therapy relationship, which is Rogers' point, Ellis does not discuss, however. Commenting on unconditional positive regard, Ellis states he has seen at least one client who was benefited appreciably when treated by therapists who "do not have any real positive regard for their patients, but who deliberately try to regulate the lives and philosophies of these patients for the satisfaction of the therapist's own desires." [62] Ellis feels that the presence of empathic understanding is the most plausible condition, but contends that clients whom he has helped by pointing out their self-defeating behavior and showing them alternative methods of behavior—after seeing their problems from their own frame of reference—have then helped friends and relatives by dogmatically and arbitrarily indoctrinating them, without any empathic understanding. Finally, Ellis claims that he has disproved in his own therapy the necessity for the client's perceiving the therapist's acceptance and empathy, in the case of paranoid patients who insisted they were not understood, but who finally accepted the therapist's frame of reference.

Ellis concludes, therefore, that while very few individuals significantly restructure their personalities when all six conditions are absent, some do. He feels that there is probably no single condition that is absolutely necessary for constructive personality change. There are a number of alternative conditions that might lead to this same result.

It might be pointed out that, as has been indicated several times in this chapter, it is not the presence of these conditions as perceived by an external observer that is necessary, but their presence as perceived by the client. Nevertheless, Ellis raises some question as to whether any one, or all, of the conditions are necessary.

A possible solution of this issue, which appears to be consistent with the general client-centered approach, is that the only necessary—but not sufficient—condition of constructive personality change is that the individual's potential for growth, as manifested in the drive for maintenance and enhancement of the self, is operating and has not been destroyed by severe organic or psychological trauma. The degree of this motivation varies, of course. When it is strong, the conditions that Rogers lists need only be present in very minimal degrees, perhaps hardly observable by an external observer, but present from the viewpoint of the client. When the basic motivation for change is weak, or when it is inhibited or threatened, then the external conditions must be present in greater degrees. They may vary in the degree to which they are present, and it may be possible that not all the conditions need to be present, although there appears to be a positive relationship among the conditions that relate to the therapist, so that if one is present, the others are likely to be present, at least to some extent. Or it may be that the only other necessary condition, which, with the client's motivation, constitutes the sufficient conditions, is the perception by the client of congruence, empathy, and unconditional positive regard in the therapist.

There are many more aspects of the client-centered theory that might be discussed, but space limitations prohibit it. As has often been pointed out, the theory is a constantly developing one, changing with experience and research. However, it appears that there has been no basic change in its assumptions or in its concept of man and the process of personality change. Changes have consisted essentially in a clarifying, sharpening, and adding of detail to the original point of view, and in the development of an integrated theory to encompass the details. The theory is one of the more detailed, integrated, and consistent theories that currently exists. Although, as indicated in the introduction to this book, we are not including a consideration of research evidence supporting the points of view treated, it must be noted that the client-centered approach has led to, and is supported by, a greater amount of research than any other approach to counseling or psychotherapy.

REFERENCES

[1] Rogers, C. R. *Counseling and psychotherapy: newer concepts in practice.* Boston: Houghton Mifflin, 1942.   [2] Rogers, C. R. *Client-centered therapy.* Boston: Houghton Mifflin, 1951.   [3] Rogers, C. R. *On becoming a person.* Boston: Houghton Mifflin, 1961.   [4] Rogers, C. R. A theory of therapy, personality, and interpersonal relationships, as developed in the client-centered framework. In S. Koch (Ed.), *Psychology: a study of science.* Study I. *Conceptual and systematic.* Vol. 3. *Formulations of the person and the social context.* New York: McGraw-Hill, 1959. Pp. 184–256.   [5] *Ibid.,* pp. 188–192.   [6] *Ibid.,* p. 191.   [7] *Ibid.,* p. 192.   [8] Rogers, C. R. *On becoming a person.* Boston: Houghton Mifflin, 1961. Pp. 90–92, 194–195.   [9] Rogers, C. R. A theory of therapy, personality and interpersonal relationships, *op. cit.,* p. 221. [10] Rogers, C. R. *Client-centered therapy.* Boston: Houghton Mifflin, 1951. Pp. 20–22.   [11] Rogers, C. R. A theory of therapy, personality, and interpersonal relationships, *op. cit.,* pp. 194–212.   [12] *Ibid.,* pp. 236–240. Passim. [13] The theory of therapy was developed first, and the theories of personality and interpersonal relationships grew out of it, in part as generalizations from it. For our purposes in this chapter, the presentation is reversed, going from the more general to the more specific. The theory of therapy is an expansion of the process of reintegration outlined earlier.   [14] Rogers, C. R. A theory of therapy, personality, and interpersonal relationships, *op. cit.,* p. 216. [15] *Ibid.,* pp. 218–219.   [16] *Ibid.,* pp. 234–236.   [17] Rogers, C. R. *Client-centered therapy.* Boston: Houghton Mifflin, 1951.   [18] Rogers, C. R. *On becoming a person.* Chap. 5, Some of the directions evident in therapy. Chap. 6, What it means to become a person. Boston: Houghton Mifflin, 1961. Chap. 5 originally appeared in O. H. Mowrer (Ed.), *Psychotherapy: theory and research.* New York: Ronald, 1953.   [19] *Ibid.,* Chap. 6, What it means to become a person.   [20] *Ibid.,* p. 80.   [21] *Ibid.,* p. 87.   [22] *Ibid.,* p. 103.   [23] *Ibid.,* Chap. 7, A process conception of psychotherapy.   [24] *Ibid.,* p. 132. [25] *Ibid.,* p. 133.   [26] *Ibid.,* p. 135.   [27] *Ibid.,* p. 138.   [28] *Ibid.,* p. 150.   [29] *Ibid.,* p. 153.   [30] Rogers, C. R. *Client-centered therapy.* Boston: Houghton Mifflin, 1951. P. 14.   [31] Rogers, C. R. *On becoming a person.* Chap. 2, Some hypotheses regarding the facilitation of personal growth. Bos-

ton: Houghton Mifflin, 1961.   [32] *Ibid.,* Chap. 3, Characteristics of a help-ing relationship. Also in *Personnel guid. J.,* 1958, **37,** 6–16.   [33] Rogers, C. R. The necessary and sufficient conditions of therapeutic personality change. *J. consult. Psychol.,* 1957, **21,** 95–103.   [34] Rogers, C. R. *On becoming a person.* Boston: Houghton Mifflin, 1961, P. 284.   [35] *Ibid.,* p. 35.   [36] Rogers, C. R. Personal communication. November 13, 1964.   [37] Rogers, C. R. The process equation of psychotherapy. *Amer. J. Psychother,* 1961, **15,** 27–45.   [38] Rogers, C. R. *On becoming a person.* Boston: Houghton Mifflin, 1961. Pp. 77–78. This and the following three excerpts are from the same client.   [39] *Ibid.,* pp. 81, 82–84, 84–85, 85–86.   [40] *Ibid.,* pp. 87–88. [41] *Ibid.,* pp. 100–101.   [42] *Ibid.,* pp. 116–117.   [43] *Ibid.,* pp. 120–122. [44] Combs, A. W., & Snygg, D. *Individual behavior: a perceptual approach to behavior.* (Rev. ed.) New York: Harper & Row, 1959.   [45] Rogers, C. R. *Client-centered therapy.* Boston: Houghton Mifflin, 1951. P. 142.   [46] *Ibid.,* p. 146.   [47] Rogers, C. R. *On becoming a person.* Boston: Houghton Mifflin, 1961. P. 154.   [48] Combs, A. W., & Snygg, D., *op. cit.,* p. 20.   [49] Beck, C. E. *Philosophical foundations of guidance.* Englewood Cliffs, N.J.: Prentice-Hall, 1963. Pp. 66–67. The quote is from Snygg, D., & Combs, A. W. *Individual behavior.* New York: Harper & Row, 1949. Pp. 130–131 n.   [50] Malcolm, N. Behaviorism as a philosophy of psychology. In T. W. Wann (Ed.), *Behaviorism and phenomenology.* Chicago: University of Chicago Press, 1964. P. 137. [51] Rogers, C. R. Toward a science of the person. In *ibid.,* p. 135.   [52] *Ibid.* [53] Rogers, C. R. *On becoming a person.* Boston: Houghton Mifflin, 1961. P. 193.   [54] *Ibid.,* p. 392. Also Rogers, C. R. Two divergent trends. In R. May (Ed.), *Existential psychology.* New York: Random House, 1961. P. 87.   [55] Ford, D. H., & Urban, H. B. *Systems of psychotherapy.* New York: Wiley, 1963. P. 439.   [56] Rogers, C. R. The interpersonal relationship: the core of guid-ance. *Harvard educ. Rev.,* 1962, **32,** 416–529.   [57] Gendlin, E. T. Client-centered developments in work with schizophrenics. *J. counsel. Psychol.,* 1962, **9,** 205–212.   [58] Porter, E. H., Jr. *An Introduction to therapeutic counseling.* Boston: Houghton Mifflin, 1950.   [59] Patterson, C. H. *Counseling and psycho-therapy: theory and practice.* New York: Harper & Row, 1959.   [60] Rogers, C. R. The necessary and sufficient conditions of therapeutic personality change, *op. cit.*   [61] Ellis, A. Requisite conditions for basic personality change. *J. consult. Psychol.,* 1959, **23,** 538–549. Also in A. Ellis, *Reason and emotion in psychotherapy.* New York: Lyle Stuart, 1962. Pp. 110–119.   [62] *Ibid.,* p. 114.

PART FIVE

Existential
Psychotherapy

17

Introduction

We have been moving, in our presentation of varying approaches to counseling or psychotherapy, from a conception of therapy as a rational or mainly cognitive problem-solving process to a conception of it as concerned with attitudes, feelings, and affects, with resulting or concomitant changes in methods or techniques. This is not to say that man is essentially irrational, or that counseling or psychotherapy is irrational in its approach. It is to say that man is more than an intellect, and that counseling or therapy must therefore be psychological rather than logical. The emphasis is placed increasingly on the counseling relationship rather than on techniques for influencing the client. The content becomes the current experiencing of the client, rather than his "problem." The therapist's concern is with understanding the experiencing of the client. He must see and know the client as the unique, specific individual that he is. He must see and know the world in which the client exists—his real world, which is unique and different from the objective world, or the so-called world of reality.

The concern with understanding the client as he exists in his world is at the basis of an approach or approaches to counseling or psychotherapy to which the adjective "existential" has been attached. The general term "existential psychotherapy" is applied to these approaches. Although they have much in common, they differ in some respects, so that it is not possible to refer to *the* existential method, but only to existential approaches. The general approach was devel-

oped independently in various parts of Europe. A number of psychiatrists, many of them trained in Freudian psychoanalysis, have been
concerned with the relation of existential concepts to psychotherapy.
These include Binswanger,[1] Boss,[2] Frankl,[3] Marcel,[4] and Sonneman.[5]
In this country Rollo May [6] has been perhaps the foremost exponent
of an existential approach to psychotherapy, though others, such as
Lefabre,[7] Van Dusen,[8] and van Kaam [9] have contributed.

The development of existentialism has been sketched by May.[10]
It is in part an outgrowth of the phenomenological movement in
philosophy,[11] with Husserl's [12] phenomenology influencing it particularly.[13] Mainly, phenomenology contributed the method of approach
to man and his world. Existential philosophy, the second major contributor, had its origins in the work of Kierkegaard [14] and Jaspers.[15]
Later existential philosophers, such as Heidegger,[16] Marcel,[17] and Sartre,[18] were influenced by the phenomenology of Husserl. Existential
philosophy is concerned with the nature of man, with his existence in
the modern world, and with the meaning of this existence to the
individual. Its focus is on man's most immediate experience, his own
existence.

Existentialism is defined by May as "the endeavor to understand
man by cutting below the cleavage between subject and object which
has bedeviled Western thought and science since shortly after the
Renaissance. . . . It arose specifically just over a hundred years ago
in Kierkegaard's violent protest against the reigning rationalism of his
day, Hegel's 'totalitarianism of reason,' to use Maritain's phrase." [19]
The individual is not a substance or mechanism but is emerging, becoming, or *existing,* and to exist means literally to stand out, to emerge.
Existence has been opposed to essence, which is an abstraction and
which has been the concern of traditional science. However, the opposition has been reconciled unwittingly, as Tillich [20] notes, by Sartre's
denial of it in his statement, "Man's essence is his existence"; that is,
the essence of man is his power to create himself.

Man, the subject, can never be separated from the object that
he observes. The meaning of objective fact depends upon the subject's
relationship to it. Man exists in a world of which he is a part—a
being-in-the-world. Existentialism focuses upon the individual's
experience—particularly the nonintellectual modes of experience
—and upon existence in its total involvement in a situation within a
world. It makes man's experience the center of things; its "frame of
reference is in man as he exists inside, in the full range of his fears,
hopes, anxieties, and terrors. . . . The fundamental contribution of
existential therapy is its understanding of man as being. . . . The
fundamental character of existential analysis is, thus, that it is concerned with *ontology,* the science of being, and with *Dasein,* the existence
of this particular being sitting opposite the psychotherapist." [21]

Nor is there a single existential psychotherapy; rather there are
numerous approaches. None of them is at present a systematic approach, and there is little attention given to methods or techniques.

Sartre's analysis is a philosophy rather than a clinical practice. Binswanger's analyses [22] are, as van Kaam notes, not examples of how to do therapy, but only suggestions that "the therapist has to foster a participation of the whole human existence of the patient in the existence of others in order to overcome his anxiety." [23]

Existentialist philosophers do not constitute a single school. There are differences and conflicts among them. Van Dusen sees them on a continuum, with some, such as Sartre, emphasizing the nonbeing end and with Marcel emphasizing the being end of the range of human experiences. One end is characterized by pessimism—darkness and death—and the other by optimism—light and life. [24]

While there is thus no single theory or approach, there are perhaps some common aspects or elements basic to all existential approaches to psychotherapy. These may include the following themes: [25]

1 The distinctive character of human existence is dasein, the being who is there, who has a there in that he knows he is there and can take a stand with reference to that fact. Human beings differ from all other animals in their capacity for being aware of (conscious of) themselves, as well as of the events that influence them and of the past, present, and future as a continuum. This makes choices and decisions possible. Man is thus responsible because he can choose. "Self-consciousness itself—the person's potential for awareness that the vast complex, protean flow of experience is his experience—brings in inescapably the element of decision at every moment." [26]

Man is thus free. He is what he makes of himself; heredity, environment, upbringing, and culture are alibis. External influences are limiting but not determining. "Man is the being who can be conscious of, and therefore responsible for, his existence. It is this capacity to become aware of his own being which distinguishes the human being from other beings. The existential therapists think of man not only as 'being-for-itself.' Binswanger and other authors . . . speak of Dasein choosing this or that, meaning 'the person who-is-responsible-for-his-existence choosing.' . . ." [27]

2 Existentialists share the "conviction that it is impossible to think of the subject and the world as separate from each other." [28] Terms such as "participation," "encounter," "presence," and "dasein" express this conviction. Man lives in three worlds simultaneously, the *Umwelt*, or the biological world, without self-awareness; the *Mitwelt*, or the world of interrelationships or encounters with other persons, involving mutual awareness; and the *Eigenwelt*, or the world of self-identity or being-in-itself.

3 Thus, the human being is not a static entity, but is in a constant state of transition, emerging, becoming, evolving—that is, *being*. Man actualizes himself, or fulfills his inner potentialities, by continual participation in a world of things and events, and always in encounters or dialogue with other men. Some qualities of being can be distinctly developed only in relation to another person. Therapy is an encounter

or a dialogue in which the client is enabled to develop certain human qualities. Being is thus not something given once and for all, but is constantly developing. The future is therefore the significant tense for human beings.

4   Man also knows that at some future time he will not be. Being implies the fact of nonbeing, and the meaning of existence involves the fact of nonexistence. Existentialism holds that death gives life reality; it is the one absolute fact of life. Man is aware of the fact that he must die, and he must confront this fact. He is also capable of choosing not to be at any instant. He is conscious of isolation, nothingness, loss of individual significance or identity, alienation or emptiness.

5   The threat of nonbeing is the source of "normal" anxiety, hostility, and aggression—normal because the threat is always present in all individuals. This anxiety (sometimes called existential anxiety) is "an ontological characteristic of man, rooted in his very existence as such." [29] Anxiety strikes at the core of the individual's self-esteem—his sense of value as a self; it is the threat of dissolution of the self, the loss of existence itself. It involves a conflict between being and nonbeing, between the emerging potentiality of being, on the one hand, and the loss of present security, on the other. It is a concomitant of freedom. Guilt is the failure to fulfill one's potentialities.

6   Being is not reducible to the introjection of social and ethical norms. The self-esteem based on a sense of being is not simply the reflection of others' views of one. Although it involves social relatedness, it presupposes *Eigenwelt,* the "own world" of a sense of self-identity or being-in-itself. Each individual, then, is not a carbon copy cut from social pressures and norms, but is unique, singular, and irreplaceable, and thus significant.

7   Man has the capacity to transcend the immediate situation, to rise above his past, to transcend himself. This capacity is inherent in the term "exist." Man exemplifies transcendence in his concept of the possible, in bringing the past and the future to bear upon the present, in thinking in symbols, in seeing himself as others see him, and perhaps most characteristically in the capacity to be aware that he is the one who is acting—to see himself as both subject and object at the same time. "Self-consciousness implies self-transcendence." [30] The capacity for transcendence is the basis of freedom, since it opens up possibilities for choice. There are, however, limits to life, to being, which must be accepted.

8   Modern man, "normal" as well as neurotic, is characterized by alienation from the world, from the community. Psychiatrists and counselors are no longer presented with the symptoms with which they were presented while Freud was developing his theories. Increasingly, the symptoms or complaints are loneliness, isolation, depersonalization, detachment. Man has lost his world; he is homeless and a stranger in a world that he not only did not make but is no longer a part of.

Ellenberger selects three concepts of existential psychotherapy as especially significant: [31] (1) the concept of *existential neurosis* (derived from Frankl [32]), according to which emotional disturbances are a result of an inability to see meaning in life rather than of repressed drives or trauma, a weak ego, or life stress, (2) the concept of the therapeutic relationship as an encounter, a new relationship opening up new horizons, rather than a transference relationship, repeating the past, and (3) the concept of *kairos,* critical points when the patient is ready for therapy, when rapid change and improvement are possible.

While these elements and concepts seem to characterize most, if not all, existential therapies, they are not sufficient to develop *an* existential psychotherapy. May feels that it would be a mistake for a special school of existential psychotherapy to be developed. Indeed, "there cannot be any special existential psychiatry. . . . Existentialism is an *attitude,* an approach to human beings, rather than a school or group. Like philosophy, it has to do with *presuppositions* underlying psychiatric and psychoanalytic techniques. The existential approach is not a system of therapy—though it makes highly important contributions to therapy. It is not a set of techniques—though it may give birth to them. It is rather a concern with understanding the structure of the human being and his experience, which to a greater or lesser extent should underlie *all* technique." [33] In addition to the fact that existential therapy is relatively new and there has not been time for a systematic approach to develop, May feels that concern about techniques is undesirable, since "it is precisely the overemphasis upon techniques, an overemphasis which goes along with the tendency to see the human being as an object to be calculated, managed, 'analyzed,' " that blocks the understanding that existentialism seeks. "The central task and responsibility of the therapist is to seek to understand the patient as a being and as being in his world." [34] Technique follows rather than precedes understanding.

Many existential therapists, particularly those influenced by Binswanger, appear to use the techniques of psychoanalysis. Binswanger essentially sees existential analysis as an "anthropological type of scientific investigation," [35] rather than as a method of psychotherapy, for which psychoanalysis is indispensable. His discussions are concerned with the analysis of cases in terms of existential concepts instead of being discussions of a therapeutic approach.

But while existential therapists appear to use many of the techniques common to other approaches, particularly psychoanalysis, in which many of them were trained, there are nevertheless certain aspects or emphases that seem to characterize existential therapies and to distinguish them as a group from other approaches. May discusses six characteristics: [36]

1   Existential therapists evidence considerable variability of technique. They are flexible and versatile, "varying from patient to patient and from one phase to another in the treatment of the same patient," depending upon what appears to be necessary "to best reveal the existence of this particular patient at this moment of his history" and "what will best illuminate his being-in-the-world." [37]

2   Existential therapists, particularly those with a psychoanalytic

background, utilize psychological dynamisms such as transference, repression, and resistance, but always in terms of their meaning for the existential situation of the patient's own immediate life.

3   Emphasis is placed upon *presence,* or the reality of the therapist-patient relationship, in which the therapist is "concerned not with his own problems but with understanding and experiencing so far as possible the being of the patient," [38] entering and participating in the patient's field. This emphasis is shared by therapists of other schools who see the patient as a being to be understood rather than an object to be analyzed. "Any therapist is existential to the extent that, with all his technical training and his knowledge of transference and dynamisms, he is still able to relate to the patient, as 'one existence communicating to another,' to use Binswanger's phrase." [39] The patient is not a subject, but an "existential partner," and the relationship is an encounter or "being-together" with one another in genuine presence.[40]

4   The therapist attempts to avoid behavior that would impede or destroy the existence of full presence in the relationship. Since full encounter with another person can be anxiety-producing, the therapist may tend to protect himself by treating the other person as "only a patient" or as an object, or by focusing on behavior mechanisms. Technique may be used as a way of blocking presence.

5   "The aim of therapy is that the patient *experience* his existence as real. The purpose is that he become aware of his existence fully, which includes becoming aware of his potentialities and becoming able to act on the basis of them." [41] Interpretation of mechanisms or dynamisms, as a part of existential therapy, will "always be in the context of this person's becoming aware of his existence." [42] Therapy "proceeds *not* merely by showing the patient where, when and to what extent he has failed to realize the fullness of his humanity, but tries to make him *experience* this as radically as possible. . . ." [43] This is important because it is one of the characteristics of the neurotic process in our day that the individual has lost his sense of being and, in the attempt to be objective about himself, has come to view himself as an object or mechanism. Simply to give him new ways of thinking of himself as a mechanism structuralizes the neurosis, and therapy that does this only reflects and continues the fragmentation of the culture that leads to neurosis. Such therapy may result in the loss of symptoms and of anxiety, but it does so because the patient conforms to the culture and constricts his existence, giving up his freedom.

6   Existential therapy helps the patient develop the attitude or orientation of commitment. Such an attitude involves decisions and actions, but not decisions and actions for their own sake. It is rather commitment to some point in one's own existence. Such commitment is necessary before knowledge is possible: "The patient cannot permit himself to get insight or knowledge until he is ready to decide, takes a definite orientation to life, and has made the preliminary decisions along the way." [44]

A seventh characteristic might be added: in the therapeutic situation existential psychotherapy focuses upon the here and now. The past and future are involved insofar as they enter into the present experience. The here and now includes not only the patient's experiences outside therapy but also the relationship with the therapist. The patient's life history may be investigated, but not in order to explain it in terms of any school of psychotherapy. Instead, it is understood as a modification of the total structuring of the patient as being-in-the-world.[45] The concern of the therapist is to provide a meaningful relationship as a mutual experience, not a relationship in which the therapist influences the patient.

These aspects or emphases of existential psychotherapy are hardly enough upon which to base a practice. The underlying concepts are, of course, of first importance, and it is significant that the object of concern, or focus, of existential therapy differs from most conventional therapies, being existence as it is experienced rather than symptoms. But it is necessary that the concepts be implemented by methods or techniques, and it would be supposed that a theory such as existentialism differs enough from other theories in its concepts and principles to lead to somewhat different methods and techniques. However, there is nowhere a thorough, systematic statement of what existential psychotherapy is and what its procedures, methods, or techniques are, particularly as they may differ from those of other approaches to psychotherapy. Lyons suggests that there is little that is new or different from other therapies.[46] However, he agrees that the approach has had an influence on the field of psychotherapy as a corrective to psychoanalysis and, as Alexander stated it, as a counterbalance to the psychoanalytic trend toward concentration upon techniques.[47]

One must still ask how the existential therapist operates, how he interacts with clients, how he participates in the therapeutic relationship. If he uses essentially psychoanalytic techniques, how does he use them, and how, then, does existential therapy differ from psychoanalytic therapy or psychoanalysis? If the therapeutic relationship is defined as an encounter, what does this mean? What does it mean to say that the therapist is authentic? If he is concerned with the mode of being-in-the-world of the client, how does he gain access to this world? And when he understands the client's mode of being-in-the-world, what does he do with this understanding? Does he interpret in terms of existential concepts? Is existential therapy an interpretative psychotherapy, then, using another theoretical system as a basis for approaching, understanding, and finally interpreting the experiences of the client? Hora contends that in existential psychotherapy special interpretations are not required, since "that which is speaks for itself, provided it is understood phenomenologically rather than interpreted in accordance with certain theoretical presuppositions. That which is understood needs no interpretation. That which is interpreted is seldom understood."[48]

Binswanger appears to reject any attempt to systematize the approach.[49] He rejects theory because he feels that it leads the therapist to try to make the client's behavior fit his theories and that it may result in his attending only to those behavioral phenomena that fit his categories of analysis, thus obstructing a full understanding of the client. But can one enter into any kind of relationship with another without being influenced by one's concepts, ideas, hypotheses, theories, or values? If the therapist is to be authentic, does not his own view of the world, his own being-in-the-world, enter into the relationship? Can one enter the world of another and view it from his point of view? Can one view things as they are or as they manifest themselves without bias or without a prior assumption (Husserl's method of pure phenomenology)?

It remains true that those who profess to engage in a form of psychotherapy that has been influenced by existentialism have not faced the problem of methods or techniques. For if they feel that techniques must be subordinated and must not interfere with the authenticity of the relationship, they should be concerned with avoiding involvement with techniques and with defining how they function in order to do so. Not only have they not dealt with this problem as a problem, they have not provided illustrations or demonstrations of how they function so that one could attempt to understand or learn their methods and procedures. These methods and procedures must exist and therefore must be given attention, unless the approach is to be considered as entirely intuitive.

Although, as Lyons points out, there are a number of existential therapists who have published articles or books on existential therapy, "as a full scale exposition of theory and practice, there is next to nothing from any of the major European figures in this movement." [50] Such a situation poses a problem in terms of the presentation of this approach. However, as Lyons also notes, there is one exception. This is Viktor Frankl. Frankl is possibly not typical (if anyone is) of the existential approach. While earlier he used the term "existenzanalysis," he later adopted the word "logotherapy" to distinguish his approach from Binswanger's existential analysis, or daseinsanalysis, and its related approach to psychotherapy. Frankl's work is more accessible to students and is less obtuse than that of most other existentialist writers. For these reasons his approach has been selected for inclusion here.

May and van Kaam note that a number of American psychiatrists and psychologists have held existential viewpoints (including William James, Adolph Meyer, Harry Stack Sullivan, Gordon Allport, Carl Rogers, Henry Murray, and Abraham Maslow). They go on to say that "what has been lacking . . . has been a consistent underlying structure which would give unity to the work of these psychiatrists and psychologists who are concerned with man and his immediate existence." But they continue: "We propose here that the existential approach, re-cast and re-born into our American language and thought forms, can and will give this underlying structure." [51]

It is not possible at this time to present an American existentialist approach to psychotherapy. There is, of course, an increasing similarity between existentialist concepts and client-centered therapy. It must have been evident to the reader that many, if not most, of the concepts discussed above characterize client-centered therapy, which has been increasingly emphasizing the immediate experiencing of the client. Gendlin, a representative of client-centered therapy who has become concerned with this aspect, indicates that "psychotherapy generally, with any type of population, seems to involve not only verbalization, but more fundamentally, the client's inward reference to and struggle with his directly felt experiencing. The individual's inward data, concretely felt, seem to be the actual stuff of psychotherapy, not the words . . ." [52]

In addition, the phenomenology represented in existentialism is probably developed and implemented in client-centered therapy— with its concern about the client's perceptions and the necessity of the therapist's entering the client's internal frame of reference—more than in any other systematic approach to psychotherapy. It would appear that client-centered therapy has been moving toward existentialism. Van Kaam, writing about "Counseling from the Viewpoint of Existential Psychology," differs very little from the exponents of the client-centered approach.[53] May recognizes the existentialist nature of client-centered therapy,[54] and Wolf notes its similarity to existentialism.[55] It may be, therefore, that we will not see a new American version of existential psychotherapy develop, but rather, in addition to its influence on other methods, the incorporation of the essential concepts of existential psychotherapy into client-centered therapy. However, a candidate has appeared as this is being written. Bugental has developed an existential approach, which, like most if not all others, is built upon psychoanalysis.[56] Like the others, also, it is not systematic and is lacking in specificity, though less so than other approaches.

REFERENCES

[1] Binswanger, L. Existential analysis and psychotherapy. In Frieda Fromm-Reichmann & J. L. Moreno (Eds.), *Progress in psychotherapy: 1956*. New York: Grune & Stratton, 1956. Pp. 144–148. Also in H. M. Ruitenbeek (Ed.), *Psychoanalysis and existential philosophy*. New York: Dutton, 1962. Pp. 17–23; Binswanger, L. The existential analysis school of thought. In R. May, E. Angel, & H. F. Ellenberger (Eds.), *Existence*. New York: Basic Books, 1958. Pp. 191–213.   [2] Boss, M. "Daseinsanalysis" and psychotherapy. In J. H. Masserman & J. L. Moreno (Eds.), *Progress in psychotherapy: 1957*. New York: Grune & Stratton, 1957. Pp. 156–161. Also in H. M. Ruitenbeek (Ed.), *op. cit.*, pp. 81–89.   [3] Frankl, V. *The doctor and the soul*. New York: Knopf, 2nd ed. 1965.   [4] Marcel, G. *The philosophy of existence*. London: Harvill, 1948; Marcel, G. *Homo Victor*. Chicago: Henry Regnery, 1951.   [5] Sonneman, U. *Existence and therapy*. New York: Grune & Stratton, 1954.   [6] May, R. The origins and signifi-

cance of the existential movement in psychology. In R. May, E. Angel, & H. F. Ellenberger, (Eds.), *op. cit.*, pp. 3–36; May, R. Contributions of existential psychotherapy. In *ibid.*, pp. 37–91; May, R. The emergence of existential psychology. In R. May (Ed.), *Existential psychology*, New York: Random House, 1961. Pp. 11–51; May, R. Dangers in the relation of existentialism to psychotherapy. *Rev. exist. Psychol. Psychiat.*, 1963, **3**, 5–10. Also in H. M. Ruitenbeek (Ed.), *op. cit.*, pp. 179–184; May, R., & van Kaam, A. Existential theory and therapy. In J. H. Masserman (Ed.), *Current psychiatric therapies.* Vol. III. New York: Grune & Stratton, 1963. Pp. 74–81.   **[7]** Lefabre, L. B. Existentialism and psychotherapy. *Rev. exist. Psychol. Psychiat.*, 1963, **3**, 271–285.   **[8]** Van Dusen, W. The theory and practice of existential analysis. *Amer. J. Psychother.*, 1957, **11**, 310–322. Also in H. M. Ruitenbeek (Ed.), *op. cit.*, pp. 24–40. **[9]** van Kaam, A. The impact of existential phenomenology on the psychological literature of western Europe. *Rev. exist. Psychol. Psychiat.*, 1961, **1**, 62–91; van Kaam, A. Counseling from the viewpoint of existential psychology. *Harvard educ. Rev.* 1962, **32**, 403–415.   **[10]** May, R. The origins and significance of the existential movement in psychology, *op. cit.*, pp. 3–36.   **[11]** Spiegelberg, H. *The phenomenological movement: a historical introduction.* 2 vols. The Hague: Martinus Nijhoff, 1960.   **[12]** Husserl, E. Phenomenology. In *Encyclopaedia Britannica.* Vol. XVII. (14th ed.) 1929. Pp. 699–702.   **[13]** Spiegelberg, H. Husserl's phenomenology and existentialism. *J. Philos.*, 1960, **57**, 62–74.   **[14]** Kierkegaard, S. A. *Either/or: a fragment of life.* Princeton, N.J.: Princeton University Press, 1944; Kierkegaard, S. A. *Fear and trembling.* New York: Doubleday, 1954; Kierkegaard, S. A. *The sickness unto death.* New York: Doubleday, 1954.   **[15]** Jaspers, K. *Reason and existence.* New York: Noonday, 1955.   **[16]** Heidegger, M. *Being and time.* London: SCM Press, 1962; Heidegger, M. *Existence and being.* Chicago: Henry Regnery, 1949.   **[17]** Marcel, *op. cit.*   **[18]** Sartre, J. P. *Existential psychoanalysis.* New York: Philosophical Library, 1953.   **[19]** May, R. The origins and significance of the existential movement in psychology, *op. cit.*, p. 11.   **[20]** Tillich, P. Existentialism and psychotherapy. *Rev. exist. Psychol. Psychiat.*, 1961, **1**, 8–16. Also in H. M. Ruitenbeek (Ed.), *op. cit.*, pp. 3–16.   **[21]** Van Dusen, W., *op. cit.*   **[22]** Binswanger, L. The existential analysis school of thought. In R. May, E. Angel, & H. F. Ellenberger (Eds.), *op. cit.*, pp. 191–213.   **[23]** van Kaam, A. The impact of existential phenomenology on the psychological literature of western Europe, *op. cit.*   **[24]** Van Dusen, W., *op. cit.*   **[25]** May, R. The origins and significance of the existential movement in psychology, *op. cit.*, pp. 3–36; van Kaam, A. The impact of existential phenomenology on the psychological literature of western Europe, *op. cit.;* Braaten, L. J. The main themes of existentialism from the viewpoint of a psychotherapist. *Ment. Hyg.*, 1961, **45**, 10–17. **[26]** May, R., & van Kaam, A. Existential theory and therapy, *op. cit.*, p. 78. **[27]** May, R. Contributions of existential psychology, *op. cit.*, p. 41. **[28]** van Kaam, A. The impact of existential phenomenology on the psychological literature of western Europe, *op. cit.*   **[29]** May, R. Contributions of existential psychotherapy, *op. cit.*, p. 50.   **[30]** *Ibid.*, p. 74.   **[31]** Ellenberger, H. F. A clinical introduction to psychiatric phenomenology and existential analysis. In R. May, E. Angel, & H. F. Ellenberger (Eds.), *op. cit.*, pp. 92–124.   **[32]** Frankl, V. *op. cit.*   **[33]** May, R. Dangers in the relation of existentialism to psychotherapy, *op. cit.*   [34] May, R. Contributions of existential psychotherapy, *op. cit.*, pp. 76–77.   [35] Binswanger, L. The existential analysis school of thought, *op. cit.*, p. 191.   [36] May, R. Contributions of existential psychotherapy, *op. cit.*, pp. 37–91.   [37] *Ibid.*, p. 78. [38] *Ibid.*, p. 80.   [39] *Ibid.*, p. 81.   [40] Binswanger, L. Existential analysis and psychotherapy, *op. cit.*   [41] May, R. Contributions of existential psychotherapy, *op. cit.*, p. 85.   [42] *Ibid.*, p. 86.   [43] Binswanger, L. Existential analysis and psychotherapy, *op. cit.*   [44] May, R. Contributions of existential psychotherapy, *op. cit.*, p. 87.   [45] Binswanger, L. Existential analysis and psychotherapy, *op. cit.*   [46] Lyons, J. Existential psychotherapy: fact, hope, fiction. *J. abnorm. soc. Psychol.*, 1961, **62**, 242–249.   [47] Alexander, F. Impressions from the Fourth International Congress of Psychotherapy. *Psychiatry*, 1959, **22**, 89–95.   [48] Hora, T. Existential psychiatry and group psychotherapy. *Amer. J. Psychoanal.*, 1961, **21**, 58–70. Also in H. M. Ruitenbeek (Ed.), *op. cit.*, pp. 130–154.   [49] Binswanger, L. The existential analysis school of thought, *op. cit.*, pp. 191–213.   [50] Lyons, J., *op. cit.*   [51] May, R., & van Kaam, A. Existential theory and therapy, *op. cit.*, p. 75.   [52] Gendlin, E. T. Client-centered developments and work with schizophrenics. *J. counsel. Psychol.*, 1962, **9**, 205–212; see also Gendlin, E. T. *Experiencing and the creation of meaning.* New York: Free Press, 1962.   [53] van Kaam, A. Counseling from the viewpoint of existential psychology, *op. cit.*, pp. 403–415.   [54] May, R. Contributions of existential psychotherapy, *op. cit.*, pp. 37–91.   [55] Wolf, W. *Values and personality.* New York: Grune & Stratton, 1950.   [56] Bugental, J. F. T. *The search for authenticity: an existential analytic approach to psychotherapy.* New York: Holt, Rinehart and Winston, 1965.

18

Frankl's logotherapy

Viktor E. Frankl (1905–) was born and educated in Vienna, Austria, receiving his M.D. (1930) and Ph.D. (1949) from the University of Vienna. He founded the Youth Advisement Centers in Vienna in 1928 and headed them until 1938. He was on the staff of the Neuropsychiatric University Clinic from 1930 to 1938. From 1936 to 1942 he was Specialist in Neurology and Psychiatry, and then Head of the Neurological Department, at Rothschild Hospital, Vienna. He became Head of the Neurological Policlinic Hospital (in Vienna) in 1946. In 1947 he was appointed Associate Professor of Neurology and Psychiatry at the University of Vienna, becoming Professor in 1955. He was Visiting Professor at Harvard University Summer School in 1961, and in 1964–1965 Visiting Professor at the Chicago Psychiatric Foundation. From 1942 to 1945 he was imprisoned in German concentration camps, including Auschwitz and Dachau. His mother, father, brother, and wife died in the camps or gas chambers.

Frankl has written a number of books in German, some of which have been translated into Polish, Japanese, Dutch, Spanish, Portuguese, Italian, and Swedish as well as English. He has made many lecture tours, speaking in South America, India, Australia, Japan, and elsewhere, as well as the United States and Europe.

BACKGROUND AND DEVELOPMENT

Frankl began his professional career in psychiatry with a psychoanalytical orientation, having been a student of Freud's. However, he became influenced by the writings of existential philosophers, including Heidegger, Scheler, and Jaspers, and began developing his own existential philosophy as well as an existential psychotherapy. In 1938 he first used the terms "existenzanalysis" and "logotherapy" in his writings. In order to avoid confusion with Binswanger's existential analysis, Frankl has concentrated on the term "logotherapy." The term "existential analysis" has continued to be used, however, and appears to refer to a different aspect of Frankl's theory and method than does logotherapy. Tweedie, who attempts to summarize Frankl's approach, notes that "these terms are nearly synonymous and refer to two facets of the same theory. While Existential Analysis is more indicative of the anthropological direction in which this theory is developed, Logotherapy is more descriptive of the actual therapeutic theory and method." [1] He goes on to say that "Logotherapy proceeds from the spiritual, while Existential Analysis proceeds toward the spiritual." [2] Later he writes that "Logotherapy . . . seeks to bring to awareness the unconscious spiritual factors of the patient's personality, while Existential Analysis is the endeavor to enable the patient to become conscious of his responsibility," and quotes Frankl: "By definition Existential Analysis aims at 'being conscious of having responsibility' (Bewusstsein des Verantworkunghabens)." [3] He goes on to another quotation from Frankl: "Beyond this it is the task of logotherapeutic endeavor to stimulate concrete meaning possibilities; this, however, requires an analysis of the concrete human existence (Dasein), the personal existence of the patient in question, in a word, existential analysis." [4] It appears that existential analysis refers to the analysis of the individual's existence, while logotherapy refers to the actual treatment. Logotherapy appears to be more generally used, however, to include both aspects, and will be so used in this chapter.

This philosophy and therapy, developed in clinical practice and teaching, was tested and strengthened in Frankl's concentration camp experiences. He saw the truth so often expressed by poets and writers, that love is the ultimate and highest goal of man and that "the salvation of man is through love and in love." [5] He became convinced that there was one ultimate purpose to existence.

Frankl recorded his experiences in a book published in German in 1946 and in English in 1959 under the title *From Death Camp to Existentialism.* A revised edition, with an added section on "Basic Concepts of Logotherapy," was published under the title *Man's Search for Meaning* in 1962. A revised paperback edition was published in 1968. This little book is one of the main sources for the present chapter. Another source is *The Doctor and the Soul,* a translation of *Ärzliche Seelsorge,* published in 1946. A second, expanded edition, with revisions and an added chapter was published in 1965. This book brought together materials published in German prior to 1946, some published in the 1930s. Frankl has published a number of books in German since then.

PHILOSOPHY AND CONCEPTS

Introduction

In spite of the apathy of the prisoners in concentration camps, which resulted from both physical and psychological causes, Frankl found that "man *can* preserve a vestige of spiritual freedom, of independence of mind, even in such terrible conditions of psychic and physical stress." [6] Opportunities for choice were many, and there were examples of heroic choices to help others rather than to preserve oneself. "The sort of person the prisoner became was the result of an inner decision, and not the result of camp influences alone. Fundamentally, therefore, any man can, even under such circumstances decide what shall become of him—mentally and spiritually. He may retain his human dignity even in a concentration camp. . . . It is this spiritual freedom—which cannot be taken away—that makes life meaningful and purposeful." [7] If there is a meaning to life, Frankl reasoned, there is a meaning to suffering, since suffering, like death, is an ineradicable part of life; without them life cannot be complete.

Only a few prisoners resisted falling victim to the prison camp's degenerating influences. The lack of any future goal or hope caused many to overlook existing opportunities to make something positive of camp life. But unusually bad external situations also give man the opportunity to grow beyond himself spiritually. To do this, however, he must have faith in the future. Without it he gives up and has no will to live. With no aim, no purpose, no sense or meaning in life, there is no point in carrying on. Frankl asked his fellow prisoners who said that they expected nothing more from life "whether the question was really what we expected from life. Was it not, rather, what life was expecting from us?" [8] Life sets tasks for each man, who in meeting them defines the meaning of his life. The tasks are different for each, and each situation is different, requiring a unique response. Sometimes man is required to accept fate or to suffer as his task. Each man's suffering is unique, and his opportunity for growth lies in the way he bears it.

The Nature of Man

Man is a unity with three aspects or dimensions. These are the somatic, or physical; the mental, or psychological; and the spiritual.[9] The first two are closely related and together constitute the "psychophysicum." They include inherited and constitutional factors, such as the innate drives. Psychoanalysis, through Freud, Adler, and Jung, has contributed to the understanding of these dimensions, particularly the psychological, but has neglected the spiritual, the distinctively human dimension.

Logotherapy emphasizes the third dimension, the spiritual. Spirituality is the first of three characteristics of human existence that distinguish man from animals. Spirituality is revealed phenomenologically in immediate self-consciousness, but is derived from the "spiritual unconscious." "Unconscious spirituality is the origin and root of all consciousness. In other words, we know and acknowledge, not only an instinctive unconscious, but rather also a *spiritual unconscious,* and in it we see the supporting ground of all conscious spirituality. The ego is not *governed* by the id, but the spirit is *borne by the unconscious.* "[10] Spirituality is the chief attribute of man, and from it derives conscience, love, and aesthetic conscience.

The second characteristic of human existence is freedom. "But what is man? He is the essence which always decides. And he again and again decides what he will be in the next instant." [11] Freedom means freedom in the face of three things: (1) the instincts, (2) inherited disposition, and (3) environment. Although man is influenced by all of these, he still has freedom to accept or reject and to make decisions. While he is not free from conditions, he is free to take a stand toward these conditions. Man thus does not simply exist; he decides what his existence will be. Since he can rise above biological, psychological, and sociological conditions, on which predictions can be based, he is individually unpredictable.[12]

The third factor in man's existence is responsibility. Man's freedom is not only freedom *from,* but freedom *to* something, and this, according to Frankl, is his responsibleness. Man is responsible to himself, to his conscience, or to his God. "Logotherapy tries to make the patient fully aware of his own responsibleness; and therefore it must leave to him the option for what, to what or to whom, he understands himself to be responsible." [13]

Psychoanalysis is concerned with man becoming conscious of his repressed experiences or drives. Individual psychology is concerned with man accepting responsibility for his symptoms. Each is one-sided and complements the other. "One might in fact state it as a basic theorem that *being human means being conscious and being responsible.* Both psychoanalysis and individual psychology err in that each sees only one aspect of humanity, one factor in human existence—whereas the two aspects must be taken jointly to yield a true picture of man." [14] Logotherapy goes beyond both, to add the realm of the spiritual *(Geistig).* Responsibility is related to consciousness through conscience.

Although each individual is unique, he would have no meaning by himself. "The significance of such individuality, the meaning of human personality, is, however, always related to community." [15] In the community each individual, because he is unique, is irreplaceable. This is the difference between the community and the "mass," which is composed of identical units. "The community needs the individual existence in order for itself to have meaning," but also, "the meaning of individuality comes to fulfillment in the community. To this extent, then, the value of the individual is dependent upon the community." [16] The mass, however, submerges the individual: "by escape into the mass, man loses his most intrinsic quality; responsibility." [17] But by becoming a part of the community, which is in itself a choice, man adds to his responsibility.

Motivation

Neither homeostasis, tension reduction, nor the psychoanalytic pleasure principle can adequately account for human behavior. The status drive of individual psychology is also an insufficient explanation, as are self-expression, self-fulfillment, and self-actualization. These, according to Frankl, are effects rather than intentions, and the same is true for pleasure. In fact, "only when the primary objective orientation is lacking and has foundered, does that interest in one's self arise, as it is so strikingly manifested in neurotic existence. Therefore the striving for self-fulfillment is in no way something primary, rather, we see in it a deficient mode and a reduced level of human existence." [18]

The primary motivation in man is not what Frankl calls the will to pleasure or the will to power, but the will to meaning. It is this that "most deeply inspires man," that is "the most human phenomenon of all, since an animal certainly never worries about the meaning of its existence." [19]

Meaning is not invented by man, as Sartre claims, but according to Frankl, is "discovered" by man. "Men can give meaning to their lives by realizing what I call *creative values,* by achieving tasks. But they can also give meaning to their lives by realizing *experiential values,* by experiencing the Good, the True, and the Beautiful, or by knowing one single human being in all his uniqueness. And to experience one human being as unique means to love him." [20] Even when these experiences are impossible, "a man can still give his life a meaning by the way he faces his fate, his distress." [21] Man realizes values by his attitude toward his destined, or inescapable, suffering. These are *attitudinal values,* as Frankl calls them, and the possibilitiy for their realization exists until the last moment of life. Suffering thus has meaning.

The will to meaning is not a driving force in the psychodynamic sense. "Values do not drive a man; they do not *push* him, but rather *pull* him." [22] They involve choices or decisions. "Man is never driven to moral behavior; in each instance he decides to behave morally." He does so, not to satisfy a moral drive or to have a good conscience, but "for the sake of a cause to which he commits himself, or for a person whom he loves, or for the sake of his God." [23]

The meaning of life is not an abstraction. "Ultimately, man should not ask what the meaning of life is, but rather he must recognize that it is *he* who is asked. In a word, each man is questioned by life; and he can only answer to life by *answering for* his own life; to life he can only respond by being responsible. . . . This emphasis on responsibleness is reflected in the categorical imperative of logotherapy, which is: 'So live as if you were living already for the second time and as if you had acted the first time as wrongly as you are about to act now!' " [24] The meaning of life is thus unique for each individual and varies with time.

Existence is transitory, but on its transitoriness hinges its responsibleness, since man is constantly faced with choices among the current potentialities. "Man constantly makes his choice concerning the mass of present potentialities." Once potentialities are actualized, "they are rendered realities; they are saved and delivered into the past, wherein they are rescued and preserved from transitoriness. For, in the past, nothing is irrecoverably lost, but everything is irrevocably stored." [25] But potentialities that are not chosen are lost.

The Existential Vacuum and Existential Frustration

A common complaint of patients today is that their lives are meaningless. "They lack the awareness of a meaning worth living for. They are haunted by the experience of their inner emptiness, a void within themselves; they are caught in that situation which I have called the 'existential vacuum.' " [26] Frankl explains it as follows: with no instincts to guide his behavior, and with the disappearance of traditions to guide his choices, but with the necessity of making choices, man doesn't know what to do or what he wants to do. "This existential vacuum manifests itself mainly in a state of boredom. . . . In actual fact, boredom is now causing, and certainly bringing to psychiatrists, more problems to solve than distress." [27] One manifestation is the "Sunday neurosis," which is "that kind of depression which afflicts people who become aware of the lack of content of their lives when the rush of the busy week is over and the void within themselves becomes manifest." [28]

The frustration of the will to meaning is "existential frustration," as Frankl calls it. This frustration is sometimes "vicariously compensated for by a will to power. . . . In other cases, the place of frustrated will to meaning is taken by the will to pleasure. That is why existential frustration often eventuates in sexual compensation. We can observe, in such cases, that the sexual libido becomes rampant in the existential vacuum." [29]

Existential frustration is not pathological or pathogenic per se. "Not every conflict is necessarily neurotic . . . suffering is not always a pathological phenomenon. . . . I would strictly deny that one's search for a meaning to his existence, or even his doubt of it, in every case is derived from, or results in, any disease. . . . A man's concern, even his despair, over the worthwhileness of life is a *spiritual distress* but by no means a *mental disease.* " [30] Philosophical conflicts and problems involving one's view of the world are psychologically, biologically, and sociologically "conditioned but not caused." It is the fallacy of psychologism "to analyze every act for its psychic origin, and on that basis to decree whether its intellectual content is valid or invalid." [31] Even if there is pathology in the individual, his philosophy or world view cannot necessarily be labeled as pathological. Psychologism, however, tends to devaluate; "it is always trying to unmask," is forever bent on debunking, is constantly hunting down extrinsic—that is, neurotic or culturo-pathological—motivations. "Everywhere, psychologism sees nothing but masks, insists that only neurotic motives lie behind these masks." [32]

The search for meaning may lead to tension rather than equilibrium. But such tension is not pathological; it is rather "an indispensable prerequisite of mental health . . . mental health is based on a certain degree of tension, the tension between what one has already achieved and what one still ought to accomplish, or the gap between what one is and what one should become." [33] What man needs in the first place is not the discharge of tension—a homeostasis or equilibrium—but " 'Noödynamics,' i.e., the spiritual dynamics in a polar field of tension where one pole is represented by a meaning to be fulfilled and the other pole by the man who must fulfill it." [34]

The Nature of Neuroses and Psychoses

Although existential conflicts may exist without neurosis, every neurosis has an existential aspect. Neuroses are "grounded in the four basically different layers (or 'dimensions') of man's being": the physical, the psychological, the societal, and the existential or spiritual.[35] The physiological bases are the constitutional (including neuropathy and psychopathy) and the conditioned (for example, the shock of a traumatic experience). The conditioned bases are probably precipitating factors. The various types of neuroses differ in terms of the relative importance of each of the four dimensions. The physiological bases cannot be reached by psychotherapy, but only by drugs, and when the physiological component is great, there is little that psychotherapy can do.[36]

NOÖGENIC NEUROSES "Noetic" refers to the spiritual dimension. "Noögenic neuroses do not emerge from conflicts between drives and instincts but rather from conflicts between various values; in other words, from moral conflicts, or, to speak in a more general way, from spiritual problems. Among such problems, existential frustration often plays a large role." [37] The disturbance is not in the spiritual dimension as such but is manifested in the psychophysicum. "Noögenic neuroses are illnesses 'out of spirit' (*aus dem Geist*), but they are not illnesses 'in the spirit' (*im Geist*)." [38]

THE COLLECTIVE NEUROSIS Although our age is often called the age of anxiety, it is doubtful that anxiety is more prevalent now than in other times. There are, however, certain characterisitcs of modern man that are "similar to neurosis" and may be designated as the collective neurosis. "First, there is the planless, day-to-day attitude toward life," with no long-term planning, which seems to be related to the uncertainty of life since the war and the atom bomb.[39] "The second symptom is the fatalistic attitude toward life. This, again, is a product of the last war." [40] It is the attitude that it is not possible to plan one's life. "The third symptom is collective thinking. Man would like to submerge himself in the masses. Actually, he is only drowned in the masses, he abandons himself as a free and responsible being. The fourth symptom is fanaticism. While the collectivist ignores his own personality, the fanatic ignores that of the other man. . . . Only his own opinion is valid. . . . Ultimately, all these four symptoms can be traced back to man's fear of responsibility and his escape from freedom." [41] Education and mental hygiene are required to cure the collective neuroses rather than psychotherapy.

THE NEUROSES   Noögenic neuroses and the collective neuroses are included under the neuroses in the broad sense of the term. In a more restricted sense neurosis involves primarily the psychic dimension of man. "Neurosis is no noetic, no spiritual illness, no illness of man merely in his spirituality. Much more it is always an illness of man in his unity and wholeness." [42] Psychological complexes, conflicts, and traumatic experiences, however, are manifestations, rather than causes, of neurosis, which is more closely related to a developmental defect in the personality structure. Anxiety is a common factor, although it is not the cause of neurosis; however, it sustains the neurotic circle. Anticipatory anxiety is a more basic element. A fleeting symptom or a momentary failure in functioning may become the focus of attention. A fear of the recurrence of the symptom arises, which reinforces the symptom, beginning a neurotic circle that includes anticipatory anxiety.

There are two major types of neurosis.

Anxiety Neurosis / Anxiety neurosis involves a malfunctioning of the vasomotor system, or a disturbance of endocrine function, or a constitutional element. Traumatic experiences act as precipitating agents, focusing attention upon the symptoms. But behind neurotic anxiety there is an existential anxiety. This existential anxiety is the "fear of death and simultaneously the fear of life as a whole." [43] It is the result of a guilty conscience toward life, a sense of not having realized one's own value potentials. This fear becomes focused upon a particular organ of the body or concentrated upon a symbolic concrete situation in the form of a phobia. A patient suffering from fear of open places described her anxiety as "a feeling like hanging in the air," which aptly described her whole spiritual situation, of which her neurosis was an expression. [44] The neurosis, existentially, is a mode of existence.

Obsessional Neurosis / Obsessional neurosis, like all other neuroses, includes a constitutional, dispositional factor as well as a psychogenic factor. But there is also an existential factor, represented by the choice or decision of the individual to go on to a fully developed obsessional neurosis. "The patient is not responsible for his obsessional ideas," but "he certainly is responsible for his attitude toward these ideas." [45] The obsessional neurotic is not able to tolerate uncertainty. He is intolerant of the tension between what is and what ought to be. His world view is one of "hundred-percentness," or a search for the absolute, a striving for "absolute certainty in cognition and decision." [46] Since it is impossible for him to achieve his total demands on life, he concentrates on a specific area; but even here he can succeed "only partially . . . and only at the price of his naturalness, his 'creaturalness.' Thus all his strivings have an inhuman quality." [47]

THE PSYCHOSES In the neuroses both the symptoms and the etiology are psychological. In the psychoses the etiology is physical and the symptoms are psychological.

Melancholia / Melancholia, or endogenous psychosis, also involves psychogenetic and existential aspects, or a "pathoplastic" factor, which refers to the freedom to shape one's destiny and to determine one's mental attitude toward the disease. Thus, "even psychosis is at bottom a kind of test of a human being, of the humanity of the psychotic patient." [48] With freedom of mental attitude goes responsibility. The anxiety present in melancholia has a physiological basis, but this does not explain the anxiety or the guilt. These are caused primarily by fear of death and of conscience, and represent a mode of existence or of experiencing. [49] "Conscientious anxiety can be understood only . . . *as the anxiety of a human being as such: as existential* anxiety," [50] not in physiological terms. Although an animal can suffer from anxiety, human psychoses involve a crucial element of humanity —of existentiality—above and beyond the organic condition.

In melancholia the physiological basis or "psychophysical insufficiency is experienced in uniquely human fashion as tension between what the person is and what he ought to be," between "the need and the possibility of fulfillment." [51] This insufficiency is felt as inadequacy and appears in various forms, bringing out fears that were present in the premorbid condition: fears of inability to earn sufficient money, of inability to attain one's life goals, of "Judgment Day." The melancholiac "becomes blind to the values inherent in his own being" and later to the values outside himself. First "he feels himself as worthless and his own life as meaningless," [52] then the world itself is seen in the same light. Guilt arising from the individual's feeling of insufficiency and "resulting from his intensified existential tension can swell to such a point that he feels his guilt to be ineradicable." [53] Life then assumes colossal dimensions.

Schizophrenia / In schizophrenia the phenomenon of feelings of being influenced, observed, or persecuted are all forms of the "experience of pure objectness. . . . The schizophrenic experiences himself as the object of the observing or persecuting intentions of his fellow men." [54] He experiences himself as if he were transformed from a subject into an object. There is an "experiential passivity" that is evidenced in the language of schizophrenics by the use of the passive mood. "The schizophrenic person experiences himself as so limited in his full humanity that he no longer feels himself as really 'existent.' " [55] Both consciousness and responsibility are affected.

THE THERAPY PROCESS

Patients repeatedly present problems concerning the meaning of their lives, that is, philosophical or spiritual problems. These problems may or may not be a sign of disease or neurosis. Neuroses and psychoses, including the organic psychotic processes, have an existential aspect as well as constitutional and psychogenetic aspects. They involve both a freedom of spiritual attitude toward the constitutional and psychological factors and a mode of existence. Therefore, treatment must be more than medical, more than psychological; it must include consideration of the existential aspects, too.

Logotherapy is directed toward such problems. Logos has the twofold meaning of "the meaning" and "the spiritual." Logotherapy thus deals with the existential and spiritual nature of man.

Diagnosis

Proper diagnosis is the first step in psychotherapy, and an important one. All emotional disturbance or mental illness involves physical, psychological, and spiritual factors: "there are really no pure somatogenic, psychogenic,, or noögenic neuroses. There are merely mixed cases, cases in which, respectively, a somatogenic, psychogenic, or noögenic moment moves into the foreground of the theoretical object and the therapeutic objective." [56] The purpose of diagnosis is to determine the nature of each factor and which is the primary factor. When the physical factor is the primary one, the condition is a psychosis; when the psychological factor is primary, it is a neurosis; and when the spiritual factor is primary, it is a noögenic neurosis.

Therapy involves the whole man, however, and may include physical (or medical) treatment, psychotherapy, and logotherapy, together or consecutively. As Frankl puts it, it is "not the aim of logotherapy to take the place of existing psychotherapy, but only to complement it, thus forming a picture of man in his wholeness—which includes the spiritual dimension." It focuses explicitly on meanings and values. A psychotherapy "which is blind to values"—for "there is no such thing as a psychotherapy unconcerned with values" [57]—is inadequate to deal with these problems.

General Nature of Logotherapy

Whereas the aim of psychoanalysis is to make the unconscious conscious, and the aim of individual psychological therapy (Adler) is to make the neurotic accept responsibility for his symptoms, the aim of logotherapy is to make man consciously accept responsibility for himself. "For the aim of the psychotherapist should be to bring out the ultimate possibilities of the patient. Not to penetrate his deepest secrets, but to realize his latent values. . . . " [58] Logotherapy fills a gap in psychotherapy; it "operates, as it were, beyond the fields of the Oedipus complex and the inferiority complex . . . beyond all affect-dynamics." It is "a form psychotherapy which sees beneath the psychic malaise of the neurotic his spiritual struggles." [59]

Philosophical and existential, or spiritual, problems cannot be avoided, nor can they be disposed of by focusing upon their pathological roots or consequences—physical or psychological. "What is needed here is to meet the patient squarely. We must not dodge the discussion, but enter into it sincerely. We must attack these questions on their own terms, at face value. Our patient has a right to demand that the ideas he advances be treated on the philosophical level. . . . A philosophical question cannot be dealt with by turning the discussion toward the pathological roots from which the question stemmed, or by hinting at the morbid consequences of philosophical pondering. . . . If only for the sake of philosophical fairness, we ought to fight with the same weapons." [60]

Psychotherapy cannot deal with philosophical questions. The neurotic's world view may be wrong, but correcting it is the function of logotherapy rather than of psychotherapy. If his world view is right, psychotherapy is unnecessary. Philosophical questions cannot be reduced to psychological terms. "Psychotherapy as such is exceeding its scope in dealing with philosophical questions. . . . Logotherapy must *supplement* psychotherapy." [61]

In actual practice, however, psychotherapy and logotherapy cannot be separated, since the psychological and the philosophical or spiritual aspects of man are indissolubly joined and can be separated only logically. Nevertheless, in principle they represent different realms. Psychotherapy uncovers the psychological background of an ideology, while logotherapy reveals the flaws in the improper bases for a world view.

Sometimes it is wise to begin with the spiritual level, even though the genesis of the problem may be in the lower layers. In other cases logotherapy follows psychotherapy of psychoses or neuroses.

Logotherapy and the Noögenic Neuroses

Logotherapy is the specific therapy for existential frustration, existential vacuum, or the frustration of the will to meaning. These conditions, when they result in neurotic symptomatology, are called noögenetic neuroses.

Logotherapy is concerned with making men conscious of their responsibility, since being responsible is an essential basis of human existence. Responsibility implies obligation, and obligation can be understood only in terms of meaning—the meaning of human life. The question of meaning is an intrinsically human one and arises in dealing with patients suffering from existential frustration or conflicts.[62] Logotherapy is thus concerned with problems involving meaning in its various aspects and realms.

THE MEANING OF LIFE AND DEATH   The normal individual can escape from a responsible life only in situations such as festivals and in intoxication. The neurotic seeks a permanent refuge from everyday society. The melancholiac seeks it through suicide. If questioned, he will deny such thoughts,

> whereupon we ask him . . . why he does not have (or no longer has) ideas of committing suicide. A melancholiac who really is not harboring such intentions or has overcome them, will answer without hesitation that he must consider his family, or think of his work, or something of the sort. The man who is trying to fool his analyst, however, will immediately fall into a typical state of embarrassment. He is actually at a loss for arguments supporting his "phony" affirmation of life. Characteristically, such dissimulating patients will try to change the subject, and will usually bring up their naked demand to be released from confinement. People are psychologically incapable of making up counterfeit arguments in favor of life, or arguments for their continuing to live, when thoughts of suicide are surging up within them.[63]

We can grasp the meaning of the universe best in the form of a "supermeaning" to indicate that the meaning of the whole goes beyond what is comprehensible. But "belief in a supermeaning—whether as a metaphysical concept or in the religious sense of Providence—is of foremost psychotherapeutic and psychohygienic importance. . . . To such a faith there is, ultimately, nothing that is meaningless."[64]

The individual is, of course, not only, or perhaps even primarily, concerned with the meaning of the universe, but is also concerned with the meaning of his own personal life. Patients often assert that the meaning of life is pleasure, "that all human activity is governed by the striving for happiness, that all psychic processes are determined exclusively by the pleasure principle. . . . Now, to our mind the pleasure principle is an artificial creation of psychology. Pleasure is not the goal of our aspirations, but the consequence of attaining them."[65] Pleasure cannot give meaning to life. If pleasure were the source of meaning, life would have little to offer, since unpleasant sensations outnumber pleasant sensations in life. "In reality, life is little concerned with pleasure or unpleasure. . . . Life teaches most people that 'we are not here to enjoy ourselves.' "[66] And those who are bent on the search for pleasure and happiness fail to find them, because of their concentration upon them.

The basic skepticism and nihilism of these patients has to be countered. "But it often becomes necessary in addition to disclose the full richness of the world of values, and to make clear the extent of its domain." [67] If the patient bewails his life for its lack of meaning, "since his activities are without any higher value . . . this is the point at which we must reason with him, showing him that it is a matter of indifference what a person's occupation is, or at what job he works. The crucial thing is how he works, whether he in fact fills the place in which he happens to have landed." [68]

In the case of a would-be suicide, the question is "whether the sum of [a] balance sheet can ever turn out so negative that living on appears incontrovertibly without value." Such a conviction is subjective and may be unjustified. "We can therefore risk the generalization that suicide is never ethically justified. . . . it is our duty to convince the would-be suicide that taking one's own life is categorically contrary to reason, that life is meaningful to every human being under any circumstances. We believe this can be done by objective argument and analysis of the problem on its own terms—by the methods of logotherapy, that is. . . . Where no psychopathological basis of motivation can be shown, and where, therefore, psychotherapy in the narrower sense of the word can find no point of departure, logotherapy is the indicated method." [69] Even in suicide "man cannot escape his sense of responsibility. For he commits the act of suicide in freedom (assuming, of course, that he is still sane)." [70]

The aim of logotherapy is to help patients "find an aim and a purpose in their existence," to help them "achieve the highest possible activation" of their lives.[71] In addition to being led to experience existence as a constant effort to actualize values, patients must be shown the value of the conviction of responsibility for a task, a specific task. "The conviction that one has a task before him has enormous psychotherapeutic and psychohygienic value. We venture to say that nothing is more likely to help a person overcome or endure objective difficulties or subjective troubles than the consciousness of having a task in life." [72]

"The factors of uniqueness and singularity are essential constituents of the meaningfulness of human existence." The patient must be shown that every life has a unique goal, which is reached by a single course. If he does not know his unique potentialities, his primary task is to discover them. "Existential analysis is accordingly designed to help the individual comprehend his responsibility to accomplish each of his tasks"; [73] the fulfillment of these assignments gives meaning to life.

The finiteness of existence also gives meaning to life. Death does not render life meaningless; rather the temporality of life gives it meaningfulness. If life were not finite, everything could be postponed; there would be no need for action, choice, or decisions, and thus no responsibility. "The meaning of human existence is based upon its irreversible quality." [74] In logotherapy this aspect of life must be put before the patient to bring him to consciousness of his responsibility. He may be encouraged to imagine he is reviewing "his own biography in the declining days of his life," and as he comes to the "chapter dealing with the present phase of his life . . . by a miracle he has the power to decide what the contents of the next chapter shall be. He is to imagine, that is, that it still lies within his capacity to make corrections, as it were, in a crucial chapter of his unwritten inner life story." [75] The categorical imperative of logotherapy applies here: "live as if you were living for the second time and had acted as wrongly the first time as you are about to act now." [76] Once a patient does this, he will realize the great responsibility he bears, the responsibility for the next hour and the next day.

Every man has a unique destiny, which, like death, is a part of life. "What we call destiny is that which is essentially exempt from human freedom, that lies neither within the scope of man's power nor his responsibility." [77] Destiny has meaning, and to quarrel with it is to overlook its meaning. Without the restrictions imposed by destiny, freedom would have no meaning. "Freedom without destiny is impossible; freedom can only be freedom in the face of a destiny, a free stand toward destiny. . . . Freedom presupposes restrictions, is contingent upon restrictions. . . . If we wanted to define man, we would have to call him that entity which has freed itself from whatever has determined it (determined it as biological-psychological-sociological type); that entity, in other words, that transcends all these determinants either by conquering them and shaping them, or by deliberately submitting to them." [78]

The past is part of man's destiny, since it is unalterable, but the future is not exclusively determined by the past. The mistakes of the past can serve as lessons for shaping the future. Man's disposition, or biological endowment, is part of his destiny, as is his situation, or external environment, and also his psychic attitude, to the extent that it is unfree. The constant struggle between man's inward and outward destiny and his freedom is the intrinsic nature of life.

Logotherapy sees destiny as "the ultimate testing ground for human freedom." [79] Biological, psychological, and sociological destiny obstruct human freedom. But the way in which the same handicaps and barriers are meaningfully incorporated into a person's life varies widely among individuals, as does the attitude or position taken toward them. Neurotics exhibit a morbid acceptance of fate and destiny, but such neurotic fatalism is only a disguised form of escape from responsibility. Patients cannot be allowed to blame childhood educational and environmental influences for what they are or for determining their destinies. This practice, and that of blaming their neuroticism for their faults, are ways of avoiding responsibility. Even the patient with an organic disorder is responsible for his spiritual attitude toward his condition.

THE MEANING OF SUFFERING   Man's responsibility is for the actualization of values. The three categories of values (already mentioned) are those that are actualized by doing; those that are realized by experiencing the world; and attitudinal values, which "are actualized wherever the individual is faced with something unalterable, something imposed by destiny. From the manner in which a person takes these things upon himself, assimilates these difficulties into his own psyche, there flows an incalculable multitude of value-potentialities. This means that *human life can be fulfilled not only in creating and enjoying, but also in suffering.*"[80] Life can obtain its ultimate meaning not only in sacrificing it, as a hero, but in the very process of facing death. Trouble and suffering guard man from apathy and boredom; they result in activity, thus leading to growth and maturity.

The destiny a person suffers is "to be shaped where possible, and to be endured where necessary." Only when man "no longer has any possibility of actualizing creative values, when there is really no means at hand for shaping fate—then is the time for attitudinal values to be actualized. . . . The very essence of an attitudinal value inheres in the manner in which a person resigns himself to the inevitable; in order therefore for attitudinal values to be truly actualized, it is important that the fate he resigns himself to must be actually inevitable."[81] Thus, every situation offers the opportunity for the actualization of values, if not for creative or experiential values, then for attitudinal values. "Cases may arise where existential analysis is called upon to make a person capable of suffering—whereas psychoanalysis, for instance, aims only at making him capable of pleasure or capable of doing. For there are situations in which man can fulfill himself only in genuine suffering, and in no other way."[82]

THE MEANING OF WORK   Responsibility to life is assumed by responding to the situations that it presents. "The response should be given not in words but in acting, by doing."[83] Consciousness of responsibility arises out of awareness of a unique concrete personal task, a "mission." The realization of creative values usually coincides with a person's work, which generally represents the area in which his uniqueness can be seen in relation to society. His work as a contribution to society is the source of the meaning and the value of his uniqueness. It is not the particular occupation upon which fulfillment depends. "The job at which one works is not what counts, but rather the manner in which one does the work."[84] Neurotics who complain that a different occupation would offer fulfillment must be shown this. It is not the occupation itself, but the expression of the person's uniqueness and singularity in the work or beyond the required duties, which gives meaning to the occupation.

For some, work seems to be only a means to the end of obtaining money to live, and life seems only to begin with leisure. There are also those whose work is so exhausting that there is no time for leisure, but only for sleep. Some devote all their time to the pursuit of wealth as an end in itself. Work can be misused, as a means to a neurotic end. The neurotic may also sometimes attempt to escape from life in general by taking refuge in his work. When he is not working, he feels at a loss, and the poverty of meaning in his life is revealed. "These people who know no goal in life are running the course of life at the highest possible speed so that they will not notice the aimlessness of it. They are at the same time trying to run away from themselves—but in vain. On Sundays, when the frantic race pauses for twenty-four hours, all the aimlessness, meaninglessness, and emptiness of their existence rises up before them once more." [85] Commercialized entertainment provides a refuge for these Sunday neurotics.

The existential importance of work is seen in what Frankl calls the "unemployment neurosis." The most prominent symptom in the unemployed person is apathy, the feeling of uselessness and emptiness. "He feels useless because he is unoccupied. Having no work, he thinks life has no meaning." [86] In neurotics unemployment becomes an alibi for all their failures and wipes out all responsibility to others and to themselves, as well as to life. But the unemployment may be a result of the neurosis rather than the neurosis a result of unemployment.

Unemployment is not an unconditional fate to which one must succumb by developing an unemployment neurosis. There is an alternative to surrendering physically to the forces of social destiny. It is possible to engage in various other activities, to use time constructively, to take an affirmative attitude toward life. Work is not the only way to give life meaning. The individual can decide what his attitude will be, whether positive and hopeful or apathetic.

Unemployment neurosis can be treated psychotherapeutically, but only by logotherapy, since it is a problem related to the meaning of existence. Logotherapy "shows the jobless person the way to inner freedom in spite of his unfortunate situation and teaches him that consciousness of responsibility through which he can still give some content to his hard life and wrest meaning from it." [87]

THE MEANING OF LOVE   The community is a rich field of human experience. The intimate community of oneself with another is the area in which experiential values are especially realizable. "Love is living the experience of another person in all his uniqueness and singularity. . . . In love the beloved person is comprehended in his very essence, as the unique and singular being that he is; he is comprehended as a thou, and as such is taken into the self. As a human person he becomes for the one who loves him indispensable and irreplaceable without having done anything to bring this about. . . . Love is not deserved, is unmerited—it is simply grace. . . . It is also enchantment," [88] which reflects upon the world and upon man's values. There is a third factor that enters into love—"the miracle of love," that is, the entrance into life of a new person, a child.

Man as lover can react differently to the three layers of the human person—the physical, the psychic, and the spiritual. The most primitive attitude is the sexual, directed toward the physical layer. The erotic attitude (commonly called infatuation) is directed toward the psychic layer. Love is the third attitude, directed toward the loved one's spiritual layer. This layer constitutes the uniqueness and singularity of the loved one, which, unlike the physical and psychological states, is irreplaceable and permanent.

"Love is only one of the possible ways to fill life with meaning, and is not even the best way. Our existences would have come to a sad pass and our lives would be poor indeed if their meaning depended upon whether or not we experienced happiness in love. . . . The individual who neither loves nor is loved can still shape his life in a highly meaningful manner." [89] But if love is lacking, it may be due to a neurotic failure rather than to destiny. Outward physical attractiveness is relatively unimportant, and its lack is not sufficient reason for being resigned to renunciation of love. Renouncing love engenders resentment, since it implies either overvaluing or devaluing love.

Emphasis on appearance or external beauty leads to devaluation of the person as such. Sex appeal is impersonal. Relationships based on sex are superficial; they are not love. Nor do those involved in such relationships want love, which includes responsibility. True love is experienced as valid forever. Man can mistake infatuation for love, but it can turn out to be error only later on.

Neurotics may fear the tensions of unhappy, unrequited love and so avoid opportunities for love. Such persons must be reeducated to be ready and receptive, to wait for the single happy love affair that may follow nine unhappy ones. Psychotherapy must bring the flight tendency into the open.

Psychosexual maturing, which begins in puberty, is subject to three kinds of disturbance, resulting in different sexual neuroses. One type occurs at the final stage of sexual maturing, when the physical sexual urge is becoming an erotic tendency directed toward a person. It may happen, perhaps after some disappointment in love, that a young person believes he will never find someone he can at the same time respect and desire sexually. He then plunges into sexuality without emotion or love, reverting to a lower level of psychosexual development. This is, according to Frankl's terminology, the "resentment type." The second type is represented by persons who have never progressed beyond sexuality to an erotic attitude and do not expect to experience love. This is the "resignation type." Such individuals maintain that love is an illusion; they include the Don Juan. The third type, the "inactive type," shuns the other sex entirely. The sex instinct is expressed only in masturbation. This group also includes young people who suffer from sexual frustration, which is the expression of a more general psychological distress. Such sexual frustration in a young person is "an indication that his sex instinct is not yet (or is no longer) subordinated to an erotic tendency and so integrated into the total system of his personal strivings." [90]

The so-called sexual frustration of youth is not solved by sexual activity, but by maturation to love. "The therapy is of the simplest. It suffices to introduce the young person in question into a mixed company of people of his age. There the young man will sooner or later fall in love—that is, he will find a partner—in the erotic and not in the sexual sense," [91] and will progress to the erotic stage of development. Crude sexuality and frustration will disappear. The person meanwhile matures, so that if and when a serious sexual relationship does develop, its sexuality will assume the appropriate form, as an expression of love. "Now, under the dominance of the erotic tendency, he can build up an erotic relationship within the framework of which sexual relations can then be considered. . . . The young man's sense of responsibility has meanwhile matured to the point where he can decide on his own and his partner's behalf whether and when he ought to enter into a serious sexual relationship with her." [92] The therapist's position on sexual intercourse between young people is that he must veto it if he can whenever it is not a part of real love. In no case, however, can he recommend it, since this is a personal moral problem and it is the responsibility of the person himself to decide. The therapist's task is to teach him to be responsible.

Logotherapy is the specific therapy for the noögenic neuroses because it directs itself toward the primary problem—their basic nature, the existential frustration or vacuum, or the lack of meaning in life and its various aspects. The therapeutic goal is to eliminate the frustration by filling the vacuum, by helping the patient achieve meaning in his life. This is accomplished by helping him to understand and accept the existential or spiritual nature of life, and to accept responsibility for himself and for the actualization of values through his responses to the demands or tasks that life presents to him.

Logotherapy as a Nonspecific Therapy of Neuroses

In the treatment of psychogenic neurotic reactions, logotherapy directs itself, not to the symptoms, nor to their psychogenesis, but to the patient's attitudes toward the symptoms. Logotherapy has developed two specific techniques for dealing with neuroses. These are described below under "Implementation."

In addition, general logotherapy, as applied in the noögenic neuroses, is also applicable, not only in the specific neuroses but in psychoses as well, in relation to the existential or spiritual problems that are present.

In dealing with neurotics, logotherapy is not a symptomatic treatment. It is concerned instead with the patient's attitude toward his symptoms. "Insofar as logotherapy does not treat the symptom directly, but rather attempts to bring about a change of attitude, a personal reversal of attitude toward the symptom, it is truly a personalistic psychotherapy." [93]

IMPLEMENTATION: TECHNIQUES OF LOGOTHERAPY

Logotherapy places emphasis upon the relationship between the patient and the therapist. "This relationship between two persons is what seems to be the most significant aspect of the psychotherapeutic process, a more important factor than any method or technique." [94] With the diversity of patients and therapists, "the psychotherapeutic process consists of a continuous chain of improvisations." [95] The relationship requires a balance between the extremes of human closeness and scientific detachment. "This means that the therapist must neither be guided by mere sympathy, by his desire to help his patient, nor, conversely, repress his human interest in the other human being by dealing with him in terms of technique." [96]

Because it is concerned with existential, spiritual, or philosophical problems, logotherapy engages in discussion of these problems. The method is not an intellectual or strictly rational one, however. "Logotherapy is as far removed from being a process of 'logical' reasoning as from being merely moral exhortation. Above all, a psychotherapist—and the logotherapist included—is neither a teacher nor a preacher. . . ." The maieutic dialogue in the Socratic sense may be used; "it is not necessary, however, to enter into sophisticated debates with the patients." [97]

The concern with existential or spiritual questions is "fraught with intricate problems, for it then becomes necessary for the doctor to take a stand on the question of values. The moment the doctor commits himself to such a 'psychotherapy' . . . his own philosophy necessarily comes to the fore—whereas previously his outlook remained hidden behind his role as doctor." [98] The logotherapist must "beware of forcing his philosophy upon the patient. There must be no transference (or, rather, countertransference) of a personal philosophy, of a personal concept of values, to the patient." [99] This is because the concept of responsibility implies that the patient is responsible for himself. The logotherapist only brings him to experience this responsibility; the logotherapist does not tell him to what or for what he is responsible—neither whether he is responsible to his conscience, to his society, or to God or whatever higher power, nor for the realization of which values, for the fulfillment of which personal tasks, or for which particular meaning of life he is responsible.

Two logotherapeutic techniques are designed to deal with conditions met in cases of the anxiety and obsessive-compulsive neuroses. Anxiety neuroses and phobic conditions are characterized by anticipatory anxiety, which produces exactly the condition that the patient fears. According to Frankl, the occurrence of the condition then reinforces the anticipatory anxiety, creating a vicious circle, until the patient avoids or withdraws from those situations in which he expects his fears to recur. This withdrawal Frankl calls "wrong passivity," which is one of the "four patterns of response" he describes.[100] In obsessive-compulsive neuroses the patient engages in "wrong activity" when he fights his obsessive ideas and compulsions. "Wrong activity" also occurs in sexual neuroses in which the patient, striving for competent sexual performance, which he feels is demanded of him, engages in responses that are inappropriate to the situation. Excessive intention makes the performance of the desired function impossible.

In such cases there is also frequently an excessive attention and a compulsive self-observation.

In cases involving anticipatory anxiety, the logotherapeutic technique called paradoxical intention is useful. This technique requires or encourages the patient to intend, if only momentarily, that which he anticipates with fear. This is a reversal of his attitude toward the situation. In addition, "it is carried out in as humorous a setting as possible. This brings about a change of attitude toward the symptom which enables the patient to place himself at a distance from the symptom, to detach himself from his neurosis. . . . if we succeed in bringing the patient to the point where he ceases to flee from or to fight his symptoms, but on the contrary, even exaggerates them, then we may observe that the symptoms diminish and that the patient is no longer haunted by them." [101]

"Paradoxical intention is effective irrespective of the underlying etiologic basis: in other words it is an intrinsically nonspecific method. . . . This is not to say that it is a symptomatic therapy, however, for the logotherapist, when applying paradoxical intention, is concerned not so much with the symptom in itself but, with the patient's *attitude* toward his neurosis and its symptomatic manifestations." [102]

Paradoxical intention is sometimes successful in severe and long-standing cases. It is particularly effective in short-term treatment of phobias with underlying anticipatory anxiety. Seventy-five percent of the patients treated have been cured or have improved. It is not a superficial method; it appears to affect deeper levels. It is "essentially more than a change of behavior patterns; rather, it is an existential reorientation (*existentielle Umstellung*)." [103] It is logotherapy in the truest sense of the word, "based on what is called in logotherapeutic terms psychonoëtic antagonism . . . which refers to the specifically human capacity to detach oneself, not only from the world but also from oneself." [104]

Excess of attention, intention, and self-observation are treated by another logotherapeutic technique, which is called de-reflection. This consists of ignoring the trouble. "Such ignoring, or de-reflection, however, can only be attained to the degree to which the patient's awareness is directed toward positive aspects. De-reflection, in itself, contains both a negative and a positive aspect. The patient must be de-reflected from his anticipatory anxiety *to* something else. . . . Through de-reflection, the patient is enabled to ignore his neurosis by focusing his attention away from himself. He is directed to a life full of potential meanings and values that have a specific appeal to his personal potentialities." [105] Paradoxical intention substitutes "right passivity" for "wrong passivity." De-reflection substitutes "right activity" for "wrong activity."

EXAMPLES

The following case is reported by Frankl.

Paradoxical intention is also applicable in cases more complex than those involving monosymptomatic neurosis. The following will demonstrate that even instances of severe obsessive-compulsive character neurosis (in German clinical terminology referred to as anankastic psychopathic character structure) may be appropriately and beneficially treated by means of paradoxical intention.

The patient was a sixty-five-year-old woman who had suffered for sixty years from a washing compulsion of such severity that she was admitted to our clinic for a period of observation in order that I might certify her for a leucotomy (which I expected to be the only available procedure for bringing relief in this severe case). Her symptoms began when she was four years of age. When she was prevented from indulging her washing compulsion, she would even lick her hands. Later on she was continually afraid of being infected by people with skin diseases. She would never touch a doorknob. She also insisted that her husband stick to a very complicated prophylactic ritual. For a long time the patient had been unable to do any housework, and finally she remained in bed all day. Nevertheless, even there she persisted in scrubbing things with a cloth for hours, up to three hundred times or more, and having her husband repeatedly rinse out the cloth. "Life was hell for me," she confessed.

In the hope of avoiding brain surgery, my assistant, Dr. Eva Niebauer, started logotherapeutic treatment by means of paradoxical intention. The result was that nine days after admission the patient began to help in the ward by mending the stockings of her fellow patients, assisting the nurses by cleaning the instrument tables and washing syringes, and finally even emptying pails of bloody and putrid waste materials! Thirteen days after admission she went home for a few hours and upon her return to the clinic, she triumphantly reported having eaten a roll with soiled hands. Two months later she was able to lead a normal life.

It would not be accurate to say that she is completely symptom-free, for frequently obsessive-compulsive ideas come to her mind. However, she has been able to get relief by ceasing to fight her symptoms (fighting only serves to reinforce them) and, instead, by being ironical about them; in short, by applying paradoxical intention. She is even able to joke about her pathologic thoughts. This patient still kept in contact with the outpatient clinic, for she continued to need supportive logotherapy. The improvement in her condition persisted however, and thus the leucotomy, which previously had seemed unavoidable, had now become unnecessary.[106]

The following case report is taken from a report of seven cases by an American psychiatrist who applied the method of paradoxical intention to twenty-four cases with successful results.

A. V., aged forty-five, married mother of one sixteen-year-old son, has a twenty-four-year history of a grave phobic neurosis consisting of severe claustrophobia such as fear of riding in cars. She had fear of heights, of riding in elevators, of crossing bridges, of collapsing, of leaving the house (when forced to do so, she would hang on to trees, bushes, anything). She also had a fear of open spaces, being alone, and becoming paralyzed. She was treated for her phobic neurosis over the past twenty-four years by various psychiatrists and received, repeatedly, long-term psychoanalytically oriented psychotherapy. In addition, the patient was hospitalized several times, received several series of electroconvulsive treatments (ECT), and finally lobotomy was suggested. During the four years before I saw her, she had been hospitalized continuously on a disturbed ward in a state hospital. There she received ECT and intensive drug therapy with barbiturates, phenothiazines, monoamine oxidase inhibitors, and amphetamine compounds—all to no avail. She had become so paralyzed by her numerous phobias that she was unable to leave a certain part of the ward which surrounded her bed. She was constantly in acute distress in spite of receiving large doses of tranquilizers. Her tension was so great that her muscles hurt intensely. She tried constantly "not to collapse," "not to get nervous," and "not to become panicky." Diagnoses of her illness, made by private psychiatrists, ranged from psychoneurosis to schizophrenic reaction, schizo-affective type. Diagnosis at the hospital, just a few months before I treated her, was schizophrenic reaction, pseudoneurotic type, with phobic anxiety and depressive manifestations. While in the hospital, she had been treated for a year and a half with "intensive analytically oriented psychotherapy" by an experienced clinical psychologist.

On March 1, 1959, all medication was discontinued and I began treatment with Paradoxical Intention. The technique was fully explained to her and we worked together, symptom by symptom and fear by fear. We started off first with removing the smaller fears, such as the one of not being able to sleep. The patient was removed from the disturbed ward and was instructed to "try to pass out and become as panicky as possible." At first, she said angrily, "I don't have to be afraid! I am afraid! This is ridiculous. You are making me worse!" After a few weeks of struggle, the patient was able to remain on a ward located on the third floor and "unsuccessfully" tried hard to pass out and become paralyzed. Both the patient and I went to the elevator to ride to the fifth floor. The patient was instructed to walk into the elevator and ride up with the strong intention of passing out and showing me "how wonderfully she can become panicky and paralyzed." While on the elevator, I commanded her to pass out, but at this she laughed and replied: "I am trying so hard—I can't do it. I don't know what is the matter with me—I can't be afraid anymore. I guess I'm trying hard enough to be afraid!" Upon reaching the fifth floor, the patient was proud and overjoyed as well. This seemed to be the turning point in the treatment. From then on, she used Paradoxical Intention any time she needed it. For the first time in many years, the patient walked outside alone around the hospital without fear, but "constantly trying hard to become panicky and paralyzed." After five months of this therapy, she was symptom-free. She returned home for a week-end visit and enjoyed her stay there without any phobias for the first time in twenty-four years. When she returned to the hospital from this trip, she was contented and stated that there was only one fear left, namely that of crossing bridges. The same day we went together in my car and crossed a bridge. While crossing, I ordered her to pass out and become panicky, but she only laughed and said, "I can't! I can't!" Shortly thereafter, she was released from the hospital. Since then she has seen me every two to three months for a check-up "because of gratefulness." It is important for me to emphasize that quite purposefully I did not familiarize myself with her past history, nor with the underlying psychodynamics.

Two months ago she wanted a special appointment. When I saw her, she was quite tense, expressing anticipatory anxiety about getting sick again. Her husband had been out of work for several months and also had been suffering from a neurological disorder which was in the process of clearing. At the same time the patient was menstruating. This pressure caused her to become anxious and she was just beginning to slide back into the vicious cycle of her previous illness. In one session, however, she was able to understand what had happened and to avoid a re-establishment of the destructive pattern of her phobias. This patient has been out of the hospital and living a full and happy life with her family for two and a half years. Recovery was brought about with no attempt on my part to "understand" the patient's symptoms in terms of psychoanalytic theory and "depth psychology."

The question might well be asked: what really goes on in the sessions? Therapy is begun with taking the case history, recording symptomatology, etc., explaining to the patient the basic principles of Paradoxical Intention, and discussing case histories of my own and some of the typical cases reported by Frankl, Niebauer, and Kocourek. This usually takes between one and a half and two hours. This will do two things for the patient: he will learn to understand what we are trying to do and he will gain confidence that this therapy is effective. I have, for instance, found it very valuable to have a patient who has been cured with this type of treatment meet with the one who is starting in therapy, both in hospital and private practice. This can be done very well individually, and also is valuable in the group psychotherapy setting. I do not deny that this sort of thing has suggestive value, but, may I ask, what doctor or psychiatrist can treat his patients without this factor? As far as the technique itself is concerned, it must not be confused with suggestion. In fact, Paradoxical Intention represents just the opposite. It does not tell the patient as Coué did, "everything will get better and better," but it instructs the patient to *try intentionally to get worse.* The logotherapist asks the patient himself to wish that the feared thing will happen to him. Frankl says very specifically that "Paradoxical Intention is most genuine logotherapy. The patient shall objectivize his neurosis by distancing himself from his symptoms. The spiritual in man shall detach itself from the psychic within him, and the patient shall call on the *Trotzmacht des Geistes,* man's spiritual capacity to resist, and by his inner freedom choose a specific attitude in any given situation." [107]

When I feel that the patient thoroughly understands the mechanism involved in the technique, we apply and practice it together in my office. For instance, the patient who is afraid he might lose consciousness is asked to get up and try to "pass out." To evoke humor in the patient I always exaggerate by saying, for example, "Come on; let's have it; let's pass out all over the place. Show me what a wonderful 'passer-out' you are." And, when the patient tries to pass out and finds he cannot, he starts to laugh. Then I tell him, "If you cannot pass out here on purpose, intentionally, then you cannot pass out any other place if you try." So together we practice Paradoxical Intention in the office over and over again; but also, if necessary, in the patient's home or wherever his neurotic symptoms appear. Once the patient has successfully used Paradoxical Intention on one of his phobias, he enthusiastically applies the technique to his other symptoms. The number of therapy sessions depends largely on how long the patient has been sick. When the illness is acute, and duration has been of only a few weeks or months, most patients respond to this therapy within about four to twelve sessions. Those who have been sick for several years, even as long as twenty years or more (in my experience I had six such cases, although more have been reported in the literature), need six to twelve months of biweekly sessions to bring about recovery. It is necessary during the course of treatment to repeatedly teach and encourage the patient to use the technique according to his specific symptoms. Since the nervous system in itself is well known for its repetitious qualities, and since our feelings are carried and expressed through nerve tissue, namely the autonomic nervous system, a once-established neurotic feeling pattern will tend to repeat itself and become a sort of reflex, even when the causes of the neurotic symptoms have been resolved and removed. Because of this repetitious quality of the nervous system, it is also absolutely essential in therapy to repeat the application of Paradoxical Intention over and over . . .

Initially, patients show very good response to Paradoxical Intention but during the course of therapy, particularly in chronic cases, patients will repeatedly suffer little setbacks. This is caused by the fact that as soon as patients *try to get better,* they enter the vicious cycle again, striving for health and providing the neurosis with new fuel. In other words, they "forget" to apply Paradoxical Intention and become worse by Coué's method of suggestion. This failure of the patient to continue to practice the technique is precisely because of the above-mentioned repetitive neurotic behavior patterns. ("I have tried to fight my neurosis for so many years the wrong way. It is hard to re-learn.") But there is another element involved here: the therapist demands from the patient tremendous courage, namely to do the things he so much fears. For instance, the patient who has the fear of blushing when in a group, is asked to do just that. Here, we appeal to the personal pride of the patient and his inner freedom in his spiritual dimension, and thus practice logotherapy in its true meaning. For all these reasons the therapist must never tire of encouraging the patient to continue to use Paradoxical Intention over and over—just as his neurosis produces the symptoms over and over. Then, finally, the neurotic symptoms will "become discouraged" and disappear. Only too often "they try to come back" but then Paradoxical Intention strangles them. "When they saw that they could not get anywhere with me any-more, they gave up completely." [108]

SUMMARY AND EVALUATION

Logotherapy is an existential approach to aiding the individual with problems of a philosophical or spiritual nature. These are problems of the meaning of life—the meaning of death, of suffering, of work, and of love. Problems in these areas result in existential frustration, or a sense of meaninglessness in life.

The meaning of life is not found by questioning the purpose of existence. It arises from the responses that man makes to life, to the situations and tasks with which life confronts him. Although there are biological, psychological, and sociological factors influencing man's responses, there is always an element of freedom of choice. He cannot always control the conditions with which he is confronted, but he can control his responses to them. Man is thus responsible for his re-sponses, his choices, and his actions.

Existential frustration may exist without neurosis or psychosis, but it may lead to neurosis, and neuroses and psychoses always have existential aspects. Logotherapy is directed toward existential frustra-tion and the existential aspects of neurosis and psychosis. It is thus not a substitute for, but is complementary to, psychotherapy. Logo-therapy is not concerned with psychodynamics or psychogenesis. It deals rather with the patient's philosophical and spiritual problems. Its aim is to bring out the ultimate possibilities of the patient, to realize his latent values, not to lay bare his deepest secrets. Self-actualization is not accepted as an end in itself. Fulfillment of oneself is possible only to the extent that man has fulfilled the concrete meaning of his personal existence. Self-actualization is thus a by-product.

Two specific techniques are described: paradoxical intention and de-reflection. The former appears to be quite similar to Knight Dun-lap's negative practice. Some other aspects of Frankl's method also resemble deconditioning. However, Frankl relates these techniques to existentialism and emphasizes effects beyond symptom removal. Nev-ertheless, there appear to be some similarities and parallels between the cases described by Frankl and those presented by Salter and Wolpe. Paradoxical intention deals with symptoms. The method en-courages the patient to enter or expose himself to feared situations, but without the expected results occurring, thus breaking the vicious circle and leading to extinction of the fear or anticipatory anxiety. Frankl, however, emphasizes the attitudinal aspects of the situation. It is the patient's attitude rather than the command, urging, or encouragement of the therapist that leads him to put himself in a situation where extinction can take place. It may be that, at the bottom, it is the changing of the patient's attitudes that is also the effective or necessary condition of other methods that lead to deconditioning or extinction, such as those of Salter and Wolpe.

For Frankl, the spiritual aspect is a separate dimension of man, different from the psychological. This is probably a result of the lack of concern for, or even rejection of, meanings and values by psychology. But it should not be necessary to consider meanings and values as constituting an independent aspect of man; they should be included as part of his psychological aspect. Nevertheless, Frankl has recognized and dealt with the concerns and distress of modern man by admitting them into psychotherapy as legitimate objects of treatment, rather than ignoring them or treating them as symptoms of unconscious or repressed intrapsychological impulse conflicts. His concept of attitudinal values is also a contribution. Ungersma feels that here Frankl "has made a profound and unique contribution to psychotherapy of all orientations . . . an insight that transcends the profoundest of Freud's contributions." [109]

While other approaches to counseling or psychotherapy emphasize self-actualization, self-fulfillment, or self-enhancement as the goal of therapy, Frankl subordinates this goal to that of the achievement of meaning. One might argue that it is the significance of events, situations, tasks, values, attitudes, etc., for self-realization that gives them meaning; they have no meaning in and of themselves, but only as they relate to the development of the individual.

It is probably unfair to judge logotherapy (or existential psychotherapy) on the basis of the techniques of paradoxical intention and de-reflection. They appear to be specific techniques for rather specific symptoms or neurotic conditions. They would hardly be generally applicable for the other major disturbances with which existential psychotherapy is concerned—existential frustration and loss or lack of meaning in life.

Logotherapy does deal with these philosophical or spiritual problems. The discussion of methods and techniques is inadequate and disappointing, however. It often appears to be combined with general psychotherapy and to utilize common methods and techniques. Frankl denies that his approach involves teaching or preaching, or that it is an intellectual or rational approach. Yet it often appears to be essentially a discussion of philosophical or spiritual problems with just these characteristics. Terms such as "reasoning," "convincing," "instructing," "training," "leading," etc., occur in the discussion of cases. Suggestion, persuasion, and reasoning appear to be part of the process.

There seems to be no question of the concern, sincerity, and dedication of Frankl. Nor does he prescribe the meanings of life for his clients, or specify their responsibilities. But he does appear to exert considerable influence in leading them to define and analyze their problems and to accept responsibility.

What, then, is the value of logotherapy? Perhaps its major value is the frank and open acceptance of philosophical problems involving goals and values as being of concern to the counselor or therapist. There is increasing evidence that modern man is troubled by problems of values and goals, the meaning of existence, and questions about freedom and responsibility. While other therapists show some peripheral concern about this area of human experience, Frankl makes it the center of his approach. This is the general center of interest of existentialism as manifested in the work of other existentialists, but Frankl's work has some advantages for students of counseling. It is not as obscure and as difficult to read as are most of the writings in existentialism, even though it is unsystematic, lacks organization, and is somewhat repetitious. It is not as abstract, or as mystical in its orientation. Nor is it characterized by the morbidity or pessimism of other existentialist approaches. While Frankl uses the word "spiritual" as a key concept, he is not using it as a synonym for "religious." In addition, although he seems to use "spiritual" interchangeably with "intellectual" or "mental," it goes beyond these, or beyond their rational aspects. Perhaps "philosophical" is the closest synonym.

While the approach of logotherapy is rather vague, with neither the theory nor the technique systematically developed or presented, it is of value to the student as an indication of the growing concern with aspects of life that are not considered, or not emphasized, in most other approaches to counseling or psychotherapy. It is possible that these aspects, related to values, goals, and the meaning of life, are today more frequently the source of problems and so-called neuroses than was true in the past. Contemporary civilization and society perhaps have changed the nature of the problems of man. In that case counseling and psychotherapy should reflect this changing or differing content. Changing conditions have brought to light a different view of man, a view that should be considered by those interested in counseling or psychotherapy.

REFERENCES

[1] Tweedie, D. F., Jr. *Logo-therapy and the Christian faith.* Grand Rapids, Mich.: Baker Book House, 1961. P. 27.   [2] *Ibid.,* p. 30.   [3] Frankl, V. E. *Logos und Existenze.* Vienna: Amandus-Verlag, 1951. P. 39. Cited (and translated) by D. F. Tweedie, Jr., *op. cit.,* p. 129.   [4] Frankl, V. E. *Das Menschenbild der Seelenheilkunde.* Stuttgart: Hippokrates-Verlag, 1959. P. 53. Cited (and translated) by D. F. Tweedie, Jr., *op. cit.,* p. 129.   [5] Frankl, V. E. *Man's search for meaning.* (Rev. ed.) New York: Washington Square Press, 1963. P. 59.

[6] *Ibid.,* p. 104.   **[7]** *Ibid.,* pp. 105–106.   **[8]** Frankl, V. E. *The doctor and the soul.* (2nd ed.) New York: Knopf, 1965. P. xi.   **[9]** It must be emphasized that by "spiritual" Frankl does not mean "religious."   **[10]** Frankl, V. E. *Handbuch der Neurosenlehre und Psychotherapie.* Vienna: Urban & Schwarzenberg, 1957. P. 674. Cited (and translated) by D. F. Tweedie, Jr., *op. cit.,* p. 57. **[11]** Frankl, V. E. *Logos und Existenze.* Vienna: Amandus-Verlag, 1951. P. 7. Cited (and translated) by D. F. Tweedie, Jr., *op. cit.,* p. 60.   **[12]** Frankl, V. E. Existential dynamics and neurotic escapism. *J. exist. Psychiat.,* 1963, **4,** 27–42. **[13]** Frankl, V. E. *Man's search for meaning.* (Rev. ed.) New York: Washington Square Press, 1963. P. 173.   **[14]** Frankl, V. E. *The doctor and the soul.* (2nd ed.) New York: Knopf, 1965. P. 5.   **[15]** *Ibid.,* p. 70.   **[16]** *Ibid.,* pp. 70, 71. **[17]** *Ibid.,* p. 72. See also Frankl, V. E. Logotherapy and the collective neuroses. In J. Masserman & J. L. Moreno (Eds.), *Progress in psychotherapy.* Vol. IV. New York: Grune & Stratton, 1959.   **[18]** Frankl, V. E. On logotherapy and existence analysis. *Amer. J. Psychoanal.,* 1958, **18,** 28–37.   **[19]** Frankl, V. E. *The doctor and the soul.* (2nd ed.) New York: Knopf, 1965. P. x.   **[20]** *Ibid.,* p. xiii.   **[21]** *Ibid.*   **[22]** Frankl, V. E. *Man's search for meaning.* (Rev. ed.) New York: Washington Square Press, 1963. P. 157.   **[23]** *Ibid.,* p. 158.   **[24]** *Ibid.,* pp. 172, 173.   **[25]** *Ibid.,* pp. 190–191.   **[26]** *Ibid.,* p. 167.   **[27]** *Ibid.,* p. 169.   **[28]** *Ibid.*   **[29]** *Ibid.,* p. 170.   **[30]** *Ibid.,* pp. 162–163. **[31]** Frankl, V. E. *The doctor and the soul.* (2nd ed.) New York: Knopf, 1965. P. 15.   **[32]** *Ibid.,* pp. 18–19.   **[33]** Frankl, V. E. *Man's search for meaning.* (Rev. ed.) New York: Washington Square Press, 1963. Pp. 164, 165–166.   **[34]** *Ibid.,* p. 166.   **[35]** Frankl, V. E. *The doctor and the soul.* (2nd ed.) New York: Knopf, 1965. Pp. 176–177.   **[36]** *Ibid.,* p. 177.   **[37]** Frankl, V. E. *Man's search for meaning.* (Rev. ed.) New York: Washington Square Press, 1963. P. 160. **[38]** Frankl, V. E. *Theorie und Therapie der Neurosen.* Vienna: Urban & Schwarzenberg, 1956. P. 125. Cited (and translated) by D. F. Tweedie, Jr., *op. cit.,* p. 95. **[39]** Frankl, V. E. *The doctor and the soul.* (2nd ed.) New York: Knopf, 1965. P. xvi.   **[40]** *Ibid.,* p. xvi.   **[41]** *Ibid.,* pp. xvi–xvii. See also Frankl, V. E. Logotherapy and the collective neuroses, *op. cit.*   **[42]** Frankl, V. E. *Theorie und Therapie der Neurosen.* Vienna: Urban & Schwarzenberg, 1956. P. 125. Cited (and translated) by D. F. Tweedie, Jr., *op. cit.,* p. 99.   **[43]** Frankl, V. E. *The doctor and the soul.* (2nd ed.) New York: Knopf, 1965. P. 180.   **[44]** *Ibid.* **[45]** *Ibid.,* p. 188.   **[46]** *Ibid.,* p. 191.   **[47]** *Ibid.,* p. 193.   **[48]** *Ibid.,* p. 200.   **[49]** *Ibid.,* p. 201.   **[50]** *Ibid.*   **[51]** *Ibid.,* p. 202.   **[52]** *Ibid.,* p. 204.   **[53]** *Ibid.,* p. 205.   **[54]** *Ibid.,* pp. 208–209.   **[55]** *Ibid.,* p. 210. **[56]** Frankl, V. E. *Theorie und Therapie der Neurosen.* Vienna: Urban & Schwarzenberg, 1956. Foreword. Cited (and translated) by D. F. Tweedie, Jr., *op. cit.,* p. 75.   **[57]** Frankl, V. E. *The doctor and the soul.* (2nd ed.) New York: Knopf, 1965. P. xi, xii.   **[58]** *Ibid.,* p. 8.   **[59]** *Ibid.,* p. 11.   **[60]** *Ibid.,* p. 13. **[61]** *Ibid.,* p. 17.   **[62]** *Ibid.,* p. 26.   **[63]** *Ibid.,* pp. 30–31.   **[64]** *Ibid.,* p. 33.   **[65]** *Ibid.,* pp. 34–35.   **[66]** *Ibid.,* pp. 36, 38.   **[67]** *Ibid.,* p. 42. **[68]** *Ibid.,* pp. 42–43.   **[69]** *Ibid.,* pp. 50, 51, 52.   **[70]** *Ibid.,* p. 53.   **[71]** *Ibid.,* p. 54.   **[72]** *Ibid.*   **[73]** *Ibid.,* pp. 55, 58.   **[74]** *Ibid.,* p. 64.   **[75]** *Ibid.*   **[76]** *Ibid.*   **[77]** *Ibid.,* p. 78.   **[78]** *Ibid.,* pp. 75–76.   **[79]** *Ibid.,* p. 82.   **[80]** *Ibid.,* pp. 105–106.   **[81]** *Ibid.,* pp. 111–112.   **[82]** *Ibid.,* pp. 113–114.   **[83]** *Ibid.,* p. 117.   **[84]** *Ibid.,* p. 118.   **[85]** *Ibid.,* pp. 127–128.

[86] *Ibid.,* p. 121.   [87] *Ibid.,* p. 126.   [88] *Ibid.,* pp. 132–133.   [89] *Ibid.,* p. 141.   [90] *Ibid.,* p. 170.   [91] *Ibid.,* pp. 170–171.   [92] *Ibid.,* p. 172. [93] Frankl, V. E. *Der Unbedingte Mensch.* Vienna: Verlag Franz Deuticke, 1947. P. 34. Cited (and translated) by D. F. Tweedie, Jr., *op. cit.,* p. 106.   [94] Frankl, V. E. Paradoxical intention: a logotherapeutic technique. *Amer. J. Psychother.,* 1960, **14,** 520–535. Reprinted in V. E. Frankl. *Psychotherapy and existentialism: selected papers on logotherapy.* New York: Washington Square Press, 1967. P. 144.   [95] *Ibid.*   [96] *Ibid.*   [97] Frankl, V. E. Logotherapy and the challenge of suffering. *Rev. exist. Psychol. Psychiat.,* 1961, **1,** 3–7. Reprinted in V. E. Frankl. *Psychotherapy and existentialism: selected papers on logotherapy.* New York: Washington Square Press, 1967. Pp. 57–58.   [98] Frankl, V. E. *The doctor and the soul.* (2nd ed.) New York: Knopf, 1965. P. 11.   [99] *Ibid.,* p. xv. [100] Frankl, V. E. Paradoxical intention: a logotherapeutic technique, *op. cit.* Reprinted in V. E. Frankl. *Psychotherapy and existentialism: selected papers on logotherapy.* New York: Washington Square Press, 1967. Pp. 161–162.   [101] *Ibid.,* p. 147.   [102] *Ibid.,* pp. 152, 153.   [103] *Ibid.,* pp. 156–157. [104] *Ibid.,* p. 157.   [105] *Ibid.,* pp. 160, 162.   [106] *Ibid.,* pp. 153–154. [107] Frankl, V. E. Seminar on logotherapy conducted at Harvard University Summer School, 1961.   [108] Gerz, H. O. The treatment of the phobic and the obsessive-compulsive patient using paradoxical intention sec. Viktor E. Frankl. *Int. J. Neuropsychiat.,* 1962, **3,** 375–387. Reprinted in V. E. Frankl. *Psychotherapy and extentialism: selected papers on logotherapy.* New York: Washington Square Press, 1967. Pp. 199–221. Reprinted here by permission of *Journal of Neuropsychiatry* Vol. 3, No. 6.   [109] Ungersma, A. J. *The search for meaning.* Philadelphia: Westminister, 1961. P. 28.

PART SIX

An Eclectic Position

19

Introduction

Eclecticism in counseling has been subjected to extensive criticism, falling into disrepute among many writers and theorists who hold to a particular school of thought. Rogers has referred to the attempt to reconcile various schools of thought as "a superficial eclecticism which does not increase objectivity, and which leads nowhere." [1] In another place he refers to a "confused eclecticism," which "has blocked scientific progress in the field" of psychotherapy.[2] Snygg and Combs wrote that "an eclectic system leads directly to inconsistency and contradition, for techniques derived from conflicting frames of reference are bound to be conflicting." [3] Thus, from the point of view of research and of practice, eclecticism has been considered as being undesirable. For research, "it is only by acting *consistently* upon a well-selected hypothesis that its elements of truth and untruth can become known." [4] In practice, a consistent frame of reference is desirable.

What is the nature of the eclecticism that has been so strongly attacked? Eclecticism in counseling has, as Brammer notes, referred to selecting, picking out, or choosing from various systems or theories.[5] Presumably what was selected was the best of each, but no criteria of what is best were stated. The choice was always an individual one. Moreover, the choices were not made and then consistently adhered to; rather choices were made as necessary or expedient in working with individual clients. Thus, no prediction could be made as to what an eclectic counselor would do—"it all depends on the circum-

459

stances or the client." The choices were not integrated or systematized into any whole or generalized into any principles. Every eclectic counselor was different from every other one. The only thing they had in common was the designation "eclectic." It should be obvious that such an approach to counseling can hardly be defined or described, and therefore, cannot be taught. No one knew what eclectic counseling was, and there are no textbooks on eclectic counseling. Eclectic counseling referred to what individualistic counselors, resistant to theory and consistency, practiced.

This seems to be a fair description of eclectic counseling; it is consistent with the brief dictionary definition. But the term is used differently by Thorne, Berenson and Carkhuff, and Brammer. Carkhuff and Berenson label their approach an "eclectic stance," which is systematic, but open, but they do not explicitly define eclecticism.[6] Thorne, arguing that all of the major theories or approaches are incomplete, attempts to incorporate them into an all-inclusive method, which he calls eclecticism, utilizing "the contributions of all recognized systems and schools of psychology according to their indications and contraindications." [7] His integrative psychology is a systematic theoretical foundation for eclectic clinical practice.

Brammer rejects attempts to "choose bits and pieces from a wide spectrum of counseling theories and methods," resulting in a "hodge-podge of contradictory assumptions and incompatible techniques," or the search for "cookbook techniques while avoiding theoretical issues." He proposes an "emerging eclecticism," developed from research and experience revealing common parameters of counseling and from a thorough study of all theoretical positions. The objective is to develop eventually a comprehensive, consistent, and systematic synthesis, "incorporating all valid knowledge about behavior." [8]

This concept of eclecticism is consistent with the definition given by English and English:

> Eclecticism. n. in *theoretical system building,* the selection and orderly combination of *compatible* features from diverse sources, sometimes from incompatible theories and systems; the effort to find valid elements in all doctrines or theories and to combine them into *a harmonious whole.* The resulting system is open to constant revision even in its major outlines. . . . Eclecticism is to be distinguished from *unsystematic* and *uncritical* combination, for which the name is syncretism. The eclectic seeks as much *consistency* as is currently possible; but he is unwilling to sacrifice conceptualizations that put meaning into a wide range of facts for the sake of what he is apt to think of as an unworkable *over-all* systematization. The formalist thus finds the eclectic's position too loose and uncritical. For his part, the eclectic finds formalism and schools too dogmatic and rigid, too much inclined to reject, if not facts, at least helpful conceptualization of facts.[9]

Thus, this newer concept of eclecticism is not atheoretical. The eclectic stance (to use Carkhuff's term) is a "recognition that no one theoretical orientation or series of techniques is adequate to deal with the complexities of multiple persons in potentially constructive interactions." [10] This statement is no doubt accurate for existing theories, but does not preclude the development of a more adequate comprehensive theory. Carkhuff and Berenson use such terms as "synthesis," "systematic," "integration," "encompassing," "comprehensive," in referring to their approach, which attempts to be systematic.

Eclecticism is thus, or should be, a systematic, integrative, theoretical position. It appears that the atheoretical, unsystematic approach to which the term eclecticism has been applied is syncretism, rather than a true eclecticism.[11]

Eclecticism differs from the theoretical positions of schools or cults in that, on the one hand, it is more comprehensive, attempting to integrate or synthesize the valid or demonstrated elements of these narrower or more restricted theories, and, on the other hand, it is a more open-ended, loose, or tentative theoretical position. There is, however, no sharp line between eclecticism and any other theoretical or systematic approach to counseling or psychotherapy. Many adherents of schools would insist that they are not rigid or dogmatic, but that they recognize the tentativeness of their approach. They are not formalists. They would feel that they are seeking a "maximum of understanding (with some loss of tightness of organization)" as English and English describe the eclectic, rather than a "maximum of rational order and over-all consistency (with resulting temporary loss in inclusiveness and explanatory power)," as they describe the formalist.[12]

The eclectic is thus not syncretistic, but is systematic; he is not atheoretical, but is a theorist. As Woods notes, "if there were no theoretical positions, there would be no eclecticism." [13] Eclecticism is simply a more comprehensive, loosely organized theory than a formal theory, attempting to be all-inclusive. If there is an underlying consistency and integration of the phenomena encompassed by an eclectic position, then, as the position or stance is developed and becomes supported by research and experience, it becomes more systematic and more tightly organized. In other words, it becomes a formal theory.

The development of an eclectic position requires the availability of a number of theoretical positions that, while lacking in comprehensiveness and inclusiveness, have demonstrated validity in terms of experience and/or research. That such theoretical systems exist today some would doubt. But one cannot, or should not, wait for complete validation of limited or part theories before attempting to go beyond them or to integrate them. Few have dared to attempt such an integration. In fact, there exists only one such attempt. That is the eclectic system of counseling and psychotherapy developed by Thorne.

Thorne was one of the first persons in the field of clinical psychology and counseling or psychotherapy to espouse the eclectic point of view in terms of a systematic position. His articles in the *Journal of Counseling Psychology*, beginning in 1945, presented this position, which was definitely stated in his *Principles of Personality Counseling* in 1950. His contribution has been inadequately recognized.

Thorne points to the rise of eclecticism in the past twenty-five years. In 1945, he notes, no members of the Division of Clinical Psychology identified themselves as eclectics. In 1970 over 50 percent so identified themselves.[14] This is impressive evidence of the change in attitude toward an eclectic position.

REFERENCES

[1] Rogers, C. R. *Client-centered therapy.* Boston: Houghton Mifflin, 1951. P. 8.
[2] Rogers, C. R. Client-centered therapy: a current view. In Frieda Fromm-Reichmann and J. L. Moreno (Eds.), *Progress in psychotherapy: 1956.* New York: Grune & Stratton, 1956. P. 24.   [3] Snygg, D., & Combs, A. W. *Individual behavior: a new frame of reference for psychology.* New York: Harper & Row, 1949. P. 282.   [4] Rogers, C. R. Client-centered therapy: a current view, *op. cit.*
[5] Brammer, L. M. Eclecticism revisited. *Personnel guid. J.,* 1969, **48,** 192–197.
[6] Carkhuff, R. R., & Berenson, B. G. *Beyond counseling and therapy.* New York: Holt, Rinehart and Winston, 1967. P. 228.   [7] Thorne, F. C. *Integrative psychology.* Brandon, Vt.: Clinical Publishing Co., 1967. P. 347.   [8] Brammer, L. M., *op. cit.*   [9] English, H. B., & English, Ava C. *A comprehensive dictionary of psychological and psychoanalytic terms.* New York: Longmans, Green, 1958. (Italics added.)   [10] Berenson, B. G., & Carkhuff, R. R. (Eds.), *Sources of gain in counseling and psychotherapy.* New York: Holt, Rinehart and Winston, 1967. P. 6.   [11] Woods, J. E. Letter to the editor. *Rehabilit. counsel. Bull.,* 1964, **8,** 18–20.   [12] English, H. B., & English, Ava C., *op. cit.* p. 168.
[13] Woods, J. E., *op. cit.*   [14] Thorne, F. C. Personal communication. January 22, 1972.

20

Thorne's eclectic system of clinical practice

Frederick Charles Thorne (1909–   ) received his bachelor's degree at Columbia College and his master's degree (1931) and doctorate (1934) at Columbia University, all in psychology. Not being able to obtain the clinical experience he desired in psychology, he turned to medicine and obtained his M.D. in 1938 at Cornell University. From 1939 to 1947 he was Director of the Brandon State School, Brandon, Vermont. Since 1947 he has been engaged in private practice. He was associated with the Department of Psychiatry of the University of Vermont College of Medicine as part-time Assistant Professor of Psychiatry from 1941 to 1953. In 1945 he founded the *Journal of Clinical Psychology*, which he continues to edit and publish. He is a Diplomate in Clinical Psychology of the American Board of Professional Psychology.

He has published *Principles of Personality Counseling* (1950), *Principles of Psychological Examining* (1955), *Clinical Judgment* (1961), *Personality: A Clinical Eclectic Viewpoint* (1961), and *Tutorial Counseling* (1965), as well as the books on which this chapter is mainly based: *Integrative Psychology* (1967), and the two volumes of *Psychological Case Handling*, Volume I: *Establishing the Conditions Necessary for Counseling and Psychotherapy* and Volume II: *Specialized Methods of Counseling and Psychotherapy*, both published in 1968. The latter constitute a revision of *Principles of Personality Counseling*, which was the basis for the chapter on *Thorne's Personality Counseling* in the first edition of this book.

463

BACKGROUND AND DEVELOPMENT

Thorne states that his interest in personality counseling originated in his search at the age of fifteen for an explanation for the stammer he had had since the age of five. He entered Columbia in 1926 to major in psychology and continued through the Ph.D. His entrance into medical school was a result of his frustration with the experimental and theoretical emphasis in psychology. He was impressed by the integration of the basic medical science into the eclectic system of practice, in comparison with the "ideological confusion of the psychological sciences in which there were almost as many schools and viewpoints as there were 'masters' who could win recognition." [1] He determined to attempt "to collect and integrate all known methods of personality counseling and psychotherapy into an eclectic system which might form the basis of standardized practice." [2] Beginning with the first volume of the *Journal of Clinical Psychology* in 1945, and also in other journals, Thorne published articles directed toward this objective. In 1950 these became part of his *Principles of Personality Counseling.*

The two volumes of *Psychological Case Handling* are based upon the system of personality developed in *Personality* [3] and *Integrative Psychology*,[4] and upon the diagnostic system of psychopathology developed in *Principles of Psychological Examining*,[5] and are to be used within the system of clinical practice presented in these books as well as in *Clinical Judgment* [6] and *How to Be Psychologically Healthy: Tutorial Counseling*.[7]

Thorne's eclectic position was no doubt influenced by the many teachers he had and others he was exposed to during his professional education and development. These included H. L. Hollingsworth, an associationist; K. M. Dallenbach, a psychophysicist; Adolph Meyer and W. H. Sheldon, psychobiologists; Alfred Adler and H. L. Ansbacher, Adlerians; Prescott Lecky and C. R. Rogers, self psychologists; Mortimer Adler, an objectivist; and William A. Marston, an integrative psychologist. He also made a personal study of Freudian psychology. His Ph.D. was taken with Robert S. Woodworth, an objectivist who was also an admitted eclectic, from whom he developed the idea of applying the eclectic method to clinical science in psychology following the pattern of Sir William Osler in medicine. He found that no single system had the complete answer and set out to develop an integration.

PHILOSOPHY AND CONCEPTS

Thorne attempts to be "rigidly scientific and eclectic" in his approach.[8] A true eclecticism is not "(a) an 'hodgepodge' of disconnected facts, (b) largely torn from context, (c) unrelated to any unifying structure, (d) lacking global perspective, (e) unsupported by valid theoretical models, and (f) barren as to research-stimulating hypotheses." [9] It is, in fact, the opposite of these, utilizing theoretical unifying principles from various schools to interrelate and integrate pertinent facts from all sources. It is inductive rather than deductive. "Instead of starting with theoretical preconceptions and then checking the fit of the facts to the model, the eclectic usually proceeds inductively, gathering and analyzing the data, and only later attempting to construct explanatory theories. . . . The main problem in all clinical work is to discover the organizational dynamics of the person under study rather than to invent one out of possible theories." [10]

While drawing upon many theorists and schools (including Adolph Meyer and Prescott Lecky), Thorne's work is not a "compilation of all standard theories," but an original contribution. He "determined to make a fresh start right from the beginning, accepting nothing on authority alone, and to formulate an eclectic system integrating all pertinent scientific information available at this time and place." [11] The model was that of Sir William Osler's work in medicine, which integrated the data of the medical sciences into an eclectic system of practice.

Recognizing that "many methods of case handling are discussed which have not been scientifically validated to date . . . at this early stage in the development of clinical psychological science, the most profitable approach appears to be to attempt an eclectic collection and evaluation of all known methods in terms of empiric experience. . . . Our main objective is to simply present an eclectic collection of methods which may be applied rationally according to their indications and contraindications. To us, this is all that clinical science can ever do. How these methods are combined and used is a function of the art of clinical practice." [12]

Philosophical presuppositions or foundations are not dealt with directly. The psychological nature of man is dealt with extensively, however, in *Personality* and in *Integrative Psychology*.

A Clinical Eclectic Viewpoint of Personality

In *Personality* Thorne does not present a single theory of personality. He attempts instead to bring together all observations and empirical data on personality. This eclectic view is not, however, unsystematic, elementaristic, disorganized, or a "rag-tag collection of miscellaneous theories and methods, resulting in a patchwork of observations and data," but is an integrated and systematic approach because personality itself is an integrated whole, and its study leads to "an inductively derived theory of personality which is rooted in empiric observations and methods." [13]

[It should be noted here that, as indicated in the beginning of the next section, the term and concept of "personality" have been replaced in Thorne's system by "person," or "behavior." Where "personality" occurs in this section, then, the reader should substitute "behavior" to be consistent with Thorne's current position.]

Thorne presents his point of view, or system, in ninety-seven postulates. It is obviously impossible to do justice to his approach in a limited space. We can only attempt to present the core or essence of his concept of personality.

Personality consists of the changing states of the total, or whole, individual living organism as it copes with the experience of interacting with its environment in the unique, individual ways that differentiate it personally and socially from others. Personality is thus a process of changing or becoming, and it is its *givenness,* existentially, that must be apprehended and that constitutes the raw data of personality. Personality can be studied only by observing the individual person in action in specific situations and, through the phenomenological method, entering into his world and experiencing it with him. The case history supplements observation by providing information about what the person has been. Since the individual is perceived differently by various other people, the results of a personality study depend upon the viewpoints or perceptual biases of the persons supplying the information or of the approach used. The competent clinical scientist is in a position to provide the most valid and reliable, or "real," picture of the individual. He does this by an eclectic method, utilizing all existing approaches to personality, since they are complementary or supplementary rather than competing or conflicting.

A system or theory of personality must provide an explanation for the whole range of behavior of human beings. The clinical eclectic viewpoint, with its incorporation of all the operational methods of other approaches, is the only method that does this. Eclecticism is a theoretical system involving "the selection and orderly combination of compatible features from diverse sources, even from otherwise incompatible theories and systems," into a "mutually consistent whole." [14] At the present time "valid methods of sufficient complexity have not been developed to permit a multivariate analysis of the inconstant qualities and quantities of factors actually determining personality status." [15] Nevertheless, the eclectic approach utilizes all existing methods, including the method of trained introspection applied in the clinical encounter. Since a personality state or status is an organized, unified whole, it can be grasped in its totality only by phenomenological methods, that is, by directly experiencing its issues and meanings. [16]

Personality dynamics involves a series of drives. There is a drive for higher organization in man, which includes man's need to maximize himself, to achieve perfect functioning, to organize his expanding experience into meaningful wholes. There is also a drive to achieve and maintain stability of organization. This includes self-preservation, homeostasis, habit systems, ideological controls, life goals and purposes, roles and statuses, and life-style. A third drive is the drive to integrate opposing functions in order to resolve imbalance (but not necessarily to avoid tensions). Personality integration is the dynamic process in which the organism strives to organize and unify all elements of the behavior field of the moment, or of the organizational status that the organism has been able to achieve. The organism strives to maintain the highest possible level of integration at all times and at all levels of functioning, from the lower psychophysiological functions to the highest psychosocial interactions. There is a "constant striving for unity manifesting itself in efforts to maintain the unity of the system of organization self-consistently." [17] Unification is a general, or master, motive,

An individual's life-style consists of his characteristic ways of attempting to achieve unification or his "distinctive offensive-defensive strategy of satisfying needs and coping with reality by use of mechanisms and expressive styles." [18] Although there is a constancy of life-style in personality, there is also constant change and flux, with multivariate etiological factors entering the hierarchical systems underlying the personality status at any particular time and place.

Consciousness is the central datum of psychology, and conscious experiences are "primary behavior data whose existential reality cannot be denied." [19] Although consciousness can be studied by objective methods, it can be apprehended only by a subjective reporter who is in a conscious state. Consciousness functions as a master sense organ or integrating function in which stimuli or momentary experiences are presented in awareness as a unified whole. "Consciousness is considered the main organizing, integrating, and unitizing mechanism determining and making possible higher level personality functioning." [20] It is the essence of being, the most unique characteristic of human beings. Consciousness is the locus of the self and of self-awareness. The contents of consciousness determine mental status, and disturbances in consciousness result in disturbances in behavior. Behavior processes that can be brought into consciousness are potentially susceptible to self-control, after appropriate analysis and practice.[21] Although there are nonconscious aspects of behavior, "they should not be postulated routinely but only when indicated by the evidence elicited in the specific case. Depth psychology should be investigated only when the possibilities of utilizing hypotheses concerning normal conscious mental life have been exhausted." [22]

The self develops in consciousness around feelings of personal identity and the experiencing of what is happening to oneself. "The *self image* is the self one *thinks* oneself to be . . . the self concept . . . is the evaluative core concept of one's own self particularly as we think it appears to others. " [23] The ego is the executive function of the self and includes the awareness of itself, evaluation of itself, regard for itself, and control of itself. The cumulation of self-knowledge and experience results in a self-apperception mass, which provides the basis for the continuity of the self and of its state of morale, or self-respect. Perceptions of personal identity and of the physical body constitute the core of the self-apperception mass.[24]

The conscious self participates in all the functions of personality and therefore becomes the organizational center of the personality. "Thus, the self becomes able to regulate the whole organism and to cause it even to do things which are against its instincts and interests, such as to kill itself in suicide." [25] In abnormal states the self may not be aware of, or able to control, certain functionings. The self-concept is important because "it operates as the functional core of being." [26]

Ideally, the individual does not react mechanistically to external stimuli or constitutional determinants, but exercises self-direction, acting purposefully, shaping his own life, and accepting responsibility. The striving for unity operates in consciousness towards self-consistency and elimination of conflicts.

Personality evolves in an irreversible sequence of statuses in the process of becoming self-actualized. Continuity exists and is present in awareness as the stream of consciousness or the stream of experience (life). Thus, while it is possible to speak of personality traits, it is more important to consider the ongoing acts of the individual in terms of the existential concept of doing something with one's life. While past experience places limits on what personality can be, "man is able to transcend the nature of his past and present existences through his ability to imagine and shape the future." [27] The self constantly strives for meaning, that is, for understanding of its experiences. There is a basic drive to organize experience into meaningful wholes: one of the highest values in life is to have meaning in one's personal existence. Meanings are determined by the whole organismic reaction of the person to his experiences. Although most meanings are acquired by social conditionings, "self-consistency theory would stress that each person should do what is best for him in terms of his own health, maturity, and growth rather than because of any artificial social meaning which may be attached." [28]

Since reason is man's greatest hope for becoming healthier and a better person, logical thinking is the best weapon in the existential struggle against blind emotion and irrationality. Therefore, "the ultimate value of man, both personally and socially, is a function of the quality of his cognitive functioning." [29]

Personality development is influenced by constitutional-biological factors, cultural factors, and self-actualization. The latter includes self-determination; thus man is not entirely mechanistically determined. The drive for self-actualization is one of the most powerful human motives and involves a dissatisfaction with self and a working toward self-improvement or perfection. The awareness of alternatives and the existence of decision making are evidences of freedom from mechanistic determination. The need to make choices introduces the need for a value system and for responsibility for one's actions. "Human living reaches its most outstanding peaks in the moments of the highest self-actualization and self-transcendence." [30] This, or the striving toward it, constitutes positive mental health.

The basic units of personality are the acts performed by the individual. These acts are organized in terms of the various roles that he plays, which are defined by his concepts of the physical and social world, perceived with himself as the center.

"From the eclectic viewpoint, personality development is regarded as a struggle to transcend affective-impulsive-unconscious determination of behavior by learning and perfecting rational-logical-voluntary control of behavior." [31]

Integrative Psychology

In his book *Personality* Thorne achieved the "break-through of postulating that behavior occurs naturally only in the form of psychological states and that these are the only proper raw data for clinical study." *Integrative Psychology* expands the theory of the psychological state, developing the psychology of integration and its clinical diagnostic implications. This psychology consists of "a basic theory of the psychological nature of man." [32] In this book "personality" is regarded as "a theoretical artifact . . . a semantic abstraction . . . an abstract generalization describing the individuality of the person." [33] Because of its vagueness and lack of clarity, the word should be avoided; the unit of study is the psychological state of being in the lives of people. The focus of concern is the person in his world, with all his situational and existential concerns.

"The basic problem of psychology is the study of factors organizing the pattern of any integration of integrates—the psychological state . . . of any particular moment." [34] The whole existence and meaning of a person could be understood if we could study his life pattern of psychological states. In general, the individual's basic goals, needs, and motivations organize the sensations, perceptions, learning, memory, feeling, and thinking that constitute his psychological state. Integrative psychology is thus holistic.

Behavior is integrated on many levels, from lower level physiological functions to high level psychosocial interactions. The organism strives to maintain the highest possible level of integration in accordance with the master motive, the homeostatic principle. Behavior is integrated by a variety of organizing principles at the different levels of the hierarchy. The more biologically primitive, lower level functions tend to be prepotent, though higher level functions may establish a transitory prepotence.

At the psychological level the master motive is the principle of unification, leading to self-consistency. The individual's "internal consistency is preserved by the selective assimilation of compatible ideas and values and the selective resistance to assimilation of inconsistent values." [35]

Organizing factors at many levels of behavior operate at the same time. It is postulated that organizers at all levels are integrated to support the dominant activity at the moment, so that the organism as a whole functions in a unified manner. Unification is inhibited under conditions of conflict. When the individual has no dominant activity or goal, behavior is at a level of random activity, and may be organized by separate lower level part functions.

"Behavior can be understood only in terms of its inner, subjective, existential meanings. . . . The psychological state of the person is the important consideration in understanding what he is doing. Integrative psychology, therefore, is concerned with phenomenological and existential considerations." [36] Integrative psychology thus rejects the behavioristic view of behavior as conditioned by the environment. The organism is striving, goal-directed, purposive. "Every person is postulated to be active, dynamic, motivated and, in general, striving for self-actualization. The primary motive of life is postulated to be self-enhancement on all levels of integration." [37]

The system of integrative psychology is presented in the form of postulates, under several major headings.

THE STRUCTURE OF INTEGRATIVE PSYCHOLOGY

Postulate 1. The central attribute of life in all its forms, and particularly of the highest human behaviors, is integration. Four corollaries develop this postulate. . . . la. Integration is an active organismic process resulting in functional unification of conflicting tendencies. . . . lb. Organization underlies integration. . . . lc. Self-consistency reflects the striving to actualize and maintain a preferred self-concept or self-status, i.e., to become and remain what one can become. . . . ld. The prime need of the organism is to organize experience consciously into psychologically meaningful integrates or wholes. . . .

Postulate 2. The psychology of integration alone is capable of clarifying the nature and causation of psychological states. . . . 2a. Complexity of integrative patterns requires an underlying complexity of etiological factors. . . . 2b. Changing patterns of integration observed phenomenologically can only be explicated by a comprehensive knowledge of etiology. . . .

Postulate 3. Integration involves the hierarchical organization of subprocesses, subfunctions, and subordinate motives into relatively unified wholes which are psychological states. . . . 3a. The highest levels are achieved only transiently, and then under optimum conditions only. . . . 3b. Homeostasis maintains integrations on sub-psychological levels. . . . 3c. On higher psychological levels, integrations are indicated and maintained consciously by deliberate self-regulation and self-control. . . .

Postulate 4. On progressively higher levels of integration, qualitatively new and different functions emerge and continue autonomously. . . . 4a. The most complex behaviors involve the "integration of integrates." . . . 4b. The most complex of integrations operate over long-term temporal intervals as complex action sequences implementing complex motivations and purposes. . . .

Postulate 5. Life in all its forms involves energy transformation systems resulting in active behaviors. . . . 5a. The upward thrust of life is towards higher and more complex patterns of organization and integration. . . . 5b. Evolutionary developments make possible successively higher level integrations, making possible broader inputs of information, and more complex outputs of coping behaviors. . . . 5c. Integration refers particularly to the organization of the sensorium making possible normal orientations. . . .

Postulate 6. Objective biologic and social conditions, past and present, provide opportunities, probabilities, and limitations to development but are not directly causal factors in the person. . . .

Postulate 7. The person cannot be considered apart from society. He is embedded in society, conditioned by it, stimulated or inhibited by society, and to some extent its product. . . . 7a. A comprehensive integrative psychology must be existentially oriented. . . .

Postulate 8. Phenomenally, conscious self-awareness is a primary attribute of humanness. . . . 8a. Consciousness is the primary mechanism of higher level integrations. . . . 8b. Consciousness is the locus or site of important mechanisms making possible higher level integrations. . . .

Postulate 9. The core of personality is the Self Concept. . . . 9a. The self concept reflects both personal and social expectations. . . . 9b. The self concept is an important integrating factor. . . . 9c. In man, who is capable of taking an attitude towards himself, the general psychological movement is expressed in striving away from a felt minus situation to an anticipated plus situation, from a feeling of inferiority to one of superiority (the striving for perfection or totality, for actualization and success). . . .

Postulate 10. The primary dynamic motive underlying all of life is self-enhancement. . . . 10a. The goal of self-enhancement is to get the most out of life in terms of the particular needs, abilities and purposes of each individual. . . . 10b. Phenomenally, every person is engaged in the business of running his life in the world to the best possible advantage. . . . 10c. Each person develops a characteristic *life style* consisting of his particular offensive-defensive strategies and tactics for satisfying needs and goals. . . . 10d. Each person knows what is best for himself under normal or ideal conditions. . . .

Postulate 11. Phenomenally, the highest levels of behavior reflect voluntary, deliberate self control in escaping from mechanistic determination from the environment. . . . 11a. Voluntary self control depends upon the ability to discriminate alternatives, to make value choices between alternatives, and then to actualize decisions by learned abilities to regulate excitatory-inhibitory processes. . . .

Postulate 12. The highest level integrations derive from factors of intelligence, making possible rational thinking and creativity. . . .

Postulate 13. Integrative psychology attempts to identify and conciliate what is valid from all the schools and systems of psychology into one unified eclectic approach. . . . 13a. The eclectic method is the only approach capable of reconciling and utilizing, according to their indications and contraindications, all the factors organizing the most complex integrations. . . .

Postulate 14. Psychopathology is largely determined by (a) factors preventing normal integration, (b) factors causing disintegration, or (c) integrations organized by maladaptive factors. . . . 14b. Organic deficits prevent integrations on higher levels. . . . 14b. Functional disorders cause disintegration through disruption of supporting functions. . . . 14c. The personality disorders are characterized by integrations organized about erroneous or socially maladaptive premises. . . . 14c. Psychological state disorders involve temporally limited disorders of integration usually limited to specific coping situations. . . .

Postulate 15. Psychodiagnosis becomes critically important to integrative psychology. . . . 15a. Psychodiagnostically, the central problem is to identify the etiological factors organizing clinically significant integrations. . . . 15b. Diagnosis should relate primarily to mental status at any existentially important time and locus. . . . 15c. Psychodiagnosis is primarily concerned with identifying the causation of phenomenological givens. . . .

Postulate 16. Psychotherapeutically, the central problem is to identify unhealthy patterns of integration and to replace them with more adaptive coping behaviors. . . .

Postulate 17. Any psychological state is an organized, integrated, unified whole which can be grasped in its totality only by phenomenological methods of directly experiencing its essences and meanings. . . .

Postulate 18. The need to balance and coordinate opposing functions so as to resolve imbalance (but not necessarily to avoid tensions) may be defined as the drive to integrate opposing functions. . . .

Postulate 19. Integration reflects the operation of the drive for higher organization in which functions and experiences are brought together in new gestalts (configurations, complexes) of increasing complexity. . . .

Postulate 20. The causal relations underlying any pattern of organizational status may be expressed in terms of an etiologic equation in which is represented the functional prepotency of the various classes of factors in the psychological field of forces existing at any particular time and place. . . .

Postulate 21. The constant striving for unity is a universal dynamic principle manifesting itself in efforts to maintain the unity of the system of organization self-consistently. . . .

Postulate 22. Consciousness functions as a master sense organ in which momentary experience is unitized, i.e., is presented in awareness as a unified whole. . . .

Postulate 23. Tests and measurements must have existential (personal) and/or situational (social) relevance to be clinically significant. . . .

Postulate 24. Phenomenally and existentially, behavior occurs only in the form of psychological states. . . .

Postulate 25. The most important characteristics of psychological states are flux and change under normal conditions. . . .

Postulate 26. Integration on many hierarchical levels is the basic process characterizing all psychological states. . . .

Postulate 27. Complex psychic behaviors depend upon the "integration of integrates." . . .

Postulate 28. Psychological states are the basic units of meaningful experience and, taken as a whole, constitute mental life. . . .

Postulate 29. Psychological states can be understood only in relation to their existential loci. . . .

Postulate 30. The primary existential need is to function well psychologically, i.e., to maintain the highest possible levels of integration while coping with life. . . .

Postulate 31. Self-actualization (potentiation) depends on achieving and maintaining the highest possible levels of integration. . . .

Postulate 32. All forms of psychopathology are characterized by a breakdown of integration manifested by defects in control. . . .

Postulate 33. The psychopathology of everyday life is largely the psychopathology of psychological states. . . .

Postulate 34. Psychodiagnostically, the primary clinical goal is to identify and diagnose the hierarchical levels and factors organizing integration in clinically relevant psychological states. . . .

Postulate 35. The most important diagnostic problem is to identify the actual integrative equation of the etiologic factors organizing psychological states which have personal-social significance. . . .

Postulate 36. Normal fluctuations of integrative status inevitably must be reflected in corresponding behavior changes and variations in psychometric status. . . .

Postulate 37. Under normal conditions, the requirements of successful coping with life result in a constantly fluctuating psychological status. . . .

Postulate 38. Under normal conditions of living, high variance of response is normal and should be expected clinically and statistically. . . .

Postulate 39. Pathological variance is caused when etiologic factors inappropriate or irrelevant to the situation become prepotent. . . .

Postulate 40. Normal invariance results from constant etiologic or motivational conditions so that constant stimulus and experiential factors produce stable response patterns. . . .

Postulate 41. Pathological invariance occurs where relatively constant etiological factors produce behavior which is reliable but irrelevant or inappropriate to normal coping. . . .

Postulate 42. Conscious mental life is the most unique characteristic of humans who cannot be understood completely except in terms of the contents of consciousness. . . .

Postulate 43. Awareness of self, the central core of psychic integration, is given only in consciousness. . . .

Postulate 44. The core of experience is a self that senses itself. . . .

Postulate 45. In a normal person, the contents of consciousness largely determine mental states. . . .

Postulate 46. Introspective reporting is the prime method for objectifying mental status and the contents of consciousness. . . .

Postulate 47. Every act in the waking state can be held in the focus of consciousness, so as to be sensed, perceived, evaluated, weighted, manipulated associatively, and considered in relation to past, present and future factors. . . .

Postulate 48. Any behavior process which can become conscious is potentially susceptible to self-control after suitable operational analysis of the necessary steps and adequate practice. . . .

Postulate 49. The self is the continuing conscious awareness of being a separate person. . . .

Postulate 50. The experiential background of the self is provided by the self apperception mass consisting of the accumulated experiential context of the self with itself. . . .

Postulate 51. Perceptions of personal identity constitute the core of the self apperception mass. Perceptions of the physical body are particularly important. . . .

Postulate 52. Instead of hypothesizing a variety of "selves" performing different functions, it is more valid to regard the self as participating in all integrative functions. . . .

Postulate 53. The importance of the self concept is that it operates as the functional core of being. . . .

Postulate 54. The validity of self-evaluatory functioning is an important determiner of psychological health. It is measured in the psychiatric concept of insight. . . .

Postulate 55. Under ideal conditions, to some degree, the self is capable of determining what it can become by imagining some future status and then acting to accomplish it. . . .

Postulate 56. Ego functioning relates to the awareness and concerns of the self with itself, i.e., with the self experiencing itself and dealing with itself. . . .

Postulate 57. The striving for unity operates on levels of conscious self-awareness in terms of the need to be self-consistent, i.e., positively to eliminate conflict and, negatively, not to create problems for one's self. . . .[38]

Therapeutic Implications of Integrative Psychology

Since all psychopathological or disturbed states involve disorders of integration, the objective of all methods of counseling or psychotherapy is to strengthen and improve the quality of the integrative process, thus fostering higher levels of self-actualization. Since the level of integration is manifested in the current psychological state of the client, the specific phenomenological goal of all case handling is to alter the existing psychological state. The focus is thus the person in the present situation, or "the psychological state of the-person-running-the-business-of-his-life-in-the-world." [39] Once the therapist determines that the client has sufficient resources for accepting the responsibility for his own life, the therapist gives him this responsibility.

The focus upon integration and the principle of unification direct clinical attention to the *integrative milieu,* or the psychological field of forces that are causative factors in the psychological state. The client's behavior in therapy reflects his psychological state and provides the data for understanding this state and its causative factors. Such understanding comes from the therapist's empathizing with the client, from the phenomenological frame of reference of the client. Since any psychological state represents the client's attempt to achieve maximum self-actualization through maximum integration, the primary question is: what and how is the client doing in managing his self-actualization? This effective management involves adequate, or optimum, control of his life, particularly his affective-impulsive life. Therapy involves the training, reeducation, or rehabilitation of the client in acquiring the controls necessary for self-regulation. Sometimes it is necessary for the client to experience a *positive disintegration* before reorganization or reintegration can occur.

Underlying every psychological state is an etiological equation (see below), which organizes the pattern of integration represented by the state. This etiological equation provides the indications or contraindications for specific interventions. Psychotherapy attempts to modify the equation or causes of disabling behavior. The eclectic approach treats each case individually. Rather than fitting the case (deductively) to a particular theory, it operates inductively from the specific case data. Specific methods of therapy, including pharmacotherapy and the various schools or systems, are appropriate for specific levels of disintegration. Eclectic therapy utilizes each of them, on the basis of the level of disintegration presented by the client.

PSYCHOLOGICAL CASE HANDLING

The term "psychological case handling" is used in preference to "psychotherapy" for two reasons. First, the effectiveness of psychotherapeutic methods has not yet been demonstrated, so that "most parsimoniously, every clinician should be regarded as only a case handler." [40] Second, the term is broad enough to include not only all methods of psychotherapy, but "all the operations conducted by competent psychologically trained personnel in helping clients to get along better in life." [41]

Elements of psychological case handling are: (1) adequate diagnostic study, (2) detailed knowledge of limitations of treatment methods, their indications and contraindications, (3) treating basic causes rather than symptoms, (4) an individual plan of treatment, (5) choice of methods on the basis of specific indications, (6) where possible the use of single methods so that effectiveness can be evaluated, (7) evaluation of results, (8) use of scientific methods in analysis of data, (9) recognition that there are no panaceas or universally applicable methods, and (10) eclecticism recognized as the keynote of modern science.[42]

Objectives of psychological case handling include: (1) prevention of worsening of the condition, (2) correction of etiological factors, (3) palliation, (4) systematic support, (5) facilitating growth, (6) reeducation, (7) expressing and clarifying emotional attitudes, (8) resolving conflict and inconsistencies, (9) catalyzing maturation and growth, (10) accepting what cannot be changed, (11) attitudinal reorganization, and (12) maximizing intellectual resources.[43] These may be summarized as catalyzing self-actualization by improving integrational status.

Psychological case handling includes personality counseling, marriage counseling, psychotherapy, psychoanalysis, pastoral counseling, child guidance, special education, vocational and educational guidance, psychiatric social work, group therapy, and hypnotherapy. It also includes educative, instructive, and advisory activities, as well as administrative activities and modification of the client's environment or removal of the client from a pathogenic environment.

Since the clinician has training and experience in all known methods,

the basic responsibility for the *direction* of all stages of case handling lies with the therapist even though some responsibility may be delegated to other persons, including the client himself. The possibility of a completely nondirective method is nonexistent, since by the very nature of the clinician-client relationship (a) the client comes to a person considered to be of superior experience and training, which establishes a relationship of dominance through prestige, (b) the case handler determines the method to be used. . . . One of the principal characteristics of the maladjusted or disordered person is the inability to resolve problems unaided. Although self-direction is the highest democratic goal and evidence of integration, the maladjusted person either asks for help spontaneously or is induced to do so for his own good. Until such time as the person demonstrates his ability to regulate his behavior within the limits of what is socially acceptable, he is subjected to varying degrees of direction or regulation from the environment. . . . While recognizing the dangers of over-regulation and over-interpretation, failure to institute degrees of direction in more serious cases may constitute grave error since the case handler has the obligation to protect the interests of the client when the client is unable to do so himself. . . . It is assumed that training and experience will provide the knowledge concerning when to be directive or relatively non-directive.[44]

But "proper case handling can make counseling and psychotherapy an interesting voyage of client discovery in which the case handler operates as a catalyst to help the client to greater insight, knowledge and competency in achieving a more individualistic life. The case handler does not have to adopt authoritarian roles to influence the client. More properly, the case handler operates as a friendly adviser. . . . primarily concerned with helping the client to work out his own problems." If he must take control when the client is unable to control himself, "the goal must always be to return ultimate control of the situation back to the client himself." [45] Since many clients are not familiar with the different case-handling methods and their objectives, it may be necessary to structure the objectives in terms of the concepts of integrative psychology.

The referents of psychological case handling are (1) the client, (2) the life situation of the client, particularly in relation to important others, and (3) the clinical encounter between the client and the case handler. The first two have been summarized in the summary of integrative psychology above.

Factors Determining the Choice of Case-Handling Methods

Case handling should be based upon an individual, rational plan for each case. The plan should include appropriate measures for beginning the relationship and discovering the problem, for dealing with pathognomonic symptoms and etiological factors, for utilizing all available methods, and for terminations.

"In general, actual direction or interference in the life of another person should be rigorously limited to the absolute minimum necessary to protect health and welfare. This implies that passive methods of counseling and psychotherapy are the techniques of choice unless definite indications exist for more active methods. Apart from this general rule, the plan of therapy will be determined by the indications of the specific situation." [46] Some of the factors, or criteria, that determine the method of choice are:

SPECIFICITY OF ACTION   A specific method is one that acts directly on the etiological factors in the disorder. There is little evidence for the specificity of action of various methods, and the therapist must depend upon clinical experience.

ECONOMY OF ACTION   The method that is most quickly and economically effective (yet safe) is preferred.

NATURAL HISTORY OF THE DISORDER   The pattern of development of the disorder must be understood for the most effective choice of treatment methods. In the prodromal stage, which is vague and nonspecific in nature, treatment should be supportive or palliative, using nondirective methods. In a syndromal stage without client insight, efforts are directed toward getting the client to recognize that he is maladjusted and to accept treatment. In a syndromal stage with client insight, the therapist has more freedom for action. Specific methods need to be applied at the optimum time in order to achieve maximum effects.

THE DISTRIBUTIVE PRINCIPLE In distributive treatment the counselor directs the treatment actively and according to a plan, adapting to the course of treatment and client progress. Problems and questions based upon the information obtained from the client are submitted to the client to assist him in developing insight and reaching solutions in selected areas.

TOTAL PUSH Every possible influence and treatment should be brought to bear in a concentrated manner.

FAILURE OF PROGRESS When a client fails to respond to treatment, more drastic methods are applied. When no rational prescription is possible, or when plans have failed, every possible method is used. While unscientific, this procedure is expedient.

CASE HANDLING AS AN ADAPTIVE PROCESS The case handler must be adaptable to the needs of each client as they develop, evaluating the indications and contraindications for various methods. This requires an eclectic orientation on the part of the counselor. Adherence to a particular school or orientation limits the counselor's adaptability.

This flexibility of approach does not mean that the counselor does not operate according to a plan. He does have a plan, based upon the diagnosis and the etiological factors of the case. But the counseling situation may change, and the plan must be changed accordingly.

ACTIVE VERSUS PASSIVE TECHNIQUES Case-handling methods may be placed on a continuum from directive and regulatory, at one extreme, to passive and nondirective, at the other. There is no agreement on the indications for various degrees of direction. The distinction between active (directive) and passive (nondirective) methods is an artifact; they are only methods to be used according to the indications of the case, not as dogmas of schools or systems. The following generalizations may be made on the basis of clinical experience:

1   In general, passive methods should be used whenever possible.

2   Active methods should be used only with specific indication, and with the minimum amount of directive interference that is necessary to achieve therapeutic goals.

3   Passive techniques are usually the methods of choice in early stages of therapy in order to permit emotional release.

4   Following the law of parsimony, complicated methods should be used only when simpler methods have failed.

5   All therapy should be client-centered; that is, the client's interests are paramount. This may require directive action.

6   Every client should be given the opportunity to resolve his problems nondirectively; inability of the client to do this is an indication for more directive methods.

7   Directive methods are usually indicated in situational maladjustment requiring the cooperation of other persons.

8   Some degree of directiveness is inevitable, even if it is only the decision to use passive methods.[47]

The case handler's activities are determined by the indications and contraindications of conditions and the situation in relation to available methods. While the statistical data based upon research are inadequate to relate indications and contraindications with methods, the clinician does not act upon whims, but upon his best information, clinical experience, and judgment.

Diagnosis

"The basic postulate of this system of clinical practice is that each step of the case handling process logically should be based on a valid diagnosis of the indications and contraindications of each clinical situation." [48] Diagnosis is not fitting the client into a classification system. "Assigning some arbitrary name or classification to a condition is less important than understanding its causation and implications. What is important is the status of the person and not how it is labeled. Until the true etiologic causes of a condition have been elaborated, no logical classification is possible. The psychiatric classification systems of the past are now known to be artifactual and invalid." [49]

Nevertheless, it is desirable to develop an etiologically based classification system. An attempt to develop such a classification system is represented in the following (abridged) classification of personality disorders, going beyond the traditional classifications (covered by the first three groups).

I   Reactions of Organic Defect
   a Genotypical (hereditary) disorders
   b Developmental-maturational disorders
   c Due to infections
   d Due to trauma
   e Toxic types
   f Due to metabolic disorders
   g With cerebral circulatory disease
   h With cerebral neoplasm
   i Presenile psychosis
   j Senile psychosis

II Constitutional Personality Inadequacy
   a Cyclothymic personality
   b Schizoid personality
   c Paranoid personality
   d Immature type

       e Inadequate type
       f Constitutional sexual deviates
       g Psychopathic deviates

III   Reactions of Physiological Deficit
       a Schizophrenic reaction types
       b Affective disorders
       c Convulsive disorders
       d Somatization reactions
       e Psychoneurotic disorders

IV   Reactions of Psychological Deficit
       a Functional disorders of sensation
       b Functional disorders of perception
       c Functional disorders of memory
       d Functional disorders of learning
       e Functional disorders of language behavior (thinking)
       f Functional disorders of self-regulation or control

V   Conditioned Behavior Disorder
       a Conditional emotional reaction
       b Colloquial patterns of expressive behavior
       c Conditioned modes of reaction to frustration
       d Conditioned conduct disorders
       e Malingering
       f Conditioned psychopathies

VI   The Attitudinal Pathoses
       a Attitudinal pathoses relating to the meaning of life in general
       b Attitudinal pathoses relating to the meaning of the individual person and the conduct of his problems in life
       c Attitudinal pathoses relating to interpersonal relations

VII   Disorders Related to Situational Maladjustment
       a Family
       b Self-characteristics
       c Work
       d Sex and marriage
       e Social adjustment
       f Education
       g Wealth and poverty
       h Religion
       i Conduct

VIII Disorders Due to Group Membership and Role Determinants
       a Minority group membership
       b Age, sex, and caste
       c Gangs, underprivileged groups

IX   Disorders Related to Lack of Self-control
       a Lack of control due to immaturity
       b Lack of control due to obsessive-compulsive emotionality
       c Lack of control due to defects of intelligence

      d Lack of control due to lack of training
      e Lack of control due to motivational factors
      f Decisions of conflict
      g Disorders of decisions of preference

X   Disorders of Style of Life
      a Mechanisms of attack
      b Mechanisms of defense

XI   Disorders of Concept of Self and Ego Formation
      a Individual differences in genetic determinants of ego strength
      b Maturational development of the ego [50]

In addition to this general outline, Thorne provides diagnostic classifications of disorders of part functions, including sensory disorders, perceptual errors, memory disorders, and semantic disorders.

Thorne has also developed a diagnostic system and nomenclature for psychological states occurring in the borderline area between mental health and psychiatric disorder. A condensation of this classification follows:

1.0   Constitutional Behavior Differences
      1.1 Behavioral Inadequacy, Constitutional Type
      1.2 Behavior Eccentricity, General Constitutional Type

2.0   Developmental Phase Eccentricities
      2.1 Behavioral Immaturity, Presocial Developmental Type
      2.2 Behavioral Immaturity, Pubertal Developmental Type
      2.3 Behavioral Immaturity, Developmental Retardation Type
      2.4 Behavioral Excess, Precocious Developmental Type
      2.5 Behavioral Inadaptability, Due to Adolescent Rebellions Reaction

3.0   Psychophysiological Habit Disturbances
      3.1 Sleep Habit Disturbances
      3.2 Eating Habit Disturbance
      3.3 Elimination Habit Disturbance
      3.4 Behavioral Inadaptability, Due to Disordered Habitual Routines

4.0   Affective-Impulsive Determined Psychological States
      4.1 Behavior Inadaptability, Temperamental Type
      4.2 Behavioral Incapacity Due to Reactive Existential Anxiety
      4.3 Behavioral Instability Due to Frustration-Hostility-Aggression State
      4.4 Behavioral Unsuitability, Due to Unacceptable Sexuality
      4.5 Behavioral Instability, Due to a Social Sexual Acting-Out
      4.6 Behavior Eccentricity Due to Incomplete Sexual Differentiation

5.0   Personality States Determined by Cognitive-Intellective Factors
      5.1 Behavior Inadequacy Due to Defects or Deficiencies of Cognitive Abilities

11.0 Psychological States Related to Poor Transactional Field Management
   11.1 Behavioral Inadaptability, Transactional Failure Due to Communications Breakdown
   11.2 Behavioral Inadaptability, Transactional Field Disorder, Due to Asocial Self-Actualization
   11.3 Behavioral Inefficiency, Transactional Failure Due to Short-Term Goals
   11.4 Behavioral Inefficiency, Transactional Field Disorder, Due to Overconcern with Materialism

12.0 Demoralization States
   12.1 Behavioral Disability, Due to Person Fatigue Reaction
   12.2 Behavioral Disability, Due to Interpersonal Demoralization Reaction
   12.3 Behavioral Decompensation, Due to Situational Demoralization Reaction, Acute
   12.4 Behavioral Decompensation, Acute, Due to Life Demoralization State [51]

In integrative psychology "psychodiagnosis refers only to the psychological state (mental status) at the time of study." [52] Since psychological states are in a constant flux and flow, "clinical diagnosis must develop methods capable of uncovering their underlying dynamics continuously. Clinical diagnosis must be capable of dealing both with constancies and with change." [53] The psychological state is determined by the integrative milieu; therefore, diagnosis must involve a study of the integrative milieu and the factors organizing it. Thus, diagnosis is a continuing process and does not have to be complete before treatment is begun. Yet partial diagnostic insights must be present in order to select methods on the basis of their indications and contraindications; otherwise—and this is sometimes necessary—case handling is conducted on a trial-and-error rather than a rational basis.

There are a number of different types of diagnosis:

DIFFERENTIAL DIAGNOSIS, OR ETIOLOGICAL DIAGNOSIS   This is the study of possible causes of a condition or psychological state. "Often the simplest method of discovering what organizes any psychological state is to ask the person what he is doing and why, or how he feels and why? Failing to secure adequate answers from such direct questions, indirect evidence must be sought that can answer the same questions." [54] Personality trait measures are useful only when the trait is clinically significant in a psychological state.

For the proper understanding and classification of any disorder, the following etiological factors must be considered: (1) primary etiological factor, (2) secondary precipitating factors, (3) preexisting personality, (4) characteristic personality reactions, and (5) situational factors and reactions.

CLINICAL PROCESS DIAGNOSIS This refers to the moment-to-moment diagnosis during the case-handling process, on the basis of which clinical judgments are made regarding indications and contraindications for the use of different methods. This involves determining the current psychological state, the integrational patterns and their dynamics and etiology, the level or levels at which disorders of integration are occurring, and the general level of global adaptive integration or the level of integration of integrates. The nature of disintegration must be considered: acute or chronic, transient or intermittent, generalized or localized—and its pattern; that is, whether it is a deficit reaction, defect reaction, conflict reaction, intrusion of affects, demoralization reaction, or a localized disintegration state, such as an organ neurosis or psychosomatic state. It is this clinical process diagnosis that is the basic diagnostic activity. It is the core of the eclectic approach, guiding the whole therapeutic intervention, which is based upon the decisions of the case handler regarding what to do about the current psychological state.

EXISTENTIAL STATUS DIAGNOSIS This is concerned with the integrative dynamics of self functioning, with attention to the self-concept (the actual self, the ideal self, and actual-ideal self discrepancies), reality contacts, self executive functions, and success-failure status. This study is accomplished within the existential or phenomenological frame of reference of the client.

LIFE MANAGEMENT DIAGNOSIS This is the evaluation of behavior in terms of social-situational requirements, determining adjustment or adaptation in the educational, vocational, sexual and marital, social, and financial management areas. The question is, what is the person doing with his life?

PROGNOSTIC DIAGNOSIS The life record is the most valid predictor of future performance. Adolph Meyer's stream-of-life concept provides the basis for the clinician's construction of a stream-of-life chart on a continuing basis. The clinician must consider external factors in making predictions by taking into consideration the probable continuance or incidence of stress factors. The persistence of equivalent psychological states indicates the continued operation of equivalent etiological factors.

The types of diagnosis given above are more important than the traditional clinical classification diagnosis.

STEPS IN DIAGNOSING PSYCHOPATHOLOGY

Step One: Is the disorder Organic or Functional? Organic disorders should always be ruled out first, since they will require psychiatric consultation and different methods of treatment.
A. If the disorder appears to be organic, is it
1 Hereditary.
2 Developmental-maturational.

3 Infectious.
4 Traumatic.
5 Toxic.
6 Metabolic.
7 Circulatory.
8 Neoplastic.
9 Presenile deterioration.
10 Undifferentiated.

B. If the disorder appears to be functional, is it a
  1 Reaction of physiological deficit.
    a Schizophrenic reaction.
    b Affective disorder.
    c Convulsive disorder.
    d Somatization reaction.
    e Psychoneurotic reaction.
  2 Reaction of Psychological deficit.
  3 Conditioned behavior disorder.
  4 Attitudinal disorder.
  5 Situational maladjustment.

Step Two: Identification of a Specific Etiologic Agent or Syndrome. If the disorder is organic, what is the specific etiologic agent, and the extent and location of the lesion? If functional, what are the primary etiologic factors? Differentiate between primary and secondary (precipitating) factors.

Step Three: Measurement of Specific Defects or Abnormal Dynamisms. In organic disorder, measure the degree of defect in mental functioning, i.e., memory defect. In functional disorders, measure emotional reactions, attitudinal factors, etc.

Step Four: Evaluate Personality Reactions to the Disorder.

Step Five: Evaluate Situational Factors. How does the disorder affect the total situation of the person-meeting-the-environment?

Step Six: Make A Diagnostic Formulation. Explain the integrative dynamics of the case in terms of all factors identified.[55]

This procedure is an ideal, since it is rarely possible to obtain complete data. At present, objective diagnostic methods are inadequate, so that major dependence must be placed on clinical judgment and intuition.

The Case History in Diagnosis

The case history consists of the direct examination of the client and any other information obtained from legitimate sources relating to his past and present status. Information from other sources is necessary because of the unreliability and invalidity of the statements of persons with psychological disorders. The client may be unable to reveal all his problems because of unconscious repression and resistance and distortion of reality. Deliberate suppression or falsification by the client may also occur. "Actually, no statement or behavior pattern should be taken at face value, whether the person is normal or abnormal, except with confirmatory evidence from external sources," because of "misperceptions of the client or informants due to different phenomenological viewpoints." [56]

The case history is useful in developing the steps in diagnosis listed above. It contributes to valid diagnosis by providing accurate information and thus avoiding diagnostic errors based upon inadequate information. When other persons are involved, it includes their side of the story. The dynamics of interpersonal and situational disturbances can be discovered. It uncovers misinformation and irrational thinking in the client. It aids in differentiating between organic and functional complaints. "An adequate case history is the most reliable source of information upon which reliable predictions of future behavior can be based." [57]

The taking of the case history can be therapeutic in itself. It assists in the building up of rapport. It provides catharsis and abreaction, as well as desensitization. It offers reassurance, impressing the client with the carefulness and interest of the clinician. In some cases the client's relating of his history to an understanding clinician is sufficient for carrying the client over temporary difficulties. Further, the eliciting of a good case history may lead to the development of insight. Finally, interpersonal misunderstandings may be resolved in the process of obtaining a case history from the client and those involved with him, particularly in a group discussion.

When blocking, resistances, or an impasse occurs during the therapy process, the case history may provide leads for exploration. When progress has not occurred after many interviews, the case history can be reviewed, and even returned to in order to explore more deeply.

THE TECHNIQUE OF HISTORY TAKING   "The therapist would do well to assume a passive, non-directive attitude during the initial contacts, interjecting only enough to elicit a coherent history." [58] The client should not be hurried. Questions should be nondirective: How? When? Where? Why? Significant or representative samples of the client's statements should be recorded verbatim. Information on the client's use of time should be obtained. Find out how the client thinks and feels about significant happenings in his life. Find out what he thinks his trouble is. An outline is useful to avoid overlooking significant areas. Areas to be covered should include birth and developmental history, medical history, educational history, emotional development, sex life, social development, work history, family life, personal habits, attitudes toward self, and socioeconomic status.

The Etiological Equation

"An *etiologic equation* is a formal statement describing all classes of causal factors and indicating their relationship." It "differentiates between primary, secondary, predisposing, precipitating, preexisting and situational factors and attempts to weigh the contribution of each." [59] The equation is based upon the diagnosis and provides the basis for treatment. Principles of primacy assert that genetic factors command priority over other factors, followed by biologically primitive factors and developmental factors. Organic factors have primacy over functional factors. Temporally earlier factors have primacy over later factors. Lower level integrations have priority over higher level integrations. The etiological equation must represent the integrational milieu, including both internal and external, or situational and organismic, factors. Since both the internal and external milieus are constantly changing, the etiological equation must be constantly revised.

Twelve classes of etiological equations are identified, in terms of the prepotent determining factor: (1) biogenetic determination, (2) constitutional determination, (3) pathological physiological determination, (4) affective or emotional conflict determination, (5) cognitive behavior determination, (6) conditioned mental context determination, (7) role-playing and social status determination, (8) self-concept and ego structure determination, (9) life-style determination, (10) interpersonal transactional determination, (11) existential status determination, and (12) social-environmental determination. Characteristic etiological equations are given in each class. As an example, the equations under (8) are as follows:

a   Low self-concept + lack of confidence = poor performance = inferiority complex (Adler)

b   Low self-concept + anxiety over failure = defensive reaction formations = existential anxiety

c   Weak ego functioning + high stress = personality disintegration caused by breakdown of controls

d   Self-damaging errors + ego deflation = lowered self-concept and guilt

e   Self-anger + frustration and aggression directly inwardly = depression and suicide

f   Lack of self-consistency + conflictual actions = neurosis (Lecky, Thorne)

These classes are related to integrative levels and to different theories and hypotheses concerning psychopathology. Direct examination is necessary to determine etiological equations; psychological tests are not adapted to the measurement of changing psychological states, and are not available to measure factors in the higher level integrations.

Every psychological state is the result of psychological fields of forces in which are represented the interactions of heredity and environment, constitutional and acquired factors, drives, needs, affective impulses, past conditionings, imaginings of the future, and various forms of self-determination. The etiological equation for the state expresses all of these factors. "The equation is given naturally, in the state, and the problem is to discover what it is." [60] The process is inductive. The clinician's task is to analyze the natural data and develop an etiological equation based upon hypotheses concerning the determination of the psychological state. "Clinical judgment is the only tool available for differentiating, evaluating and weighting all the various classes of factors etiologic to a psychological condition." [61]

The Clinical Encounter

"In the existential sense, every interview should be a genuine *clinical encounter* in which clinician and client *experience* each other and themselves more completely and meaningfully. . . . It is now well established that all productive case handling depends upon the creation of positive, accepting interpersonal relationships between counselor and client." [62] Factors that contribute to a therapeutic relationship include personal warmth and liking, unconditional positive regard, nonjudgmentalism, nonimposition, permissiveness, empathy, and genuineness. These factors reduce defensiveness and provide a safe environment in which the client can be and experience himself more completely and constructively.

Usually, the client has had no previous experience in counseling or psychotherapy, and often has a different viewpoint from the case handler's. Although it is only by experiencing the process that the client can come to know what it involves, some structuring can reduce differences in viewpoints. The client, impatient for quick relief of symptoms and to find happiness and success, can be helped to understand that it is necessary to discover and modify basic etiological causes, and that this may require weeks or months of hard work.

Most clients are ambivalent about coming for help. They do not know what to expect. Some orientation is necessary to obtain the client's cooperation. "The permissive nondirective relationship is desirable if it works, but unfortunately many clients are so disturbed that they may not remain in the situation unless external pressures are brought to bear." [63] Once contacts are initiated, a relationship can usually be developed.

Communication must be established at the client's level. Rapport, which is defined as *"the harmonious relationship and mutual responsiveness which results from heightened suggestibility and emotional transference occurring where people have confidence, trust and esteem for each other,"* [64] involves a number of factors. The client expects help and ascribes prestige to the counselor, who responds with warmth, acceptance, permissiveness, respect, genuineness, empathy, and self-disclosure. Rapport is maintained by the counselor's avoidance of criticism, moralism and judgmental attitudes, insincerity, and any suggestion of ulterior motivation. Rapport creates a sense of security in the client, which is conducive to learning.

The counseling relationship develops most favorably when the counselor is passive at the beginning, while the client is becoming familiar with the situation at his own rate. However, with clients who are doubting, negative, and resistant, more active methods may be necessary.

Terminating Case Handling

Ideally, counseling concludes naturally, with the client gradually resuming independent self-regulation. In many instances, however, factors enter that either terminate counseling before the desired objectives have been reached or prolong it.

The closing phase of counseling is characterized by the achievement of an understanding of the nature and origin of the maladjustment, the reduction of tension and defensive reactions, and the development of a rational approach to dealing with the maladjustment or problems. The client is freed from affective-impulse behavior and is able to use his intellectual resources in problem-solving behavior. Clients with good intellectual resources may be able to reach their own solutions by themselves, and counseling may terminate before specific solutions have been arrived at. With clients of lower intelligence, counseling may continue, with the counselor contributing more actively or directively to the solution of problems. The first, and longer, part of counseling consists of release and clarification of emotional problems, with the counselor in a passive and nondirective role. In the second, and shorter, part of the counseling process, the counselor participates more directively in the intellectual problem-solving process.

Most counseling relationships come to a natural termination by mutual consent. The client begins to feel he can get along by himself and may skip an appointment to try himself out. Or the counselor may suggest that the client now seems able to become independent and should try to get along on his own to see how it goes.

Although the counselor should respect the client's feelings and wishes about terminating counseling, the counselor has a responsibility to prevent premature discontinuance of counseling. Clients sometimes desire to terminate counseling after experiencing symptomatic relief, but before getting at the etiological factors. There are other clients who want to terminate when they experience the discomfort of facing painful memories or insights. The client may also desire to terminate prematurely when the counseling reaches the point where action on new insights is required, which the client may not be ready to accept or implement. Clients may also want to discontinue counseling because of external problems such as financial difficulties or changes in residence. Finally, poor handling by the counselor, including inability to establish rapport (which may not, however, always be the counselor's fault), failure to structure adequately, overdirectiveness, and improper handling of the transference, may lead to premature termination.

Whether the counselor should take action to prevent premature termination depends upon the nature of the individual case. In some cases the client may be told simply that the counselor feels that treatment should continue, but persuasion or threat should not be used. The counselor should handle resistance by accepting, reflecting, and clarifying the client's feelings. A client who is known to be at an acute crisis of conflicts must not be allowed to terminate treatment until all resources fail. When termination is due to incompatibility of the client and the counselor, referral should be attempted.

The counselor must be concerned about premature termination resulting in undertreatment, because of possible serious consequences to the client. When a client develops further difficulties, which presumably might have been avoided with adequate treatment, the counselor may be blamed for poor clinical judgment, with consequent damage to his reputation and his future effectiveness. The counselor should, therefore, be very careful about abandoning treatment too easily. He should be sure that he has recognized and dealt with all pathological processes. He should abandon passive methods for more active methods when the former are ineffective, and he should not be afraid to attempt drastic treatment methods. The counselor should follow up clients to see that they carry out instructions and that appropriate actions are taken.

While counseling may continue for long periods of time, sometimes for years, there are some clients who would continue indefinitely if allowed to. The counselor should avoid overtreatment of such cases. There are also cases where the counselor holds clients in treatment for unnecessarily long periods. In private practice the financially insecure counselor may become dependent upon the fees of a client and keep him longer than necessary. Sometimes the counselor may be overconscientious or overanxious and lacking in confidence in the client's ability to become independent. While it is desirable to prevent undertreatment, this danger may be minimized by follow-up checks, and overtreatment should be avoided.

The closing phase of counseling involves the terminating of the transference relationship in cases where it has developed. In some cases this termination occurs spontaneously, but with dependent clients separation may become a problem. Such clients may attempt to delay termination. The counselor may bring the relationship to a close by interpreting the transference and indicating why termination is desirable.

Counseling should be concluded with some type of summary of the process and its accomplishments. Counseling is a slow and gradual process, with many small gains or insights. Bringing these together gives an overview and clarifies what has gone on for the client. With verbal clients it may be desirable to ask them to summarize. This enables the counselor to evaluate the accuracy of the client's conclusions. Some clients are unable to make an interpretive summary, however, and the counselor must summarize. Such summarizing is useful at various points in counseling as well as at its conclusion.

METHODS OF PSYCHOLOGICAL CASE HANDLING

Dealing with Presenting Complaints and Symptoms

While psychotherapy or counseling is directed toward removing or remedying the causes of the client's disturbance, it is desirable to give the client relief from symptoms and to improve his general condition by supportive therapy and reassurance. In general, symptomatic and supportive therapy are used when deep psychotherapy is not indicated or possible. While the methods are superficial and not major methods of therapy, they are useful either when other methods are not possible or in conjunction with other methods.

SYMPTOMATIC THERAPY   Symptoms deserve attention because, to the client and to those who are concerned about him, they constitute the complaint and may be their only concern. If symptoms do not improve or disappear, treatment may not be considered useful or successful.

Many maladjustments or disorders terminate spontaneously with the passage of time. Palliative methods, that is, methods of reducing the client's suffering by relieving his symptoms, are useful while the natural recuperative processes are functioning. In addition, these methods are useful in the absence of more specific methods. Although symptoms may disappear with other methods of treatment, such as nondirective methods, they should be dealt with directly. Such treatment of symptoms does not interfere with more specific treatment directed to the etiological factors.

Indications for palliative methods include the following:

1 *Major crises in adjustment*   Clients sometimes are in a state in which they are unable to approach their problems constructively, being too excited or agitated. Their behavior may only make their condition worse. In such situations palliative actions alleviate the condition until other approaches can be used.

2 *Minor periods of instability*   Most people have periods of difficulty that resolve themselves spontaneously. During those periods palliative measures help the client until the period passes or the environmental conditions improve. In periods of temporary instability or indecisiveness, plans or actions may be suggested to the client, or he may be supported in postponing decisions or actions until conditions change or he is sure of what he wants to do.

3 *Insoluble problems*   When reality prevents any satisfactory solution, support may be provided to give the client relief.

4 *Distressing symptoms*   It may be desirable or necessary to palliate distressing symptoms before dealing with the basic problems.

5 *Dangerous symptoms*   Symptoms of organic disorders, symptoms of desperation and panic, suicidal threats, uncontrollable sexual impulses, homicidal ideas, and paranoid delusions must be dealt with actively to safeguard the client and society.

Techniques of symptomatic therapy include the following:

1 *Structuring the process* This consists in leading the client to understand the relation of the symptoms to causes, the distinction between symptomatic and specific therapy, and the results to be expected from symptomatic therapy.

2 *Avoiding symptom fixation* Encouraging client action that antagonizes symptom formation or enables the client to control the symptoms may prevent the fixation of symptoms.

3 *Maintaining morale* Attention, sympathy, and encouragement provide the emotional support and hope that may be necessary in order for the client to continue, and they thus make more specific therapy possible. They may also make an insoluble problem bearable.

4 *Masterful inactivity* This technique involves the postponement of action without disturbing rapport or losing the client's confidence. In effect, it consists of putting the client off with plausible excuses, explanations, or vague assurances of later action.

5 *Suggestion* Suggestion has long been used, and although it has been widely criticized, it has a use in certain situations, such as dealing with functional or psychogenic symptoms.

6 *Nondirective methods* While nondirective methods are primarily suited for counseling normal people, they may be used for palliative purposes with neurotics, psychotics, and mental defectives, pending the application of more suitable active methods, including hospitalization.

SUPPORTIVE THERAPY Supportive therapy consists of nonspecific techniques used for their constitutional or psychological effects, and includes both physical and psychological methods. The former were used in early psychiatry, illustrated by S. Weir-Mitchell's rest cure, but have come into disrepute. Nevertheless, they may be useful in restoring or building up the organism, so that it may function adequately in everyday living and develop resistance to disturbances.

Among the factors involved are the natural functions of the body, including eating and sleeping; economic support; and satisfaction in work, family, social activities, and recreation. The correction and improvement of these factors may increase the client's threshold of personality disorder.

Physical methods of supportive therapy include medical treatment, rest, improved nutrition, physiotherapy, hydrotherapy, chemotherapy, material (financial) security, and hospitalization. It is desirable for every client exhibiting any psychosomatic symptoms to have a complete physical examination, and the counselor should consult with a physician at frequent intervals. When a medical examination indicates no organic disease, this information may help the client to recognize the psychological nature of his disturbance.

Psychological supportive therapy includes healthy habit routines, environmental manipulation, occupational therapy, diversional therapy, bibliotherapy, changing attitudes in the environment, and reassurance, suggestion, and advice.

Reassurance is an important supportive method. Reassurance strengthens positive attitudes and healthy behavior by acting as a reward. It is an antidote for fear, worry, doubt, uncertainty, and insecurity, and is one of the oldest and most widely used methods of psychotherapy. Even though it may be superficial and its effects transient, it is a valuable method of treatment, although it is sometimes misused. Reassurance is indicated in cases of mental deficiency, in combating anxiety, in feelings of inferiority and inadequacy, in reinforcing new adjustment patterns, and in child guidance. It is contraindicated when it is necessarily false and the client knows the truth, when it allows the client to shift responsibility to the counselor, and when it may lead to overconfidence or aggressiveness.

Reassurance is of several types. There may be reassurance that the client is not unique or unusual, that the nature of his condition is known and has a cause, that the symptoms may be annoying but not dangerous, that something can be done, that the condition will not lead to insanity, that relapses occur and are not an indication that the condition is getting worse, and that the condition does not indicate sinfulness or blame.

Reassurance may be freely used when it is true; too free and too early use, however, may give premature and superficial relief, which may block further progress. The client should first be allowed to express his fears, and the counselor should recognize, accept, and clarify the need for reassurance before reassurance is given. Reassurance may be either verbal or behavioral. The counselor should use both, and they should be used consistently.

High fees, impressive surroundings, an air of confidence, and pomp and ceremony are reassuring in that they meet the need of the client to feel that he is getting the best treatment from a competent therapist. "An effective personality and a quick, dignified mode of speaking and acting are very reassuring to most patients. Successful clinicians inspire such utter confidence that their clients are reassured that they are receiving the best possible treatment." [65] These methods may be justified, even though they have no direct effect upon therapeutic outcome, in persuading the client to continue treatment until other techniques become effective.

Reassurance is most effective when it involves factual information rather than opinions. When a client raises questions about which he could be reassured by one of the methods listed above, to be nondirective and to tell him nothing may increase his anxiety and lead him to conclude that his condition must really be bad if the counselor cannot tell him about it. Yet, when the condition or prognosis is actually serious or unfavorable, this should not usually be revealed to the client.

Conditioning and Behavior Therapies

"The whole process of case handling must be regarded as a learning situation in which suitable conditions for reconditioning are provided for the client to unlearn maladaptive behaviors and acquire more healthy patterns." [66] The specific methods of the behavior therapies, however, "treat the patient like a mindless animal organism which is subjected to an authoritarian reconditioning instigated by a directive therapist who assumes the responsibility of knowing what is wrong with the patient and what should be done for him without securing his permission or even his cooperation." [67] Whether any changes in personality integration or life-styles occur is yet to be demonstrated.

When the affective component of a disorder is primary, it must be dealt with first, and learning methods will not be effective. When it is secondary or reactive, methods of learning and retraining may be effective. Moreover, since motivation is necessary for learning, the client's need systems and motivational status must be studied in order to determine effective incentives and rewards.

Tutorial counseling, in which specific problem areas are discriminated and formulated in psychological terms that the client can understand, followed by tutoring and training exercises in the solution of the problems, utilizes retraining involving conditioning methods.

Life Management Analysis and Tutoring

Many simple adult maladjustments are situational in nature. Some situations contain pathogenic factors stimulating maladaptive reactions in even "normal" persons. The case handler must have knowledge of such situations, particularly those of a local nature. Analysis of the extent of situational factors in maladjustment is part of diagnosis.

Observation and operational analysis of the client's behavior in the situation should be made. The observation should involve empathically living through situations with the client. The client's role-playing skills in the major roles of student, worker, financial manager, sex and marriage partner, parent, and social person in the community should be evaluated.

After the counselor has diagnosed what the client is doing wrong in the situation, this is communicated to him, with techniques of situational adjustment, and intensive tutoring in the requisite skills is carried on. Tutorial counseling is dealt with in detail in the book entitled *Tutorial Counseling.*[68]

Circular and chain reactions may occur. Here, in addition to strengthening the person's ability to deal with situations whenever possible, the external factors should be dealt with or modified. This is particularly relevant in problems of childhood, with mental defectives, in marriage and family problems, and with problems of the aged.

"Failure to recognize the situational determination of many simple adult maladjustments may constitute an important source of diagnostic and therapeutic errors." [69]

Methods of Therapeutic Influence

Methods of directly and actively influencing the client have been in disrepute, but this is mainly because they have been abused, appearing to be ineffective because they have not been used in accordance with specific indications, and because they are inconsistent with the prevailing orientation of psychotherapy. Nevertheless, there are many clients who are unable to move toward goals by their own efforts alone and who require active intervention and direction.

SUGGESTION   Suggestibility is a universal phenomenon, entering into all psychogenic disorders and all therapy. Therapeutic results are often ascribed in error to other factors when in actuality they are the result of suggestion. Suggestion is the influence of the ideas, feelings, or actions of another without direct command or appeal to intellectual functions. Hypnotism appears to be based upon suggestibility, and suggestibility is related to positive transference.

Suggestive techniques are indicated to achieve limited objectives, such as (a) antagonizing the effects of negative suggestions, (b) stimulating positive attitudes, (c) catalyzing desirable actions by the client, and (d) removing symptoms known to have been produced by suggestion. Suggestion is effective with children, mental defectives, and immature personalities. It should not be used when it is not likely to succeed or to result in symptom disappearance.

The technique of suggestion may be facilitated if (a) it is kept to a minimum and used only when indicated, (b) it is not used too early or too often, (c) positive ideas are emphasized, (d) negative suggestions are avoided, (e) benevolent rather than dictatorial authority is used, (f) suggestions are repeated often, (g) the client is prepared to accomplish the suggestion, (h) the truth (but not necessarily all the truth) is adhered to, and (i) the counselor is cheerfully reassuring. Reflections of the client's feelings may provide suggestion if the counselor selects elements and word responses in a suggestive manner.

PERSUASION AND ADVICE   Persuasion appeals to reason and intelligence. It involves a counselor-client relationship in which the counselor is wiser and more mature, and teaches, educates, or advises the client. Advice consists of opinions or recommendations to the client, usually on the assumption that the counselor knows better what to do than the client does. Persuasion and advice imply dependence and lack of responsibility in the client. These methods have fallen into disrepute as being limited to symptom removal and ignoring emotional elements. However, when some directive action is indicated, persuasion and advice may be useful in obtaining the cooperation of all concerned. When an immediate, clear solution is available, persuasion and advice are methods for influencing clients in the simplest, quickest way. They are indicated, therefore, in mild conditions where intellect is intact and rapport and cooperation are easy to obtain, in emergency situations, and to secure limited objectives such as symptom removal. They should be used for client-centered purposes and should be avoided when they might interfere with major psychotherapy.

Techniques of persuasion include pointing out the facts of the situation to the client, explaining causal relationships, showing why the client should change his attitudes or habits, pointing out future consequences of maladaptive behavior, substituting knowledge for emotions, outlining rules of mental health, encouraging the facing of reality and the practice of problem-solving techniques, and introducing alternatives for action.

Since clinical judgment is generally unreliable and invalid, "persuasion and advice should not be used indiscriminately but only after intensive case study when specific etiologic findings indicate specific directive advice. . . . Too early application may destroy rapport and transference. Too frequent application may stimulate undesirable reactions of negativism or dependency." [70] They are justified in life management situations where outcomes can be predicted statistically by the case handler.

PRESSURE, COERCION, AND PUNISHMENT   Although early treatment of mental patients included punishment, the pendulum has swung to the opposite extreme of rejecting any punitive methods. Nevertheless, there appear to be situations where the suppressive methods of pressure, coercion, and punishment are useful. Such techniques are to be used with a firm, kind, understanding authoritarianism.

Restraints and punishments are necessary in dealing with the behavioral excesses of immature and asocial personalities. Absolute permissiveness leads to excesses. In psychotherapy pressure and coercion are used to achieve therapeutic objectives of training or retraining, or correction or control of unacceptable or dangerous behavior, which have not been achieved in the home or the school. The therapist may have thrust upon him the task of making a plan to control deviant behavior. It is desirable that he accept the role of a reasonable, paternalistic authority, so that the client can learn to accept limits and authority.

The indications for the use of pressure and coercion include: the dependent person needing a "push"; the "spoiled" person; persons escaping reality; persons who are constitutionally inadequate; domineering clients; persons creating an intolerable or dangerous emergency situation; temporarily emotionally uncontrolled persons; the client who will not or cannot act by himself; the indecisive, wavering neurotic; the sociopath; and the failure of other methods.

These methods have probably been misused more than any other methods of influencing behavior, and they may have lost their effects with some clients; they may lead others to react negatively or to react in other unconstructive ways, such as with anxiety, defiance, hostility, or aggression. Such clients require careful handling and more coercion or punishment will not be effective. "In general, the use of pressure, coercion and punishment is contraindicated unless there are specific reasons for its use." [71] The general approach is to begin with permissiveness in order to see how much responsibility the client can take for controlling his behavior, then as necessary, progressing to pressure (suggestion), coercion (requirement), and finally punishment.

Pressure and coercion may be necessary to make clients conform to the limits of the counseling situation or to keep them in treatment. Punishment, as such, is rarely if ever used in psychotherapy, but as an incentive to learning it may be effective. However, it should be used only when rewards have proved ineffective. In emergency situations, shock methods, withdrawal of love, withdrawal of privileges, and rejection and ostracism may be used, not by choice, but for want of better methods.

Drastic methods of coercion and punishment are indicated only for the protection of the client and of society.

Dealing With Emotional Factors in Maladjustment

"Much of behavior is determined by subconscious emotional factors which must be dealt with first before the higher mental functions can be released in problem-solving behavior. . . . There is no attempt to slight or minimize the importance of emotional behavior, particularly on subconscious or unverbalized levels. On the contrary, we reaffirm that the handling of emotional factors constitutes one of the most important problems in all psychotherapy because of the significant role played by early childhood conditionings in later maladjustments." However, "affective-impulsive factors are not the only, or even necessarily the most important, cause of disorder." [72] Although emotional factors constitute only one kind of primary etiological factor, clinical experience indicates that they should ordinarily be dealt with first. Methods for dealing with affective-impulsive factors are derived primarily from psychoanalysis and nondirective therapy, with the addition of conditioning methods.

A distinction is made between *primary emotional states* and secondary *emotional reactions.* The former are related to temperament and are largely constitutionally determined, and thus not usually modifiable by psychotherapy. Secondary emotional reactions result from frustration, conflict, and stress, and may be prevented by preventing these causes, and can be modified by reconditioning. There are different types of emotional disorders, and thus there is no single therapeutic method that is suitable for all. Emotional reactivity constitutes a continuum from overexpressiveness to underexpressiveness, with different methods being required to deal with the extreme patterns.

EMOTIONAL CONDITIONING AND RECONDITIONING "Since most reactive emotional patterns are acquired by known principles of learning, they may be modified by appropriate methods of retraining." [73] Emotional retraining utilizes varied methods to create situations in which the client may learn new emotional responses to replace neurotic responses to stimuli. Affective reconditioning makes use of the classical learning methods of positive reinforcement, extinction, reciprocal inhibition, desensitization, and positive reconditioning. Reassurance involves these methods and is effective with normal situational fears. Giving examples of others who have solved similar problems and the setting of a series of tasks are effective methods for situational complaints, usually in conjunction with other (deeper) methods. Positive reconditioning (associating an unpleasant experience with a pleasant state or condition, or introducing an experience of success) is useful in cases where traumatic experiences have created a chronic fear. Graduated experiences over a long period of time may be required. The clinical relationship constitutes a reconditioning experiment. Sublimation, that is, finding creative, socially acceptable outlets for emotional needs, may be effective, with the counselor assisting the client in choosing outlets. Techniques of muscular relaxation may reduce the muscular tension associated with emotional states.

These methods involve an active, directive role, with the case handler "authoritatively assuming the responsibility for actively manipulating client integration levels by deliberately breaking up and removing neurotic integrative patterns and replacing them with more healthy and adaptive patterns. Basically, such methods regard the client as a psychophysiological mechanism which can be tinkered with to get it running right. All this places great ethical responsibilities on the case handler to improve conditions for the better." [74]

PROBLEMS OF EMOTIONAL OVEREXPRESSIVENESS Clients with these problems include persons who have failed to acquire normal degrees of control, or inhibition, of emotional responses. In some cases the disorder may be constitutional (as in cyclothymic personalities, constitutionally inadequate or immature types, constitutional sex inversion, or the affective psychoses), but in many cases it is a conditioned reaction, including some psychoneurotic reactions, uncontrolled rage and fear reactions, and acquired sexual deviations. It is the latter that are of concern here. Emotional overexpressiveness interferes with integration.

When the undercontrol is due to lack of early training, treatment consists of informing the client of the nature and etiology of his condition and pointing out the steps in controlling behavior, with graded exercises and rewards for success. Emotional overexpression in the neurotic client is not encouraged; instead, the client is directed to perform normal daily activities, and the hysterical symptoms are interpreted. With clients showing continued agitation, crying, and hostility over a period of time, the interview may be discontinued, or the counselor may leave until the client regains control.

In children and in institutionalized adults, excessive emotional reactions can be treated by isolation when warnings and other methods have failed. Excitement and temper tantrums usually subside in three or four days, and counseling may then be effective. In immature adults uncontrolled emotional behavior usually subsides. If it continues for unreasonably long periods, a few days of hospitalization may dissipate it, or electroshock may be used in severe reactions. Panic states are usually self-limiting, or with a calm and reassuring counselor the client may be able to talk himself out of his state.

FACILITATING EMOTIONAL EXPRESSIVENESS   Repression or suppression of emotional complexes leads to overcontrol, and in such clients emotional release must be facilitated so that the conflicts may become conscious and neutralized or redirected. Several methods may be used to achieve this.

1 *Passive listening*   Simply listening to the client's story or complaints may be all that is necessary with clients who have superficial disorders, and this may be the method of choice when it is inexpedient to use more active methods. In serious disorders it may do no more than give temporary emotional release.

2 *Silence*   Silence on the part of the counselor exerts pressure on the client to talk and thus may lead him to go deeper into his problems. The effects of silence may be detrimental with insecure or hostile clients.

3 *Free association*   When the client doesn't have anything particular to talk about, free association may be used to uncover emotional complexes.

4 *Catharsis*   In catharsis the counselor actively stimulates the client to talk himself out. It is effective only with relatively superficial problems; in the case of more serious disturbances it may not even give symptomatic relief, but may reinforce the tension. Catharsis probably should not be prevented unless it becomes repetitious, but more active methods may be initiated also.

5 *Abreaction*   In contrast to catharsis, which is talking out, abreaction is a reliving, with emotional accompaniment, of previous experiences. Abreaction is related to the transference relationship and may be facilitated by the counselor's providing or suggesting "acting out" experiences, such as activity or play therapy.

6 *Acceptance*   The counselor's acceptance of the client as a person, in spite of or including his negative aspects, relieves the client of the need for being defensive and allows him to express feelings that he was unable to express before. Acceptance may be expressed in a natural, nonjudgmental attitude; extreme effusiveness, cordiality, or friendliness are less effective than quiet friendliness.

7 *Recognition and reflection of feelings*   Reflection by the counselor of the client's feelings ed lead the client to recognize his emotionally determined behavior. Reflection should be limited to verbally expressed feelings, since expression by the counselor of his diagnostic insights might result in the client's becoming anxious, guilty, depressed, or panicky.

8 *Clarification*   Clarification of feelings goes beyond simple reflection and may be a summary or integration of a long or confused expression given by the client; but, unlike interpretation, it does not go beyond what the client has expressed.

9 *Semantic reorganization*   Reflection and clarification that are clothed in a different, richer, and more varied vocabulary than that used by the client may help him understand and communicate his feelings more adequately.

10 *Active uncovering techniques*   When the client is unproductive, cause-effect probing by the counselor may lead to the exploration of emotional reactions by the client. How? Where? Why do I get upset? are questions he is encouraged to ask himself. With training, most clients can analyze the causes of their emotional reactions.

11 *The "What If" Technique*   The client may be asked to explore what it would be like if he could have the feelings or emotions that he is lacking.

12 *Active techniques of emotional release*   Although encouraging the client to go out and engage in social, recreational, and other activities is widely advocated, this method is usually not successful, since the client is generally unable to concentrate on such activities.

The objective of these methods is to prevent affectivity from becoming isolated and from blocking higher levels of integration.

TRANSFERENCE AND RESISTANCE PHENOMENA   While personality counseling, unlike psychoanalysis, does not foster the development of transference, the counselor must have an understanding of transference, since a transference relationship may develop in counseling that is intensive and of long duration. Transference is the projecting of emotional attitudes originally directed toward significant figures in early life onto the therapist. Positive attitudes result in positive transference, and negative attitudes in negative transference.

The fact that many clients have strong unmet needs for love and affection, and that they find the therapist accepting and noncritical, often leads to emotional attitudes toward the therapist that create problems in counseling. The counselor must be careful to prevent the development of unhealthy emotional attachments in his clients. Similarly, counselors must be prepared to handle reactions of fear, hate, hostility, and anger resulting from negative transference.

Since those without psychoanalytic training are not competent to resolve the transference, they should not allow a classical transference to develop. However, the counselor must terminate the dependency relationship that develops.

Resistance is the natural defense of the client against the pain and unpleasantness of recognizing and accepting insight and change. Resistance may be manifested in various ways: negative attitudes toward therapy and the therapist, failure to keep appointments and attempts to avoid or end treatment, lack of production or irrelevant productions, intellectualization, failure to carry out prescriptions, failure to pay for treatment, emotional blocking, and demands upon the counselor to attempt to control the situation.

Methods of handling resistance include the following:

1 *Passive listening* Expressions of resistance and hostility tend to be self-limiting and tend to dissipate when allowed expression in a nonthreatening atmosphere.

2 *Acceptance, reflection, and clarification* When resistances continue, they may be openly recognized and responded to by acceptance, reflection, and clarification.

3 *Neutral conversation* When resistance is too open or strong, or leads to an impasse, temporarily leading the counseling away from sensitive areas may be desirable.

4 *Analysis of resistance* Analysis and interpretation of the causes of resistance may help the client face the nature of the resistance.

5 *Termination of treatment* When resistance cannot be modified, counseling may have to be terminated, or the client may be referred to another counselor, who may not be the object of such strong resistance. The client may break off the relationship because of resistance.

FRUSTRATION AND CONFLICT RESOLUTION Conflict normally provides a motive for change. But excessive conflict either blocks integration or produces disintegration. Conflict is a cause of frustration. In such cases disabling conflicts involve two incompatible reactions, which are intense and approximately equal in strength. An objective of case handling is conflict resolution.

The disintegrating effects of frustration induced by conflict can be neutralized by increasing the client's frustration tolerance through training in tolerating tension and in rejecting immediate need gratification and by his learning through conditioning to "take punishment."

A first step in conflict resolution is to make the conflict and its opposing forces conscious through interpretation. Then plans can be formulated for coping with the forces and helping the client carry out the plan through tutorial counseling.

THE THERAPEUTIC USE OF CONFLICT The absence of conflict may be pathological; normal conflict is a motivating or corrective factor, stimulating creativity and achievement and leading to desirable changes in behavior. It may thus be desirable for the clinician to create conflict, so that the client can recognize the need for change and be motivated toward change.

Conflict may be induced by bringing into consciousness inconsistent and conflicting attitudes. When the client becomes aware of the inconsistency, he will be motivated to resolve it. The desirable effects of punishment may be the result of induced conflict.

"The use of induced conflict as a technique in therapy must be handled with great caution. Conflict should not be used promiscuously or indiscriminately. . . . It must be emphasized that the efficacy of the technique depends upon the clinical sagacity of the case handler, who must be able to guide the therapeutic process in positive directions, keep the conflict focused on inconsistencies in the client's attitudes, and avoid any attempt of the client to introduce interpersonal conflicts which would conceal the real issues." [75]

Maximizing Intellectual Resources

Education attempts to develop intellectual resources by improving sensory functions, perceptual training, memory training, and semantic training. Defects of sensation, perception, memory, learning, and the use of verbal symbols may be important causes of maladjustment and may be remedied by retraining methods. These methods are aimed at training the client to think straight and to correct illogical thoughts that are the basis of maladaptive behavior. It cannot be assumed that the client can resolve his problems logically or intellectually simply by the removal of emotional blockages. He needs direct assistance or formal training in intellectual problem solving.

SENSORY PROBLEMS AND COMPLAINTS Remedying of organic sensory defects is not a function of the personality counselor, but he should be alert to their occurrence and make appropriate referrals. Personality reactions may, however, require counseling. In addition, there are sensory complaints or peculiar sensory experiences that have a functional basis. These include frequent headaches; eyestrain; hypersensitivity to light, noise, and other stimuli; muscular and joint aches and pains; cardiac palpitation and arhythmias; "nervous stomach," etc. Diagnosis of these difficulties and differentiation from organic disorders is a medical function.

These sensory experiences are present in the normal individual, but he has learned to accept or ignore them, or to become less concerned about them than the psychoneurotic. The counselor must accept the reality of the symptoms. Reassurance may be given that they are not dangerous, that they are due to emotional disturbance, and that they can be treated. Psychosomatic information and explanations may be given. Peculiar sensations may be ignored or treated symptomatically, since they will disappear with psychotherapy directed at the etiological factors. Behavior therapy may be used for desensitization and elimination of symptoms diagnosed as functional.

PERCEPTUAL RETRAINING "Perception is organized by and makes its relevant contribution to the functional needs of the prevailing psychological state. . . . Clinically, we are interested in the study and remediation of factors interfering with the normal processing and integration of sensory input. . . . Pathologically, disorders or defects of information processing at perceptual (discriminatory) levels produce disturbances of reality testing and other perceptual errors. Since informational input is essential to keeping abreast of the times, perceptual disorders are an important cause of psychopathology." [76]

When client misperceptions become evident, attention is called to them, with an explanation of their nature. "When defects in reality testing in the client become apparent, it may be indicated to conduct diagnostic studies to discover their origin so that they may be corrected. Standard types of perceptual errors may be explained to the client with appropriate demonstrations as to how they may be corrected. The client may be tutored in more systematic reality testing by routinely analyzing maladaptive perceptual sets." [77] The client's perceptual field can often be reoriented by introducing new elements.

The client's perceptions of himself are important in his perceptions of his world and of others, and thus must be systematically evaluated. Delusional thinking and paranoid ideas can be corrected in their early stages by "pointing out their erroneous nature to the client, explaining the underlying projection mechanisms, and admonishing the client to try to correct such thinking himself." [78] Full-fledged paranoid complexes do not usually respond to counseling, however.

THE IMPROVEMENT OF MEMORY FUNCTIONING Memory deficits and pathological forgetting impair integration by preventing past experiences from entering into the process. Memory deficits due to incomplete learning may be corrected by the use of remedial learning methods (increasing motivation, grouping of materials into meaningful combinations, spaced practice, overlearning, special cues, and verbalization during learning). Pathological forgetting may be treated by the psychoanalytical methods of free association, dream analysis, and symptom analysis.

The intrusion of undesirable memories and minutia may interfere with adequate functioning. Ventilation through repeated catharsis and deliberate recalling of traumatic experiences are standard methods for reducing the affective charge of such experiences.

SEMANTIC REEDUCATION General semantics is concerned with the use of language and symbols in the thinking process. Semantic disorders include vague, fuzzy, and illogical thinking and inaccurate and unclear use of language, which interferes with communication.

The case handler should evaluate the client's language functioning from the beginning and undertake semantic reorientation through careful definition of psychological terms, which are often not understood clearly by clients.

Informal semantic reeducation consists of correcting semantic errors as they occur in counseling, thus helping the client to become clearer, more accurate, and more articulate in his use of language. Clients who are highly intelligent and verbal, and who have basic emotional stability, may be given formal semantic training. This may include reading and exercises aimed toward the objective of dealing with their problems logically and scientifically. Semantics underlies all methods of improving intellectual resources and is also relevant to methods of developing emotional release and clarification, which may be regarded as preparation for intellectual problem-solving behavior.

Methods of Ideological and Attitudinal Reorientation

Ideas and attitudes integrate the highest levels of human behavior. Many disorders are the result of lack of knowledge, erroneous knowledge, and logical or semantic failure to use symbols validly. It is thus necessary to evaluate the client's ideological beliefs and values. The neurotically or emotionally determined ideas and values that are involved require deep psychotherapy. Most ideas are acquired normally, and ideological disorders then reflect a pathological environment rather than pathology in the person. Methods of ideological reorientation are then necessary.

IMPARTING PSYCHOLOGICAL INFORMATION The counselor has a responsibility to provide helpful psychological information to the individual who needs it for more efficient functioning or in problem solving. The giving of psychological information is indicated when it is lacking and when it will be necessary or useful to the client. It is contraindicated when it would have threatening or destructive effects and when there are unhealthy motives for seeking it. The kinds of information that may be given include material concerning the nature of the disorder and its prognosis, information concerning alternative courses of action, information necessary to forestall unwise action, and information concerning the attitudes of others toward the client. In some cases, when scientific knowledge is not available, opinions may be offered.

Information should be given, not in the form of a lecture, but as needed and in relation to the problems of the client. The language should be adapted to the client's background. References to books and other sources may be used. Information should be selective and presented objectively, in a manner that does not intimidate or threaten the client. The counselor should check to see whether the client has understood or assimilated the material.

Systematic psychological tutoring may be provided to impart the latest basic scientific psychological information. The book *How to Be Psychologically Healthy* [79] may be assigned to clients when appropriate; in selected cases (clients who are too directive and authoritarian or who have to deal with authoritarian people) study of the theory and practice of nondirective methods can be valuable.

THE METHOD OF INTERPRETATION One of the major goals of psychotherapy is the development of insight by the client. The method of interpretation, one of the most widely used and misused techniques of psychotherapy, is the most specific and the simplest method of transmitting insights from the therapist to the client. Interpretations are attempts to provide understanding of the nature and origin of the maladjustment.

Indications for interpretation are difficult to specify; mature clinical judgment must be relied upon. In general, there must be reason to believe that the client can use the interpretation constructively. Interpretation is indicated when the client is unable to reach the insight alone and when therapy would be speeded up by the providing of an insight long before the client could achieve it by himself. Interpretations should not be used when, although true, they are threatening, when the client is unable to do anything about them, when they may create more conflicts than they solve, and when the client is not able to comprehend them.

Interpretations should be made cautiously and sparingly, at the optimum moment (not too soon), and tentatively, even though the counselor will make an interpretation only when he is convinced it is valid. The counselor must be truthful, nonjudgmental, and simple in his interpretations. Methods of interpretation include sympathetic or understanding comments, reflective comments, focusing comments, facilitating comments, comforting comments, and connecting comments. The interpretation of symbols in psychoanalytic terminology should be avoided in general. The counselor should make certain that the client understands the interpretations by having him reformulate or summarize them.

IDEOLOGICAL AND ATTITUDINAL REORIENTATION   Many normal people have adjustment problems related to unhealthy or untenable attitudes acquired in the normal learning process. Disorders of this kind are called attitudinal psychopathies and consist of a constellation of pathological attitudes. They are differentiated from the psychoneuroses and psychoses in which pathological attitudes are secondary to an underlying disorder. Pathological attitudes are those that are so deviant, erroneous, or untenable as to cause maladjustment.

Reorientation requires first the analysis of the constellation of attitudes and the identification of core attitudes. Reorganization is achieved through the introduction of conflicting (healthy) attitudes, requiring the reduction of inconsistency. Repetition is necessary, as well as emotional and intellectual reinforcement of the new attitudes. The process of change is usually slow, often with resistance, so the counselor should be prepared for a long-term process. However, sudden and complete changes can occur when a nuclear or core attitude is displaced.

Caution must be used in attempting to reorganize the attitudes of older people and those whose whole way of life is based upon questionable beliefs, such as certain religious beliefs.

The Self

Many client complaints relate to perceived disorders of self functioning. Self functioning represents the highest level integrations. Positive mental health and complete self-actualization depend upon the normality of self functioning.

THE SELF AND ITS STATUS   The evaluation of self functioning is an important part of the examination of the client's mental status. The client constantly reveals self status throughout case handling. The Q sort provides an objective measure. Dissatisfaction of the client with the self status is necessary for effective counseling, providing the motivation for change. Discrepancies between the concept of the self and that of the ideal self are the source of many adjustment problems, and important goals of case handling are to remove these discrepancies and to strengthen the self-concept.

THE IDEAL SELF Attempts to influence the client's concept of the ideal self are based upon the argument that good character is essential for mental health. There are a number of systems of character building, including the theological. Spiritual counseling can be helpful for those who can accept its assumptions, and the case handler should utilize this as a referral resource.

Character rehabilitation is one objective of case handling. Moralistic judgments must be made in a nonauthoritarian and nonrejecting manner to avoid alienating the client. Psychological tutoring is one method of character rehabilitation.

When the ideal self is unattainably higher than the actual self, frustration is inevitable, until the ideal self becomes realistic and thus attainable.

SELF EXECUTIVE FUNCTIONINGS The highest levels of integration are characterized by purposive, voluntary, conscious integration. "It is also postulated that the ability to exert self-control, conscious volition or to utilize intellectual resources optimally is not instinctive or innate but is learned by training and experience." [80] Feelings and emotions exist involuntarily (unconsciously), but they may be controlled and channeled. Defects or disorders in learning control are involved in behavior disintegration from frustration and stress. Diagnosis of such disorders is thus important.

Factors contributing to control include emotional stability, the capacity for adequate discrimination of alternatives, adequate symbolic representation, a positive attitude or "mental set" toward control, ability to direct or withhold conscious attention selectively, acceptance of the possibility of self-control, and adequate self-signaling devices. These factors are integrated slowly in a learning process that is specific for differing situations.

"Many clients are completely undisciplined and out of control when they first come for help. . . . One of the first steps in case handling may be to persuade and train the client to adapt to the general requirements of cultural conformity. This may involve going back to the simplest exercises in self-control which should have been acquired in early childhood." [81] In states of heightened affectivity the client must be taught how to deal with psychophysical reactions. With clients who have problems of interpersonal conflicts, tutoring in nondirective methods of handling hostility and aggression may be very effective.

TRANSACTIONAL ANALYSIS AND SOCIAL PSYCHIATRY Transactional analysis focuses upon interpersonal relations. The integrational state of the person influences his social transactions. Eric Berne's classification of ego states into the child, the parent, and the adult is oversimplified, but can be expanded to do justice to all the factors organizing integration levels. Games, following Berne, consist of a transactional unit or series of unified interactions, with a beginning and an end, involving ulterior motives in the players, with a payoff for each. While games are only one kind of social transaction, they are important because of the effects on the loser. In addition, the person engaged in gamesmanship, while he may be a "winner," develops personally and socially unhealthy relationships.

"It is indicated to indoctrinate the client with a working knowledge of normal probabilities, gamesmanship and good sportsmanship to teach the client a philosophy of life which will support him in times of need." [82] The person who is being victimized can be taught to avoid this by refusing to play the game, by neutralizing moves with countermoves, or by withholding the payoff.

THE HANDLING OF EXISTENTIAL PROBLEMS   With the increasingly difficult conditions of living, more clients are coming for help on problems that are existential in nature, that is, involving the meaning of life in a confusing world, in which values are being questioned and are often inconsistent. The counselor enters into the consideration of alternative values and their alternative consequences or costs with the client.

The primary existential motive is self-enhancement or self-actualization. Anxiety is the result of the threat or the actuality of failure to become actualized. An effort to cover up failure results in lack of authenticity and genuineness, with resulting anxiety. The case handler should have a pretty realistic understanding of what life can be expected to hold for any particular client. Clients with great unrealized possibilities for self-potentiation may be stimulated toward greater efforts and more aggressiveness in wresting for themselves what life has to offer. With clients of lesser potentialities, it may be indicated to discourage unreasonable expectations and to encourage acceptance of the status quo.

Maladjustments result from the failure to achieve a realistic and tenable *Weltanschauung*. The individual's *Weltanschauung* may be too rudimentary and incomplete; it may be inadequate to handle the inconsistencies of life; it may fail to evolve and thus become outdated; an adequate *Weltanschauüng* may be insufficient to meet extreme adversity; or the individual may have insufficient experiential resources to build a satisfactory *Weltanschauüng*. Though there are no objective methods for evaluating the client's *Weltanschauung*, it becomes apparent over a period of time. Misconceptions and unhealthy attitudes are dealt with realistically as they occur. Alternative attitudes may be discussed, but no attempt is made to argue the client out of his attitudes. When the client's *Weltanschauung* is the focus of concern, the case handler assumes the position of an educator who presents "the concentrated experience of mankind" to avoid the client having to learn by the trial-and-error method. The case handler "attempts to overhaul and bring up-to-date the client's world conception in the light of the most advanced information. . . . Ideally, the client might be allowed to work through his problems nondirectively. . . . Practically, however, more or less direction is indicated, since the achievement of an adequate *Weltanschauung* is upon a broad cultural background which is beyond the education and experience of large segments of the population. The assumption of responsibility by the therapist for modifying a person's world conception assumes a genuine wisdom and years of experience." [83]

EXAMPLES

Thorne includes many excerpts in his book, illustrating the application of specific methods. However, he notes that "the case reports in this book are not exact transcriptions of any particular case but have been extensively edited and revised to describe general situations rather than specific cases." [84]

The following is an excerpt in which the counselor interprets resistance in terms of what had previously come out in counseling, in an effort to prevent premature termination.

CLIENT   I don't see as we are getting anywhere. Here I have been coming for almost five weeks and I don't feel any better than when we started. Sometimes I think maybe I feel worse.

COUNSELOR   Sometimes you get discouraged and feel that you are wasting your time.

CL   We . . . to be frank, yes. You just sit there listening to me and never say anything. I sometimes wonder if I wouldn't do better talking to the wall. You never answer any of my questions.

CO   It makes you mad because I don't tell you what to do, but just reflect the question back for you to solve for yourself.

CL   Why shouldn't I just talk this over with my husband? He says, "Why do you keep going there and seeing that doctor? He never seems to do anything for you."

CO   Sometimes you feel upset because you are wasting your time and money just talking things over when you feel that more should be done.

CL   I don't think I will come anymore. We seem to be at a standstill. I don't see where we are getting. I could use the money better somewhere else.

CO   I think we have discovered from these interviews that whenever we are coming to something important, you seem to become blocked emotionally and have trouble getting it out. You remember last time, it took you quite some time to express feelings of hostility toward your mother. It was so painful to you that you would almost rather break off the interview than talk about it. I wonder if your present feelings of discouragement are related to the fact that we are getting close to something else.

CL   What do you think it could be?

CO   I don't know. That is something you will have to discover for yourself. All I know is that as long as you continue to feel bad, your problems aren't solved. There was something you started to tell me last time but never got it finished. Do you remember? You started to tell me something that was upsetting you very much but somehow you couldn't bring yourself to.

CL   Oh, that. I don't see as that had anything to do with it. I am not sure I want to talk about it. I felt like talking for a minute and then it passed away.

CO   It's something which made you feel upset even to think about it.

CL   Yes, but it hasn't anything to do with this.

CO   How can we tell until we find what it is?

CL   I can't bring myself to say it. (cries) Sometimes I am afraid of myself.

CO   M'hm.

CL   You're going to think I'm awful.

CO   You're afraid I might reject you if you tell bad things about yourself.

CL   But this is bad.

CO   M'hm.

CL   I see you are going to get it out of me so I might as well tell it. Maybe you'll say I should be put away when you hear it. It's just this. The other night I had an impulse to choke my baby. It just came into my mind. It upset me so I didn't know what to do. There he lay, the dear little thing. Sleeping so peaceable. It was all I could do to keep from doing it. I had to run out of the room. I woke my husband and he said, "What's the matter anyway?" I was afraid to tell him, I just said I was lonely and would he love me a little bit. I guess people like me should be put away.

CO   Having such a thought frightened you.

CL   I'll say it did. I don't think I would have done anything but suppose I did. Do you think I am safe to have around?

CO   Have you ever had other thoughts like that?

CL   Once or twice I had funny thoughts. Knives bother me. I have had impulses to pick one up and stick it into sombody.

CO   Who?

CL   My mother for one. I don't understand it. She has done everything for me. Maybe too much. And I still feel like that.

CO   Sometimes people feel like this if they have unconscious resentments against people. They can love a person and hate them at the same time. It is all right to consciously admit that you love somebody, but most people don't want to face the fact that they have negative feelings to somebody they should love. It makes you feel guilty if you feel that way. Do you know what I mean?

CL   You mean that maybe I have hateful feelings way down inside me and they take this way of coming out. But why on my innocent child that I love so much?

CO   Probably most of the time you love him dearly but once in a while he upsets you. Maybe you are feeling tired or sick and it's just too much.

CL   Of course he does get on my nerves sometimes. I guess maybe I'm not a good mother.

CO Again, it makes you feel guilty to have these thoughts. I want you to understand this and come to accept your own feelings. Probably if you could express what you feel more and not bury it deep inside you, it would not come out in these devious ways.

CL Whew. It makes me feel better to get that out. Do you think I am safe to be around? I would be willing to go away if I thought anything would happen.

CO I don't think there is any danger as long as you keep coming for a little to talk these things over. I want you to promise that you will come and talk with me anytime these things get to bothering you. Get them off your chest.

CL All right, I will.[85]

In the following excerpt the client is a young girl, twenty years old, talking about her emotional feelings toward her mother. It is illustrative of semantic reorientation:

CL I suppose if I really faced the fact I would have to admit that I have never loved Mother. There is something about her which rubs me the wrong way. I think this has always been so. I can remember as a little girl being closer to my father. I know it's awful to say this but it's so.

CO You have never felt easy with your mother.

CL No. We never seem to understand each other. I know she tries her best to do things for me but I never know how to take her.

CO In a way you are a little afraid of her.

CL I wouldn't say that I was afraid of her, or am I? She can be quite cutting in her remarks. When I was a little girl I would try to be doing something and she would laugh at me.

CO You were afraid that she would make fun of you.

CL Sometimes she did. In a nice way, of course.

CO It makes you feel guilty if you think bad thoughts about your mother.

CL We-e-ll, anybody should be loyal to their mother. Think of all the things she has done for me.

CO But still little hostile feelings come into your mind and then you feel guilty.

CL I love my mother.

CO I know you do. I didn't say anything about not loving her. I merely said that occasionally you feel upset by what she does and then you have hostile thoughts. That is perfectly natural. Nobody likes any other person 100 percent. We are all mixed in our feelings. There is a word for it—ambivalence. When you're ambivalent, you hold positive and negative feelings toward a person at the same time.

CL You mean part of the time I love my mother and part of the time I don't like her so well. I never thought of it that way but I guess it's true.

CO Many people are confused over these mixed feelings.

CL I guess I've felt that way for some time.

CO Can you remember when you first began to have mixed feelings toward her?

CL   I can remember there was always some jealousy and fighting with my brother. It seems that Mother always used to take his part and be on his side.

CO   It made you feel upset because you didn't feel she gave you an equal amount of attention.

CL   That's it. I remember that she used to let Bob get away with a lot of little things. Like when it came out that she had been giving him more spending money. I also used to notice that he got the best helpings of meat. She served him first.

CO   You felt resentful because he seemed to always get the best.

CL   Not always but most of the time. It didn't do any good for me to say anything, because if I did my mother would say, "You're just a jealous little girl."

CO   M'hm.

CL   And then if I said anything she would get mad. It seemed that she was always getting mad at me. Hardly a meal went by without her and I getting into a squabble. But it always ended up all right.

CO   Even now it upsets you to think about it.

CL   It still bothers me if it comes up. I live at home and he doesn't. When he comes to see us, Mother always makes a big fuss. You'd think he was something unusual. Of course he is something nice. I think a lot of him.

CO   You like your brother all right but it upsets you when your mother makes such a fuss over him. That is a very common situation. Most mothers are closer to their sons and fathers are closer to their daughters. That seems to be a natural thing in the world.[86]

The following excerpt relates to "feelings of personal/social adequacy which tend to arise in every client and are handled within the eclectic method by the standard techniques of helping the client recognize and give up maladaptive defense mechanisms, to recognize and accept feelings of inadequacy, not to be incapacitated by anxiety reactive to fears of failure, and to learn new coping methods which promise some degree of success":

. Joan G., aged nineteen, had just returned home in the middle of her first semester at college in a state of high anxiety, crying and protesting that she could not bear to return to school. The client trembled and cried the first fifteen minutes of the initial interview.

CO   I see that you feel pretty bad today.

CL   Yes. Everything is awful. (cries)

CO   How is that?

CL   I have made a failure of everything. Now I can't go back.

CO   You feel terribly embarrassed and ashamed about things.

CL   I just feel terrible.

CO   Do you want to tell me about it?

CL   There's not much to tell. I just didn't make it up there. I made a terrible mess of things.

CO   M'hm.

CL   I was so happy and hopeful when the term started, but then the first two weeks were horrible. Things started to go bad. I went to class like a walking zombie. My body was there, but my mind was somewhere else. I just couldn't concentrate on anything. The instructor would ask a question, and my mind would just go blank. I must have seemed like a fool. They were all so kind, but I just knew they thought I was some kind of a screwball. I started staying away from classes and going for long walks in the town. I just couldn't stand to face it. Then last weekend I just decided to give it all up and come home for good. I just couldn't take it anymore. If I try, I fear something terrible will happen.

CO   What is your worst fear about what might happen?

CL   Oh, I don't know. My head feels kind of funny, tight like, as if it might blow up. And I feel as in a daze, as if I was losing my mind. I was never like this before. What can be the matter with me? I don't understand myself. This is not me.

CO   This has shaken your confidence badly so you don't like yourself so much any more.

CL   Who would?

CO   How about before you got to college? Did you have much confidence in yourself?

CL   Oh, yes. I was always very popular and had a lot of dates and was considered one of the most popular girls. Most of the time it was very easy.

CO   How about the school work itself?

CL   I never had to work very hard. It all seemed to come very easy. I never studied too much—was always too busy having a good time. I would just listen in class. I have a good memory.

CO   But it was not so easy in college where you had to get the material yourself from outside readings?

CL   I couldn't seem to settle down and dig it out. I had several embarrassing experiences in class where I was supposed to know something and didn't. One instructor in particular seemed particularly tough. He went right after me and I felt like a fool.

CO   Your little ego has taken quite a beating, is that it?

CL   I guess so. I feel as if I have hardly any ego left.

CO   Well, you must understand this is an experience which many young people go through. In high school, you were a prima donna but now you find yourself in the big time where the competition is tougher. At first, it makes you anxious and discouraged, fearing that you haven't got the stuff. You develop an inferiority complex, and the easiest thing would be just to fold your tent and disappear.

CL   That's just what I did. I can't take it any more. I am developing a terrible inferiority complex.

CO   So what? You and everybody else. If you only knew it, most of your classmates in the freshman year are going through the same experiences. They all feel uncertain and shaky. Let me ask you something. Do you feel that it is best to do nothing rather than risk failure? Or, it is better to try and try again until you succeed?

CL   Right now, all I want is peace. I don't care whether I fail or not. I just want to be left alone. I'll just go somewhere and get a job on my own level.

CO   Well, you might do that but first, though, I want you to understand a few things about yourself. These terrible feelings you have are what we call anxiety, which is caused by fear of failing. You can't stand to mess up things, so, you get very upset emotionally, and then your mind does not work, and you feel like dropping out. You must believe that what you are experiencing is simply upset emotions. So what? Your emotions are upset, is that any reason to give up?

CL   But how can I go on like this? I can't trust myself. I might cry right in class.

CO   All right. So you feel bad a few minutes? So what? You can't give up on life whenever you feel bad. This is like the boys in the war who got combat fatigue. They felt just like you do. All to pieces and ready to give up. Those who gave up became neurotically disabled. Those who stayed in the situation and overcame their fears lived to become better men. Don't let the first big obstacle in your life stop you. I can assure you that nobody ever died from feeling upset emotionally. You may feel like it, but you won't.

CO   I am not going to ask anything superhuman of you, but simply that you regroup yourself and edge back into the situation. Go back up next Monday and resume as if nothing had happened. I will give you the name of a counselor you can look up, or you can always come back and talk to me if you get too upset.

CL   What will people think? What will the Dean say?

CO   She is a good friend of mine. I'll just call her up and tell her you got a little tense and were worried about yourself and now you are going to settle down. Nobody will say anything to you. But suppose they did, what will you say?

CL   Oh, tell a lie and say that I had a date at home and act as if nothing happened.

CO   Why create more to feel defensive about? The best defense is no defense. Just tell the truth. Just say that you felt a little discouraged. That is true, isn't it?

CL   I hate to admit anything like that about myself.

CO   Why? Everybody has things they are sensitive about. The best defense is no defense. If you feel inadequate about something, don't hide it but instead come right out and admit it. Nobody is going to take advantage of you. They will like you just as much because they have things they are sensitive about too.

CL   I just don't think I can do it. The way I feel now, I just want to go to bed and stay there.

CO   I know it. But this is a key point in your life. You have got to lick this or it will lick you. My judgment tells me that you have the stuff to go back.[87]

SUMMARY AND EVALUATION

The attempt to integrate all empirical psychological knowledge into an eclectic system is a tremendous undertaking. Some would consider it to be premature. The spotty, scattered, and inexact nature of psychological knowledge makes it a difficult if not an impossible task at the present time. Psychology is perhaps below the level of medicine in Osler's day as far as validated empirical knowledge is concerned. Thorne repeatedly admits the lack of experimental, empirical, or actuarial data regarding indications and contraindications for clinical methods or procedures. Thus, it is not surprising that Thorne's system may leave one doubtful that he has convincingly demonstrated the relation of specific methods to specific problems. The system consists essentially of assumptions and opinions rather than the integration of empirical facts or validated knowledge. In place of nonexisting empirically validated data, Thorne has used his wide clinical experience and extensive knowledge of various psychological systems and theories. Thorne is not, of course, responsible for the state of affairs in psychology. He must be admired for his courage in attempting the task of integration of all existing knowledge in psychology. The result is impressive. It is without doubt the most comprehensive system of behavior and its psychopathology and treatment in existence. Thorne would no doubt agree that it is only a first approximation to a final eclectic system.

Thorne's concept of clinical case handling goes beyond the usual definitions of counseling or psychotherapy. He is concerned with the entire range of disturbed, abnormal, or psychopathological behavior, from disturbed psychological status often classified as "no psychiatric disorder," emotional immaturity, or "simple adult maladjustment" to frank psychotic states. Also included are maladaptive attitudes and the existential problems of living. Thus, one finds Thorne visiting clients who take to bed for psychological reasons in their homes. Again, since many of his clients do not come on their own seeking help, he becomes involved in attempts to help or work with involuntary and resisting clients. This, of course, extends the range of methods of psychological case handling beyond the methods of office counseling or psychotherapy.

The range of disorders dealt with also lends support for a diagnostic system that attempts to classify clients or problems for more specific treatment. It may be questioned whether the detailed system of diagnostic classification developed by Thorne is particularly useful. Thorne himself, however, minimizes the value of a diagnostic classification system, and his methods of case handling are not organized on the basis of this classification. Rather it is the etiological equation that is to be the basis of treatment, and these equations are unique to each client and are to be constantly revised on almost a moment-to-moment basis. Thus, it is presumably etiological equations that are classified and related to treatment indications and contraindications. A broad or general classification of samples, or illustrations, of diagnostic equations is presented. It is not clear just how the equations are derived, except that it is a process of clinical judgment. This is, of course, the best that can be done at our present stage of knowledge. There is no specific instruction on assigning weights to the elements of the equations, though relative weights are assigned to different major kinds of etiological elements, as indicated above. Presumably a client may have a complex problem or a number of different problems, and thus require a number of etiological equations. Thorne appears to select a single—or what he considers the major—problem and work on that, apparently moving on to other problems later. It is difficult to know just how the entire process of treatment might be handled, since the numerous case illustrations are brief and represent only a part of the total treatment. The impression of clear-cut discrete problems may be misleading, since the examples, as noted, are not actual cases but reconstructions. It should be noted, however, that this approach to diagnosis is not the standard method of psychiatric classification and is certainly an advance over that method. The concept of etiological equations, related not only to the unique individual but to changing psychological states, would appear to be a fruitful one.

The impression that one gets from reading the examples and illustrations is that Thorne's practice is highly didactic or tutorial. This approach is advocated for certain kinds of problems, but it seems to permeate his treatment of all clients. The general approach to problems is a rational, logical problem-solving approach. To the criticism that rational elements are emphasized, Thorne replies that "it is only because we believe that reason is man's ultimate resource, and that only by maximizing rationality can man cope with an increasingly complex reality." [88] While this is no doubt true, the disturbed individual is in no condition to enter into a rational or logical problem-solving process. Thorne does, of course, recognize emotional factors in disturbance. While the goal is rationality, the cure for unreason may not be reason. However, forcing the client to talk and think rationally may have some value, and apparently Thorne has found it to be effective. Again, one must remember that the excerpts in his writings may not represent exactly how Thorne operates. They also, of course, do not, and cannot, present the personal, psychological context of the counseling.

This leads to a comment on the extent to which Thorne's eclectic system incorporates elements of the major schools of counseling or psychotherapy, or what is coming to be recognized as basic common elements of all systems or approaches. The three major elements, or "core conditions" as they are called by Carkhuff and his associates, are empathic understanding, respect and warmth, and genuineness. There is now considerable research supporting these conditions as necessary (and sufficient in many if not all cases) for successful counseling or psychotherapy. Thorne recognizes these conditions, but they do not receive the emphasis or attention that they appear to deserve. There is no doubt that they are present in Thorne's practice, and in fact it may be that his success is due more to the presence of these conditions, and less to his specific techniques, than he recognizes.

The emphasis upon self-actualization, self-enhancement, and

self-consistency as the primary dynamic motives underlying all of life and as the highest level of integration brings Thorne's position into agreement with perceptual-phenomenological-existential systems, and also with the gestalt approach. This provides an organizing principle, which is necessary for a truly integrative system.

Thorne has attempted a Herculean task, to use the phrase of one reviewer, who goes on to say:

> He has brought together a large variety of methods and procedures and has offered what he believes is a comprehensive and organized system. However, it is this reviewer's opinion that the attempt, while valiant, is not quite successful. The reader does not really get a concise or integrated system for practice. The scheme offered tends to be abstract, and the diagnostic system and the methods of case handling are not tied together in a really functional way. While the author has attempted to meet previous criticism of his eclectic system by offering an attempt at an integrative theory or substructure, I do not believe the venture has succeeded. It still remains, essentially, a loosely tied together eclectic system, and one is not able to derive a formulation clearly and then to select the appropriate method of case handling.[89]

All this may be true. Yet I believe that Thorne's work is more than a valiant try. If our goal is to integrate all psychological knowledge into a comprehensive system—and, certainly, this is the goal of science and of psychology as a science—then Thorne is moving in the right direction. Certainly, proponents of, and experts in, various schools, such as psychoanalysis, client-centered therapy, gestalt therapy, or existentialism, may feel that he has not adequately recognized or utilized their formulations. And certainly, the result of any integration at this point in time will not be a completely satisfying or finished product. Perhaps no one man can achieve this at any time. But Thorne has set an example and made a beginning which he and others can continue to build on.

Thorne has begun work to identify the factors organizing the various levels of integration. In 1965 he designed a series of Integration Level Tests measuring eight levels of organizing factors. Factor analyses of two of these (the Sex Inventory and the Ideological Survey) have been completed, and factor analyses of the remaining tests and a second-order factor analysis are now in process. Preliminary results indicate that self- and existential concern factors are the major second-order factors.[90]

REFERENCES

[1] Thorne, F. C. *Psychological case handling.* Vol. I: *Establishing the conditions necessary for counseling and psychotherapy.* Brandon, Vt: Clinical Psychology Publishing Co., 1968. P. vi.   [2] *Ibid.*   [3] Thorne, F. C. *Personality.* Brandon,

Vt.: Clinical Psychology Publishing Co., 1961.   [4] Thorne, F. C. *Integrative psychology.* Brandon, Vt.: Clinical Psychology Publishing Co., 1967.   [5] Thorne, F. C. *Principles of psychological examining.* Brandon, Vt.: Clinical Psychology Publishing Co., 1955.   [6] Thorne, F. C. *Clinical judgment.* Brandon, Vt.: Clinical Psychology Publishing Co., 1960.   [7] Thorne, F. C. *How to be psychologically healthy: tutorial counseling.* Brandon, Vt.: Clinical Psychology Publishing Co., 1965.   [8] Thorne, F. C. *Psychological Case Handling.* Vol. I. Brandon, Vt.: Clinical Psychology Publishing Co., 1968. P. v.   [9] Thorne, F. C. *Personality.* Brandon, Vt.: Clinical Psychology Publishing Co., 1961. Pp. 42–43. [10] *Ibid.,* p. 43.   [11] Thorne, F. C. *Psychological case handling.* Vol. I: Brandon, Vt.: Clinical Psychology Publishing Co., 1968. P. v.   [12] *Ibid.,* pp. vi–vii.   [13] Thorne, F. C. *Personality.* Brandon, Vt.: Clinical Psychology Publishing Co., 1961. P. xiii.   [14] *Ibid.,* p. 40.   [15] *Ibid.,* p. 41. [16] *Ibid.,* p. 54.   [17] *Ibid.,* p. 65.   [18] *Ibid.,* p. 68.   [19] *Ibid.,* p. 74. [20] *Ibid.,* p. 92.   [21] *Ibid.,* p. 92.   [22] *Ibid.,* p. 101.   [23] *Ibid.,* p. 102. [24] *Ibid.,* p. 108.   [25] *Ibid.,* p. 110.   [26] *Ibid.,* p. 111.   [27] *Ibid.,* p. 141.   [28] *Ibid.,* p. 159.   [29] *Ibid.,* p. 163.   [30] *Ibid.,* p. 181.   [31] *Ibid.,* p. 184.   [32] Thorne, F. C. *Integrative psychology.* Brandon, Vt.: Clinical Psychology Publishing Co., 1967. P. vii.   [33] *Ibid.,* pp. 22–23.   [34] *Ibid.,* pp. 1, 2.   [35] *Ibid.,* p. 14.   [36] *Ibid.,* p. 20.   [37] *Ibid.,* p. 22. [38] *Ibid.,* pp. 25–85, 158–185. Passim.   [39] *Ibid.,* p. 315.   [40] *Ibid.,* p. 350.   [41] Thorne, F. C., *Psychological case handling.* Vol. I. Brandon, Vt.: Clinical Psychology Publishing Co., 1968. P. 23.   [42] *Ibid.,* pp. 11–12. [43] *Ibid.,* pp. 12–13.   [44] *Ibid.,* pp. 30–31.   [45] *Ibid.,* p. 36.   [46] *Ibid.,* p. 59.   [47] *Ibid.,* p. 69.   [48] *Ibid.,* p. xi.   [49] *Ibid.,* p. 129.   [50] Thorne, F. C., *Principles of psychological examining.* Brandon, Vt.: Clinical Psychology Publishing Co., 1955. Pp. 96–106.   [51] Thorne, F. C. Diagnostic classification and nomenclature for psychological states. Monograph Supplement No. 17, *J. clin. Psychol.,* 1914; also in F. C. Thorne, *Integrative Psychology.* Brandon, Vt.: Clinical Psychology Publishing Co., 1967. Pp. 86–157. [52] Thorne, F. C. *Psychological case handling.* Vol. I. Brandon, Vt.: Clinical Psychology Publishing Co., 1968. P. 46.   [53] *Ibid.,* p. 104.   [54] *Ibid.,* p. 111.   [55] *Ibid.,* pp. 130–131.   [56] *Ibid.,* p. 132.   [57] *Ibid.,* p. 139. [58] *Ibid.,* p. 140.   [59] *Ibid.,* p. 81.   [60] *Ibid.,* p. 87.   [61] *Ibid.,* p. 99. [62] *Ibid.,* p. 53.   [63] *Ibid.,* p. 152.   [64] *Ibid.,* p. 176.   [65] *Ibid.,* p. 221. [66] *Ibid.,* p. 232.   [67] *Ibid.,* p. 238.   [68] Thorne, F. C. *Tutorial Counseling.* Brandon, Vt.: Clinical Psychology Publishing Co., 1965.   [69] Thorne, F. C. *Psychological case handling.* Vol. I. Brandon, Vt.: Clinical Psychology Publishing Co., 1968. P. 261.   [70] *Ibid.,* p. 292.   [71] *Ibid.,* p. 305. [72] Thorne, F. C. *Psychological case handling.* Vol. II: *Specialized methods of counseling and psychotherapy.* Brandon, Vt.: Clinical Psychology Publishing Co., 1968. P. 347.   [73] *Ibid.,* p. 357.   [74] *Ibid.,* p. 373.   [75] *Ibid.,* pp. 452, 453. [76] *Ibid.,* pp. 468–469.   [77] *Ibid.,* p. 477.   [78] *Ibid.,* p. 485.   [79] Thorne, F. C. *How to be psychologically healthy.* Brandon, Vt.: Clinical Psychology Publishing Co., 1965.   [80] Thorne, F. C. *Psychological case handling.* Vol. II. Brandon, Vt.: Clinical Psychology Publishing Co., 1968, p. 615.   [81] *Ibid.,* p. 621.   [82] *Ibid.,* p. 640.   [83] *Ibid.,* p. 671.   [84] *Ibid.,* p. 346. [85] Thorne, F. C. *Psychological case handling.* Vol. I. Brandon, Vt.: Clinical

Psychology Publishing Co., 1968. Pp. 175–176.   **[86]** Thorne, F. C. *Psychological case handling.* Vol. II. Brandon, Vt.: Clinical Psychology Publishing Co., 1968. Pp. 402–403.   **[87]** *Ibid.,* pp. 585–587.   **[88]** Thorne, F. C. Personal communication. June 2, 1967.   **[89]** Garfield, S. L. A valiant try. (Review of *Integrative Psychology,* and *Psychological case handling,* Vols. I and II. *Contemp. Psychol.,* 1969, **14,** 131–133.   **[90]** Personal communication. January 22, 1972.

PART SEVEN

Conclusion

21
Divergences and convergences in counseling or psychotherapy

The preceding chapters have summarized a number of approaches to counseling or psychotherapy. At least an equal number of other approaches, including orthodox psychoanalysis and neoanalytic approaches, could have been included. The picture, at least on the surface, is one of diversity. The various points of view appear to differ considerably not only in methods or techniques, but also in their goals and in their basic concepts and philosophical orientations.

This diversity, and even disagreement, has led some observers to despair about the state of counseling or psychotherapy. Ungersma writes as follows: "The present situation in psychotherapy is not unlike that of the man who mounted his horse and rode off in all directions. The theoretical orientation of therapists is based upon widely divergent hypotheses, theories, and ideologies. . . . Individual practitioners of any art are expected to vary, but some well-organized schools of therapy also seem to be working at cross-purposes with other equally well-organized schools. Nevertheless, all schools, given favorable conditions, achieve favorable results: the patient or client gets relief and is often enough cured of his difficulties." [1] This equal success of apparently widely differing approaches constitutes a problem requiring some explanation.

Some years ago Carl Rogers, who had hoped that therapists

521

would be able to come to agreement on what constitutes psychotherapy, expressed his disillusionment. Whereas he had previously felt that "we were all talking about the same experiences, but attaching different words, labels, and descriptions to these experiences," he then wrote that he felt that "we differ at the most basic level of our personal experiences." He concluded that "the field of psychotherapy is in a mess," although he felt that the confusion provided a healthy climate for new ideas, theories, concepts, and methods.[2]

Is there any reason to believe that the situation is any different now from what it was a decade ago? Is there less confusion, less divergence? Has the field of psychotherapy coalesced, or shown evidence of converging toward a common, generally accepted theory or system? It appears that while there has been some progress in agreement upon some common elements of psychotherapy, this has been limited mainly to those approaches that are currently labeled as "traditional," that is, those methods or approaches that are not included among the behavior therapies. The past decade has been the period of the development of learning theory approaches, as the 1950s seemed to be the decade of client-centered therapy. This development has introduced new diversity into the field, to the point where it has appeared to some that two inconsistent and irreconcilable approaches were developing.

Kanfer and Phillips state that not only do clinicians disagree in the theories that they hold, but "their practices and beliefs reflect even deeper inconsistencies and contradictions." Limiting themselves to the behavior therapies, Kanfer and Phillips recommend that "instead of accepting the goal of more refinement of the numerous specific procedures, it may be more useful to strive for their eventual integration into a more comprehensive behavior system. . . . The first step toward such a framework lies in efforts to find the common elements and the differences among the variety of techniques used." [3]

We ended the last chapter by suggesting that while Thorne's eclectic system was not the final answer, some systematic integration of the various, apparently divergent, approaches to counseling or psychotherapy is the ultimate goal. Thorne's eclecticism, while the most comprehensive to date, is not a satisfying integration of current theory and knowledge. Its major weakness appears to be that it fails to reflect adequately the two major current positions, behavior therapy and client-centered or relationship therapy. Nor does it (nor perhaps does any current approach) adequately incorporate social psychological theory and research relating to attitude change, interpersonal attraction, social influence, role theory, expectancy, etc.

It is perhaps beyond the ability of one person to master the vast amount of theory and research relevant to the development of an integrative eclectic system. Such a system would require for its base the development of a theory or system of human behavior. Certainly, the writer would make no pretension of being able to accomplish this. Yet this book would be incomplete without some attempt to integrate the various approaches, at least to the extent of identifying some commonalities (if they exist) and pointing the way to a reconciliation of divergences. That some consistent theory and system is possible is an assumption of the scientific endeavor, and progress toward its development is made through the method of successive approximations. In this chapter we shall attempt to present, not an eclectic system, but a foundation or a framework for such a system.

There have been a number of attempts to discover or define common elements among various approaches to counseling or psychotherapy.[4] An obstacle to the discernment of similarities is the striving of theorists to be unique and different. This leads to the creation of new and different terminology, though the concepts represented by the terminology may not be new or different. Differences are focused upon or emphasized. New techniques are presented without reference to the total process in which they are used or of which they are a part. Presumably all those theories or approaches that have gained wide acceptance or have persisted have some degree of truth. Their differences may be more apparent than real, representing different perceptions and descriptions of the same phenomena, or emphasizing different aspects of the same process. "Indeed, by and large the various theories are not logically incompatible and often neatly supplement and indirectly prove one another." [5] To the extent that they are based upon extensive experience in practice it would be expected that there would be commonalities, agreements, and mutual support.

COMMONALITIES AND DIFFERENCES

Philosophy and Concepts

It would seem to be difficult to find a common philosophy, or even a single common concept, among the points of view covered in this book. Concepts relating to the nature of man and the nature of emotional disturbances vary considerably. There would seem to be little, if anything, in common between a concept of man as determined by his environment or by his internal needs and drives, on the one hand, and the concept of man as a person capable of making choices and free to do so, on the other hand; or between the concept of man as essentially an organism to be manipulated by rewards and punishments, on the one hand, and, on the other, as having the potential for growth and development in the process of self-actualization.

Nevertheless, as minimal as it may appear, there is agreement in the view of man as capable of changing or at least of being changed. He is not hopelessly predetermined, but at any stage may still be pliable. A learning theory approach actually may assume that man is infinitely susceptible to change. Skinner expresses this as follows: "It is dangerous to assert that an organism of a given species or age cannot solve a given problem. As a result of careful scheduling, pigeons, rats, and monkeys have done things in the last five years which members of their species have never done before. It is not that their forebears were incapable of such behavior; nature had simply never arranged effective sequences of schedules." [6] And, regarding the possibility of molding personality, he states: "Give me the specifications, and I'll give you the man." [7]

Other approaches may not be so optimistic about the changeability of personality or behavior, but clearly they assume change is possible; otherwise there would be no point to engaging in counseling or psychotherapy.

There is at least one other common element, and that is the recognition that (a) the presence of a neurosis, a disturbance, a maladjustment, a conflict, an unsolved problem, "symptoms," or disordered behavior is unpleasant and painful for the client, and (b) such a state of affairs is undesirable and warrants attempts to change it.

A third possible common element is the recognition of the influence of the future—or of anticipations, hopes, or expectations related to the future—on present behavior. This is an element that appears to tie together approaches as different as operant conditioning and existentialism. In other words, the recognition that behavior is not entirely "caused" by the past but is also influenced by future consequences, or expectation of consequences, seems to be accepted in most points of view. Lindsley states it as follows, referring to operant conditioning: "The discovery that such [voluntary] behavior is subject to control by its consequences makes it unnecessary to explain behavior in terms of hypothetical antecedents." [8] May, presenting the existentialist position, writes that "the future, in contrast to the present or past, is the dominant mode for human beings." [9]

Goals and Objectives

Mahrer opens his book on the goals of psychotherapy with the statement that "The literature on psychotherapy has little to offer on the goals of psychotherapy—their identification, significance, and organization. On this point, clinicians, researchers, and theoreticians have been curiously inarticulate." [10] Many therapists have given their attention to the matter of goals, however, and the insistence of the behavior therapists on specifying the objectives of treatment has directed attention to the consideration of goals.

When one examines the goals that are discussed by the theorists represented in this book and by the contributors to Mahrer's book, one finds an amazing range and variety. Some speak of personality reorganization, others of curing a disease or illness, others of adjustment to the environment, society, or culture. Still others are concerned with such things as the development of effective biological and social functioning, unlearning unadaptive and learning adaptive habits, reduction of anxiety, or relief from suffering. Some, particularly the client-centered or humanist therapists, talk of the meaning of life, facilitating growth or optimal functioning, or the development of self-actualizing persons.

It would appear to be more difficult to find commonalities among goals than among concepts or techniques. Much of the problem with regard to goals, however, is that the stated goals represent different levels of specificity or generality. Parloff recognizes this when he distinguishes between mediating and ultimate goals.[11] His mediating goals are steps, or stages, in the counseling process, which lead to the outcome or ultimate goals. There seems to be a need for another level of goals in addition to the mediating goals and the ultimate goal considered as a long-term or general goal. Thus, there might be three levels: (1) immediate, or goals for the process, (2) mediate, or rather specific outcome objectives, and (3) ultimate goals.

If we accept this concept of levels, we can find some agreement among the various approaches. The behaviorists stress specific goals as direct outcomes of the treatment process. Other therapists emphasize long-term or ultimate goals, and although they express these goals in somewhat different ways, the concept of self-actualization seems to represent them. Maslow's description of self-actualizing people, which results from his research, would constitute a provisional definition of the concept.[12] Rogers' description of the fully functioning person is similar.[13] Many of the more specific goals of the behaviorists would be acceptable to client-centered or existential therapists, either as aspects of the self-actualizing person or as subgoals or steps toward the ultimate goal.

The behavior therapists, though they emphasize the removal of symptoms as an objective goal, also seem to recognize and accept a broader goal. They apparently expect the client to feel better, to function better in life and its various aspects, and to achieve at a higher level—in short, to live up to his potential. Salter speaks of freeing the individual by "unbraking" him.[14] Wolpe used as criteria of improvement not only symptom removal, but "increased productiveness, improved adjustment and pleasure in sex, improved interpersonal relationships and ability to handle psychological conflict and reasonable stresses," [15] although these were not the specific targets of treatment. Thus, the behavior therapists are interested in broader, more general changes, which can be considered aspects of self-actualization.

The Counseling Process

The therapy process is viewed differently in the various approaches. Psychoanalysis stresses insight in relation to the past, achieved by skillful interpretation. For Kelly therapy is the process of loosening old constructs and reconditioning personal constructs. For Ellis it is a matter convincing the client that he has been functioning irrationally and teaching him a more rational structure to live by. The client-centered approach conceives of the counseling process as the experiencing, in a psychologically safe relationship, of feelings that have previously been too threatening for the client to experience freely and fully. Behavior therapy views counseling as the process of eliminating undesirable behavior through desensitization, extinction, and reconditioning. Existentialists see counseling as the subjective encounter of two individuals in an affective relationship.

The organization of this book is based upon a continuum in terms of the various concepts of the counseling process. The continuum varies from highly rational approaches at one end to strongly affective approaches at the other end. In the rational approach the counseling process tends to be planned, objective, and impersonal. In the affective approach it is considered as being warm, personal, and spontaneous. One approach emphasizes reason and problem solving; the other, affect and experiencing. Although there are probably no pure forms of either approach, the above distinction appears to be one that is supported by an examination of the various points of view. In fact, it appears that there may be two divergent trends in counseling —one toward a more cognitive approach and the other toward a more affective approach—so that there may be a bimodal distribution, or a dichotomy, in the making.

Another differentiation of approaches in terms of process is the insight-action dichotomy of London.[16] He includes under the insight therapies client-centered therapy and existential analysis, as well as the various schools of psychoanalysis. Although there are differences among the insight approaches, London sees these as insignificant in comparison to their commonalities. There are two commonalities that stand out and dwarf other likenesses as well as differences: "1. The single allowable instrument of the therapy is talk, and the therapeutic sessions are deliberately conducted in such a way that, from start to finish, the patient, client, analysand, or counselee does most of the talking and most of the deciding of what will be talked about. 2. The therapist operates with a conservative bias against communicating to the patient important or detailed information about his own life, that is to say, the therapist tends to hide his personal life from the patient." [17] Techniques such as free association and permissiveness lead to exposure of the repressed or unconscious material, which is then responded to by means of reflection, empathic understanding, or interpretation by the therapist, leading to insight on the part of the client.

Action therapies, or behavior therapies, on the other hand, are not concerned with verbalizations, or talk, but with behavior, actions, or symptoms. The action therapist operates on behavior, and "he cares not a whit what the patient does or does not say about himself or even know about himself except insofar as such *behaviors* have concrete and demonstrable value for producing change." Two characteristics of the action therapist, according to London, are: "1. The therapist assumes a much greater influence over the detailed conduct of the treatment sessions, and possibly over the outside life of the patient, than Insight therapists would. 2. The therapist is much more responsible for the outcome of treatment, that is, for whatever changes take place in the patient, than are Insight therapists." [18]

Ullmann and Krasner propose essentially the same dichotomy in their distinction between evocative or expressive therapies and behavior therapy, although they recognize that there are overlappings in techniques.[19] While learning theory concepts are present in expressive therapy, in behavior therapy they are applied systematically.

Sundland and Barker studied the differences in orientation in a group of 139 psychotherapists who were members of the American Psychological Association, using a Therapist Orientation Questionnaire containing sixteen subscales.[20] These scales included, among others, Frequency of Activity, Type of Activity, Emotional Tenor of the Relationship, Spontaneity, Planning, Conceptualization of the Relationship, Goals of Therapy, Theory of Personal Growth, Theory of Neurosis, Theory of Motivation, and Criteria for Success. The therapists distributed themselves over the range of scores from "strongly agree" to "strongly disagree" on most of the scales. The therapists were classified into three groups—Freudians, Sullivanians, and Rogerians—and compared on the scales. The three groups differed significantly on nine of the sixteen scales, with the Sullivanians being in the middle position in eight of these comparisons. The Freudian group, compared to the Rogerian group, believed that the therapist should be more impersonal, plan his therapy, have definite goals, inhibit his spontaneity, use interpretation, conceptualize the case, and recognize the importance of unconscious motivation. These results support those of Strupp.[21] Only one difference was found between therapists grouped by levels of experience: While most of the therapists accepted an innate self-actualization theory of personal growth, the less experienced group indicated greater acceptance than did the more experienced group (significant at the .05 level).

A factor analysis of the sixteen scales yielded six factors. A general factor cut across most of the scales, providing a major single continuum upon which therapists vary. One end is labeled "analytic" (not simply "psychoanalytic") and the other is designated as "experiential" by Sundland and Barker. The "analytic" therapist emphasizes conceptualizing, planning therapy, unconscious processes, and restriction of spontaneity. More therapists tended toward the "analytic" approach than toward the "experiencing" approach.

Wallach and Strupp obtained similar results from factor analysis of the ratings of two groups of therapists on a scale of Usual Therapeutic Practices.[22] The major factor was called the maintenance of personal distance. Four groupings of therapists—orthodox Freudians, psychoanalytic general, Sullivanian, and client-centered—were compared, with the first group being highest in the personal distance factor, the second group next highest, and the remaining two about the same but lower than the other two.

McNair and Lorr studied the reported techniques of 192 male and 73 female psychotherapists (67 psychiatrists, 103 psychologists, and 95 social workers) in forty-four Veterans Administration Mental Hygiene Clinics, using an instrument developed on the basis of the Sundland and Barker Therapist Orientation Scale.[23] They hypothesized three dimensions to be measured by AID scales: (A) psychoanalytically oriented techniques, (I) impersonal versus personal approaches to the patient, and (D) directive, active therapeutic methods. All three dimensions emerged in the factor analysis of the forty-nine scales included in the analysis. High scores on the A factor represent traditional psychoanalytic techniques. High scores on the I factor represent a detached, objective, impersonal approach, while low scores represent emphasis on therapist personality and the therapist-patient relationship. High scores on the D factor indicate therapist setting of goals, planning of treatment, and leading of the interview, and acceptance of social adjustment as a major goal. Low scores indicate lack of therapist direction of the interview and belief in patient determination of therapy goals. While the three factors are intercorrelated, McNair and Lorr consider them to be independent.

These studies support the existence of differences among therapists. The Sundland and Barker study provides evidence for the rational-affective continuum or dichotomy. The McNair and Lorr study also supports this ordering or classifying of approaches or techniques. In addition, McNair and Lorr found a factor (D) that may indicate support for London's dichotomy. Neither the Sundland and Barker nor the McNair and Lorr study would support London's classification of client-centered and existential approaches with psychoanalysis in a homogeneous insight therapy group. None of these studies included behavior therapists, and the results would no doubt have been different if they had. With the advent of behavior therapy, a new dimension has been added to psychotherapy and counseling, and it is the difference between this approach and all other approaches that now seems to present the major problem for the future.

The most widely known studies of commonalities among schools of psychotherapy in terms of process are those of Fiedler.[24] Fiedler found that therapists from different schools agreed upon the nature of the ideal therapeutic relationship, and that factor analysis yielded one common factor of "goodness" of therapeutic relationships. But how are these results to be interpreted in view of the studies referred to above, which found important differences? The answer seems to lie in the nature of the instruments used in the studies. Sundland and Barker developed their instrument by eliminating items that therapists agree on. Fiedler, on the other hand, appears to have assembled a group of items that therapists agree on. Sundland and Barker point out that the items they discarded because they did not result in a distribution of responses were similar to the items used in Fiedler's studies. These items were concerned with empathy. There appears to be evidence, therefore, that therapists agree upon the importance of empathy and understanding, although the behavior therapists seem to deny or minimize the presence and importance of empathy. Nevertheless, it would appear that a minimum of empathic understanding is necessary for the continuation of the interaction of the counselor and the client; it is also a factor in effecting change, as will be demonstrated later. That is, it appears that a relationship characterized at least to some extent by interest, acceptance, and understanding is basic to influencing others therapeutically. Other factors may direct change along the lines the therapist desires, but it is the relationship itself that makes any influence possible.

Our concern in this book is with individual counseling or psychotherapy. In this process it would appear that all approaches utilize the private interview, in which verbal interaction is the major component. The techniques of conditioning, which are a major aspect of behavior therapy, may be used outside the interview situation, of course, but the point here is that behavior therapy utilizes the interview. It is also true that the methods and techniques of other approaches may be applied in other situations than the counseling interview.

There are some behavior therapists who are interested in the application of conditioning techniques outside the interview situation. The control of the client's environment outside the interview is much more difficult than the control of the interview environment, however. It might also be maintained that the application of any of the methods or techniques of counseling or psychotherapy outside the interview situation does not constitute counseling or psychotherapy. The increasing use of the term "behavior modification" by those interested in behavior change through the use of conditioning techniques indicates their broader interests. Wolpe, however, wishes to retain the term "behavior therapy" and to consider this a method of psychotherapy.

In addition to the common element of a personal relationship in the interview, there appears to be a number of other aspects of the counseling process that most, if not all, approaches share. Among these are certain characteristics of the counselor or therapist and of the client or patient. The first characteristic of the therapist is a genuine interest in, and concern for, the client, a strong desire to help him, to influence or change him. Not only do counselors or therapists accept the possibility and desirability of client change, they are genuinely and strongly interested in being the agent of change in their clients. If they were not, they would not be engaged in counseling or psychotherapy.

Furthermore, all counselors or therapists expect their clients to change. This expectation may vary in its degree, in some instances approaching a highly optimistic or even enthusiastic expectation, while in others it may be minimal. But it is always present. There is always an attitude of hope and expectation of change. Again, without this expectation therapists would not continue in such work. A factor that may not be independent of, or separate from, those already discussed is an acceptance of, or respect for, the client as a person, an individual, which is present in spite of his problems and difficulties or his disagreeable characteristics. In other words, acceptance or respect is not conditioned upon the client's evidencing behavior that the counselor feels is desirable, good, or healthy. Acceptance does not preclude, therefore, disagreement with the attitudes, beliefs, and behavior of the client; it does not mean approval of them. It is a respect or even liking for him in spite of his unlikable characteristics. It is the unconditional positive regard of client-centered therapy. It would appear that this must exist, at least to a minimal degree, or a counselor could not continue the relationship with a client. Counselors do not continue to work with clients when this condition does not exist; clients are therefore selected on the basis of the possibility of the existence of acceptance or respect.

Another element that appears to be common to all approaches is given various designations. In the client-centered approach it is referred to as "therapist genuineness" or "self-congruence." Others refer to it as "sincerity," "honesty," or "openness." The existentialists use the term "authenticity." Some approaches (such as that of Ellis) do not refer specifically to this characteristic, but it is apparent in the discussions of these approaches, and particularly in their protocols, that this element is present.

There is a final characteristic that unites therapists of widely differing approaches. This is the fact that each therapist believes in or has confidence in the theory and method that he uses. If he did not feel it was the best method or approach, he would not use it, but would adopt a different one. It might be hypothesized that success (or at least reports of success) bears a strong relationship to the degree of confidence the therapist has in his approach. The failure or inability of the therapist to commit himself to an approach apparently limits his effectiveness and makes of him a technician, or makes him technique-oriented. A common aspect of therapy thus appears to be the therapist's commitment to a particular method or approach.

Most, if not all, approaches therefore seem to include a relationship that is characterized, on the part of the counselor or therapist, by a belief in the possibility of client change; an expectation that the client will change; interest in, and concern for, the client, including a desire to help, influence, or change him; sincerity and honesty in the therapy process; and confidence in the approach used to achieve client change.

It is necessary to add one other point. This is that the crucial aspect of the therapist's impact or contribution is not his actual personality or behavior, or even his intent in the relationship. It is the client's perception of the therapist that determines the therapist's characteristics and contribution. Thus, the client's characteristics, his attitudes and set, are important aspects of the relationship.

Some common aspects of individuals who come to counselors or therapists for help are apparent. First, as indicated above, they "hurt"—they are suffering or are unhappy because of conflicts, symptoms, unfulfilled desires or aspirations, feelings of failure or

inadequacy, or lack of meaning in their lives. They are therefore motivated to change. Clients who are referred may not always be aware of
their "hurt" or, if they are, may not feel the need for help or may not
want it from a counselor or therapist. It may, of course, be maintained
that everyone "hurts" in some respect and so could benefit from
counseling.

Second, clients also believe that change is possible and expect
to change, to be helped. Frank has emphasized the universality of this
factor in clients.[25] Cartwright and Cartwright indicate that this is a
complex factor: there may be belief that improvement will occur, belief
in the therapist as the major source of help, or belief in himself (the
client) as the major source of help.[26] These writers feel that it is only
the last belief that leads to improvement in a positive linear manner.
The other beliefs are probably present to some extent in all clients,
however. The client must feel that the counselor is interested, concerned, and wants to help him. This belief appears to involve a complex of attitudes on the part of the client. The client must have some
trust and confidence in the counselor and his methods, or he would
not enter counseling.

Third, the client must be active in, or participate in, the process.
He is not a passive recipient, as is the physically ill patient being
treated by a physician. All learning (behavior change) appears to require activity (whether motor, verbal, or intellectual) on the part of
the learner. This kind of behavior in counseling or psychotherapy
includes self-analysis or self-exploration. Truax and Carkhuff refer to
it also as intrapersonal exploration or self-disclosure.[27] Jourard [28] and
Mowrer [29] also speak of self-disclosure. It appears that the client, as
well as the counselor, must be genuine, open, and honest in the therapy process.

Thus, all approaches seem to deal with clients who are in need
of help, recognize this need, believe they can change, believe that the
counselor can help them change, and engage in some activity in an
attempt to change.

All approaches, then, appear to involve a relationship between
a counselor and a client in which each contributes certain characteristics that lead to client change.

AN ATTEMPT AT INTEGRATION

Although there are many similarities, there also appear to be many
differences among widely differing approaches to counseling or psychotherapy. Perhaps the greatest divergence is between the behavior
therapies, on the one hand, and the existentialist approaches (including client-centered therapy), on the other. In spite of the similarities
or agreements noted above, it appears that these two points of view
are perceived by their adherents and by others as inconsistent and
contradictory. The behavior therapies appear to be objective, impersonal, technique-oriented, and mechanical. The existential ap-

proaches may be seen as subjective, personal, and not concerned with technique. Is it possible to reconcile these apparently inconsistent approaches? Rogers, recognizing these divergent trends not only in psychotherapy but also in psychology, has stated that they "seem irreconcilable because we have not yet developed the larger frame of reference that would contain them both." [30]

It is suggested that a possible reconciliation of the divergent views of man may be derived from a consideration of the different models of man delineated by Allport. Allport writes: "The trouble with our current theories of learning is not so much that they are wrong, but that they are partial." [31] It may be said, then, that the trouble with the behavior therapy or conditioning approach is not that it is wrong, but that it is incomplete as a description or theory of the nature of man and of his behavior and its modification. It is a "nothing but" approach. There can be no question about the existence of conditioning, about the fact that man is a reactive being who can be conditioned and reconditioned. But man is more than this. He is also an active being, an initiator of action. His behavior influences his environment, as well as being influenced by his environment.

He is not merely a mechanism or organism who is controlled by objective stimuli in his environment or subjective stimuli from within. The concept of operant behavior recognizes that man operates upon his environment. He selects or defines, through his perceptions, the stimuli that he will respond to. He is thus a being who lives, or exists, who thinks and feels, who interprets or defines his environment and himself in certain ways. His world is determined in part by his perceptions, not solely by the objective nature of stimuli. This is a "something more" approach.

As noted above, there appears to be agreement on the necessity of a relationship in counseling or psychotherapy. It is a complex relationship, with various aspects. It is not simply a cognitive, intellectual, impersonal relationship, but an affective, experiential, highly personal relationship. It is not necessarily irrational, but it has nonrational aspects. The nature of man's ties to his fellowman is essentially affective.

Evidence seems to be accumulating that the effective element in counseling is the nature of the relationship established by the counselor. Goldstein, reviewing the literature on therapist-patient expectancies in psychotherapy, concludes: "There can no longer be any doubt as to the primary status which must be accorded the therapeutic relationship in the overall therapeutic transaction." [32] The behavior therapists appear to be unconcerned about the relationship or to minimize its importance. However, it appears that the relationship is of greater significance in their methods than they admit. It should be apparent that the characteristics of the counselor or therapist and of the client discussed above are manifested in, or manifest themselves in, a relationship.

The counseling relationship always involves conditioning aspects. The accepting, understanding, nonthreatening atmosphere of the therapy situation offers the opportunity for the extinction of anxiety or for desensitization of threatening stimuli. In this relationship, where external threat is minimized, anxiety-arousing ideas, words, images, and feelings are free to appear. Moreover, they appear in a sequence that resembles the kind of hierarchy established by Wolpe, that is, from least anxiety-arousing to most anxiety-arousing. Thus, in any nonthreatening therapy relationship desensitization may be achieved in the same manner that it is by Wolpe. The relationship, by minimizing externally induced anxiety, makes it possible for the client to experience and bring out his internally induced anxieties or anxiety-arousing experiences at the time and the rate at which he can face and handle them in the accepting relationship.

In addition, operant conditioning serves to reinforce the production of verbalizations that the therapist believes are either therapeutic or necessary in order for therapy to occur. The therapist rewards these verbalizations by his interest and attention or by explicit praise and approval. At the beginning of therapy, negative elements may be rewarded—for example, the expression of problems, conflicts, fears, and anxieties; and negative self-references. As therapy progresses, the therapist may reinforce positive elements—for example, problem-solving efforts; positive thoughts, attitudes, and feelings; and positive self-references. The therapist expects progress of this kind and is sensitive to its expression in the client.

The question to be faced, to quote Jourard, is: "What conditions foster output of a kind of operant behavior in the *therapist* that we call 'patient-growth-fostering'? That is, what conditions serve to increase the rate at which the therapist will emit behavior which, in turn, serves as stimuli which evoke growth-conducive behavior in the patient?" [33]

Conditioning principles have contributed to an understanding of the nature of the therapeutic process and the therapy relationship. But the conditioning that occurs is not the mechanical conditioning of a rat in a Skinner box. It is instead an aspect of the therapy relationship, and it takes place in, and is influenced by, the relationship. There is considerable evidence that the rate and extent of conditioning is influenced by the personality and attitudes of the experimenter and by his relationship to the subject.[34] This relationship involves characteristics of the client—his interest, motivations, thoughts, attitudes, perceptions, and expectations—as well as those of the counselor. It is also affected by the situation or setting in which the relationship occurs—what are called the demand characteristics in a research experiment. As Ullmann and Krasner note, "both the subject's and the examiner's expectancies, sets, and so forth have a major effect on the individual's response to the situation," and "the best results are obtained when the patient and the therapist form a good interpersonal relationship." [35] The relationship, therefore, cannot be ignored, even in behavior therapy. Krasner points out that Skinner classified attention as a general reinforcer.[36] The most powerful influences on behavior—or, in conditioning terms, reinforcers—are the respect, interest, concern, and attention of the therapist. The demonstration through research of the effects of these generalized reinforcers supports the theory of the importance of the relationship in counseling or psychotherapy.

There is a further point emphasizing the importance of the therapy relationship. Many, if not most, of the problems or difficulties of clients involve interpersonal relationships. It is being increasingly recognized that good interpersonal relationships are characterized by honesty, openness, sincerity, and spontaneity. Psychotherapy is an interpersonal relationship that has these characteristics. It is therefore a situation in which the client can learn good interpersonal relationships. In fact, therapy would be limited if it tried to influence the client's interpersonal relationships by providing a different kind of relationship. And if it attempted to influence interpersonal relationships by avoiding the establishment of a therapeutic relationship, it would seem to be inefficient. Teaching, or conditioning, individual behavior in a mechanical manner would not appear to offer much hope of generalization to personal relationships outside of therapy. The therapist provides a model of a good personal relationship for the client.

London sees Mowrer as offering a solution to the inadequacies of insight therapy, on the one hand, and action therapy, on the other.[37] But Mowrer's approach, though not yet systematically developed or presented, is a relationship therapy.[38] Mowrer, recognizing that personality is a product of interpersonal relationships, emphasizes the therapeutic value of openness and self-disclosure in interpersonal relationships. However, although he feels that such openness may begin in a relationship with an individual therapist, he states that it is seldom that more than one or two interviews are necessary. He feels that the client should move quickly from the group of two to the larger group of significant others in his life (to use Sullivan's phrase) or to the primary groups in his life (to use a sociological term).

There is thus no basic or necessary contradiction between behavior therapy and relationship therapy. One emphasizes the shaping or changing of specific aspects of behavior by specific rewards or reinforcers. The other emphasizes more general behavior changes (including changes of attitudes and feelings), achieved by the use of generalized reinforcers. Both utilize the principles of learning—one rather narrowly, emphasizing conditioning, the other more broadly, emphasizing what might be called a social learning approach.[39] The behavior therapists are, as Ullmann and Krasner point out, systematic in their application of specific learning concepts.[40] But it might also be said that relationship therapists are also systematic in the application of generalized reinforcers. The conditioning or behavior therapy approach is supported by research evidence, including laboratory or experimental research. The relationship approach is also supported by research, including some of the research on conditioning. It is interesting and significant that both groups are coming to the same conclusions, one from laboratory work in conditioning, the other from experience and research in counseling or psychotherapy. It is important, however, that behavior therapists come to recognize the complexity of the learning process and its social or relationship aspects, and also that relationship therapists be aware of the conditioning that is an aspect of counseling or psychotherapy. The total process, although it may be learning, is a complex one, involving various kinds of learning and not simply operant or classical conditioning. It includes perceptual, cognitive, and affective elements, all of which are important in behavior and behavior change. The difficulty of providing a therapeutic relationship, with its necessary affective aspects, is greater than that of providing a laboratory conditioning relationship, or even a rational, problem-solving relationship in an interview.

The complexity of the process and the importance of the therapist's interest, concern, and understanding have an important implication. The process cannot be mechanized, routinized, simplified, or controlled in the sense of programing or of objective, planned manipulation of rewards in terms of expressing interest, concern, etc. This is because the therapist's behavior is only effective when it is sincere and spontaneous, not when it is a contrived technique. The therapist is most effective when he is a person—when he is, as it is termed in the client-centered approach, "genuine" in the relationship. While the behavior therapists strive for effectiveness by attempting to reduce treatment to the essentials of technique, it would appear that to be most effective the therapist must be a real, human person. The most effective influence is that of another person offering a genuine human relationship.

Jourard's comments are relevant here:

> I believe we are on the brink of discovering that when an experienced therapist eschews technique, and just is *himself* in the presence of his patient, then he is in fact accomplishing the following things: 1. He is actually providing a condition which elicits real-self-being, that is, spontaneous, uncontrived self-disclosure in his patient. This is analogous with priming the pump, or showing the rat how the lever works. 2. He is providing a powerful reinforcement to real-self-being in his patient. Real-self-being begets real-self-being. 3. By spontaneously responding to the patient's output, the therapist not only fosters real-self-being in the patient, but he is also extinguishing many of the sickness-fostering responses emitted by the patient. 4. He is avoiding the therapy-defeating behavior of contrivance, seeming, and impersonal manipulation of himself and his patient. Rather, he is providing the patient with a role-model of honest, healthy behavior.[41]

The evidence seems to point to the establishment of a particular kind of relationship as the crucial element in counseling or psychotherapy. It is a relationship characterized not so much by what techniques the therapist uses as by what he is, not so much by what he does as by the way that he does it. Rogers notes that "some of the recent studies suggest that a warmly human and genuine therapist, interested only in understanding the moment-by-moment feelings of this person who is coming into being in the relationship with him, is the most effective therapist. Certainly there is nothing to indicate that the coldly intellectual, analytical, factually minded therapist is effective." [42] Much of what therapists do is superfluous or unrelated to their effectiveness; in fact, it is likely that much of their success is unrelated to what they do, or even occurs in spite of what they do, as long as they offer the relationship that it appears therapists of very differing persuasions do provide. To some extent at least, even the most extreme behaviorists provide such a relationship.

TWO QUESTIONS

The conclusion that the essence of counseling or psychotherapy consists in a genuine human relationship characterized by interest, concern, empathic understanding, and genuineness on the part of the therapist leads to two questions.

1. What is there that is unique about this relationship? How does it differ from all good human relationships? If the answer is, as should be obvious, that there is nothing unique or different, then what is there that is special about the practice of counseling or psychotherapy? Fiedler concluded from his studies that "a good therapeutic relationship is very much like any good interpersonal relationship." [43]

This view may be opposed by those who feel that it deprives counselors or therapists of unique powers, who fear that "it leaves the practitioner without a speciality." [44] But it should not be surprising that the characteristics of psychotherapy should be the characteristics of all good human relationships. Nor does it follow that if such characteristics are not limited to counseling or psychotherapy, they are not relevant or specific. The essence of emotional disturbances is disturbed human relationships. The individual has become estranged from others, has become detached from the community of men. His relationships with others have been ruptured or have been placed on an insecure, false, or untenable basis. He needs to reestablish good relationships with others.

But often he cannot do this alone for several reasons. He may not be able to change the behavior that contributes to the poor relationships. He may not know what behaviors are involved. Others may not provide him with the opportunity to change, or even if he changes, they may not recognize, accept, or believe in the permanence of the change. Their behavior, stimulated in part at least by his behavior, contributes to the vicious circle of poor relationships. Such a situation is not conducive to change; the individual is, or feels, threatened by others and reacts in turn by threatening them.

There is a need, then, for someone who can accept the disturbed individual, with all his disturbed, irritating, threatening behavior, and offer him a nonthreatening relationship in which he can respond in an open, nonthreatening way. Therapy offers the opportunity for learning how to relate to others in a different and more effective way. It utilizes or embodies the principles of good human relationships, which although they appear to be simple, are not widely practiced outside of therapy. If such relationships were practiced generally, there would presumably be no emotionally disturbed people, except those whose disturbances were of organic origin. Perhaps the difficulty of providing such relationships within the confines of the patterns of many human interrelationships is the basis for the practice of the therapist avoiding relationships with clients outside the therapy relationship. While there is merit in Schofield's analysis of psychotherapy as the purchase of friendship,[45] therapy is, however, more than the offering of friendship, at least in the usual sense of the word. While the viewing of psychotherapy as something dark and mysterious classifies the therapist with magicians and witch doctors, viewing it as bought friendship places him in the same category as taxi dancers, gigolos, and call girls.

2. The characteristics of counseling or psychotherapy that have been developed above have frequently been considered nonspecific elements. It is often assumed that they are not related to the specific nature of the client's disturbance, and that while they may be considered as necessary conditions of therapy, they are not sufficient. Further, such characteristics as attention, interest, concern, trust, belief, faith, and expectation are part of what is called the placebo effect in the treatment of physical diseases. While it is not usual to insist that these effects be eliminated from counseling or psychotherapy, it is generally accepted that, as nonspecific factors, they are not sufficient, and that other methods or techniques must be included to deal with the specific aspects of the disturbance. It is generally argued that any method or technique must produce greater effects than those obtained by placebo elements in order to be considered useful.

The placebo effect is a psychological effect. When the interest or concern is with determining the physical or physiological effect of a drug or medication on a known physical disease or disturbance, it is reasonable to consider this effect as extraneous and nonspecific. Even here, however, it is of interest to recognize and study the effects of such psychological factors on physical functioning.

But the concept of the extraneousness of the placebo effect may not be applicable in counseling or psychotherapy. Here, the disorder or disturbance is psychological. Is it not logical that the specific treatment for a psychological condition should be psychological? Should it not be reasonable to suggest that the specific treatment for disturbed human relationships is the providing of a good relationship? Is the placebo effect, as Rosenthal and Frank state, "a nonspecific form of psychotherapy"? [46]

It has long been known that any new form of treatment of emotional disturbance, from electric shock to tranquilizers, meets with great success when it is first introduced, but that its success declines with time. This is because when it is first used, it is expected to be successful—there is hope and expectation on the part of both the therapist and the patient. Patients become the object of increased interest and attention. But as time goes on, as the procedure becomes routine, as doubts or questions arise because it is not always successful, its effectiveness decreases. Its early success was the result, in whole or part, of the placebo effect. It is only reasonable, again, that in evaluating the results of an experimental treatment, this effect should be considered nonspecific. But we might also look at the apparent success of behavior therapy in the same way. How much of its success is actually the heightening of the placebo effect? Should it not be required that this effect be eliminated in order to evaluate the real effect of conditioning?

It is strange that with all the evidence of the power of the placebo effect, it has not been recognized as the most effective approach to the treatment of psychological problems. As Krasner and Ullmann put it, "Whereas the problem had previously been conceptualized in terms of eliminating the 'placebo effects,' it would seem reasonable to maximize placebo effects in the treatment situation to increase the likelihood of client change. The evidence is growing that 'placebo effect' is a euphemism for examiner influence variables." [47]

The placebo effect, as a psychological effect, includes a wide variety of elements—all the elements of a psychological relationship, in fact. In addition to the relationship variables emphasized above, it also includes therapist behaviors that enhance his prestige, status, and authority, as well as direct or indirect suggestion—elements that appear to be very prominent in behavior therapy. These factors have been demonstrated to be effective in placebo studies involving drugs. The extent to which behavior therapy is successful because of the presence of these factors has not been evaluated.

A CONTINUUM OF HELPING RELATIONSHIPS

The recognition of the basic commonalities among all approaches to counseling or psychotherapy, focusing upon the relationship, is important. But that differences exist must not be ignored, and it would appear that some attempt to develop a model or theoretical structure that would accommodate these differences should be made. Such a model would minimize the tendency to dichotomize, to state an either/ or position, as represented by London's "insight" versus "action" therapy, the "disease model" or "medical model" versus the "learning model." Such distinctions, as Lazarus notes, are oversimplified.[48]

Other writers suggest that, rather than there being a single model or a dichotomous solution, there are a multitude of separate methods or approaches. The proliferation of theories, methods, and techniques has led to a resurgence of a recurrent proposal that techniques must be matched to problems and clients. Ford and Urban, in their review of psychotherapy for the *Annual Review of Psychology* noted a growing emphasis on differential treatment.[49] Krumboltz stated it as follows: "What we need to know is which procedures and techniques, when used to accomplish which kinds of behavior change, are most effective with what kind of client when applied by what kind of counselors." [50]

Blocher similarly writes: "The old questions of, 'Is counseling effective?' or 'Which counseling theory is correct?' are seen as largely rhetorical. They give way to questions of, 'Which treatments in the hands of which counselors can offer what benefits to particular clients?' " [51] Paul writes: "In all its complexity, the question towards which all outcome research should ultimately be directed is the following: *What* treatment, by *whom,* is most effective for *this* individual with *that* specific problem, and under which set of circumstances?" [52] And Strupp and Bergin, after reviewing hundreds of references, state: "The problem of psychotherapy research . . . should be reformulated as. . . . What specific interventions produce specific changes in specific patients under specific conditions?" [53]

This approach appears to be empirically sound. As a research program it is practically impossible, however, certainly at present. It would require (a) a classification system for clients and/or client problems, (b) a classification of counseling approaches and treatments, and (c) a classification system for counselors. After several hundred years of effort, psychiatry has not yet achieved an acceptable diagnostic system, and it may be questioned whether it ever will. A reading of the preceding chapters in this book will make it clear that we do not have a system for the classification of treatment methods. Research on counselor characteristics has just begun.

It is possible, however, to make a beginning, in terms of broad differences in treatment methods and clients. Part of our difficulty at present is that the word "counseling," particularly, and increasingly the word "psychotherapy" have come to be used so broadly that they cover a wide variety of activities. It would be desirable if we could delimit the terms in some way or agree upon the existence of different kinds of counseling or psychotherapy. Failing this, perhaps we can distinguish between behavior therapy and what might be called relationship therapy. In addition, it might be helpful if we thought in terms of a continuum of helping relationships. An even broader concept is that of helping methods, which would include methods of helping others that do not involve any relationship between the participants, such as environmental intervention or social engineering. However, this goes beyond our concern here, which is to attempt to introduce some order into the variety of helping relationships involving personal contacts, such as counseling or psychotherapy in the usual, or traditional, usages of these terms.

The following figure presents such an attempt. Several of the variables underlying the continuum of helping relationships are indicated. The first three are continuous, not dichotomous, variables; the fourth and fifth are perhaps dichotomous.

This model provides a basis for "diagnosis" or classification of client problems and of treatment measures, in a broad, general sense. Treatment is then specific. It is interesting that in this respect, the relationship is, as Wolpe and others have suggested, nonspecific in behavior therapy, but is the specific treatment in relationship therapy. Relationship therapy is the specific treatment for those clients whose problem is the lack of facilitative interpersonal relationships. Thus, the relationship is necessary and sufficient for such a problem. But for other problems, it is necessary but not sufficient. A client who lacks information or skills needs more than a relationship; he needs information or instruction. It is of course possible, indeed likely, that many clients have a number of different problems requiring several methods of treatment. The counselor or psychotherapist—or, to use a generic term, the helper—must decide upon the section(s) of the continuum of helping relationships in which he desires, and is competent, to function. Helpers would appear to have the right to limit themselves quite narrowly, if they desire, referring clients who need other kinds of help for particular problems.

A CONTINUUM OF HELPING RELATIONSHIPS

information giving	instruction in subject matter (education)	behavior modification (education)	behavior therapy (reeducation)	relationship therapy
Cognitive ←				→ Affective
Impersonal ←				→ Personal
Specific ←				→ General
Learning ← (response not in repertoire)			→ Performance (response in repertoire)	
Relationship as medium ←			→ Relationship as essence	

The concept of a variety of kinds of helping relationships, all involving the variables of a good human relationship, though to different (minimal) degrees, with some involving other variables, including the methods of behavior therapy, appears to offer a foundation or structure for the development of a general system or theory of helping or therapeutic behavior.

REFERENCES

[1] Ungersma, A. J. *The search for meaning.* Philadelphia: Westminster, 1961. P. 55.   [2] Rogers, C. R. Psychotherapy today or where do we go from here? *Amer. J. Psychother.,* 1963, **17,** 5–16.   [3] Kanfer, F. H., & Phillips, Jeanne S. A survey of current behavior therapies and a proposal for classification. In

C. M. Franks (Ed.), *Behavior therapy: appraisal and status.* New York: McGraw-Hill, 1969. Pp. 445–475.   **[4]** Patterson, C. H. *Counseling and psychotherapy: theory and practice.* Chap. 12. Common elements in psychotherapy: essence or placebo? New York: Harper & Row, 1959.   **[5]** Perls, F. S., Hefferline, R. F., & Goodman, P. *Gestalt therapy.* New York: Julian Press, 1951. P. 280. **[6]** Skinner, B. F. Reinforcement today. *Amer. Psychologist,* 1958, **14,** 94–99. **[7]** Skinner, B. F. *Walden two.* New York: Macmillan, 1948. P. 243.   **[8]** Lindsley, O. Free operant conditioning and psychotherapy. In J. Masserman and J. L. Moreno (Eds.), *Current psychiatric therapies.* New York: Grune & Stratton, 1963.   **[9]** May, R. Contributions of existential psychotherapy. In R. May, E. Angel, & H. F. Ellenberger (Eds.), *Existence.* New York: Basic Books, 1958. P. 69.   **[10]** Mahrer, A. R. (Ed.), *The goals of psychotherapy.* New York: Appleton-Century-Crofts, 1967. P. 1.   **[11]** Parloff, M. B. Goals in psychotherapy: mediating and ultimate. In A. R. Mahrer (Ed.), *op. cit.,* pp. 5–19. **[12]** Maslow, A. H. *Motivation and personality.* (Rev. ed.) New York: Harper & Row, 1970. Chap. 12.   **[13]** Rogers, C. R. *On becoming a person.* Boston: Houghton Mifflin, 1961. Chap. 9.   **[14]** Salter, A. *Conditioned reflex therapy.* New York: Capricorn, 1961. P. 24.   **[15]** Wolpe, J. *The practice of behavior therapy.* New York: Pergamon Press, 1969. P. 275.   **[16]** London, P. *The modes and morals of psychotherapy.* New York: Holt, Rinehart and Winston, 1964. **[17]** *Ibid.,* p. 45.   **[18]** *Ibid.,* p. 78.   **[19]** Ullmann, L. P., & Krasner, L. (Eds.), *Case studies in behavior modification.* New York: Holt, Rinehart and Winston, 1965. Introduction.   **[20]** Sundland, D. M., & Barker, E. N. The orientations of psychotherapists. *J. consult. Psychol.,* 1962, **26,** 201–212.   **[21]** Strupp, H. H. An objective comparison of Rogerian and psychoanalytic techniques. *J. consult. Psychol.,* 1955, **19,** 1–7.   **[22]** Wallach, M. S., & Strupp, H. H. Dimensions of psychotherapists' activities. *J. consult. Psychol.,* 1964, **28,** 120–125.   **[23]** McNair, D. M., & Lorr, M. An analysis of professed psychotherapeutic techniques. *J. consult. Psychol.,* 1964, **28,** 265–271.   **[24]** Fiedler, F. The concept of an ideal therapeutic relationship. *J. consult. Psychol.,* 1950, **14,** 235–245; Fiedler, F. A comparison of therapeutic relationships in psychoanalytic, nondirective, and Adlerian therapeutic relationships. *J. consult. Psychol.,* 1951, **15,** 32–38.   **[25]** Frank, J. D. The dynamics of the psychotherapeutic relationship. *Psychiatry,* 1959, **22,** 17–39; Frank, J. D. *Persuasion and healing.* Baltimore: Johns Hopkins, 1961; Rosenthal, D., & Frank, J. D. Psychotherapy and the placebo effect. *Psychol. Bull.,* 1956, **53,** 294–302.   **[26]** Cartwright, D. S., & Cartwright, Rosalind D. Faith and improvement in psychotherapy. *J. counsel. Psychol.,* 1958, **5,** 174–177.   **[27]** Truax, C. B., & Carkhuff, R. R. Client and therapist transparency in the psychotherapeutic encounter. *J. consult. Psychol.,* 1965, **12,** 3–9.   **[28]** Jourard, S. M. *The transparent self.* New York: Van Nostrand, 1964.   **[29]** Mowrer, O. H. *The new group therapy.* New York: Random House, 1961. p. 85.   **[30]** Rogers, C. R. Divergent trends. In R. May (Ed.), *Existential psychology.* New York: Random House, 1961. P. 85. **[31]** Allport, G. W. Psychological models for guidance. *Harvard educ. Rev.,* 1962, **32,** 373–381.   **[32]** Goldstein, A. P. *Therapist-patient expectancies in psychotherapy.* New York: Macmillan, 1962, P. 105.   **[33]** Jourard, S. M. On the problem of reinforcement by the therapist of healthy behavior in the patient. In F. J. Shaw (Ed.), *Behavioristic approaches to counseling and psychotherapy.* Tuscaloosa, Ala.: University of Alabama Press, 1961, P. 14.   **[34]** Ullmann, L. P., & Krasner, L., *op. cit.*   **[35]** *Ibid.,* p. 43.   **[36]** Krasner, L. The therapist as a social reinforcement machine. In H. H. Strupp & L. Luborsky (Eds.), *Research in psychotherapy.* Vol. II. Washington: American Psychological Association, 1962. P. 67.   **[37]** London, P., *op. cit.*   **[38]** Mowrer, O. H., *op. cit.* **[39]** Murray, E. J. Learning theory and psychotherapy: biotropic versus sociotropic approaches. *J. counsel. Psychol.,* 1963, **10,** 251–255.   **[40]** Ullmann, L. P., & Krasner, L., *op. cit.,* p. 37.   **[41]** Jourard, S. M., *op. cit.,* pp. 15–16. **[42]** Rogers, C. R. *On becoming a person.* Boston: Houghton Mifflin, 1961. P. 269.   **[43]** Fiedler, F. The concept of an ideal therapeutic relationship. *J. consult. Psychol.,* 1950, **14,** 235–245.   **[44]** Mowrer, O. H. *op. cit.,* p. 235. **[45]** Schofield, W. *Psychotherapy: the purchase of friendship.* Englewood Cliffs, N.J.: Prentice-Hall, 1964.   **[46]** Rosenthal, D., & Frank, J. D., *op. cit.*   **[47]** Krasner, L., & Ullmann, L. P. (Eds.), *Research in behavior modification.* New York: Holt, Rinehart and Winston, 1965, P. 230.   **[48]** Lazarus, A. A. *Behavior therapy and beyond.* New York: McGraw-Hill, 1971. P. 10.   **[49]** Ford, D., & Urban, H. B. Psychotherapy. *Ann. rev. Psychol.,* 1967, **18,** 333–372.   **[50]** Krumboltz, J. D. Promoting adaptive behavior: new answers to familiar questions. In J. D. Krumboltz, (Ed.), *Revolution in counseling.* Boston: Houghton Mifflin, 1966. Pp. 3–26.   **[51]** Blocher, D. What can counseling offer clients? Implications for selection. In J. M. Whiteley (Ed.), *Research in counseling: evaluation and refocus.* Columbus, Ohio: Merrill, 1967.   **[52]** Paul, G. L. Strategy of outcome research in psychotherapy. *J. consult Psychol.,* 1967, **31,** 109–118. **[53]** Strupp, H. H., & Bergin, A. E. Some empirical and conceptual bases for coordinated research in psychotherapy: a review of issues, trends, and evidence. *Int. J. Psychiat.,* 1969, **7,** 18–90.

INDEX OF NAMES

543

INDEX OF SUBJECTS

547

73 74 75 76   9 8 7 6 5 4 3 2 1